Child and Cross

The Western Learning Tool in 14 Stations
from Nazareth to Gaza.

Konrad Yona Riggenmann

Child and Cross

The Western Learning Tool in 14 Stations
from Nazareth to Gaza.

Bibliographical information by Deutsche Nationalbibliothek:
German National Library registers this publication in German National
Bibliography; detailed bibliographical date are accessible via
http://dnb.dnb.de.

Production and editor:
BoD – Books on Demand, Norderstedt, Germany.

ISBN 9783752824582

In memoriam

Elisabeth Riggenmann, née Ritter (1922-2015),
who as a retired teacher of Catholic religion supported her son's stance and
efforts against state-ordered classroom crosses.

Johann Riggenmann (1920-2004),
who in 1937 painted a wayside devotional picture deliberately giving Mary
and her baby Jesus, instead of blond Germanic, the pitch-black curls of cloth
merchant Jakob Koschland, the Jewish friend of my grandfather.

Jakob Koschland (*1896) and Emma Koschland, née Maier (*1901),
Peppi Lore (*1931) and Justin Koschland (*1934),
all deported to Poland on Thursday before Holy Friday, April 1, 1942.

Auschwitz, May 1944: Edith, the 22 years old
non-Jewish nanny of Jolan Wollstein's family, going to the "showers" together with Jolan
and her four children Dori (11 years), Judith
(5 or 6) and Erwin (8), carrying the youngest,
Naomi (2 years) on her arms.

Content

Preface: Searching keys

"Good evening neighbor. Just saw you searching the ground and thought I could help, what are you looking for?" – "My house key." – "Are you sure you lost it here under this street lantern?" – "No, I lost it in the garden, but here the light is brighter."

"This harmless crucifix? What a sissy would bother about that? Simply overlook, forget it, okay?"
Yes, exactly that's how it works. One tries to forget it because it depicts the cruellest way of execution mankind ever invented, and just as the impression keeps working inside unconsciously, one of its expressions were to be the "six million crucifixions" a honest Pope and rescuer of thousands addressed precisely.
Serious research in whatever field should examine evidence and come up with the most parsimonious explanation. Viewing the crucifix as the stark key and learning device to Jew-hate is not a new concept by any means. Søren Kierkegaard yet in his 1850 book *Training in Christianity* explained how the learning of Jew-hate works with the crucifix. In 1935, Richard von Coudenhove-Kalergi repeated his insight just more concisely. The big acting out began three years later in a pogrom whose horrors have been told in many idioms and whose childhood roots concealed in all of them.
Starting from a traumatized child in Nazareth, this book questions the graphic picture of his mortal torture as a bizarre and fatal intrusion of infantile world-view, yielding a textbook lesson about the power of visual images and subtle psychological mechanisms overlooked, belittled and forgot too easily even after Shoa by many educators. Ever listening to the little ones who are known to tell the truth as drunkards do, the fourteen chapters defend the following seven theses:
A. As crucifixion is mankind's cruelest execution method, the crucifix is the cruelest, most hurtful symbol mankind ever invented, depicting the worst thing human beings can do: to torture a fellow to death.
B. Children, as the most vulnerable human beings, by looking at and musing about this piercing, pity arousing symbol learn "rightful anger" against the cruel torturers of Jesus.
C. All historically operant anti-Jewish stereotypes root in the Passion texts, in synergy with the picture of Jesus' crucifixion.
D. In the persecution of Jews, grown-up Christian children performed "just punishment" of Jesus' alleged torturers and reenacted the Jewish crime in the vain attempt to free themselves from the hurting impacts of their childhood encounter with the crucifix.
E. Muslim anti-Zionism, as resistence against a mainly Christian European project, builds on Christian imagery but is basically incomparable – a hopeful finding – with cross based Western antisemitism.

F. While the torture of the Lamb on Cross underlies the stereotype of Jews acting cruelly also towards animals, the rightlessness of objectified animals in western culture bases broadly on the reification of suffering in the wooden victim, on the function of the Lamb on Cross in atonement for human violence against animals, and on the absence of animal-friendly words in the New Testament – strongly contradicting the vegetarian Jesus whose last action tackled animal sacrifice.

G. Waiver of crucifixes will not only make this earth a more human place but also bring Christians closer to the rabbi and rebel Jesus bar Miriam bar Abbas who put children in the midst.

Anyone who would object the first thesis I'd like to ask where on this earth and at what point of its history a more awful, more cruel and more inhumane symbol existed.

The theses B to G are the main subject of this book, which has a strong relation with my biography. It is written with the passion of an educator who during three decades of teaching in public school used to start his didactic reflections with the question: How will children take it up? Therefore, and very naturally, this book starts with how children perceive the picture in Chapter 1: "Mommy, this man has boo-boo".

Reviewing this man's life is a precondition for deconstructing the symbol he is built into – a man-made symbol which developed its own dynamics from the beginning. Going back to the very beginning of his life, this book empathizes in biographical deepness and sympathizes on strictly human grounds with the man whose cruel death the sign reminds. The next four chapters focus on him and his suffering.

Chapter 2, "Born by Mary the victim", deduces from highly acknowledged sources that Jesus in his mother most probably was a victim of Roman soldiers from the beginning, before ...

Chapter 3, "Suffered under Pontius", describes how he again became a victim of Roman soldiers in the end. Searching for the authentic earthly Jesus the Son-of-Man, this book assesses all his words according to critical theologist Gerd Lüdemann's comprising work "Jesus after 2000 years", marking all words Lüdemann deems authentic by bold type, for instance "The Sabbath was made for humankind, and not humankind for the Sabbath" (**Mark 2:27**), a statement Lüdemann regards as characteristic for Jesus' Jewish and human thinking.

Chapter 4, "Crucified, died, overcome" about the practise and technique of crassly cruel crucifixion is necessary to realize what the children of this world, with their sensitive eyes and unhardened souls, suffer by pictures showing what this man had to suffer.

How could this expression of sadism transform to a symbol of salvation?

Chapter 5, "Revised by Paul" analyzes the newcomer apostle's seizure-born distortions of this Jesus he never knew and their lasting effect on this world.

Chapter 6, "And daily killed in kindergarten", investigating what the cruel eye-catching symbol triggers in mind and heart of children, is the pedagogical heart of this book, aptly followed and deepened by the subsequent ...

Chapter 7: "Paternal love", focused on the child's relation to the most important male person of his young life, a bond exemplified in the traumatical ties of many German sons with harshly educating fathers; ties that took effect in their later hate against the religion of the old divine father.

Chapter 8, "Roles of Character" illustrates how the plastic and dramatic presentation of mankinds most cruel and most-displayed execution became the starting point for all established anti-Jewish stereotypes, before ...

Chapter 9, "Chosen" shows how the secular racism of modernity sprang from the inquisitorial *limpieza de sangre* statutes aiming at the chosen-victim people.

Chapter 10 is titled "Reenactments" since it reviews the bloody replays by which European children tried to act out their childhood imprints, stretching from the first child-crucifixion ascribed to Herod's people up to the reenactment of cross-way station No.10 "Jesus is robbed his clothes" with Jewish men, women, children as naked as the crucified rabbi.

Chapter 11, "The cross is the nerve" shows that beneath the surface of political correctness Germany's well-hibernated anti-Judaism is enhanced by a secondary antisemitism that will never pardon the Jews for Auschwitz, and protected by a taboo on its religious roots which, for instance, have a liberal Munich newspaper rather falsify a Jewish actress's memory of classroom mobbing than trespass political cross correctness.

Chapter 12 ("Cruzionists") attempts to prove the following four theses:
- Middle-Eastern Jew-hate is generally a European export in various product lines;
- Europe's import of Holy Land news corresponds to the continent's key images;
- Muslim anti-Zionism quotes Christian imagery but differs crucially (a hopeful outlook) from Christian Jew-hate;
- Zionism is mainly an occidental project and endangers Judaism.

Chapter 13, "The Lamb on cross" starts from the place of animals in Rabbi Jesus' religious tradition that still in our days keeps being rated as cruel to animals; and it ends with their place in a Western culture bone-deeply informed by the salutary slaughter of a Holy Lamb and its objectivation as a wooden soulless entity of sacrifice for man's sake.

Chapter 14 presents a very modern Passion Play enacted by a corrupt Roman media Caesar: The Strasbourg Passion, a Kafkaesque court performance which legalized state ordered crucifixes in all European classrooms.

Finally, the "Exam: Why Johanna fed him vanilla cake and other child's play questions" resumes the book in poignant questions to failing theologians, returning to its first and foremost subjects: children.

Before the attempted final solution, German historian Theodor Mommsen classified antisemitism as "a horrible epidemic, like cholera – one can nei-

ther explain nor cure it": After Shoah, survivor Esther Jungreis opined that "we mortals have no way of comprehending why, for it is only in retrospect – sometimes not even in our lifetime – that people can hope to gain a glimmer of understanding."[1]
I dispute this inability with the same argument Yehuda Bauer uses: If the Shoah was committed by human beings, human beings can find out why. And like John Weiss I emphasize how fatal incomprehension would be: Incomprehensible means inevitable.[2] How humans could assume that an accusative and stark cruel symbol would not result in cruelty is hard to understand; that it did so is easy to grasp. "Let violence be far from things" the great educator Jan Amos Comenius demanded 300 years ago, urging that violence be far from education. Today we all know how decisive the experiences, learning processes and images of early childhood are. One must not be a media designer to know how efficiently images work psychologically. What I do in this book is viewing childhood vulnerability synoptically together with visual power and millennial evidence, leading to insights that for the sake of human society should not be ignored. The "crucial task" in historical and psychological inquiry is always, "to lay bare the roots", says Yerushalmi, adding: "Truth is often very improbable."[3] The crucifix as cause of *"sei miglione crocifissione"* in the honestly disclosing words of Pope John XXIII, seems improbable only to those who still underrate the power of early learning.
Those who shun books about Shoah because the theme is scaring are right in their feeling, but the crucifix is scaring daily. Those who suggest we should stop reminding Auschwitz and those things should question a crucifix industry that daily reminds a barbaric crime committed two millennia ago that on grounds of falsified accusations led to millionfold crime. Those who denounce a "holocaust industry" should question a crucifix industry whose best customers are European public schools and kindergartens.
Nowhere in this book I ask the reader to believe me and I won't do that also in the following assertion: This is a thoroughly religious book – since the term *religio* is not derived from *religare*, to link back (in this case believers would have *religatio*), but from *relegere*, to read again, consider, pay attention. My old Latin dictionary defines the term *religio* by the first notions "scruples, doubt, concern" and illustrates its meaning by the locution *religioni mihi est*, that is, to make something a matter of conscience. To warn against dangers in public space – for instance a hole in the sidewalk – is a civil duty. How could I, as an educator who researched the deep dangers of this picture during two decades now answer for not writing this book? "Indeed you said you suffer from not being able to help Jesus down from the cross" my school director disclosed triumphantly, in front of forty colleagues. Well, I admit, its true. I've always been a *sensibelchen*. However:

---

1 As to Mommsen: Pulzer, Peter G.: The Rise of Political Anti-Semitism in Germany and Austria. New York 1969, p.299 (quoted by Perry/Schweitzer, p.107); Jungreis: 2006, p. 243.
2 Weiss 1997, Preface, p.ix.
3 Yerushalmi, p.17.

"Who lends me a ladder?" Generations of Marranos sang this line knowing well that helping Jesus down would bring Jew-hate down, and in vain Frank Andermann after Auschwitz promised his Jesus: "I'll take you down one day. I'll help you down from the cross of shame."[4] Though Andermann's and Riggenmann's strong sympathies for the rebel won't draw out those nails he has to hang on, the reader will notice that many faithful Christians are looking for ladder and pincers already, in step with Irving Greenberg's insight "that the religion that is most able to correct itself is the one that will prove itself to be most true."[5]

The most successful one, however, is the cross religion, and cross-shaped were in 1600 the mighty vanes of windmills in the land of crypto-Jew Cervantes, and all the more appreciative might the reader be wherever in the 14 chapters of this quixotic book the wind has happened to blow in a Jewish joke. Recall, for instance, the Jewish master tailor who finds his monied modern thinking customer in a slightly disgruntled mood when he delivers his made-to-measure trousers after ten days instead of one week as arranged. "Well, didn't your God make a whole world within one week?" – "Well, look at the world, and look at these trousers!"

---

4 Andermann, p.43.
5 Greenberg 2004, p.145.

I   Mommy this man has boo-boo

On a playground in a German town, during the 1920s.
"My mummy said I shouldn't play with you, Sarah."
"Why not?"
"Mummy says you Jews have killed good Jesus."
Sarah drops her sand-filled cake-pan and runs home furious. Ten
minutes later she's back. "Listen, Peter. I didn't do it, Mummy
didn't do it, Daddy didn't and Aunt Betty didn't do it anyway. It
must have been the Cohns from second floor."

While this book is about the crazyness of adults and great men of world history, its kingpins are children from A to Z, from Sarah with the cake-tin to Johanna with vanilla cake; it focuses on the question how they experience the cast metal or wood-carved issue "Jesus crucified"; what they learn at this icon and how it mints their minds.

Exactly this was what I asked myself when I, in late summer 1993, prepared my classroom for my future third grade pupils: a reading corner with couch, self made pinewood bookshelves, colorful pictures. On the side wall, above the door, hung the obligatory cross: dark beams with carved corpus and painted blood. I took a pupil's chair, sat down right in front of the sculpture and asked myself: What's this symbol giving to my pupils? – "Surely nothing positive" was my answer after long consideration. I took down the death symbol, went home, pasted a beautiful poster from Misereor (a Catholic third-world solidarity NGO) on a pinewood panel: two hands, one white, one black, sharing bread in front of the blue planet. This, I opined, could visualize Christian human ethics much more adequately to my children than the picture of an execution.

Wrong by far. Next spring, one day a pupil, on behalf of his classmates, addressed me about replacing the bread-sharing hands by the crucifix. "But tell me why", I answered, quite perplexed. "Cause the Jesus may help us during math tests" was their only one halfway non-theological answer. We sat down in a circle, listened to one another, and but now I recognized their teacher of Catholic religion, the village parson of Pfaffenhofen, as their request's initiator. Bewildered by their earnest, perceptibly coached reasonings I didn't want either to display my knowledge nor to infringe my duty of religious neutrality. Let's vote. A clear majority, one steadfast young dissident, one "I-don't-mind" Turkish Alevite, one French girl whose parents told me later how alienated they felt when they nevertheless had let their daughter vote with the foreseeable majority. I took down the bread-sharing hands and hung up the nailed-on-wood hands. And since the wooden Jesus during his sojourn in the cabinet had lost his right hand, I told my pupils about a crucifix that had lost both arms during a bombing raid and after the war was accompanied by a signboard saying "I have no hands but yours". However, the parson's successful intervention via pupils' votes had

shocked me. The question got a hold on me: How do children see the man on the cross? Only now I realized that this crucifix indeed was ordained by public school regulations: a manifest offence against our constitution, but tolerable to my opinion at least insofar as "the Nazis", so we were told, had tried to remove crucifixes from public schools.

Two years later I saw the word "Kruzifix" in bright sunshine, in the headlines of half a dozen German newspapers at a news-stand. By strange coincidence this news-stand was exactly within the former Jewish ghetto of Prague. The journals reported a judgement of German Constitutional Court, in favour of Bavarian family Seler: "The mounting of a cross or crucifix in the teaching-rooms of a state-run obligatory school that is not a denominational school, offends article 4 of Basic Law."

My goodness! The German state of rights, I thought, is working still! I took the next train home to support the Supreme Court's judgement that was under heavy fire already. The shortest one of my letters to the editor had only three sentences: "When the Nazis wanted to remove the crosses from the classrooms, a stormwind of outrage aroused among Bavarian population. The crosses remained. Removed were the Jewish pupils."

In December 1995 the Christian-conservative majority in Bavarian *Landtag* parliament passed a new law that clears everything yet in its first sentence: "In every classroom a cross is to be mounted." Surely, this law admits exceptions in case of "serious objection". I applied, with 22 pages of serious objection, for the removal of the crucifix in my classroom. Munich ministry of education replied with a circular, stating that, different from parents, teachers were not entitled to objection. Tongue-in-cheek, however, officials told me: "You surely can sue". For which Bavarian teacher would dare to sue against the holy picture?

"Don't you have better pastimes?" This was the final question of the presiding judge at Augsburg administrative court, his jury having rejected my claim for detaching tortured Jesus, albeit recognizing my "credible and convincing" rationale. I led my class of teenagers to their final exams in summer 1998, took a one year grant leave, made my M.A. in Pedagogy; and when the court still delayed my trial, I continued with my PhD including a 479 pages thesis about John Dewey's influence in Brazilian education. And while the court still had no time for my case I found an editor for my 448 pages book about *Kruzifix und Holocaust*.

In December 2001 finally, when the authorities had not achieved to drop me out of the proceedings neither by patient starving nor by a tricky order of relocation, I won at the appeal court amidst of Munich. "Church is Raging" the tabloid Bild-Zeitung headlined, and "*Der Mann muss raus, raus, raus!*" the Christian Party's secretary general ranted on TV, urging to bump this man out of school. Almost daily now the postman delivered new murder threats, apt to correct the court's outrageous judgement that, by way of exception, had conceded to me, being classified as an "atypical singular case", the right to teach in a cross-free classroom. What made me "atypical" was my "intense Christian faith", the judges claimed. I protested against

this distortion that pigeonholed me with the anonymous bigots who urged me to shove off, but the presiding judge replied that there was "no space" for changing the judgement's text, and maybe I could find comfort, Judge Thomas wrote, in the fact that the court itself had received "letters of likely reviling content". Anyhow, besides of the psychologically interesting insults and menaces I received by phone and mailbox or while walking or bicycling in my home district, I also got strong support by courageous Christians. For instance by Munich resident grandmother Lisa Wanninger, who told me in her letter:

"Only when, some 15 years ago, my then **three-year-old grandson** viewing a wayside cross with the crucified one asked me: 'Grandma, does this not hurt that man?' I became aware of what barbaric symbol I often had admired in Gothic style, Baroque et cetera. And what this symbol causes in tender souls of children. I thank you very much for your engagement and your refractoriness against this inhuman sign."

Obviously, Grandma Lisa understood how a child tries to grip this sign internally: What's that – a man – naked but has kind of pants okay – hands up, clings on this bar – but can see all fingers so how can he hold fast and does not slip off – why? – must look closer ... Oops! – Grandma ...

Strong support also, for example, by parson Ludwig Dallmeier, not the only one Bavarian cleric who sympathized with me. He had removed the big black crucifix from his Catholic kindergarten already before the scandal that my Munich judgement triggered, and after it he dared to go public. "Crucified One Undue to Children" Munich tabloid tz quoted him in its headline.[6] "It is the brutal presentation of a maltreated man" he explained to the readers and pointed to his key moment four years before "when one of the nurses of the kindergarten told him that the little ones are afraid of the crucified one". His courageous confession created a stir; he asked me for my juridical reasoning and wrote back that during reading it "the scales fell from my eyes ... Yes, as a child (I was born in 1940) I viewed the Jews as murderers of the Godson! ... For decads I didn't recall these feelings of my childhood, also cannot remember my school lessons in religion, but this my dislike for the Jews now suddenly was so present to me as if all happened just yesterday!" The parson annexed supportive letters he had received as replies to his reader's letter which Dingolfing Journal had published under the heading "Must it be a cross absolutely?" Here a schools inspector calls the parson's courage a "sign of hope", there a school director grants him his staff's support, while a teacher of religion agrees completely to his opinion: "Da muss mehr Leben rein!" (We must get more life into that!). And an observant Catholic lady told him: "As one of the attending mothers I was close by when during rehearsal for Thanksgiving celebration a **Greek kindergarten child** suffered a shock when she saw the crucified one for the first time! The girl just cried and cried and no one could calm her, she was in panic really! ... Why is there a dead man being prayed to in the churches?

---

6   Tz München (Munich tabloid daily), January 19/20, 2002, p.1.

... Your words in the article, saying 'it is the brutal presentation of a tortured man', I emphasize completely!!!"

A case for the child therapist? "Kruzifix, Kind, Angst" – by this keyword combination, google presented the following childish questions reported by their helpless parents; questions of little ones having come to this planet just two or three years ago:

"Hello Mummies, **my daughter (two-and-a-half-year-old)** frequents kindergarten since September. Having been with a day care mother before, she was accustomed to being attended by other women. But since she goes to kiga she always says in the morning that she's afraid of the big cross in kiga. The "man with the nails" gives her a fright. Meanwhile I don't know any more whether I should react and what I should say to begin with. They definitely won't remove it because of her. All my appeasements and explanations just come out making it more serious. I have to add that the cross in kiga is truly a monstrous ugly thing in two-meter-size and hanging exactly on children's eye level (with a real Christ figure). As a small child I probably would be frightened by such an item, too. Can anyone give me advice how I should deal with my child? Whose child has fear of crosses, too?" ("huxe 91", on netmoms.de)
Remark: When a child of two and a half years is frightened so strongly by the nails in Jesus' hands, we may suppose that this child has already watched how one drives nails into wood. This handwork – one of the first "true adult" tasks children try themselves – stands out for children as an archetype of handicraft and of physical force: trying to drive with noisy hewing, striking, hitting, knocking, beating a sharp metal pin into flesh-like brown material. And you'll hurt yourself badly if you fail the nail and hit your thumb.

"Hallo and a beautiful Saturday afternoon altogether. Somehow you're already wont you should be well prepared to always have in stock some sense giving answers to a **three-and-a-half-year-old daughter**. But yesterday she had us seriously challenged by her question why Jesus hangs on the cross and why he bleeds? And this just 5 minutes before sleeping time!" (Mac, on chefkoch.de/forum)
Instead of giving advice to daddy Mac, forum user Syldron adds own memories: "I still remember how **my little brother** was afraid of the cross in the bedroom when we were visiting our Catholic relatives. Fortunately, we didn't have to visit them so often."

"**My granddaughter is four years old** and has angst of the crucifix", writes grandmother Christa who was born in 1939. "The church in our neighborhood has a big cross outside. She refuses to pass by that site saying she's afraid of the crucifix. She cries because the man is aching and bleeds. How can I explain that to her, child-adequately? Greetings, Christa.

Grandma Christa's question triggers a debate between a mother with high emotional IQ but modest diction who calls herself SubsTanz and a more rational, more eloquent man who chose the codename Adept.

SubsTanz: "I once had this problem myself and could understand my child easily. In rather all churches there hangs a cross on which hangs a tortured man. ... There's no legal protection of the young with regard to such images and stories. The man is hanging there with nails in hands and feet that have been rammed through his flesh. Would you confront your granddaughter regularly with a picture showing an almost naked woman hanged on a tree by other humans, fixed cruelly by nails? Imagine this through a child's eyes! Why don't we show this to our children of three or four years? Perhaps because this is not a religious picture but only a sadistic one?"

Adept: "According to Christian conviction the one who was nailed to the cross has overcome death, too. So no one has to be afraid of him."

SubsTanz: "Aha, guess I got it ... and that's why you may show to children this picture and not the picture of the tortured woman."

Adept: "You surely know that crosses are art works whose effects are not comparable to a real scene by any means. In the cross representation the crucified one is by no means the man of suffering only, but also already the conqueror of death, this being expressed formally in his upright position fixed on the cross. For Christians, the reality of the cross is bearable by the reality of resurrection. To someone who doesn't share the faith in resurrection I wouldn't recommend to confront his children with the death on cross.

SubsTanz: "Oha ... so if the parents are pious, children can bear it. If they are not pious, it makes the children afraid and they suffer too much in feeling with him?"

Adept: "If parents are pious, they should be able to tell their children something about cross and resurrection. One may even assume that atheistic or non-Christian minded parents will be able to familiarize their children with their own view of the Christians' symbol. I can't grasp the advantage of styling oneself or one's offspring as victims in this regard. Or do you have a victim-complex?"

SubsTanz: "Laughlaugh, no. As to complexes, I don't have any, but a victim of Catholic Church I for sure have been. Once I had to kneel down at the altar for punishment and pray the Our Father ten times with the crucified Jesus before my eyes who injected more than angst into me, cause I was a **sensibelchen**, I had so much compassion with the poor man and also disgust because this crown of thorns still stuck in his head and the blood ran over his dying face. Those nails in hands and feet, I always tried to avert my look from them. I refused to look at them and that's how it started ... If you shun, [he said] you will be punished severely for your sins in hell and so on and so on ... and when he menaced that if my parents would not come to church more often they too would be punished, after that I gave in and did it ... And now, would you show a picture of a woman nailed on a tree, to a child of four years, and explain to her: She suffers for you and your sins? I also might put the question whether one should nail a child to a tree and show that to

another child. Hard thought, isn't it? Such cruel things one shouldn't even think about, right? I don't give up. (Nov. 4-8, 2011, spin.de/forum).

I do hope this mother will not give in anymore like she was forced to in her childhood; no matter if the mainstream keeps smiling at those squeamish sensibelchen who suffer by the sight of crosses. Are they such queer and rare exceptions really? A cautious approach to this question is given by German Wilhelm-Griesinger-Institut in a web text in which I mark the quantitative aspect by italics:

"*Many adults* report that they themselves at the age of three or four years were afraid of crosses they had seen in a church or in the house of relatives who had crosses on their walls. For *most people*, the cross is a Christian symbol standing for the resurrection [sic!] of Jesus Christ. Since younger children *mostly* don't dispose of the religious background, *far from rarely* the cross represents something uncanny and threatening to them, all the more so if the cross contains a Jesus-figure that visualizes the sufferings of Christ. This childlike angst of crucifixes might *not at all events* be understandable for adults, because to them it is an everyday religious symbol. There is *not much use* in minimizing the child's fear saying 'Jesus protects you' or the like, because *for children* it is not understandable in their world that someone of whom they don't have any more detailed knowledge and who suffers visibly on the cross should protect them. The fear of crosses however vanishes *mostly* by itself when the children are grown somewhat older and have understood the religious background of cross and crucifixion at least roughly."

Remark: In physics nothing vanishes; it but transforms.

How childhood crosses may cause late after effects on sensitive, intelligent adults is revealed by a **student of pharmacy**, who relates his case on the psychological website "suite101.de". His dream sequence might represent uterus (cavern) and phallus (crucifix), but more concisely it appears to stage the sequence in Catholic creed, where the *born of ...* is followed immediately by the *suffered under ...*

"I have such terrible nightmares. They come to me since my childhood: I live in a big cavern. All around me is darkness only. In far distance I see a small light. Suddenly I feel that I am fastened on a cross and see terrible figures approaching me. They scourge me hard. There's a chain put across my face. I feel helpless and have terrible angst of those merciless figures' strokes. I wake up with my heart beating excitedly and have to start finding my way in the darkness before I realize that I am lying in my bed."

I cited this student's case as an example of long term cross effects on sensitive, intelligent adults – since I want to encourage the reader to practise civil courage, that is, not to be afraid of appearing as a fearful hypersensitive. Concerning the relation of intelligence and sensitivity, Kierkegaard stated yet in 1848 very shortly: "The less intellect, the less fear."[7] Andrea Brackmann stresses the "strong feeling of justice" and the "pronounced delicacy"

---

7 Kierkegaard: "Der Begriff Angst"; in: Kierkegaard 1982, p.377.

of highly gifted children. Two examples: "If **Ina** witnesses how someone is treated unjustly, she is so bewildered and afflicted that she does not recover for a long time, remaining all churned up inside, unhinged and terrified." – "In kindergarten there was spoken about Easter and Holy Friday. By the fact that Jesus was crucified, **Ben** was so appalled that he cried again and again during the holidays, asking 'Why did Jesus have to die?'"[8]

This does not mean that only highly gifted children suffer by crucifixes. My former pupil Stefan Gassner told me about his work as educator in a special school for mentally handicapped children: "Once **Karin** told me: 'This Jesus I don't like.'" Karin's Jesus is the crucified one who, hanging tacid in the classroom, is meant to explain also to mentally disabled children how nailing a man on beams has brought salvation to mankind. Who, actually, is disabled here?

1847: "**Children who hardly can stammer a word**", a Christian mother complains, "learn to detest the name *Juden* like a demon", and very early they are taught "that those nasty *Juden* had nailed the Lord on the cross."[9]

1893: **Little Dov Berkovitz** had, like all Jewish children in Poland, been inculcated to turn his face away at every roadside crucifix, not to have his eyes defiled by the idol. But one day he wants to know it – and turns his face to it! "What's that to mean? Is that he? ... The impression was ... uncanny, terrifying in its strangeness ... But then a peasant on a horse-cart came passing by, stopped and made the cross-sign on his body. When he saw me standing there, he uttered a curse and tried to hit me with his whip."[10]

1925: **Little Michael**, son of a Nobel-Prize awarded novelist, was afraid of the little man hanging on the cross. Had this fear to do with the Jewish ancestors of his mother, or even of his father's Brazilian mother? Anyhow, the time-proven German "child-must-cope-with" therapy went this way: "The crucified naked one the father nailed above the pillow of his bed, explaining that 'this is part and parcel of our western culture and the boy has to get used to this'."[11] It is the boy's sister Elisabeth who remembers this educational act. Her brothers Michael and Klaus died by suicide: too soft for this cross-world puzzle or for this German father Thomas Mann?

1938: **Little Victor**, a descendant from the many Pereiras who escaped Spanish inquisition, grew up in Guatemala cosseted by his seventeen-year-old

---

8   Brackmann, p.22, 48 and 59.
9   Erika Weinzierl: Stereotype christlicher Judenfeindschaft; in: Jüdisches Museum, Die Macht der Bilder, p.131.
10 Lapide 1985, p.17.
11 Roggenkamp, p.125. Viola Roggenkamp supposes that the masculine body with its "loose loincloth" could "signify something homosexual" to the bisexual Thomas Mann. Of course this aspect for viewers of both sexes is taboo. See also the chapter "Kruzifixus" in Michael Degen's novel about the Mann family (Familienbande, Reinbek 2011, p.11-21).

nanny: "Chata, a Catholic Maya from a highland village of Cobán, was determined to save my Jewish soul from perdition; she often sneaked me into the cathedral, where she had me kneel at the foot of the crucified Christ and recite the Ave Maria. My senses reeled from the mingled scents of incense and Chata's blouse as she pressed her firm breasts against the back of my neck; this was her way of allaying my fright of the terrifying naked figure on the cross."[12]

In 1967 she had been **a girl of four years**, the teacher of arts and mother of two daughters who told me in 2002 that back then she used to view the holy cards in her mother's prayer-book nosily. "One picture ... stuck deeply in my mind: the punctures of the crown of thorns, the pierced hands with fingers bent in pain, the face streaming with blood. I could not fall asleep then. My mother took that for theater, but she wouldn't let me view the holy cards again. Actually I felt very much pity with Jesus Christ and big guilt at the same time because he had died 'for us'. Sometimes when we were too noisy in our children's bedroom I had to sleep in my parents' bedroom, but there hung a crucifix above the bed. Stylized indeed, but it instantly reminded me on the cruel holy card and all came up again. I started crying but my mother thought it was for the chuck. When I recently asked my mother about this childhood experience, she opined that back then she had taken down the crucifix so I could fall asleep. But even after she had taken down the cross, it had kept haunting me so much that I pressed away the wrinkles in the feather bed because in their round arch form they reminded me on Mary the mother, as I sketched her with four or five years, and on the fate (?) of her son."

1970: "I can remember from a very early age the experience of being in a church – I must have been about five years old – and when I looked up to the cross, I was very aware that I was struggling in my acceptance of Jesus as God. I was afraid of Jesus on the cross. I was afraid of it because it was very graphic, but it was my secret and I kept it to myself." The little girl chose the name **Shlomit** years later when she converted to Judaism.[13]

1985: Housewife Terry Kallet was more than astonished when one day her son **Nathan** at age three came home from preschool and said, "Protect me from Daddy!" I said, "Why, why, what happened?" His preschool teacher had told him that the Jews killed Jesus and that Jesus was the son of a Jew. "So my own son went home thinking that because his father was Jewish and he was the son of a Jew, therefore Daddy was going to kill him. This whole conversation happened while I was preparing a seder!"[14]

---

12 Perera, p.231.
13 Myrowitz, p.193.
14 Myrowitz, p.72. The Seder is the dinner table celebration on the eve of Passover, with the children's active participation.

1993: "For as long as someone is not allowed to see something, he will have to overlook, misunderstand, to ward it off in any way", says Jewish-Polish born Swiss psychotherapist Alice Miller.[15] The same surname bore the faithful Catholic carpenter **A. Miller** at whose local saw mill I bought some roof laths for theatre sidescenes when he, by no perceivable motive, went on telling me a story that visibly lay on his heart: "'Take that crucifix out of this room', the young woman said when she came to the hospital for delivery. 'I don't want my baby have to look at that when it comes to this world', she said. And when the baby had come to world, it was – blind!"
May I interpret the unsaid feelings of this loving father and grandfather A. Miller this way: "The cross is awful. But God wants it. And woe to those who avert their eyes"?

2001: Preparing for the trial in Munich, the Bavarian government's attorney had reproached me for reasoning "pedagogically", this being "not the plaintiff's task" since pedagogical reasoning is "unfit to support his legal claim". So as a teacher I have the duty to act pedagogically responsible but not the right to?

2010: The far from revolutionary staff and director of Röfingen primary school, near Suebian town Günzburg decided to remove a huge crucifix from the entrance hall because its view was "not bearable for first and second grade children". The scandal was made public by the parson during Corpus Christi holiday procession; only the director and one female teacher resisted the ensuing pressings. In a web forum, a mother of 40 years who describes herself under the codename **Dembara** as "Roman-Catholic, conservative", comments the pedagogical issue: "My son (3 years) needs a crucifix to recognize the person Jesus. If Jesus is represented another way my boy is in trouble because he doesn't know the Bible already. I never noticed him being especially shocked by bleeding Jesus. However, yes, it's true: I know churches which, due to numerous presentations of martyrs, really resemble a chamber of torture more than a holy room. But I also think truth may be required to put up with. I think that 99.9 percent of all crucifixes are a more than embellished presentation of this torture technique and thus one may suppose they are endurable even for children. A crucifix is grotesque only if one doesn't know what it means. In this case Christendom suddenly looks like a sadomaso chamber. But because 'earlier on' ordinary people knew why Jesus is presented this way, they had no problems with it. Today there are many who even don't know that Jesus is a historical person. Thus, the crucifix inevitably becomes an evil torture-fairytale, à la Hansel and Gretel. So, it's not as important to redesign the crucifixes in a more harmless style or to fade them out than rather to point people to the backgrounds of this presentation. For, behind the cross", Dembara knows, "is standing our *redemption*" – whatever this final word, and final image, may mean to children.

---

15 Miller 1983, p.24.

Does her son understand redemption? How should a girl age two, a boy age three like Dembara's son, a first grader age six be able to integrate this Pauline concept into his innocent, young, vulnerable outlook on this world? And if all the children cited in this small sample are more sensitive than average – who would be that naïve to say that the more robust children will simply overlook the hurting man, storing no tiny trace of him in their innermost? And when all these children, those with fine aerials as well as the overlookers – have accustomed to the sight: everything's OK then? Or will the "man-with-nails-emoticon" remain stored in the amygdale, every nail and thorn working as a synapse ready to transmit an electric impulse whenever the child, the adult, the aged one will hear the name of those Jews who racked this man with nails and thorns?

Considering this man's life and death, surveying all the facts and falsities around his globally displayed ordeal, we should walk the humble but honest way Hyam Maccoby suggests for reconstructing the historical Jesus (and his brother Judas): "We have to read between the lines in the documents that are available to us, catching hints from passages that seem to have survived from earlier accounts. This enquiry is not merely academic and theoretical. It helps us understand how myths arise, and it helps to dispel prejudices still remaining from myth-derived indoctrination. Even if we are left finally with a question-mark and a theory that reaches only to the probable, we nevertheless strengthen the rational approach that aims primarily to the probable, and eschews the bigoted certainty of minds imbued with myth and fantasy."[16]

Paixão de Cristo: During a passion play in a small Brazilian town an ignorant child, spontaneously succouring Jesus, disrupts the studied drama by his true, childishly active compassion (*compaixão*).

---

16   Maccoby 1992, p.128.

II   Born of the victim Mary

"Tremble, Jews!" exclaimed the monk,
"fear the God whom you with scourges,
with a crown of thorns have tortured
whom into his death you've chasen.

His murderers, revengeful people,
That's what you have been, the Juden –
Always do you kill the Saviour
Him who comes for you, redeeming ... " Heinrich Heine, Disputation

Heine's monk describes the one who makes Jews tremble in a triple way: as God, as redeeming Saviour – and as victim of the Jews.
Only one of these roles was ascribed to Jesus by the Ebionites, this early Christian community led by people who must have known the ropes: Jesus' biological relatives. To them, their crucified brother, uncle, great uncle was just "the Righteous One (saddiq), the only man who has completely fulfilled the law [and therefore] been appointed to be the Christ ... 'If another man likewise would have fulfilled the precepts of the law, he too would have become Christ'" as reports Church Father Hippolytus (ca.170-235). "Jesus, moreover, fulfilled the law as man, not as Son of God (*huios theou*) but as Son of man (*huios anthrópou*). He was consecrated for Messiahship and endowed with the power of God not through real preexistence but through the act of adoption which was announced in Psalm 2:7 ..."[17]
In this psalm verse, God Himself affirms "You are My Son, I have fathered you this day" towards the same King David to whom he elsewhere promises "I will be a father to him, and he will be a son to me"; the same King David who will answer him in another psalm: "You are my father, my God, the rock of my deliverance" (Ps 2:7; 2 Sm 7:14; Ps 89:27).
This King of the people that in Exodus 4:22 is called "my firstborn son" by Yahve himself and "children of Yahve Elohim" in Deuteronomy 14:1, this royal ancestor of Jesus however is not regarded as a "genuine" Son of God by any Christian or Jew. The most appropriate answer to the question when and where Yahve sired His Son with the Virgin would be: about 50 CE, shortly before Damascus, in the head of Saul. This eager tracker of the Christian sect by order of the Sadduceans during his investigation surely had gained and gathered all information available (place of birth, father, mother, brothers ... ?) concerning Jesus. All this huddled and mingled in Saul's head, together with all the myths of divine sons provided by his Greek education, those famous Osiris, Attis and Adonis, Heracles and Dionysus. Note that these self-sacrificing sons of mystery religions were "all human-divine figures. Frequently the necessary mixture of human and divine in the sacrifice was achieved by the arrangement that one parent of the victim was

---

17 Schoeps 1969, p.61, referring to the Church Fathers Origenes, Epiphanius and Hippolytos.

human and the other divine."[18] All those pied parts for a patchwork-myth garment just had to be sewn together and put onto the naked man on cross who used to talk so much about his father. The sewing happened some miles before Damascus, when suddenly the glinty needle or rather "a light from heaven flashed around him", Saul heard a voice and fell to the ground blind (Acts 9:3), but three days later the scales fell from his eyes (9:18) and Saul, now having romanized himself as Paul, proclaimed in synagogues that "this one be the Son of God" (9:20).

Why exactly this one?

Before Paul, never in the 1800-years-biography of Yahve Elohim, the invisible, unseizable "I will be who I will be" (Ex 3:14) had anybody tried to link Him to attitudes of the kind the Greeks enjoyed to tell about their Zeus, who himself was a son of Cronos and father of many a semi-divine offspring of his diverse earthly love affairs.

To ascribe such things to Yahve obviously was difficult to Paul the Jew. To the Romans he wrote yet in the letter's first sentence that Jesus "was descended from David according to the flesh", but to the Galatians he specified with new formula (4:4) that "when the fullness of time had come, God sent his son, born of a woman". Fifteen years later, the first gospel knows nothing about a virgin Mary but describes the Nazarene's "act of adoption" as Son of God à la David in quite an Ebionite way: "And a voice came from heaven, 'You are my Son, the Beloved ...'" (Mark 1:11). Again fifteen years later Matthew and Luke relate the Saviour's virgin origin in two very different conception narratives which agree in few more details than that, in Matthew's words, "the child conceived in her is from the Holy Spirit" (1:20). From their simultaneous but obviously independent narrations, Reza Aslan concludes that "the tradition of the virgin birth was an early one, perhaps predating the first gospel, Mark."[19]

Aslan is right, of course: The "early one" is Paul's vision which became prevalent here after three decades of tradition.

In this world of causality, nothing comes by chance. Were there, in the Nazarene's CV that Paul had studied eagerly, any odd indices propitious to see in him the son of super-natural begetting? Was there a thread in his biography fitting and robust enough to sew up the strange Greek-Hebrew couture design?

There were. In the sixth chapter of the earliest gospel, written probably in Rome around 70 CE by a non-Jewish Roman named Mark, the former neighbors of Jesus in Nazareth ask themselves: "Isn't he the carpenter, the son of Mary and a brother of James, Joses, Judas and Simon?"

Son of Mary? No father mentioned? Every Jew then had it clearly: Oops, an illegitimate. And at that, his brothers, one, two, three, four counted and still he is just son-of-mother?

Fast forward: "If my good friend Dr Gasparri says a curse word against my mother, he can expect a punch. It's normal. It's normal. You cannot pro-

---

18 Maccoby 1992, p.171.
19 Aslan, p.36.

voke."[20] The man who would defend his mother's honor so manly is Latin American Pope Jorge Mario Bergoglio. He made this comment referring to the twelve journalists of French satirical magazine Charlie Hebdo who however didn't die by punches and not because they insulted someone's mother. Which curse word could the good Dr Gasparri have said to make Pope Francis lose his temper? Or which insult could hit all honest men more deeply, if applied to the one female person to which their whole life refers from its very beginning? *Figlio di troia! Son of a bitch! Filho da Puta!*

Of course, nowhere in the gospels Jesus is called a son of a bitch, at least not directly. And let me state my view already at this point very clearly: He was no harlot's son and his very honest mother was, just like Pope Francis' mother, never a whore, hooker, harlot, prostitute or whatever vulgarism men have coined for those usable despicables. But: What would be so inacceptable in that? Let's remember that Jesus' predecessor Moses, the *"meshiakh fun knekht"* (messiah from slavery)[21] was the by-drifted child of an illicit sexual relation (Ex 6:20) between aunt and nephew; that the incest between Lot and his daughters (Genesis 19) is a detail of the Messiah's pedigree; that the Messiah's low birth was the essence of Luke's manger story. And let's recall, on the following pages, that Matthew's gospel points to no less than four "disreputable" grandmothers of Messiah Son of David, exactly in Mary's genealogy.

Matthew: Jesus' great mothers

"Book of descendance of Jesus Christ, the Son of David, the Son of Abraham: Abraham begot ..." and so on. This passage (Matthew 1), presenting the transition from the "Old Bible" to the "New Testament", counts down 40 old ancestors of Jesus. But scanning this congregation of long-bearded patriarchs exactly, five female headscarfs gleam among them:
"Judah begat Perez and Zerah by Tamar ..."
"Salmon begat Boaz by Rahab ..."
"Boaz begat Jobed by Ruth ..."
"David begat Solomon by the wife of Uriah ..." whose name was Bathseba.
"Jacob begot Joseph the husband of Mary, of whom was born Jesus, who is called Christ" (Matthew 1, verse 16). The husband of Mary who elsewhere and doctrinally rates but as Jesus' stepfather is here the indispensable link in the genealogical chain from Abraham to Mary's son. So was Jesus begot by Joseph ben Jacob? No, for immediately after the whole chain of ancestry follows the disclaimer: "When his mother Mary was betrothed to Joseph, it happened that she, before they lived together, had conceived from the Holy Spirit" (Matthew 1, verse 18). Here Joseph is definitely not the natural father, having not yet lived together with Mary.

---

20   Polly Toynbee, "On Charlie Hebdo Pope Francis is using the wife-beater's defence". The Guardian, January 16, 2015.
21   Avrom Reisen / Michl Gelbart: Shvimt dos kestl afn taykh. In: Shura Lipovsky: Moments of Jewish Life (CD), Schiedam, Netherlands, 1992.

26

Textual contradiction or careless edition? One shouldn't take Matthew, the probably only Jewish one of four gospel authors, for silly. Of course he was completely conscious of the contradiction within one and the same chapter of his text. Completely consciously he had copied the line of David's forefathers from the first book of Chronicle (1-2) and modified the line of David's offspring to get to a neat three-fold symmetry of 14 generations up to David, 14 up to Babylon and 14 from Babylon to Jesus – provided, however, that Mary is counted as a man's equivalent. Matthew's new edition is completely intentional. But what is his intention? Did he, who "writes among Jews for Jews"[22] intend to hint his Jewish readers, by introducing the four Davidian grandmothers, at an open secret in his Jewish ambience, a vital biographic detail of the fifth Jewish mother, Mary of Nazareth? What detail this might be, we can find out by taking a close look at the four uncommon women Tamar, Rahab, Ruth, Bathseba, those special mothers Matthew deemed worthy to stand in line with 40 virile patriarchs.

Tamar screws the chief: Jacob's fourth son Judah had migrated to Canaan and become the husband of the Canaanite woman Shua in mixed marriage. She bare him three sons named Er, Onan and Shelah, who grew up to – so he hoped – give Judah grandsons, and "Judah took for his firstborn Er a woman named Tamar." But Er dies early. Now the second son is obliged to marry the widow to deliver offspring to his dead and childless brother. Not very romantic, and no wonder Onan now starts to do not exactly what is termed referring to his name but coitus interruptus, every time, "and let his semen drop to earth." Because this is not healthful and "Yahve disagreed of what he did", Onan also dies. Now Tamar has to wait until Judah's third son Shelah advances up to marriagable age to be given to her as her third husband. In vain she waits. Her father-in-law Judah, meanwhile a widower himself, makes no arrangements to give his third son to his two sons' black widow. After the mourning period, widower Judah journeys to Timnah for sheep shearing. At the entrance to the village Enayim he catches sight of a veiled harlot, and for the price of a he-goat she agrees. But since he-Judah has no he-goat at hand, he asks the harlot if she will accept his signet-ring, cord and rod as pawns? Okay, she does, they do.

Three months later Judah gets alerted: "Your daughter-in-law has gone astray and become pregnant due to her sin." Well, with such a woman the chief will make short trial: "Take her out. She shall be burnt!" But the condemned young woman puts three objects in front of the patriarch's eyes: Signet-ring, cord and rod. Accused by those objective objects Judah confesses: "She's in her right against me. Why did I not give her as his wife to my son Shelah?" (Gen 38:26). And the child of shame and incest is named Perez and becomes one of the Messiah's great-grandfathers.

---

22 Arenhoevel et al., Jerusalemer Bibel, p.1364.

Rahab whores and helps: While Jesus' great~grandmother Tamar had to play the harlot just for a short time to win her case against the patron, seven generations later his great~grandmother Rahab is right in the service and probably not lacking clients in Jericho. Into this capital of Israel's enemies, two spies are sent by Joshua son of Nun. They stay in Rahab's house during the night, but raise suspicions and Madame is asked by her compatriots to deliver her strange customers. They're gone already, Rahab says, but if you hurry you'll catch them! Alone again, she goes up to the roof where she has hid the two spies beneath stalks of flax. Here she requires them to promise that her father, her mother, her brothers and sisters will be treated merciful when the city gets conquered. On a chord she lets the two James Bonds climb down out of the brothel's window, "for her house was at the city's wall (Joshua 2:15). Short time later, God's people advances to take Jericho. Joshua orders the tabernacle to be carried seven times around the walls and seven priests to blow on seven ram horns; and on the seventh day at first the walls come tumbling down and second the citizens are slaughtered.

For the walls are falling down
And the town is flattened to the earth alike
But one cheap hotel is shunned from every strike
And they ask what VIP is living there?
And this very noon there will be silence in the harbour
When they ask themselves now: Who will have to die?
And then everyone will hear me saying: All them!
And when the head drops down I just say: Hoppla!
And the ship with eight sails and fifty big cannons
Will vanish with me.

No, Rahab doesn't order "them all" to be killed and she doesn't comment with *Hoppla* as Bertolt Brecht's *Pirate Jenny* does. But Rahab-Jenny of Jericho, together with "her father, her mother, their brothers and all who belonged to her" is escorted from her happy house out to a "safe place" and she "remained living in Israel up to this day" (Joshua 6:25). In her new life Rahab the hooker first became an honest housewife, then a mother, grandma and Ruth's second mother-in-law. Matthew has no problem integrating the former harlot into the Messiah's maternal line: "Salmon begot Boaz from Rahab and Boaz begot Jobed from Ruth."

Ruth pulls the honest whoreson: "In the days when the chieftains ruled, there was a famine in the land; and a man of Bethlehem in Judah, with his wife and two sons went to reside in the country of Moab". The women of Moab, descending from Lot and his elder daughter, are famous for their beauty. No wonder that both sons of the migrant family marry soon, the happy brides' names are Orpah and Ruth, but again both husbands die. Their father Elimelech had passed away yet before them, and his widow Naomi, having heard that in the land of Judah rain, milk and honey are flowing

again, sets out to return to her people. Both daughters-in-law shed tears, "but Ruth clung to her" and insists on going with Naomi. "For wherever you go, I will go; wherever you lodge, I will lodge; your people shall be my people, and your God my God."

Arrived in Bethlehem, Ruth takes on the kind of bread-winning open to the paupers: Gleaning ears of grain on harvested fields. All by chance she comes to the field of Boaz, who all by chance just arrives from Bethlehem and asks his reapers' foreman: "Whose girl is that?" – "She is a Moabite girl who came back with Naomi", the servant tells him. "She has been on her feet ever since she came this morning and rested but little in the hut." Boaz is impressed with the Moabite belle's good references. "Don't go to glean in another field", he greets her. "I have ordered the men not to molest you. And when you are thirsty, go to the jars and drink some water of that the men have drawn." Mealtime gives occasion to get closer: "Come over and partake of the meal, and dip your morsel in the vinegar", he invites her with lavish compliments of fragrant, crispy roasted grain.

When Ruth comes home to her mother-in-law at night with amourousness beaming out of every buttonhole, Naomi asks her knowingly: "Daughter, I must seek a home for you, where you may be happy. Now there is your kinsman Boaz, whose girls you were close to. He will be winnowing barley on the threshing floor tonight. So bath, anoint yourself, dress up ..." After the early summer work peak Boaz, son of Rahab, "ate and drank, and in a cheerful mood went to lie down beside the grainpile." And so decently the Bible describes how a strong woman – all without seduction – gains her ends: "Then she went over stealthily and uncovered his feet and lay down. In the middle of the night, the man gave a start and pulled back – there was a woman lying at his feet! "Who are you?" he asks with male naivity. "I am your handmaid Ruth. Spread your robe over your handmaid, for you are a redeeming kinsman." Boaz, however, is but the second-ranking redeemer, his obligation on the distant cousin's inheritance including his widow depends from another kinsman's will. When this first redeemer renounces, due to material considerations, on the economically unsexy match, Boaz marries Ruth "and the Lord let her conceive and she bore a son. Naomi is happy, gracefully listening to the women's congratulations: "He will renew your life and sustain your old age; for he is born of your daughter-in-law, who loves you and is better to you than seven sons."

The grace of female beauty – with which Tamar was blessed maybe poorly, Rahab profession-adequately and Ruth most surely – this attraction may be found in Jesus' fourth foreign grandmother, at King David's times, in most infatuating power:

Bathseba bathes and succumbs: "The woman was very beautiful" – the young woman whom King David, strolling on the roof of his royal palace, sees bathing in another man's dominion. Spontaneously, the *voyeur royale* sends messengers to this cherry in neighbor's garden; spontaneously he layes with her and she – having taken this fateful bath to purify herself after

29

her period – conceives. In order to make the fruit of love appear legitimous, David orders her husband, General Uriah, to come home from military front and almost coerces him to meet his wife. But Uriah, too ascetic or too well informed, refuses and prefers to sleep outside the gate in his troop's camp. Plan B: "Place Uriah in the front line where the fighting is fiercest", David writes to Joab. "Then fall back so that he may be killed."

And thus the angel of death meets Uriah, and David marries Bathseba, who now bears him a son. No sooner than wise Nathan tells the king a story of the "only one ewe lamb" heeded like a daughter by the poor man but slaughtered and put roasted on the table for his guest by the rich man (2 Sam 12:4), no sooner than David falls in rage against this man who "did this and deserves to die" and Nathan says: "That man is you!" – no sooner than now David breaks down, confesses, repents. Nathan, taking God's position, replies: "The Lord has remitted your sin; you shall not die" – but the child will. David fasts, sleeps on the stone floor, and ends his self-punishment no sooner than on the seventh day, when his servants dare to tell him that the baby boy has died. "Now that he is dead, why should I fast? Can I bring him back again? I shall go to him, but he will never come back to me." Then he consoled his wife Bathseba, he went to her and lay with her, she bore a son and named him Solomon.

Four women, four questionable, but child-bearing encounters: Why did Matthew spread this four-cornered basis of Jesus' maternal ancestry before he put Mary on top of it?

American theologian Jane Schaberg emphasizes that all four prefigurants of Mary were born non-Jewish. "Rahab and probably Tamar were Canaanites, Ruth a Moabitess, and Bathseba probably a Hittite like her husband." According to the later Jewish rule that became valid in Jesus' times and based being Jewish on being born from a Jewish mother, the four women's sons were not Jewish and nevertheless were to become Solomon's forefathers.[23] Mary, however, was a Jewess. Did Matthew want to intimate gently that this time not the mother, but the father was outlandish?

Jane Schaberg considers the four indecent women to have four common features;[24] four similarities that I, taking into account especially the perspectives of Brazilian rabbi Nilton Bonder in his book "Our Immoral Soul", will formulate with slight modifications:

1. All four find themselves outside patriarchal family structures, struggling with, and wronged or thwarted by, the male world's rules: Tamar and Ruth are childless young widows who achieve their rights by seducing elder men; Rahab a prostitute who achieves to safe her family just by her male-dominated, males-dominating profession; Bathseba is an adulteress between two warriors, and then a widow pregnant with her lover's child, advancing her lively inheritance into the center of social power.

---

23 Schaberg, p.21.
24 Schaberg, p.32-33.

2. In their sexual activity all four risk damage to the social order and their own condemnations.

3. All four are wronged or thwarted by the male world but achieve to turn depreciated relations with men into socially and individually positive, life conserving conditions.

4. In this task, all four are helped and their situations righted by men who acknowledge guilt and/or accept responsibility for them.

From these common features, Schaberg proceeds to the gospel writer's intentions: "Mention of these four women is designed to lead Matthew's reader to expect another, final story of a woman who becomes a social misfit in some ways; who is party to a sexual act that places her in great danger; and whose story has an outcome that repairs the social fabric and ensures the birth of a child who is legitimate or legitimated. That child, Matthew tells us (1:1), is 'the son of David, the son of Abraham'."[25]

But there's a second quartet of features: One could say that the four cases of illegal begetting combine to a rather complete painting of deviant sexual behavior: Incest (Tamar), prostitution (Rahab), calculated seduction (Ruth) and adultery (Bathseba). What still misses is the most repugnant form of illegitimate sexual encounter: intercourse by force.

In Joshua Sobol's drama "A Mentsh", young Sheindl enters scene with her dress tore.

Gebirtig:	*Sheindl? What happened?*
Sheindl:	*Dead!*
Gebirtig:	*What?*
Sheindl:	*A policeman caught me at selling bagels, he dragged me to an abandoned backyard.*
Gebirtig:	*Stop talking ... All that counts is you're alive!*
Sheindl:	*I'm all dirty.*
Gebirtig:	*You're all clean, Sheindl. Dirty – is he.*
Scheindl:	*If I become pregnant, then ...*
Gebirtig:	*I am the father. Your child is my child ...*

In this case, the carpenter, poet and composer Mordechai Gebirtig is the man who helps the woman to have her situation righted; but Sheindl's situation differs from those of Tamar, Rahab, Ruth, Bathseba as basically as the case of Miriam of Nazareth. If Miriam became pregnant by a Roman act of violence, as Schaberg assumes, the features 1 and 2 do not apply to her: Whatsoever she suffered by men, it was not due to patriarchal structures; and Miriam was not active, took no risk. Quite possible or even probable, however, is that, in line with Schaberg's features 3 and 4, she, too, is helped by a carpenter in creating "life conserving conditions" out of what began with being "wronged" by the violent rules of warriors' world.

---

25 Schaberg, p.32-36.

31

Nazareth, a warm spring day, 4 BCE. The troops marched in shortly before noon, two cohorts. At late afternoon, when they marched off again, fourteen women and eight girls had been raped, of whom five months later, fortunately, only three carried a Roman's child in her belly. Miriam, Joseph's fiancée, was one of them.

That's how it could have happened.

In his Christmas play "Bariona or the Son of Thunder", French philosopher Jean-Paul Sartre has his rebel say: "Soldiers will enter our village like last year in Hebron? They will rape our women and take our animals with them?"[26]

That, too, is how it could have happened.

Historically and verifiably, what happened is this:

"It was in the period of the Roman invasion of Palestine that the Jews made an important modification in their jurisdiction. Having hitherto observed a patrilineal tradition in which rights, titles and identity were passed from father to child, Judaism at this point turned matrilineal, establishing the relations between one generation and the next one now between mother and child. In view of Judaism's strong adherence to patriarchal text tradition, there must have been very significant reasons to justify such a radical amendment with this amount of implications" explains Brazilian Rabbi Nilton Bonder. The shift to maternality occurred not incidentally during[27] but "just because of Roman occupation. Violent in the treatment of vanquished peoples, Roman legions were infamous for their praxis exercised already during earlier occupations: rape. For the Roman army, the power to take the nation's daughters implied the symbolical meaning to make use of this nation. The defilement of the family, the assailant expropriation of continuity, the wombs of Israel inseminated by a foreign people: this was to Judaism an all too frontal attack on survival. That those girls' wombs would present to the world the gift of sons of Rome meant more than only the looting of the present time and the erasing of the past of Israel. It meant to incorporate Israel's future."

The Jewish antidote: "Matrilinearity meant the legal solution for the status of these fatherless children of Israel and safeguarded that they would form the continuity of a people that would not submit. Particularly in the cases of rape where the children had the status of bastards, a new symbolical understanding of the situation was necessary." The problem was "children without fathers. Someone had to assume fathership for these sons who were not marginalized by any means, but contrarily represented the hope that tragedy would turn into a wonder. The task of assuming fathership would fall to no one else than God, the creator ... This is the perspective of the power of the humble ones present in Hebrew culture: the lowest one, the

---

26   Sartre, J.P.: Bariona or The Son of Thunder. A Christmas Play, written in PW camp 1942; 2nd scene.
27   Lisa Katz (judaism.about.com/od/whoisajew/whoisjewdescent.htm) claims it happened before 70 CE: "Sometime during the Roman occupation and the Second Temple period, a law of matrilineal descent, which defined a Jew as someone with a Jewish mother, was adopted."

weakest one, the one who experienced the hardships of life most deeply is the superman actually ... Not the intact family, not correct behaviour engender the species' best individual, but the orphan, the widow, the stranger, the sick one, the whore." Moses, for instance, arose from the incorrect, incestuous marriage of Jokhebed with her nephew Amram (Ex 6:20); he was saved by the disobedience of the midwives Shifra and Puah; drifted to the Pharao's daughter who disobeyed her father in pity for the Hebrew child, while this boy's cunning sister Miriam watched the rescue and hastened to recommend a very apt wetnurse – Jokhebed herself – thus closing the circle, completing the chain of five life-saving women, five like in Matthew's save-the-messiah chain concluding with the other Miriam, the one of Nazareth. "It is the woman's obligation", Bonder comments, "to preserve the semen, even by employing strategies that contradict the dominant morale. In this perspective of preservation, the Messiah figures in humanity's picture album as the subversive, renegate, heretic. In all these cases [from Eve and Lot's daughters to Shifra, Puah, Jokhebed, Miriam and the Pharaoh's daughter; and from Tamar, Rahab, Ruth, Bathseba to Miriam of Nazareth] the woman, by and through her deviation, opens the path of humanity ..."[28]

To his Jewish and his many female followers, Jesus' impure, violent Roman origin may have been a well-known or even confirming fact. Being a Roman's rape son would not hinder but enhance his messianic message of non-violence, in an era of sexual violence Judaism tried to cope with by "identifying the son of *some father* as son of *The Father*" and "transforming the illegitimous son into the most legitimous".[29]

Luke: Rising from humility
The perspective of low birth and highest importance, of holiness from humble origin is stressed in the gospel to which Christian folklore owes the newborn surrounded by sheep, ox and donkey. As companion of Paul, the physician Luke displays his prowess for idyllic poetry in the Christmas story with shepherds at their campfire, guided by an angel to find "Mary and Joseph, and the child lying in the manger" (2:16).

The highest man in lowly animals' manger: Luke's love of vertical tension helps understand what he wanted to intimate by those two contrasting conception stories he prefixed to the Christ-animal-contrast. In the first story the angel Gabriel tells the old priest Zachary that his old wife Elizabeth will conceive of him. In the second story the same Gabriel deeply terrifies a young woman announcing she will conceive a son "who will be called the Son of the Most High. The Lord God will give him the throne of his father David." Mary hurries to the mountains. But this is no post-traumatic escape from a bunch of soldiers; just "in haste" she hikes to meet her elder yet pregnant cousin, "and when Elizabeth heard the greeting of Mary, the baby leaped in her womb". And this latish mother Elizabeth sings the "Magnificat",

---

28   Bonder 1998, p.88-98.
29   Bonder 1998, p.123 (italics: K.Y.R.).

praising the one who "looked with favour on the humiliation [ταρείνωσιν, tapéinosin] of his servant"; who "brought down the powerful" and "lifted up the lowly". Remarkably, the word that the oldest Greek translation of the Bible (the "Septuaginta") employs here for humiliation, namely ταρέινοω ("tapéino-o", to make low, humiliate, weaken)[30] signifies in Genesis (34:2) for Dina, the daughter of Lea, as well as in Judges (19:24-20:5) for two other victims, and also in Lamentations (5:11) for the virgins of Jerusalem explicitly "the sexual humiliation of a woman".[31] Dina had gone out "to visit the daughters of the land. Shechem son of Hamor the Hivite, chief of the country, saw her, and took her, and lay with her by force" – a crime that ends in a bloodbath of revenge. In the book of Judges, an old resident of Gibea, in order to protect his guests by satisfying the "depraved lot" of the town, goes as far as offering his virgin daughter to the riffraff, and his guest gives them his concubine, and "they raped her and abused her all night long ..." The ensuing carnage of revenge is Homeric in its dimension.

Elisabeth's destiny is the happiest possible contrast to those rapes. In her Judean mountain village she had been called the barren one. Childlessness was commonly understood to be the woman's fault. The barren womb is spoken of as punishment for sin (Lev 20:20-21) or at least as caused by God having "forgot" the woman (see I Sam 1:11). Why did Luke prepare Mary's conception story by the low-high-journey of a much elder cousin? Because, explains Jane Schaberg, compared to an old wife's childlessness "the humiliation of a betrothed virgin who was seduced or raped, and who became pregnant by someone other than her husband, was far worse ... In contrast to the humiliation of the barren woman (see Isaiah 54:1-3; 1 Sam 2:5), this kind of humiliation was never explicitly promised reversal."[32] The womb of this woman humiliated by barrenness would bear the forerunner John the Baptist; the birth of the cosmic redeemer from Mary's womb inescapably required a much deeper degree of previous humiliation.

Much higher value, however, Luke places on Jesus' pure and sinless pedigree: 15 generations longer than the Matthean register, mentioning David, Boaz, Perez, Juda but no woman, this genealogy ends in the top three men "Seth, son of Adam, son of God". Thus Luke clarifies, that Jesus is the son of God in the same sense as David et ceteri, in the same sense as all sons of Adam, and God could not have done anything more absurd than, kind of refreshing his own genome, to intervene anew now, impregnating the fiancée of Joseph, the earthly man upon whom the whole ladder builds with supposed firmness in the initial verse 3:23: "Jesus, when he began his ministry, was about thirty years of age, being the son, as was *supposed*, of Joseph ..."

30 Langenscheidt's Pocket Dictionary Classical Greek – German, 1990.
31 Schaberg, p.100; cf. p.95 and 138.
32 Schaberg, p.103.

Mark: Jesus ben Miriam

"Your firstborn is supposed to be the son of ...": What would this sentence mean in antique or modern social context and for the addressed woman? However, what Mark has her Nazarene neighbors state about her when her son starts preaching in his home town is hardly less offensive: "Isn't this the carpenter? Isn't this the son of Mary and the brother of James, Joseph, Judas and Simon? Aren't his sisters here with us?" (Mk 6:3).

Since in Palestine's male-dominated society a man used to be presented in the way of "Josef-ben-Jacob" or "Simon-bar-Yona", in any case as Son-of-Father, the notion "son of Mary" is uncommon – maybe intentionally degrading, too? "There is no certain evidence", Jane Schaberg admits, that identifying a man by his mother was already in Jesus' days "a customary way of designating illegitimate children or sons of prostitutes. But it is a later Jewish legal principle that a man is illegitimate when he is called by his mother's name, for a bastard has no father."[33] German scholar Gerd Lüdemann is more outspoken: "Historically we have to conclude that the mark of Jesus as 'son of Mary' was already used against him in his home town. Thus the mark is to be termed a sneer which put the finger on a sore spot of Jesus' origin."[34]

If this home town rumour had spread until 70 CE together with the growing faith, no one has to wonder why this passage in Mark's gospel remained of all canonical pages the only occasion where the Son of God is addressed as "son of Mary". Expectably, the ensuing gospels correct the troublesome "son of Mary" in an increasing thoroughness. Matthew (13:55) amends the first gospel's text discretely, in order to identify Jesus correctly by his father: Now the people's first question "Isn't this the carpenters's son?" introduces the father so elegantly that the subsequent son-of-Mary-question becomes completely honest: "Isn't his mother's name Mary?" Maintaining the question form, Luke (4:22) fights remaining doubts by inserting the *as was supposed* father's name in a noncommittal way: "Isn't this the son of Joseph?" And the last gospel of John (6:42) has the honest family of lower middle class perfected in a slightly awkward question: "Isn't this the son of Joseph, whose father and mother we know?"

John: But you were!

Surprisingly, this last, least carnal and most spiritual gospel, written four generations after Jesus birth, in its verse 8:41 contains the most carnal allusion to the Nazarene's dark origin, in an argument with Pharisees that escalates this way: "We are descendants of Abraham" – "I know you are but ..." – "Our father is Abraham." – "If you were, you would do the works of Abraham" – "We were not born of fornication" (*Hýmeis ek pórneias ou gegennémetha*). As alien as the point-blank term *pórneias* is to the context, as strongly the assertation points to what remains unsaid: "... but you were!"

---

33 Schaberg, p.160-162; cf. Lüdemann, p.60-61.
34 Lüdemann, p.61; cf. his pages 157-160 as to the five women in Jesus' lineage.

The passage is delicate enough to produce a variety of translations: "We are not illegitimate children" (New International Version, 2011); "We of whoredom have not been born" (Young's Literal Translation); "We were not born of sexual immorality" (World English Bible). Jane Schaberg dryly resumes: "The Jews meet Jesus' challenge to their religious or spiritual legitimacy by a challenge to his physical legitimacy."[35]

In the non-canonical gospel of Thomas (whole text written ca.100-110, fragments dating back to 40-70 CE) the logion 105 has Jesus say: "He who knows the father and the mother will be called the son of a *pornē*" (πόρνη, whore). Lüdemann comments: "Here Jesus speaks about himself and his special relationship to his father and mother. His statement concerning his father and his mother is literal and symbolic at the same time [and ...] obviously refers to the tradition that stands behind John 8:41 and whose content has been directed by non-Christian Jews against the procreation and birth of Jesus, imputing illegitimacy, from the beginning." The renowned gospel expert does not suppose the words of Thomas' logion 105 to relate authentic words of Jesus. "But they reflect historical facts."[36]

Traces of these facts are recorded by very canonical authors. Writing his texts around 197 CE, North African Church Father Tertullian, himself born as son of a Roman officer, mentions Jewish assertions saying that Jesus was the son of a prostitute (Quaestuariae Filius; De Spectaculis 30:6). Tertullian, an enemy of theatre and a believer in eternal infernal torture, chilled down his rage against this slur by imagining how some day Jesus would punish the Jews for the offense: "I ... would prefer to turn an insatiable gaze on those who vented their rage on the Lord. 'This is he,' I will say, 'the son of the carpenter and the harlot ... This is he whom you purchased from Judas, this is he who was struck with the reed and fist, defiled with spittle.'"[37]

Italian Church Father Origen (185-254), who emphasized the humanness of Jesus and objected to Tertullian's teaching of eternal torture, felt obliged to reply at least to the most well-known and philosophically qualified one of those "harlot's not David's son" attacks, cited in the culture comparative work of renowned philosopher Celsus who wrote in Alexandria around 178, critical of Jews and Christians. This work's last copies were burnt after Christendom's establishment as state religion, but the philosopher's assertions remained preserved in Origen's polemic writing *Contra Celsum*.[38] Concerning Mary, skeptic Celsus had reported that she was "a poor country woman who earned her living by spinning". When this woman was corrupted or seduced and became pregnant by another man, a soldier named Panthera (1:69), she "was driven out by the carpenter to whom she was betrothed, since she was convicted of adultery" (1:32). Wandering forlorn, she bore her boy child secretly, writes Celsus not too different from Mohammed

35 Schaberg, p.157.
36 Lüdemann, p.807.
37 Efroymson: Tertullian's Anti-Judaism, p.125 (quoted by Michael, p.26).
38 Giuliana Lanata (ed.): Celso. Il discorso vero. Milano 1987, p.10-13 (I quote her from wikipedia page "Kelsos"); cf. earlychristianwritings.com/text/origen161.html.

in his Sura 19, where Miriam retreats to a remote place and goes into labor under a date tree, above a rivulet.

Origen's responses to Celsus' attacks are ambiguous. He first gives it as an opinion that "all these things worthily harmonize with the predictions that Jesus is the Son of God (1:28). He appears to accept Celsus' portrait of Jesus and Mary as outsiders par excellence, as "quintessential aliens", conceding everything but the conclusion that Jesus's claim to the title of God is unwarranted. What the spinner woman's son did not dispose of – noble ancestry, distinguished parents with the necessary means to provide their child a good formation – all this was but the dark background which made Jesus' aureole just radiate the brighter. Jesus, "with all these things against him" has yet been able to shake the whole world (1:29). His reputation is victorious over "all causes that tended to bring him into disrepute".

In 1:32, however, Origen (maybe afraid of his own courage?) sounds the counterstrike: "Let us see whether those who have blindly concocted these fables about the adultery of the Virgin with Panthera ... did not invent these stories to overturn His miraculous conception by the Holy Ghost: for they could have falsified the history in a different manner, on account of its extremely miraculous character, and not have admitted, as it were against their will, that Jesus was born of no ordinary human marriage." The concoctions could have been different, that is, more prudent, since "It is not reasonable", as Origen argues, "that he who did so much for the human race should not have had "a miraculous birth, but one of the vilest and most disgraceful of all" (1:33; cf. 6:73). Origen, well-known for his believe in pre-existence of souls, continues asking whether it weren't much more reasonable "that a soul, when being inserted into a body according to certain secret laws, will take her dwelling according to dignity and with regard of her former character?" Jesus' great soul, he says, "merited a body in conformity with its character; whereas a body produced by an act of adultery such as that between Panthera and the virgin would have produced "some fool" to do injury to humanity, a teacher of wickedness (1:33; cf. 6:73).

Good advocacy sounds different. Resorting to a supernatural deduction to counter the rumors about Jesus' earthly nature, Origen rather reflects than rejects the Jewish defamation that Jesus' wickedness was caused by his impure conception. According to the Toldoth, teachers played a decisive role in the personal development of this sensitive Galilean teenager, confronting him with how his body had been produced.

Toldoth Yeshu: Cheeky bastard, expelled from school
"*Ze sefer toledoth Adám*" – this is the book of Adam's offspring" is the first verse of Genesis' fifth chapter, and already the book's title "Tol(e)-doth Yeshu" appears to be a bitter Jewish irony against a nebulous rabbi whom the dubious Paul had presented as a second Adam (Romans 5). Celsus knew the Toldoth certainly, Martin Luther despised this "family history of Jesus" as a Jewish provocation, Diderot mentioned the book assertively

in his Encyclopedia,[39] Pinchas Lapide recognizes in this "anti-Christian denigration" a scheme "as primitive as the embellishments in the gospels"; and nevertheless, Lapide admits that this Jewish "Story of Jesus" might date back to oral traditions of first century CE.[40] Jane Schaberg assumes an even earlier starting point: "It is likely that the basis of the tradition does stem from the family of Jesus, probably from Mary or from the brothers or sisters of Jesus". Rumours spread rapidly, you won't retell it, in small towns like Nazareth. "If the story of how and when Jesus was conceived was a family tradition, it is unlikely it would have been communicated to many. Rather, it would naturally have been kept secret. But leakage and rumor were possible, especially in the home town, and its spread can be easily imagined during the ministry and afterwards, especially on the lips of those who did not accept either the claims Jesus made or those his followers made for him."[41] Not accepted: that's exactly what, according to the Toldoth, young Yeshu was. On one side, the Nazarene teenager no doubt was a good pupil – maybe because a child's "early fright" is often "compensated by overly discipline and high performance"?[42] On the other side, alas, he obstructed his own possible normal career by blunder like lacking reverence and defiant pertness against his honorable teachers. This, too, would fit into the symptoms of an unwanted, early traumatized and verbally outcast child.

The Toldoth begins with his birth. "Miriam brought forth a son and named him *hoshua*, that is Joshua, after the name of his mother's brother. But when *kilkulo* was revealed, that is the blemish of his birth, he was called Yeshu, that is Jesus. And his mother gave him to a *Bes Hamedras*, that is a house of study, and he learned ... and became very wise in Torah and Talmud." Trouble was to come from the custom that among the learned scholars "neither a *Bachor* (student) ... nor a youngster" must encounter the old masters with uncovered head, "but had to stand with covered head *ki avél*, that is like mourning, his eyes fixed to the ground". One day, imagine, at the gate of the yeshiva, this intelligent pupil passed by the reverend teachers "with straight neck and bare head and did not pray for the peace of every one of them". Impertinent! When one of the scholars censures him, the pupil Hoshua even dares to raise his score by a self-willed, non-hierarchical interpretation of the scripture: "How can Moses be the greatest of all prophets if he himself asked Jethro for counsel?"

Young rebel Hoshua paid dearly for his chutzpah. "How does he make head against us?" the scholars grumble. "Let's investigate him!" By hearsay, examination and asking around, they find out some incriminating details. Mainly their colleage Rabbi Shimeon ben Shetach still knows a lot from Yohanan, the then-time fiancé of Miriam. This Yohanan, his rabbi remembers, had come to him one morning and told him what had happened to his fiancée last night: How one of her neighbors, the lascivious Joseph

39 Weiss, John 1997, p.23 (Luther) and 41 (Diderot).
40 Lapide 1974, passim.
41 Schaberg, p.153-155.
42 Janus, p.49.

ben Pandera, had entered her house drunken, pretended in the darkness to be her fiancé and distressed her. Indeed she had refused: "Don't you touch me, I have menstruation." But nevertheless the deceiver had imposed his will. When later on, right after midnight, he himself, Yohanan, had knocked at his betrothed one's door also, Miriam astonishedly had replied: "This has not been your custom since the day I was betrothed to you, that you come twice to me in one night." Weeks later, it became visible that she was pregnant and both betrothed ones had been betrayed like Alkmene and her husband Amphitryon. While Alkmene's spouse adopts the mailman's child, i.e. Zeus' strong son Herakles, Mary's ashamed fiancé, this God-fearing student Yohanan, runs off to far away Babylon, as Shimeon ben Shetach remembered. Now that "the shameful deed was made public" Miriam's half-grown son had to leave his home town Nazareth at once.[43]

The fact that Rabbi Shimeon ben Shetach lived in the first century BCE does not make the whole Toldoth unreliable. Travers Herford emphasizes the repeating figure of a rebellious student Jesus and his harsh treatment by his teachers in the few and questionable Talmud passages that mention Jesus. Reliable seems at least one Rabbi Eliezer, who said that he "conversed with a disciple of Yeshu ben Pandira". Eliezer was a pupil of Rabbi Yohanan ben Zaccai, who "must certainly have seen and heard Jesus."[44]

Great Spanish poet Judah Halevi (who died in Jerusalem 1142) affirms that Jesus had been a student of Rabbi Joshua ben Perahyah who belonged to the school of Hillel.[45] The wise and famous Hillel distinguished from his equally famous contemporary antagonist Shammai by his kindness and down-to-earth humanity. While Hillel summarized the whole Torah in the shortest possible way – "What is odious to yourself, don't do to no other one. The rest you have to learn" – Jesus in **Mt 7:12 (Lk 6:31)** said "Do to others as you would have them do to you. This is the law and the prophets."

Back to Pandera, the Latin panther: A predator tom cat's name wouldn't be too inapt for a sword-and-dagger-armed legionaire assailing female prey. Anyhow, Christian scholars have kept interpreting "Pantera" as a bowdlerized Greek "pártenos" (virgin), i.e. a Jewish attack against virginal conception – though yet in 1859, Rhenanian construction-workers had come across a stone-hard evidence: a tombstone for a Roman soldier, with the effect that the theological virginization of Pantera "will no longer hold up".[46] For here was chiselled, with a tool of first century CE, the very name mentioned by Celsus, by the Toldoth and the Talmud in the second to fourth century.

Jane Schaberg resumes the present state of knowledge: "Panthera was a common Greek proper name, found in many Latin inscriptions of the early Empire, especially as a surname of Roman soldiers. An inscription found on an epitaph in Germany, for example, mentions a Sidonian archer, Tiberius Julius Abdes Pantera, who was transferred in 6 C.E. from Syria."[47]

---

43 Callsen et al., p. 41-49.
44 Travers Herford, p.52-53 and 352.
45 Patterson, David, p.162.
46 Nicholls, p.14.
47 Schaberg, p.167.

Just five miles distant from Nazareth, the antique Hellenic city of Sepphoris (Zippori) was destroyed by Roman troops in 4 BCE in response to an insurrection led by Judah ben Hezekiah against the pro-Roman Herodians after Herod the Great's death. Historians Horsley and Silberman shed light on the fall of Zippori:

In March of 4 BCE, the Rome-dependent 69-year-old King Herod, having never been accepted by many Jews due to his Idumean origin, had succumbed to his long-term illness. His son and successor Archelaos reacted to the immediate uprises with all hardness. His cavalry slaughtered thousands of temple pilgrims in Jerusalem at Passover time. But when the news of the Jerusalem rebellion spread, messianic leaders in all regions rose up, each one hoping to be proclaimed the new king. Rebel nests formed in Judean villages. "In Galilee, a certain Judah, son of a famous gang leader executed years before by Herod, led his followers in a raging attack through the streets of Sepphoris, invaded the well-sorted arms depot and took treasures as well as luxurious furniture out of the governor's palace. The Romans reacted with expectable hardness. Syrian governor Quinctilius Varus set out immediately with two legions southward, supported by the mobilized armies of the Hellenist cities and the other loyal princes of the region. In autumn, the Roman army had already combed out many of the country's cities and villages, raping, killing and destroying almost everything that came to their eyes. In Galilee, the centers of rebellion were suppressed brutally; the rebel-held city of Sepphoris, burnt down and all surviving inhabitants sold into slavery."[48]

Thus Roman commander Publius Quinctilius Varus extinguished the rebellion with blood, crucifying 2000 Jews all over Palestine. Having flattened Zippori and defeated the Jewish rebels, he was to suffer his own defeat 13 years later in Germania's dark forests. Would Panthera, well in his thirties, now run escaping from fierce German warriors instead of raping Jewish girls? Could Jesus' father have survived the defeat of three legions healthy enough to continue serving the army, drinking Rhine and Moselle wine, to die with 62 years and be buried with military honors? Does it matter whether he merited this honors or if, by strange coincidence, just he among the numerous Panteras in Roman legions (yet in 1906 Adolf Deißmann confirmed 6 Panteras but in first century CE) had been the father of this Jesus he never knew? Anyhow, James D. Tabor[49] can itemize some indices that confirm at least the Pantera hints of Celsus and Rabbi Eliezer:

- Epiphanius (~320 – 403), this zealously orthodox bishop born near Beit Guvrin south of Jerusalem, ascribes a certain credibility to the Jesus-ben-Pantera tradition, however viewing "Jacob Panthera" as Jesus' grandfather.
- Abdes is the latinized form of aramaic *ebed*, signifying "servant of God"; the surnames Tiberius and Julius are *cognomina* he acquired in later years,

---

48   Horsley/Silberman, p.18-20 (cf. Carroll, p.83).
49   Tabor, p. 86-94; Adolf Deißmann: Der Name Panthera. In: Orientalische Studien, Gießen 1906, p.871-875 (quoted by Tabor, p.429 and his website).

giving evidence that he was not a Roman citizen by birth, but maybe a released slave who was given citizenship by emperor Tiberius, due to his military service.

- His Libanese home region of Sidon (to which Jesus made a short visit according to Mark 7:24) is situated less than 50 miles from Sepphoris and 60 miles from Nazareth;

- His cohort of archers was transferred in 6 CE to Dalmatia and 9 CE to the region between the river Rhine and affluent river Nahe.

Location Bonn (60 miles north of Bingerbrück): Tombstone of the Iberian PINTAIVS PEDILICI Filius, SIGNIFER CHO · V · ASTVRVM ANNO XXX STIPendio (standard bearer of cohort 5 of Asturians, in service for 30 years).
As suits the Signifer, he is wearing a predator's skin, the animal's head covering his helmet, its fore-paws crossed upon his breast.

Location Bingerbrück (region of Roman Bingium) on Rhine: Tombstone of Roman legionary TIBerius JULius ABDES PANTERA [from] SIDONIA, [died] ANNO LXII [62 years old], STIPENdio XXXX MILITIS [in service since 40 years], EXS [Exsignifer, former standard bearer?], COH I SAGITTARIORUM [cohort I of archers]. H · S · E [Hic Situs Est, here he lies].

Anyhow, Nazareth and Mary were within one historical focus of Roman rape raids. Tabor's Panthera theory does not explain how the victim got notice of the rapist's name. Marauders don't use to be great narrators. Still, the Lebanese legionary spoke Mary's language; his comrades could have called him by his name; as a standard bearer he at least at parades would dress a predator's skin; maybe he had been infamous already in the small village of some hundred families. The Bingerbrück Pantera surely was acquainted if not with Mary, so with the region, and looked back to a long life in the Legion, when he, shortly after the legion-crucified Son-of-Man, shut his eyes on father Rhine's western embankment.

Young Mary's old Joseph

This is something that drives Pinchas Lapide furious: "Don't those Greek gospel writers know that there is no worse insult in Israel than degrading a man to but a care-father or foster-father and thus humiliating him concerning his own children? And the five sons and at least two daughters whom Miriam bore to Joseph (**Mk 6:3**), aren't they more than sufficient prove that he was in full possession of his virility? And yet he is presented in thousands of churches and hundreds of museums as a weak old man appearing to be Mary's grandpa."[50]

With equal indignation as Lapide, also Klausner and Andermann reject the label "only foster-father" applied to Joseph. Even some Christian sources, particularly Matthew's gospel in the Codex Syrus Sinaiticus (a 4th century Syrian Bible compilation found in the Catharine Monastery on Sinai) grant Joseph his paternal honour: "Joseph, who Mary the virgin was betrothed to, begot Jesus."[51] For all these authors it was a challenge to their common sense that while Mary had a marriage-like relationship with Joseph he was not the father of her baby. The awkward answer of artists was to olden Joseph, creating an odd couple of young woman and post-sexual senior which arouses exactly the suspicions that appear in the old Jewish anecdote about the old man who marries a swinging and pretty young woman. When she soon gets pregnant, neighbors comment: "If it's a wonder, it's a wonder. If it's no wonder, it's no wonder." Why didn't the gospel writers eschew these problems by simply leaving Joseph away?

Because there was a strong oral history that confirmed Joseph's existence. In 62 CE, Jesus' brother James had been executed and the Christian community of Jerusalem had to elect a successor. "All with one consent" according to Church Father Eusebios "pronounced Symeon, the son of Clopas, of whom the Gospel also makes mention, to be worthy of the episcopal throne of that parish. He was a cousin – at any rate so it is said – of the Savior; for indeed Hegesippus records that Clopas was the brother of Joseph." He also was Mary's husband, in the writings of the Anatolian Church Father Papias (ca.70-140), who wrote extensively about Christian oral tradition. By these strong evidences, James Tabor argues that Joseph's brother Clopas became the second husband of Jesus' mother – according to the law of levirate marriage which however would only apply in case of a childless widow. All this points to the probable family situation that Jesus was not Joseph's son; that Joseph died early; and that his brother Clopas begot four sons and two or more daughters with Jesus' mother Mary.

Lapide supposes that Joseph, too, died on the cross of rebels. "We cannot exclude that Joseph belonged to those pious partisans who joined the liberation movement of Judas the Galilean until General Varus scattered them, destroyed their houses und had 2000 of them crucified – when the son of Joseph was still a boy."[52] In my view, we cannot exclude any better that

50 Lapide 1988, p.91.
51 Vermes, p.30.
52 Lapide 1988, p.102.

Mary in those terrible years – Varus raged in 4 BCE – was traumatized twice by the Romans who gave her an unwanted pregnancy and took away her fiancé. Double reason for Joseph's brother Clopas to marry her and become the father of the children, who are counted by their Nazarene neighbors in **Mk 6:3**: "Isn't this Mary's son and the brother of James, Joseph, Judas and Simon? Aren't his sisters here with us?" Also David Flusser assumes that Joseph died early, "maybe he died when Jesus was still very young". The Jewish historian states that there "seems to have existed a certain tension between Jesus and his family." Apparently, this psychological fact "whose reasons we don't know" had effected a certain influence on his personal and "for mankind so highly important decision".[53]

In search for the reasons of Jesus' go-aheaded risking – or subconscious seeking – crucifixion, we have but one source: his proper statements about himself.

Telling words of an intruded child

In 1993, the Canadian theologian William Nicholls noted: "Even if Jesus was actually conceived as the son of a Roman soldier, especially as a result of rape or seduction, that would not make him illegitimate by Jewish law, since he was born of a Jewish mother and not as an offspring of adultery or a prohibited marriage."[54] When one year later Nicholls' colleague Jane Schaberg defended the thesis that Jesus probably was the result of rape suffered by Miriam, she hardly could have exposed herself in a more lonely way within predominantly male theologian circles. One of the few colleagues who dared to stand by and protect her was Donald Capps:

"What I believe is occurring here is a not-so-subtle form of verbal shaming. Schaberg is being told by her colleagues in the field of New Testament that she crossed a line that she ought not to have crossed, that, in fact, she has committed a shameful act. Her critics undoubtedly miss the irony here, *for this is precisely* what her book is about: the shaming of a woman and the power of a patriarchal system to protect its own interests."[55]

And not too unprecisely this is the verbal form of what Roman warriors – in Schaberg's and my view – did to Miriam physically. What this meant mentally for the collaterally produced children is a question that could be answered by thousands of children who meanwhile are adults in Bosnia: living souvenirs of modern khaki and Kalashnikoff Pantheras, of machos who had applied "single, group and continuous rape"[56] as defiling means of ethnical cleansing. Those happy ones of these forced-into-being babies who had not been killed soon after birth were raised, according to a UNICEF study, as a "particularly vulnerable ... hidden population", either in children's asylums or "at home" by their mothers. "In one family, the child was coerced

53 Flusser, p.23.
54 Nicholls, p.15.
55 Capps, p.125 (italics: K.Y.R).
56 Classification by Human Rights Watch, quoted in: "Sie wollten uns zerstören, aber wir haben überlebt", SZ-Magazin, Süddeutsche Zeitung, 10/2013.

to comprehend his life as a mistake" and had to present himself to guests confessing: "I am the product of my mother's violation." In the 2004 war movie "A Boy from a War Movie", Alen Muhic is shown playing cheerfully with his classmates and scrambling with his adoptive father, and he also tells how he got knowledge of his real origin from a talkative classmate, how he ran to his "father" immediately and how this honest man told his adopted son the truth.

What the movie does not render is Alen's hurt when the neighbors suddenly called him "Pero" – a Serbian name – and how he desperately tried to meet his mother, who however rejected him roughly.

What the movie does not tell is "Pero's" attempt to commit, because of this rejection and the ongoing classroom mobbing, suicide.

What is not shown is how he for several days kept crying and rioting at his adoptive parents' home. "Why have you deceived me?" he shouted at his foster mother. "You said you've carried me here!" and pointed to her womb.[57]

What kind of relation can a woman who has conceived in this traumatic way develop to *her* and the rapist's child? If we trust the Toldoth narrative that her son's good school education was important to her, Miriam did not reject him, and not at all roughly. Apparently she loved him and stood by him, in spite of the evil primary memories. But how did he, her son, experience the time between conception and birth, while his small body grew from two to two trillion body cells?

Modern science has proved with stringent evidence that already embryos perceive their mothers' feelings; that all of us yet since the act of procreation carry within us the vitally decisive judgement whether we are welcome or rejected, invited or intruded; the judgement that will model the process of our life.[58] Having grown for nine long months into this "rejecting womb",[59] as literally em-pathic, in-feeling inner listeners to their mothers' frights, complaints and heartbeats, as part-takers of all that she is forced to gulp, undesired children start to show conspicuous behaviour as soon as they are born. At this stage, one third of their mothers regret to have foregone aborting what has grown inside them.

Many parents of unwanted children are inclined to ill-treatment "out of rage and helplessness" – or to overcare their children in order to compensate for self-reproaches after intermittently intensive feelings of hate. Among their classmates, the unwanted ones often go for "deviants" or "cowards" and, contrarily, as daringly go-aheaded. Grown up, the unwanted ones suffer permanently of relational problems, are social misfits, twice as often criminal and not rarely lifelong incapable of happiness.[60] They tend to al-

---

57 George Jahn, AP: "Leben mit der grausamen Wahrheit", in: Südwestpresse Ulm, May 25, 2005.
58 Häsing/Janus, p.117.
59 cf. Kafkalides, Athanassios: The Knowledge of the Womb. Heidelberg 1997 (quoted by Janus, p.17).
60 Feature "Ein Leben lang unglücklich", Augsburger Allgemeine ca. 1991; cf. the studies of Gerhard Amendt and Michael Schwarz, as well as Czech and Swedish studies described

cohol and drug abuse, but also to life-endangering sports like skydiving or motorcycling, this being no surprise considering their generally higher rate of suicide. Ultrasonic scans of modern days can visualize – as US-scientist Jeanette di Pietro proved – the little in-belly-human's distinct reactions even to such trifles as encumbering thoughts passing through the mind of the "surrounding" mother.[61]

How should children not perceive those encompassing emotions? How would undesired fruits of the womb try to understand their superfluous existence? How many cumbering thoughts had passed through brain and heart and belly of a rape-impregnated girl of Nazaret? How many of those thoughts and tears and sighs and cries had her baby overheard, and how did they inform his later feeling, acting, speaking out?

On the other side, traumatized mothers can give their children forces with a vengeance. A two-phase study of Alexandra Piontelli with pregnant women and their then born children showed: "A mother's fantasies, hopes, and emotions for a fetus in the womb affect the infant's coming into the world and modalities of being."[62]

So mothers yet prenatally give orders to their children? In his Fate Analysis, Leopold Szondi writes that "every human being comes to this world with a life plan which under guidance of hidden inherited elements determines our fate-forming actions of free choice unconsciously."[63]

Is this true also for Jesus' life and fatal end?

During the 1970s, German rallies for legal abortion used the darkly intuitive rhyme "If Mary'd done abortion, she'd spared Him gruesome portion." We can try to intuit the feelings and motives of her son who was not spared his portion only out of what He most probably really said, passing all the words He is said to have said through the filter of a rigid historical criticism. Just fifteen percent of all gospel-words eventually pass through Gerd Lüdemann's sequence of seaves as authentic words of Jesus. This extract of what Jesus carried inside and spoke out is like scattered shards of a broken vessel, enabling us to compare the vessel's engravings with the scars disclosed by children of later times and mothers. I will classify this emotional patchwork according to three relations: first, to life (acceptance, confidence, joy of being); second, to sexuality; third, to father.

1. **Life**. Alfred Adler wrote in 1937: "The child should perceive his entrance into the world as a kind invitation. A child who doesn't feel kindly invited, lives like in a foreign country."[64] A child like this "cannot arrive at the other ones", American therapist Barbara Findeisen said in 1997; this child "can't find a place on earth ... and cannot settle down". Nests and caverns are archetypes of prenatal comfort for discomforted ones.

in Janus, p.111-112.
61 Alberti, p.76.
62 Piontelli, From Fetus to Child, London 1992, p.1-25 (quoted by Schwab, p.141).
63 Szondi, p.20.
64 Levend/Janus, p.112.

*"Foxes have dens and birds have nests, but the Son of Man has
no place to lay his head." (Mt 8:20; Lk 9:58; Thomas 86:1-2)*

Barbara Findeisen speaks about the "melody of life" we learn in the womb.
If this melody whispers only *piu triste* and *ritardando* because what lacks
is the feeling of being welcome, the weakly connected ones "will be rather
shy in their relationships". Since any separation recalls the child's pain of
feeling abandoned, any later lovelornness "mixes with the whole despair of
the child we once have been"; of a child who for all his life will nevermore
"obtrude" on someone, be nobody's "burden" any more – as this child once
had perceived to be in a harbouring-rejecting body.[65]

*"When his family heard it, they went out to restrain him, for
people were saying: 'He has gone out of his mind'" (Mk 3:21)*

Frequently, the unwelcome intruders bear "a feeling of guilt of having been
born at all". In his essay "The Unwelcome Child and his Death Impulse",
Sandor Ferenczi wrote: "The child must, by immense amounts of love, tenderness and care, be induced to excuse the parents for having him brought
to this world; otherwise, soon the destructive drives will stir." Destroying
what? "In later life", Ferenczi notes concerning two patients, "relatively tri-
fling occasions were enough to want to die, even if this was compensated by
strong efforts of will. Moral and philosophical pessimism, scepticism and
disconfidence became their conspicuous traits of character."[66]

*"If anyone comes to me and does not hate father and mother,
wife and children, brothers and sisters – yes, even their own
life – such a person cannot be my disciple." (Lk 14:26)*

The Latin verb *linquere* means to leave back, desist from, abandon; and often this feeling of being left back and abandoned ends in the delinquency
of a "disoriented" adolescent.[67] Responding to his feeling of being left, he
tends to leave the patriarchal order. Miriam's son, for instance, defied the
teachers of tradition and was put outside of traditional order, "outed" by
them as a *"mamser"* (bastard). Should anyone be surprised if the intelligent
thoughtful teenager would be uncertain about his identity, asking:

"Who do people say I am?" (Mk 8:27-29)
"But you? ... Who do you say I am?" (Mt 16:15)

If a mother rejects her pregnancy, she shuts herself off from moments of joy
and joyous anticipation. Biochemically, she and her child will lack the "hor-

---

65 Cf. Janus 2000, passim; Findeisen, B. in her article about long-term psychic consequences of pre- and perinatal experiences, in: Janus, Ludwig and Haibach, Sigrun (ed.):
Seelisches Erleben vor und während der Geburt, Neu-Isenburg 1997.
66 Ferenczi, p.253-254.
67 Alberti, p.72.

46

mones of joy", serotonin and oxytocin. What her mind lacks at the moment, and maybe her child will lack for all his life is the feeling of the "world's rightness"[68]. Such persons often are very thin-skinned, feeling to be "too permeable, too unprotected in their essence, oversensitive and delicate". Searching for the roots of their being different, they become introspective – and keep contact with their "inner child":

> *"Whoever doesn't receive the kingdom of God as a little child will never enter it."* (**Mk 10:15**)

2. Sexuality: Would it be astonishing if a rape-conceived child should develop an "unbiological sharpness ... against man's sensual desire" as historian Will Durant (married almost 70 years to his former student and co-author Chaya Kaufman) observed in Jesus?[69]

> *"But I tell you that anyone who stares at a woman with lust for her has already committed adultery with her in his heart."* (**Mt 5:28**)

If, according to the above quoted studies of Alexandra Piontelli, "a mother's fantasies, hopes, and emotions for a fetus in the womb affect the infant's coming into the world and modalities of being",[70] would it come as a surprise if this child emphasized women's rights against irresponsible, abandoning men?

> *"Anyone who divorces his wife and marries another woman commits adultery against her."* (**Mk 10:11**)

And if to him sexuality remained connected with the womb-feeling of a young girl who had been impregnated violently?

> *"For there are eunuchs who from the mother's womb were so born."* (**Mt 19:12**)

3. Father: What answer should we expect, if the force-made fatherless one is solicitated by one of his activists: "Sir, permit me to bury first my father"?

> *"Follow me, and let the dead bury their own dead."* (**Mt 8:22; Lk 9:60**)

Should we be surprised if this son, in sharp contrast to this negative image of a "father, bad, gone somewhere" (... but all too present in the Roman oc-

---

68 Alberti, p.31 and 103; in German: "Richtigkeit der Welt".
69 Durant, p.638.
70 Piontelli, From Fetus to Child, London 1992, p.1-25 (quoted by Schwab, p.141).

cupators) would develop a contrasting, consoling image of a "father, good, caring, responsible, up there"?

> *"Father in heaven, may your name be kept holy."* (**Mt 6:9** *and* **7:11**; **Lk 11:2** *and* **11:13**)
> *"So if you who are evil know how to give good gifts to your children, how much more will your Father in heaven give good things to those who keep on asking him!"* (**Mt 7:11**)
> *"But your heavenly Father already knows all your needs."* (**Mt 6:32**; **Lk 12:30**)

What will an unwanted child undertake who grew up with feelings of alienation and homelessness in this world, yearning for the homey sheltered safety he missed yet in the womb?

> *"I will set out and go back to my father ..."* (**Lk 15:18**)

Wouldn't this fatherless child dream of a father who cares especially for this one lost child among hundred and who will come certainly to get him out of here?

> *"Suppose a man has 100 sheep and one of them strays. Won't he leave the 99 sheep in the hills to go on searching for the one that has strayed? And if he finds it, I tell you the truth, he will rejoice over it more than over the ninety-nine that didn't wander away! In the same way, it is not the will of your Father in heaven that even one of these little ones should perish."* (**Mt 18:12-14**; **Lk 15:4-6**)

All those gospel-words of Jesus speak of the same sufferings and symptoms unwanted children relate until today. All put together, those puzzling word-protocols of the synoptic gospels, presenting Jesus as his family's misfit and enfant terrible – all these words are badly fitting a perfect heavenly father but perfectly a bad primal scene in Jane Schaberg's and my view. All these words Gerd Lüdemann assigns as authentic, and as authentic are the symptoms they point to and the more valid is the thesis of Jesus' origin having been violent. "I cannot think of any need in childhood as strong as the need for paternal protection", writes the same Sigmund Freud who states that "the origin of the religious attitude" incontrovertibly can be traced back to "the infant's helplessness and the longing for the father aroused by it."[71] On grounds of this "longing for the father", US-theologian Donald Capps is right in a very deep sense when he, "against the tendency to minimize the impact of childhood experience", propounds the total anti-thesis "that virtually everything that Jesus said and did as an adult is traceable, in one way or another, to his awareness of being an illegitimate child". This awareness

---

71 Freud 2010, (Civilization and Its Discontents), p.25.

could explain "what is commonly judged to be the core of his own religious experience and public message, his unusually close and personal relationship to God whom he called 'my father'."

"Would it be merely happenstance", Capps asks, "that an illegitimately conceived child, a child raised by an adoptive father, not only addressed God as father, but did so in an unusually intimate manner?" And more exactly, in a very personal, idiosyncratic manner which is "diametrically opposite to his perception of his natural father"; in a strident and world-historically important case of "image-splitting"?[72] In a surreal scene, reported in all synoptic gospels (Mk 5:1-17; Mt 8:28-34; Lk 8:26-39) Jesus asks a demon-obsessed man for his name. "My name is legion", the madman replies, "because there are many of us inside this man". And the legionary's rape-son commands the whole legion of demons into an absurd herd of two thousand pigs – the epitome of impure, foreign, sexually uninhibited beings. This crazy fantasy suggests that Mark personally knew more than he reveals in calling Jesus the son of Mary; enough about Jesus' gentile, legionary, sexually impure origin to be able to perceive what was "inside this man" and to see what Capps would see much later: "His 'pathology' is that he has the genes of a Roman, and is therefore occupied by a foreign element that can only be exorcized by replacing this inner demon with a new internalized father, the one he affectionately calls 'my father'."[73]

The image-splitting is bipolar: the more violent, careless and abandoning this father of back then, the more worth confidence, the more helpful and sincere the father of the future would have to be. Just believe strongly. Faith can move mountains and remove bad fathers. "His awareness of his illegitimacy and his deeply personal experience of God as father ... would enable him to transform the self-endangerment caused by his illegitimacy into a new sense of self-empowerment and inner freedom, one that challenged the negative self-image resulting from awareness of his illegitimacy."[74]

Jesus' father-image-splitting would result in a split duality of his biographic options. First, the illegal Alpha of paternal violence would be followed by the high Omega of paternal help: Legion pigs would run mad to drown themselves in the Galilean sea – whereas the son of humiliation would be raised to power by father's strong hand and outstretched arm! (Psalm 136:12) Second, the brilliant student of the scriptures, as the Toldoth describes him, must have studied Isaiah's anti-hero, God's suffering servant: "I will give him the honors of a victorious soldier, because he exposed himself to death. He was counted among the rebels. He bore the sins of many and interceded for rebels. "Sing, O childless woman, you who have never given birth! Break into loud and joyful song, O Jerusalem, you who have never been in labor. For the desolate woman now has more children than the woman who lives

---

72   Capps, p.108-115.
73   Capps, p.120; Schützenberger (p.76), citing her colleague Jean Guyotat, notes that "when difficulties occur on the level of instituted filial relationship – an illegitimate child, uncertainties about the father ... it weakens the instituted axis and tends to exalt the imaginary axis in a kind of dialectic relationship between the two."
74   Capps, p.108-109.

with her husband,' says the Lord." (Isaiah 53:12-54:1 in King James/New Living Translation). High-flying Isaiah would suit well as Jesus' favorite prophet, most deeply maybe in his verses 49:1-5: "The Lord appointed me before I was born, he named me while I was in my mother's womb ... And now the Lord has resolved, he who formed me in the womb to be his servant, to bring back Jacob to himself ..."

Already when his nerved teachers called him a *mamser* from the womb, the boy whom his mother had named "God will save" could refer the passage of God-wanted passion for the liberation of many and intercession for rebels to himself. Twice seven years later it erupted from the man who had to say to himself: "My semen is legion."

A case of literally self-fulfilling prophecy?

No, this is nonsense, the famous Jerusalem scholar Joseph Klausner might comment. In his view, the gospels contain "not even the faintest indication concerning heathen blood rolling in Jesus' veins ... The truth is, that Jesus, like every other child in Galilee, descended from honest Jewish parents, for also in this province betrothed girls were supervised sternly, if perhaps indeed not all as strictly as in Judaea."[75]

The psychological truth is that Klausner's idyllic view, completely alien to Jesus' visibly traumatized personality, rather exemplifies Lüdemann's statement that "theological interpretation on golden ground is one thing. Another thing is the partly brutal history in this earth's dust that Jesus came to know in boosted amount. Since his appearance in his home-town Nazareth he was attacked referring to his being a bastard without legal father; hence the scorn-word 'son of Mary'... Maybe herein consists one root of his later concern for despised people, for whores, tax collectors, sinners ..."[76]

While this concern for despised women is highly regarded by Christians, the exposure of its root – Jesus' coming into this world by a violent sexual act – is utterly inacceptable to many Christians. At least on first glance. On second glance they could detect that this lowest possible way of getting sired, while not doing any harm to the human dignity of the man who emphasized the human dignity of whores, thoroughly fulfills the criterion "he humbled himself" (Philippians 2:8), and fulfills it much more authentically, incarnates it, brings it to this planet much more physically than Luke's child in the monger between animals, since "God chose what is low and despised in the world" (1 Cor 1:28). And this humblest possible origin not even contradicts the God-sonship of Jesus Bar Abbas if one lends an ear to Paul, in Romans 8:15: "When we cry, 'Abba, Father!' it is that very Spirit bearing witness with our spirit that we are children of God."

75 Klausner, p.316-317.
76 Lüdemann, p.879-880.

III   Suffered under Saint Pilate

"I have a daughter: Would any of the stock of Barabbas
Had been her husband, rather than a Christian!"

Shylock, in Shakespeare's Merchant of Venice, Act 4, Scene 1

When thirty-year-old Jesus began preaching in the upper Jordan valley, he
became known not only by his healings and his personal radiation – Geza
Vermes calls him a "charismatic hassidic healer in rural Galilean tradition"[77]
– but also by his peculiar bond with the divine father he called Abba. Why
the poet of the *Our Father* was the loser in the casting against the *Son of Father* (Bar Abbas) is a major subject of this chapter about their final struggle.

The breaker

What did Our Father demand of him?
When his baptizer John was already in prison, Jesus had proclaimed his program: "From the days of John the Baptist until now the kingdom of heaven
suffers violence, and *biazetai* take it by force." (**Mt 11:12**). Greek biazetai
means people who "coerce, enforce ... rape ... penetrate by force".[78]
And Lüdemann leaves no doubt: "The 'violent ones' refer to Jesus and his
disciples, since only thus the time-wise positioning 'from the days of John'
becomes plausible."[79] At the day he spoke about biazetai, Jesus was on the
road with his disciples "to teach and preach in their cities" and probably
referred to what Micah had written about the breaker (*poretz*, פֹּרֵץ): "I will
gather Jacob, you all, yes, gather the remnant of Israel, joint like the flock
of Boz-rah amidst of its pasture, noisy by men. The breaker goes up before them; they will break and pass through the gate and go out. Their king
marches before them, the Lord at their head." (Micah 2:12-13). Zechariah
provided the man so close to God, heading for God's holy mountain, with a
rather complete program, starting with instructions for "the zenith of Jesus'
political career",[80] his entrance to the city: "Shout in triumph, O daughter
of Jerusalem! See, your king is coming to you. He is righteous, and able to
save (*ve nosha),* humble, riding on an ass, on a donkey foaled by a she-ass.
He shall banish chariots from Ephraim and horses from Jerusalem ..." (9:9-
10). "On that day the Lord their God will rescue his people" (9:16). Superior
Roman forces? No problem: "In that day, a great panic from the Lord shall
fall upon them ... and everyone shall raise his hand against everyone else's
hand" (14:13). Zechariah reminds him of a low point: the city captured, "the
houses plundered, the women violated" but right in the next verse he tells

---

77 Geza Vermes, thus quoted by Nicholls, p.56.
78 Verb βιάζω, Langenscheidt's Pocket Dictionary Ancient Greek – German, 1990.
79 Lüdemann, p.225.
80 Maccoby 1996, p.91.

him where the final battle would be started: "Then the Lord will come forth and make war on those nations ... he will set His feet on the Mount of Olives, near Jerusalem on the east, and the Mount of Olives shall split across from east to west ..." After the battle, "all who survive of all those nations that came up against Jerusalem shall make a pilgrimage year by year to bow low to the King Lord of Hosts" (14:2-16). In other words: The nation of Panthera, tamed in due time, would bow low to the good father.

If not now, so when? The advent of the Messiah would be announced by an unequalled fertility of nature as the prophets had said: "Fig tree and the vine shall give their fruits" (Joel 2:22). The day after having been welcomed with Hosianna, on the morning of his primal attack on the Temple's sacri-business, he saw a fig tree and expected to find figs on it, yet "found nothing but leaves, for it was not the season" (Mk 11:13). So what? Good reason for cursing the tree but not for stopping himself heading for the Temple.[81]

The abolisher

He was angry *because of* the Temple. One of his most eloquent Jewish con-temporaries, historian Flavius Josephus, describes the flood of sacrifice ani-mals, merchants and consumers surging against Jerusalem Temple at Passo-ver: "Desirous of informing Nero of the power of the city, Cestius entreated the high priests to take, if possible, the number of their whole multitude. So these high priests, upon the coming of that feast which is called the Pass-over, when they slay their sacrifices, from the ninth hour till the eleventh, found the number of sacrifices was 256,500; which, upon the allowance of no more than ten that feast together, amounts to 2,700,200 persons."[82]

Even supposed these sums were puffed up ten times the real size, the settled numbers paint a troubling image of the holiday reality which Jesus would neither want to nor be able to see at Passover 30 CE: Jerusalem, the dwel-ling-place of about 50,000 people, drowning in a swashing tide of 270,000 pilgrims in and around a temple that was dripping from the blood of 25,000 sacrificial lambs, in a place as crowded "as Jerusalem is filled with sacrificial sheep during her festivals" (Ezekiel 36:38). "The profits that these activi-ties yielded were vast. The temple of Jerusalem was the most gainful sacral enterprise [and slaughterhouse] in the whole Roman world."[83] Was it this booming blood-and-barbecue-business that the Galilean rebel planned to stir up by overthrowing tables of pigeon-merchants and money-changers in the temple's outer court? If yes, due to which item of his rebellious doctrine? The last lines (14:21) of Zechariah's prophecy contain another element fit-ting into Jesus' program of abolishing temple sacrifice: "And every caldron

---

81 See Maccoby 1996, p.92; Lüdemann (p.106) seems to overlook this Messianic aspect of Jesus' untimely expectance of figs that to my opinion, together with the logion's strange-ness, confirms its authenticity in its core. However, Lüdemann may be right in explaining how this core was transformed into "radical anti-Judaism" by linking its interpretation to Jeremiah 8:13.
82 Josephus, The Jewish War, 6.9.3.
83 Tabor, p.243.

in Jerusalem and Juda shall be holy to the Lord of Hosts: and all those who sacrifice shall come and take of these to boil in, and in that day there shall be no more traders in the house of the Lord of Hosts."
Zechariah's prophecy proposes to bypass sacro-business in the temple by making every caldron, every kitchen, every Jewish home a holy place – exactly what Roman destruction and rabbinic innovation achieved to realize after 70 CE until today. Was it this what Jesus headed for in 30 CE and deemed the most important thing? "Tell me what is the most important commandment", Jesus had been asked few days before by a scholar who did not hesitate to praise his answer: "Well said, rabbi. You are right in saying that God is one and there is no other but him. To love him with all your heart ... and to love your neighbor as yourself is more important than all burnt offerings and sacrifices." (Mark 12:32-33).
In Matthew's version (22:40), Jesus himself explains: "On these two commandments hang all the law and the prophets" – which combines with Hillel the Elder's famous formula: "That which is hateful to you, do not do to your fellow. That is the whole Torah, now go and learn." – "Go and learn what this means: I desire mercy, not sacrifice", Jesus demands in Matthew 9:13, quoting Hosea 6:6. In my view the two parallels between Hillel and Jesus weaken Lüdemann's opinion that Mark's quoted passage is too tipical for a "Greek Judeo-Christian community" which "had disengaged from temple cult" to be authentic. For just this disengagement by abolition of animal sacrifice was part and parcel of the rebel's coming kingdom, much more essentially than it had been for many prophets. "You do not desire sacrifice and ... burnt offering", David says to God in Psalm 40:6, and in Psalm 50 Yahve himself ridicularizes the human attempts to serve him by slaughtering animals: "Do I eat the flesh of bulls, or drink the blood of he-goats?"
After David came the prophets who inveighed against the profitable lamb turnovers: "What need have I of all your sacrifices?", Yahve asks in Isaiah around 700 BCE, giving the answer himself: "I am sated with burnt offerings of rams, and suet of fatlings, and blood of bulls and I have no delight in lambs and he-goats ... Who asked that of you? Trample my courts no more" (1:11-13). Micah's equation (6:7) is equally poignant: "Will the Lord be pleased with thousands of rams ... with ten thousand rivers of olive oil? Shall I offer my firstborn for my transgression, the fruit of my body for the sin of my soul?" Jeremiah (7:22) has God correct historical errors: "When I brought your ancestors out of Egypt, I did not tell them anything about burnt offerings and sacrifices."
In a settled, static, statist Judaism the mobile tabernacle had turned into a sacral slaughterhouse, and Amos (5:22-25) tells how a disgusted God compares this urban center of sacrifice with the non-sacrificial God-people-relationship during the nativeness of exodus: "I loathe, I spurn your festivals ... If you offer me burnt and meal offerings I will not accept nor will I heed your gift of fattened calves ... Did you bring me sacrifices and offerings forty years in the wilderness, people of Israel?" Make the change, demands this

blood-despising God: "Let justice flow like water and righteousness like an unfailing stream."

At the unfailing waters of Jordan, Jesus had met an ascetic Temple opponent who was believed by some to be Elijah returned and whose imprisonment he had commented with those already cited words German theology dubs the *Stürmerspruch* (stormer's quote): "From the days of John the Baptist until now the kingdom of heaven suffers violence, and *biazetai* take it by force." John had been beheaded by Herod. Now it was Jesus' turn.

"This conscious working toward death"

Regardless of whether he intended to be the breaker through the occupier phalanx of Roman superpower or the abolisher of highly profitable Jewish temple sacrifice: Didn't he have to suppose that he himself would be his project's most predictable victim?

That Jesus' fanatism "bordered to insanity" David Friedrich Strauß had asserted yet in 1864. In 1910, Dr. Charles Binet-Sanglé published his book *La Folie de Jesus* diagnosing Jesus' illness as "religious paranoia" on grounds of seven gospel-related details which he classified as halluzinations. In 1912, prominent New York psychiatrist Dr. William Hirsh agreed with Binet-Sanglé's opinions and pointed to Jesus' "megalomania, which mounted ceaselessly and immeasurably". Hirsh concluded that "everything that we know about him conforms so perfectly to the clinical picture of paranoia that it is hardly conceivable that people can even question the accuracy of the diagnosis."[84]

In 1933, the Alsacian theologist, brillant organ player and famous "jungle doctor" Albert Schweitzer wrote in his book *Die psychiatrische Beurteilung Jesu* (The Psychiatric Diagnosis of Jesus), that "this conscious working toward his death can by no means be interpreted, as Binet-Sanglé seems to be inclined to, as a morbid self-sacrifice ...". Rather, indeed, this victimal death "represents a necessary element of Jesus' messianic thinking and acting."[85]

In Schweitzer's view, Jesus wanted to take the birth pangs of messianic age on himself, believing strongly in the big bang, the final clash initiating the kingdom of God – yet before the barley harvest. "As preparation for this he sent out his disciples to warn his fellow Jews. He was convinced that his disciples were going to suffer in this task. When they returned uninjured, he was constrained to bring God, so to say, into a compulsion-to-move situation. Therefore he himself stepped into foreground, not only as messenger of God's kingdom, but also as God's suffering servant."[86]

During his hearing by the high priest, Jesus could have saved his life "by keeping silence", Schweitzer supposes. "But he didn't want to, for he had

84   Havis, Don: An Inquiry Into the Mental Health of Jesus: Was He Crazy? In: Secular Nation, 2/2001, San Mateo, CA (sfatheists.com).
85   Schweitzer, p.36-37.
86   De Rosa, p.179 and Nicholls, p.25.

come to Jerusalem with the determined intent to die, and had also disclosed this to his disciples (Mk 8:31; 9:31)."[87] In Dr. Schweitzer's view, Jesus behaved "totally different from a persecuted paranoid", since he didn't stay inactive and defensive but by provoking actions attempted "to enforce an intervention against himself". The thesis of his colleagues Binet-Sanglé and Hirsh that Jesus suffered from a *"relationship mania* insofar as Jesus related the prophets' messianic passages to himself" Schweitzer counters similarly to Maccoby, interpreting this behaviour of Jesus "in an adequate historical consideration of his standpoint [as] a thoroughly normal psychological performance".[88]

One century later, critical exegesis confirms Schweitzer's viewpoint. Rightly he weakened the diagnoses of his colleagues Binet-Sanglé and Hirsh by stating that "three quarters of their material stem from the fourth gospel" – whose author could with more reason be diagnosed as somewhat otherworldly. Concerning the remaining third, Hirsh's and his colleague's diagnoses are flawed by their reference to mostly non-authentic gospel material. What remains as proofs of Jesus' mental suspiciousness cited by the mentioned authors is his cleansing of the temple (**Mk 11:15-19**), his ethical rigorism in **Mt 5:22a** ("But I say you that if you are angry with a brother and sister you will be liable to judgment"), his indifference concerning familiar duties ("Let the dead bury their own dead", **Lk 9:60**); the statements of his contemporaries about his madness (**Mk 3:21**) and his call for self-mutilation which reminds on borderline-syndrom ("For there are eunuchs who have been so from birth, and eunuchs made by others, and self-made eunuchs", **Mt 19:12**). All of these authentic quotations are in Schweitzer's view "by far insufficient" to diagnose insanity.

As to my view that they point to childhood trauma, right here Hirsh's viewpoint does come to grip: "We have here a boy with extraordinary mental talents, who however is predisposed to psychic disturbances and who by and by develops fixed ideas. His complete leisure time he uses for the study of 'holy' texts, whose reading certainly contributed to his mental illness."[89] Did he read the story of Jephthah, the strong warrior – and son of a harlot – who was first expulsed by his stepbrothers, then called back and put to the top of a victorious army as "their commander and chief" (Judges 11)? Did he identify with Samson, this archetype of suicide attacker figuring also in the book of Judges (13-16)? Samson's story starts with the angel of Yahve announcing to a barren Danite woman: "You will conceive and bear a son ... and he will be the first to deliver Israel from the Philistines".

Whereas Samson was famous for his physical strength, the charismatic Galilean preacher Jesus (who according to Celsus, the church fathers Justin Martyr, Ambrose, Tertullian und Ephrem Syrus was small, according to a disputed Roman source but 150 centimeters tall)[90] was himself surprised and

---

87   Schweitzer, p.22.
88   Schweitzer, p.15 and 30.
89   Schweitzer, p.22.
90   Eisler, Robert: The Messiah and John the Baptist, London 1931 (quoted in Wikipedia article "Race and appearance of Jesus"; Roman source: Lehmann, p.10-11.

impressed by the healing effects of his mere presence, of his layed-on hands or the mere touching of his garment by health-seekers; that is, by "thin membrane" qualities found frequently in people with prenatal trauma.[91] Did he, who apparently could heal all illnesses by expulsion of demons – did he deem himself able to deliver Israel from the Roman legions?

On Mount of Olives: Two swords against one legion

"He himself, Jesus of Nazareth, was the person to whom the prophet directed his orders; the Messiah who should arrive in Jerusalem on the foal of a donkey and should stand in the 'Valley of the Hills'... to see the appearance of God's glory on the Mount of Olives. He would see the Romans be stroken by a plague and should lead 'Judah' in the battle against them." And afterwards he would rule as a peace-loving king in Jerusalem and all peoples should beg: "Let us go with you, for we have heard that God is with you" (Zechariah 8:23). This is how Hyam Maccoby interprets the post-Maccabean Jewish rebel's worldview. "One could object", he admits, "that this report makes Jesus appear insane. Can he really have expected that Zechariah's prophecy would fulfil so literally in just this night on Mount of Olives?" Maccoby's diagnosis, closer to Dr. Schweitzer's than to Dr. Hirsh's, describes Jesus as "maniac typus", i.e. a man "who was able to persist over long periods in a condition of great enthusiasm and euphoria. This enabled him to perform his wonder healings and to impress his companions to such an extent that they could never let his memories go down."[92]

With the Mount of Olives, his favorite place (cf. Lk 22:39), the wonder rabbi connected strong reminiscences – biblical and personal. King David had gone up to here "where people would prostrate themselves to God" (2 Samuel 15:32). Here Jesus himself, in a little town on the Mount of Olives, had been anointed almost like a next king David, with precious oil of nards poured on his head by a woman (Mk 14; Mt 26; Lk 7; John 12), in a scene of doubtful historicity that anyhow "quite probably reflects Jesus closeness to a probably ill-reputed woman in Galilee."[93] No Galilean woman's generosity but "God's glory" had appeared here on the mountain east of the city to Ezekiel (11:23). Here Isaiah's call "Come, let us go up to the mountain of the Lord, to the house of the God of Jacob" would realize: "He shall judge between the nations, and shall decide disputes for many peoples; and they shall beat their swords into plowshares, and their spears into pruning hooks" (Isaiah 2:3-4). "Come, let us go up to the mountain of the Lord", Micah had summoned the people to the hilltop where "he shall judge between many peoples, and shall decide for strong nations far away; and they shall beat their swords into plowshares, and their spears into pruning hooks; nation shall not lift up sword against nation, neither shall they learn war anymore" (Micah 4:2-3). "Arouse the warriors to ascend", Joel had called, "prepare for

91 Alberti, p.172.
92 Maccoby 1996, p.100-101.
93 Lüdemann, p.127-128 (quoted here) and 387-390; cf. Lapide 1988, p.37-40.

battle!" (3:9). Again the iron is battered, but this time from plowshares into swords and from pruning hooks into spears, and after the victory the Lord will dwell on the holy mount. Precisely the Mount of Olives would be the place, so Jesus believed, where the fight had only to be started; just the first spark had to be stroken to make "Judah like a flaming brazier among sticks and like a flaming torch among sheaves" (Zechariah 12:6).

Just start, just strike the spark! A spark from two swords only: "They said: 'Lord, look, here are two swords.' He replied: 'It is enough.'" (Luke 22:38). "A sword for the Lord and for Gideon!" This was the battle call of Gideon's elite troops who had, with nothing else but torches and shofars, defeated the joint armies of Midian, Amalek and Kedem (Judges 6-7). Hadn't Gideon reduced his 22,000 men to 10,000 by sending home the fearful ones, and then reduced the 10,000 to an elite of 300, and hadn't Yahve kept his promise "I will put Midian into your hand by the three hundred"? 310 followers, according to the Toldoth, accompanied Jesus to Jerusalem.[94] And when the Midianites with their allies had panicked in a darkness flickering of torches and resounding of hornblows, hadn't the Lord "turned every man's sword against his fellow" (Judges 7:22), as also Zechariah (14:13) had foreseen in the "great panic from the Lord [that] shall fall upon them"? And hadn't Zechariah assured that "On that day, He will set his feet on the Mount of Olives" and all will change forever, since "the Mount of Olives shall split across ..." (14:4)? It was Zechariah's prophecy "on which Jesus relied especially" in Maccoby's view, and the glory seen by Ezekiel "on the hill east of the city" was the glory of God "for which Jesus, too, was waiting".[95] The two-swords-episode is related by Luke though it doesn't fit at all to his image of Jesus as a self-sacrificer who not only unswervingly performs "what is written" (Luke 22:37) and "as it has been determined" (22:22), but also performs it "just as my father has conferred on me ..." (22:29). Only Luke refused to leave away the all too sharp swords-detail. Only Luke dares to mention that the apostle Simon "was called the Zealot" (6:15, Acts 1:13), thus attaching him to a paramilitary resistance movement founded in 6 CE and united in the credo "that even a militarily hopeless revolt might bring a catastrophe in which the Messiah would be bound to intervene."[96] Himself neither being a zealot nor a Guerrilla leader, "Jesus was convinced that this was the night when God would appear in his glory and destroy the foreign invaders of his Holy Land." The battle, chanceless without the Lord, just had to be started some way, so full of confidence in God that "two swords would be enough. The miracle would be even greater than with Gideon."[97] But don't the two swords run afoul of the famous, and probably authentic "if anyone strikes you on the right cheek, turn the other also" (**Mt 5:39b-42a**)? – No, since "Let him offer his cheek to the smiter" is verse 3:30 of the Lamentations, and it is followed by the outlook on a speedy turn of tables:

94 Goldstein, Morris, p.148-154.
95 Maccoby 1996, p.98; Ezekiel 11:23.
96 Nicholls, p.54.
97 Maccoby 1996, p.81-82 (no zealot) and 99.

"For the Lord does not reject forever ... To wrong a man in his cause – this the lord does not choose" (3:31-35). Rather than preaching passive renounce of life and dignity, Jesus' ominous words in Matthew 5:39-42 are the credo of this rebel who put all his eggs in one basket, who also by offering his cheek to the smiter tried to create a compulsed-move situation, thus coercing his Abba, good father, to intervene and make it right against the Romans.

To modern thinking, Maccoby admits, "it must appear frenzied to reckon with destroying Rome without a regular army and with only two swords, just because of some obscure phrases in a book that was written 500 years before the birth of Jesus. But the Christian presentation has Jesus appear even more frenzied. According to this presentation, Jesus thought himself to be one of the three persons of the Trinitary Almighty God who had descended from the immensities of the world of light to sacrifice Himself for mankind. Such a combination of megalomania and suicidal phantasy was completely alien to the Judean and Galilean societies at Jesus' times. They had their own apocalyptic eccentricities, but this kind of Hellenistic schizophrenia was completely outside of their experience and comprehension." The maniac charisma of Jesus however "followed the standard that is determined for such temperaments in prophetic Jewish tradition" and must have appeared to his contemporaries "breathtakingly bold, but completely reasonable".[98]

Sacrifice objector sacrificed?
Breathtakingly bold – and significant in two overthrowing details – was also his provoking action against temple sacrifice, when he "overturned the tables of the money changers and the seats of those who sold doves" (**Mk 11:15**). Why he started his "violent" activism just at bird cages is the first de-tail, posing an interesting question that could reveal a lot about his motives as a sacrifice opponent and therefore is shunned by Christian theologians. Money changers, well, this role has always fit the Jews, and filled the Chris-tian screen right to the frame, so the doves could fly away unseen from the scene of Jewish greed. Second detail: When the angry activist asks "Is it not written 'My house shall be a house of prayer for all the nations'?" and declares "But you have made it a ...", he takes the term "... a den of robbers" from Jeremiah (7:11), coming very close to, and maybe quoting also, the nearby verses 7:21-22, sarcastic verses that Paul's co-worker Mark would not have liked to mention: "Add your burnt offerings to your other sacrifices and the meat! For when I freed your fathers from the land of Egypt, I did not speak or give them orders about burnt offering and sacrifice." One week after he had called the temple which resembled more a slaughterhouse[99] a den of robbers, the overturner of birdcages was dead.

The fact that Jesus was the baptized disciple of a vegetarian sacrifice-aboli-tionist and that some of his own disciples were vegetarian opponents of ani-mal sacrifice (see chapter 13), together with the profitability of temple sac-

98 Maccoby 1996, p.101.
99 Akers, p.103 ("butcher's shop")

rifice and the power of the established caste raises a startling question: Was Jesus bound to die because he fought against the corruption of Judaism by sacrifice business and had become a naughty guy for branche insiders? Were priestly circles standing behind, or at least conniving at his crucifixion? "Jesus' conduct concerning the temple may have been the reason for the Jewish authority to deliver him to the Romans", Gerd Lüdemann assumes, giving space to old and new versions of Jewish guilt and conspiration.[100] This space, however, depends on the three coordinate questions whether (1) the rebel really presented a serious threat for those circles' income sources; whether (2) Pilate was a loyal representant of Roman jurisdiction or rather a hardliner who didn't hesitate for a wincing to liquidate a potential stress-maker before the most explosive days of the year; and (3) whether the chief of Roman occupation forces in his task of fighting criminal elements would really have depended on the temple-establishment's collaboration.

The latter two points are disproved by the chronicle of Pilate's term of office as well as by his work's schedule on the eve of Passover. Together with Jesus he ordered to crucify two *lestái*. Flavius Josephus uses this term *lestes, lestái* generally to point out Zealots. Also in these two forever anonymous cases of crucified rebels, the complete trial-plus-judgement time seems to have been much shorter than the victims' time of agony; and anything like treason and extradition by Jewish hands was utmost redundant.

Point (1) was dissolved in smoke every year at Passover by the lamb meat craving Jewish population's appetite, as Flavius Josephus' above cited calculation proves. Now just this Galilean itinerant preacher should succeed in what so many prophets together had not achieved, namely to make unpopular or even to abolish the sacrifice of animals? After the destruction of Jerusalem in 70 CE, the rabbis debated seriously whether now the time had come to renounce completely on wine and meat, while ascetic celibatarian groups already had started this eschewal after the catastrophe. The rabbis denied this option by two reasons. First, to beware of those ascetic somatophobic tendencies so alien to Judaism's this-worldlyness; and second, Rabbi Ishmael ben Elisha argued: "Since the destruction of the temple, we should renounce wine and meat. But we shouldn't make an order out of it as long as the community isn't able to live according to."[101] The former British chief rabbi J.H. Hertz stated that had Moses not instituted sacrifices, "his mission would have failed, and Judaism would have disappeared". Rabbi Milgrom adds: "Many prophets sharply criticized the sacrificial system ..., but their lonely isolation in this respect and the positive evidence of the folk literature make it amply clear that the people themselves were convinced that meat met their spiritual needs."[102] As late as 2010, a study of Matthew Ruby proved that in many cultures meat is a symbol of wealth and that women, though they classified vegetarian males as more attractive and smelling bet-

100 Lüdemann, p.107; cf. Akers, who also blames the temple's meat lobby for Jesus' death.
101 Isaiah Berman, Shechitah, p.33 (cit. by Louis A. Berman in Kalechofsky 1992, p.151).
102 Kalechofsky 1992, p.225 and 87.

ter, regarded meat eating men to be "more masculine".[103] In his concept of "Carno-Phallogocentrism", French philosopher Jacques Derrida expresses the common assumption that a person, in order to be fully recognized, must eat meat, be a man and have the word.[104] In the patriarchal order of 30 CE, the action of a man engaged for women's rights, a man who until today is painted in feminine or androgyne softness, would hardly be supposed to change a male dominated, meat accustomed society. His liquidation was a routine order-keeping provision on behalf of an occupational power being just slightly more nervous before a holiday of Jewish masses.

Caught and cleft: Jesus Bar Abbas

Roman routine: seizure of the popular man by military forces, his gang fails to protect him, marching off, examination by the man of power, short court martial? No, in the story told to billions on every Holy Friday, the masses meet the might in a dramatic showdown: "Now at the festival" the noble Roman "used to release a prisoner for them, anyone for whom they asked. And there was one called Barabbas who was in prison with the rebels who had committed murder during the insurrection".

Fast forward: In his documentary film "Shoah", producer Claude Lanzmann interviews, on the holiday of 'Mary's Birth', a group of Polish Catholics in front of their new-gothic church in Chelmno where from December 1941 to spring 1943 and again from June 1944 to January 1945 the Jews, after a night in church, had entered the *Vergasungswagen*. Now 40 years later, the only survivor Simon Srebnik has come back from Israel to stand here amidst his old friends and playmates of childhood. When Lanzmann asks them: "What do you think why this could happen to the Jews?" forward steps one Mr. Kantarowski who then had given "bread and cucumbers" to the Jews. Energetically he tells a story in which a rabbi – with the SS-officer's permission – had explained to his waiting community how, long time ago, the Jews had condemned Christ, who was completely innocent, to death and said his blood shall come upon us and our children. And now, the rabbi said, this time has come, "so let's do what we're required to, let's go!"

Lanzmann: "Ah, the rabbi has said this!"

Kantarowski: "When Pilate washed his hands he said: 'This man is innocent, I don't want to have to do with this story', and he sent Barabbas. But the Jews shouted 'His blood shall come upon us!'" – Short silence. Then ...

Kantarowski: "That is the end, now you know everything."[105]

By the way, the surname Kantarowski, probably reminding the cantor of a synagogue, owes to 212 Shoa victims registered in Yad Vashem, Jerusalem.

Back to this city: The "abba, father", (Mk 14:36; Mt 23:9; Rom 8:15) inserts a personal note into the gospels, as abba is one of their few words from Ara-

---

103   Frankfurter Allgemeine Zeitung online, December 18, 2012.
104   Adams, p.6.
105   Lanzmann, p.17-19 and 132-137.

maic, the everyday language of Jesus. The strange coincidence that this *Bar Abbas*, literally *Son of Father*, bore the first name *Jesus* had startled already Church Father Origen (185-254). Can a robber, he asked himself, bear such a holy name? During the following centuries, the name "Jesus Barabbas" was suppressed in most of the handwritten gospel copies. Why? Meticulously my Catholic German "Jerusalemer Bibel" of 1968 hints in a tiny footnote to Matthew 27:16 at the "Other reading (here and v.17): Jesus Barabbas". Actually and literally, in the Greek original text of Matthew 27, the two verses read: *Eichon de tóte desmion epísmenon legómenon Iesoun Barabban* – "At that time they had a notorious prisoner, called Jesus Barabbas." Now Pilate asks the Jewish people: *Tina thélete apolýso hymín: Iesoun ton Barabban e Iesoun ton legómenon christón* – "Whom do you want me to release for you, Jesus Barabbas or Jesus who is called the Messiah?"
And as Pilate's motive Matthew adds: "For he knew that for envy they had delivered him." (27:18). If so, shouldn't he have foreseen clearly that they would decide against this Jesus whom he could save much easier by a simple word of command, playing the casting game instead with the two "robbers" he anyway would crucify besides the loser of the casting?
Much more telling than this Freudian slip of Matthew is, however, the Jesus Barabbas. Yet in 1946, and by timely reasons, Jules Isaac had hinted gently to this reading: "Why should I conceal the suspicion that obtrudes on me against my will and foreshadows ... that it's been the one and real Jesus for whose pardon the Jewish crowd entreated?"[106]
How the twin question "Jesus the Barabbas or Jesus the Messiah" was born, Hyam Maccoby explains: "All gospels get embarrassed because in the earlier part of the story they have emphasized Jesus' general belovedness so much. This inevitably led to a stumbling transition when later on they wanted to underscore the whole Jewish people's guilt in the crucifixion of Jesus. In the original gospel, Jesus never at all was rejected by the Jewish people or their religious leaders, the Phariseans. His enemies among the Jews were the Sadduceans and the Herodians."[107] That Jesus himself belonged to the progressive, popular group of intellectuals called the Pharisees may be seen yet in his exclusively Pharisaic title "rabbi" which, contrary to the collaborant Sadduceans with their hereditary titles of Levites and Cohanim, signified wisdom acquired by learning.[108] At any rate, the scission between Jesus and the Pharisees was rather harmless compared to the Jekyll-Hydean scission between Jesus and Barabbas.
Purpose and construction of the dramatic element "Enter Barabbas" Maccoby explains this way: "When Jesus was in Pilate's prison, the crowd surrounded the building and called for his release. This was quite a natural thing for them, just continuing their fervent support for him during his triumphant entry and later on. This fact could not be suppressed completely since it based on a strong tradition, but it posed a big problem for later gos-

---
106 Isaac, p.393.
107 Maccoby 1996, p.114.
108 Ben-Chorin 1980, p.185; Lapide (1987, p.111) counts 14 NT mentions of Jesus as rabbi.

pel editors who wanted to show Jesus as being rejected by the whole people. They could not deny that the Jewish people called for Jesus' release but they found a clever solution ... Since the embarrassing tradition related that the crowd called for 'Jesus Barabbas', it was a simple task to imply that this was not a variant name for Jesus but a different man."
Changing Jesus Barabbas to Jesus or Barabbas was to Jesus' scribes as featherlight as it was weighty for Barabbas' kin.

Within his crowd: Barabbas, painted by James Tissot (1836-1902)

But why had Jesus been nicknamed Bar Abbas? In his well-known Father-verses of **Mt 6:9/ Lk 11:2** (Our Father prayer) **Mt 7:11/ Lk 11:13** (If you give good gifts ... how much more your Father), **Mt 6:32 / Lk 12:30** (Your Father knows ...) and the already quoted **Mt 18:14** (... not the will of your Father in heaven that one of these little ones ...) he never refers to *his*, but always to *your* father, stubbornly denying the Son-of-God role Paul would make out of his salient habit of relating to God as Father. "There are some examples of other rabbis in the Talmud who called God 'Abba', but Jesus maybe has made a tantamount conspicuous habit out of this that he came to be called 'Barabbas' by nickname, marking his close relationship with God."[109] Maccoby's view is plausible, but since his proofs (Mk 14:36; Mt 23:9; Rom 8:15; Gal 4:6) are scarce, the more convincing seems how Rabbi Bonder relates the name Bar Abbas to the times of Roman raids when *someone had to assume fathership for these sons who were not marginalized by any means*: "The Aramaic name Bar Abbas or bar-ha-aba literally means Son of Father ... Individuals without a confirmed father could name themselves 'Son of the father', either in the sense of a 'divine fatherhood' – or even in ironic form. This denomination, central to the messianic tensions of redemption of the fatherless sons who threaten Jewish continuity, is very significant." So Bonder, living in a land with so many *mães solteiras* (single

---

109 Maccoby 1996, p.115.

mothers) puts the accent quite different from Maccoby when he strongly backs the British scholar's reading of Pilate's judgment, "... that there were not two to be judged but only one – Jesus, the *bar ha-abba*, the son of the father."[110]

The editorial cleaving between Jesus and Barabbas was not very smooth, however. The rapidness with witch the "Hosianna!" was followed by the "Crucify him!" has become proverbial (notably in Germany) for an abrupt ungrateful revulsion. A disloyal bunch that had welcomed him a week before as "a very large crowd" with palmtree-branches (Mt 21:8); a crowd that in the quantity of "all the people" short time later came to meet him in the temple (John 8:2); a crowd that also Luke terms "all the people", that was "spellbound by what they heard" from his lips (Luke 19:48) and later as "a large crowd of the people and of women who were mourning and lamenting" accompanied him with solidarity on his last walk (Luke 23:27) – this very bunch and what's worse, "all of them" (Mt 27:22), i.e. the "people as a whole" (Mt 27:25) in between is heard shouting for his crucifixion and his blood to come upon them.

Rather, says Maccoby, not the people as a whole but an alarming crowd had gathered in front of Pilate's palace – to call for what? The two details that this "notorious prisoner" (Mt 27:16) named Bar-Abbas "had been thrown into prison for an insurrection in the city" (Lk 23:19) and that the people wanted this selfsame Barabbas to be freed, are two well-linked puzzle parts which now fall to the right place: the place of an insurrector, well-loved by a people that in front of the Prefect's windows had chorused the name of their man of hope, preferring his nickname since it sounded much more rhythmic and aggressive: Je-shú ha Bar-Abbas, Bar-Abbas ha Bar-Abbas! To no avail – or even with a vengeance? The Roman does not yield to *vox populi*, just speaks three words to him, if any: "*Ibis in crucem!*" You'll go to the cross. And thus it happened that this Bar-Abbas who one week before, celebrated by the people, had entered the city through the eastern gate riding over green branches of hope; and who had paced the eastern gate again to pray on the Mount of Promise, was to leave Jerusalem again through the northern gate with a timber on his shoulder.

The last walk of a man whom many had taken for the Messiah: "So much had he relied on the expected miracle on Mount of Olives that his complete apocalyptic system of redemption was broken now."[111] The gospel reports about his increasing taciturnity during the examinations are thoroughly plausible to Maccoby, "not because of surrender to death or the wish for crucifixion but out of total despair and deception." His last cry "Eli, Eli, lama sabachthani? – My God, my God, why have you forsaken me" – is the first verse of Psalm 22. Matching the voluntary self-sacrifice à la Paul like a dementi, this verse of Mark (15:34) is rather a "product of the community" which knew crucifixions, and it "reflects the true tragedy of his situation."[112]

110 Bonder 1998, p.101.
111 Maccoby 1996, p.107.
112 Lüdemann, p.146 ("product of the community"); Maccoby 1996, p.107 ("reflects ...").

One more failed Messiah. *Awanim u meshugaim* – "stones and loonies" are abundant in Jerusalem, a Jewish proverb rightly states until today. In 2008, the city's police central had to take care for the new record number of more than 200 male tourists who right here became convinced to be Jesus. Jerusalem is located high: this happens not for too much heat. Rather for too much cruelty on crosses anchored in young souls and now erupting from grown-up men right here where countless croaked on them.

Less harmlessly, already one generation after the real rabbi Jesus had been cleared by Rome's routine crucifier Pilate, in 66 CE anew enough *meshuggene Rebellen* had assembled to put all chips on one number. "In messianic reveling they moved in masses through the streets, in their naïve conviction that God would intervene to counterbalance Rome's overwhelming military superiority." Fanatics burnt down the grain stock in order to baffle the endurance of a long siege and thus make their fellow-citizens ready for battle. Rabbi Yohanan clearly foresaw how this would end. As truly stinking fake corpse he let himself be smuggled out of the city, had a meeting with General Vespasian, prophesied him that he would become the emperor. Grateful for this career-tip, the arch-enemy rewarded him by his permission to establish a new center of Jewish life in Jaffa. When Jerusalem was defeated and the temple destroyed, the rabbi consoled a disciple who cried after the animal sacrifices in the good old temple: "My son, don't mourn. We have a new sacrifice: acts of charity. Doesn't say God: 'For it is acts of compassion that I seek, not sacrifice; knowledge of God instead of burnt offerings'?" (Hosea 6:6). And concerning Messiahs, Yohanan henceforth kept to be reserved: "In case the Messiah comes when you're just holding a young plant in your hand, first plant the tree, then go and greet the Messiah."[113]

Saint Pilate
When the Greek original verse of Matthew 27:17 has Pilate ask the Jewish people "Which one do you want me to release, Jesus Barabbas or Jesus who is called the Messiah", this generosity of the powerful is as authentic as the later option "Che or Guevara" for Latin American, or "Nelson or Mandela" for African peoples.

Rome's rough-job-man had exercised a strong hand and drastic hardline style since his installation in the rebel people's capital in 26 CE. Wantonly – and maybe testing the limits – he had challenged the Jews yet by his first official act, bringing images of the divine emperor to Jerusalem. All too well he knew that the recognition of the Torah's ban of idols belonged to the privileges Rome had granted to the Jews since Emperor Augustus. Having protested in vain, the Jews reacted with non-violent resistance. Five days and five nights they maintained their sitting blockade in front of his house. Then, Pilate ordered troops to enter; and at a prearranged signal they drew their swords. In this moment the Jews, instead of fleeing in panic, threw themselves to the ground as if on secret order, and offered their necks to

113 Telushkin 2001, p.136.

the swords – prepared to rather die than betray their law. What did Pilate? Calculating quite pragmatically, he not only withdrew the troops but also the idols. To start his presumably highly gainful term of office here with a massacre seemed hardly expedient to the new governor. Anyhow, Emperor Tiberius was not amused with Pilate's stress-test. Philo reports that upon reading the Jewish letter of protest, Tiberius "wrote to Pilate with a host of reproaches and rebukes for his audacious violation of precedent and instructed him to take down the shields at once and have them transferred to Caesarea."[114]

What did end bloody was a second non-violent rally Flavius Josephus reports: "When Pilate raised another disturbance, by expending that sacred treasure which is called Corban ... the multitude had indignation; and when Pilate had come to Jerusalem, they came about his tribunal, and made a clamor at it. Now when he was apprized aforehand of this disturbance, he mixed his own soldiers in their armor with the multitude, and ordered them to conceal themselves under the habits of private men, and not indeed to use their swords, but with their staves to beat those that made the clamor. When he gave the signal from his tribunal, many Judeans perished either by the stripes they received, or trodden to death by their fleeing compatriots; the horror about the sad fate of the killed ones soon silenced the people."[115]

A third massacre is related by Luke (13:1-3): "Now there were some present ... who told Jesus about the Galileans whose blood Pilate had mixed with their sacrifices. He asked them, 'Do you think that these Galileans were more sinful than all the other Galileans because they suffered like this? Absolutely not, I tell you! But if you don't repent, then you, too, will all die'."

Some weeks later albeit, face to face with captive Jesus, this "man of a very inflexible disposition, and very merciless as well as very obstinate", this Roman ruler known for "his corruption, and his acts of insolence, and his rapine, and his habit of insulting people, and his cruelty, and his continual murders of people untried and uncondemned, and his never ending, and gratuitous, and most grievous inhumanity"[116] would melt his heart. Right now this Pilate at last should ripen to become this sympathetic, "milquetoast-like"[117] nobleman who rightly earned his canonization in the Coptic Church by having resisted the evil Jewish conspirators so valiantly until he bent in at last. For "they kept urgently with loud shouts that he should be crucified", and thus the Roman world power's rock-hard outpost gives in, more cowardly than any Sheriff in Wild West confronting a local lynch mob, "... and he handed Jesus over as they wished" (Luke 23:23-25).

German lawyer Weddig Fricke quips that this process would come as "juridical buffoonery number one in world rankings" if it had actually taken place.[118] Pinchas Lapide proves in twelve items how the related trial which

---

114 Philo, On the Embassy to Gaius, Book XXXVIII, p.299–305 (wikipedia, Pilate).
115 Flavius Josephus, The Jewish War, 2.9.4.
116 Philo, op.cit. (en.wikisource.org/wiki/On_the_Embassy_to_Gaius#XXVIII); cf. Maccoby 1996 (p.26) and Perry/Schweitzer (p.33).
117 Rudin, p.33.
118 Fricke, p.321.

for Nicholls is "so improbable as to border on the ludicrous",[119] contradicts the Jewish penal laws and procedural regulations to a grotesque extent. The distortion-opera's finale chord (John 19:16) resounds when Power-Pilate hands the Rebel-Rabbi over "to be crucified", to no one else than to the Jews. "Only one who can imagine the thousands of Roman crosses onto which Pilate, his predecessors and successors, ordered innumerable Jews to be nailed can understand the bloody irony of these lines which try to mock the humane judicature of Israel, to which crucifixions are unknown."[120]
Having condemned Jesus at some day amidst of his term of office, in 36 CE Pilate triggered his own dismissal by his last and bloodiest massacre, which sheds light backwards on his Gethsemane to Golgotha schedule:
At Mount Garisim, the holy site of Samaritans, a group of Samaritans had been persuaded by a preacher to ascend the mountain in order to see sacred artifacts allegedly buried there by Moses. Pilate sent in "a detachment of cavalry and heavy-armed infantry, who in an encounter with the firstcomers in the village slew some in a pitched battle and put the others to flight. Many prisoners were taken, of whom Pilate put to death the principal leaders and those who were most influential."[121] In their complaint filed with Vitellius, the Governor of Syria, the Samaritan council of elders avered that they had gathered at Garisim "not to revolt against the Romans but to escape the violence of Pilate". When Pilate was ordered back to Rome to give report about this clampdown, his files were already filled with what Philo notes apart from his character traits ("vindictiveness and furious temper ... naturally inflexible ... a blend of self-will and relentlessness") and what was intolerable for Roman reputation as a state founded on law, namely "the briberies, the insults, the robberies, the outrages and wanton injuries, the executions without trial constantly repeated, the ceaseless and supremely grievous cruelty."[122]
During his ten years term of office Pilate had sent about 6000 Jews to crosses.[123] That means, just doing business as usual he at an average made 11 men per week croak on the cross. Amidst of these six thousand the condemnation of Jesus had been nothing but "an insignificant act of police", as theologian Maurice Goguel soberly states.[124] His own condemnation Pilate is said to have evaded by suicide.[125] Not even this end did impede his veneration by the Coptic Church, while the Greek-Orthodox Church sainted his first lady Procula who seems to have been sleeping well before her husband's normal workdays but had cautioned him against this special crucifixion: "Have nothing to do with that righteous man; for last night I suffered a great deal because of a dream about him" (Mt 27:19).

---

119 Nicholls p.107.
120 Lapide 1987, p.79.
121 Josephus, Antiquities of the Jews 18.4.1.
122 Lapide 1987, p.72 (Vitellius); Philo, Message to Gaius, XXXVIII (cf.wikipedia, Pilatus).
123 Lapide 1987, p.73: "by conservative estimate roughly sixthousand Jews ... "
124 Isaac, p.337.
125 Lapide 1987, p.72, referring to church historian Eusebios.

Both her and his canonizations were side-effects of the successful little distortions by which early Christians managed to shift the guilt of Jesus' crucifixion from the Romans – under whose authorities they lived – to the Jews. Quite probably, however, the stories about Jesus' trial have been inspired by Paul's trial (Acts 22-24) at the court of Pilate's successor Felix, with its first hearing at the Sanhedrin, with Jewish conspiracy and the bonhomie of a Roman governor who "wanted to grant the Jews a favor" (24:27). While this triple analogy speaks for an early dating of Acts, until 62, decisive was the year 64: After the conflagration of Rome, up to 300 Christians, i.e. one of ten Christians in the capital, were crucified, burned alive, thrown to animals et cetera, since according to Tacitus (Annals 15:44) the imperator Nero, himself suspected as the big arsonist, put the blame on the Christians "and inflicted the most exquisite tortures" on them.

So it was in a very real fear of cross and flames that Mark wrote his gospel around the year 70, in the understandable attempt to avert suspicions of anti-Roman enmity from the young sect. Life-threatening were three points: Jesus (a) belonged to the rebel people of the Jews; condemned (b) by a Roman he had died the typical (c) cross death of a rebel. Wiping off three dangers with one sweep? By shifting! Guilty had to be – in spite of the undeniable procurator – the Jews. Thereby Jesus was extracted from the Jews, Pilate excused, the cross explained.

Significant for this shifting is the Greek word *lestes*, plural *lestai*: Barabbas was a lestes, but in Christian shift of meaning he became a robber. Actually lestai were but those who stole and agitated for political reasons, and Josephus used this word exclusively when referring to revolutionaries, as the Greek word was commonly used for "guerilla fighters against Rome, who were either 'terrorists' or 'freedom fighters' depending on one's point of view. Their presence in the story reminds us that crucifixion was used specifically for people who systematically refused to accept Roman imperial authority."[126]

Mark accepted. How vehemently must or should we accuse him and his epigones of falsifying history? "In its origins and first moments, that Christian propaganda was fairly innocent", the distinguished trial-of-Jesus expert Dominique Crossan admits. "As long as Christians were the marginalized and disenfranchised ones, such passion fiction about Jewish responsibility and Roman innocence did nobody much harm. But once the Roman Empire became Christian, that fiction turned lethal. In the light of latter Christian anti-Judaism and eventually of genocidal anti-Semitism, it is no longer possible in retrospect to think of that passion fiction as relatively benign propaganda. However explicable its origins, defensible its invectives, and understandable its motives among Christians fighting for survival, its repetition has become the longest lie, and for our own integrity, we Christians must at least name it as such."[127]

---

126 Stephen Mansfield: Crucifying Terrorists. Huffingtonpost, July 14, 2013.
127 Crossan, p. xi-xii and (repeating) p.152.

Lübeck born Haim Cohn (1911-2002), Supreme Court judge in Israel, delegate to UN-Human Rights Council and judge at International Court in Den Haag, found it "depressing to realize that the Jewish canon, prohibiting the study of the New Testament, so long delayed an impartial investigation of the judgement of Jesus". Here's his own assessment: "I dare to say that the rapporteurs themselves who primarily wrote for the propaganda of their faith could never have imagined which immense and ineffable sufferings they would invoke by their ficticious reports ... Everywhere in the Christian world the Jews have been accused of a crime that neither they nor their ancestors had committed. Worse even, through centuries and millennia they had to suffer all kinds of torture, persecution and humiliation due to the role their ancestors were said to have played in the trial of Jesus, in which these ancestors not only didn't take part by any means but also did everything that was feasible by human standards to save this Jesus, whom they loved as one of theirs, from his tragic end in the Roman oppressors' hands. If we can find anywhere a grain of comfort for this perversion of justice, then in Jesus' own words: 'Blessed are those who are persecuted for justice's sake, for theirs is the kingdom of heaven.'"[128]

Last not least, William Nicholls resumes: "We do not know if the device" – the Roman-friendly falsification of history – "worked to save Christian lives in the dangerous times of the first century. We do know that it cost countless Jewish lives in the subsequent centuries."[129]

Succinctly, for Jesus' cross the Jews got Auschwitz, the Romans the Vatican. What historical scholarship permits us to assume with certainty behind all fiction is for Nicholls this: "Jesus of Nazareth was a faithful and observant Jew, who lived by the Torah, and taught nothing against his own people and their faith. He did not claim to be the Messiah and may even have denied outright that he was. The Jews did not conspire to kill him and were not responsible for his death. He met his end on a Roman cross, condemned by a Roman official for a Roman offense. The myth of the Christ-killers lacks a basis in history. The story it tells of Jewish rejection and malice is not true. The Romans, not the Jews, were the Christ-killers."[130]

Still in 1960, the Catholic Religion Booklet for Primary Schools in Augsburg Diocese informed me and my classmates: "The Jews however shouted even louder: 'Crucify him, crucify him!' So Pilate was frightened. He spoke the sentence of death and handed Jesus to the Jews to crucifixion." About the meaning of this last term, the bleeding Jesus in our classroom left no doubt. And that's the point. The gospel texts just channel emotions of just revenge, emotions whose anchor and generator is the crucifix. The channelling works safely. Just punishment never hit Italians for the nails which their legionaries knocked through hands and feet of two equally suffering, equally desperate, equally naked Jewish mothers' sons Signor Pilato ordered to crucify aside of Jesus. Since they were just lestai.

---

128 Cohn, Haim, p.342-345.
129 Nicholls, p.108.
130 Nicholls, p.xxvi.

IV   Crucified, died, overcome

*"If the God of love and mercy, just out of his compassion, could not stand
seeing that Abraham wanted to slaughter his son – how could he have
permitted that his own son was killed away, and at that in the most cruel,
most inhumane way on earth?"*   Martin Buber[131]

Civilized Greek and Roman authors classified crucifixion as a method of
barbarian peoples. Anyhow, in its combination of purposes, the technique
was almost as genial as brutal. A low-cost high-profit device for high-power
low-scruple machos, providing high visibility, supreme cruelty, outstanding
isolation, excellent terrorizing effect at the low cost of one to two rough
beams and three to four nails: "At relatively small expense and to great public effect the criminal could be tortured to death for several days in an unspeakable way."[132] No wonder that the cheap method was applied for thousand years, from 600 BCE to 400 CE, by Indians and Assyrians, Scythians
and Taurians, Celts and Seleucids, Persians, Numidians and Macedonians
– and particularly by Carthaginians from whom the Romans learnt, as Cicero says, *istam pestem,* "that pestilence" which probably by Roman model
spread to Britons and Germans, and by Christian model as far as to Japan
where it was still practised around 1865.
No wonder so far that this expression of unrestricted power in form of
unrestricted cruelty found its largest application in the "first totalitarian state
in history".[133] During the first century CE the Roman Empire was dominated
by a plutocracy of 600 senators who owned probably half of the 500.000
slaves living in the Roman capital while of Italy's 13 million inhabitants
almost five million were slaves.[134] *Crucifige et impera!* Crucifixion technique
was applied against rebellious slaves within Italy (Crassus, who crucified
6000 Spartacists in 71 BCE, had gained enormous wealth by slave-trade)
– and "excessively to 'pacify' rebellious provincials", whom Roman law
did not regard as enemies but as *latrones* (robbers).[135] By Jesus' time, the
cross "was the primary form of punishment for 'inciting rebellion', the exact
crime with which Jesus was charged."[136]
Tacitus reports that at the execution-place near the gate of Esquilin outside
of Rome an area was reserved especially for the crucifixion of slaves, which
gave reason to Horace for giving the vulture a new name: Avis esquilinus.[137]
The vertical beams stood there, allegedly in the quantity of a small forest,
ever ready to take up the vertical beams which the arriving slaves carried on
their shoulders, their hands maybe already nailed onto them.

---

131   Buber, Martin (ed.): Aggadat Bereshit. Vilnius 1925, p.31 (by Lapide 1988, p.58-59).
132   Hengel, p.22-23 and 87; complemented by wikipedia-entry "crucifixion".
133   A.N.Wilson, British historian, quoted by Carroll (p.80).
134   Wikipedia, slavery in ancient Rome; unrv.com/empire/roman-population.php.
135   Hengel, p.66 and 47.
136   Aslan, p.220.
137   Hengel, p.54.

Telushkin estimates the total number of crucified anti-roman Jewish *latrones/lestai* at 50.000 to 100.000.[138] Were Jews more pain-resistant than other peoples? Hardly so, considering how Roman general Bassus defeated the fortress of Machaerus: When a heroic and defiant young Jew named Eleazar was captured off the walls, Bassus "ordered that he should be taken up naked, set before the city to be seen, and sorely whipped before their eyes". Perceiving how the Jews "were terribly confounded, and the city, with one voice, sorely lamented him", Bassus commanded "to set up a cross, as if he were just going to hang Eleazar upon it immediately; the sight of this occasioned a sore grief among those that were in the citadel, and they groaned vehemently, and cried out that they could not bear to see him thus destroyed." Eventually, the whole city surrendered for one man, in exchange for safe conduct granted to all of them including Eleazar, "who himself had pleaded them not to abandon him to suffer this most cruel kind of death."[139] In 1968, archaeologists discovered in the northeastern part of Jerusalem the remains of one Jehohanan ben Hagkol, who had been crucified in the first century CE. The remains included a heel bone with a nail driven through it from the side. The tip of the nail was bent, perhaps because of having stroken a knot in the upright beam. The nail's length of less than 12 cm (4.5 inches) suggests that in Jehohanan's case the heels were nailed to opposite sides of the upright beam. "Crucifixion was usually intended to provide a death that was particularly slow, painful, gruesome, humiliating, and public, using whatever means were most expedient for that goal." Because it was often "performed to terrorize", Wikipedia adds, "victims were left on display after death as warnings to others who might attempt dissent."

What kind was the mind and soul of those hangmen who placed the nail tip on trembling flesh and swung the hammer? Josephus relates the siege of Jerusalem, where "they caught every day five hundred Jews; nay, some days they caught more ... The soldiers, out of the wrath and hatred they bore against the Jews, nailed those they caught, one this way and one that way, to the crosses, by way of jest, when their multitude was so great that room was wanting for the crosses and crosses wanting for the bodies."[140]

However, one should not think too badly of the legionaries. They, too, were capable of compassion, could often stand no more to watch the endless perishing, to hear the cries and howls of victims hanging on their nails probably not much higher than eye-level. Besides, the guards could only leave the site after the poor guys had died. To put an end they lighted dry brush beneath them to choke the delinquents, or they practised the crurifragium, smashing the victim's legs and arms with clubs so the body collapsed and death by suffocation came soon.

Quite a different intention was embodied in the "sedile", a plug to sit upon, and the "suppedaneum" to stand upon: relieving pain and giving minimal comfort, but just to prolongate the suffering, not to let the victim escape too

138 Telushkin 2001, p.507-508.
139 Josephus, The Jewish War, 7.6.4.
140 Josephus, The Jewish War, 5.11.1.

soon to where there is no crucifixion. Physicians still debate where the hand nails had to be placed to avoid tearing out, and where the foot nails were hammered down for a better cost-benefit ratio. The benefit: submission by fear of similar torture.

Few artists (among them Michelangelo und Brunelleschi) dared to present the crucified one in the way that was required by the purpose of utmost humiliation: stark naked. Sueton relates that "with his proverbial clemency, Caesar had the pirates' throats cut before crucifixion in order to spare them suffering". In the dramas of Plautus, the *maxuma mala crux* translates as "cross, the utmost evil" for the slaves, while Cicero, who demanded that "the very word 'cross' should be far removed not only from the body of a Roman citizen but also from his thoughts, his eyes and ears", had to invent a new word to express his abhorrence: "crudelissimum *teterrimum* supplicium", literally signifying the "cruellest utterterrible torture" possible. To his contemporary Varro yet the word expresses pain: "As gentle the word 'voluptas'[joy, lust] is to our ears, as scratching is it when we say 'crux', ... the very word's scratchiness concording with the scratching pain effected by the cross ... Are we not barbarians", the satirical writer asks, "when we fasten humans to the cross"?

Stoic philosopher Seneca points to the basic message of crucifixion – We have the power to make dying your desire! – when he rhetorically asks why someone hanging on his wounds should not hope for death during torments "in which the only comfort is the outcome of the execution" after a protracted agony "limb by limb and exhaling life drop by drop"?[141]

Based on these and other diligently compiled statements of antique authors, German theologian Martin Hengel resumes: "Crucifixion was widespread and frequent, above all in Roman times, but the cultured literary world wanted to have nothing to do with it, and as a rule kept quiet about it ... The extraordinary paucity of the theme of crucifixion in the mythical tradition, even in the Hellenistic and Roman period, shows the deep aversion for this cruellest of all penalties in the literary world ... No ancient writer wanted to dwell too long on this cruel procedure." None except those famous four: "We have very few more detailed descriptions, and they come only from the Roman times: the passion narratives in the gospels are in fact the most detailed of all."

Socio-psychologically, Hengel extrapolates four motives of antique crucifixion which are not too antique: "The chief reason for its use was its allegedly supreme efficacy as a deterrent; it was, of course, carried out publicly ... There was doubtless a fear that to give up this form of execution might undermine the authority of the state and existing law and order. At the same time, crucifixion satisfied the primitive lust for revenge and the sadistic cruelty of individual rulers and of the masses." Altogether, crucifixion is "a specific expression of the unhumanity dormant within men ... a manifesta-

141 Hengel, p.7-10 (Plautus, Cicero, Varro ...); Sueton: The Twelve Caesars, ourcivilisation.com; Cicero: Pro Rabirio Perduellionis Reo 5:16; Seneca, Epistle 101 to Lucilius, quoted by freerepublic.com.

tion of trans-subjective evil, a form of execution which manifests the demonic character of human cruelty and bestiality."[142]
Only with the last word I cannot agree, considering that the Latin noun *bestia* stands for "animal, beast of prey, rapacious animal". No beast of prey would do what human brutes did to their victims on the cross and what Maurice Goguel calls the "peak point of torture art".[143]
One can rightly argue that the thousand-years-long use of crucifixion as the non-plus-ultra of cruellest possible execution was not characteristic for the soul-condition of populations at that time but always the work of single brutished individuals capable of, and useable for, everything; and that the abolition of crucifixion was the long-term success of outspoken, humanely feeling individuals like Cicero, this marking a progress of humanity.
But then, in what barbarity the Christian occident has remained since Constantine? Yes, Constantine the Great, who abolished crucifixion as Roman method in 320, openly confessed the Christian faith when he had conquered autocratic rule in 324, dominated in 325 the Nicean council especially in having it adopt the creed of the Son's one substance with Almighty Father – and ordered the murder of his son in 326! "A father who slays a son! A father who slays his son in righteousness! ... One needn't be a Freudian", James Carroll says, "to sense the new power that the myth of the cross would have had over him ... If God can kill his son, so can God's coregent." Few people today know this son's name Crispus, fewer don't connote the other son's name Jesus with cross nails, and Carroll asks for the consequences this "pathological culture of holy violence" had for other victims: "Can it be a coincidence that attacks on Jews ... become a notable pattern of Christian behavior only after the cult of the cross is established ...?"[144]
Can it be a coincidence that still in the 1940s workmanlike crucifixions were performed in a suburb of Munich? About these "controlled tests" French Catholic surgeon Pierre Barbet relates at length:
"We can cite the depositions of two former inmates of the Lager Dachau who several times have seen how this kind of execution was applied and have kept it in terrible reminiscence ..." I spare the reader details, the finale says enough: "After one hour of hanging, the pullups became more and more frequent, and weaker and weaker. The witness describes that the chest was puffed up to the highest limit, the belly sunk in deep. The legs hung down stiffly and didn't move ... The skin became violet. Sweat broke out of the body abundantly, running to the ground and wettening the concrete floor. Particularly during the last minutes before death it flew extraordinarily plentiful; hair and beard were literally soaked. And this at temperatures near zero degrees Celsius ..."[145]

142 Hengel, p.87; previous citations: Hengel p.7, 8, 80, 42, 10, 36, 30-31, 38, 14, 25.
143 Goguel, M.: Jesus and the Origins of Christianity, Vol.II. New York 1960, p.535 (Haim Cohn, p.242).
144 Carroll, p.203-204 and 191.
145 Barbet, p.126.

In Munich, the heart of the "national Bavaria" which Hitler in 1923 held proudly against "Bolshevist northern Germany",[146] the Landtag in 1995 ordered crosses into all public primary schools. In Vienna, where the pamphlets of fanatic ex-monk Lanz von Liebenfels made Hitler a Jew-hater, the Supreme Court's judges in 2011 legalized crucifixes in *public kindergartens*. The presentation of the "most barbarous execution that has ever been employed by a state"[147] in kindergartens, classrooms, courtrooms and on countless mountaintops of both countries seems to express an extroversion inherent to the symbol: "Crucifixions were always carried out in public – at crossroads, in theatres, on hills, or on high ground – anywhere where the population had no choice but to bear witness to the gruesome scene."[148]
The crucifix is not the symbol of death, but of death defeated, of resurrection and new life. So Christians say. In Pauline and common Christian doctrine, Jesus by his breakthrough ultimately vanquished death and granted afterlife for all humans, or rather: all believers. "Do you believe in afterlife, heaven or hell, or reincarnation?" A poll around this question, performed in 2011 by Ipsos Global Advisory, yielded the following percentages of believe in life after death: Behind mainly Muslim Turkey with 80 percent ranked the mainly Christian countries Brazil (74) and USA (69), before mainly Muslim Indonesia (65) and mainly Hinduist India (57). The culturally Buddhist countries South Korea, China and Japan ranked at the end with 39, 34 and 27 percent believing in afterlife, together with the 37 percent in cross-abundant Germany with its 58.7 percent Christians.[149] Obviously, the picture of his death-defeating death gives Christendom no edge in global believe-in-afterlife championship, and neither does Paul's assertion that "as all die in Adam, so all will be made alive in Christ" (1 Cor 15:22).
How do the gospels relate this resurrection? In the earliest gospel, "When the Sabbath was over, Mary Magdalene, Mary the mother of James [as well as of Jesus, Judas, Simon] and Salome bought spices, so they might go and anoint him." When they arrive at the grave, the shutter stone is rolled aside, the grave is empty, save for a young man dressed in a white robe explaining: "He has been raised. He is not here. Look, there is the place they laid him. But go, tell his disciples and Peter that he is going ahead of you to Galilee; there you will see him, just as he told you."
Why do the three women who had been so close to Jesus in his lifetime now flee from the tomb, as "terror and amazement had seized them and they said nothing to anyone, for they were afraid"? And why does Mark's final chapter in his authentic form end so mundanely without any actual witness of resurrection, whereas yet some fifteen years earlier Paul had assured the Corinthians (1, 15:4-8) neatly: "He was raised on the third day in accordance with the scriptures and appeared to Cephas, then to the twelve. Then he appeared to more than five hundred brothers at one time ... then to James,

---

146 Hitler, speech on September 5, 1923; Boepple, p.87.
147 Nicholls, p.110.
148 Aslan, p.155.
149 ipsos, April 25, 2011; the share of 58.7 % was summed up by the author from all the 65 Christian denominations listed by Wikipedia ("Religionen in Deutschland") for 2011.

then to all the apostles. Last of all, as to one untimely born, he appeared also to me"? The explanation of the discrepancy resides within Paul's last words: Just as Jesus had "appeared also to me" more than ten years after his crucifixion, namely in a non-physical but spiritual vision, thus Paul alleges Jesus to have appeared to the leading figures of the Jerusalem community. Paul's spiritual, visionary interpretation of Christ's resurrection – note that according to Paul so far no female sinful being had seen the raised redeemer – contrasts strikingly with the sober report of the three Jewish women who never claimed to have seen the person so dear to them in his lifetime newly alive now after his death on the cross.

How did they have spent, or better say come through the Sabbath after his crucifixion and burial? Sabbath is not for sadness. How not get drowned in depression after his death? What to read in order to gain new hope? What did *he* use to read? Maybe Hosea, chapter 6? "Come, let us return to the Lord. He has torn us to pieces; now he will heal us. He has injured us; now he will bandage our wounds. In two days He will make us whole again; *on the third day* he will raise us up ... *His appearance* is as sure as *daybreak* ... for I desire goodness, not sacrifice; knowledge of God instead of sacrifice." *On the third day*, at *daybreak*, his sister Salome, his mother Mary and his friend Mary from Magdala went to the tomb. *His appearance*? The tomb is empty.

Crossan disputes the empty tomb as an historical fact, but Geza Vermes argues that this emptyness is rooted too deeply in tradition to be dismissed as untrue, since within the passion narratives this empty tomb is rather "the one solid fact underlying all these stories".[150] Matthew enshrouds this *solid fact* into one more plot story including this time an angel in white clothing and Pilate's dumbstruck guards bribed by the Jews to spread the lie of the stolen corpse. Luke hasn't heard that rumour, but he replaces the one white angel by two men in white and the *solid fact* confirmed by the third man Peter who "ran to the tomb ... and looking in, he saw the linen cloths by themselves". Contrarily, John is moved by *the one solid fact* to provide, among all gospels, the historically most correct description of the then common burial customs of the Jews, in a rock tomb typical of Jesus' time.

Historical fact is that these tombs were made for a two-steps-burying: The embalmed corpse remained stretched-out therein until one year later its dried bones were put into a small ossuary to remain in the tomb together with other ossuaries.

If we suppose a vanished corpse had been the starting point of all these visions (as the majority of scholars assumes), we are left with two interpretations: Either the corpse was removed or put into another tomb – what Matthew (28:11-15) disputes by means of ascribing bribery to the usual suspects. Or, the crucified one was not really actually truly dead which John (19:33-35) denies by means of physical evidence (broken legs, side wound, embalming).

---

150   Nicholls, p.117.

Flavius Josephus, who died in 100 CE, in his biography (section 75) remembers a friend who really rose from crucifixion: "I saw many captives crucified, and remembered three of them as my former acquaintance. I was very sorry at this in my mind, and went with tears in my eyes to Titus, and told him of them; so he immediately commanded them to be taken down, and to have the greatest care taken of them, in order to their recovery; yet two of them died under the physician's hands, while the third recovered."

In Jewish jurisdiction, the fact that a man had been seen hanging on the cross was not taken for a valid proof of his death. According to the Talmud, the spouse of a crucified man could marry newly only if trustworthy witnesses had stated her husband's death or he himself from high on cross had agreed to divorce. For tradition has cases of crucified ones who hung up to five days on beams and life – persevering long enough "to obtain their pardon from the Romans by means of bribe and, taken down from cross, to be nursed to health again."[151]

"Nursed to health" is a metaphor of enticing humaneness. However, neither will I indulge in speculation about a happier end of Jesus' life, nor do I subscribe to Crossan's worst case scenario in which he explains the empty tomb, as well as the fact that "of all other thousands of Jews crucified around Jerusalem in that terrible first century ... we have found only one skeleton and one nail", with "the dogs again, at worst".[152] The best case scenario probably would start with "the richest matrons among 'the dear women of Jerusalem' who, as we read, attended crucifixions and by bribing soldiers and officials sometimes achieved to have a still respiring victim taken down from the cross."[153] And best case could finish, since the ends of Mark's, Matthew's and John's gospels point to Galilee, with the "grave of Jesus tradition" to which the famous 16th century Kabbalist Isaac Luria refers and that in any case expresses high esteem: Luria says that Jesus lies buried near Galilee's mountain top city of Safed, and counts his grave among "the burial places of the righteous".[154]

151 Lapide 1984, passim; cf. Lapide 1988, p.84.
152 Crossan, p.188.
153 Cohn, Haim, p.239.
154 Tabor, p.295-300.

V   Revised by Paul
Make the rebel teach submission

*For I would have you know, brethren, that the gospel which was
preached by me is not according to man. I received my message
from no human source, and no one taught me. Instead, I received
it by direct revelation from Jesus Christ.*   Paul, Galatians 1:12

"One who has visions should meet his doctor". This advice was given by
a Sephardic Jew's German grandson, i.e. the Protestant Federal Chancellor
Helmut Schmidt (1918-2015), to all politically engaged citizens.[155] Ironically
enough, European citizens' political views were molded by a Roman citizen
who dedicatedly spent his post-conversion life converting Roman Empire
to his visions, instead of meeting his doctor. His personal visions about a
man he had never met transformed this man into the son of a being that no
one had ever seen: God. The fact that Paul had chosen just a son of this odd
people for the role of a perfect God-man hardly makes his visions more
credible to Jews. And his promotion of a rebel to a teacher of obedience
reminds me on a Berlin citizen who in 1937 applied at NSDAP party bureau
and put on the desk a page of Nazi gazette *Völkischer Beobachter* in which
he had marked with a pencil the job offer "Young, strong man wanted for
storeman work".
"Good man, how old are you?" the staff manager asks. "Fifty-nine." – "And
where have you lost your right arm?" – "At Verdun in 1916." – "And what's
that funny cap you've on your head?" – "My kippah." – "So you happen to
be Jewish?" – "Right." – "And why did you come here?" – "Just to tell you
that you shouldn't count on me."

Saul, why do you persecute me?
But Paul counted on Jesus, who could not decline the offer. "After his death
he fell into the hands of the pagans who didn't understand neither his aims
nor his inner essence. They cut him off of his roots and transformed him
into a forceless angel and finally into an object of adoration. This happened
in the interest of a world-negating philosophy he would have hated. It was
part of a compromise and an agreement with the very power he had attacked
at the price of his own life; since thanks to a paradoxon that he would have
understood very well, a world-negating philosophy always means an aban-
donment of the world, and the only philosophy which enters into relations

---

155   His father Gustav Schmidt (1888-1981), the illegitimous son of a waitress with banker
Ludwig Gumpel, was adopted by a dockworker family. Only his mother, behind his father's
back, had told him "the story" in 1934. As a front-line officer, "I didn't know anything about
the genocide of Jews, like many people then", Schmidt said in 2005. Counting Anwar Sadat
and Henry Kissinger among his greatest friends, Protestant Schmidt confessed his lack of
religious faith since "God let Auschwitz happen" (FAZ, April 9, 2005 and Wikipedia).

with worldly powers and fights against them is a philosophy which affirms this world."[156]

Though I doubt whether an early traumatized Jesus bar Pandera was very affirming to his own life which he threw into the battle, for the rest I agree with Maccoby's view. Against the worldly power of Pilate's empire, Jesus had fought with the Jewish concept of a this-worldly redemption from slavery, of an authonomy which grants that "everyone will sit under their own vine and under their own fig tree, and no one will make them afraid" (Micah 4:4), a concept which affirms the body and its needs, including sexuality which played a certain role in all human procreations for millions of years except for – in Christian view – but one of all these beings: the Son of Man. This son of a Jewish mother suffered a Kafkaesque conversion, getting remodelled to a quasi Alien, an icon of absolute purity and celibatarian body-aversion, in favor of an idealism hovering above this dirty world, and against Judaism which is "a religion of the body. Even immortality is Jewishly conceived in terms of the resurrection of the body, not in terms of a so-clean wraith-like soul floating clear from the contamination of matter."[157]

Such down-to-earth a Jewishness Hyam Maccoby attributes to this man who in Richard E. Rubenstein's view "in truth was a great prophet – a teacher and activist with important contributions to the tradition of Isaiah's and Jeremiah's era six centuries before"; a prophet who since then, by his message of non-violent resistance, "inspired modern prophets like Gandhi, Martin Luther King and Nelson Mandela". The praxis of Jesus was to extend human respect on "the less important ones among you: women, children, slaves and all those who, by virtue of their anonymity and powerlessness, were denied respect and dignity ... But when, three centuries after his crucifixion, the new faith became the state religion of Roman empire, the latter's hierarchy of power was adopted by Christendom together with its insensitivity against the weak ones and with exactly that injustice, inhumanness and violence which the prophets had condemned."[158]

According to Sidney Ahlstrom, Christian doctrine is but "a series of footnotes to Paul"[159] – and Paul was Roman. Small wonder hence that the term "Romans" occurs but one time in all four gospels, namely in John 11:48 where High Priests and Pharisees fear that at the end "everyone will believe in him, and the Romans will come and destroy both our holy place and our nation ... So from that day on they planned to put him to death."[160] James Tabor deems the four gospels and the New Testament on the whole "hardly more than the literary legacy of the apostle Paul". However, Tabor finds in the New Testament "two completely different and separated 'Christianities'. With the first one we are well acquainted; it became the one 'version' of Christian belief which during the last two millennia was professed by billions of human beings. The initiator of this version was the myth-creator

156 Maccoby 1996, p.111.
157 Maccoby 1987, p.19.
158 Rubenstein, Richard E., p.131-139.
159 Sidney Ahlstrom, ed.: Theology in America. Indianapolis 2003, p.23 (by Rudin, p.47).
160 Maccoby 1996, p.8.

Paul. The other Christianity fell almost completely in oblivion, and as early as at the turn to the second century it had been largely marginalized and oppressed by the first one."[161]
But let's turn towards the winners first, as usual. Their master-mind is the probably most famous convert of world-history. Considering his immensely powerful influence, some oddities of Paul are worth mentioning here. From the Jesus-sect's merciless persecutor in charge of the collaborant priestly caste of Sadduceans, Saul turned into the vision-legitimized Jesus-disciple who almost like a young cuckoo pressed Jesus' brothers out of the nest in which he spread. For just to spreading aimed his program, outflanking the proselytist universalism of the pharisees, towards an empire-wide pagan target group. He presents himself as a Jew "of the tribe of Benjamin" (Romans 11:1; Philippians 3:5), though already after the end of the Babylonian exile (536 BCE) all tribal lines (except the tribe of Levi) had been blurred and in first century BCE no Jew knew any more whether he descended "from Rachel or Leah", not to speak of Bilhah and Zilpah, the other two matriarchs of the twelve tribes. Paul allegedly speaks Hebrew (Acts 22:1), calls himself a "Hebrew of Hebrews, in regard to the law, a Pharisee" (Philippians 3:5), but takes all his 160 biblical quotations from the Greek translation of the Hebrew Bible[162] and presents himself, a little too rich, as a disciple of great scholar Gamaliel (Acts 22). He pretends to be a Pharisee but persecuted the Jesus community by order of the decidedly anti-Pharisaic Sadduceans.
"For the sake of knowing Jesus I have discarded everything else" he assures the Philippians (3:8), but the Corinthians he reminds of "your aforepromised bounty, that should be ready as a matter of bounty, and not of extortion" (2 Cor 9:5). He justifies his "material benefits" and his refraining from work on the ground that whoever tends a flock should get some of its milk and one who threshes should have "a share in the crop" (1 Cor 9:3-10). And with amazing regularity he talks about donation money (Rom 15:26; 1 Cor 16:2; 2 Cor 8; Phil 4). Even the Roman governor Felix "hoped that money would be given him by Paul, and for that reason he used to send for him very often and converse with him" (Acts 24:26).
These talks between Paul and Felix "who was rather well informed about the Way" (Acts 24:22) however did not take place until Paul had passed a decisive parting of the ways.
Having caused a tumultuous "outcry" in the temple by his touting speech – centered in his Damascus vision – to the "Jews of Jerusalem", a Roman tribune orders him to be examined by flogging. Not earlier than when the soldiers have already "tied him up with tongs", not earlier than he has made up his decision, he asks the bystanding centurion: "Is it legal for you to flog a Roman citizen ...?" Immediately, the centurion calls the tribune, who asks Paul: "Are you a Roman citizen?" – "Yes." – "It cost me a large sum of money to get my citizenship." – "But *I* was born a Roman citizen".

---

161 Tabor, p.338 and 326.
162 Maccoby 2007, p.79.

Really? As a "Jew from Tarsus in Cilicia" Paul had introduced himself before the temple sermon (22:3). In her study *Romanisierung in Kilikien*, Susanne Pilhofer "found during the first half of the first century but three Cilicians with Roman citizenship.[163] Paul, his father, mother and sister would be four already – and Jews at that! This outing as a Roman citizen is decisive in two ways. On one side, from now on Paul is well protected. The Romans escort him with 470 well-armed legionaries to Roman-named coast city Caesarea (Acts 23:23), and in his letter to the faithful in Philippi (4:22), a place where Roman citizenship was in great demand, Paul greets "all the saints, especially those of the emperor's household": a compromising greeting which Catholic *Jerusalemer Bibel* tries to blur by the addition that "*emperor's household* had a very large meaning". Maccoby supposes that Paul acquired Roman citizenship not earlier than shortly before his journey to Jerusalem – by donation money. "Not for his personal advantage, but weighing priorities on which would depend the future of Christianity." Which priorities? "As soon as Paul had outed himself as a Roman citizen, his problematic relationship with the 'Church of Jerusalem' was broken. This message must have been not a little shock for James and the other Jerusalem community leaders. In its essence, the movement of Jesus had been a throughout anti-Roman movement ... By that, a Roman citizenship was the last thing which an adherent of this movement would have deemed desirable."[164]

Paul had taken his decision. Rather than breaking with the Jewish undivided worldview and "religion of the body", he mentally sneaked back to the Hellenistic dual worldview separating between the chimerical world of physics and the true celestial, mythical region. So strongly rooted was he in this world of myths, that even in his vision of Jesus, Paul's subconscious mind illudes a detail of Greek myth: "I heard a voice speaking to me, and saying in the Hebrew tongue, Saul, Saul, why dost thou persecute me? It is hard for you to *kick against the pricks*." (Acts 26:14, Jubilee Bible 2000). Obviously, this metaphor was inspired lesser by the Aramaic speaking rabbi Jesus than by Greek poet Euripides who, in the third chapter of his Bacchae, has the earthling Pentheus be warned by virgin-born semi-god Dionysus: "I say you shouldn't go to war against a god ... Better to yield him prayer and sacrifice / Than *kick against the pricks*, since Dionyse is God, and thou but mortal." To which Pentheus replies: "I'll sacrifice all right / with a slaughter of women's blood, just as they deserve / in the forests on Cithaeron."[165] A female human sacrifice: this is the Iphigeneia in the famous tragedy which the same Euripides wrote around 405 BCE. Here too a Greek visionary plays the key role. In the port of Aulis the Greek fleet is unable to depart due to a strange lack of wind. The seer Calchas clears the original sin: Goddess Artemis had once been insulted as a subprime hunter by fleet commander

163 Pilhofer, p.175-225.
164 Maccoby 2007, p.178-180.
165 The translation by Gilbert Murray (gutenberg.org/files/35173/35173-h/35173-h.htm) is combined here with Ian Johnston's (records.viu.ca/~johnstoi/euripides/euripides.htm; Malaspina University-College, Nanaimo, BC).

Agamemnon who also brought down a hind in Artemis' holy holt and now must sacrifice his firstborn daughter to solve the problem and let the fleet sail to Troy to take revenge on Paris, the Trojan who had abducted Helena, the wife of his then host Menelaos who is Agamemnon's brother. Lured into the army's camp by a kind of betrayal, Iphigeneia eventually by her own choice accepts the role of sacrifice for her people's success in its genocidal expedition. At the end of the drama, however, a messenger relates that Iphigeneia was saved by the goddess Artemis who instead of the virgin put a hind on the altar.[166] In other versions the father performs the sacrifice. The parallels to Jesus, Isaac and the ram are evident. Euripides solves the moral problem the same way as, probably at least one century before him, the redactors of Genesis did: by intervention of Yahve resp. Artemis, by non-human proxy. This option was not available to the visionary Paul once he had decided to present a charismatic man who had died ten years before now as the sacrificed Son of God. But what was it that caused him to make this fusion? As psychic conditions I discern three elements:

(1) Syncretism of sacrificed sons
The ingredients of the mixture in the myth-maker's mind came not only from the cult of god-son Heracles, who was sired by Zeus fooling Alkmene in her husband's appearance and who ended lifted up to Olympos after his painful death had reconciled the goddess Hera, the jealous wife of Zeus. They came also from the myth of rock-born Mithras, whom a father god had sent to save the world, who after a last supper with twelve disciples died and rose again; his western cult center in the first century BC was Tarsus.[167] But Paul's home region was also close to Phrygia, the syncretic center of two cults Euripides joined in his Bacchae: the cults of Mother Cybele and her partner, the wine loving Dionysus, whose flesh was eaten by his titanic killers and whose resurrection celebrated every springtime in Delphi. The godsons Heracles and Dionysus suffer terrible deaths which correlate to the gratuitous cruelty that the Hellenic gods exercise in the satisfactive punishments of Sisyphos and Tantalos, of Niobe and Cybele's musician Marsyas, the latter getting hanged on a tree and flayed alive by Apollo. Paul's linking of cruel sacrifice with the divine is obviously one more influence of his Greek education, and Franz Rosenzweig is right in his remark that "Prometheus hung in the rock face already half a millennium before the cross was raised on Golgotha".[168]

(2) Sexual trauma
The amphitheatre of Tarsus, where young Saul may have experienced impressing presentations of Euripides' plays, is still a sightseeing point. The subconscious anchorage of Paul's vision in Greek drama might shed no murky light on his positions concerning women, as well as on his parents

---

166 See full text on perseus.tufts.edu; Friedrich Schiller's translation ends with sacrifice.
167 Deal, p.117; Wikipedia (Heracles, Mithras, Dionysus).
168 Rosenzweig, Third Part, Second Book, paragraph 395 (p.418).

who in a way "sacrificed" their sensitive son who never mentioned his parents, but obsessively dealt with obedience. His suppressed homosexuality, channelled into a "homoerotic relationship to his Christ that becomes commendable for millennia"[169] is in Friedrich Heer's view the key to Paul's obsession with this Jesus who couldn't escape his visionary transformation to the sex free, cosmically atoning son of the most high.

From Jesus he hadn't learnt that. For while Paul ascribed his psychopathic view of expiation to a godhead "who did not spare his own Son, but offered him as a sacrifice for all of us", as a "sacrifice of atonement" because he is "our Passover lamb / delivered for our offences" (Rom 8:32; 3:25; 4:25; 1Cor 5:7), forgiveness for offences had been a very different thing for Jesus: The sinful woman's "certificate of debt" is not cancelled bloodily by "having nailed it to the cross" (Col 2:14) but by the signs of her love that Jesus explicitly enumerates: tears, kisses, ointment (**Lk 7:36-47**). In Jesus' way, the gate to the Kingdom of God consists in receiving it "like a little child" (**Mk 10:15**; **Mt 18:3**; **Gospel of Thomas 22:1-2**). In Paul's way the entrance ticket is to have "crucified the flesh with its passions and desires" (Gal 5:24). "Lord, come soon" the early Christians prayed, hoping for the speedy return of the Messiah Jesus. But now "in Paul, this call of the young Christian community becomes the essential of his life. Make use of this short time until the Lord comes back: this is the challenge now – in tireless missionary service, in relentless struggle against the sin, the carnal lust."[170]

Significant for his "homoerotic relationship to his Christ" is Paul the matchmaker's bizarre declaration of love in his second letter to the Corinthians (11:2): "I feel a divine jealousy for you, for I promised you in marriage to one husband, to present you as a chaste virgin to Christ." Jesus the asexual, chaste teacher of self-possession replaces the rebel against oppression; the Roman execution method ends in inner self-crucifixion, punishing the flesh. Advice to Titus (2:9-10): "Tell slaves to be submissive to their masters and to give satisfaction in every respect. They are not to talk back, not to pilfer, but to show complete and perfect fidelity, so that in everything they may be an ornament to the doctrine of God our Savior." In his Letter to the Romans, Paul the Jew proposes the new temple rite "to offer your bodies as living sacrifices that are holy and pleasing to God, which is your spiritual worship" (12:1), while Paul the Roman gives the term slavery a new meaning: "We know that our old natures were crucified with him so that our sin-laden bodies might be rendered powerless and we might no longer be slaves to sin" (6:6, International Standard Version). The battle continues being deadly, without attacking any Roman forces: "If you live according to the flesh, you will die; but if by the spirit you put to death the misdeeds of the body, you will live" (8:13).

Again the question: Was Paul's model of paying by pain in any accordance with Jesus' intentions? Yet Bar-Abbas' prayer to the father (**Mt 6:9-13** without 10b; **Lk 11:2-4**) confirms the opposite in the simple plea: "And forgive

169 Heer 1990, p.66-67.
170 Heer 1990, p.66-67.

us our debts"; the opposite since this forgiving requires no cross-torture here, but only that "we also have forgiven our debtors". This is exactly the condition of Jewish Yom Kippur: Reconciliation with God only after (and by) reconciliation with fellow humans.[171] "Which one of you, if his son asks him for bread, will give him a stone?" Jesus asks in **Mt 7:9**, long before Matthew has him ask the father, in a good Pauline and futile way, for much less than bread: for no wine of pains (Mt 26). Consequently, in his parable of the prodigal son (**Lk 15:11-32**), Jesus praises a human father who does not put any value on reconciliation by atoning sacrifice nor at that by bloody sacrifice or even bloody human sacrifice.

If in Christian-Jewish relations "the Jewish conviction that no good arises from human sacrifice, and the Christian faith that only out of such may be gained salvation, represent the core of conflict" as Gunnar Heinsohn points out,[172] the two antagonists in this conflict are exactly Jesus and Paul, and up to the death camps, those altars of holocaust. Death is the salvator: salving man from sin and mankind from the Jews: This death in sacrifice is the selector, the artist, the race breeding master, the *Meister aus Deutschland*, and Rabinovici says nothing new: "The myth of quasi sacral, necessary sacrifice – Christ's crucifixion – stands at the origin of Christian antisemitism."[173]

Not by accident, Paul's position within early Christianity might be called anti-Jamesism, anti-Simonism and anti-Jerusalemism: His main opponents were the Jerusalem Church with its leaders James and Simon Kephas (Peter). Yet in his second letter to the Corinthians, Paul mocks at those "hyperapostles" (ὑπερλίαν ἀποστόλων, hyperlian apostolon, 11:5/12:11), whom he in between calls "false apostles" (11:12) just because they lead astray from the "sincere and pure devotion to Christ" just like the serpent led Eve astray" (11:3). "You foolish Galatians!" he snarls. "Who has bewitched you, before whose eyes Jesus Christ was publicly portrayed as crucified ...?" Exactly this is what the Jamesians obviously didn't, and in the next sentence (3:2) Paul counters the Jamesian-Jewish teaching with his own: "The only thing I want to learn from you is this: Did you receive the spirit by doing the works of the law or by believing what you heard? Are you so foolish? Having started out with the Spirit, are you now ending up with the flesh? But he who troubles you will bear his judgment, whoever he is" (Galatians 5:10). Even if the troublers are Jesus' brothers James and Simon?

"Those who belong to Christ Jesus have crucified the flesh with its passions and desires" (5:24). The master in this exercise is Paul; he is Christ's true messenger, nay, he's almost Christ himself: "I have been crucified with Christ" (2:20) And at the letter's end, Paul shows how bodily the cross controls his world view: "May I never boast except in the cross of our Lord Jesus Christ, through which the world has been crucified to me, and I to the world ... From now on, let no one cause me trouble, for I bear on my body the marks of Jesus."

---

171 Cf. Greenberg 1993, p.212.
172 Heinsohn, p.86 (here quoted according to Ley 2002, p.166).
173 Rabinovici 2001, p.94.

(3) Stigma by traumatic violence

The latter remark suggests that Paul was the first stigmatized Christian. This is highly meaningful, for the second stigmatization is related not until 1224 from Assisi. Saint Francis and the hundreds of Christians who after him developed physical marks of Jesus' wounds did this only after the spreading of crucifixes and precisely on grounds of the picture's psychic effects. This is overwhelming reason to suppose that Paul himself was deeply affected by the view of crucified victims. Strong evidence also hides in the fact that he enshrines in this one and only letter to the Galatians three very personal orientations that would dominate two Christian millennia: the cult of cross ("for our sins"; 1:4), power of faith (3:2-14) and mortification of the body ("crucified the flesh with its passions and desires"; 5:24). Triple basis is the execution gear Paul uses as vertical vanishing line, out of the dirty body, out of political ground combat, up to the pure high spheres of spirit, accessible not by this-worldly justice but faith in the one he had "clearly portrayed as crucified" before the "very eyes" of those "foolish Galatians" (3:1).

Such apolitical acquiescence serves whom? Who would gladly promote it among slaves, subjects, subliterates? But still one element of convenience is missing, an element extremely helpful for the spreading of Paul's vision within Roman Empire as well as for the millennial synergy between state and cross; an element that suitably is found most strongly in his letter to the Romans. "Everyone must submit to the governing authorities, for there is no authority except from God, and those that exist are instituted by God. Therefore whoever resists authority has opposed the ordinance of God; and those who oppose it will bring judgment on themselves" (13:1-2). Tabor attributes this core element of Pauline doctrine to a childhood trauma of little Saul. According to Church Father Hieronymus, Paul was not born in Tarsus (as he claims in Acts 22:3) but in Galilean town Gishala, just 25 miles from Sepphoris. When the whole province was devastated by the Romans, young Paul, so Hieronymus reports, was captured together with his parents "and in the course of large-scale deportations of Galilean Jews was sent to Cilician Tarsos".[174] The genuinely traumatic incident in this occurrence – so I suppose – was not the deportation but the picture that from now on held him captive: little Saul nevermore being able to forget the sight of stark naked rebels crucified after their defeat in 4 BCE by order of commander Varus, dying cryingly on 2000 crosses. My main argument is that, on closer inspection, Paul's interpretation of Jesus' death on cross quite precisely renders the childlike crucifix-effect that Kierkegaard (see chapter 6) was to describe in 1850: "What effect, to your opinion, will this story have on the child? ... Probably the child would sink into the deepest amazement about why God in Heaven had not done everything to prevent that this has happened; or why it happened without God having ... in the very last moment, to prevent his death, ordered fire pouring down from heaven."

Four decades later, Saul the seer found the answer to his rebels-on-cross trauma: God had not done anything because it had to be: The son had to be

---

174 Tabor, p.323.

crucified. For our redemption. This solution also resolved Paul's personal problem: Paternal power up there must remain a loving one.

State power is divine

After the Jewish people's thorough punishment in twentieth century, it has been argued they brought it on themselves since antisemitism existed already in pre-Christian antiquity. Investigating the issue, Menachem Stern found that among 161 Greek and Roman authors who dealt with the Jews, 133 wrote respectfully about the high age of Judaism, its well documented history and literary grandeur, its emphasy on family and community; they praised the monotheism of the Jews, their rejection of all God-images and their high codex of morale. However, 28 expressed negatively on them. Main point of the critics was that Jews were different and bothersome, because obstreperous, rebellious, insubordinate.[175] In modern terms: "Attention! Name?" – "Private Cohn." – "Man, there's a button missing on your uniform!" – "Herr General, *your* sorrows I would like to have."

Impossible conduct. To historian Yehuda Bauer, writing in his nineties a book about "The impossible people", mainly three fundamental principles maintained by the Jews separated them from other peoples:

1. All humans are free;
2. All humans are equal;
3. All humans have the right to criticize the power.

And Bauer adds: "If the peoples of antiquity had taken over these principles, their empires would have collapsed."[176]

Not so with Paul's modifications:

1. Freedom? While Paul does not get tired of speaking about the Christian freedom from law, he warns the Corinthians that "we take every thought captive to obey Christ. We are ready to punish any disobedience ..." (2 Cor 10:4-6).

2. Equal rights for all humans? No, but equal obedience for all subordinates: "Wives, submit yourselves to your husbands as to the Lord", writes the author of Ephesians, "for the husband is the head of the wife as Christ is the head of the Church ... Children, obey your parents in the Lord, for this is right ... Slaves, obey your earthly masters with respect and fear, in singleness of heart, just as you would obey Christ." (Eph 5:22; 6:1-5); Paul's all-embracing hierarchy of obedience centers in the one who "taking the form of a slave ... humbled himself and became obedient to the point of death, even the death on a cross" (Philippians 2:7-8).

3. Criticize the power? As befits to Roman saints, both Pilate and Paul did their share to fight dangerous Jewish insubordination. Both used the cross as learning device for submission: Pilate in the brutish, Paul in the subtle way:

175 Stern, Menachem: Greek and Latin authors on Jews and Judaism. Jerusalem: Israel Academy of Sciences and Humanities, 1984.
176 Bauer, Yehuda: "Anti-Semitism as European and World Problem" in: Patterns of Prejudice, Vol.27 n°1, London, Institute of Jewish Affairs, 1993, p.15-24; cited by Fucs Bar, Jayme, in Judaismo humanista (judaismohumanista.ning.com), February 26, 2013.

"For just as by the one man's disobedience the many were made sinners, so by the one man's obedience the many will be made righteous" (Romans 5:19). "Who are you, man, to argue with God?" Paul asks the same community in Rome (9:20) and adds the correct answer quickly: "Whoever rebels against the authority is rebelling against what God has instituted". Follows an affidavit that eventually throws the right light on the Pilate-Jesus issue: "For rulers are not a terror to good conduct, but to bad" (13:1-3).

Paul's sanctification of obedient submission was momentous to the point of millionfold death. *"Befehlsnotstand"* – coerciveness of order – was the defense argument of thousands of perpetrators examined after 1945. "Civil courage was not ordered by our instructions" (*Von Zivilcourage stand nichts in unseren Vorschriften*), chief extermination manager Adolf Eichmann, with his *"streng protestantisch"* education, shuffled during his trial in Jerusalem. To Eichmann's contemporary Erich Fromm, son of a rabbi and himself a sociologist, "the one man's disobedience" caused by his silly spouse named Eve was by no means a lapse requiring atonement by obedient crucifixion of the flesh, but an eye-opening, necessary and willed by God act of humanization: "For centuries kings, priests, feudal lords, industrial bosses and parents have insisted that obedience is a virtue and that disobedience is a vice. In order to introduce another point of view, let us set against this position the following statement: human history began with an act of disobedience, and it is not unlikely that it will be terminated by an act of obedience." While in Paul's view Adams sin of disobedience brought death to mankind, and Christ's obedience into death brought life (1 Cor 15:22), in Fromm's view "the prophets, in their messianic concept, confirmed the idea that man had been right in disobeying; that he [she] had not been corrupted by his [her] 'sin', but freed from the fetters of pre-human harmony".[177]

Disobedience generally challenges ruling powers, majorities, traditions, and is a vital factor in societal innovation, just as obedience bows down to power and brings offers to tradition, particularly the sacrifice of the intellect. Maccoby has Paul in mind when he states: "The Christian myth is a powerful version of a means of exorcising guilt that had been practiced by mankind since Neolithic times. Judaism is a revolutionary religion that attempted to eschew both human and divine sacrifice, and sought to lay moral responsibility on the community itself and on the individuals who compose it."[178]

However, Paul's letters of obedience were to prevail, though he had a hard time against the "pillars" of the Jerusalem communities, led by Jesus' brother James. While Paul writes that "a man is justified by faith apart from works of law" (Romans 3:28), the readers of James' Epistle (2:14-20) well knew who was this untold *one of you* whom James attacks: "Can faith save you? If a brother or sister is naked and lacks daily food, and *one of you* says to them: 'Go in peace ... and yet you do not supply their bodily needs, what

---

177 Fromm 1993; English version: eqi.org/erich_fromm_on_disobedience.htm.
178 Maccoby 1992, p.13.

is the good of that?" And more outspoken, James concludes: "Do you want to be shown, *you senseless person*, that faith apart from work is barren?" In spite of Paul's doctrinary claims, the Jerusalem community remained authoritative even after James' death in 62 CE – until eight years later when the Empire of cross-inforced obedience put an end also to the Jerusalem Church, cutting Christian diaspora from the "Jesus dynasty" (wording of James Tabor) and safeguarding Paul's victory.

At the same time (70 CE), Paul's Roman cooperator Mark wrote in Rome the first gospel on which later Matthew (around 80 CE) and Luke with his gospel as well as with his Acts of the Apostles (80-90) relied. Based on a Roman citizen's vision, woven to a basic text in Rome, written for citizens of Roman empire, the core of Christian teaching – Jesus' crucifixion – was better cleaned of Roman guilt with each new gospel text, and in John's gospel (120 CE), the Roman gentleman Pilate finally hands over Jesus to the Jews who do the crucifixion now themselves.

Brazilian psychoanalyst Davy Bogomeletz comments: "During this era – who studies history knows that – the kingdom of hardness, the land of non-compassion had a name: Rome. Exactly the same Rome that crucified Jesus; the same Rome against which he had preached; ... with a genial realpolitical break, Christianity acquitted the hangmen and condemned the victims."[179] The most crucified people became a people of crucifiers, the Roman cross a reminder of evil Jewish deed – and the living Jews now turned into a reminder of evil crucifixion: "The Jews are for us the living words of scripture, for they permanently remind us on what the Lord has suffered. They are dispersed all over the world so that by expiating their crime they may be everywhere the living witnesses of our redemption". The famous monk and order founder Bernard de Clairvaux wrote this in protective intent, for "if the Jews are utterly wiped out, what will become of our hope for their promised salvation, their eventual conversion?"[180]

In Christian view, until final conversion their misery was well-deserved by non-submission to the order "Believe!" which biblically starts with Eve's interest in special fruits and her disobedient disbelieving disregard of divine prohibition. *Sapere aude!* Dare to test, don't fear the costs. "Look! The man has become like one of us in knowing good and evil" the prohibitors themselves praise Eve's courage to shed obedience for sapience (Gen 3:22), holding the fruit in her hand.

Holding the crucifix in his hand, just one day before his visit to the cemetary of German Army and SS troops at La Cambe, Pope Joseph Ratzinger said in the cathedral of Caens that even Nazi-German government "led by a criminal" nevertheless had the right "to call in the citizen's obedience to law and respect for the state's authority".[181] In this handy crucifix, Jewish philosopher Ernst Bloch finds "exactly the subversiveness of the Bible bro-

179 Bogomeletz, Davy: A Epopéia Hassídica e a Reconstrução da Identidade Judaica. In: Fuks, p.129.
180 Saperstein, Marc: Moments of Crisis in Jewish-Christian Relations. Philadelphia 1989, p.9 (cited by Carroll, p.271, Wilensky, p.101 and Michael, p.69).
181 Die Tagespost (Catholic German triweekly), June 14, 2004 (quoted by Posener, p.82).

ken down the last time by the myth of the sacrificed lamb; a breakdown in order to sanctify the so-called patience of the cross, this patience so recommendable to the oppressed ones and so comfortable for the oppressors; and generally the unconditional obedience to the authorities, established by God."[182]

When Asher Norman supposes that Paul the sect-prosecutor "continued to work for the Romans while acting as an apostle of Jesus",[183] this suspicion is valid at least so far: What Paul made out of Jesus almost never was inconvenient to authoritarian and totalitarian states. "The Christendom as Paul taught it from the beginning contained well-fitting premises to let it become the state-religion of Roman Empire; for nothing comes in more useful to an imperial power than a religion that preaches submission to its subjects and hold still. It is symptomatic that Paul, the creator of the teaching which was to make this career, had made himself a Roman citizen."[184] And it is no less symptomatic that the Eucharist blessings "Take and eat. This is my body ... This is my blood ..." are the only words of Jesus that Paul ever quotes: words that Jesus said but in Paul's vision.

Albeit, concerning the defamation of the Jews as Christ-killers, Paul was innocent. Of Judas's treason Paul knows and tells as much as of Jews machinating Jesus' condemnation or a Jewish self-curse: nothing. The real crucifiers he points to are the "rulers of this world [or age; 1 Cor 2:8]", a term that may be seen as a cautious cue to the Roman Empire. His only verse which addresses the Jews as perpetrators (1 Thess 2:15), discloses itself clearly as a post-70 insert by the subsequent verse: "But God's wrath has overtaken them at last."[185] Though the vision of Jesus as God's incarnated son is his very own copyright, the virginity of Mary is not Paul's issue; rather, this dogma was a consequence of his Son-of-God vision. In a similar way, the crucifix was unimaginable to this Jew who during his stay in Athens "was deeply distressed to see that the city was full of idols" (Acts 17:16) and who warns the faithful of Rome (1:23) of those who "exchanged the glory of the immortal God for images made to look like a mortal human being".

Familiar ideas

To understand a historical idea, one should look at the community this idea lived in, as British moral philosopher Mary Midgley recommends. In the case of Jesus, of his ideas and the history of "his" religion, Hans-Joachim Schoeps stresses the "self-evident duty ... to study the statements of the vanquished groups as carefully and to take their value as evidence as seriously as one does those of the canonical New Testament."[186] Having returned from Swedish exile in 1946, as chairholder for the history of religions at Erlangen University (near Nuremberg) Schoeps since 1947 searched for

---

182 Bloch 1973, p.186.
183 Norman, p.136.
184 Maccoby 2007, p.180.
185 This view is shared by Nicholls, p.134 and 155-156.
186 Schoeps, Hans-Joachim, p.4.

vestiges of Jesus' ideas within the Ebionite community, because this early Jewish-Christian group was closely related to Jesus concerning ideas as well as family ties: Their highest authority was Jesus' brother James, killed by stoning in 62 CE. Church Father Eusebios reports that "after the death of James as a martyr, and the soon following conquest of Jerusalem, the then still living apostles and disciples of the Lord convened with the physical relatives of the Lord, for also some of the latter ones then still were alive." Unanimously they elected as James's successor the man we heard of already: "Simon son of Clopas, whom the gospel mentions". More precisely, it is John's verse 19:25 that unites "his mother, and his mother's sister, Mary the wife of Clopas, and Mary Magdalene" under Jesus' cross, in neat accordance with Papias and with Eusebios' plain remark that "according to Hegesippos, Clopas was the brother of Joseph" and "an uncle of the Lord". We already noted how the puzzle parts of Jesus' family fall onto their places if, according to Tabor's view, after Joseph's early death his brother Clopas had married his widowed sister-in-law Mary in a so-called levirate marriage to "build up his brother's house (Deuteronomy 25:9);[187] when according to Tabor's convincing view, the brothers James, Joses, Judas and Simon listed in Mark 6:3 were all sons of Clopas and stepbrothers of Jesus; and if in Mark's trias of "Mary Magdalene, Mary the mother of James, and Salome" who in 16:1 together went to Jesus' tomb, this Salome was simply, naturally and lovingly a stepsister of Jesus, and sister of this Judas whose grandsons Jacob and Zocher (Zechariah) Palestinian Church Father Eusebios, the "father of church history" (~260-340) honors this way:
"On Domitian's order to execute the descendants of David, according to an old report some heretics denounced the descendants of Judas, a natural brother of our Saviour, saying they were the lineage of David and relatives of Christ. Hegesippos literally relates: 'From the Lord's family still the grandsons of Judas were alive, who is said to have been a natural brother of the Lord ... [During interrogation] they replied that their assets consisted in a field of but 39 acres which they tilled ... proving by the hardness of their skin and the weals on their hands due to their arduous work that they were manual workers ... After manumission they achieved, as professors and relatives of the Lord, leading positions in the *Church*" which in Schoeps' reading means "congregations in Galilee" during the epoch from emperor Domitian (81-96) until Trajan (98 to 117).[188]
The ostracism of their grandfather started around 70. While Mark (**6:3**) counts Jesus' four brothers as "James, Joseph, *Judas* and Simon", Matthew (**13:55**) tellingly shifts him to the end: "Is not his mother called Mary, and his brothers James and Joseph and Simon and Judas?" In both gospels, the register of apostles (Mk 3, Mt 10) includes only one Judas, namely the Iscariot. Luke, however, and whyever, in verse 6:16 discerns literally one "Judas

187 Hegesippos in Eusebios, Historia Ecclesiastica 3.11; 4.22 (unifr.ch/bkv/kapitel50-21. htm; cf. Tabor, p.105; Wikipedia article "Klopas").
188 Schoeps, Hans-Joachim, p.30; Eusebios, Historia Ecclesiastica, 3:19-20. The names of Judas' grandsons are mentioned by church historian Philip of Side (ca. 380-431).

of James" (his brother or son?) and one "Judas Iscariot, who became betray-er" (*Ioudan Iakobou kai Ioudan Iskarioth, hos géneto prodotés*).
In John's gospel (7:3-5), "his brothers" are the ones who wheedle Jesus that he, since "no one who wants to be widely known acts in secret" should "leave here and go to Judea". Come on, brother, "If you do these things, show yourself to the world." Rather awkwardly, John explains: "For not even his brothers believed in him." Later on, in chapter 14, John puts the same advice – persuading Jesus to make himself a public figure – precisely on whose lips? "Judas (not Iscariot) said to him, 'Lord, why do you intend to show yourself to us and not to the world?'"
John provides no register of apostles. But the one who was "going to betray him" in his gospel and who in the three earlier gospels had figured as Jesus' brother and James' brother and James's son, is here named the "Judas son of Simon Iscariot" (6:71), outing Mary's second husband Simon bar Clopas as a radicalist if we assume that the word Iscariot is derived from the militant "sikarii". Two partisans of this, so to say, "Zionist" rebel group were also the apostle brothers James and John, whom Jesus nicknames "Boanerges, which means sons of thunder" in **Mk 3:17**, while he blesses and addresses "Simon Peter" as "Simon Bariona" in Mt 16:17. Bariona harmlessly is translated as "Son of Jonah", though the highly charged political background should be well-known: In a rabbinical text, a certain Abba Sikrah is labelled "resh barionei", signifying in Aramaic language nothing else than head-man of "Zealots" or "Sikarians". What's the use of these odd nicknames or *nomes de guerre* among Jesus' disciples? Hyam Maccoby remembers a group that in 164 BCE ventured a defiant but successful rebellion against the Seleucids who attempted to Hellenize the temple. The leader of this group of Maccabeans was Judas ha-Maccabi. This name itself yet announced no tender aims, meaning "the hammerer"; and the other members of the band had nicknames too, as Flavius Josephus (Antiquities, XII:266) confirms. "I am not suggesting that Jesus was himself a Zealot", Hyam Maccoby clarifies. "But he was the leader of a band in constant danger of arrest and execution ... His charisma attracted men who had previously belonged to armed bands engaged in guerrilla resistance. [...] Jesus' band was similar to that of Judas Maccabaeus, in its hopes, in its companionship and in its use of nicknames". There was one fact, however, that gave this Maccabean companionship "the solidity of a rock: They were all brothers."[189] Unfortunately, a Jesus with biological brothers and sisters was hardly compatible with the post-Pauline necessity of the Godson's adequate, i.e. virgin mother. The Eastern Churches solved the problem by declaring the undeniable brothers to be his step-brothers, not sons of Mary of course, but sons of Joseph with another wife. Roman Church unobtrusively made them Jesus' cousins. Thus, the difficult but indispensable dogma of Mary's virginity resulted in a grossly distorted image of Jesus and his group, a band that before and after his death was led by the sons of this not to be underestimated mother Mary.

---

189 Maccoby 1992, p.146.

One could argue that a politically so rebellious Jesus-group can hardly be squared with the rather passive Jerusalem group after Jesus' death. But exactly this chastened reaction after the terrible end of their brothers' go-getting courage appears to be psychologically very plausible. Not only the shock of a cruel execution was paralyzing here, but: If the brothers had quasi persuaded him into the role of Messiah (**Mk 8:29**; **Mt 16:15**) and afterwards had pushed, cajoled or just encouraged him to publicly display his charisma for "self-promotion"[190] – what amount of guilt feelings would they then have to cope with, after they had seen their elder brother on the cross and realized what they had driven him into? How readily would they now accept everything that allowed them to believe in his resurrection and his later comeback in glory? How alleviating must now appear to them the continuation of his wrecked project and the shouldering of leading functions in a quasi Rabbi-Jesus-Foundation, in honor of his memory and in resumption of his message?

Such was the situation of the primitive community, when Saul first tried to destroy the movement and then succeeded in changing its direction completely. Paul as the first author of New Testament (before 60 CE) mentions "the brothers of the Lord" as a group with particular authority, standing out from the "apostles" (1 Cor 9:5). But this loquacious Paul would waste no word about a plot, a traitor, a process or Jewish guilt. Instead, he assures the Corinthians (1 Cor 15:5) that the risen Jesus first appeared to Peter, then to "the Twelve" – i.e. to all of them including Judas. Also the "Gospel of Peter" which Bishop Serapion had mentioned already in 200 CE, leaves Judas within the company. A fragment of this gospel, found in 1886 in the tomb of an Egyptian monk, ends this way: "Now it was the last day of the unleavened bread, and many were going forth, returning to their homes, as the feast was ended. But we, the *twelve* disciples of the Lord, wept and were saddened: and each one, being grieved for what had come to pass, departed to his home ...".[191]

As in the cases of "son of Mary", of "Mary of Clopas", of "Jesus Bar-Abbas" and his "brothers and sisters", also concerning this Judas Perfidias the very gospels transpire a very different story of a very human son of Mama Maria and member of her family.

While Jesus Barabbas was divided into only two opponents, in the case of Judas orthodox theologians actually have to assume four persons. All gospels have the ominous Judas Iscariot whom John (6:71) names "Judas son of Simon Iscariot"; Judas the brother of Jesus is presented by **Mark 6:3** and **Matthew 13:55**; whereas **Luke 6:15** adds a Judas son of James.[192] The fourth one is the author of the doubtlessly canonical Epistle of Judas, completing a quartet Maccoby comments with British humour: "This proliferation of Judases is itself a curious phenomenon."[193]

---

190 Maccoby 1992, p.149.
191 Maccoby 1992, p.88.
192 Lüdemann (p.373; 38-39) deems the mentioned names (as in Mark 3:16-19) historical.
193 Maccoby 1992, p.175.

The number of Judases shrinks if we read the Greek original texts. In Luke's gospel actually Jesus does not name a "Judas son of James" but a *Ioudan Iakobou*, literally "Judas of James", and indeed was Judas the brother of James. John's actual Greek words are *Elegen de tón Ioudan Símonos {Iskarióten · Iskariótou}*, literally "He spoke of Judas Simonos, {from/of Iskariót}", and indeed Judas Simonos was the son of Simon(os) Clopas, as was his brother James. Remarkably, this Judas Simonos is confirmed in Coptic versions of John's gospel as "Judas the Zealot",[194] which maybe sheds light on why his father's brother Joseph – Jesus' stepfather and Judas' uncle – probably died early. All said, the texts of the very gospels, of the very Church Fathers and the early Christian communities together let the puzzle parts fall on their place: Judas is Jesus' stepbrother, he is the son of Mary and Simon Clopas and a nephew of his late uncle Joseph. Together with his brother James and Simon Clopas, Judas remained a leading figure of the Jerusalem Church after Jesus' crucifixion, and his sons Jacob and Zocher became prominent in the Ebionite community. After Jesus' demise his family around the central woman Mary lived in danger for generations, but their structure and solidarity were almost boringly normal, without virgin mothers and betraying brothers. The blinder that prevented this very human view of Mary's family was the vision of an outlandish Jew convincing himself that Jesus was in a Greek way the Son of God.

Paul's Jewish-Christian opponents were the "Ebionites", this being the later name for the Nazoreans or Nazarenians, who themselves were the successors of this "primal Church" of Jerusalem. They viewed Jesus as a purely human prophet like Moses, as a messianic reformer of Mosaic Law. They believed in resurrection from death and hoped for the return of Jesus: They practised non-violence including refusal of military service. True to their master, they rejected animal sacrifices and replaced the fire of the altar by an extinguishing element: the water of baptism. And clear as water was the reason why they had to reject decisively Paul's teaching of redemption with its concept of Jesus as bloody sacrifice of atonement: In their view, "Jesus had established baptism as a means of purification and atonement in the place of the bloody animal sacrifices. In so doing he merely accomplished what yet Moses had desired: the abolition of the animal sacrifices. [...] Christianity had been freed from the Jewish sacrificial worship not through the universally efficacious sacrifice of the son, as the Church which followed Paul believed, but rather through the water of baptism whereby Jesus had extinguished the fire of the sacrificial cult."[195] In Ebionite view, Jesus had even prophesied the destruction of the temple – as the end of animal sacrifice. His programmatic statement "Do not think that I came to abolish the Law or the Prophets; I did not come to abolish but to fulfill" (Matthew 5:17) reads different in the Gospel of the Ebionites: "I have come to annul sacrifice, and if you will not cease to sacrifice, the wrath will not turn from you." In Schoeps' view the "dogmatic vegetarianism" of the Ebionites "undoubtedly represents an

---

194 Maccoby 1992, p.134.
195 Schoeps, Hans-Joachim, p.60 and 83.

intensification of the Mosaic food laws." The Jewish-German scholar admires the Ebionites' shrewd historical judgment, anticipating what today is well-known: "... that it was the post-Deuteronomic Priestly Code which introduced the many sacrificial commandments into the Torah ... wrongly giving Jewish religion a cultic character".[196] The Ebionites already in second century CE condemned the sacrificial regulations within the books of Moses, written hundreds of years after him, as fictions. From the fourth book of Moses (11:33), where the Israelites get sick and die of the flesh of quails, the Ebionites concluded "that vegetarianism is God's expressed will". Consequently, they portrayed Peter and James as vegetarians, while "Jesus himself became a vegetarian when, according to the Ebionite 'Acts', he declined the suggestion that he eat meat at the Passover." Instead of being a son of God and a virgin, the Ebionite Jesus was the "Son of Man" in the meaning of the Book of Daniel as well as Psalm 2:7 ("He said to me: 'You are my son; today I have become your father.'"). They contested Jesus' descendance from bellicose King David whom they opposed as critically as Salomon the polygamous temple-builder. To build a temple of stone appeared to them as a "Baalization of Yahve", since the God of the wandering people demanded nothing than a mobile tabernacle and did not need a permanent residence as was suitable for a stone-formed, blood-dripping Baal.[197]

When Paul wrote "Eat whatever is sold in the meat market" (1 Cor 10:25) and abolished the law including circumcision, kashrut and purity regulations, he literally made Jesus tradeable. And yet he must have known that this Jesus he presented as an atoning sacrifice for the carnal sins of mankind would have rejected a meat market no less than temple sacrifice and the sacrifice delusion itself. For when Paul adviced the Romans that "If your brother or sister is being injured by what you eat, it is good not to eat meat or drink wine, or doing anything else that makes your brother upset" (14:21), he knew that the Christian vegetarians – who according to Augustine were "without number" still in his fifth century – referred to Jesus' teachings.[198] Paul surely had long talks with Peter whom the vegetarian Church Father Clement of Alexandria calls a vegetarian.[199] And he probably had even longer talks with James, whom he apparently tried to hit with his skit "the weak eat only vegetables" (Rom 14:2). If, referring to second century Christian historian Hegesippus, scholars agree in deeming James a vegetarian, what does this fact say about Jesus? "Who and whatever James was, so was Jesus" is Robert Eisenman's short answer.[200]

The belief of many Christians that Jesus was a habitual meat-eater derives mainly from his miraculous multiplications of bread and fish (Mark 6; Matthew 14; Luke 9; John 6). Paradoxically, these narrations rather prove the contrary, since the miracle is obviously inspired by the story of the prophet

196   Schoeps, Hans-Joachim, p.100 and 84.
197   Schoeps, Hans-Joachim, p.101 and 86.
198   Augustine, On the Morals of the Catholic Church, p.33 (Akers, p.132).
199   Clement of Alexandria, Homilia XII, 6, respectively. Paidagogos II, 1.16.
200   Eisenman quoted by Kamran Pasha in "Was Jesus a Vegetarian?", Huffingtonpost, Nov. 17, 2011.

Elisha who (modestly by comparison) fed hundred men with twenty loaves, "and when they had eaten, they had some left over" (2 Kings 4:44). So why did Mark and Matthew add fish here while later on in their gospels, both Mark (8:18-20) and Matthew (16:9-10) remember only five breads, seven breads – and no fish? Why did early Christian authors Eusebius (260-340) and Arnobius (-330) in both miracle reports speak of bread only? Why did Luke (24:43) and John (21:13) have the resurrected Christ put fish on his flatbread? If their anti-docetist intention was to prove him as not just spiritually but corporeally present, bread would have done the job. The issue seems fishy, the more so as in his life Jesus never had shown appetite for fish or meat. Were these fish'n-Jesus-stories meant to take the bread out of the mouth of those annoying Ebionite vegionites, for the sake of Paul's normative eat-whatever-meat doctrine?

While Jesus used to argue "a fortiori" (don't swear and don't divorce at all; love even your enemy), typical of *Paul* was a marketing strategy "a leviori": lenience concerning rules that could deter new adherents; release from the law, blurring of distinctions, adapting to the pagan ambience: "For though I am free from all men, I have made myself a slave to all, so that I may win more. To the Jews I became like a Jew ...", to those with law a lawyer, to those outside an outsider, to the weak a weaker and so on, and all this just "for the sake of the gospel" (1 Cor 9).

Whose gospel? In Simone Weil's view, "la verité", the truth, is the "fugitive from the camp of the winner". The vegetarian-pacifist Ebionites who were, in Schoeps' view, "the physical descendants of his first disciples", died out in sixth century; and winning was their arch-enemy, the *senseless person* who recommended to crucify the flesh and buy anything on the meat-market, in favor of a larger target group; who taught slaves submission in favor of their owners (1 Cor 7:20-22; Eph 6:5; Titus 2:9); who introduced the "belief in the miraculous power of the mass" which Spanish conversos considered apt to "keep people from seeking effective earthly solutions to their problems".[201] While the Ebionites aimed "against the slack conformation to slavery and oppression" and to "humanization and concern for this world",[202] this very world was "only a shadow of what is to come: the reality that is Christ's body" for the man who backs the Colossians against anyone who'd "judge you in regard to meat or drink" and in the same paragraph (2:16-18) warns them of a type of charismatic he knows quite well – one who is "taking his stand on visions he has seen, inflated without cause by his fleshly mind." A last illustration of Pauline mind-inflation and its disastrous outcome seems suitable.

Washing is bosh
"For the Pharisees and all the Jews do not eat unless they thoroughly wash their hands ... and they do not eat anything from the market unless they

---

201 Gitlitz, p.152.
202 Maccoby 2007, p.201.

wash it; and they observe many other traditions, such as the washing of cups, pitchers and kettles." Thus Mark prepares to his non-Jewish readers a strange teaching of Jesus. When the Pharisees criticize that his disciples eat with unwashed hands, Jesus summons the people. "Listen to me, all of you, and understand", he addresses the Jewish crowd. "Nothing that goes into a person from outside can defile him, but the things that come out of a person are what defile him" (**Mk 7:15**). Strangely, Lüdemann takes the fact that kosher regulations were "unreservedly valid" in early Christendom as an indication for the authenticity of this provoking word, of course without the additional verse 7:20: "Thus he declared all foods clean". Also my Catholic *Jerusalemer Bibel* assumes this concluding carte blanche to be a later insert and cogently affirms this view by three Pauline references: First this pompous dream of Peter who views a table-cloth sailing down from heaven, filled with "all kinds of fourfooted beasts and creeping things of the earth and birds of the air" and hears the order "Get up, Peter. Kill and eat", as Paul's friend Luke relates in Acts (10:9-16). Paul himself, second, wrote to the Colossians the above quoted licence "Let no man therefore judge you in meat, or in drink", as well as, third, to the Romans (14:14): "I know, and am persuaded by the Lord Jesus, that there is nothing unclean."

Any food is good, and all is clean! Could Jesus ever have drunken enough wine to utter such utter nonsense?

Nine centuries after his death, the 100.000 Muslim-Christian-Jewish citizens of Cordoba boasted of 700 mosques and 3000 public baths.[203] When Christian Europe was infested by epidemics after 1300, it may well be that in the emerging resentments against the Jews "their relatively higher standards of hygiene played a part. Such practices as the obligatory washing of hands before eating could not fail to keep down the spread of many infections"[204] – during an epoch where the normal lane of a normal Christian town indeed was (using Mother Courage's expression) a "Shit Lane", in which so many pigs ran around that during fifteenth century cities like Ulm, Frankfurt and Nuremberg set a limit of 24 pigs per citizen, thus reacting to the complaints of aldermen who didn't arrive clean at the townhall, and clerics who couldn't walk to the cathedral without stilts.

At the same time, the queer attention to personal cleanness sufficed to the *inquisitores* of Spanish Dominican order to convict a suspect of clandestine practise of Judaism or Islam.[205] Around 1660, New Mexican inquisitors duly noted that Doña Teresa de Aguilera "washed her face; even in bad weather, when it was snowing" and that "she never failed to wash herself and change her clothes, as it was Friday".[206]

Meanwhile Paul's sentence about "the reality, that is Christ's body" increasingly characterized sacral art. While primitive nomads around 1000 before Pauline era were ordered to "remove from camp ... anyone defiled by a

203   Gerber, Jane, p.28.
204   Nicholls, p.247, ref. to Abba Eban: My People. New edition, New York 1984, p.183.
205   Cecil Roth: History of the Marranos, p.105.
206   Hordes, p.155-156.

corpse ... so that they do not defile the camp in whose midst I dwell" (Num 5:2-3), the morbid worship of a dead corpus in wooden materiality soon drew real dead bodies into churches, as venerable objects. In Trento, for instance, Bishop Hinderbach proudly led the Papal Nuncio to the corpse of little martyr Simon (crucified by Jews), which was being exhibited in the cathedral since six months, and the papal nuncio wrote in his report to Rome: "When the bishop curiously examined the shin-bone and moved it, a stench sprang up of such a kind that I got a colic ... strong enough that I could have vomited at any time."[207]

Examining corpses: Twice daily the medical students of Professor Ignaz Semmelweis in Budapest performed clinical sections on the corpses of mothers who had died of childbed fever. In between, with unwashed hands, the future doctors examined women during their delivery. The midwifery students of the second department didn't come into contact with corpses, didn't perform vaginal examinations, and much fewer young mothers died in their department.

When Semmelweis therefore instructed his students to disinfect hands and instruments after the section of corpses, the rate of mortality decreased from 12.3 to below 3.0 percent. After he additionally had required disinfection of the hands before each examination, he succeeded in lowering the rate to 1.3 percent in 1848. Again he was awarded with scorn and derision, but the attacks became more malicious. His students deemed cleanness simply unnecessary, his colleagues knew it was waste of time, the famous professor Virchow referred the puerperal fever to weather influences, and freaky professor Semmelweis died on August 13, 1865, two weeks after having been hospitalized, in a lunatic asylum.

Poor lunatic, aborted wisenheimer! What a contrast to Paul with his sin therapy in three steps: "When we are grown together [sýmphytoi] with the image of his death ... and our old self is crucified together [synestáurote] ... the body of sin may be destroyed that we no longer are enslaved to sin" (Romans 6:5-6)!

Also these verses evidence that a picture held Paul captive, ingrown in his amygdale since days of childhood; a picture Christian Europe exposes so ubiquitary that no child in occident escapes. However, the somatophobia radiating from the picture, in Paul's psyche being adnate with the picture itself as much as with repressed homoerotic bents, in modernity faded down slowly, thanks to the increasing light of social and scientific progress.

Modern medicine must not reject old biblical experience: "Hand washing is the most important thing one can practise in order to protect himself and others from infections", stresses Dr. Ernst Tabori, the director of German Counsel Center for Hygiene in Freiburg and namesake of Cornelius Tabori (1879-1944) who with the gentle deference "Please after you, Herr Mandelbaum" upheld his level of normal human respect – and Jewish humour – still at the entrance to the gas chamber.

---

207 Hsia, p.103.

VI   And daily killed in kindergarten

"An attitude as unforgiving and permanently hateful as the Christians' attitude concerning the Jews because of the alleged execution of a Jew has no parallel in history."   Avi Primor[208]

This chapter presents the core thesis of this book: The Christian child's compassion with the innocent one on the cross turns into ingrained but subconscious, punishment-prone anger against the perpetrators.

To start with, keep in sight that 80 percent of our sensory stimulation comes in through the eyes.[209] Even for goats, who rely much more on their noses than we do, visual imprints have a fateful force. In an ethically questionable animal test of British neuroscientist Prof. Keith Kendrick, male goat kids who as newborns had been forcedly adopted by ewes, in adult age "were attracted to ewes whose facial structure resembled that of their adoptive mothers".[210] And faces, mammal or human, are structured by one vertical line and two eyes on a horizontal beam, as the mask of the hot-cross-loving German Klanman (2012) shows not badly.

The probably most well-known psychological test method bases exactly on the activation of subconscious motives by simple visual images. Hermann Rorschach's form interpretation test uses nothing but left-right-symmetrical folded inkblots which trigger the gestalt-psychological archetypes of our visual perception. If we are shown two circular spots symmetrical to a vertical line, our brain will produce the interpretation "face". Eyes with dark pupils or palms with dark nails – the cerebral scan program recognizes the same mathematical relation of equidistance to the vertical axis, no matter if the object is a Rorschach inkblot or a human face or an inhuman crucifixion.

Children's eyes and childish questions
After the child-abuse scandal around 2010, Pope Benedict XVI admonished the (Irish) Church that "in order to recover from this deep wound, it is essential to admit the besetting sin against children openly in face of God and others".[211]

---

208   Primor / von Korff, p.213.
209   Aron, p.55.
210   Gabriel Bukobza: Beyond Cupid: The secret of human relationships; in haaretz, October 11, 2013.
211   Kathrin Zeilmann, in: "Die Kirche hat ihre Krise noch nicht überwunden",

Which wounds are left in defenceless children by throwing crucifixes on their eyes?

A highly experienced primary school colleague with diploma for Protestant religious education told me that for decades she had (illegally) removed the crucifix from her classroom, because regularly her new first-graders during their first school days used to ask her "What is that on the wall there with the man?" and when she tried to explain crucifixion to them as careful as possible, the little ones regularly burst into tears. Why on earth?

Because children feel what men have done to this man, here on this still unknown earth in which they live not always secure. Beware of bad people, mummy said. I remember having asked my mother at age four, looking at a map of Germany: "Mama, bad people are not here, right?" Her answer "Yes, there are" was unsettling. Here, too?

The cross as map: Where are the bad people who make such things? Can't see them. Who did it? Who has, and why have they (it's always "them") done that, with real fat nails at that?

This triple void – Who's done it? Why? And why so cruelly? – is the invisible part and background of every crucifix. Man is an eye-animal and links his emotions to visual impressions. In the central region of the amygdala he stores emotional memories. The store's opening is triggered by acustic, tactile, olfactoric stimuli: Sounds, touches, smells suddenly recall emotions which at some time had been stored together with these stimuli. The highest amount of associations however is produced by visual triggers. We vividly re-imagine images and sounds, but hardly ever smells. We dream mainly in sequences of images. We speak in visual metaphors. We react on images, and most emotionally at that.

A detective movie, for instance, mostly starts with pictures of the committed crime: Fear-filled eyes, shouts, a shadow pursuing the victim, quick chase, a body prostrated, blood. After this motivational phase, emotionally and dramatically it's all about one thing: to catch the perpetrators, to have them fettered and extracted (not to say extirpated) from our peace-loving human society and justly punished for their crime.

The image of their crime: Blood running from painful head wounds, from hands and feet pierced for fixation in most painful posture. A stripped victim hanging on nails. So far the Christian motivation phase since thousand years.

Adult human beings, of course, are accustomed to the picture of the man whom so many Christians want to see hanging. In one scene of their *Film-preis* awarded movie *Almanya – Willkommen in Deutschland* the Kurdish born producers Yasemin and Nesrin Şamdereli show in 2011 how six-year old Cenk suffers nightmares by the classroom symbol he is welcomed with in his new German school. But any child in Christian cultural space once views the crossmurder-puzzle for the first time, tries to understand, and seems to accustom quickly, forgetting unsolved questions. To which ques-

Südwestpresse Ulm, December 22, 2010, p.3.

tions has the God-image got connected when it was first downloaded to the infant soul, and processed and classified *transacted*? What is obvious to the child is that others people have done to this man something really bad. The notion that every event must have its cause is part of the child's acquired world order already. Were *them* human beings who nailed him on? Who else? What kind of people? May one do that? The child says "No!" Can't help saying no, knowing quite well "I'm small, the big ones can do me good – and harm." The sadism of a crucifixion goes beyond the child's imagination of harming someone intentionally. Children are caring, and piercing hands with nails is the stark ungraspable opposite of caring for someone. But the child's "No!" does not prevent that the image remains in his or her memory as an unresolved issue. "The key to trauma bonding is this: the human personality experiences something that the conscious mind cannot explain, so the experience goes directly to the unconscious part of the personality."[212]

According to the Perception-Action-Model of empathy proposed by **Stephanie Preston** and **Frans de Waal** in 2002, "viewing another's emotional state automatically and unconsciously activates one's personal associations with that state, causing one ... to react to another's experience as one would to one's own."[213] Is viewing the other the key? Or, are mice who empathize with writhing cage mates just triggered by specific odors, or by ultrahigh-frequency moans emitted by the victim? Researchers destroyed the bystander mice's hearing and smelling capacities, but as long as they could see the suffering fellow, the animals remained empathic – and prone to help: If a rat was kept imprisoned in a transparent tube, another rat viewing this situation from outside became visibly anxious, and if this second rat had the option of liberating her tube-fixed fellow rat by pressing a lever, the rodent did this without any training or reward.[214]

Rats pity suffering rats. Human children punish human perpetrators: At Leipzig *Max-Planck-Institut für Evolutionäre Anthropologie*, in 2010 scientists wanted to find out to what extent three-year-old children apprehend the behaviour of others or even their intentions. The research team around **Amrisha Vaish** confronted 100 three-year-old children with four different scenes: First, the little ones watched helpful adults repairing a drawing which another adult had rent to pieces wantonly. Second, the children observed how someone intentiously tore the drawing made by someone else. Third, the children watched someone who obviously tried to rend a drawing but did not succeed. And finally they watched persons who unintentionally destroyed someone else's drawing.

---

212 Swaim 2013, p.31.
213 Preston, S.D., and F.B.M. de Waal, "Empathy: Its ultimate and proximate bases", in: Behavioral and Brain Sciences (2002) 25: 1-72; thus resumed by Nicole M. McDonald & Daniel S. Messinger, in: The Development of Empathy: How, When, and Why. University of Miami. (psy.miami.edu).
214 Mice: Herzog, p.231; rats: Sezgin, p.32, citing a study by Inbal Ben-Ami Bartal, Jean Decety and Peggy Mason at University of Chicago, published in *Science 9*, December 2011, Vol.334, no.6061, p.1427-1430.

Subsequently, adults and children together played a game during which the young ones should help the adults. The research team observed that the children behaved helpfully toward adults who themselves had helped others before or harmed others just unintentionally. By contrast, those adults who with conscious intention had harmed somebody were offered no helping hand by the children, who punished in the same way those adults who had intended to harm someone but failed to accomplish their mischievous intent. As the last result shows clearly, for children yet in this early age it is not the action itself but the intention that makes the difference. "Our study yields information about the development of morale in children", Mrs. Vaish resumes, "and it questions previous assumptions which contended that little children make no difference and help everyone likewise."[215]

Fine, but where's the link to crucifixes in children's retina, as the ill-intending adults are not visible in the Jerusalem *them-harm-him-badly*-scene? Once again: What is visible in crucifixes yet for children at age three is the (extremely!) mischievous intent. At this "I-do-age", when curious children want to do everything themselves, they perceive that this man surely did not single-handedly stick nails through his hands and then through his feet; the terrible thing was done to him, against his will. This perception arouses punishment-prone anger immediately; and the triple complex of *perceived evil intention* + *compassion with the victim* + *desire to punish* is stored in the child's amygdala, ready to be linked with the notion "Jews" as soon as the child – incessantly eager to learn who's done it – comes to know it's been the Jews. While in the test situation the children punished bad-intentioned adults just by not helping them, there have been other options for cross-accustomed grown-up children in European history.

The fact that children of three years have eaten already of the tree of knowledge, enabling them to feel into other human beings and judge their good or bad intentions, is referred today to the "mirror-neurons" of which the human brain disposes in an incomparably greater number than the brains of our next relatives among the apes. Mirror neurons "reflect" the feelings which we observe in bodily expression and behaviour of other human beings. Triggered by observations of the outer world, the neural cells start to "fire" automatically and to send electrical impulses in a pattern which corresponds "like mirrored" to the patterns in the neural systems of the observed persons. Imagine how these mirror-neurons which mark the origins of empathy – and for some scientists even the basis of morale – were discovered in 1992. The setting: Hungry monkey sitting in the test chair with a crown of electrodes, sweet-toothed Italian scientist grabbing for a raisin. Incidentally the scientist glimpses at the monitor which shows the monkey's brain waves with, right now, hosts of neurons firing as if he, the monkey, would grab the raisin himself.[216] Obviously, the brain of the observing person performs the

215   Vaish, A., Carpenter, M., & Tomasello, M. (2010). Young children selectively avoid helping people with harmful intentions. *Child Development, 81(6)*, 1661-1669 (eva.mpg.de/psycho/staff/vaish/publications.php).
216   Sezgin, Hilal, in: Die Zeit, February 7, 2014.

same proceedings it would perform if the observing person herself would be the actor, able to achieve the tempting – or flee the threatening – aspects of a situation. Today it is "evident that this mirroring is a basic principle", says Christian Keyser of the Netherlands Institute for Neurosciences in 2013. "If persons observe disgust, pain or joy in other persons, this activates brain areas that become active also if someone senses these emotions himself. So we do not only *know* that somebody else feels pain, we *feel* it really."[217] Sensorial cells in the brain, whose task is to react on signals of own pain, "fire" also if the individual observes another individual being pricked with a needle. What will happen in children's heads if children's eyes see not sweet raisins but dozens of pointed thorns prickling the skin above the good son's eyes and one nail punching his feet, two piercing his hands? What *did* happen in history is the already mentioned "coincidence, that attacks on Jews, both rhetorical and physical, become a notable pattern of Christian behavior only after the cult of the cross is established."[218]

What unaccustomed children think and what they feel perceiving a crucifix, is the basis for "one of the most efficient education processes of history", by which they, as Hyam Maccoby stated after Shoah, "had been conditioned to regard the Jews as the source of all evil."[219] The efficient education process was made possible by a historical loss of memory: "The Christians of antiquity still had such a deep fear of crucifixion that they never presented Christ on the cross."[220] By this reason, after Constantine's abolishment of crucifixion as method of execution in 320, two centuries or seven generations had to pass before the first cross representations emerged and displaced the previous presentations of the Redeemer as the Good Shepherd. Why and where did the fearful avoidance of the cross give way to its acceptance and later on to its expressive emphasis?

Advance in art and hatred

From a modern point of view, what art-historically happened between the 8th and 14th century appears as a slow and sneaking approach to the dreadfulness of crucifixion. Still no crucifixes had existed when Clovis, king of the Franks, converted to Catholicism around 500 CE, after a victorious battle near Cologne. When he was told how much Christ had suffered, he remarked: "Would I have stood in front of my brave Franks, I would have revenged his wounds." However, Clovis' Jewish contemporaries – a Jewish community existed in Cologne since the first century CE – remained as unharmed as the succeeding twenty Jewish generations: "The year 1000 found Jews in conditions reasonably stable for the time", Catholic cleric Edward Flannery remarks. "Two centuries later they were almost pariahs, in three, they were terrorized."[221] What had changed?

---

217 Kai Kupferschmid: Die Macht des Mitgefühls. Tagesspiegel.de, December 20, 2013.
218 Carroll, p.191.
219 Maccoby: The Sacred Executioner, p.175 (quoted by Ley, p.134).
220 Schönberger/Pleticha, p.230.
221 Flannery, p.91.

The following triple sequence of crucifix paintings almost appears as a biography of the symbol. The Irish book painter swaddled his crucifixus in protecting diapers – covering the grown-up Christ-child's nakedness between his cautiously hinted wounds. The Italian master of 13th century bestows honor on the crucified king, decently covered and unmoved by pain, his head but slightly inclined – while master Grünewald's scourge-torn expression scourges the viewer ruthlessly.

From the first crucifixes of 8th century until after 1000 CE, wretched human pain was deemed not suitable to the Lord of the Universe, contradictious to his almightiness and absolute divinity. The Romanic crucifixus is a victorious king who has overcome the world's evil. The Romanic-Byzantine "Christos Pantokrator" lacks the deepness of pain as well as of space. Earnest and calmly he looks down, the sublime and eternally unmoved cosmic mover, having performed his plan of mankind's redemption. Legs closed and stretched, arms spread for a comprising blessing, palms painlessly open like in the Roman "Salve!" gesture, this sovereign remains an unmoved mover who calmly keeps the whole world in his pierced but blessingly outstretched hands.

  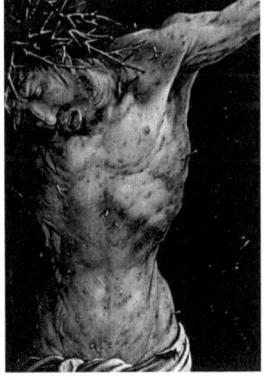

Irish book painting, 8th century;
Lucchesian master, Italy, around 1250;
Matthias Grünewald, Isenheim Altar, Alsacia, 1506-1515.

No earlier than around 12th century, a poignant and meaningful change happens. Just when artists learned to add spacial deepness to their flat two-dimensional paintings, compassion now acquired its third dimension, opening a soul-space whose converging lines aim to utmost pain. Now real life comes into the lethal scene. Body postures become more variable and individual, anatomically more natural. Painters study human bodies more exactly, they perceive emotions in body motions and learn to express their perceptions with increasing skill. The art-historical trends towards realism, perspective,

human life, individuality and corporeality are detainable in cultural evolution no easier than the same trends might be repressed in the development of teenagers, and in renaissance they come to a maturity which manifests a very advance of human culture: a progress in the logic and precision of man's comprehension of this world as well as in the sensitivity of emotional communication. The epoch of the first fire arms forged visual weapons too, and sometimes painters went too far in their newly acquired skills of hurting on distance. In 1306, the bishop of London ordered to remove a so-called mystician-cross – because of significant reactions: The total impression of this extreme, fork-like type of cross, sculptured unchangingly with salient ribs, gaping side wound, crooked body, cramped fingers and distorted mouth "was so much awe-inspiring that believers were put into fear and terror."[222] But good painting must be strong (German: *stark*) in its expression, and twenty generations of central-European artists got inspired by Grünewald's man of stark pain: Covered with scourge-torn wounds, with tense sinews and muscles, fingers cramped around the nail in their midst, head fallen down, the tortured man has opened his mouth for his last cry of suffering. His suffering, which was whose guilt? Starting in ninth century, conical hats, "Jewish" noses and long beards became details of a generally understandable iconology. Rarely, however, the Jews were explicitly presented as hate objects, for this was not the artists' aim of expression. Moreover, around 1100 just ten percent of all Jews globally lived in non-islamic Europe,[223] while Mediterranean Jews at least visually hardly distinguished from their Christian and Muslim compatriots.

It happened shortly before this 12th century that for the fanatic crusaders, setting out for the Holy Land, the who-has-done-it-void suddenly got filled. The outset of (according to reserved estimates) more than hundred thousand enthusiasts during the first wave was experienced by Jewish eyes this way: "They taunted us from every direction. They took counsel, ordering that either we turn to their abominable faith or they would destroy us 'from infant to suckling'. They – both princes and common folk – placed an evil sign, a horizontal line over a vertical one, upon their garments, a cross." Another witness noted the motives of the mostly illiterate believers who yet advancing towards Rhenanian town-walls asked if this now were Jerusalem at last. "When they passed on their way through the cities where Jews lived, they said to one another: 'Behold, we travel the long way to visit the tomb of Jesus and to take revenge on the Ismaelites [the Muslims] and behold, here among us live the Jews whose fathers have killed and crucified him, the innocent one! So let us first take revenge on them and exterminate them from the peoples ...'."[224]

222 Wikipedia, search term "Gabelkreuz".
223 Malka, p.24.
224 This quotation combines a) the statements of "Mainz Anonymus" and Solomon bar Simson, both cited by Carroll, p.237; and b); Neubauer, A. / Stern, M.: Hebräische Berichte über die Judenverfolgungen während der Kreuzzüge. Berlin 1892, p.82-83 (Rohrbacher/ Schmidt, p.228).

By coincidence, this 12th century that had the great cathedrals, these "religious and social encyclopedias, intelligible to the masses" adorned with the Crucifixion story on their pediments "in increasingly realistic detail",[225] this 12th century was also the one which produced more works of anti-Jewish polemics than all centuries before; and just as coincidentally this 12th century marks also the beginning of the socio-economic change "that was to characterize the predominant occupations of Jews in the countries of Europe for the next centuries".[226]

It happened in exactly this 12th century of emotionally enhanced paintings that a dark-red reproach spread over Europe: rumors of bearded Jews killing Christian infants, reenacting crucifixion and using their blood to bake their Matzot. And this complex was "combined with the belief in a secret and mysterious Jewish society, a conclave of sages holding its sessions somewhere in a remote country and choosing by lot the place where the sacrifice was to be performed ..."[227] Thus the two most disastrous derivates from crucifix that are used against the Jews until today – Blood Libel and Elders of Zion – were conceived in the minds of crucifix-viewers in exactly this 12th century.

Six centuries had to pass until sensitive persons described the psychic transformation that happened between view and deed, between the receptive retina of children and the sword-wielding hands of crusaders.

Early learning

"Imagine a child you want to rejoice ... and so you show him all kinds of pictures to the child's ineffable delight, and you arrive at one that has been put between deliberately, showing the crucified one. The child, not understanding this picture at once, will ask what that means, why this man is hanging on such a beam. You explain to the child that this is a cross, and hanging on it means being crucified, crucifixion having been the most painful death penalty in this country ..." Thus the Protestant philosopher **Søren Kierkegaard** (1813-1855) in his work *Training in Christendom* began to describe the childhood training in Jew-hate, just viewing and feeling in children's shoes: "How, then, will this affect the child? The child will feel strange, he properly will wonder how you came to place such an ugly picture among the pretty ones ... For just as against the Jews's will above his cross was written 'The Jews's King', so this picture which is published newly every year, to this nation's defiance is a reminder they never can get rid of ... and it will be as if the present generation had crucified him every time just to explain to the child of next generations what's going on here in this world; and the child will ... feel afraid and anxious of the elder ones, this world, and of himself ... Meanwhile the child, eager to learn as children always are, will go on asking who is he, what has he done, you know? ... Tell the child that he is love; that

225 Poliakov, Vol.I, p.56.
226 Anti-Jewish polemics: Cohen, p.86; Jewish occupations: Novinsky 2013, p.26.
227 Poliakov 2003, Vol.I, p.58.

he came to this world out of love, to love the human beings and to help them ... Then tell the child how he has fared in life, how one of those few who have been standing close to him had betrayed him, the few others disowned him and all others scorned and scolded at him until they finally fastened him to the cross – as shown in the picture – and wished that his blood shall be on them and on their children. What effect, to your opinion, will this story have on the child? First of all he'll probably forget all other pictures ... And then probably the child would sink into the deepest amazement about why God in Heaven had not done everything to prevent that this has happened; or why it happened without God having ... in the very last moment, to prevent his death, ordered fire pouring down from heaven. – By and by, however, if the child continued thinking about this story, he'd probably get ardent more and more; he'd think and speak about nothing else but war and weapons – for this the child would have determined inwardly for later on when he'd grown up: to smash to pieces all those godless people who had behaved so wickedly against the one man full of love, against whom they had shouted "crucify him, crucify him!"; this the child would have determined, in childish way forgetting that more than 1800 years have passed since they have lived."[228]

These lines Kierkegaard wrote down in Copenhagen, in 1850. In 1941, on a summer day in Radzilow, a survivor observed the Poles beating whole Jewish families to death amid crowds of laughing Polish men, women and children, under surveillance of *Gestapo Einsatzgruppe B* and after "propaganda ... coming out from the higher echelons of society which influenced the mob, stating that it was time to settle scores with those who had crucified Jesus Christ ..."[229]

"It is but natural to want to punish every injustice that is done to us or to those with who we feel compassion."[230] In 1863, **John Stuart Mill** (1806-1873), one of the most important "social philosophers" of 19th century, labelled this compassion-born desire for just punishment as "empathic anger" which he defines as "the natural desire for avenge ... that is expressed by reason and compassion and refers to those offences which hurt us by hurting others". This sensation is to Mill the "sentinel of justice".[231]

Catholic Austrian **Richard von Coudenhove-Kalergi** (1894-1972) drew on his own childhood experiences. Born in Tokyo to a Japanese mother and an Austrian diplomate, he hated the Jews for they had crucified Jesus. Not until the avidly reading teenager came to know that not the Jews were Jesus' murderers, he began to question Christian teaching as a whole. Emphasizing the impact of "covered childhood impressions", he in 1925 rephrased Kierkegaard's insight concisely:

"The child views a crucifix and asks for its meaning. He receives the answer that the man on the cross is the dear Saviour (whom he loves and reveres as the "Christ child") being tortured to death by the Jews. In the child natural-

---

228 Kierkegaard 1951, p.167-170.
229 Perry/Schweitzer, p.261-262, citing Gross, Jan T.: Neighbors, p.65.
230 Mill, p.248-249 (Utilitarianism, chapter 5: Of the Connection between Justice and Utility, Part 2).
231 Mill, thus cited by Goleman, p.138-139.

ly awakes a deep compassion with the Saviour, connected with an equally deep abhorrence of his enemies and assassins: 'the Jews'. If later on he hears about Jews or sees Jews, he associates them spontaneously with the Christ-killers ... With this antipathy inside, the child grows up and treats those Jews he comes into contact with in a prejudiced, distrustful and hostile way; this behaviour of course encounters reciprocity and thus goes on providing anti-Semitism with ever fresh sustenance."[232]

Was Chriftus
über die Juden fagte

Right: Down to the valley's darkness? Watercolor by young Adolf Hitler, interpretable (*Le style c'est l'homme*).

Left: "What Christ said about the Jews", from the Nazi children-book "Der Giftpilz" (The Poisonous Mushroom), 1938. Caption: "If you view a cross, think on the gruesome Jewish murder on Golgotha". In the book's textpage: "He said to them, that their father was the Devil!" The mother went on talking: "And because this man knew the Jews and proclaimed the truth to the world, he had to die. They drove nails through his hands and feet, hung him on the cross and let him die. In such a dreadful way the Jews took revenge."

In 1935, Coudenhouve-Kalergi edited his work together with his father's essay *Judenhass von heute* (Jew-hate of today) newly with the introducing remark: "Since the takeover of National Socialism, the Jewish question advanced to the focus of world affairs." Three years later the unrefrained discharge of "empathic anger", the "smashing to pieces" of the "godless people", became real in the encounter of well-armed cross-educated child-

---

232 Coudenhove-Kalergi, p.35-36; cf. Ben-Chorin 1962, p.6.

ren with the wicked crucifiers in Eastern European *shtetls* from Vilnius to Sebastopol.

Born in former Austrian-Hungarian, today Ukrainian Zastavna, ten years after the discharge the Jewish-American philosopher **Dagobert David Runes** (1902-1982) in his fulminant essay "The Jew and the Cross" put it bluntly: "The cross is for the Jew the symbol of pogrom, ... hate and condemnation. [...] No religion except the Christian has woven into its theology such a cruel chapter ... No other religion, be it Buddhism, Hinduism, Confucianism or Taoism, Islam or Shintoism, no faith in the world has built into its teachings such a gruesome pattern of outrageous hatred ... It is the only one religion which made the gallows a symbol of love. All the manifold flowers of poison sprout from the same seed, the Christian religious anti-Semitism. The Christian child drinks his Jew-hate in Mother Church. This first impression of the grisly crucifixion stories is never to be forgotten [...]. Indeed, cross and crucifix are the constant reminders of the deviltry of Jews, the God-hated murderers of his son."[233]

In 1966, the Auschwitz-Trial in Frankfurt had just ended when the Hamburg and Oldenburg chairholder of pedagogy **Hans Jochen Gamm** (1925-2011) dared to speak out: "If the pupil hears the gospel reports in the religious education lessons, he is prompted to recognize *die Juden* wholesale as the guilty ones of Jesus' death, not different from what the New Testament itself intends ... The cross and the bleeding hanged one on it refresh permanently the Jewish role of 'opponents' in God's plan of salvation, besides of the shock which the child obtains from the passion story's general circumstances ... Here at any rate a problem exists which not earlier than after the European *Judenkatastrophe* is being perceived now by some theologians and teachers of religious education."[234]

In the same year, young **Melvin J. Lerner** started a series of experiments that investigated observer responses to shocking paradigms of victimization and led him to his well-known "Just-World-Hypothesis". Four decades later, Lerner and **Susan Clayton** conclude from studies of **Carolyn Hafer** that the responses to injust treatment of a victim are so automatic that they "appear to be scripted". Hafer had confronted all her test persons with the same "vividly compelling report of injustice: Another student had been robbed and severely beaten". Subsequently, "some of the participants were informed that the perpetrators had been apprehended and punished, so that justice had been at least partially restored, while others were told that the perpetrators had gotten off scot-free." With this difference of information, both groups were tested for their delay in reacting to coloured stimulus words, which is significant for the extent to which a person is inwardly occupied with weighing the content of the word (justice, fairness, deservingness ...) instead of reacting quickly to its colour. Those who believed that the perpetrators had escaped unpunished showed a strong mental occupation – with what? Lerner stresses that the participants had no awareness that their commitment to

233 Runes, p.82-92 and 67.
234 Gamm, p.89-90.

justice and deservingness had generated their "automatic and preconscious" justice-restoring reactions to the injustices they had observed. "If asked, they would have been unable to consciously retrieve these processes. The strength of the emotional response to injustice is heightened by the fact that the assessment of justice is automatic and lies outside of conscious awareness."
Especially notable in view of the abused one on the cross, "witnessing some injustices inflicted on others may create a greater imperative to punish the perpetrator than does directly experiencing the same undeserved fate." In another test constellation, the participants at first rated the extent of anger they experienced while watching a tape recorded bullying. In a second experiment they responded to several incidents in which someone by negligence caused harm to others. "The angrier they were to the first injustice, the more punishment they assigned to the second negligent perpetrator of undeserved harm." Employing the videotape of a very moving incident of bullying, James J. Gross and Robert W. Levenson (1995) "vividly demonstrated the persistent preconscious influence of these ... automatic justice-driven imperatives on the person's behavior."[235]

Oftern   **Auferstehung**

The crucifix in Julius Streicher's hate sheet *Der Stürmer*;
Left: Easter walk in 1933. Accompanying text: "The Jews have nailed Christ to the cross and believed him to be dead. He has risen. They have nailed Germany to the cross and deemed it dead and it has risen more glorious than before."
Right: *Auferstehung* (Resurrection), Issue 13/1929: Old Jew beneath the crucifix, SA-troopers saluting, or pointing to his crime.

When Lerner started his studies in 1966, **Jean Piaget** (1896-1980) was looking forward to his 70th birthday in Genéve. His research on how children learn, develop and come to grips with this world had made the Swiss biologist

---

235 Lerner/Clayton, p.41-44; 49-51 (here citing Gross, J.J./ Levenson R.W.: Emotion elicitation using films. In: Cognition and Emotion, 9/1995, p.87-108); 58 and 242-243.

the leading developmental psychologist of twentieth century. What Piaget wrote down at age 77 was the quintessence of his observations made on innumerous children – including his own two daughters and their younger brother – as well as of the studies of Russian developmental psychologist **Helena Antipoff** (1892-1974) who emigrated to Brazil in 1929 and until her death worked there with lasting effects for child-centered school reform, promoting ecological awareness yet in the 1950s: "Among the instinctive inclinations, especially those to revenge and compassion are to mention here. Both indeed develop independently from adults' pressure ... However, as Mrs. Antipoff has demonstrated very well in a short remark about compassion, the inclinations to revenge may get 'polarized' very early under the influence of sympathy: While children, due to their amazing ability to empathy and emotional identification with the suffering one, suffer themselves, they feel the desire to avenge the unhappy one, like themselves, and sense a certain malicious joy about the suffering done to the originator of someone else's pain."[236]

Within the same study, Piaget points to the amazing severity and hardness, even cruelty, with which children wish to punish all evildoers: If they themselves can choose the "just punishment" for transgressions, they "almost always recur to expiation, and their choice is of amazing rigor."[237] In Goethe's words, "all children are moral rigorists".[238] Kierkegaard grasps this rigor sensitively in the child's desire to "smash to pieces" – a wish as rigorous as recurring through the centuries. In 1673, Padre Torrejoncillo regards the crucifixion of daily 500 Jews before the walls of Jerusalem back in 70 CE just justified: "And all this occurred to them as castigation for the words they had spoken against Christ our Lord: *Crucifige, crucifige, sanguis eius super nos*.[239] In his work about Hitler's Willing Executioners, Daniel Goldhagen proved abundantly clear "that to the Germans, on all levels, the point was first and foremost to inflict pain on the Jews; their work compared with this was side issue". January 1945: "The cruelties in Schlesiersee did not confine to exposing the women to bad weather during work without protection. The guards flogged them as soon as they just tried to warm up." A witness: "It was bitter cold in Schlesiersee and we were dressed poorly; some of the women took the only blanket they possessed and wore it outside at work. Three or four times all women were controlled when they came back from work and all those who got caught with blanket wrapped around were punished with 25 lashes."

Was this behaviour of "first and foremost to inflict pain" modelled on Europe's foremost symbol? "The ideal which oriented the behaviour against the most hated inmates of the Lager world – the Jews – was a world *of boundless torture* that should lead to their *death*. The life of a Jew had to be

---

236   Piaget 1973, p.259-260; I translated German "das Kind" (singular, neutral) with "children" to avoid he/she/it for child); cf. Antipoff, Helena: Observation sur la compassion et le sens de justice chez l'enfant. Archive de Psychologie, Vol.XXI, 1928.
237   Piaget, p.238.
238   Krogmann, p.13.
239   Torrejoncillo, p.173; "sanguis eius super nos" means "his blood upon us".

but hell on earth, *incessant torment, endless pain without comfort and assistance.*"[240] If the Lager reality "scorned the Christian values of charity, compassion and sympathy with the oppressed ones", this lack of mercy might be ascribed to Nietzsche's anti-Christian, supermannish counsel "Be warned about compassion!"[241] The preferential treatment of the Jews, however, this relentlessness of punishing sprang from German children's never forgotten compassion and sympathy with the victim hanging at all cold seasons naked on those beams *"of boundless torture* ending in his *death"* after *"incessant torment, endless pain without comfort and assistance".*

In a diligent translation, the child transforms the visual input of the crucifix into a "severe, but just" output of later punishment. Childish rigor and desire for boundless torture surfaced already during the Dreyfus affaire: "Criminal scum, honest workers and noble ladies of the Salons united in speculations about the ways how the Jews should die: whether they should be hacked to death, thrown living into boiling water, fried in oil or pierced with needles; the most radical ones proposed to 'circumcise them up to their necks'."[242] A certain Abbé Cros donated three francs for a bedside rug made of "Yid's skin to trample, on morning and evenings."[243] As likely as Spanish, French and German grown-up children recurred to *expiation ... of amazing rigor*, as equally the one diagnosis applies to both: In head the nails of Jesus, in hand the whip Jesus was scourged with.

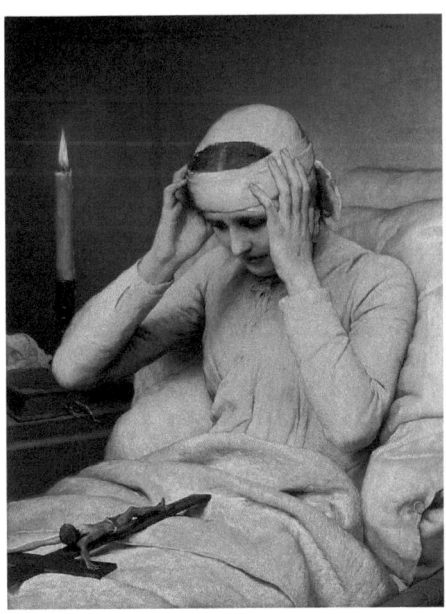

Facing the crucifixus:
Anna-Katharina Emmerick, 1885.
Dreyfus at court martial, 1894.

---

240   Goldhagen 1996, p.391 and 535.
241   Friedrich Nietzsche, Thus Spoke Zarathustra, chapter "Of the Compassionate Ones".
242   Nazário, Luiz: Nacionalismo e Judeofobia na Europa dos seculos XIX e XX. In: Fuks, p.282.
243   Michael, p.4.

Sometimes – in sensitive persons prone to turn aggression inward – the piercing impression works so strongly inside a viewer that the body tries to relieve by physical expression: Saint Francis of Assisi and the Spanish Marrano-daughter Theresia of Avila are the most famous ones of about 400 historically noted Jesus-centered persons whose bodies uttered the inner compassion by blood-red stigmata. In the case of the highly sensitive Francis, compassion with the crucified one had also another side-effect: In order not to defile himself, he even refused to but pronounce the word "Jew". [244] Anna-Katharina Emmerick (1774-1824) heard in her meditations the terrible shout "His blood be over us and our children", saw "uncanny threatening clouds in the sky, of blood's colour, sending swords and arrows over the shouting crowd". Having shocked her parents by the decision to enter a monastery just when a marriage seemed upcoming, the sensitive young nun's ecstatic visions were accompanied by nail wounds on her hands and a cross stigma on her breast which had the shape of the extremely frightening fork-shape variant. [245]

These wounds, pediatrician Jim B.Tucker argues, are not supernatural wonders but psychosomatically restaged impressions, resulting from the phenomenon that "the mental image of the wounds of Christ in the head of a particularly susceptible person can evoke on her skin specific alterations which reproduce the image".[246] The reproduced lesions of course do not replicate the actual injuries of Jesus, but their painted replicas: Usually the stigmatically hurt persons, for instance the 1972 Jewish born and Catholic encultured German anthroposopher Judith von Halle who now reveals the *Secrets of Way of the Cross and Grail's Blood* and meditates the *Our Father*, feature a wound on both palms as seen on the crucifix, whereas Roman hangmen used to drive the nail between the bones of the carpus or between ulna and spoke bone – to prevent a tear-out.

Agreeing with Tucker's diagnosis, Professor Gerd Overbeck, chairholder of Psychosomatic Medicine and Psychotherapy at Frankfurt Goethe-University, views the stigmatisations as religious dramas on the proper body's stage. "These persons experience Mount Calvary with the whole shebang. They sense the sufferings of Christ on their own body. They hear the hammer blow, see the cross in front of them, feel the whiplashes and the crown of thorns pricking. On Holy Friday their stigmata begin to bleed intensively ... But this suffering, to be sure, is desired by them. (...) We had 20 cases from the Rhine-Main-region up to Würzburg and Fulda, among them 18 women and two men. The youngest was 17 and the oldest 50. Most of them came from a religious, rural ambience."[247]

In this ambience people use to draw the cross sign in four wound points onto their bodies: "In the name of the Father (head), the Son (breast), the Holy (left side) Spirit (right side)."[248] Even without these repetitions, and even in

244 Michael, p.94.
245 Cohen, p.130 and wikipedia.
246 Tucker, p.64-65.
247 Süddeutsche Zeitung, Munich (SZ-Magazin, 13/2012, Easter issue).
248 Possibly the Christian symbolical crossing oneself as a gesture of blessing is derived

lesser susceptible, stable persons able to slackly overlook all crucifixes, the wounds in Jesus' limbs are subliminally stored and always present – in the cerebral body map which resonates in every gesture of the hands and every step of feet. No wonder since the antique torture gear was adapted to human body shape from the beginning (form follows function), corresponding to the cross-shaped body structure in which man, as any other vertebrate, is embedded since hundreds of millions of years, and which is present in his body-memory with an equally inveterate tradition. In German language where cross (*Kreuz*) signifies also the backbone, the locution "*Das haben wir im Kreuz*" signifies: This is inside us, strong and unremovable.

"He often wanted to clasp these two good musicians in his arms", French novelist Romain Rolland recalls a music teacher who had two gifted Jewish pupils. "But then he remembered that they had crucified God and didn't know how to arrange his troubled feelings."[249] Does it suit to mention here that the gene which controls the positioning of the human arm exists in all vertebrates and even insects?[250] Arms (French: *bras*) stand polyglot and archetypically for *embrasser, embrace, abraço*, this archaic gesture of opening up, accepting, giving shelter and social contact. In sudden danger, children of apes and human mothers instinctively stretch both arms upward, reaching for mother's fur. And even photos of soldiers in the moment of being hit by a lethal bullet show steel helmet men throwing their hands above where mother's helping arms had always been. This very basic reflex is followed yet in early infancy by another instinctive reflex in case of danger: Running away. Be it kicking babies, running apple thieves, a panicking crowd, or a grenade-struck soldier walking away on legs with no feet: Legs and arms are our instinctive means of movement, of fortunate escape and playing chasey; of shaking hands and showing the way, and above all of social contact, gentle touch, caressing, comfort. On the cross, they are fixed with nails. Keeping this in mind, the following results of psychological research become palpable:

"Do you remember a situation where you had to view another person who inadvertently had caused to herself a deep cut with a knife?" – Freiburg University Professor **Joachim Bauer**, in his book "The Body's Memory" (Das Gedächtnis des Körpers, 2004), gives his question a general answer: "The experience of most people is that they as (normally unwilling) observers in such a situation sense 'kind of pain' themselves; in fact a pain which runs weirdly deep into us and sticks in our minds as an impression for a long time vividly. Pictures or accounts of an accident often trigger ... the same strong *sym-passion* of pain in us. The pain we are talking about has a strong emotional component. It is an emotional pain (close to feelings of horror and angst) and likewise linked to what could be called compassion or empathy."[251]

---

from the Jewish custom of drawing the Hebrew letter Beth [ב] with which Torah begins in Genesis 1:1 (B'reshit bara ...) on one's body at the beginning of a prayer.
249 Rolland: Jean-Christophe, IV, La Révolte (cited by Isaac, p.305).
250 Gerald Schroeder, cited in judaismohumanista.ning.com, December 14, 2012.
251 Bauer, p.154-155.

Empathy researcher **Tania Singer**, director of Max-Planck-Institute for Cognition and Neuro Sciences in Leipzig, put test persons in situations in which people normally react with empathy. For example, she watched on the MRI scanner what happens in the brain of a person whose partner gets a pulse of current through his hand. The result: In the test person who sensed no pain, the same cerebral regions became active as in the partner who just got the electric shock. Not the entire regions, to note. From the partner's piercing pain, the observer gets, as Singer says, the "end note", the feeling "Ouch, that hurts".[252]

What Bauer and Singer relate seems no surprise in view of mirror neurons. In a modified test situation, Tania Singer however obtained results in line with the fact that Nazi perpetrators were mostly male. Now before the test Singers probands played a game with determined roles: Some had to behave always fairly, others were instructed to play especially nastily; but afterwards the persons of both groups, visible to their partners, got the same painful pulses of current. When the victim had played fair, both men and women showed heightened activity in two brain areas associated both with processing one's own pain and with empathy toward the pain of others. When the victim had played unfair, the female observers still seemed to experience the same empathetic response to the victim's "deserved" pain. The male observers, however, no longer showed increased activity in their pain-processing regions but a slight rise in the nucleus accumbens, which is activated when, among other things, we receive rewards.[253]

Only boys had access to Bavarian gymnasiums with their crucifix adorned classrooms when Albert Einstein (*1879) at Munich Luitpold Gymnasium had an experience he still in his old age told his biographers Rudolf Kayser and Carl Seelig. In one of the religious education lessons, the Catholic priest had presented a giant iron nail to the pupils, saying: "With such nails Jesus was crucified by the Jews." All eyes turned towards the only one Jew in the classroom, who felt very embarrassed" and "for the first time in his life sensed the appalling poison of anti-Semitism."[254]

Einstein escaped the giant punishment, but his French contemporary Jules Isaac (*1877) relates another school experience: "A girl, a little black-eyed Jewess, has entered as 'new classmate' into a Paris highschool; during re-cess she shyly approaches to another girl she takes to be sympathic, and invites her timidly and friendly to play with her. "No", this girl replies, "I don't want to play with you. You have crucified God.' This little Jewess who had crucified God, was ... deported to Auschwitz and there ... killed by men who surely were baptized and had not crucified God; by men with whom many righteous well baptized French surely would have liked to play."

She was killed by men who had read the *Stürmer* hate sheet, edited by a for-mer *Volksschul* teacher who thus remembered his school days in Bavarian public school: "The parson explained to us how the Jews had fought Jesus

---

252 Kai Kupferschmidt: Die Macht des Mitgefühls. Tagesspiegel.de, December 20, 2013.
253 beinghuman.org/article/schadenfreude-and-sexes.
254 Jammer, p.21.

fiercely and eventually crucified him. Back then I realized for the first time that the nature of the Jew is different."[255]
In 1946, the year this teacher and editor Julius Streicher was hanged in Nuremberg, Jules Isaac heard a French educator say: "It would be better to be grateful to the people that crucified Jesus for everything marvellous and true they gave to mankind, instead of hating them." Jules Isaac views this "laudable intention" as completely ineffective: "The people that crucified Jesus: This suffices to call up hatred."[256]
The ways how modern German religious educators circumnavigate the question who has done it shows how clearly they know where Jew-hate starts. For instance Prof. Albert Biesinger who in April 2009 answered children's FAQs concerning Easter in liberal Frankfurter Allgemeine Zeitung. "Why did God allow that his son was nailed to the cross, did he not love him?" – "Yes, he did love him even very much" and so on. Answering children's questions is an examen rigorosum, Kierkegaard knew.[257] But what counts here is how Biesinger circumscribes who's done it:
"Jesus has been threatened on this world from the beginning, already King Herod tried to kill him when he was still a baby – that's why his parents fled with him to Egypt ... There have been around Jesus very evil people who feared that he would become too mighty, that he would mix up everything with his speeches, and they have killed him."[258]
Very evil people, very punishable. The final punishment in genocide no sooner could take place than when technical options of modernity (i.e. means of transport, chemistry and electronics) were available to modern men whose compassion born desire for just punishment was incited by an image of antique Roman *brutalitas*. No one else has understood this zoom effect from crucifixion to killing in concentration camps better than an Italian peasant's son born 1881 who in the 1940s saved the lifes of thousands of Jews by, for example, tricking the German Jew-search-engine with masses of falsified baptismal certificates. He also didn't shun from passing off Hungarian Jews as pilgrims to Paul's now Turkish home town Tarsus. This Papal Nuncio in Turkey, Angelo Giuseppe Roncalli who, as new Pope John XXIII, in his term of "six million crucifixions" left no emergency door open, described the zoom from infant compassion to grown-up mass murder in a prayer of atonement he shortly before his death in 1974 addressed to Jesus: "Forgive us the curse we wrongly attached to the name of the Jews. Forgive us that we crucified You in their flesh the second time."

Forgiveness is appropriate: The killers were children when they learned empathic anger against Biesinger's *very evil people*.

255 Bytwerk, p.2.
256 Isaac, p.304.
257 Kierkegaard, "Image of mother love", in: Kierkegaard 1982, p.185.
258 faz.net, April 11, 2009.

VII   Paternal Love

I love you like a father, said the Czar to the peasants and ordered the Czarevitch's beheading.

Soldier Simon, in Bertolt Brecht's Caucasian Chalk Circle

Hard-hitting love is not the exclusive domaine of father Czar. And the peda-gogical approach of the previous chapter remains fragmentary as long as we don't examine the childhood impact of the male key figure in most human lives, which is highly influential even if the child grows up fatherless. Commemorating Swiss childhood psychologist and Shoah survivor Alice Miller (1923-2010), in autumn 2010 a young Catholic wrote in leftist German *graswurzelrevolution*: "The God of the Old Testament is like the father of Black Pedagogy: greedy for power and revenge, swift to take offence, bossy, brutal ... Jesus names and shames that and proclaims real love, means one that comes straight from heart. Jesus is the Bible Rebel. In fact, Old and New Testament should not be printed together. And the Church absurdly acts until today as if Jesus stood in her center – while she still ticks more like Herod. Or like old short fuse Yahve" – who, by the way, is labelled "one of the most unpleasant figures of world literature" by British atheist Richard Dawkins. And this is quite a gentle wording in view of the outrageous pas-sage of Samuel where selfsame Yahve commands to punish "Amalek" for an assault three centuries back: "Now go, attack the Amalekites and ... kill alike men and women, infants and sucklings, oxen and sheep, camels and donkeys.'"

Of course the question here to ask is not why God orders genocide but why a human author ascribes such inhumanity to Him. Einstein, another atheist, regards this literary figure as "the attempt to base the moral law on fear, a lamentable inglorious attempt. But it seems to me that the strong moral tradition within the Jewish people has widely disengaged from this fear."[259] Sigmund Freud sheds light on the beginnings of this fear: "We can trace back the origin of the religious attitude in clear outlines to the childhood feeling of helplessness ... I'd not be able to indicate another childhood born necessity as strong as that of paternal protection." And withal, atheist Freud is able to rate this strong protector as if he'd met him personally: "The father of pre-history was certainly terrible and capable of extreme aggressivity."[260]

A Father God of genocide?

In historical times, this divine-paternal ambiguity shows up when the military commander Joshua, after having exterminated "man and woman, young and old, ox and sheep and ass" in Jericho, also proscribed Makkedah

---

259   Einstein, Mein Weltbild, p.101.
260   Freud 2010, p.25 and 102.

"leaving none that escaped", and captured Libnah and put "all the people in it to the sword, letting none escape", and then Lachish and Eglon and he continues, same procedure, the conquest of the promissed land in Hebron, putting "all the people that were in it to the sword", and then cleaning Debir, and the Neeb, the Shephelah, and the slopes, the whole country, and still he "let none escape, but proscribed everything that breathed – as *Yahve, the God of Israel, had commanded* " (6:17-21; 10:28-40).

This leaves me, the reader, with two options: Either God is sick or the scribe is. In the first case honest people shouldn't bestow more honour on this genocidal Lord than on Herr Hitler, who on October 22, 1939 allegedly told his generals that he had given orders to his Death's Head Units "to send to death mercilessly and without compassion, men, women, and children of Polish descent and language. Only thus shall we gain the *Lebensraum* we need. Who, after all, speaks still today about the annihilation of the Armenians?"[261] In the second case, it follows pars pro toto that all Bible texts are doubtful narrations of doubtable authors with dubious political intentions.

As to the exterminations of defeated tribes and cities, archeological evidence refutes that those genocidal horrors ever happened. Equally strong disproof comes from the literary evidence of much more human encounters: Whereas the scribes declared that Yahve required to doom the "Hittites, Girgashites, Amorites, Canaanites, Perizzites, Hivites and Jebusites ... to destruction" (Deuteronomy 7:1-3), the sons and daughters of those "Canaanites, Hittites, Amorites, Perizzites, Hivites and Jebusites" matched so gaily with the Hebrew teens and twens in Judges 3:5-7 that Shlomo Sand does not refrain from quipping: "Strange though it seems, God first ordered the complete extermination of the local population and then issued instructions not to marry those who had been annihilated."

Both orders came from the power seeking priests who alone had ears good enough to hear the God who back then on Sinai so clearly had demanded *Lo tirza* (Not murder) demanding now, in whatever godly voice, to murder women, children, every life of Amalek's tribe (1 Sam 15:2-3). A backward God of olden times? Shlomo Sand remarks that the book of Joshua was until relatively recently the favoured text in many Zionist circles, and still is part of the curriculum of students nine and ten years old in Israeli schools. "The Ministry of Education has never found it necessary to distance itself from such schocking parts of the Bible, and instead facilitates its instruction without any censorship." Is there a connection between modern Zionists' faible for old tales of ethnic cleansing and the old authors' situation? Sand assumes that those Bible passages that threaten Israel with getting "scattered among the nations" (Lev 26:33-39; Deut 4:27; Nehemiah 1:8, Jeremiah 9:15) reverberate the Babylonian exile from which the inteligentsia had just returned to Palestine. "Here the pioneers of Western monotheism assembled in small Jerusalem and began to cultivate their new faith [...] By comparison with them, the inhabitants of Canaan were ignorant, corrupt and inclined in

---

261 Friedrich-Ebert-Stiftung, Netz-Quelle: Die NS-Bevölkerungs- und Vernichtungspolitik für Osteuropa (1939); cf. armenian-genocide.org/hitler.html.

idol worship. Contempt for and alienation from the autochthonous population were ultimately translated into disturbing literary descriptions of their expulsion and extermination."[262] Disturbing whom? "Dear God! Why are you doing this to us? If we have sinned, take us, but why are you permitting this to happen to innocent newborn babies? Why? Why? Why?" Thus He is asked by Ben Edelbaum in the ghetto of Lodz in 1942, in view of SS guards throwing babies alive out of the upper windows of the hospital. In March 1943, the same SS enacted in Piotrkow a "Purim Play" and hung the Jewish watchman of the cemetery and his wife next to the already selected eight other Jews because back then in Persia ten sons of Haman were "impaled on the stake": all the ten sons of this Haman descendant of Agag the Amalekite, this Haman who had divulged, in the name of his lord, the Persian King Ahasveros, a decree ordering to "exterminate all the Jews, young and old, children and women, on a single day ..." (Esther 3:13).[263] Scheduled to some war years, Haman's plan was implemented by SS-man Eichmann, and considering his, in his own words, "extremely pious" upbringing, one may ponder if the well-versed son of Protestant parents had read about the hanging of Haman's sons and Samuel's extermination order in young years and already at this point developed, analogous to a Jew-hate out of pity for Jesus, a Jew-hate out of pity for the innocent children of the Amalekites; a desire for expiation showing the same "amazing rigor" Piaget attested to empathetic children, a rigor that deemed the killing of children and women quite justified if they were Samuelites, members of the same tribe as those, in Sand's view, "by comparison" civilized creators of Western monotheism with their civilized God of child murder, sending His people out with orders for genocide.

Anyhow, I'd like to widen Sand's political view by aspects of developmental psychology, starting from another disturbing Bible passage. Why does Isaiah (13:13-16) associate war atrocities of raped wives and "babes dashed to pieces in their sight" to "the fury of the Lord of Hosts on the day of his burning wrath?" Whence the pervasive tendency of antique world-view to interpret whatever collective sufferings as castigations, imposed by godheads displaying those furies, wrathes, rages which children archetypically first experience with their parents? Or rather, how could things be different, since parents are, in good or bad, the primeval God-figures, the first and foremost providers of love and food, uplifting and pressure, rejection and protection? Since from time immemorial parents used the whole gamut of beating and caressing, giving and denying, promise and punishment for educational purpose, how could anyone's view of God or moral instance not be coined by her or his childhood experience with the elder attachment figures?

262   Sand 2012, p.74-83.
263   Gilbert, p. 442 (Ben Edelbaum) and 553 (Joseph Kermish).

Offspring's obsession

"Judaism was fated to remain a 'Father-religion'", Sigmund Freud noted in his last work in 1939, terming Christianity the *"Son-Religion*, in which the Son was deified and he, in effect, usurped and displaced the Father."[264] Léon Poliakov, referring to the "odious father image" of the "Protocols of the Elders of Zion", stresses the Christian "fear of the Jews, these 'fathers' endowed with superhuman faculties, these 'wise men' who impose their laws on the Christians, these mentors whose very existence makes them intolerable". And he hints like a tour guide in a haunted castle: "We are in the presence of the anti-Semite's major obsession."[265]

Norman Cohn surveys the connection-wires between the father-reconciliation-cross and conspiration myths: "Indeed and obviously, the Elders of Zion are father figures, as already their name indicates. And what they do to nations corresponds exactly to what the 'wicked' father in phantasy does to the son ... First and foremost they own the monopoly of power. Mysterious and unfathomable, they manipulate and harrow the human masses who in their hands are as help- and clueless as infants."[266]

Cutting fathers! Left: The Circumcision of Jesus. Book Painting, Neustift convent, South Tirol. Right: Photo Album of Police Battalion 101 (witty note on the photo's backside: "He'll work, alright, but shaved he must be").

The Elders' profile doesn't sort ill with the Father who didn't soften when his son, sweating blood and water, implored his Dad to spare him from crucifixion. Hearing this nightly scene in Gethsemane (Matthew 26:39-44), what does a Christian child feel? The odd relationship is described with bitter irony by Theodor Weißenborn (born 1933): "Since he had my brother crucified in order to reconcile with me I know what to think of my father."[267] To Eugen Drewermann the view that God should have to kill a man to reconcile with the world "doesn't make God trustworthy but lets him appear

264 Freud: Moses and Monotheism, translated by James Strachey, 1939, p.135-136 (quoted by Yerushalmi, p.38; italics K.Y.R.).
265 Poliakov 2003, Vol.IV, p.61 (Vol.VII, p.78 in the German edition).
266 Cohn, N., 1969, p.334.
267 Weißenborn in: Berg, S. and H.K. (ed.): Wege nach Golgatha. Biblische Texte verfremdet. Munich 10/1989, p.82 (quoted by Mynarek, p.176-177).

bloodthirsty, brutish and barbarous." With the insight of his long professional practice as psychiatricist, the ordained Catholic priest Drewermann speaks out: "Why should the horrid torment of cross and execution be necessary to atone for any guilt toward God? What moloch of a God would need such atoning sacrifice?"[268]

The moloch-likeness, however, must be kept aloof from Jesus' heavenly father who for mankind's sake required his sons's sacrifice. So the faithful of the Son-religion ever pushed this moloch back into the time before the birth of Christ, i.e. the Old Testament, where he quickly melded with the old "eye for eye and tooth for tooth" dictator. Shifting hate from the father to his people, the son can stay the good son who honors the father and does his will. "My father I honored, my mother I loved" the beaten son of Alois Hitler balanced. Describing how the father reacted to his proposal to become a painter – "The alte *Herr* was embittered and ... I, too" – he doesn't fail to insert the father-fearing line "... as much as I, however, loved him".[269] And lifelong he remains the loving-hating, obedient son of the fatherly ruler: "Defending against the Jew, I struggle for the work of the *Herr*."[270]

Catholic historian Friedrich Heer explains: "The shifting of the repressed hostility concerning one's own father towards external 'fathers' and 'overfathers' benefits antisemitism. Not by chance Judaism is viewed as the religion of the father and Christendom as the religion of the son. The most pathetically charged image of the Jew, the 'Ostjude', bears traces of the 'Old Man', the ancient in his beard, the degenerated father. German army propaganda pictures of second World War display young German soldiers cutting the beards of old Jewish fathers, making them impotent."[271]

Those dirt sacks of German sons

Martin Luther is a prime example for the interaction of father image, crucifix and Jew hate. In his 1523 pamphlet *That Jesus Christ Was Born a Jew* he is one of the few who dared to take a stand for Jews at that time: "They are friends by blood, the cousins and brothers of the Lord ..." Twenty years later, disappointed in his hope that they would join his Bible-centered version of the Son-faith, in *On the Jews and Their Lies* he railed against the bunch: "Instead of letting us participate" in the Messiah, they would rather "crucify ten more Messiases and strike dead God himself ... Therefore, wherever you view a real Jew, with a clear conscience you can make the cross sign and say: There goes a devil in the flesh." Some months later, Luther's childhood emotions peak in his last work *Of the Unknowable Name and the Generations of Christ* (1543). The justice imperative shows up in the self-reproach "so it's our guilt that we don't avenge the blood they shed of our Lord ... and, to this day, of children, by beating them dead"; and it escalates in the wishful

268 Drewermann, Eugen: Das Markusevangelium – Bilder von Erlösung. Olten 1987, p.72 (quoted by Mynarek, p.177).
269 Hitler, p.16 and 7-8.
270 Hitler, on July 29, 1921 in Zirkus Krone, Munich (Heer 1989, p.193).
271 Heer 1967, p.460.

thinking "that the lanes flow full of blood, that one count their dead not by hundred thousands but by ten hundred thousands."[272]
In all his rage against the crucifiers of his son, the father who required his crucifixion remains unimpeachable: "The destruction of Jerusalem was cruel and lamentable", Luther sighed in his table talks. "But even for God it was too much to see his only son crucified outside of town."[273] It was too much for Luther, we may conclude. In order to defend a Godhead fitting to his own soft heart against Paul's crucifying God the Father, Luther, as any Christian, had to charge the hard and cruel Jews – as every Christian is, with cross in mind, inclined to do.
May we analyze Luther on base of the anti-Jewish couch talks of his late life? German theologian Heiko Oberman did so, and interprets one key passage in Luther's late table talks where the great reformer remembers that once, when little Martin had pilfered a nut, he was beaten "unto the blood". By his mother! Oberman asks: "A mother punishes her son unto the blood ... Doesn't this make for a plausible anamnesis for a frightened and depressive son?" No, says Oberman: the mother-centered view did not prevail, because "Margarete Luder [original spelling] recedes completely behind her impressive husband who kept his son under his thumb so perfectly that reformation can be explained as an act of self-defense, as a protest against merciless fathers, call them Hans, Pope or God."[274] And this father Hans Luder bate hard, and one time hard enough that the scared, unhinged son but slowly found back to him. Martin draws his personal conclusions as to the education of his own son, baptized Hans again: "One shouldn't thrash the children too hard, for once my father thrashed me so much that I fled him and he was apprehensive until I had accustomed to him again. I also wouldn't like to beat my Hans so hardly, lest he become dumb and hostile to me ..." – as hostile, to wit, as Martin was to his father and the old God of the Jews.
Carl-Heinz Mallet elaborates stringently how Luther's pedagogic concept evolves from his never overcome childhood; how his catechetical method was implemented adequately even in Catholic ambience and how his adamant request of obedience is operant in Germany until today. "From the time of Luther, obedience has been the national virtue",[275] and not by chance: Citing ever handy Bible verses, Luther leaves no doubt that only loveless, spoiling parents "spare the birch" (cf. Proverbs 13:24) and fail to thrash their "dirt sack of a child" many times, "justly earning hell" for this lamentable failure in child rearing. Morton Schatzman views Luther's educational recipes as the basis of the "conspiracy of the German parents against their children". This educational rigor resulted in the massive "shift of repressed hostilities" from the own onto the 'superfathers'" which eventually found its outlet "in hate against Judaism as the religion of the father".[276]

---

272 Luther: Vom Schem Hamphoras ... (1543); in: CW Vol.53, p.579.
273 Isaac, p.290.
274 Oberman, p.92.
275 Poliakóv 2003, Vol.III, p.159.
276 Mallet, p.37 and 216; Schatzmann, passim; Heer 1967, p.460; cf. post-war Germany born Gabriele Schwab (p.178): "Germany has a strong tradition of harshly authoritarian and

Defiant children should be killed, Luther concludes from Exodus 21:15, translating verse 17 with trenchant steeliness: "Who curses father or mother shall be killed, head cut down, head away with no delay, lest the land get full of godless ones."

But this tough defense of ironclad paternal venerability, equating father with god and punishing verbal offence with capital castration, is the adult psychic armor of a sensitive child: When in 1528 his little daughter Elisabeth dies, Luther wonders about his "almost womanish heart": "... so much I'm filled with sorrow. Never before I'd have believed that a father's heart might be so soft toward his children."[277]

Luther's utterings remind the words of another sensitive child: "Should we say that God is unjust when he punishes in anger? By no means!" Paul assures the Romans (3:5). "For how, then, could God judge the world?" And Paul concludes: "So anyone who rebels against authority is rebelling against what God has instituted, and they will be punished." (13:2, New Living Translation). "What would you prefer?" the big boy asks the Corinthians (I, 4:21): "Am I to come to you with a stick, or with love in a spirit of gentleness?"

Both beaten boys, Luther and Paul, were energetic persons, dedicated to their aims and claims. Elias Canetti's following observation points to their childhood source of energy:

"The recipients of orders given the rawest deal are children. It appears miraculous that they do not break down under the charge of orders, that they survive the actions of their educators. That they, no less cruel than them, will pass all this to their own children is as natural as biting and speaking. But what, time and again, will come as surprise is the completeness in which orders from earliest childhood have been preserved. They are on the scene as soon as the next generation sends ahead their victims ... Any child, even the most common one, neither loses nor excuses any order that was part of his maltreatment ... The reconstruction of those early situations, but in reversion, is one of the great sources of psychic energy in the life of man. The 'goad', as we say, to achieve this or that is the deepest urge to get rid of orders one received at one time."

Canetti stresses that only an order which was actually carried out will leave its goad in the one who followed it. "The 'free' person is but the one who achieved to sidestep orders ..."[278] And exactly here German culture had a deficit I will illustrate in two major guides of German education.

Johann Gottlieb **Fichte** (1762-1814) probably had been the obliging cause for his parents' dutiful marriage; seven brothers and sisters followed. Working as a cattle herding boy, he impressed his landlord repeating by heart the pastor's whole Sunday sermon; as a philosopher, he interpreted the concept of duty (highly important for Germans) according to John's gospel.[279] Fichte

---

cruel childrearing" which "helped to forge the culture of obedient German citizens unwilling or unable to question the Nazi regime."

277 Mallet, p.37 and 216.
278 Canetti, p.339.
279 Hirschberger, p.153.

asserted that only the Germans' blood contains the blood of Christ which is refreshed by transsubstantiation in the Eucharist, wherefore it is the Germans' divinely ordained task to establish a spiritual world empire, against the usual plotter gang's resistance: "Through almost all countries of Europe spreads a mighty hostile state which is at war with all others steadily and in some of them presses heavily on the citizens: It is the *Judenthum*."[280]

In his *Speeches toward the German Nation* where he claims the German people's "divine mission", Fichte demands a "new education" which will have to consist "just in this: that on the soil whose reworking it undertakes, it entirely destroys the freedom of will."[281]

Fichte's proposal suggests that he had enjoyed a similar education as Luther. Since his mother "never showed unusual tenderness to me" as she "saw in her firstborn a child of shame and let him feel it", the "good, warm-hearted, upright father" was a counter-image to the boy – until one day a book, a present of his father, landed in the brook, and the book-thrower was "punished severely" by his father. The son had thrown the book away because it thrilled him too much and restrained him from learning – but this he could not explain to the father.[282]

Erikson's diagnosis of the German soldier applies to Fichte safely: "In him, unity by blind obedience was brought to proof, and disproved any aspirations toward democratic diversity."[283] Anticipating the merciless benevolence of totalitarian power addressed by Kafka and Orwell, Fichte's "free obedience consists therein that children, without means of coercion and without fear of them, do voluntarily what parents order and avoid voluntarily what parents forbid, just because they ordered or forbade it". In this political pedagogy Fichte explicitly refers to Luther: to the man whose unresolved conflicts of his childhood, as Jewish psychologist Erik Erikson saw it, came to surface in late adult age and brought him to the border of psychosis[284] – but who in Fichte's view was a paragon for subsequent generations, having won freedom for God's children.[285]

Luther's and Fichte's recipes for education peaked in famous Dr. Daniel Gottlieb Moritz **Schreber** (1808-1861), the physician, author and inventor of the *Schreberscher Geradhalter*, an upright holding orthopedic device for German children. Schrebers educational brochures stressed the necessity of taming the rebellious savage beast in the child to transform the young ones into productive citizens. Of his own five children whom he taught to revere their father like a God, the first son ended in suicide, the second and one daughter in psychosis. In the *Memoirs of My Nervous Illness* authored by his

---

280 Ley/Schoeps 1997, p.19; citing Fichte from his "Anleitung zum seligen Leben", Hamburg 1983, p.100, and from Dantine, Wilhelm: "Frühromantik – Romantik – Idealismus"; in: Rengstorf/ Kortzfleisch (ed.): Kirche und Synagoge, Vol.2, p.214-215.
281 Fichte, J.G.: Reden an die deutsche Nation, p.28.
282 Jacobs, p.8-9.
283 Erikson 1950/1999, p.345.
284 Erikson, Erik H.: Young Man Luther: A Study in Psychoanalysis and History. London 1959 (passim).
285 Schatzman, p.203-206.

younger son, court president Daniel Paul Schreber, Morton Schatzman finds eery traces of a German education. For example, what the son describes as the "miracle" of increasingly tight chest compression actually reenacts the upright holder experience, while the "freezing miracle" mirrors Moritz Schreber's advice to place the infant in a bath of ice cubes beginning at age 3 months. Schatzmann deems father Schreber a key figure in the mentioned "conspiracy of the German parents against their children" and attests him to have created "the basis for a system of child persecution, not child education". Elias Canetti paints Schreber even larger: "Some decades later ... his political system came to high honors and became, in a somewhat cruder and less sophisticated version, the credo of a great people."[286]

"All creating ones are hard"
... said Nietzsche.[287] How did he come to this opinion? Artistical creation he could not mean with this formula, or does any kind of armor ease composing, painting, poetry? In *Education After Auschwitz*, Theodor Wiesengrund Adorno recalls "that the terrible Boger during the Auschwitz Trial had an outburst culminating in a eulogy on education for discipline by hardness, necessary to produce the right type of man in his view. This leitmotiv of *Härte* in which many might believe without pondering on it is perverse to the core. The view that manliness consists in a maximum of endurance has long since become the cover picture of a masochism which – as psychology has showed – all too easily converges to sadism. The praised hardness to which education should lead means disregard for pain plainly, without precise distinction between one's own pain and that of other persons. One who is hard against himself acquires the right to be hard against others also and takes revenge for the pain he, since its expression was forbidden, had to repress."[288]
In the following six prominent cases the leitmotiv of hardness is not by chance connected with hard fathers, with education under crucified sons and harsh attitudes against the people of the Ancient in his beard.
"If I go home I get a beating by father but can not play. If I stay away I can play for an hour and the beating takes no longer than five minutes." The boy who made this cool calculation concerning his "*alten Herrn*", shortly afterwards became a choir singer and altar boy in the Benedictine monastery of Lambach, and on May 1, 1939 he prayed into the Volks-receiver microphones: "*Herr, wir lassen nicht von Dir. Nun segne unseren Kampf für unsere Freiheit ...*" (Lord, we do not cease from you! Now bless our struggle for our freedom.).[289] His secretary Christa Schroeder was trustworthy enough in **Adolf Hitler**'s eyes to trust her with another secret: "As to my father, I

286 Canetti 1994, p.502-503.
287 Nietzsche, Thus Spoke Zarathustra, chapter "The ugliest man".
288 Adorno 1971, p.96.
289 Hitler as boy: Schaake, p.21; Hitler as Führer, May 1, 1933: Heer 1989, p.263.

did not love him, but feared him all the more: He was swift to anger and coldcocked straightway. My poor mother then always was afraid for me."[290] Christa Schroeder was one of his ersatz mothers, and to her he confided many years later a key scene with world-historical sequels. "As a child, he told her, he had read in an adventure novel that it is a token of courage not to show one's pain. So 'I set out not to utter any sound at the next spanking. And when this happened – I still remember my mother standing anxiously outside at the door – I kept counting every spank that went down on my butt. The mother thought I had gone bonkers when I proudly told her: Thirty-two spanks the father has given me!'"[291] From that point on, the Führer told his secretary, the father had not touched him any more.

Father defeated? Sadly, no. In 1938, when the Führer of the German Reich stood skyscraping above the late Austrian Customs Oberoffizial Alois Hitler, the villagers of Döllersheim witnessed strange events. "That happened all so suddenly: In March was Hitler's march-in to Austria and in May the military vehicles already drove around, officers standing inside with general staff maps in their hands. We didn't know what's going on. What are they doing over here?"[292]

On order of Hitler, Döllersheim and surroundings were transformed into a military training area, his father's birthplace shot to pieces and crushed by Wehrmacht tanks. A prelude to the great production? "By all appearances", Friedrich Heer concludes, "the extinction of Döllersheim ensued directly on Hitler's order – out of insane hate against his father, who maybe had a Jewish father."[293]

Father buried? Was Adolf's sister Paula right when she recalled: "All attempts of his father to beat the pertness out of him and to make him choose the profession of a state official were futile"?[294] Quite the contrary, the father visited his son, now the fatherland's supreme state official, in Berlin Reichskanzlei! Adolf's confidant Rauschning marvelled about the Führer's nightmares: "Someone of his most intimate environment has told me that he wakes up at night with screaming fits. He cries for help. He sits on the edge of his bed, unable to move. Dread shakes him, the whole bed vibrates. He gasps as if he feared to suffocate. The man told me a scene which I could not believe if it wouldn't hail from this source. Teetering he had been standing in the room, darting around like mad. 'He! He! He's been here', he'd have wheezed. His lips were blue, sweat trickled down from him. Suddenly he'd start reciting numbers to himself. Completely meaningless ... Then he'd be standing all still again, moving his lips. They rubbed him, instilled something to drink. Then suddenly he bellowed: 'There, there! In the corner! Who's standing there?' He stamped his foot, he shouted as one

---

290 Schröder, Christa: Er war mein Chef. Munich 1985, p.63 (in Hamann, p.31).
291 Miller 1983, p.185, citing Toland; cf. Toland, p.12-13.
292 doellersheim.at/doellersheim/Das_Buch/warum_hier_/warum-hier-.HTM.
293 Heer 1967, p.384-385.
294 Stierlin, p.23.

is used with him. They showed him that there was nothing uncommon and then he gradually calmed down ..."[295]
After all, the reciting of numbers had stopped at spank number 32.
And who was the He standing in the dark corner? Big He was 23 years the senior of his wife Klara who called her husband "Uncle Alois" since he was her cousin of second degree. He was age 52 when Klara delivered her fourth child – the first one she would not have to bury early. She was the third wife of Alois Hitler, whose unwed grandmother Anna Schicklgruber had become pregnant at age 41. Who by? Nobody knows. By a Jew of Graz named Frankenberger? This rumour has one miller: Hans Frank. Hitler's juridical counselor who later became "one of the main architects of the extermination process in Poland"[296] had surveyed the subject, as is said, on Hitler's order yet in 1930. Is said who by? By Frank himself, in his book "In Face of the Gallow", written in 1946 before his execution and after his rueful return to Catholic faith.
Indeed there was a butcher's family Frankenreiter in Graz, but no Jews had been living there since 15th century because they were forbidden to settle in the whole Styria region until 1849. Anna Schicklgruber was not listed in any municipal register, neither in the servants' nor the citizens' book of Graz. And Frank himself stresses on page 331: "Adolf Hitler himself knew that his father did not descend from the Schicklgruber's sexual relationship with the Jew of Graz. He knew it from the narrations of his father and his grandmother." Indeed Anna Schicklgruber (1796-1847) had passed away age 51, just 42 years before the birth of his mindfully listening grandson Adolf.[297] Frank's survey seems to clarify but one thing: that the origin and person of the Schicklgruber's *Schandkind* were dark spots on Adolf's brown shirt.
Proudly the Döllersheimers had renamed their *Hauptplatz* (Main Place) in *"Alois-Hitler-Platz"* after the annexation of Austria. Now two years later when their homes were pancaked, they must assume that Hitler chose exactly this region as a military training place in order to blur his paternal lines of descent, or palimpsest the page with tank treads.
The fact that Hitler assures in *Mein Kampf* that from his father's mouth, in spite of his "staunchest national stance", he never had heard the word "Jew" raises Friedrich Heer's suspicion: Who is cloaking here "the Jew"?[298]
In Hitler's favourite Wagner opera it is Lohengrin, the "God-sent man" who warns Elsa: "Never shall you dare to ask me, whence to here has led my task me, nor ever query for my kin, about my name, my origin." The probable fact that Hitler, as well as 20 % of Ashkenazi Jews, genetically belonged to the north-african Y-DNA haplogroup E (more exactly, to Albert Einstein's and Napoleon's haplogroup E1b1b) is hardly a proof of Jewish descent, as some 9 % of Austrian and German populations belong to this haplogroup and just one in five of these persons (1.8 %) are associated with Jewish

295   Miller 1983, p.204-205, quoting Rauschning, Gespräche mit Hitler, Vienna 1973, p.273.
296   Hilberg 1982, p.144.
297   Holocaust-Referenz, h-ref.de; siehe auch Hamann, p.77.
298   Heer 1981, p.385-386.

ancestry. The fact that Hitler suffered from Parkinson disease doesn't add a 20:1 probability since while the genetic mutation responsible for this disease indeed is twenty times more frequent in Ashkenazi Jews, it also is ten times more common in North-African Arabs than in average Europeans.[299] While these facts by no means evince that Alois Hitler was paternally a *Halbjude* (half Jew), "the point of overriding psychological and historical importance is not whether it is true that Hitler had a Jewish grandfather; but that he believed that his father had Jewish blood. This father Alois Hitler was "saugrob" (literally sow-gruff) with his wife and "Frau Klara had nothing to smile about", as a neighbor attested still in the 1950s. Hitler had sketched her on deathbed, between the morphine injectures by Dr. Bloch. On Christmas Eve 1907 he stood at her grave for a long time after the sisters had left. "In my whole career I have never seen anyone so prostrate with grief as Adolf Hitler", Dr. Eduard Bloch remembered. "I shall be grateful to you forever", young Adolf assured the family's Jewish physician. Four months later, in April 1908, he joined an antisemitic society.[300]

35 years later, psychiatricist Walter Langer who had studied in Germany and witnessed the *Anschluss* in Vienna, was commissioned by American secret service with a long distance analysis of Hitler. In 1943 Walter Langer attested the Führer a Messias-complex which fully deployed after his nine months arrest in Landsberg Fortress (1924): "As time went on, it became clearer that he was thinking of himself as the Messiah and that it was he who was destined to lead Germany to glory. His references to the Bible became more frequent, and the movement began to take on a religious atmosphere. Comparisons between Christ and himself became more numerous and found their way into his conversation and speeches. For example, he would say: 'When I came to Berlin a few weeks ago and looked at the traffic in the Kurfuerstendamm, the luxury, the perversion, the iniquity, the wanton display and the Jewish materialism disgusted me so thoroughly, that I was almost beside myself. I nearly imagined myself to be Jesus Christ when he came to his Father's temple and found it taken by money-changers. I can well imagine how He felt when He seized a whip and scourged them out." Some years later, one of the large art shops on Berlin's Unter den Linden avenue had Hitler's portrait in the center of its display window, "entirely surrounded, as though by a halo, with various copies of a painting of Christ."

But Langer distinguishes precisely: "As a matter of fact, Hitler has very little admiration for Christ, the Crucified ... This kind of Christ he considers soft and week and unsuitable as a German Messiah. The latter must be hard and brutal if he is to save Germany and lead it to its destiny." The man who prided himself "on his hardness and brutality", who despised "the Jewish Christ-creed with its effeminate pity-ethics" and seemed to have a "violent dislike for going to bed or being alone" would not admire the weak defeated loner hanging on the beams at father's behest. On father's order? No. Just

299 wikipedia.org/wiki/Medical_genetics_of_Jews.
300 Langer, p.128, 256, 260, 264 and (R.G.L.Waite, afterword) p.265; as to Dr. Bloch, Hitler kept his promise insofar as he helped him to emigrate to New York in 1938.

as to Luther, also to Hitler the father above the cross is unimpeachable. To both beaten sons, their earthly fathers' spanks but reinforce the following cross-maths rule of three: Jesus (1) is innocent; the *big father* (2) must not be charged since he is the loving antagonist to the earthly spanker-father and the son wants to keep his conscience free of hate against his father. One subject remains for shifting guilt, and the bunch in the temple (3) doesn't merit the whip alone. This ascription of shifted guilt is the common denominator in the three themes Langer found in "almost all" of Hitler's speeches before coming to power: (a) the November traitors of 1918, (b) the Marxist rulers and (c) the world-dominating Jews. Are they Hitler's themes, or whose? His former "leftist" party companion Otto Strasser, whose brother Gregor was murdered in the Röhm cleansing, observed: "Hitler responds to the vibrations of the human heart with the delicacy of a seismograph ... enabling him, with a certainty with which no conscious gift could endow him, to act as a loudspeaker proclaiming the most secret desires, the least permissible instincts, the sufferings and personal revolts of a whole nation."[301]

The father is taboo, but safely Führer and nation can hate the *Volk* of big bad *Vater*: the people that fits perfectly into the void beneath the cross and whom they identify with the severe Old God of Old Testament. Shifting hate from *old Vater* to *old Volk*, Germans get alright again with German fathers. As for example young Adolf who was nearly beaten to death by Herr Zollamts-Oberoffizial Alois Hitler; who feared the father but liked to go shooting rats with the Flobert-gun his father had given him as a present; who rejected the proposal of his *"alter Herr"* to adopt the career of civil servant as too bourgeois a living, but more than fulfilled his Oberoffizial father's wish by becoming Germany's oberhighest civil servant and best paid public official.

Hitler's attempt to come to good terms with his *alten Herrn* by hating *das alte Volk*; his self-image as a Jesus-like "instrument of God" commissioned to achieve "by holocaust the healing, of Germany and the world"[302] resounds in a series series of revealing quotes, varitations of one theme.

In 1921, the recently discovered rhetoric talent gave a cheery speech to the small Rosenheim group of NSDAP: "Once a man in Galilee stood up, and his movement was small, but today it dominates the whole world."[303]

On July 29, 1921, in Munich Circus Krone arena the thirty-two-year-old Hitler-son uttered a winged word that later appeared on German calendars and served the SS as one weekly *Motto der Woche* in 1938: "By fending off the Jew, I fight for the work of the Lord."[304] Nine months later, on April 12, 1922, Hitler fervently professed: "I would not be a Christian but a real devil if I wouldn't feel compassion and ..., as once our Lord two thousand years ago, stand up against those who rob and plunder this poor people today. [...] My

301 Langer, p.38 (Kurfürstendamm), 62 (shop window), 33 (brutality), 38-39 (Messiah), 50 (Strasser) and 78 (going to bed alone).
302 Ley, p.168.
303 Ernst Piper in "Die Religion des Adolf Hitler", ORF (Austrian Radio and Television).
304 Heer 1989, p.193; use for calendars, posters, SS-motto: Michael, p.169. "Woche" means week.

feeling as a Christian leads me as a fighter to my Lord and Saviour. It guides me to the very man who once in his solitude, surrounded by few followers, recognized the Jews as what they were and called the men to struggle against them and who, God's truth! – was greatest not as man of sufferings but as a fighter. In boundless love, as a Christian and as a man, I read through the passage which tells us how the Lord at last rose in His might and seized the scourge to drive out of the Temple the brood of vipers and adders. Two thousand years later I bow down deeply in face of the unequalled struggle he fought against the world, against the Jewish poison, and I state that this was the reason why he had to die on the cross."[305]

Above: A young man of fascist Slovakian Hlinka Guard (which acted under a cross emblem) cutting a Jewish father's beard during a deportation at Stropkov, 1942.

Left: Advertising poster for the *Stürmer*'s special issue "*Judentum gegen Christentum*" in 1937. The text reads: "2000 years ago, Christ was nailed to the cross by the Jews on Golgotha. He died under their scornful laughter. This death on cross was the greatest ritual murder of all times. Why did it happen? Why do the Jews persecute Jesus with their hatred? Why do they scold him until today? Why do the Soviet Jews burn down churches? Why do they torture clerics to death? Why do they extirpate Christianity everywhere they can? The answer to these questions is given by the special Easter issue of the Stürmer, 'Judaism against Christendom. The Jewish battle of extermination against Christian Church.' In this special issue, the Stürmer proves that Christ led his struggle only against the Jews ..."

At Novemberputsch 1923, when Hitler's temple-cleansing founders in the pathetic March on Feldherrnhalle, the failed overturner tells the Landsberg

---

305 Rohman, p.75; cf. Langer, p.39; Charles Bracelen Flood: Hitler. The Path to Power. Boston 1989, p.261-262; Ley/Schoeps, p.71-72; Wistrich 1987, p.251-252, referring to Boepple (see bibliography).

prison psychologist: "This pack of *Volk* and smartasses! For them one ventures his life in holiest intention and then one is betrayed by them. Afterwards they always shout their crucifige, crucifige! They are not worth one's sacrifice."[306]

Shortly before Christmas Eve, in December 1926, Hitler declared himself – feigning or true – to be a great admirer of the Nazarene: "The birth of this man which is celebrated on Christmas is of highest importance for National Socialists. [...] Christ was the greatest fighter by nature who ever lived on earth. [...] The struggle against the power of the capital was his lifework and his teaching, for which he was nailed by his archfiend, the Jew, on the cross. The task Christ has begun but never brought to end, I will complete."[307]

And in 1938, advanced now in his mission thanks to massive sponsoring by capitalists like Siemens and media baron Hugenberg, by arms producers Krupp and Thyssen, Hitler now residing in the Reichskanzlei is even more outspoken: "In the gospels the Jews called out to Pilate, when he refused to crucify Jesus: 'His blood come upon us and our children's children!' Maybe it's me who has to execute this curse."[308] In 1940, George Orwell commented about Hitler's face: "It is a pathetic ... face of a man suffering under intolerable wrongs ... In a rather manly way it reproduces the expression of innumerable pictures of Christ crucified, and there is little doubt that that is how Hitler sees himself."[309]

In view of all this evidence, what's the point of Langer's diagnosis that "it was not only Hitler, the madman who created German madness, but German madness that created Hitler"? It tells much about the German readers of *Mein Kampf* that Hitler could disclose to them the following – obviously his own – experiences without compromising himself: "There is a boy, let us say, of three. This is the age at which a child becomes conscious of his first impressions. In many intelligent people, traces of these early memories are found even in old age. [...] When the parents fight almost daily, their brutality leaves nothing to the imagination ... Those who are not familiar with such conditions can hardly imagine the results, particularly if the differences show up in brutal attacks on the father's part toward the mother or assaults due to drunkenness. The poor little boy, at the age of six, senses things which would make even a grown-up person shudder. [...] When he finally comes home ... drunk and brutal ... then God have mercy on the scenes that follow. *I witnessed all this personally* in hundreds of scenes ..."[310]

What the Nazi Strasser called Hitler's ability to respond to "the sufferings and personal revolts of a whole nation ... with the delicacy of a seismograph", antiauthoritarian educator A.S.Neill perceived in other pointer deflections: "I saw how in 1935 a hundred thousand obedient, fawning dogs

306 Maser, p.18-19; cf. Gritschneder, p.35.
307 Wistrich 1987, p.252.
308 Heer 1981, p.387; Bailey, p.179.
309 Swaim 2013, p.207.
310 Langer, p.154 (madman); 159-161 (three quotings from Mein Kampf, Langer giving but p.38); italics: K.Y.R.

on Tempelhofer Feld in Berlin wagged their tails when big trainer Hitler shouted his commands."[311]
Exactly this willing submission Langer traces back to a general "structure of the German family" which, albeit "not nearly as marked" as in Hitler's case,[312] was centered in a fearsome father role palpable in the gloomy motherly warning "Just wait till Dad comes home!" that was proverbial up to the 1990s. In a virtuoso manner, Hitler took up the common obsession of all those beaten sons, and healed them in his own way: channelling their repressed and fearful father feelings towards the bearded Jews who had crucified this paragon of innocent overpowered sons. The target was convenient in Europe's "most churchgoing nation" 95 percent of which payed church-tax in 1940 while further 3.5 percent auto-defined as *gottgläubig* (God believing), confessing the religious minimum Himmler required of every member of SS.[313]
Fear of father coming home: If Saint Paul and insane Adolf join in anything, it is just this childhood fear. Concerning Paul, theologist Johannes Lehmann concludes: "In his search for a 'merciful God' he discards the Law and his own pharisaic past, and one almost could assume that everything he writes and does serves but for overcoming his past ... [and] that he used the case of Rabbi J. but for resolving the case of Paul."[314] Concerning Adolf, Langer concludes: "Unconsciously, he is not dealing with nations composed of millions of individuals but is trying to solve his personal conflict and rectify the injustices of his childhood."[315]
This holds true equally for a boy born in Baden-Baden in 1900 who was known for his strong justice imperative: "If I was wronged by some injustice I did not cease until this – in my view – was expiated. In this I was relentless and feared by my classmates."[316] His favorite place was the Black Forest farm of his grandparents: "Here I acquired my love of agriculture, nature, animals. I passed for a placid, sensitive boy ..."[317] And future farmer? No, since God, or a pious, twice wounded veteran of German colonial army, had other plans. "My father educated me according to rigidly military principles." A future soldier? No, since "as often as his time-schedule allowed to, he travelled with me to the places of pilgrim and mercy in our home region, as well as to Einsiedeln [the Swiss "Black Mary" pilgrim place] and to Lourdes in France. Fervently he implored heaven to give me his blessing, so I would once become a God-gifted priest" – a priest like those bearded Africa-missionaries who on father's invitation so often visited his home and whom the son admired so devoutly. When after the father's death his guardian tried to coerce him to study theology, the son waived the inheritance,

---

311 Neill, p.110.
312 Langer, p.166.
313 Runes, p.79 ("most churchgoing nation of Europe"); percentages: Wilensky, p.143-144.
314 Lehmann, p.108-109.
315 Langer, p.173.
316 Broszat, p.26.
317 Gilbert, M.: The Psychology of Dictatorship. Based on an examination of the leaders of Nazi Germany. New York 1950, p.242 (cf. Deselaers, p.40).

joined the army, acted in Palestine age 17 and next WW became the Lager commander of Auschwitz who ordered to throw living children in the fire during a lack of petrol; who in the garden of his family home just outside of the barbed wire raised vegetables and splashed with his four children on hot summer days.[318] These CV details are mentioned by a Catholic priest in his theological dissertation: Manfred Deselears, PhD, who caretakes a memorial site in Auschwitz, finds in the behavior of **Rudolf Höß**'s father the main cause of the son's end as a schizoid, authoritarian mass murderer. This father's religious attitude, says Deselaers, is "atheist, godless, because loveless", since he assigned his son to lifelong celibate.

And not to death on cross, for mankind's redemption.

"Mein alter Herr himself had Jewish friends ... By this I just want to say that by my upbringing I was free of any Jew hate since the whole education by my mother and my father was rigidly Christian."[319] Born in Westphalian Solingen and grown up in Austrian Linz as son of an "extremely orthodox" Protestant family who yet in childhood had him registered for YMCA, this man noted in 1961 for a British journal: "I remembered in deep gratitude the assistance by Catholic priests during my escape from Europe and decided to honor Catholic faith by becoming a honorary member."[320] His sons were born in 1936, 1940, 1942, and the youngest one in 1955 in Argentine where their father, who in his self-image was an "idealist", confessed to German friends in 1957: "I have to tell you very honestly, if of the 10.3 million Jews which Korherr as we now know has calculated, we would have killed 10.3 million, I would be satisfied and would say well, we have destroyed an enemy."[321] For from 1942 to 1945 this father of three sons, according to his subordinate Rudolf Höß, "with downright obsession espoused the total annihilation of all attainable Jews"[322] Why the "special treatment" of Jews was an ideal to him and why, in Hannah Arendt's words, "his conscience brought him to this relentless stance", he revealed in little verbal sparks. "It was probably the truth when he said ... that he only did his duty. He said he also wouldn't have hesitated to send his father to the gas chamber if he had been required to."[323] In January 1941, when the Wannsee Conference decided the "final solution" – he proudly claims to have coined this term – **Adolf Eichmann** felt alleviated: "In this moment I felt a kind of Pilate-like satisfaction; for I felt pure of any guilt."[324] His fourth son Ricardo Eichmann, professor of middle-eastern archeology, is today the Director of the section Orient at German Archeological Institute in Berlin, and a pacifist.

---

318 Deselaers, p.177.
319 Arendt, p.58.
320 Klee 1991, p.25.
321 Stangneth, Bettina: Eichmann vor Jerusalem. Das unbehelligte Leben eines Massenmörders, Zurich 2011, chapter "Nachspiel" (The Korherr-Report consisted in statistics Himmler in 1943 had charged the statistician Richard Korherr with); cited from Einsicht 05, spring 2011, fritz-bauer-institut.de.
322 Höß quote: Broszat, p.128-129.
323 Askenasy, p.24-25.
324 Stangneth, p.31 (concerning the term final solution); Heer 1967, p.472.

"We know well, that we expect of you something 'superhuman'; we require you to be 'superhumanly inhuman'." The author of this quote grew up in Munich as the son of a grammar school director whom his pupil, the Munich lawyer and author (see bibliography) Otto Gritschneder remembers as "Rex the just", whereas Gritschneder's classmate Alfred Andersch portrays this educator from a different viewpoint, asking in his story *Der Vater eines Mörders* if it wasn't just inevitable that "such a father would produce such a son?" No, Gritschneder says, stressing that it was this father's wife who exacted their three sons' "active participation in church life [and] attached so much importance to establishing their Catholic faith that their father felt he must warn her against taking such things too far". The three sons were "subject to a system of rules and prohibitions, while their father monitored their obedience precisely and at times pedantically". In 1914, the school-report of the middle son who "in religious education ... was always graded *sehr gut* extols: "An apparently very able student who by tireless hard work, burning ambition and very lifely (*sehr lebhafte*) participation achieved the best results in the class. His conduct was exemplary."[325] Twenty-five years later, this model student, now "Reichsführer SS", wrote in his diary: "I will always love God and pray to him and belong to the Catholic Church and defend it, even if I should be excluded from it".[326] He almost fainted at a shooting when a piece of brain hit his black lapel[327] but advised his elite guards in their skull-decorated black uniforms to draw encouragement for their difficult, historically necessary duty from the awareness that they "serve a task occurring only once in 2000 years".[328] Why exactly 2000, someone could have asked this soft-faced man **Heinrich Himmler**?

"In the evening we watched the film 'Rebell' produced by Luis Trenker. A top performance of cinematic art! This way one can imagine the movie of the future, revolutionary with very big mass scenes, thrown onto the screen with a tremendous vital energy. In one scene, in which a giant crucifix is carried by the rebels out of a chapel, the audience is moved in the deepest way ... A nationalist outset. Very big mass scenes ... Hitler is fire and fat."[329] In 1942 the same former art reviewer confided to his diary: "From the *Generalgouvernement* the Jews are now, beginning at Lublin, getting deported to the East. Here a rather barbaric and not specifiable treatment is applied and of the Jews themselves not much remains ... On the Jews a tribunal is performed that indeed is barbarous but which they fully deserve", as the diarist knew from childhood on.[330] For he had been raised in Cologne by a Holland-born mother and an earnest, deeply religious father, whose severe manners were fortunately tempered by his Rhenanian humour, but who very seriously wished to see his son once in the priestly robe. During

325 Longerich, p.11-19.
326 Longerich, p.34. According to Wilensky (p.236), Himmler's godfather had been the Bishop of Bamberg.
327 Peuschel, p.134.
328 Arendt, p.139.
329 Joseph Goebbels, diary entry, Jan. 19, 1933; critic.de/film/bergblut-2486/ - Im Cache.
330 Joseph Goebbels, diary entry, March 27, 1942, quoted by Fraenkel/Manvell, p.274.

six semesters their highly intelligent, slightly physically handicapped son received a scholarship by the fostering *Albertus-Magnus-Verein* to which Chaplain Dr. Mollen had provided, "due to his religious and moral behaviour, the best recommendation". Freshly graduated, the young PhD wrote a Christ drama titled "Der Wanderer", which unfortunately was never staged or published. But as Minister of Propaganda, **Dr. Joseph Goebbels** had lots of opportunities to display his dramatic gift in service of the man with whom he shared an early constellation: "Hitler has gone through almost the same youth as I did", Goebbels wrote. "The father a home tyrant, the mother a source of love and goodness."[331]

Paternal terror

The five boys had more in common than their career-end in 1945. "Among all leading figures of the Third Reich I have not found a single one who would not have been educated hardly and severely", Alice Miller resumes. And they all had become hardworking members of society, just as, by the way, all the pupils of that German teacher who, due to his diligent book-keeping, could balance in 1934 that during his professional life he had educated his pupils with 911,527 cane strokes, 124,000 whiplashes and 1,115,800 bitchslaps. "Do you think that the Nazi Lagers would have been possible, if psychic terror in the sense of beatings with sticks, carpet beaters, cane sticks and strap whips would not have been the rule in German child rooms?" This is what a 37-year-old post-war mother wrote to Alice Miller, confessing that she still did not succeed in "ousting the aggressively punishing father from my inner structure or rather to humanize him". Anyhow, she can finish her letter with the statement that she grew up "in well-ordered conditions: My father is a parson."[332]

This "ousting the aggressively punishing father" failed differently in the case of US soldiers who committed war crimes in Vietnam. David Mark Mantell's study points to the fact that under their armor of emotional endurance, these elite warriors hid a deep hate against their parents and particularly their fathers; an overproportional number of them came from pithily Catholic homes.[333]

But "Catholic" is not the point. In his 1950 work "Childhood and Society" Erik Erikson finds in Hitler and the typical Germans a "peculiar mixture of idealistic rebellion and obedient submission" towards fathers, with the idealized image of a "pure mother ... who would not betray her son to the monster, the father [...] The German is hard with himself and others" and in-clined to "blind conviction, cruel self-denial and extreme perfectionism."[334]

In 1970, Vienna-born American psychoanalyst Leopold Bellak performed observations on playgrounds in Copenhagen, Frankfurt and Milan. While

---

331 Fröhlich, Elke: Die Tagebücher von Joseph Goebbels. Teil I. Munich 1993-1995, Vol.2, p.681 (quoted by Hamann, p.22).
332 Miller 1983, p.84 (leading figures ...); rest of paragraph: p.269-270.
333 Mantell, D.M.: Familie und Aggression. Frankfurt on Main 1978.
334 Erikson, quoted from the German edition, p.328-329.

Danish and Italian parents committed no aggressive acts against their children, the observers counted 73 by German parents. German children committed 258 aggressive acts against other children, as opposed to 48 by Italian and 20 by Danish children. "One is inclined", Bellak resumed, "to formulate as the story's morale, that Germans maltreat their children more often than Danish or Italian adults, and that the children vent that on others." Bellak titled his research "Why I fear the Germans".[335]

No doubt, the fearsome Germans feared their fathers. But where's the link to the fearsome superfather figure of Jewish Bible critizised by Gudrun the German Catholic and Richard the British atheist?

Is the crucifix a learning model for discipline-enhancing hardness toward oneself and others, for discipline by fear of crucifying fathers?

Albert Einstein opined that in the Jewish Bible one could neatly observe "the progress from fear-religion to moral religion, which found its continuation in the New Testament."[336] A contrarious view is given by Jacob Dolinger, the Brazilian scholar of international law: "In order to emphasize the importance of Christ, the divine son, the God of Old Testament, who at the same time is the Father of divine Trinity, was construed as a 'severe' God, thus easing the task of inculcating to pagan minds the idea of an entirely good Jesus the Son. Unfortunately, I would say that the shot backfired, because the result of this epistemological operation was that Christians came to have a strong fear of the figure of God the Father – something totally alien to Jews. The Jews fear God, obviously, but never with such a *sentimento de terror* of a persecuting figure ..."[337]

But Dolinger leaves in darkness where this fear of God the Father comes from. A Spanish converso named Santacruz spoke out clearer when at a Castilian passion play in 1494 he muttered much too loudly: "He was the son of God? What Father would put his son through this?"[338] And it was Brazilian Marrano descendant Chico Buarque[339] who during Brazilian military dictatorship (1964-1985) was inspired by Paul's image of the paternal prosecutor to compose, together with Gilberto Gil, a song which identified the strong men of military junta and the "*realidade morta*" of their torture terror system precisely with the silent God of the pleading Jesus. Most every Brazilian then knew their subversive song "Calice", and everyone who heard it grasped its critical meaning, untouchably codified by and within the key story of Brazil's Christian tradition and the assonance of "calice" (chalice) with "Cale-se!"(Shut up!).

Pai, afasta de mim esse calice	*Father, remove from me this chalice*
Pai, afasta de mim esse calice	*Father, remove from me this chalice*
Pai, afasta de mim esse calice	*Father, remove from me this chalice*

---

335 Moor, p.385-386.
336 Einstein, Mein Weltbild, p.19.
337 Jacob Dolinger: O Patriarca Jacob e a Identidade Judaica. In: Fuks, p.38.
338 Gitlitz, p.140-141.
339 Dória, Francisco Antonio: Os Herdeiros do Poder, Rio de Janeiro 1995 (according to Paulo Valadares, in judaismohumanista.ning.com, July 27, 2013).

De vinho tinto de sangue. [...]	*filled with wine, redded by blood.*
Como beber dessa bebida amarga	*How to drink of this bitter potation,*
Tragar a dor, engolir a labuta	*take up the pain, swallow the grind?*
Mesmo calada a boca resta o peito	*Mouth is shut but breast remains.*
Silencio na cidade não se escuta	*No silence is heard in this city.*
De que me serve ser filho da santa?	*Of what avail is being the santa's son?*
Melhor seria ser filho da outra	*Better be a son of the other*
realidade menos morta	*reality, the lesser dead one.*
Tanta mentira, tanta força bruta. [...]	*So big lies, so much brutal force.*
Como é difícil, pai, abrir a boca	*Father, it's so difficult to open the mouth*
Essa palavra presa na garganta.	*with this word caught in the throat*
Esse pileque homérico no mundo [...]	*this Homeric tipsyness on earth.*
Quero perder de vez sua cabeza	*I want to lose your head just one time*
Minha cabeza perder teu juízo	*and my head get rid of your judgment.*
Quero cheirar fumaça de ólio Diesel	*Want to smell the fume of Diesel*
Me embriagar até alguém me esqueça.	*and to enebriate until someone forgets me.*
Cale-se!	*Shut up!*

Does the Homeric tipsyness allude to how Hellenic Paul transforms Jesus into a sacrificed Greek godson and his blood into wine? And the Diesel fume to Austrian Gustav Wagner who suicided in São Paulo in 1980, having killed in Sobibor 250.000 persons using the fume of a captured Russian tank? The comparison between spared Isaac and sacrificed Jesus is a textbook case about the redaction of holy texts, about retouching God's image according to human progress and regress. In Genesis 18, four chapters before Isaac's sacrifice, Abraham rebukes a Yahve who plans to destroy Sodom: "Far be from you such a thing, to kill the righteous with the wicked ... Far be it from you! Should not the judge of all the earth do what is right?" And Yahve replies: "If I find fifty righteous people in Sodom, I will spare all ..." While this text of human chutzpah towards God obviously was written by the "Yahwist" author, the beginning of God's inhuman test ran from the pen of the scribe who by his usual term of God is called the "Elohist": "They arrived at the place of which Elohim had told him. Abraham built an altar there; he layed out the wood; he bound his son Isaac; he laid him on top of the altar, on top of the wood. And Abraham picked up the knife to slay his son." And now who holds back his hand? Not so much God as rather the mentioned Yahwist who simply can't stand the behavior of the "judge of all the earth" and amends it thus: "And an angel of Yahve called to him from heaven: 'Abraham! Abraham!' And he answered, 'Here I am'. And he said, 'Do not raise your hand against the boy, or do anything to him.'"
Sceptically Richard E. Friedman mentions the interpretation "that in the original version of this narration Isaac was sacrificed actually, and that the intervening four verses have been inserted later, at a time when the idea of human sacrifices was rejected (inserted maybe by the scribe who assembled the Yahwist and Elohist sources).[340] But indeed, as soon as the E-scribe is allowed to go on amid of verse 22:16, Elohim praises Abraham "because you

---

340   Friedman, R.E., p.345.

have done this and not withheld your son". And soon after, the E-version ends when "Abraham returned to his servants, and they departed together for Beer-Sheba" – obviously without Isaac.

And Sarah, who had named her son *itzchak*, meaning *he will laugh*? The Elohist mentions neither Isaac nor Sarah anymore but has Abraham marry ersatz woman Keturah who gives her God-fearing husband six ersatz children (25:1-6). Also the Yahwist mentions Sarah nevermore. The priestly P-author (Genesis 23) has Sarah die five verses after Abraham's return and get buried in Hebron. Epitaph by humanistic rabbi Edward Klein: "Sarah leaves Abraham, never to rejoin him or speak another word to him until her death, which may well have been caused by what happened to Isaac."[341]

What impact God's test had on the two male test persons Kierkegaard describes in four versions. In the first one Abraham, while Isaac's eyes still bewilderedly gaze at the knife, whispers to himself: "Lord in heaven, I thank you; better he deems me a monster than he'd lose his faith in You." The second: "From this day on Abraham became old, he could not forget that God had required that from him. Isaac thrived as before, but Abraham's eye was darkened, he did not see the joy anymore." In the third version, Abraham, prostrating on his face, "begged God to forgive him the sin of having wanted to sacrifice Isaac, that the father had forgotten the duty towards his son". And the fourth ends this way: "Isaac saw that Abraham's left hand cramped in desperation, that a tremor ran through his limbs, – but Abraham brandished the knife. They returned home and Sarah hastened to meet them, but Isaac had lost his faith."[342]

But even Elohim is not mere obedience but also audience, able to hear. "Elohim heard the cry of the boy" (Gen 21:17), namely the son of Haggar the maid, expulsed to the desert by the boy's father Abraham on request of jealous Sarah. Elohim saves Ishmael. And requires Isaac's killing. And Yahve, or better the Yahwist, saves Isaac by the new conclusion of a story that is marked by Abraham's threefold *Hineni* – "Here I am" answer to his son, and by two stages of a God who slowly learns how He will be:

Elohim: "Abraham!" – *"Here I am."* – "Take your son and sacrifice him!"
Isaac: "Abi!" – *"Here I am, my son."* – "Where is the sheep for sacrifice?"
Yahve: "Abraham!" – *"Here I am"* – "Do not sacrifice him!"

Thrice the father listens in obedience: to cruel tradition, to his son, and to a God who slowly learns how He should and would like to be but who five centuries later, in Paul's doctrine of human sacrifice, in the garden scenes of the Synoptics regresses to his Moloch phase. To the thrice entreaty of his son "Father, remove this cup from me" this father replies in thrice a silent Sacrifice!!! that resounds from Golgotha to the stakes and gas chambers.

---

341 Edward J.Klein, "My Jewish Odyssey", in: Humanistic Judaism, No.1, 2105, Farmington Hills, Michigan, p.40-41. Klein differs from R.E.Friedman (p.330, 331, 345) in ascribing Gen 22:11-16a not to P, but to the Yahvist J-source.
342 Kierkegaard 1982, p.244-247.

In a "prayer" that according to Gunda Schneider-Flume is "revisited again and again" in Germany, therapist Tilmann Moser reminds God of his lenient attitude towards Isaac: "Next, towards your own son you've been more unbothered and gave free rein to your sadism. They tried to cheat me into believing that with the sacrifice on cross you wanted to ring in the covenant of love [...] How bad must I be that an enactment like this is necessary to redeem me? Strangely, none of the preachers ever smelled a rat that maybe there's something wrong not with us but with you if by your love for mankind you had to have your boy child slaughtered."[343]

Just as to Luther and Hitler, also to French theologian Dom Guéranger (1805-1875) the father is sacrosanct. The sacrifice is done by others. "They lay the heavy cross on his shoulders ... The place, where the new Isaac is burdened with the cross for his own sacrifice, is the second station ... The Jews must be afraid that their victim dies before arriving at the place of execution."[344] The Jews? No, the Christians must fear that. Suppose Jesus had died yet on the way: No cross, no salvation, no crucifix – where would we have come to? What would Michelangelo have painted in Sixtine Chapel, instead of the Salvator Mundi who with a resolute gesture of his pierced hand sweeps the condemned half of mankind into millions of years of torture?

"The Church established, in one of her hardest tenets, eternity of hellish punishment. Exactly the new God of Love", Ernst Bloch remarks, "harbored in this place a much deeper pool of cruelty ..."[345] None of the alleged words of Jesus concerning the Christian hell complex is authentical, including the passage of Matthew 25:41 that underlies Michelangelo's gargantuan panorama and faintly reminds selection in Auschwitz: "Then he will say to those at his left hand, 'You that are accursed, depart from me into the fire ...'"

The Third Man

As in Michelangelo's, also in the Last Judgements of Hans Memling and other painters of his epoch the condemned ones hold balance with the redeemed ones. Fifty percent: this lamentable coefficient of Jesus' redeeming self-sacrifice renews the question why the almighty needed his son's sacrifice. Paul's explanation that the father had to sacrifice him in order to reconcile his own offended majesty with the offspring of disobedient Eve is like a comic that shows the Almighty explaining to his victim via speech bubble: "Sorry, you know how much I hate those things but alas, He insists on it."

On a philosophical level, Ernst Bloch wonders: "Evidently, thereby the lamb, as gentle as it was, most ungently was slaughtered here. As if there were above it, imagined and real, still but a terrible juggernaut who only by bloody baptism may be appeased ... This backfall into most barbarous times

343 Gunda Schneider-Flume in Zimmermann/Annen, p.163.
344 Isaac, p.430.
345 Bloch 1985, p.1330.

and means is startling, but more astounding is the regression from hallowing the name to such a barbaric god-image."[346] If God "did not withhold his own son, but gave him up for all of us" (Romans 8:32), why did he have to, to begin with? If he disliked what he had to do – as one should suppose – what coerced him to sacrifice his son? Who extorted the Highest? Who stood behind him, pressed the gun in the Almighty's back?

When in a radio broadcast I put this question to Catholic theologian Dr. Langhans, he replied that God probably "had reasons to organize things" this way. Langhans defended the same God as did Dean Heinrich Grüber and Rabbi Ignaz Maybaum. Dr. Grüber was asked by Richard Rubenstein: "Was it God's will that Hitler destroyed the Jews?" And this clergyman answered: "For some reason, it was part of God's plan that the Jews died." In Rabbi Maybaum's view, the Shoah was but a "small anger" of God; in Auschwitz the Jews suffered for the sins of mankind, and the Jewish people is "mankind at it's goal. We have arrived. We are the first fruits of God's harvest."[347] While the Rabbi lost two sisters in KZ Auschwitz, the Dean had paid, during interrogation in KZ Dachau, with all his teeth for his audacity of publicly confronting antisemitism.

Both don't see their blasphemy, their backslide to the moloch old Abraham had abolished. Their "Judge of all the earth" did not bother about killing the innocent with the guilty ones. Their all-knowing almighty One makes plans whose stupidity imply the lamentable side-effect of fifteen-hundred-thousand innocent children murdered. Their God used Hitler as His helper and gas for gathering His harvest. Some people prefer blasphemic reverence whenever they hear atheism knocking on the door.

Listening to Grüber's approval of God's plans, Rubenstein recalled Erich Fromm's description of the authoritarian personality in *Escape From Freedom*. "All the clergymen", Fromm summarized, "had asserted the absolute character of God's Lordship over mankind and of mankind's obligation to submit unquestioningly to that Lordship". In Dean Grüber's view, the unquestionable fatherly ruler smashingly punished even his instruments of punishment: "I know that God is punishing us because we have been the whip against Israel. In 1938 we smashed the synagogues; in 1945 our churches were smashed by the bombs."[348]

As to the profile of this punishman in background, Canetti's already cited view sheds no dim light on him: "Any child, even the most common one, neither loses nor excuses any order that was part of his maltreatment ... The reconstruction of those early situations, but in reversion, is one of the great sources of psychic energy in the life of man. The 'goad', as we say, to achieve this or that is the deepest urge to get rid of orders one received at one time."

346 Bloch 1973, p.184-186.
347 Maybaum, p.35-36 and 67-68 (cf. Cohn-Sherbok, p.231-232).
348 Rubenstein, Richard L., p.53-55.

Here we have the triple structure in the sequence of three generations, the passing on of orders and maltreatments: execution on order of, on order of, on order ...

"It is important to know that never any order will get lost; never is the issue over with its execution; it is stored forever." [349]

Paul had no children to whom he could pass on the suppressive orders of his childhood. Instead, he channelled them into a "homoerotic relationship to his Christ"[350] and the personal myth of sacrificing one's body in order to win big father's favour. Since this myth touches upon very common emotions of our childhood – emotions working in Canetti's reconstruction of early maltreatment, in Sándor Ferenczi's introjection of, in Anna Freud's identification with the adult aggressor – it found wide acceptance and concretization in the most awful and violent symbol mankind ever created.

Search for the Third Man: Hieronymus Wierix (1554-1619), a flamish painter quite obsessed with crucifixion, has God the Good Father, in a triangle with Mother Mary, having to squeeze their good son in the salvific wine press.

349 Canetti 1994, p.338-339.
350 Heer 1990, p.66-67.

VIII Roles of Character
Nine jobs, one center

> *"Only the terrible accusation, known and taught to every Christian in earliest childhood, that the Jews are the killers of the Christ can account for the depth and persistence of this supreme hatred."*   Richard L. Rubenstein[351]

In January 2011, the Palestinian, Freiburg resident psychoanalyst Gehad Mazarweh was asked by Edith Kresta of leftist Berlin Tageszeitung: "As a Muslim you identify with Freud who was a Jew?"
"Actually, yes. I am sure my fascination for Freud has to do with what I experienced in Europe ... and I see his doctrine also as a part of the exclusion he experienced himself. His belonging to a minority to which one imputes everything bad. On which one dumps the proper ugliness."[352]
Europe's dumping worked quite well, loading the chosen players with seven villain roles which are as strongly linked to Jesus' ordeal as the "Seven Sorrows of Mary". To name these roles is the first aim of this chapter. The second: Demonstrating how these seven roles are connected to three nails and four wooden ends I attempt to clarify that not the alleged "social envy" reasons are what led allegedly "exploited" Europeans to persecute and liquidate the Jews, but rather the Christian children's ressentiments stemming from the cross-shaped beams in their eyes and brains. "The central charge", Nicholls repeats, "is the killing of Christ, all else follows from this."[353]

Betrayers
Sitting next to a Jew in a wagon compartment of Austrian railway, an officer of Austrian imperial army uses the opportunity to educate his aptly named fox terrier with commands like "Sit, Moses! – Beg, Moses! – Fine, Moses, good dog!" At last the Jew can't help commenting: "A fine dog!" – "I say." – "And so well trained!" – "No doubt." – "Pity his name is Moses." – "Pity, why?" – "Otherwise, he could have become an officer."
As to the French officer Capitain Dreyfus, the national Catholic author Maurice Barrés (1862-1923) expressed the common viewpoint this way: "That Dreyfus is capable of treason I deduce from his race."[354] Not by accident untrustworthy Judas stands for the people of Moses with its enduring non-access to trust-requiring professions in Europe: "In the Bible, the whole is often named after the part: As Judas was called a devil and the devil's workman, he gives his name to the whole race."[355] This *pars pro toto* rule was given out by Pope Gelasius I (492-496). In 1969, the question "Was Judas

---

351 Rubenstein, Richard L.: After Auschwitz, p.20.
352 Tageszeitung (taz), Berlin, January 22/23, 2011, p.16.
353 Nicholls, p.211 and more extensive on p.220.
354 Poliakov 2003, Vol.IV, p.51.
355 Maccoby 1992, p.6.

Jewish?" was answered with "Yes" by 44 percent of Protestant and 47 percent of Catholic Californians. "Were the other apostles also Jewish?" Yes: 13 percent of the Protestants, 16 percent of Catholics.

Two years earlier, in Germany 56 percent had agreed to the statement "God exists", and 91 percent to "Judas betrayed Jesus to his enemies", urging pollster Werner Harenberg to comment: "Those who hardly believe anything anymore, still believe that Judas betrayed Jesus to his enemies."[356]

So what? This prejudice does not hurt anybody, since no mother would name her son Judas today, okay? Anyhow, this Jewed-ass, this evil incarnate, who "traditionally personified the Jewish people"[357] and "was transformed into the symbol of the Jew"[358] most probably (see chapter V) was no one else than Mary's fourth son, the stepbrother of Jesus and brother of James and Simon. Confirming his opinion by quoting six Christian and Jewish scholars who wrote already between 1909 and 1921, Maccoby supposes "that the name 'Judas' was deliberately chosen in preference to the name of any other Apostle for a diabolic role, as part of the anti-Semitic campaign within the Pauline Church, which had cast the Jews as people of the devil and enemies of the incarnate God".[359]

So who made Jesus' brother his betrayer?

As to the tensions between Jesus and his brothers (**Mk 3:21**: "He has lost His senses"; **Mk 6:4**: "A prophet is honored everywhere except ..."; **Lk 14:26**: "Whoever does not hate his brothers and his sisters cannot be my disciple"), Tabor, Akers and Maccoby suggest that these passages might document attempts of the Pauline entourage to denigrate the opponent party of the "Brothers of the Lord" (*desposynoi*) as people who never understood their brother but had quarrelled with him; as people who were close to him as to their roots but distant in ideas. Thus Judas suited twice – first as a member of this denigrated group of Jesus' this-worldly oriented relatives and second by his name – for a downward career from disciple and misunderstander to betrayer and agent of the negative power in cosmos.[360]

On grounds of this disputed reputation of the "Brothers of the Lord" and after the Jewish catastrophe of 70 CE, the Roman author Mark probably plucked the whole story of conspiracy, betrayal, kiss and process out of the Roman capital's air, choosing the name of Judas who fit so well to the Greek word *Ioudaios* as it would to German *Juden*. The thirty silver coins, however, were Matthew's creative contribution, borrowed from Zechariah's verses (11:12-13) "So they weighed out my wages, thirty shekels of silver ... and I took the thirty shekels and deposited it in the treasury of the Temple" – a verse that also inspired Matthew to give this man who "better ... had not been born" a scenic exit: "Throwing down the pieces of silver in the temple,

356 US poll: Charles Y. Glock and Rodney Stark: Christian Beliefs and Antisemitism. New York 1969, p.49 (in Maccoby 1992, p.126); German poll: Harenberg, W.: Was glauben die Deutschen? Munich 1968, p.89 (in Fricke, p.165).
357 Friedman, Saul S., p.173.
358 Sorj, p.60.
359 Maccoby 1992, p.29.
360 Maccoby 1992, p.149-150 and passim; Akers, p.179; Tabor, p.103 (only ref. to Luke).

he departed; and he went and hanged himself" (26:24-27:5). Luke doesn't add much more than Jesus's question to his perfidious brother: "Judas, with a kiss do you betray the Son of Man?" Judas the greedy villain and money grabber incarnate is revealed in the last gospel. Where Mark (14:4-5) had reported of "some" disciples discussing about the woman's costly ointment of nard, which "could have been sold for 300 denarii", meaning good money that could be given to the poor instead of poured on Jesus hair, John (12:6), puts this "materialist" critique exactly in Judas' mouth and explains: "He said this not because he was concerned about the poor, but because he was a thief, and as he had the money box, he used to pilfer what was put into it." Even John's last mention (13:29) of Judas is about money: "Buy what we need for the feast", Jesus commissions him, and "Judas left at once, going out into the night."

But morning comes. "On Easter Saturday, Catholic Youth hauled heavy logs to the morning service, piled them up in the church yard and lighted them. The parson spoke a benison and sprinkled holy water over the Easter Fire; eventually the boys took the charred logs, ran across the village and with the shout '*Der Jude ist verbrannt!*' (The Jew is burnt) bate on doors and shutters of the houses where Jews lived."

This folkway was practised in Viernheim (Hesse) still in 20th century but understandably ended around 1940. In 1956, however, Bavarian ethnologist Hans Moser found "present evidence for the Jew Fire" in the Bavarian regions of Aichach, Schrobenhausen and Dachau. "Till this day", writes Bernhard Dieckmann still in 1991, "in Allendorf (North Rhine-Westphalia) a Judas is burnt in Easter Fire."

Judas is the first object of cross-created punishing anger, in the gospels as well as in real life. He figures pars pro toto for the *Juden, Juifs, Judéus, Židom, Jews, Judíos*, as first choice dummy for the punishing reenactments chapter X will focus on. A striking aspect of the following folkloristic pay-backs to Judas is how educationally they announce the techniques used in the holocaust.

Dieckmann quotes a Bavarian observer around 1850: "At the burning of the straw man always great rejoicing arose, as if this way the Lord's betrayer in person were punished." Coevally, the Silesian folkway of *Judenstürzen* consisted in throwing live cats and goats from church towers, while the *Jaudesjagen* was not lethal at least: "After service in the church, a church servant with a rattle appeared from behind the altar. A boy with red waistcoat had planted himself already at the church door. No sooner than the sign was given, the boy in red waistcoat ran away. The mustered children, equipped ... with rattles and ratchets, loudly yelling chased him out of town where he surrendered in the so called rod alley and was beaten mercilessly by the boys because he had sold the savior."[361]

In modern South America, for instance, a Chilenian boy explains the traditional children's game during *Semana Santa*, the Holy Week before Easter:

---

361 Dieckmann, p.94-99, ref. to Dinzelbacher, P.: Judastraditionen. Vienna 1977, p.43.

"When the Judas burns, the hot coins fall out of him."[362] In Brazil, where the verb *"judiár"* until the present signifies "to torture, maltreat, use badly", this game for Holy Saturday is simply called "Threshing of Judas" (*malhação de Judás*) and goes this way: "The believers tinker a puppet of fabric which presents Judas. The puppet is bound to a stake, stoned around noon and burnt subsequently."[363] From German Black Forest village Grünmettstetten, a young reporter of *jungle-world* at Easter 2003 flabbergastedly reports a "rustig graduation fest for highschool pupils" at the end of which one pupil, peering at the burning wallet-equipped puppet, gives three grounds for burning in one sentence: "This *wanker* has *betrayed* our *Jesus*."[364]

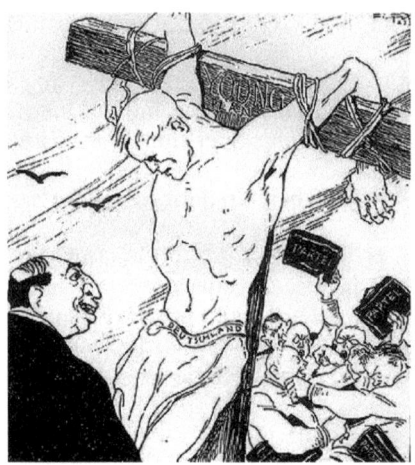 

Judas crucifying Germany: In *Der Stürmer*, August 1930: Blond Deutschland crucified on "Young-Plan", democratic deputies struggling in the background. Subtitle: "They scramble and the Jew smirks."
Right: *Der Stürmer*, after Hershel Grynszpan's deadly 1938 Paris assault on German diplomat Ernst vom Rath. Heading: "Kreuzigung" (Crucifixion). Writing on the cross beam: "Krieg" (War). Subtitle:
"Will the world again through Judas' power / dare to crucify its vigor's flower loose their best blood yet anew, / and see triumphing the sadism of the Jew?"

Money mongers
"Money is the zealous god of Israel, beside which no other god may stand." This attack on Jewish moneytheism was written in 1843 by a 25-year-old German who six years before had titled his essay for gymnasium exam "The Unification of the Faithful in Christ" and happened to be the grandson,

---

362 German TV documentary about Chile after dictatorship, 3Sat TV, October 16, 2005.
363 Levy, Vera, p.37-38; concerning the question whether "judiação" means maltreatment *of* or *by* Jews, Sergio Rodriguez (Veja, São Paulo, 29.01.2015), referring to the author João Ribeiro, confirms the former meaning.
364 Tobias Bezler in "jungle-world", Berlin 2003, cited in Südwestpresse Ulm, Easter Saturday (April 14) 2001.

great-grandson and so on of rabbis on both parental sides.[365] Is there a quasi genetical link from the money changers Jesus drove out of the temple to those who Marx so zealously characterized by their God Mammon? Or to the twenty Jews that Forbes lists among the fifty most successful capitalists in 2009? Or to the Jewish 11 percent of world's billionaires in 2013?

If genetical, the money gene began to thrive in Jewish genepool not until Christian era. From the 2nd century BCE through the Roman Empire of Jesus' days and until the 8th century, when Judaism was "a dynamic and proselytizing religion" and "the fervor of proselytism was indeed one of the most distinctive traits of Judaism",[366] also their trades and occupations were "extremely varied", as Poliakov states, adding: "In the Dispersion, as in Palestine, they gained their livelihood chiefly by the sweat of the brow ... In Egypt and Asia Minor they were generally agricultural colonists; elsewhere, they were widely represented in all the trades of the period, particularly weaving and dyeing, which they virtually monopolized in certain regions." Though they dominated textile manufacture, "what the Jews are most frequently criticized for is not being covered with gold but rather with filthy rags ... No pagan author has ever characterized them as merchants; nowhere do we come upon that identification of Judaism with business that, a few centuries later, will seem so natural."[367]

Essential to this "natural" identification with bargain was the fact that Christian doctrine praised poverty from the beginning, apparently following Jesus' teachings. "Go, sell everything you have and give to the poor, and you will have treasure in heaven. Then come, follow me." This is the ultimate advice Jesus gives to a young man who said he observed all the commandments, but is saddened by Jesus' counsel "because he had great wealth". (**Mk 10:17-22**). Whereas he radically fights the merchants in the temple, overthrowing their exchange tables (**Mk 11:15-16**), rather pragmatically he answers the Pharisees as to tax money: "Give Caesar what belongs to Caesar, give God what belongs to God" (**Mk 12:17; Th 100:1-3** adding: "... and give Me what is Mine"). In Luke's gospel, surprisingly enough, Jesus recommends to calculate the costs before starting to build a tower (**Lk 14:28-32**) and has a woman "light a lamp, sweep the house and search carefully" for the lost one of her ten silver coins (**Lk 15:8-9**), which somewhat reminds on Scottish or Swabian parsimony. And in his puzzling parable of the dishonest manager (**Lk 16:1b-7**) he even recommends to "shrewdly" commit frauds against the "rich man" in order to make friends with his debtors.

As all passages cited here rank as authentic, they give an impression about how Jesus rated money: not as unimportant, but secondary with respect to "God" and his kingdom, both figuring as paragons of social justice. This justice, not poverty per se, is Jesus' aim. Once Christianity had become the Roman state religion, poverty in this world became the token for otherworldly remuneration (in whose best interest?) and the basis of serious God-

365 Marx, On the Jewish Question (1844); exam essay: Weischedel, p.248.
366 First quote: Sand 2012, p.13; second: Ostrer, p.23.
367 Poliakov 2003, Vol.I, p.5-11.

searching. Thisworldly Judaism, never having appreciated poverty, was assigned to – and accepted – the role of the antagonist, the dealer with stinking money in Christian Europe.

Contrarily, the Jewish colonies in China probably date back to the first centuries CE, and a Chinese stele written in 1512 by a Mandarin states that the Jews in China "excel in agriculture, commerce, law, and the military arts; they are greatly esteemed for their integrity, their loyalty, and their piety".[368] So far the Chinese Jew-image of 16th century.

"Three thousand ducats: well?" This is the English Jew-image of 1596. The four words Shakespeare has Shylock say when the Merchant of Venice enters stage cristallize the psychological connections between the crucifix and the money Jew who mercilessly insists on his contract that entitles him to cut a pound of flesh out of his debitor's body, "near at his heart" where the spear pierced Jesus' body. An eye for an eye, a pound for a pound, it's very Jewish, right?

Not so much. In European tales "the theme of the 'pound of flesh' had hitherto presented, in all its various forms, a pitiless creditor who was either a resentful slave or the incarnation of the Devil. Around 1378, however, the Florentine author Ser Giovanni Fiorentino, in his tale *Il Pecorone*, decided to transform the character into a Jew."[369] Shakespeare's flesh-for-debt idea perhaps was inspired also by a tooth-after-tooth punishment: In 1210, King John had demanded so exorbitant a contribution that the English Jews were unable to comply. Hence the King arrested a great number of them, and being one of the wealthiest, Abraham of Bristol was jailed in a dungeon where one of his teeth was torn out every day. On the eighth day he committed suicide.[370]

Anyhow, Shylock of Venice combines no less than seven reminders of the crucifix that now dominated European minds: (1) Jew attacking Christ(ian), (2) wound in Christ(ian) body, (3) eye for eye mercilessness, (4) Judasic greed for money, (5) Jewish cruelty, and (6) a process which this time ended with the Jew's defeat, the more happy an end since Shylock, as the reader knows, concerning his future son-in-law tends to a cross related lineage (7): "I have a daughter; would any of the stock of Barabbas had been her husband, rather than a Christian!"

As to the ominous 30 silverlings of Judas the betrayer which Shakespeare splendidly joins with the 300 denars of Judas the stingy cashier in Shylock's blood-extorting loan of 3000 ducats, Jewish history admits:

It is true that in trade and money market business of Christian occident Jews were mostly represented overproportionately. This shift of professions had been promoted already by the *privilegia odiosa* curtailing the Jews' free choice of professions in the Codex Theodosianus (438 CE).[371] By and large the Judases were barred from European craft guilds and agriculture, from

368 Poliakov 2003, Vol.I, p.14.
369 Poliakov 2003, Vol.I, p.126.
370 Poliakov 2003, Vol.I, p.78.
371 Flannery, p.56-58.

army and administration until Enlightenment, while their access to the professions of physician, pharmacist and lawyer was restricted in many regions even hereafter. It is true also that before the Spanish pogroms of 14th and 15th century, as well as before the Eastern European Chmielnitzky-Pogroms (1648-1656) many Jews had made their living as tax-collectors for the (ever more demanding) feudal lords – and thus had worked as hate-collectors in the poor villages of serfs and peasants.

It is true that Jewish money-lenders often demanded high, usurious interests – from failing Christian farmers to whom Christian bankers would not lend a penny anymore, hence the Hesse-Darmstadt secretary Baron du Bos du Thil noted at the beginning of 19th century: "One might perhaps state generally, that the Jews in the cities and in rural areas nowadays are cheated as often as the Christians, for in order to gain something they dare the damnedest. [...] Where no one wants to lend any more, the Jew still lends."[372]

It is true that "under these circumstances, money finally acquired for the Jew a quasi-sacred significance"; circumstances visible in the following lines which a feudal landowner, who used to sell writs of protection to Jews, wrote to his *vetter* (cousin): "What profit does Herr Vetter estimate that I draw from them year-round? From their Synagogue alone 25 Reichstaler hard cash yearly / if one dies / so I have 1 Gulden / Every Newyear they have to donate some spice and sugar for the kitchen / to the women and to me besides a silver cup or else something: I estimate in total at least some 100 Gulden that I yearly gain from them."[373]

Yet in 13th century France, the Jews merited the title *"eponges a phynances"*, and their function in feudal society truely was to become that of financial "sponges for Europe".[374] Here's the user's manual: Press sponge with well-dosed pressure onto the lower classes, allow to soak up liquid, then hold sponge over the feudal jar and press once more. Repeat procedure if necessary. Discard or burn after use.

Still the enlightened Prussian King Frederick the Great (1712-1786) was taught by his father: "If you need something for your pleasure, then put all the Jews down for 20.000-30.000 thalers every three or four years, in addition to the protection money they must give you. You must squeeze them for they betrayed Jesus Christ, and must not trust them, for the most honest Jew is an arch-traitor and rogue."[375]

It is true that these often expelled people (thrown out of the city of Mainz, for instance, four times between 1420 and 1471) acquired a predilection for gold and jewels. When in hot August of 2007 a strange flying object landed on Jeff Larsens Farm in Minnesota, thanks to their language computer he quickly got into a conversation with the visitors: "Do all of you have this dark green skin colour?" – "No, our children are light green." – "Do all of you have those two antennas on their head?" – "No, our women have three."

372 Rohrbacher/Schmidt, p.121-122.
373 Rohrbacher/Schmidt, p.121-122.
374 Poliakov 2003, Vol.I, p.106; Nicholls, p.234.
375 Poliakov 2003, Vol.III, p.16-17.

– "Do all of you have a diamond wristwatch and three golden rings and a jewel necklace?" – "No, only our Jews."
On our blue planet, however, the Jewish jewel-mania can be traced back. First, the Talmud states that Jewish husbands are obliged to make their wives beautiful. And second: "The developments that began with the First Crusade led many Jews to convert their property into possessions that could be concealed [and transported] easily in case of danger – that is, into gold and silver."[376] In July 1915, the state comptroller Kharitonov, in a Russian cabinet conference devoted to the lifting of anti-Jewish restrictions, made the black joke that the abrogation of restrictions would make a police strike inevitable – as the protection money which policemen squeezed from Jews for not enforcing legal restrictions was estimated 6 million rubles annually for the city of Saint Petersburg alone.[377]
It is surely not a lie what Peter Abaelard, the open-minded French scholastic, wrote down as a rare document of Christian tolerance in 12th century: "Maltreating the Jews is deemed to be a pleasing act to God ... If they want to travel to the nearest town, they have to buy with high amounts of money the protection of the Christian princes who in truth desire their death to seize their property."[378]
It is true, no doubt, that success in the trade professions has something to do with the educational level, with knowledge of language and mathematics and training in abstract thinking: all these being skills which the average clerical and feudal men of power hardly deemed their subjects's most indispensable priorities. So the Jews were just too cunning? "In reality", Léon Poliakov points out, "disputes over the Jews generally pitted their 'owners' – princes or municipalities who derived a certain profit from their presence – against the mass of citizens, who derived no profit and who hoped to benefit from the Jews' disappearance."[379] On the other hand, after the mass expulsion of the Jews from France in early fourteenth century, the poet and chronicler Geffroi de Paris wrote: "*All the paupers now complain / The Jews, they say, used to be fair / much more in making their affaires / than all the Christians who today / take guarantees, pledge, mortgage 'way / extorting everything to pay / and pluck you first before they flay ...* "[380] Under these conditions it is hardly surprising that the decree of July 28, 1315, the readmission of the Jews, corresponded to the demand and "common outcry of the people". The deep religious pretext for economically advantageous expulsions emerges in the Bavarian city of Regensburg, where the municipality, supported by the bishop, attempted to expel the Jews in 1476 following a charge of ritual murder. The Jews appealed to Emperor Frederick III., arguing that since

376 Poliakov 2003, Vol.I, p.74.
377 Poliakov 2003, Vol.IV, p.113.
378 Kühner, p.134-135.
379 Poliakov 2003, Vol.I, p.119.
380 Poliakov 2003, Vol.I, p.80; French-English translation: K.Y.R.; French text: "Tout pauvre gent se plaint / Car Juifs furent débonnaires / beaucoup plus en faisant leurs affaires/ Que ne sont maintenant les Chretiens. Garanties ils demandent et liens / Gages demandent et tout extorquent / Que les gens plument et écorchent."

the Jews "had been living in the ancient city even before the birth of Jesus Christ, they could in no way be held responsible for his crucifixion."[381]

Schemers

The "Jews before Jesus" who settled in the Roman colony of Regensburg, this border and bridge city on river Danube, were merchants as well as those Jews who coevally settled on the coasts of India and China. The later Christian image of a far-stretched, cobweb-like Jewish network derived in a quite realistic sense from the business travels and relationships which Jewish merchants, as pioneers of mercantilist "globalization", actually knit and undertook. But this drawing was mythologically colorized and what's more, it was emotionally charged by the conspiracy network of the passion stories with their backstage meeting, backstage planning and backstage money transfer plus treacherous deliverance "when no crowd was present" (Luke 22); charged also by the Jewish backstage pressuring of a decision maker who was lobbied offensively by touching upon his loyalty to the Emperor (John 19:12); and it was charged by the notions of opinion making spin doctors who successfully "stirred up" this crowd to shout their "crucify him" (Mk 15:11-14).

Shady characters in background: the void beneath the crucifix is the place where all mycelia of conspiracy are grounded in; so much so that to British historian Paul Johnson "anti-Semitism is the father of all conspiracy theory".[382] Nothing stimulates creativity better than an empty white canvas, yet Picasso and Dalí have known this. But as long as the crucifixes were relatively moderate in their radiation of pain, Jewish plotters were punished moderately. For instance in early medieval Bordeaux, where Jewish conspirators – who else? – must have invited the Normans to their looting raids. Indeed the city's Jews were looted also, but considering that "one of the Temple guards standing nearby slapped Jesus across the face" (John 18:22), for 300 years on every Holy Friday the head of the Jewish community was given a bitch slap in front of the cathedral for public exhilaration.[383]

Hilarity was over when after the turn of the millennium the crucifixes were fashioned increasingly pain-expressive and the bad intentions of the evildoers perceived in living Jews. The variety of their conspirative actions is impressing: In 12th century, Jews had "started the crusades in order to weaken Christendom and Islam", as an Egyptian newspaper found out in 2001; Jews had founded Protestantism in 1517, as Turkish ex-president Erbakan blew in 2007. Jews had managed the Peasant's War of 1525, as already Luther's contemporary Erasmus of Rotterdam suspected;[384] English and American civil wars had been their works as well as French Revolution, according

381 Poliakov 2003, Vol.I, p.120-121.
382 Paul Johnson in his article "Marxism versus the Jews", in: Curtis, Michael (ed.), Antisemitism in the Contemporary World, London 1986, p.39 (by Perry/Schweitzer, p.98).
383 Kühner, p.98.
384 Crusades: Lewis, p.194; Protestantism, Erbakan: Wistrich 2010, p.827; Erasmus: Ley 2002, p.38, ref. to Oberman, Heiko: Wurzeln des Antisemitismus, Berlin 1981, p.48.

to a prestigious Egyptian weekly in 2001. In Russian October Revolution 1917, in Germany's defeat in 1918 (Jewish stab-in-the-back), in the outbreak of WWII ("*internationales Finanzjudentum*"): Jews pulled the wires. Their killing of charismatic persons hadn't stopped with Jesus. The US-presidents McKinley, Lincoln and Kennedy were their victims, while evil persons from Darwin and Al Capone up to Arafat were discovered by conspiration experts to be of Jewish extraction. Guilty of the schism of Islam in Sunnites und Shiites; guilty of the Tsunami in South-East-Asia in 2005 (caused by Israel's submarine nuclear tests); guilty of chemical warfare and the destruction of the ozone layer and the environment in general,[385] Judaism self-evidently was behind the global finance crisis around 2010, since the debt-crisis was, according to Bishop Seraphim of Piraeus, a Zionist plan for the "enslavement of Greece and orthodox Christianity". In his TV interview shortly before Christmas 2010, the Bishop proclaimed that Hitler had been "a tool of Zionism", since the Rothschild family had sponsored him to force the Jews to leave Europe and "establish their new empire" in Palestine.[386]
Meanwhile they had attempted for generations to destroy European culture by Liberalism and Darwinism, Marxism and psychoanalysis, by movie, porno and *entarted* art, by "Negro Jazz" and Popmusic, Chernobyl and alcohol, mad cow and avian flu – behind all that: the Jew.[387]
The intellectual level of these charges might correspond to the following dialogue: "You Chinese have assailed Pearl Harbour!" – "Excuse me, Sir, that's been the Japanese." – "Chinese, Japanese, what's the difference!" – "And you Jews have sunk the Titanic!" – "What? That's been this iceberg!" – "Iceberg, Goldberg, what's the difference?"
Intelligence: German philosopher Friedrich Gentz (1764-1832), whom Poliakov regards as "one of the best political brains of the period", already knew that "all the misfortune of the modern world ... comes manifestly from the Jews, they alone made Bonaparte emperor" – which also means that even Napoleon's genius was insufficient without shrewd Jews in the background. And Gentz expressly points to this shrewd-devils-core of all conspiration myths and Jew-hate in general: "Intelligence – that is the mortal sin of the Jews. All of them are more or less intelligent; but only let one be born in which a spark of heart, a spark of true feeling can be found! The curse that is pronounced on them and pursues them to the ten-thousandth generation, is that they can never leave the sphere of intelligence ... but must make endless circles in it until their black souls descend into hell."[388]
In order to win over the Jews and make them controllable, Napoleon, who was already recognized as the "enemy of Europe" and Anti-Christ incarnate, had convened a new "Great Sanhedrin"; a faithful replica (same number of members, same titles) of the Jerusalem Sanhedrin which had ceased to

---

385 Civil wars, French revolution, communism, world wars: Wistrich 2010, p.810; assassinations, Darwin, Al Capone, Arafat: Lewis, p.214, 215 and 266; schism, Tsunami, ozone layer, environment: Wistrich 2010, p.174.
386 thelede.blogs.nytimes.com, December 22, 2010.
387 Wistrich 2010, p.50, 162 and 793.
388 Poliakov 2003, Vol.III, p.296-297 (cf. Ley, p.72).

exist in 70 CE. The pompous opening took place on February 9, 1807, in the secularized chapel of Saint-Jean, in the former Rue des Piliers, now Rue du Grand-Sanhedrin. But behold! Was not the Sanhedrin the Jewish tribunal that had made the deal with Judas and paid him thirty silverlings? Was it not the Sanhedrin where "that scene of unspeakable outrage took place when the son of God was insulted, covered with spittle and abuse", as the Jewish born convert Abbé Lemann brought to conscience? Still at the beginning of 1807, in Moscow the Holy Synod ordered a proclamation against Napoleon to be read in all Russian churches: "In order to complete the degradation of the Church, he has convened the Jewish synagogues in France, restored the rabbis to their dignity, and laid the foundations of a new Hebrew Sanhedrin, the same infamous tribunal which once dared to condemn our Lord and Saviour Jesus Christ to the cross." Count Chaptal, Napoleon's former Minister of the Interior, relates in his *Souvenirs* how, at a dinner given by Napoleon, his mother's stepbrother, Corsica born Cardinal Fesch entered "looking very worried, which struck the Emperor." Bewildered, his stepnephew Bonaparte asked: "What's the matter with you?" – "Do you want the end of the world to come?" – "Why?" – "Do you not know that the Scriptures foretell the end of the world the minute the Jews are recognized as forming a nation?" Anyone else, Chaptal notes, "would have laughed at this outburst by the Cardinal. But the Emperor's expression changed and he seemed worried. He rose from the table, went into his study with the Cardinal, and only emerged an hour later. Two days after, the Sanhedrin was dissolved." However, with his attempt of reconstruction Napoleon had installed "perhaps ... the primary source of the Protocols of the Elders of Zion".[389]

While the French royalist and son of a slave-trader François-René de Chateaubriand warned that the Sanhedrin would result in "world finances falling to the Jews' stalls", Bavarian freethinker Franz von Spaun, who expiated his Yes to the French revolution in ten years of prison, foresaw "circumcised kings on the thrones of Europe".[390] In spite of the Sanhedrin's early abortion, these fears were the point where two generations later (1868) a German novelist made his contribution: "When all the gold of this world is ours, all power will be ours. [...] Gold is the new Jerusalem – it is dominance on earth: It is power, revenge, pleasure – all that man fears and desires. This is the secret of the Kabbalah, the teaching of the spirit who governs the world, of future! For eighteen centuries the people of Israel has been fighting the battle for the dominance which was promised to Abraham and which the cross has wrenched from us. Eighteen centuries belonged to our enemies – the new century belongs to Israel ..." Thus spoke the *Welt-Oberrabbiner* at his secret nightly meeting with his twelve rabbis of twelve tribes in the old Jewish cemetery of Prague – overheard by Friedrich Goedsche und unbosomed in his novel "Biarritz". Goedsches concoction of golden calf and cross and Sanhedrin made "Biarritz" a bestseller; a Russian translation was published in 1872, Czech, French und Swedish editions followed.

---

389 Poliakov 2003, Vol.III, p.228-230 and 278-283.
390 Poliakov 2003, Vol.III, p.285-286.

Goedsche, whose pen name was John Retcliffe, drew on his own well-applied skills of scheming. The low-level Prussian post-officer was a high-end denunciator: In the aftermath of liberal March Revolution of 1848 he had submitted to the authorities some letters which proved that the leading leftist-liberal politician Benedikt Waldeck was planning nothing less than the overthrow of constitution and murder of the king. When the letters turned out to be fakes and Goedsche to have known this, he had to retire from post office and from now on could focus on his work as redactor of "Neue Preussische Zeitung", better known as "Kreuzzeitung" (Cross Journal).[391]

Yet with his conspirative meeting of 13 rabbis Goedsche, after Napoleon with his Sanhedrin, provided the second source for the infamous "Protocols". The third script was found in the brilliant "Dialogues" of French Democrat Maurice Joly: Fictive conversations between Montesquieu und Macchiavelli – in hell. This book was heisted by Russian secret agents burglaring Joly's house. Joly died in 1878 by suicide and could not prevent that Pyotr Rachkowski, based in France from 1885-1902 before becoming chief of secret service in Moscow, exploited his book in order to deflect public attention from Russia's growing social problems.

The Jewish conspirators pursue a greater aim: the overthrow of all thrones and religions, the destruction of all states – preconditions for the establishment of a Jewish world empire reigned by an emperor of David's line. Important tools for this purpose are democracy, liberalism and socialism. The Jews have stood behind all historical upheavals and have always supported the call for individual freedom. All political murders and all major strikes have been organized by Jews. They seduce the workers to alcoholism and Marxism and attempt to bring about chaotic political conditions by raising food prices but also by spreading infectuous diseases. Right now they already constitute a secret world government; yet since their power is still uncomplete, they set the peoples against one another in order to unleash a world war.

"The responsible ones, however, are those 300 Rathenaus of whom each one knows each other, who control the fate of the world over the heads of kings and presidents of states ...", Hitler warned in his speech of April 13, 1923. One week later, on Friday, April 20, 1923, three weeks after Holy Friday, Hitler celebrates in Munich his thirty-fourth birthday with a good resolution: "We want to avert that also Germany suffers death on cross."[392] One year later, in *Mein Kampf* he praises those "infinitely hated by the Jews, 'Protocols of the Elders of Zion'. They are based on a forgery, groans the Frankfurter Zeitung over the whole world, proving perfectly they are authentic ... It doesn't matter anything which Jewish head these disclosures hail from. What prevails, however, is that with downright gruesome veracity they reveal the nature and activity of the Jewish people."[393]

---

391 Cohn, N., 1969, p.42-43.
392 Boepple, p.48-49 and 56; cf. Wistrich 1987, p.131.
393 Hitler, p.337.

Still more revealing is how Austrian parson Arbogast Reiter worded his approval of the czarist pamphlet: "Why does Israel bear such a grudge against the protocols? Because they reveal to us the giant plan for the erection of a Jewish world empire, a humongous global conspiration ... The question is not whether true or false but simply whether there is still a chance of salvation from Ahasver's hands clawed deeply in our flesh already." This review figures in Reiters work *Das Judentum und die Schatten des Antichrist*, published in 1933 by the Graz-based Publishing House of Styrian Catholics. Not too coincidentally, the Catholic Parson's mind map of Jewish world dominion reminds on non-fiction monocratic structures of Catholic hierarchy: "At the top of these secret organizations stands the Exilarch, the common Jewish world-head in New York; by his side the three Wise Men, and as their wire pullers on whole earth the so-called 300 Adepts ... Step by step, decade by decade in Europe, America, Asia, Africa and on all the islands" Jewish seizure of power is being prepared. "Does this happen really without a guiding hand, without supreme control? A fool who still believes this, a blind doter who does not see the wires which already have spun the whole world in! The giant *cross spider* sits in New York."[394]

One could do away with the *cross spider* as a classic Freudian slip, but reminding the common German metaphor of *"Hirngespinst"* (figment; literally "brain web"), I would rather say that *cross spider* is this Austrian parson's brain scan: All the synapses, like the spider's long feet, striding from the cross-marked power unit in the center. Highlighting the cross-like feature of an animal that humans are genetically inclined to perceive as dangerous and ugly, the parson sheds light on his relation to the cross – and reminds another analytical remark made by the aforementioned Chateaubriand. As for the exciting question "why the women of the Jewish race arc more beautiful than the men" Chateaubriand elucidates: The son of God was denied, martyred and crucified by the men alone, while "the women of Judea believed in the Savior, loved him, followed him, comforted him in his afflictions".[395] In daily view of "the unspeakable crime of Jesus's crucifixion ... attributed to all Jews collectively ... for medieval Europe there was no crime which the enemy of mankind was not capable of potentially."[396] In this diagnosis Robert Wistrich does not shift the year 1938 back into the Middle Ages, but rather refers to Uri Avnery's simple wisdom that "in politics, it is irrational to ignore the irrational".[397]

As to the rational and all too real political intrigues which members of the mainstream faith could enact all the better behind the backdrop of the common "Caution, Jews conspiring!" scenography, only one example: Before 1933, the Vatican had negotiated with democratic German governments for a new Reichskonkordat – to no avail. Now, when Hitler was the new Reichskanzler, Papal Nuntio (and later Pope Pius XII) Eugenio Pacelli

---

394 Heer 1989, p.211-216.
395 Chateaubriand in his essay "Walter Scott et les Juives", Oeuvres completes, Paris 1861, Vol.XI, p.764-766 (quoted by Poliakov 2003, Vol.III, p.326).
396 Wistrich 2010, p.90.
397 tikkun.org, April 22, 2013.

urged the Catholic Zentrum Party to support the National Socialists – who offered a new concordat according to the Vatican's wishes. Prelate Ludwig Kaas, the leader of the Zentrum and close confidant of Pacelli, arranged with Hitler the firm promise of this contract – for a small service in return: The Zentrum would vote for the Enabling Act. So it was the connection Hitler-Pacelli which for a money bag called concordat would hand over a country and almost a world to the curse-executer.[398] No one confirmed this transaction more outspokenly than Munich Cardinal Faulhaber in a sermon of 1937: "At a time when the leaders of most of the world's nations faced the new Germany with cool restraint, the greatest moral power on earth confessed its confidence in the new German government by the concordat. This was an act of immeasurable importance for the new government's reputation abroad."[399]

Poisoners

"They still have the bitterness of their parents, who gave the Lord gall to eat and they are old by the vinegar they gave him to drink [...] They themselves, to wit, are bitter like gall and sour like vinegar, because to the living bread they handed gall and vinegar. [They are] degenerated wine of the prophets, filled with the injustice of this world like a vessel, with a heart like a sponge, deceitful so to say by holey and crooked lairs."[400] Saint Augustine's poetic text evinces his skill in reframing profane household tools and liquids metaphorically, turning them against "them". What "they" actually offered to the victim on Golgotha was a pain and thirst allaying drink: Wine with myrrh before nailing, in Mark's gospel; wine with gall (taken from Psalm 69:22) for the victim hanging on nails, says Matthew; vinegar before dying, as all four gospels report. The pronoun "they" primarily denotes the soldiers of the crucifixion unit. While the vinegar was a cheap thirst-quencher, Mark's "wine spiced with myrrh" points to a custom mentioned in the Talmud: Noble women used to ease the victims' awful fate by narcotic drinks. While Matthew has the sour wine offered to Jesus by "one ... of the bystanders" who soaked the wine with a sponge he then sticked on a cane, Luke turns mercy into malice: "The soldiers also mocked him, coming up and offering him sour wine" (23:36).

There's no gospel word of poison-giving Jews: Their defamation in this case is mostly the work of later writers and painters, and once more we can observe, as in the cases of Jesus versus Barabbas and Judas Iscariot versus Judas the "not Iscariot" (John 14:22), an artificial polarization, this time between Roman and Jewish soldier.

Before examing the next pictures, let's review the Irish bookpainting in chapter 6: One of the soldiers has a moustache. What is his job? And his

398 Ley, p.122-124.
399 Lewy, Günter: The Catholic Church and Nazi Germany. New York 1965, p.78/86 (quoted by Weiss, Hamburg 1997, p.314).
400 Lapide 1987, p.46.

colleague's? This soldier with the Holy Lance was given the Roman name Longinus in early Christian legend. The story says that he was originally blind (a blind soldier in action, beat that!) and his blindness was cured by the holy blood dripping from Jesus' wound (hit blindly!) down on his eyes. He converted, became a bishop of Cappadocia and a martyr – all this triggered by the holy blood. So the unholy red vinegar must be whose job?

In both bookpaintings below, the reader will notice that the decent moustache has grown to a full beard, a sign of Jewishness confirmed by the bearded one's conical hat in the picture of 9th century, while the bookpainting from the Monastery of St. John of Zagba emphasizes the gall giver's "Jewish" nose even to Syriac viewers.

Jewish poison-givers: Left: Crucifixion folio (detail) from the Rabbula Gospels, Syria, completed in 586 whereas French orientalist Edgard Blochet (1870-1937) dated the folios no earlier than 10th century. Above the Roman soldier reads his name ΛΟΓΙΝΟΣ (Longinos), while the drink-giver excels by his hooknose. Right: Bookpainting, late 9th century. Here Stephaton, putting the sponge of vinegar on his cane, is marked as Jewish also by his conical Phrygian cap.

In paintings which combine the couple Longinus/Stephaton with the equally contrastive female couple of Ecclesia/Synágoga, this Longinus, no surprise, is always close to Ecclesia. If the female couple is alone, the speaking attributes of sponge and jar are close to, guess it, the Jewess. An act of compassion by Jewish women or Roman soldiers thus was transformed into the taunting toxicity of Jews.

This is understandable by two reasons. First, Jewish pain relievers dont't agree with the Jewish tag of crucifiers. Second, the Eucharist as the most wholesome act of eating and drinking wine must have its poisonous contrast in the acting of those "doctors of incredulity"[401] whose mere presence is toxic for Christian faith. Already in 1265, the *Siete Partidas* legal code of Spanish King Alfonso X marks the Jews as prone to poisoning, stipulating

---

401 Poliakov 2003, Vol.IV, p.68.

that a Christian could take medicine from a Jew only if a Christian physician was acquainted with the contents. Hadn't a physician who was burnt as Jew in Llerena confessed under torture to have poisened several persons? On this base around 1530 the counselors of Portuguese king João III begged him to prohibit *Cristãos Novos* the sale of any medicine.[402]

The economic background reasons of the poison slander that are transparent at both times in between showed up genocidally. In February 1349, the Strasbourg municipality proceeded to hold an investigation concerning the charge of Jews having poisoned the wells, and concluded that the Jews were not guilty. Quickly the municipality was overthrown by a coalition of patricians and guilds, and now all went blow on blow: "On Wednesday one swore the new council, on Thursday one swore in the garden, on Friday one caught the Jews, on Saturday one burnt the Jews, who numbered about two thousand as one considered." The chronicler leaves no doubt about the kind of poison: "What one was indebted to the Jews was quit, and all pawns and bonds they had of debts were passed back. As to their cash assets, the council took and apportioned them to the guilds prorated. That also was the poison that killed the Jews."[403]

Martin Luther warns in 1546 of the Jewish physicians, who with devil's help master a special art "of fetching one a *Gifft* [german: giving/poison] on which he in one hour, in one month, in one year, yes, in ten or twenty years must die. This art they do master."[404] In 1610, the Vienna Faculty of Medicine proclaimed the caring indication that Jewish physicians are bound by law to poison every tenth Christian patient.

In 1822, authorities in Bavarian district of Lower Franconia feared attacks against the Jewish population, which was imputed with "poisoning of wells and [worse still!] poisoning of the hop used to brew beer". Three years later, authorities were alarmed anew, when Jews were charged with having "killed children by dispensing of poisoned comfit".[405]

Hitler, the WWI-private affected by "Yellow-Cross" poison gas, exhorted the Germans still on April 29, 1945 in his testament "to merciless resistance against the world poisoner of all peoples, *das internationale Judentum*".[406] In 1953, his eastern colleague Josef Stalin, beaten for hardness by his father and educated in the Georgian Orthodox Spiritual Seminary in Tbilisi, outlined the "Doctor's Plot" that allegedly attempted to kill Soviet officials. Most of the physicians were Jewish; Stalin ordered accused physicians to be tortured "to death", and wrote to Nikita Khrushchev he should incite anti-Semitism in the Ukraine, instructing him that "the good workers at the factory should be given clubs so they can beat the hell out of those Jews."[407]

---

402 Spain 1265: Gerber, J., p.111; Portugal ~1530: Kayserling, p.212 (original edition p.170).
403 Rohrbacher/Schmidt, p.198 and Poliakov 2003, Vol.I, p.111.
404 Sermon about Matthew 11:25-27 given at Eisleben, February 15, 1546. In: Luther, CW, Vol.51, Weimar 1914, p.195 (quoted by Cohn, N., 1969, p.336).
405 Rohrbacher/Schmidt, p.200-201, referring the Bavarian fact to: Staatsarchiv München, RA 22044.
406 Jäckel: Hitlers Weltanschauung, p.88 (by Goldhagen 1996, p.197).
407 Pinkus, Benjamin: The Soviet Government and the Jews 1948–1967: A Documented

Crossadists

"Oh you cruel Jew! Pilate teaches you, that your character is rougher than the pig's character; the pig at least knows mercy."[408] That's how Luther's mentor Johannes von Staupitz (1465-1524) saw it – citing pigs and Pilate (him of all people) to link Jew with cruel. The later association of Jude+Sade is inherent to all the roles discussed here, and particularly in the alleged Jewish cruelty against animals chapter 13 will deal with. The present paragraph surveys why this connotation anchors yet in children's minds.

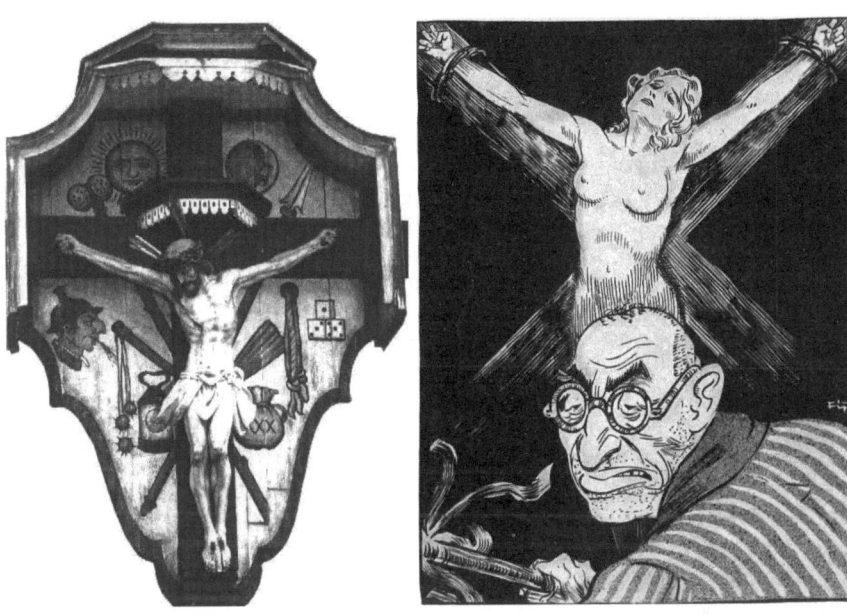

Jews enjoying cruelty: A 19th century wayside cross in German Black Forest region combines a spitting Jew with a sack of money (XXX for 30 silverlings), dice (for raffling Jesus' clothes, see Mk 15:24; cf. Mt 27:35; Lk 23:34; John 19:23-24) and torture tools. Right: From the (undated) book *Der Jude als Rassenschänder* (The Jew as race defiler). Subtitle: "The Nuremberg Jew Otto Mayer used to crucify his victims. He fixed them stark naked on a home made wooden cross and raped them as soon as blood ran from the wounds."

Jews considered blood to be "a drink like milk"; concerning the extraction of blood, the Jew always must take care to not only murder Christian children but to make sure that they die "in the most painful way possible.[409] This was stated by Jesuit father Paolo Silva in his order's gazette "La Civiltá Cattolica", in 1914.

Study, Cambridge University Press 1984, p.107-108; Stalin's torture: "Beat them to death", Novaya Gazeta, 2008 (Wikipedia).
408   Von Dohna, Lother (Graf zu) and Wetzel, R. (ed): Staupitz, Sämtliche Schriften. Berlin 1983, Sermon X (according to Michael, p.106).
409   Kertzer, p.314.

When on October 1941 in the Belarussian district of Mogilev 2273 Jews had to be shot, Viennese police secretary Walter Mattner did his job impeccably. In his letter of October 5, 1941, Mattner wrote to his wife: "At the first truck my hand was still trembling when I shot, but one gets used to this. When it comes to the tenth truck-load I already aim calmly and fire surely at the many women, children and babies. Considering that I also have two toddlers at home, which these hordes would treat just the same way *if not ten times worse*. The death we were according them was *a fine, short death*, compared to the *infernal torments* of thousands upon thousands in the dungeons of the GPU. Newborn babies were flying high through the air and we picked them off in flight, before they fell into the pit or the water." [410]

Mattner attempts to justify himself in the usual way, imputing guilt to his victims; as this works bad with babies, he identifies them with the "hordes" of Jews and recurs to their *höllisch* (infernal) cruelties. "Do you know who the devil is?" Julius Streicher had asked his audience of 2000 Nuremberg children in a Christmas speech in 1936, and "*Der Jud, der Jud*", was the echo resounding from thousand children's throats.[411] Devil is in hell. But there's no death in hell. With the "*fine, short death* we gave them" Mattner clearly contrasts the *long and cruel death* those Jewish hords exacted shouting "Crucify him". And the toddlers Mattner "picked off in flight" indeed had a short death compared with Mary's toddler in the manger, on the crosses Austria abounds with.

"Dear, good Uncle Hitler", the Führer was addressed in 1933, in a letter from "Your little 13 ¾-years old niece" living in East-Prussian Memelland. "The Jews not only take us here our bread away, but also slaughter Christians at Easter. Every child is afraid before Easter to go to a Jewish shop. That's awful really."[412]

Two days before Easter the manger child of Christmas dies on cross. Cruelties are perceived as more awful if the victims are children. Does this apply also to another paschal motive of fear, to wit Yahve's angel of death on his way through nightly Egypt, killing the first-born of the Egyptian mothers but passing by the houses of the Hebrew families with the blood-red signs on the doorposts? Driving home from a Passover Seder, Shlomo Sand's five year-old daughter challenged her daddy, the distinguished historian, with poignant questions that give insight in children's perception of adults' cruel narrations: "'What exactly did 'the first-born' mean? Did it include just boys, or were girls killed as well?' When I assured her that only boys were singled out, it had a calming effect on her, and her subsequent silence persuaded me that she'd gone to sleep. But suddenly there came a final 'shock' question from the back seat: 'Did God also kill the little babies, if they were the first born in the family?'"[413]

410   Klaus-Michael Mallmann, Volker Rieß and Wolfram Pyta: Deutscher Osten 1939-1945. Darmstadt 2003, p.27-28; cf.: yadvashem.org/untoldstories/database/germanReports. asp?cid=234&site_id=196.
411   Goldhagen 2002, p.184.
412   Eberle, p.134. Of course Hitler was but the girl's fantasized uncle.
413   Sand 2014, p.66.

Would Christian children who are told this story identify with the Hebrew or with the Egyptian children or with children in general, fearing and hating the murderous Jewish God? Will children quieten down if they are told that the angel's death raid was the punishment for Pharaoh's order to kill the first-born of the Hebrews, and that little Moses barely escaped this mass murder? More than thousand years after this fictive story of fearsome Pharaoh, the Roman Senate very really adopted the resolution to order all children who would be born next year (63 BCE) to be killed. Why? Astrological auguries had announced that nature was "pregnant with a king for the Roman people". Only by the intervention of senators whose wives were expecting, this resolution was not forwarded to treasury and thus not ratified, as Julius Marathus and Sueton relate. Both chroniclers were intimates of the physically small but politically outstanding Emperor Augustus who happened to be born in exactly this year 63 BCE.[414]

The nearly forgotten Roman episode turns up 150 years later in a worldwide well-known remake by Paul's co-worker Matthew – a story about astrologers and a massacre in Betlehem, about a Jewish King who wants to ferret out the "newborn king of the Jews ... and when you have found him, bring me word, that I too may come and worship him". Wait till Herod comes! The abysmally contrastive perfidy (worship – murder) of this Jewish textbook villain returns in the equally contrastive perfidy (kiss – betrayal) of villain Judas, but the former leaves an even deeper impression, deeper even than the death of those little Egyptians, in children ever dependent on king-like adults. Matthew's principal narrative aim, however, was rather homey: By letting little Jesus, thanks to a warning angel and the quickly acting Joseph, escape to Egypt, in his verse 2:15 Matthew can place the rescued little Jesus besides the rescued little Moses and apply the second half of Hosea's verse 11:1 to the new redeemer: "When Israel was a child, I loved him, and *out of Egypt I called my son.*"

This return from Egypt Jewishly begins at Passover. While the Christian Easter holiday as well as Luke's manger narration date back to the first century, the celebration of Christmas on December 25 is documented not until 336 in Rome. Eleven years later Saint Chrysostom (347-407) was born who, having lost his father early, clung to his mother strongly and in his youth often secluded himself to a cavern to read the Bible. This sensitive Church Father was the first one to view Jesus' death as a child murder: "If someone had murdered your son, could you abide his sight or his greeting? Wouldn't you flee him as if he were a vicious demon, as if he were the devil himself? The Jews killed the son of your Lord ... Do you want to dishonor him by ... consorting with those who crucified him?" One who loves Jesus boundlessly, must not set bounds to himself "in the battle against those who hate him."[415]

---

414   Cf. Lüdemann, p.171.
415   Weiss, Hamburg 1997, p.25.

That's what you were born for:
Above: Workshop Leonardo da Vinci, Madonna dei fusi, 1510-1540; right: Russian Icone, 19ᵗʰ century, photographed in a Bavarian wayside chapel.
Below: Lorenzo Lotto, Nativitá, 1523; I.A.M. of Zwolle (Johan van den Mynnesten), Madonna sitting with Christ child holding a cross, around 1480.

The connection of manger and cross was for Chrysostom, and is for Christian children to this day, the product of a simple but inevitable learning process. While cross and manger never enter stage together, they partner yearly in a catchy rhythm: born at winter solstice, killed at spring equinox, the ba-

158

by's diaper turns to bloody loincloth, year in year out. Eight centuries after Chrysostom, Bishop Berthold of Regensburg (1210-1272) bizarrely disclosed the child-cross link in his brain, explaining that crucified Christ, though present in the wafer, keeps invisible in the bread, for "who would like to bite off the little head, or the little hands, or the little feet of a little child?"[416] Little child, big crucifix: Catholic church rooms usually contain both biographic points, but in different places. Few artists put both into one picture like Raffael did in his Alba Madonna (1510) and Lorenzo Lotto (1480-1557) in his "Birth of Christ", with an anachronistic crucifix hanging between the naked child and naked flying putti, besides the entrance of the stable like in Italian farmhouses. Here it is Joseph who shields his child from the cruel sight, while in Lotto's "Madonna with Saint Gerome and Saint Saint Anthony" Mary protects her son – who visibly dislikes the monk – with her motherly body from the crucifix the old monk musingly holds in his hands. In his "Saint Joseph charpentier", Baroque painter George de La Tour (1593-1652) has the carpenter set his auger on a beam, looking with somber premonition at his little helper whose fingers are pierced for now just by the candle light. Russian Madonnas have the child on their lap and two angels with cross, lance, sponge behind them, while in Brazilian presepios of 18th century the *Menino Deus* lies lovely in his manger, a cross beside him.
No evil Jews here on the scene. But the humane intolerability of the inevitable mental connection between the manger boychild and his crucifixion found its pressure valve in the projected picture of Jews crucifying children. The emotional synergy of the son in the manger on Xmas (note spelling!), the sons massacred by Herod (few days after Xmas) and the son on cross (few months later) resulted in which phantasm of eight centuries?
Still in 1942, the March issue of Civiltá Cattolica charged the Jewish "Christ-killers" with ritual murder.[417] On May 19, 1943, Bavarian Catholic Heinrich Himmler instructs the chief of Gestapo and Einsatzgruppen, Ernst Kaltenbrunner: "Of the book 'Die jüdischen Ritualmorde' I have ordered a bigger quantity and let it be distributed up to *Standartenführer* level. I send you several hundred exemplars so that you can distribute them to your *Einsatzkommandos*, but mainly to the men who deal with the Jewish question."[418] For instance Walter Mattner?

Outsmarters
"We are standing against a people that thinks. They survived 2000 years of pogroms not striking back, but thinking. They invented and successfully promoted Socialism, Communism, human rights and democracy so that persecuting them would appear to be wrong, so they may enjoy equal rights with others. With these they have now gained control of the most powerful countries and they, this tiny community, have become a world power. We

---

416 Trachtenberg, p.14; cf. Prager/Telushkin, p.86.
417 Phayer, p.8.
418 Hilberg 1982, p.693; cf. Perry/Schweitzer, p.2.

cannot defeat them by strength alone. We too have to use our brain."[419] For this and other statements, Malaysian Premier Mohamad Mahathir earned standing ovations on October 16, 2003, at the Tenth Islamic Summit Conference in Putrajaya, Malaysia.

The almost fearful words of Mahathir (himself a well-achieved physician and politician, the successful son of low-status parents) adumbrate how much anti-Semitic conjuration theories are feeding on the image of the clever Jew. "The wicked Jewish intellectual and sophist is a last portrait of the Pharisee, designed in Christian sermon and religious instruction", Friedrich Heer declares.[420]

Indeed, the forcedly baptised Marranos who had escaped the Spanish inquisition, at their new places of residence soon excelled as the most famous physicians, the most innovative entrepreneurs and "played a rôle which was altogether out of proportion to their numbers in the trade of Western Europe", while at the same time quite a few ex-Jewish converts in Spain soon girded episcopal purple though already being family men.[421] The lawyer and statesman Pedro de Caballería was asked by a Jewish scholar how he could justify having converted to the Christian faith. "Imbecile", he snarled, "with the Jewish Torah what more could I have ever been than a rabbi? Now, thanks to the little hanged one, I have been given all sorts of honours. I am in command of the whole city of Saragossa, and I make it tremble."[422] His son Alfonso de la Caballería, the vice-chancellor of the kingdom of Aragon, was so attached to Judaism that the inquisition trialled him for nearly twenty years. "Despite the overwhelming evidence collected against him" he was finally acquitted in 1501 "on orders from the papacy".[423] Historian Angel Alcalá estimates that the majority of authors and mystics in Spain's *siglo de oro* (golden age) came from converso families – at a time when out of 100 Spaniards but 20 were able to write their names and even out of these, few ever read a book.[424] Portraying "the Jew" in general, Mark Twain in 1897 states that "his contributions to the world's list of great names in literature, science, art, music, finance, medicine, and abstruse learning are also away out of proportion to the weakness of his numbers" and warns that this headstart boosts hatred: "I am persuaded that in Russia, Austria, and Germany nine-tenths of the hostility to the Jew comes from the average Christian's inability to compete successfully with the average Jew in business – in either straight business or the questionable sort."[425]

An example of this Jewish cleverness is the physician who had given his patient at the longest three more months to live, but had not got his bill paid after three months: He gave him three more months. The explanation of anti-semitism as "the socialism of the witless guys" (a term falsely accredited

419   Anti-Defamation League, archive.adl.org/...; Primor/von Korff, p.34.
420   Heer 1981, p.461.
421   Trade: Roth, p.233; purple: Gerber, p.124; Moreno de Carvalho in: Fuks, p.235.
422   Cohn-Sherbok, p.83.
423   Poliakov 2003, Vol.II, p.192.
424   Yovel, p.241-242 and 266.
425   Twain, Mark, Concerning the Jews: Wikipedia, cf. Gilman, p.38.

to German Social Democrat August Bebel who himself attributed it to the Austrian politician Ferdinand Kronawetter) anyway points to a function they both knew well: racism as a "feel-good-strategy to cope with the unpleasant experience of envy".[426] Is there a real reason for this fear of being inferior which Alfred Adler labelled with the typically German well-sounding term *minderwertigkeitskomplex*? Since the first awarding of the Nobel Prize in 1901, among the 555 prize winners (until 2012) more than 18 percent belonged to a people whose estimated 13,8 million members represent 0.2 percent of the whole world population that anyhow, believe Mahathir, is reigned by them.

Before WWI, Christian states like Poland or Russia, but also the US administration, used access restrictions to keep Jewish students off the universities into which they funnelled in highly disproportionate numbers. German universities and secretaries of culture succeeded halfway in avoiding Jewish postgraduations, to the effect that, in 1900, only 7 of 1000 German citizens and 50 of 1000 professors, but 125 of 1000 students were Jewish, while 500 of 1000 physicians in Berlin (590 of 1000 in Vienna) were of "Mosaic persuasion", whereas in Paris 600 of 1000 Jews died *pauvre* in 1870 and in Vienna 660 of 1000 were "destitute" in 1880.[427]

Worldwide, among the authors of the most cited books of twentieth century 30 percent, and among all chess world champions 47 percent are Jewish.[428] It has been said that the "people of the book" excels mainly in verbal and rational disciplines while due to the prohibition of images the visual arts are alien to Jews. However, even there you find names like Chagall, Segal, Kahlo, Lichtenstein, Liebermann, Beckmann, Spiegelman, the Marrano painters Velazquez, Pissarro, Modigliani, not to speak of the world of moving pictures, while Jewish success in physics and chemistry, drama and comedy, medicine and psychology is hardly reducible to bookish behaviour. So to what? The amazing number of Jewish masters of the violine who grew up in Odessa (Igor and David Oistrach, Jakob Lichtman, Itzhak Perlman, Alexander Schaichet, Nathan Milstein, Klara Berkovich ...) once made one of them suggest it must be due to Odessa's water. In the USA, a Jewish population of 2 percent bore 27 percent of US Nobel Prize winners, 23 percent of the wealthiest 400 citizens and 80 percent of comedians. Not bad for a group that in an intelligence test performed in 1913 by eugenicist Herbert H. Goddard (1866-1957) in the immigration center of Ellis Island had evinced as feebleminded and that in mass tests of army recruits beginning in 1917 ranked at the end of an intelligence scale whose top was occupied by Nordic race.[429]

---

426 Kaye/Kantrowitz, p.23.
427 Weiss, Chicago 1997, p.134 (universities); Entine, p.237 (physicians); Perry/ Schweitzer, p.85, 134 (poor people).
428 Telushkin 1992, p.19, 43 and 75. Comedians: Estimate by Woody Allen; Nobel Prize: Raphael Patai, The Jewish Mind, New York 1977, p.339-342; wealth: Forbes Yearbook. Most frequently cited authors and chess world champions: Sacks, p.207.
429 Sussman, p.85 and 102.

This result gives me just one more reason to mention genetical causes (1) but shortly among the four reasons for alleged Jewish intelligence argued below. During the 1980s, when less than five percent of Bavarian population were Turkish, I taught a class of rather intelligent but mostly Turkish children in a Bavarian school for educationally impaired children to which these children had been committed on base of intelligence tests. "Experts say these tests are culturally neutral", my colleague Georg Spiegler explained. "But they aren't." The more my working class and migrant children taught me during three decades to mistrust the selection rituals of a retarded school system, the stronger I view giftedness as effect of cultural nurture instead of genetic nature. Jewishly, this gifting is less genetic than gynetic, female conditioned by the yiddishe mame's prescient ministration, as may be seen in the following afternoon dialogue in New York Central Park: "Hallo Mrs Levy! Nice to see you! We haven't met for years, did we? And your gorgeous two boys! How old are they?" – "The surgeon is five and the lawyer two."

1. Focussed on genetics is for instance the Cochran hypothesis: In the densely populated ghettoes Jews acquired and forwarded the so called LSD, i.e. lysosomal storage diseases (Gaucher, Tay-Sachs, Niemann-Pick disease ...) as well as the breast cancer related gene BRCA1, all of which have tragic outcomes if the individual inherits the "defect" genes from both parents, but otherwise enhance her/his brain development if only one of the parents carried the gene. The ghetto-mutated lysosomes might have been positively selected "in Jews for the intelligence putatively required to survive recurrent persecution and also to make a living by commerce, because Jews were barred from the agricultural jobs available to the non-Jewish people", Jared Diamond suggested in 1994.[430] In 1885, when social Darwinist eugenics was popular science, Australia born Joseph Jacobs had asserted: "Jewish mind was never fettered, and eventually the weaker members of every generation were sifted out by the persecution that seduced or coerced them to convert to Christianity, and thus the Jews of today are the survivors of a long process of unnatural selection, which seemingly has prepared them perfectly to the struggle for spiritual existence."[431] Zeitgeisty typical is also Coudenhove-Kalergi's hymn of 1925: "By a martyrdom of two millennia the Jews ascended to their present-day greatness. Excluded from most professions and under living conditions aggravated in many ways, they had to sharpen their wits tenfold just to save their existence through the Middle Ages. Only the most able ones survived and procreated", thus bringing forth "a particularly precious branch of humanity steeled by suffering and ennobled by thinking". Notably, since Jews rated as "the most feminine of all nations" (to Vienna rabbi Adolf Jellinek in 1869), as effeminate in general (Vienna Jewish antisemite Otto Weininger) and as responsible for the feminist movement (in the eyes of German *Kaiserzeit* antisemites), the Jewish people

---

430 Entine, p.318.
431 Jacobs, Joseph: Studies in Jewish Statistics, London 1891; Men of Distinction (1916); Contributions to Civilization (1919); according to Gilman, p.102-103.

shines as the most feminine and most steeled one of all peoples.[432] Among this people's *weaker members* in Jacobs's diction was also Heinrich Heine who had taken baptismal water as the "entrée-billet to European culture" and with sarcastic irony (paraphrasing Mark 9:43-49) wrote to the open-minded husband of early feminist Rahel Varnhagen, née Levin, about a more costly entrée-billet: "If your eye troubles you, pluck it out. If your hand troubles you, chop it off ... and if your reason troubles you, turn Catholic."
What Charles Darwin in 1874 had called the "Catholic degeneration", geneticist Ernest van den Haag reworded in 1969, asserting that Christians sacrificed their "good" genes almost on schedule. "The Church has offered the sole career in which intellectual gifts were rewarded independent from the owner's social origin ... but priesthood had a price: celibacy. That meant that the most intelligent section of the population had no offspring; their genes, generation after generation, were skimmed off by the Church and not restored to the gene pool of the world or even the Church."[433] However, Brazilian anthropologist Gilberto Freyre, with his not unproud remark that "over here a priest staying chaste was a rarity, most of them contributed generously to the growth of population and begot highly intellectual sons and grandsons",[434] puts all those breeding theories down to mother earth again.

2. But also on the Middle-Eastern earth of Jewish patriarchs, the story of intellectual sons and grandsons starts in a womb that conceived from a man ordained for sacrifice: Rebecca's. Yet her pregnancy is problematic. She suffers from the fact that her twins bandy yet in her belly. At delivery, the strong one comes out first: Esau, red and hairy like a fur coat, and clutched at his heel by his loser brother. "As the boys were growing up, Esau became skilled at hunting and was a man of the outdoors, but Jacob was the quiet type who tended to stay indoors ... Isaac favored Esau because he had a taste for game, but Rebecca favored Jacob", her little softy.
Ironman or homebody, wild game or granola? The showdown is tipped by a lentil gruel, smelling sweet enough for hungry hunter Esau to sell his birth right for the vegan dish: a literarily rare victory of the soft, cunning, feminine Isaacson against dragon-blood-steeled Siegfrieds? In 1938, when Germany was almost ready steeled, Freud wrote: "The primacy which during about two millennia was granted to spiritual efforts in the life of the Jewish

---

432   Coudenhove-Kalergi, p.75. As to "most feminine ..." see Rabbi Adolf Jellinek: Studien und Skizzen. Erster Teil: Der jüdische Stamm. Vienna 1869, p.19 (Gilman, p.96). This Jewish trait was stressed by Jewish Vienna anti-Semite Otto Weininger (1880-1903) who had considerable influence on misogynic Jew-hater Lanz von Liebenfels and his "Ostara-Hefte für arische Männerrechtler", avidly read by young Hitler. Lewis (p.273) states that "in Wilhelminian Germany, anti-Semitism and antifeminism were closely linked, and Jewish responsibility for the feminist movement was a frequent theme in anti-Semite propaganda."
433   Darwin, Charles: The Descent of Man and Selection in Relation to Sex. New York 1874, p.160 (cited by Gilman, p.127). Ernest van den Haag: The Jewish Mystique. New York 1969, p.13-25 (cited by Gilman, p.125-126). This genetical rationale is supported also by Arthur Ruppins, Salcia Landmann and, even more precisely, by Nathaniel Weyl (The Creative Elite in America, Washington 1966).
434   Freyre, p.409-410.

people naturally has had its effect; it helped to curb the crudeness and inclination to violence which usually ensues where the development of muscle
power is a people's ideal. The harmony in the formation of spiritual and
physical activity which the Greek people achieved has eluded the Jews. In
the conflict leastwise they opted for the higher-value good."[435] Opted in the
way Rebecca opted for the introvert thinker Jacob against his extrovert mus-
culous brother? In this perspective Léon Poliakov points to a criterion that
may be seen as characteristic for a culture's mind-body-politics: consume of
alcohol. In 1925, a study revealed that Jews in Warsaw were 68.6 times less
likely to be alcoholics, and in 1931 New York state hospitals registered, out
of one million persons of each ethnic group, 256 Irish, 78 Scandinavians,
48 Italians, 43 British, 38 Germans and 5 Jews admitted for alcoholic psy-
choses. "There is no question", N.Glazer muses, "that a people's relation to
alcohol represents something very deep about it; so deep, however, that it is
not easy to find a very good explanation of just what it is."[436] Maybe it is just
the basical connection of Jewish religion, rite and rhythm (Sabbat, Pessach,
Purim) to wine on dinner tables that renders alcohol subject to control and
moderation from the beginning. Or are ethanol and mythanol two non-Jewish ways of shirking problems instead of solving them rationally? Endorsing this view not badly, Michael Ley's explanation for the Jewish love of
reasoning could also help explain the proverbially strong Jewish presence
in psychotherapy which stresses active human clearing on the ground (or on
the couch) instead of hoping for help from on high: "As Jewish monotheism,
by its renouncement of sacrifice, compels to sublimate destructive impulses,
rational ways of overcoming frustrations and psychological strain have to
be found."[437] Italian Jewish therapist Silvano Arieti (1914-1981) relates the
"creativogeneous culture" of Judaism primarily with its openness for cultural impulses and emphasis on *becoming* instead of *being*.[438] This leads us
back first to Moses' God who introduced himself as "I will be what I will
be", and second to Sigmund Freud who in *Moses and Monotheism* (1939)
interprets the specific Jewish spirituality as the result of the Second Temple's destruction – and of that second Mosaic commandment which is "more
significant than one recognizes at first. It is the prohibition to make an image
of God ... For it implied a triumph of intellectuality by prompting man to
acknowledge 'spiritual' powers in the first place; powers which cannot be
perceived by the senses but nevertheless exert indubitable and even overly
strong effects ... Hence also the discovery of soul was given, as the spiritual
principle in the individual person."[439]

3. This soul is sick by original sin, says Paul, and healable neither by works
nor reason but just by the cross. Christ's healing message, he says, should
be preached "not with wisdom and eloquence, lest the cross of Christ be

435 Freud 1990, p.116.
436 Poliakov 2003, Vol.I, p.304; Warsaw: Prager/Telushkin, p.34.
437 Ley, p.32.
438 Gilman, p.274.
439 Freud 1990, p.114-115.

emptied of its power ... Has not God made foolish the wisdom of the world? ... Jews demand signs and Greeks look for wisdom, but we preach Christ crucified" (1 Cor 1:17-23). Hence, "We destroy arguments ... and take every thought captive to obey Christ" (2 Cor 10:5).
A feminist woman gives Paul short shrift: "Mythology blocks clarity: You could almost say that's its job."[440] And Paul's myth-based program was anything but a training of intelligence. While to the Jew "the ignorant cannot be pious",[441] the non-authentic "Blessed are the poor in spirit, for their's is the kingdom of heaven" in Matthew's Pauline gospel (5:3) was always gladly heard by feudal princes in the sense of "our servants need not be book-worms". While as early as in Jesus' lifetime rabbis prompted all communities to establish public schools for children of age six to seven and limited class size to twenty-five pupils per teacher; while yet in 2nd century CE a Jewish regulation determined that no one must impede school instruction in his street because of noise annoyance, no sooner than in 1592 the Calvinist Johann I made his duchy of Palatinate-Zweibrücken the first state in the world with compulsory school attendance, and Calvinist was also the pragmatic Friedrich Wilhelm I of Prussia who in 1717 made retired army sergeants teach in the village schools of his kingly domain manors.
Already in 5th century the Babylonian Talmud had admonished communal authorities to make certain that poor children receive a free public school education: "Neglect not the children of the poor, for from them shall come forth Torah."[442] A twelfth-century monk and student of great Abaelard reported: "A Jew, however poor, if he has ten sons, would put them all to letters, not for gain, as the Christians do, but for the understanding of God's Law, and not only his sons but his daughters."[443]
In 1918 a Christian Russian official noted: "Their entire population studies. Girls too can read, even the girls of the poorest families. Every family, be it in the most modest circumstances, buys books, because there will be at least ten books in every household." Ruefully, the official contrasted the standards among even poor Jews to the bookshelves in Christian rural population: "Most of those inhabiting the huts in villages have only recently heard of an alphabet book."[444] At a Berlin book-burning on May 28, 1933, Joseph Goebbels combined his belief that "the era of an exaggerated Jewish intellectualism has ended now" with the ominous announcement that "revolutions, if they are genuine, stop nowhere".[445] Six decades later and with nicer prospects, a New York Times article on the training of real estate brokers noted the guidelines to approach potential clients: "If they are rich,

440 Kaye/Kantrowitz, p.35.
441 Lévinas 1996, p.26.
442 Nedarim 81 a (according to Telushkin 1994, p.430).
443 Smalley, Beryl: The Study of the Bible in the Middle Ages, p.52 (quoted by Prager/Telushkin, p.32).
444 Entine, p.232.
445 Goebbels' speech was published in Nazi Party gazette Völkischer Beobachter, May 12, 1933 (de.wikipedia.org/wiki/Bücherverbrennung_1933_in_Deutschland).

tell them about the country club. If they're a young couple, emphasize low property taxes. If they're Jews, tell them how good the schools are here."[446]

4. "Seems this man's got weak nerves" leading Christian-Democrat politician Wolfgang Schäuble told a female journalist about the cross-dissenting teacher Riggenmann.[447] A telling quip, for its ostentatious toughness reveals that crucifixes in primary schools are for strong nerves. When in its portrait of the cross-dissenting teacher Munich Süddeutsche Zeitung mentioned that I have been a paratrooper in military service, a male friend remarked: "So at any rate people get aware that you're not that sissy." And a man with healthy hardness sent me the following anonymous type-written letter, one of the most respectful ones I received from classroom-cross defenders in 2002:

"Despite your upscale education maybe soon the casket lid will close over dear Konrad. Then he will be able to complain to 'heavenly daddy' for His line of action 2000 years ago. Apropos, also to present-day effeminate education (behind every other German a couch doctor!) applies the verse of 1 Corinthians 1:23 f.:
'But we proclaim Christ crucified, a stumbling block to Jews and foolishness to Greeks; But to them who are called, both Jews and Greeks, Christ the power of God, and the wisdom of God.'
No offense, and with more intelligible greetings,
From an old veteran, relict of Second World War."

Obviously, it's the old man himself who wants to complain about the heavenly father's line of action. Yet he accepts it with German obedience and the justification that the cross is a device of hard and healthy, toughening and manly education that helped him survive the hard times of the war. *Upscale education* gets squeezed down by *the casket lid; effeminate education* finds its cure in the *crucifix.*
Mother Nature seems to have a different cure in mind. For if we can perceive in evolution from protozoon to human being any pervasive trend at all, it is the trend to more sensitivity in sensory organs as well as in our soul. Not a very German trend: The student Margit Boeckle considers Germany to be an especially difficult country for the sensitive ones.[448] She left her Swabian hometown and went to San Francisco, where she met Elaine Aron whose psychological concept describes the mental otherness of between 15 and 25 percent of any population. In the brains of these individuals, neuronal nets charged with the attenuation of emotions are lesser developed; therefore, fewer sensorial impressions are filtered out; more stimuli are classified as important and thus reach consciousness. This is advantageous for the whole population, since these sensitive individuals are more cautious and by their tenderer strings also quicker to perceive new dangers than the hard rock phenotypes of their species. Highly gifted children generally don't

---

446   Cf. Telushkin 1992, p.46-47; Prager/Telushkin 2003, p.30-33.
447   Der Freitag weekly, Berlin, February 2002.
448   Streitbörger, Wolfgang: Die Supersensiblen – eine übersehene Minderheit? (The super-sensitives – an overlooked minority?), in: texttransfer.de/sensible.html.

belong to the robust ones. All psychic traits of highly gifted children listed by Augsburg University chairholder Wolfgang Michaelis[449] show up in Elaine Aron's list concerning adult highly sensitive persons (HSP). While Michaelis concisely states that highly gifted children are "mostly very sensitive observers", Aron ascribes to HSPs being "enormously aware of the suffering of others", an "elevated pain-sensitivity, ... high level of empathy and fine antennas for other people's psycho-social affectivities, moods and emotions, besides their intensive experiencing of art and music". While according to Michaelis gifted children "develop high concepts of morale" and "think about all kinds of moral problems early on", highly sensitive adults according to Aron are characterized by "pronounced altruism and sense of justice ... need of harmony, high scrupulosity ... thinking in greater contexts" and "multilayered fantasy and reasoning".

Andrea Brackmann resumes the "connection between high introversion, high intelligence and high sensitivity" in the formula "Giftedness means more of all: more feeling, more thinking, more perceiving."[450] Michaelis' observation that highly gifted children "have *realangst* and environmental angst from the beginning" agrees with Aron's HSP traits as well as with Brackmann's observation of those children: "They feel above average apprehension for others and early on start pondering about environment, social problems and death"; they "not only are highly responsive on a rational, but also highly sensitive on an emotional and sensory level."[451]

Surely, crucifixes nurture neither gifted minds nor "*sensibelchen*", to say the least. Sensitive people "have thinner boundaries separating them from other people's emotions and from the tragedies and cruelties of the world. They tend to have unusually strong consciences. They avoid violent movies ..." Today's high-tech brain scanners picture the cerebral effects of cruel pictures: When these people who "can't help but feel what others feel" are exposed to "pictures of scared faces, accident victims, mutilated bodies, and polluted scenery, the amygdala – the part of the brain that plays such an important role in processing emotions – becomes strongly activated". In children's theater, little Julian "wants to run onto the stage to intervene if something evil happens" – "Rahel couldn't stand viewing anything sad or scary ..." – "If Ina witnesses someone being treated unjustly, she is shaken, unhinged and appalled". Fortunately, "a strong sense of dry humour" seems to be a special trait of gifted children, too.[452] For instance Michael: "As a pupil of a Bavarian school, for thirteen years I stared with mixed feelings at the crucifix on our classroom wall ... All laws aside, in the face of the God-son our seasoned teacher castigated his wayward pupils either with the ruler or ('Huber, glasses down!') – by hand. It wasn't my symbol properly. But

---

449 Michaelis, W., oral teaching in his seminary "Hochbegabung", Augsburg University, Summer 99; Arons p.xxi-xxii, 126-129, passim and her homepage.
450 Brackmann, p.167 and 111; see also p.15-16, 137; Brackmann confirms (p.92) the elevated pain-sensivitiy and remarks that "in a strikingly high ratio gifted persons ... are strict vegetarians".
451 Brackmann, p.16 and 48.
452 Cain, p.137-138; Brackmann, p.47-48 (Julian, Rahel, Ina) and 101 (humour).

then again, in the presence of the crucified one I could enjoy being not the only Jew in this classroom."[453]
One of those two Jews today is teaching Judaistik at Munich University, the other one still whatsoever in all Bavarian grade school classrooms. Unfortunately, robust people hardly can imagine the impact of crucifixes on highly sensitive children. Granted, these children partly can protect themselves – by dimming down their sensitivity; by complying with a culture of blunted feelings and sacred cruelty, of emotional repression and rationalized hypocrisy. Hitler's "intensive experiencing of art and music" is but one of Aron's HSP indices that apply to this man whose favourite and self-describing terms *"eiskalt"* and *"hart wie Kruppstahl"* cannot hide the fact that he had neither been an insensitive child nor an ungifted artist by any means.[454]
His either more sensitive or less beaten, in any case more gifted painter colleague Nicolas Poussin (1594-1665) shunned the *eiskalt* way of deadening emotion. He was age 52 when he, having just finished a crucifixion painting, decided not to begin the next tableau "Jesus bears his cross" any more. To a friend he wrote why: "I don't have enough joy and health any more to create such themes. The crucifixion has sickened me. It became so onerous to me. To paint Jesus now bearing his cross would kill me."[455]
Poussin lived on for 19 years, but painted no more crucifixion.

Life spoilers
"Oh, Ernie," Golda said, "you know them. Tell me why, why do the Christians hate us the way they do? They seem so nice when I look at them without my star." Golda's fiancé Ernie, the *Last of the Just* in the same name novel of gas-chamber-orphan André Schwarz-Bart, can't explain it either: "It's very mysterious ... They don't know exactly why themselves. I've been in their churches and I've read their gospel. Do you know who the Christ was? A simple Jew like your father. A kind of Hasid."
The pious Rabbi Jesus – Magdalene even called him tenderly "Rabbuni" – differed from normal pharisean Rabbis in a very human point: "Every man who has no wife is no man actually" the rabbis wrote in their great collection of debates, the Talmud (Jewamot 83 a).[456] Among the famous rabbis of two millennia only one remained unmarried – his wife had died early. And the rabbis declared it to be every man's duty to have at least two children; a man could neither be a high priest nor a member of the high court unless he had children, "it being the Jewish sages' belief that raising children humbled, humanized and increased a judge's wisdom".[457] Maccoby adds that the rabbis had "very great respect for the body" and there was kind of bodily machismo in the Talmud world at that. "Since they regarded sex as an important aspect of life, they even boasted about what huge penises

453 Michael Brenner: Wir da und die da. Süddeutsche Zeitung, Munich, January 10, 2002.
454 As to "eiskalt" see Picker, p.86.
455 Ranke-Heinemann 1994, p.340.
456 Much, p.152.
457 Prager/Telushkin, p.39.

the Rabbis had. Now this, of course, you would never find in the Christian tradition – no one talks about what huge penis St Jerome had, or St Thomas Aquinas."[458]

Not to speak of Rabbi Jesus.

What will be the effect on young people with blossoming sexuality and lots of butterflies in belly, if a handsome twenty-something who instead of flirting with a dark-eyed Madeleine or scoring goals heads straightforward to atoning sacrifice is presented to those young ones as a role model to be followed submissively? "The hatred against Judaism on its deepest level is hatred against Christianity."[459] In this analytic statement of 1939, Sigmund Freud's agrees with survivor Frank Andermann's remark of 1970 about the "Jesus-haters called Christians". More precisely: "The cult of the cross. This is the core of the clod ... The Jesus-hatred keeps the clod together from time immemorial, it dominates the Christian world."[460]

It rules a Christian world that places crucifixes above conjugal beds since Paul defines the "enemies of the cross" as those "whose god is their appetite, and whose glory is in their shame, who set their minds on earthly things" (Philippians 3:19). If the Catholic authors of the *Jerusalemer Bibel* are right with their assumption that "shame" in this verse signifies the "penis on which circumcision was done", Paul's "enemies of the cross" were just those who take as important exactly what to Yeshayahu Leibowitz "constitutes human life", namely "1) kitchen/dinner table; 2) sex/marriage; and 3) work ... The one who twisted this to an expression of ignomy was the apostle Paul."[461]

His tool of distortion was the Galilean who died so wife- and child- and joyless, so alien to laugh and carnal love that Christian anti-Semites "must spit on the Jews as 'Christ-killers' because they long to spit on the Jews as Christ-givers", as Maurice Samuel explains. How can you love a loser who by his defeat redeemed you, while this unmerited grace requires you to emulate him in similar humiliation, "carrying around the death of Jesus in our bodies" (2 Cor 4:10)? The dutiful mental gratitude for His sacrifice along with the deeply physically felt rejection of His cross yoke transforms to additional physical hatred against the crucifiers. In Franz Rosenzweig's words: "Whenever the pagan within the Christian Soul rises in revolt against the yoke of the cross, he vents his fury on the Jew."[462]

Here's what Golda's fiancé Ernie answers: "The Christians say they love him, but I think they hate him without knowing it. So they take the cross by the other end and make a sword out of it and strike us with it! Do you get it, Golda?' he suddenly shouted. 'They take the cross and turn it round, they turn it round, my God ... Poor Jesus! If he came back on earth and had to see how the pagans make a sword of his cross to slay his own brothers and sisters ... And maybe he does see it ..."[463]

458 Maccoby 1987, p.92.
459 Strauss Feuerlicht, p.37.
460 Andermann, p.61-62 and 100.
461 Leibowitz, p.84.
462 Samuel, The Great Hatred, NY 1941 (Flannery, p.293); Rosenzweig: Eckardt p.28-29.
463 Schwarz-Bart, André: The Last of the Just, p.323-324; cf. Lapide 1988, p.87.

IX   Chosen
By whom, what for?

*"There cannot be two chosen peoples. We are the people of God ...
Two worlds are opposing each other! Godman and Satanman!
The Jew is the counterman, the antiman. The Jew is the creature
of another God. He must have grown from another root of the
human stem."*   Adolf Hitler[464]

In 1837, the doctor of medicine Georg Büchner, a social rebel prosecuted
by Hesse authorities, died in Zurich at the age of 23 years, doing research
on an infectious disease whose pathogen science had not discovered yet:
typhus. In his tragedy fragment *Woyzeck* the young genius Büchner left a
paradigm for this era of rolling progress and receding myths. The soldier
Woyzeck is the human guinea pig of his doctor, allowed to eat *"nothing but
peas, cruciferae, mark this well! We'll have a revolution in science, I blow it
up. Urea 0.10, ammonium nitrate, hyperoxydul – Woyzeck, must he not piss
again?"*
In the tavern, Woyzeck listens to the journeyman's sermon:
*"Truly, I say to you: Of what should the peasant, the cooper, the doctor have
made his living if God had not created man? Of what should the tailor have
made his living if God had not implanted man a sense of shame? Of what
the soldier, if God had not equipped man with the need to strike dead one
another? So don't doubt it – yes, it's lovely and fine, but all worldliness is
evil, even the money passes into putrefaction. To finish, my beloved hearers,
let us piss cross-over as yet, in order that a Jew dies!"*
If Woyzeck's urine is examined by the doctor, okay, that's comprehensible.
But why can two urine jets kill a Jew if running cross over? The irrational
reason for such little-boy-games does interest science just as much as the
welfare of a guinea pig named Woyzeck interests the doctor. The dietary
pea-test leaves Woyzeck with delusional ideas. At the Jewish broker's shop
he buys a cheap knife, since the drum major with whom his fiancée Mary
two-times him "shall have an economic death". But who is to die cheaply in
the end is Woyzeck's philandering Mary and then he himself. Cap shut, ape
dead, science proceeds forward. Economic disparity? Economists research
upon. Who dies or survives? Darwin's theory explains. Why do Jews make
trouble, since 1800 years? Racism clarifies, and economic killing works already in the slaughterhouses.
"If the Crusaders possessed the same organization and technology of death
as the Nazis, they would have achieved a final solution", Robert Michael
deems, while Lawrence Swaim terms the holocaust an "application of the
industrial method" to Christian pogrom and asserts that Christians would
have performed this project "long before the 1940s if they'd had sufficient

---

464 Hermann Rauschning: Gespräche mit Hitler. Zurich 2005, p.227-228.

technology"[465] Both views are doubtful by at least two reasons. First, a (despite of so much) ethically founded Christian ecclesia whose favorite element was not fire but the water of baptism, had successfully applied this tool for 1900 years; and second, she needed the Jews – as genial French mathematician and mystic Blaise Pascal (1623-1662) explains in his *Pensées*: "It is an amazing thing, and worthy of particular attention, to see this Jewish people existing so many years in perpetual misery, it being necessary as a proof of Jesus Christ both that they should exist to prove Him and that they should be miserable because they crucified Him."

Pascal starts out from the doctrine of Augustine who presented the Jews as the tools of Satan in the savior's crucifixion – reliable forever in their denial of Jesus'victory. Therefore they had to be kept living; the age of wholesale killing had to be prepared by a saeculum which substituted faith by science, replaced mythical believes by rational approach – while old holy images still dominated life and education so pervasively that Pascal's compatriot Sartre stated after 1945: "The Antisemite chose the Jew as object of hate because of the religious abhorrence he always instilled ... From earliest on the killing of Christ rests with him. Has one ever thought about the unbearable situation of people who are condemned to live amid of a society which adores the God they allegedly have killed?"[466]

"But Christianity alone could not produce a Holocaust": Accepting this not too relieving judgement of John Weiss[467], this chapter however holds the twofold thesis that cross-faith-rooted religious anti-Judaism was the sociopsychological foundation not only of secular "antisemitism" but also of eugenic racism plainly, and that the scapegoat was chosen on grounds of the goat's annoying, genetically incarnate stubbornness against good old sacrifice delusion. And that whereas the secular killing under crooked crosses continued to happen "over cross", Pascal's postulate had to be crooked but in two points: "It being now unnecessary that they should exist to prove Him; and that they should die miserable because they crucified Him."

Little boys had come to this yet long before. The Spanish variant of Büchner's pissing-out trick usually started with one boy asking the age-old question: "Who killed Jesus?"
"The Jews" was the correct answer.
"And what does one do with Jews?"
Now the boy would spew some spittle on the floor and smear it with one foot drawing the sign of the cross ... *Los judios mataron a Jesus y había que aplastarlos.*"[468]

---

465   Michael, p.183; Swaim 2013, p.162. For a synopsis of anti-Jewish measures of the Church and the Nazi Government see Hilberg 1982, p.15-17; Czermak, p.294-299 and Prager/Telushkin, p.88-89.
466   Sartre (p.142, 158) wrote this in 1946, praising the Jews' "wonderful role in the resistance", where they, "yet before the communists started action, made up the main cadres".
467   Weiss, Chicago 1997, p.viii.
468   Bonnin, p.99: *"The Jews killed Jesus and one had to crush them."*

While the little Spaniards never had any doubt about the reason of hating Jews, great thinker Immanuel Kant had to find a secular motive. Judaism "excluded the whole humankind from his community", Kant asserted in his 1794 critique of religion. "They regarded themselves as the chosen people of Jehova, a fact that incited the hostility of all peoples."[469] In an editorial of November 27, 1919, the British Times utters the same charge now based on contemporary racist relining: "The essence of Jewry is, above all, a racial pride, the believe in a superiority, the faith in the final triumph, the conviction that the Jewish brain is superior to the Christian brain; summarized, an attitude corresponding to the innate persuasion of the Jews being the chosen people, destined to become the regents and law-givers of human race."[470] In his London exile, Sigmund Freud in 1939 retraces the feelings of exclusion put forth by Kant and Times to sibling jealousy: "I dare to assert that till this day the other peoples still have not outgrown the jealousy against the people who impersonates itself as the first-born, favorite child of God the Father."[471]

However, what Freud, Kant, Times undervalued is how tightly the feeling of chosenness belongs to the "healthy self-confidence" of almost all "important" peoples. Concerning the British, their later Premier Cecil Rhodes noted in 1877: "I claim that we are the first race in the world and that it is the better for the human race, the more we inhabit of the world."

The well-travelled author of the whaling novel "Moby Dick" said it flat out: "We Americans are the chosen people – the Israel of our times. We carry the tabernacle with the liberties of this world ... God has predestined great things for us." Some five generations later, President Ronald Reagan successfully reactivated the Melville-like view whose core content Harvard historian Paul D. Erickson describes in *Myth America*, namely "that we are the chosen people, blessed by God, and that we work on earth as his agents." Polish author Adam Mickiewicz in 1832 viewed Poland in the center of nations, being politically crucified as Jesus was bodily. Just like His holy suffering, Poland's suffering served as sacred offering for the whole mankind; Poland's national resurrection would redeem all nations, as Poland is the "Jesus among the nations".

During the 1990s, the Metropolitan (archbishop) Ioann of St.Petersburg did not grow tired emphasizing that "the whole fire of hatred of this nation of God-killers" were "in a logical and inevitable way focussed on the nation which carries God in herself" – i.e. the Russian nation.[472]

It may be mere coincidence that all these pompous national self-inflations have white authors; as incidental as that just the antiracist Abraham Lincoln praised his nation, tongue in cheek, as "almost chosen people" or that multicolored Brazilians would not expect their divine compatriot to use one of their ever overcrowded busses: "Deus é Brasileiro – mas não pega ônibus."

---

469 Kant 1793, Third Piece, Second Compartment (humankind = Menschengeschlecht).
470 Finguerman, p.16-17.
471 Freud 1990, here as quoted from CW, Vol.XIII, Frankfurt on Main 1997, p.197 by Primor / von Korff, p.190.
472 Wistrich 2010, p.172.

Hardly incidental is the deadly serious attitude in which the quoted four white *enlarge-your-people*-efforts combine a racial-national with a Christian-religious component. Already Justin the Martyr (born around 100 in Palestine and died in Rome 165) asserted that the true people of Abraham, Isaac, Jacob and Judah were those "whom the crucified one guided to God."[473] On that note Richard Wagner, the most musical of all Jew-haters, composed a rather pompous aria of *deutschvölkisch* chosenness: "In the German people, world's oldest primordially legitimate royal house has survived. It hails from a God-Son who by his kin is called Siegfried and by the rest of earth's peoples is named Christ ... The Germans are the oldest people, their blood-relative king is a Nibelung, and reigning on their shoulders this king has to maintain world-dominance", and so on.[474]

The aversion against the cross-averse people, audible yet in Justin, gets *forzato* in Wagner, and it shrills in Hitler's confrontation of "Godman and Satanman". Was this aversion the well of racism? Or was the myth of races rather a reflex against the "racism" of Jewish exclusiveness? Heinrich von Treitschke (1834-1896), German historian and creator of the slogan "The Jews are our misfortune" saw their only virtue in having kept their race "relatively pure".

It was, however, the Christian white United States where for purposes of purity marriages between Blacks and Whites were forbidden in 19 states in 1913. Eleven years later Hitler, under strong influence of Treitzschke but also of US-racists, wrote in *Mein Kampf* about the Jew: "Thus he uses all the knowledge he acquires in the other one's schools only in the service of his race ... While he seems to overflow with 'enlightenment', 'progress', 'freedom', 'humanity' and so on, he himself practices the most rigorous seclusion of his race. To be sure, he sometimes attaches his women to influential Christians, but he keeps his male lineage always pure. He poisons the blood of the other ones but safeguards his own."[475] This is the psycho couch talk of a man who was obsessed with the suspicion that his own hated father, sired by a Jew, had poisoned his mother's blood and his own. It sounds more credible if French philosopher and resistance fighter Simone Weil asserts "the Jewish" to be "the only one racist religion ... For they have as godhead a race". But here the daughter of a Russian Jewish mother and an Alsacian Jewish physician succumbs to zeitgeist and her Catholic studies which however did not lead her to the baptismal font of universal faith. "To her, alone the bonds of spirit counted", explains her biographer, counting "Homer, Platon, Kant, Marx, Alain" as spiritual ancestors of *La Sainte Simone* and wondering: "Her physical genealogy starts to fade in murkiness yet beyond her great-grandparents. This is the more unsatisfying as Simone Weil herself says that the most precious property of man in temporal dimension is the continuity forth and backwards.[476] This physical, sexually transmissive continuity does

---

473 Michael, p.24.
474 Wagner, Richard: Die Nibelungen. Leipzig 1907, p.137 (acc. to Primor / von Korff, p.193-194).
475 Hitler, p.346.
476 Krogmann (p.11 and 101), quoting Weil, S.: Lettre a un Religieux, Paris 1951, p.15.

matter to Jewish "religion of the body". Races are a racist construct, as was proved by Franz Boas whose Jewish family tree did not fade beyond his great-grandparents. Jewish racists do exist galore, but a Jewish race no more than a Catholic or Sunnite one since getting Jewish was easy before the cross became the separator.

Yet in the exodus starting from Egypt "a mixed multitude went with them" (Ex 12:38). Karl Marx had this in mind when he, in a letter to Friedrich Engels, sneered at the alleged negrois features of Ferdinand Lassalle, the pioneer of German social democratic movement: "It's quite clear to me now that he, which also is proved by his cranial formation and his hair, descends from the Negroes who joined the journey of Moses out of Egypt."[477] With his Cushite, i.e. black Ethiopian wife (Num 12:1) Moses himself may be typical for this *miscige*-nation. "Foreigners will join them and unite with the descendants of Jacob", Isaiah (14:1) prophecies 700 years before Jesus. "I am dark, but comely, o daughters of Jerusalem" says, around 400 BCE, the bride in Song of Songs, "don't stare at me because I'm swarthy, because the sun has gazed upon me". Modern genetics ascribes 3 to 5 percent of Jewish ancestry to sub-Saharan Africans, thanks to an exchange of genes approximately 72 generations or about 2,000 years ago,[478] that means around the same first century BCE when after the conversion of Queen Helena of Adiabene in present-day Kurdistan also many Kurds became Jewish; almost at the time when Great Hillel the Elder, at whose death in 10 CE Jesus was some fourteen years old, eased conversion by teaching the whole Torah while the hurried convert-to-be kept standing on one leg: "What you dislike, do not to others, now go and learn." Few decades later, Matthew has Jesus criticize those phariseans who "travel over land and sea to win a single convert" (23:15).

Small wonder that in 5th century Italy, for example in Emperor Theodosius' new capital Ravenna, every third Jew was a descendant of pagan converts.[479] This was minatory: Becoming Jewish mostly happened informally, joining in Jewish domesticity. Constantine prohibited conversion in 315; it became a capital offence in 407, and as from the synod of Orleans in 541 there hardly was any council that did not menace the most severe punishments for turning Jewish. Getting classified as lunatics or candidates of eternal hellfire would not deter the renegades, but death penalty threatening the convert as well as the hosting community urged Judaism to internalize this ordered exclusiveness and curl to the hedgehog stance by which it "adopted the attitude of the Jews' oppressors".[480] Far from Rome, however, between Black and Caspian Sea, still in 8th century the ruling house of the Khazars and parts of this Turk people converted to Judaism.

By the late 19th century, in the debate about Jewish skin colour, "ethnological literature" had modulated into a general consensus "that the Jews were

---

477   Marx to Engels, 1862 (MEW 30; 257), acc. to Wikiquote (German); cf.Lewis, p.112.
478   Gianna Palmer: Genes Tell Tale of Jewish Ties to Africa, The Forward, Aug.12, 2011.
479   Dimont, p.213; Dennis Prager in Epstein, p.90.
480   Dennis Prager in Epstein, p.92.

'black' or at least 'swarthy'". But when a German study of 1870 yielded that the rate of "pure blond" versus "black-haired" was 11 to 42 among Jews and 32 to 14 among Christians and that the "mixed types" made up 47 percent among Jews and 54 among Christians, the German Anthropological Review reduced these data to the simple statement that there are less blonds among Jews.[481]

In 1922, the later on celebrated "Rassen-Experte" Hans F.K. Günther (nick-named *Rassengünther*) defined the Jews, against Treitzschke and Hitler, as an "oriental-anatolian-nordic-hamitic-negroide race mix".[482] To León Polia-kov they are "just the contrary of a race",[483] while Shlomo Sand views pre-sent-day Judaism as the "product of a dynamic religion which spread in the antique and medieval world. In line with this, the biological provenance of the Jews is rich and variegated."[484] To this diversity belong for instance the Semitic language culture of the Ethiopian Falash, or the Lemba in South Africa and Simbabwe among whom, presumably due to their descent from Yemenite Judaism, the famous "Cohen gene" is more frequent than in Israel. Yet in third century CE, Rabbi Ulla criticized the purist attitude of his friend Rabbi Yehuda bar Yechezkel: "Do we know for sure that we ourselves do not descend from those pagans who during the siege of Jerusalem have raped the virgins of Zion?"[485] Wolf Mankowitz considers that "the original Semitic stock of the Jews has been adulterated out of recognition in the millennia of Jewish history" and points to the same violent factor: "Countless Jewish women were raped in the course of Gentile persecutions, and every child born in this way was brought up as a Jew and treated as a full Jew in every way."[486] When Rap poet Y-Love, born from Puertorican-Ethiopian parents in New York, complained to the director of his Jerusalem Torah-school about having overheard his fellow students talking about the "nigger", the Rabbi told them the Why of Jewish whiteness: "The sages of the Bible were dark-skinned. Moses was dark-skinned. The only reason for your white faces is that your great-grandmothers were raped by some Cossacks ..."[487]

In largely chronological order I will set forth below that race and racial pu-rity are originally rather Christian concepts, emerged from Christian-Jewish conflict and Spanish *limpieza de sangre*.
In his letter to the Romans (9:7-12) Paul prepared the issue by re-defining God's people in a non-physical but spiritual way: "Not all of Abraham's children are his true descendants, but [quoting Gen 21:12] 'It is through Isaac that descendants shall be named for you'. This means that it is not the

481 Kaye/Kantrowitz, p.15; referring to Sander Gilman: The Jew's Body, p.172.
482 Hans Friedrich Karl Günther: Rassenkunde des deutschen Volkes, Munich 1922, p.453; thus cited by Karl-Josef Müller, Jüdische Zeitung, June 2008, p.27; as to Treitzschke, see Weiss, Chicago 1997, p.133.
483 Poliakov/Delacampagne 1979, p.184.
484 Sand 2010, p.18.
485 Coudenhove-Kalergi, p.135.
486 Maccoby 1987, p.73.
487 Jüdische Zeitung, June 2008, p.17.

children of the flesh who are the children of God, but the children of the promise are counted as descendants." A breathtaking argument, since Isaac had offspring just because he – contrarily to Jesus – was not sacrificed in his bachelor years. But Paul goes on with Isaac's sons, deviding them into one Jewish Esau and one Christian Jacob: "'The elder shall serve the younger.' As it is written: 'I have loved Jacob, but I have hated Esau'. What then are we to say?"

I say: A masterpiece of Pauline argumentation (brashly misusing Maleachi 1:2-3) and a basic example of the formidable cleaving method we saw in Jesus/Barabbas, Judas/Iscariot, father/sacrificer. Paul's disciple Matthew transforms his teacher's cleaving into a dreadful verse (27:25) which offers the racist key terms *Volk – Blut – Erbe* (nation-blood-heritage) so handily: "Then the *whole people* answered: His *blood* be on *us* and our *children!*" Where did Matthew take this "blood-on-head" metaphor from? "*Dam'ekha al rosh'ekha ki pi'ekha aná* ..." Thus reads David's condemnation of the mourning young Amalekite who had killed the defeated King Saul on Saul's own demand: "Your blood be on your head", said David, "since your mouth has testified against you when you said 'I put the Lord's anointed to death'" (2 Samuel 1:16). Matthew takes this phrase by which David condemns the unvoluntary, tragical executioner of the suicidal, depressive, failed Messiah Saul; he takes it from the mouth of David and puts it on the lips of the Jewish people to have them condemn the failed anointed one Jesus.

Around 386, Church Father Chrysostom took the word συνάγογή (synágoge, meeting) literal: "Where Christ-killers meet, the cross is being offended." He calls the synagogue "a house of whores, a theatre, a den of robbers, lair of wild animals" and applies a verse of Luke (19:27) against them: "If animals aren't good for work, they are marked for slaughter ... That is why Christ said: 'But as for these enemies of mine, who did not want me to reign over them, bring them here and slaughter them before me'."

Taking up Paul's fission of physical Esau and spiritual Jacob, Church Father Jerome (347-420) paints the "children of the flesh" as Judases altogether, as innately evil creatures who betrayed the Lord for money. Innately Jewish means marked forever, as Isidore of Seville (560-636), quoting Jeremiah (13:23), proves with two examples of unchanging nature: "Can the Cushite change his skin or the leopard his spots?"[488]

Unaware of this unchangeability, in 1096 the crusaders gave free choice to the Hebrews of Mainz: "Either the Jews convert or they will be wiped out totally, they and their children down to the last toddler at the breast." For guilty they were altogether: "Behold, the time has come to avenge the crucified one whom their forefathers murdered. Now leave no one over and let no survivor escape, also no child and no baby in the cradle."[489]

488 Sussman, p.31 and 33.
489 Stern, Moritz: Hebräische Berichte über die Judenverfolgungen während der Kreuzzüge. Berlin 1892, p.176 and 169; Eidelberg: The Jews and the Crusaders, p.102; Chazan: European Jewry, p.57 and 247 (cited by Michael, p.63-66).

When in 1130 the well-baptized Anacletus II was elected to the Holy See, Bernard of Clairvaux called it "an insult of Christ that the son of a Jew occupies the chair of Peter". (At that, Anacletus had but one Jewish great-great-grandfather). When the plague raged in 1349, Berthold, bishop of Strasbourg and president of a Council of Alsacian Towns, demanded that all Jews be killed off *"mit Kind und Kegel"* i.e. kith and kin and, once again, sparing no one, not even "the children nor the infant in the crib". Although the burgomeister Conrad of Winterthur and others tried to help the Jews, it happened: On a Sabbath coinciding with Valentine's day the Jews, under the pretext of expulsion, were led out of town to a makeshift wooden house and burnt to death in flames they however could escape through water, since "those who would accept baptism one let live, also many young children were taken from their resisting mothers and fathers, and baptised."[490]

In 1458, Alfonso de Espina, a Franciscan monk and confessor to Henry IV, wrote a parable that foreshadowed selection at Auschwitz, giving free choice to the chosen people. In the friar's fantasy about how the king of England solved the problem of converted Jews who had "occupied all posts" and "enslaved the Christians" in the kingdom, "God then put wisdom into the heart of the king, and he rid his kingdom of these serpents, in the following manner. He pitched two tents on the sea-shore. In one tent he placed a scroll of the Law, and in the other a cross. Then he sat between the two tents on the royal throne, and courteously summoned the converted Jews to indicate the religion they would rather choose. All the Jews, with their womenfolk and children, then ran joyfully into the tent where the Torah was. As they came into the tent, they were slaughtered one by one and their bodies were flung into the sea. Thus the land was purged and an end was put to this affliction."[491] Equally radical, in 16th century the French poet Ronsard back-projected his cross-related destruction fantasy *Je n'aime pas les juifs* onto the Roman troops of 70 CE:

I do not love the Jews, for to the cross they nailed
the Messiah our Christ who wipes what we have failed
You Vespasian's son, Titus the great, destroy their town destroy their race
Don't leave them time nor spell nor space
to elsewhere spy for other dwelling place.

Citing this poem, Luiz Nazario explains how Jesus' nails entered Jewish genes: "The doctrine transformed the political accusation into a hereditary assertion, as if the repudiation of Christ's godliness and the guilt of his crucifixion were curses magically transmitted by blood."[492]

Could baptismal waters really cure this blood-transmitted curse? For more than 200 years, Spanish Church had made this attempt by more or less

490 Rohrbacher/Schmidt, p.197-198; Michael, p.93, refers to Graetz, H.: The History of the Jews, 4:108; Rohrbacher and Schmidt quote Haverkamp, A. (ed.): Zur Geschichte der Juden im Deutschland des späten Mittelalters und der frühen Neuzeit. Stuttgart 1981, p.30.
491 De Espina: Fortalitium Fidei, cited by Liebman Jacobs, p.24-25.
492 Nazario, p.38 and 51.

coerced conversions. But yet in 1449, the first defense against conversos was promulgated in Toledo. In 1495, Pope Alexander VI formally ratified a statute of *limpieza de sangre* (purity of blood), barring all conversos from membership in a Spanish order; in 1515, the archbishop of Seville went on to barr second generation descendants of conversos from ecclesiastical office; in 1530, the bishop of Cordova banned even the admission of *cristiano nuevo* choirboys, since their impure blood was credited with an irresistible tendency to heresy.

At the same time in Germany Martin Luther buried his hope that many Jews would become "enrapt to Christ" like the Rabbi Jakob Gipher who had accepted baptism in 1519 and now was teaching Hebrew in Wittenberg. Frustrated in his expectations and upset by the news about those "judaizing" Sabbatarians in Moravia, Luther in a sermon of September 1539 declared that Jews undergo no significant modifications by baptism. Hence, "to settle the issue once for all, the Jews should be expulsed from Christian community altogether. An end to the curse of mankind."[493]

With logical coerciveness, the decrease of faith in the spiritual force of baptism led to (at first but anti-Jewish) racism as the belief in the power of physical biology. The Spanish priest Augustín Salucia warned in 1599, that for racial defilement one Jewish great-great-grandfather sufficed even if the rest of fifteen great-great-grandparents were "extraordinarily pious and noble Christians".[494] In Padre Salucia's Spain the cult of *limpieza de sangre* became so obsessive that in 16th century all religious orders except the Jesuites required Jew-free certificates of descent from their novices. Ignatius López de Loyola, the founder of Jesuite order, was the non-racist exception: When he was accused of having partly Jewish ancestry, he replied, "If only I did! What could be more glorious than to be of the same blood as the Apostles, the Blessed Virgin, and our Lord Himself?" Some of Loyola's closest collaborators, as for instance his successor Diego Lainez, were of Jewish descent.[495] Nevertheless, in 1592 the order gave in, expelled its New Christians, falsified the pedigree of Lainez posthumously,[496] and in 1608 his successors mandated that every novice had to prove his pure descent back to the fifth generation – a rule that remained valid until 1946, eleven years after the Nuremberg Laws. The contiguity, however, between *limpieza de sangre* and *Ariernachweis*, between stakes and ovens is evident yet in the "Warning Call Against the Jews" published by Fra Francisco de Torrejoncillo in 1673: "To be an enemy of the Christians and of Christ, it is not necessary to have a Jewish father and mother; one pa-rent would suffice. It makes little difference if the father is not; it is enough that the mother be. And it means nothing if she herself is not entirely; half would be enough. Even less. A quarter

493 Trachtenberg, p.218, here cited from Shoham, p.166.
494 Hering Torres, Max S.: Rassismus in der Vormoderne? Die ‚Reinheit des Blutes‘ im Spanien der frühen Neuzeit. Frankfurt on Main 2006, p.221 (quoted by Junginger, p.29).
495 Donnelly, John Patrick, S.J.: Antonio Possevino and Jesuits of Jewish Descent. Marquette University 1986; elvis.rowan.edu/kilroy/JEK/07/31b.html: Ignatius Loyola, Mystic, Educator, Preacher, and Founder of the Jesuits.
496 Poliakov 2003, Vol.II, p.226.

would do it. One eighth. And now the Holy Inquisition has discovered that Judaism is practiced to the twenty-first generation."[497] Consequently, until the beginning of 20th century the Chuetas of Mallorca were required to sit in a special pew in their Catholic church, wearing a yellow jacket, the mark of their Jewish ancestors who survived the great auto in 1691. Padres with Chueta blood were not allowed to say mass in the island's cathedral until the 1960s.[498]

While in Catholic Spain *limpieza de sangre* became "the first example in history of legalized racism" and in 17th century Brazil many aspirants for military or religious orders were rejected because of their "*sangue judeu, mouro, ou negro*",[499] the concept of "racism" still had to be invented. Bernard Lewis remarks that "the word *race* was for example normally and even officially used in Britain to denote the four elements – English, Scottish, Welsh, and Irish – that together composed the British nation."[500] Max Hering Torres points to Spanish Archbishop Silíceo, who in 1547 was probably the first to use the word *raza* in relation to limpieza de sangre – stating that clerical office was accessible but to Old Christians "without race of a Jew, Moore or heretic".[501] What caused the change from the "ethnic" to the "racist" notion of race?

The enlightened philosopher and would-be Church eraser Voltaire, famous for his "*Écrasez l'infame*", was engaged in various and not always very enlightened financial enterprises. The most relevant was a large-scale investment in a slave-trading enterprise out of the port of Nantes, which according to contemporary witnesses made him "one of the twenty wealthiest persons in the kingdom." In his *Traité de Metaphysique*, Voltaire has his narrator observe that white men "seem to me superior to Negroes, just as Negroes are superior to monkeys and monkeys to oysters." Obviously, Voltaire – and European society – in order to preserve their self-image needed a makeshift moral justification for their immoral but enormously profitable trade with abducted Africans: hierarchical racism. "New rationalizations had to be made to justify mistreating the peoples Europeans encountered and new theories formed to explain their place in the universe."[502] John Locke (1632-1704) indeed maintained the creatural equality of Eve's offspring and their natural rights, which however did not apply to American Indians since they did not use their land appropriately. "Slaves are necessary, otherwise sugar would become too expensive" said Baron de Montesquieu (1689-1755), prone to sweat black workforce for white sweetness. The Africans are "black from head to toes", the Baron observed, and one could hardly understand "how God could send a soul into an entirely black body [since it is] so natural to

---

497 Torrejoncillo, p.62. Ariernachweis = Aryan certificate; limpieza ...: = purity of blood.
498 Carvajal, p.188 and 287.
499 Legalized racism: Poliakov 2003, Vol.II, p.221; as to "Jewish, Moorish, Negro blood", Novinsky (2013, p.17) is quoting here verbatim from the "Apontamentos sobre Inquirições no Santo Officio" of Arquivo Nacional da Torre do Tombo, Lisbon.
500 Lewis, p.33.
501 Hering Torres: Rassismus in der Vormoderne, p.220-221 (quoted by Junginger, p.29).
502 Sussman, p.12.

think that skin color constitutes the essence of humanity."[503] David Hume (1711-1776) ventured to disagree with the Bible, ascribing non-white humans to separate roots different from Eve's womb and concluding "that the negroes and generally all other species of humans ... are naturally inferior to the white." Immanuel Kant (1724-1804) taught geography at the coast of Baltic Sea by means of descriptions of travellers like one Father Labat who in 1724 quite respectfully had described the household of a black carpenter in Santo Domingo. Kant turned the monogamous Negro into a polygamist and asserts: "This guy was wholly black from head to feet, a clear prove that what he said was silly."[504] As further prove Kant takes Hume's bet that no one could cite a single example in which a Negro has shown talent.[505] Not before 1795, the now 71-year-old Kant in "To Eternal Peace" would criticize the "oppression of the natives" considering that "the Sugar Islands, this site of the most cruel and sophisticated slavery, give no good returns".[506]

If antisemitism is "the socialism of the witless guys", the scientific returns quoted above confirm Yirmiyahu Yovel's quip of racism as the "science of the witless guys". The European racist elite's level of reasoning hardly surpassed the standard of their younger colleague Dr. Samuel Morton (1799-1851), well-known for his technique of measuring the volumes of crania by filling them with peppercorns. "We of the South should consider him as our benefactor, for aiding most materially in giving to the negro his true position as inferior race" Morton's friends wrote in his obituary, abusing Jeremiah's popular biologism: "We believe the time is not far distant when it will be universally admitted that neither can the leopard change his spots, nor the Ethiopian his skin."[507]

Exactly this unchangeability – the basic axiom of racism – Christian Europe had learned in the attempt to convert Jews against their will to faith in the cross. The statutes of limpieza de sangre not only were heretical in their contradiction to universal Christian ethics; they also proved, as "first racist theory of modern times"[508] the defeat of the spiritual-cultural (baptism, faith, doctrine) against the sexually inherited corporeality discounted by Paul. Baptism made no Jew a faithful Christian and no Negro a free man. "African Blacks were sold as slaves even when baptized; in their case, too, holy water could not purify the blood."[509]

Cui bono? The social construct of race serves whom? "Fecit cui prodest" is Poliakov's reply: The maker is the profiteer. Racism as the ideological tool of Western bourgeoisie, "intended to justify the black slave trade and colonial depredation"[510] reveals its origin in its technique of separation: In-

503   Ch. de Montesquieu, De l'esprit des loix; Œuvres complètes. Paris 1950, Vol.I, p.330.
504   Monika Firla: "Rassismus und Kulturalismus", in: Mitteilungen des Instituts für Wissenschaft und Kunst, Vienna 1997, Vol.52, issue 3, p.7-17.
505   Sussman, p.28.
506   Kant, in his essay Zum ewigen Frieden, p.23.
507   Sussman, p.31.
508   Yovel, p.73.
509   Yovel, p.222.
510   Poliakov 2003, Vol.III, p.125.

quisitors found in Brazil "1/2 New Christians" and even the "1/5 cristã nova" Ana Gertrudes de Bragança. In the US of 1900, "octoroon" Blacks were accepted as Whites, in Germany of 1935 "quarter Jews" as Aryans; the later "one-drop-law" of the US, declaring that a single black ancestor made all his outwardly white descendants black[511] is the equivalent to Torrejoncillo's judaizing of the blood up to the twenty-first generation. "The cross between a white man and a Negro is a Negro ... and the cross between one of the three European races and a Jew is a Jew", big racist and big game hunter Madison Grant (1865-1937) wrote in 1918. In 1924 he wisecracked in a letter that Harvard University was now paying the price of liberalism by having to create "kykological tests to save herself from being swamped."[512] The term "kykological" is an eerily funny derivate of Kikes, i.e. the Killers of Jesus Krist, i.e. the same people of whom Torrejoncillo knows: "Some writers say that this bad smell or stench is common to all of them, the descendants of those who were complices in the killing of our Lord Jesus Christ."[513]
In his *Centinela contra judíos*, Padre Torrejoncillo also refers to the first "racial" classification of mankind as the tripartite offspring of Noah's three sons: "Sen [Sem] conquered Asia, particularly the eastern part of Syria; Can [Ham] seized Africa, Judea, Egypt und Arabia; and Japhet the rest, which was Europe."[514]
On grounds of Genesis chapter 10, Christians like Torrejoncillo, and to a lesser extent also Muslims and Jews, believed that Noah's sons Sem and Ham represented the eponymous ancestors of Hebrews with their various cognates (Semites) and the dark-skinned peoples of Africa (Hamites), while Japhet was the ancestor of the Medes, the Greeks, and the Persians/Iranians from Eryana, the land of the Aryans. The simplification went on when in 1781 German philologist A.L.Schlözer coined a new name for a group of languages that Gottfried Wilhelm Leibniz had named "Arabic" languages: "The Syrians, Babylonians, Hebrews and Arabs were one people", Schlözer asserted. "Even the Phoenicians, who were Hamites, spoke this language which I might call the Semitic."[515]
The term gained acceptance among linguists. In 1860 the French historian, critical theologian and expert of Semitic languages Ernest Renan was attacked sharply when in his opus magnum *"La Vie de Jesús"* he presented the Nazarene as a man posthumously called divine. Renan reproached the "Semites" – in his view Arabs, Muslims, Jews – with being alien to military, political, scientific and spiritual progress, while their conceit of chosenness incurred hatred on them *since 1800 years* (!). Altogether, Renan stated the "dire simplicity of the Semite spirit". When Jewish-German scholar Moritz Steinschneider, who translated the Koran to Hebrew, worked in Ox-

---

511 Novinsky 2009, p. 176, 186, 187, 219; Tobin/Tobin/Rubin, p.43; Sussman, p.73.
512 Sussman, p.89 resp. 206, here quoting Spiro, J.P.: Defending the Master Race. Burlington 2009, p.331.
513 Torrejoncillo, p.169.
514 Torrejoncillo, p.125.
515 August Wilhelm Schlözer, in J.G. Eichhorn, ed.: Repertorium für Biblische und Morgenländische Litteratur [sic], Leipzig 1777-1780, 8: p.161-163 (cited by Lewis, p.44).

ford every summer, headed a Jewish girls' school and was deemed "the most universal Jewish scholar of his time"[516] objected and called Renan's assessments "anti-Semitic", this word was seized quickly. The atheist-anarchic German journalist Wilhelm Marr who in 1873, 1874 and 1877 had divorced from (probably too intelligent) Jewish wives, substantivized the term and made use of its academical appeal in founding his *Antisemiten-Liga*. "We have among us an elastic, tenacious, intelligent tribe who knows to bring to bear abstract realism in all forms" Marr wrote in his essay about "The victory of *Judenthum* over *Germanenthum*, as seen from a non-confessional viewpoint"[517] of which yet in the same year 1879 twelve editions were sold and avidly read by a German audience that obviously imputed to their half percent of Jewish fellow citizens and economic rivals anything but dire simplicity.

Just because Marr's neologism hides the confessional, cross-related motives of Jew-hatred it went down well and prevails up today. Well received was also his essay *Goldene Ratten und rothe Mäuse*, presenting the interesting variant of Jewish conspiracy where they control capitalism and communism synchronously. In his old age however Marr renounced the whole schmontzes and returned to the anarchist ideals of his youth – having masked old motives with secular newspeak successfully.

There was clerical newspeak also. The gospels repeatedly have Jesus address his Jewish contemporaries with a collective term given as *genea* in the Greek original, *generatio* in the Latin Vulgata and *génération* in French. For instance in Mark (9:19): "You unbelieving *generation*, how long shall I be with you?" Or in Matthew (12:39; 16:4): "A wicked and adulterous *generation* asks for a sign!" And in Luke (21:31): "This *generation* will be held responsible for the blood of all the prophets that has been shed since the beginning of the world". Jules Isaac verifies how French theologists during 20th century proceeded from *génération* to *race*: "God's avenge will strike without mercy this deicidal *race* and demand an account for all blood injustly shed." Or "Jesus speaks his condemning judgement over the murderers of the prophets, their sons, the present generation and the whole *race* of Israel." And "Israel ... will pe punished as a whole people for their crimes ... this is the fate that waits for this perfidious *race*."[518]

What crime had made this *race* a mean and mighty collective was no question for the readers of those theological texts. What secular antisemites endeavoured to express in a modern, non-religious way, Hitler could reveal to his German audience in traditional diction: "Thus he [the Jew] continues his doom-laden way, until another force confronts him and in gargantuan wrestling throws the heaven-stormer back to Lucifer."[519] In January 1942, ten days after holocaust planning *Wannseekonferenz*, the Führer, again referring

---

516 Stemberger, G.: Geschichte der jüdischen Literatur. Munich 1977, p.191 (Wikipedia).
517 Wilhelm Marr, Der Sieg des Judenthums über das Germanenthum, Bern 1879, p.32 (gehove.de/antisem/texte/marr_sieg.pdf).
518 Isaac, p.216 (Hebert Roux, Protestant); 263, 267-268 (P. Lagrange); 381 (P. Prat); moreover Calvin (p.379).
519 Hitler, p.751 (cited by Ley 2002, p.5).

to Revelation, announced in Berlin Sportpalast: "The hour will come when the most evil universal enemy of all times will have played his part for at least thousand years."[520] Why just thousand years? "He seized the dragon, that ancient serpent, who is the Devil and Satan, and bound him for a thousand years ... so that he would not deceive the nations no more, until the thousand years were ended" (Revelation 20:2-3).

In European folklore, ranging from Grimm's fairytales to Strawinskij's *The Soldier's Tale*, temporary superhuman power of mortal beings used to have one ever-working explication: pact with the devil. Now in 1930, with an above-average presence of Jews in academic professions and journalism, in art and commerce (75 percent of German big stores being "Jewish"), rational reasons of Jewish success like assiduous work or intelligence were hardly acceptable to German middle and lower classes who the more avidly grabbed at the mythic explications shooting forth evergreen from fertile irrational layers: By which ruthless deed, by which heinous sale had the Jews acquired their uncanny force? Who were they in league with? Who else could have chosen them than "the spirit that ever denies"?[521]

That "the world is controlled by good and evil forces" and the Jews thereby incorporate the "evil principle" – this was, according to Eichmann's proxy, the former student of theology Dieter Wisliceny, the basic idea of Nazi antisemitism.[522] And here we arrive at the commonalities of "secular" racism and Christian anti-Judaism: Both of them claim first the existence of fundamentally different types of humans, and second the fundamentally different quality of these genetically fixed groups. Third point: Blacks did not need black badges since any child saw who was black. Jews needed yellow badges, but any child had seen their dark atrocity at crosses. And fourth, both darknesses were ancestral inheritance, requiring legal ban of their transmission.

Racial hygienic exclusion chose native American, black, and chosen people. In 17th century, padre Gregorio Garcia claimed that the índios were of Jewish descent since like the Jews "they are lazy, unbelieving in the miracles of Jesus Christ and ungrateful to the Spaniard for all the good they did to them".[523] Still in December 2016, holocaust denier and Imperial Wizard David Duke declared that "Jews are not white". Presumably his cross loving Ku-Klux-Klan would accept a Jewish Groucho Marx ("I don't want to belong to any club that will accept me as a member") as eagerly as a black and gay James Baldwin who stated in 1987: "The crisis taking place in the world, and in the minds and hearts of black men everywhere, is not produced by the star of David, but by the old, rugged Roman cross on which Christendom's most celebrated Jew was murdered. And not by Jews."[524]

520 Weiss, Chicago 1997, p.375, ref. to Gilbert, Martin: Holocaust, p. 285; holocaust-chronologie.de/chronologie/1942/januar/24-31.html.
521 Mephisto in Goethe's Faust, study room scene : "Ich bin der Geist, der stets verneint!"
522 Wistrich 1987, p.22 and 250; (alleged) ex-student of theology: Wikipedia.
523 Galeano, p.68.
524 Final sentence of Baldwin's essay "Negroes Are Anti-Semitic Because They're Anti-

All differences between anti-Black and anti-Jewish racism notwithstanding, the Christian imagery of Satan is dark and phallic, and rightly the feminist Melanie Kaye/Kantrowitz points to the very physical background of genital-genetically defined rejection: "Racism of either sort inevitably conspires with contempt for the flesh and fear of its desires, projecting all sexual impulse onto the racial other." Significantly, while in the US Negroes (and Jewish Leo Frank) were lynched for alleged rape of white females, "the Nazis were avid students of United States eugenics doctrine"[525] and Julius Streicher's *Der Stürmer* engaged in denouncing "Jewish girl defilers" with pornographic detailedness since "in Europe, the Jews were traditionally regarded as deviant from sexual standard."[526]

Burning of chief Hatuey, Cuba 1512 – Klan and cross, 1922 – Jews and Jazz, 1938

But the sexual deviance of God's antagonist is but one rather folkloristic and voyeuristic aspect of demonic otherness. When in 1961 Adolf Eichmann stood trial in Jerusalem, his defending lawyer Dr. Servatius suggested that the death of the six million had been "part of a 'higher purpose' and retaliation for an earlier and greater crime against God, whereby the attorney linked the modern trial in Jerusalem with another one having occurred twenty centuries before". It is Richard L. Rubenstein who recalls this causa prima, and in this context he also remembers his Protestant dialogue partner, the resistance fighter and concentration camp inmate Heinrich Grüber who between 1938 and 1940 had saved probably 1138 baptized Jews. Rubenstein in 1966: "What made the visit with Dean Grüber so worth remembering and interesting was the fact that here a German who paid his efforts for the Jews almost with his life – the Nazis knocked out his teeth and one time he was transported out of the camp as dead – nonetheless was unable to view

White"; New York Times, April 9, 1967.
525   Kaye/Kantrowitz, p.9 and 16, quoting Nancy Ordover (American Eugenics, Minneapolis 2003, p.41) concerning the link between Nazi and US eugenics.
526   Sander Gilman, in: Jüdisches Museum der Stadt Wien, Die Macht der Bilder, p.174.

the Jews simply as normal people, with the same span of vice and virtue as every other group."[527] Normal people? No, the God-bringer and God-killer people must be cosmically evil, their killing part of God's plan. In 1940, Hitler spoke of a "satanic power that had taken possession of our whole people" and ascribed omnipotence to it: "Almighty *Judentum* declared war on us back then ..."[528] Exactly this mythical construction of their diabolic otherness preordained the Jews to be apt objects of what Hitler considered to be "the art of all great national leaders of all times", that consists "not in dividing the attention of a people, but in concentrating it upon a single foe".[529] This "scapegoat for all" enabled Hitler to address low-class voters sympathetically without annoying his main clientele from middle and upper class, as well as his sponsoring tycoons like Krupp, Flick and Hugenberg who provided for a war and a Shoah that, in Dean Grüber's view, was part of God's plan. "I could not possibly believe in such a God", Rubenstein concluded, "nor could I believe in Israel as the chosen people after Auschwitz."[530]
If the Jews "attract on themselves, in theory and practice, the will to extermination which the false societal order produces out of itself", and if "thus, they indeed are the chosen people", as Horkheimer and Adorno remarked in 1947, what is the error in the false order? Maybe the acceptance of sacrifice? "All de-mythologizing has the form of the unstoppable experience of the futility and expendablity of sacrifices", Horkheimer and Adorno state. "All human acts of sacrifice, performed methodically, belie the God to whom they are offered. They put him under the primacy of human ends, dissolve his power, and the fraud against him seamlessly passes over to the fraud the faithless priests perform against the faithful community."[531]
About one third of mankind cultivates the religion of atoning sacrifice and clings to its voluntariness to evade the insight that this offering of the other is the epitome of lawlessness, inequality, abuse of power and ethical corruption. To choose an innocent for sacrifice corrupts the offering collective in its equal solidary basis and changes this society along the lines of its divine despot, Big Sacrificer. As the first abolishers of human sacrifice, the Jews were also pioneers of equal human rights.
Egalité, as the basis of lawfullness, in Judaism starts with the descent from one human couple, granting equal nobility. But man becomes human only "hearing the other and responding to him" (Lévinas)[532]. Significantly, Abraham heard Isaac, but God did not reply to Jesus, his sacrifice. Obedience was called for here, the waiving of rights, the victim's right of living to begin with. "Nobody respects or cares for one who does not fight for his rights", wrote Einstein who did not believe in a personal God and also did not recognize anything "chosen" in that people whose "love of justice bordering

527 Rubenstein, Richard L., p.53-57.
528 Völkischer Beobachter, Northern German issue, Nov. 10, 1940 (Hilberg 1982, p.21).
529 Hitler, p.118 (cited by Weiss, Chicago 1997, p.202).
530 Rubenstein, Richard L., p.46-57.
531 Horkheimer/Adorno, p.177, 57 and 61.
532 Lévinas 2008, p.64, resp. 2005, p.XIII.

on fanaticism" he appreciated so deeply that he regarded as a "present of heaven" to belong to it.[533]
"Which legal system will a person choose *before* she knows which social role (rich or poor, man or woman, black or white, handicapped or gifted) she will act out in this legal system?" With this question starts John Harsanyi's thought experiment named "veil of ignorance" on which John Rawls built his own moral philosophy. In a legal system worth to be chosen, Rawls concluded, two principles must hold. First: Equal basic liberties for all. Second: Social unequality is bound to two conditions: In the obtainment of advantageous positions, fair equality of chances must be valid, and the social unequality must serve "the greatest advantage of the least favored fellow human beings". [534]
Is it by sheer coincidence that John Harsanyi, whose genial experiment my low level secondary school pupils grasped easily, descended from "a people that for two thousand years had made justice the cornerstone of its spiritual and communal existence"?[535] Or rather 2700 years, since it is Isaiah who wrote about the chosen one: "Here is my servant, whom I uphold, my chosen one, in whom I delight ... He will not falter or be discouraged till he establishes justice on earth" (Isaiah 42:1-4).
This justice of equality builds on the compassion Nietzsche warns against, the German philosopher who concerning law-abidingness opined that "in world history all comes down to the great criminals" and who wrote in *The Antichrist* to whom it wouldn't come down: "We wouldn't chose for company first Christians any more than Polish Jews: ... They both don't smell good." Moral law is not a Jewish but a universally human achievement. Jewish, however, is the choice of justice as Summum Bonum, by the "reason pronouncing justice, reason that had risen to the concept of the one god",[536] and Jewish is the chutzpah with which the right as an interhuman issue is defended against all authorities, including God; for in Jewish liturgy "no trial is authentic without putting God on trial".[537]
He wasn't put on trial for having sacrificed his son. Whereas Europe's majorities chose beatific faith, the chosen people had to choose exclusion whenever necessary: "You shall not follow the majority to do evil, and not turn after the mighty to pervert justice" (Exodus 23:2).
There were reasons not to come along with Paul's psychic path of cosmic sacrifice; this choosing of dissent being vital and historically indispensable. Someone had to take the role of the child who speaks out that the moloch's new clothes are but Paul's vision-web; and to pass on this chutzpah just as Michael Chlenov was taught by his father: "Judaism is a tool of resistance."[538]

---

533 Quoted from: Kligsberg, p.128; God/chosen: Einstein's letter (January 3, 1954) to Erich Gutkind (Wikipedia); justice: gemeinden.judentum.de/muenchen/vhs/juedische-0506.htm.
534 Rawls, John: Justice as Fairness: A Restatement (2001), §13 (Wikipedia).
535 Hannah Arendt, in "Magnes, the conscience of the Jewish people", 1952, acc. to Karpf (ed.), p.94.
536 Adorno, Minima Moralia 151 (Thesen gegen den Okkultismus), p.321.
537 Greenberg 1993, p.213.
538 Michael Chlenov, in: Pearl, p.23.

X   Reenactments
Who plays victim?

> *"The origin of these images ... is to be found in the crucifixion of Christ – in the very event which throughout all times was held against the Jews and updated in various seasonable transformations, as the founding myth of a whole civilization."* Dan Diner[539]

Civilization: "What had we done to deserve this hurricane of evil, this avalanche of cruelty? Why had all gates of hell opened up and spit the furies of human baseness on us? What crimes had we committed for which this would be the catastrophic punishment? Where, in which moral codex, be it human or divine, exists such excruciate a crime requiring innocent women and children to expiate it by their lives in tortures no Torquemada dreamed of?" Thus asks Alexander Donat, who survived the Warsaw Ghetto and four Lagers, who afterwards found his wife again (she had passed through Auschwitz and Ravensbrück) and also his son who had been saved by Polish Christians.[540]
Why? In Christian Europe the question for the motives of Shoah is commonly resolved – if put at all – referring vaguely to "social reasons". But take whatever societal upheaval (France 1789, Santo Domingo 1791, Russia 1917...) and whatever genocide (Indians, Aborigines, Armenians, Cambodians, Tutsi ...): never the victim group met as abysmal a hatred as the Jews in all medieval pogroms including Chmielnitzky, Nazis and Kielce 1946. "Don't give them anything to eat, they're Juden", an SS-guard cautioned German villagers against his emaciated death march prisoners. "And so I got nothing to eat. German children started throwing stones at us." These German children of 1945, Goldhagen comments, "whose knowledge about Jews consisted exclusively on what society had taught them, knew how to behave."[541]
Historians who deny or play down the cross-learned hatred acquired in early childhood should try to explain why nationalist German decision makers on all levels, at all their sober calculations, regarded supporting their national army and rescuing German civilians secondary to tormenting Jews; why they employed increasingly scarce capacities of vehicles, fuel, personal and ammunition in late 1944 rather to transport 400.000 Hungarian Jews to Poland than to save fleeing German soldiers and civilians; and why during the death marches in April 1945 the SS-guards, yet in eyeshot of US-tanks, kept on shooting exhausted prisoners who were not able to march on?[542]
All these irrationalities point to one origin: the driving psychic force of the committed cruelties can not be found neither in economical or social rea-

---

539   Dan Diner: Der Sarkophag zeigt Risse. In: Rabinovici/Speck/Sznaider, p.320.
540   Donat, p.100-101.
541   Goldhagen 1996, p.429.
542   Römer/Erlanger, p.62.

sons, nor in metaphysical evil or the perpetrators' diabolic wickedness, but in the long-lasting effects of a childhood trauma bond, in the mental violation by a picture that assails children with inscrutable, sanctified cruelty. This chapter "Reenactments" confronts the mode and manner of, as Donat says, *such excruciate a crime* attributed to the Jews, with mode and manner of their punishment by cross-taught children. Three psychological motives of the "avengers" must be distinguished here.

First, the desire to apply a punishment matching with the crime, as Abbot Peter of Cluny exposes in the eve of the second crusade: "Since this slavish, miserable, fearful, whining people shed the blood of Christ, they richly deserved a punishment *fitting to the crime.*"[543]

Fitting in detail, to wit. Remembering that Jesus on the cross bled from five wounds (two hands, two feet, one heart), a bunch of crusaders marau-ding through Troyes ripped up a Torah scroll in Rabbi Jacob Ben Meir's face and promised: "On you we'll take revenge because of him who was hanged, and we'll wound you just like you Jews have slain him five wounds." With five wounds commemorating the main wounds in Jesus' body, the rabbi was rescued by a passing chevalier who promised the crusaders that he would either convince him to convert to Christ or return the rabbi to them.[544]

Second, the retribution must be a severe one. In this requirement, the playful crusaders as well as the former kidmonk who now was Abbot Peter of Cluny, wishing to have the Christkillers punished "fitting to the crime" (i.e. extremely cruel), hardly differred from the children of Geneva whom Piaget observed in the 1950s and who, if asked how to perform just punishment, "almost always recur to expiation, and their choice is of amazing rigor."[545] Léon Poliakov reports an attempt of five schoolboys to "replay the Golgotha drama in reverse"; the incident of 1928, which the local school authorities at first had tried to hush up, was published by a Moscow newspaper in detail: "Yid, you crucified Christ. Now we are going to crucify you", the five told their classmate before they bound him to a tree at the edge of frozen Lake Seliguer near Oshtakov. Merciful enough, they changed their minds and freed their victim, probably saving him from a slow death.[546]

Exactly the happy end of the boy-group's passion play shows the third motive for reenactment: the subconscious desire of the (young or grown-up) Christian children to free themselves from the traumatizing cross compassion of their childhood years. "One can see that the children repeat in play whatever in their lives impressed them strongly; that in this they abreact the power of the impression and make themselves, so to say, the masters of the situation. This endeavor", Sigmund Freud notes in 1921, "could be ascribed to a drive of overcoming which makes itself independent of whether the reminiscence in itself was joyful or not." Its painfulness not always renders an experience impractical: "When the doctor has looked into the child's

---

543 Peter the Venerable, Epistola XXXVI (cited by Michael, p.71); italics mine.
544 Michael, p.73. The Rabbi was the son of great Rashi.
545 Piaget, p.238.
546 Poliakov 2003, Vol.IV, p.318 and 402.

throat or performed a small surgery on him, this terrifying experience will certainly become the subject of the next game ... Passing over from the passivity of the experience onto the activity of playing, the child inflicts the painful thing that happened to himself now to the playmate, taking revenge on the proxy's person."[547] The proxy may even be an animal. Lloyd deMause relates an incident from the times when European parents used to educate their children by having them witness public executions. One such boy who had been forced to view a hanging at the gallows "awoke at night screaming and hanged his cat."[548]

In 1926 Freud declared: "We know that the child behaves toward all painful impacts by reproducing them in play; in this way of passing over from passivity to action, the child attempts to master the impressions of life mentally."[549] In 1931 Freud emphasized even more generally that in every area of psychic experience "a passively received impression provokes in the child the tendency to an active reaction. The child attempts to do himself what before has been done to him or with him."[550]

Sixty years later, the American psychologists Reiker and Carmen warned: "Confrontations with violence challenge one's most basic assumptions about the self as invulnerable and intrinsically worthy and about the world as orderly and just." This statement of 1986 strikingly reminds Kierkegaard's insights of 1850 concerning this "reminder they never can get rid of ... and it will be as if the present generation had crucified him every time just to explain to the next generation's child what's going on here in this world; and the child will ... feel afraid and anxious of the elder ones and the world and of himself". How important "the elder ones" are to the child, the trauma researchers Reiker and Carmen expose quite clearly: "The child needs to hold on to an image of the parent as good parent, in order to deal with the intensity of fear and rage which is the effect of the tormenting experiences". In the "acting out" of these experiences, the children's "anger directed against the self or others ... is seldom understood by either victims or clinicians as being a repetitive reenactment of real events from the past."[551]

But may we interpret adults' brutal reenactions really as an acting out of childhood impressions?

Play it again

A social practice not of extreme brutality but popular hilarity similar to the folkway practised in Bordeaux (see chapter 6) was reenacted also in Tou-

547 Freud, S., Jenseits des Lustprinzips (Beyond the Pleasure Principle), 1921, chapter II.
548 deMause, p.31.
549 Freud, S., Hemmung, Symptom und Angst (Inhibitions, Symptoms and Anxiety). Leipzig/Vienna/Zurich 1926, Appendix concerning anxiety, p.128
550 Freud, S., Über die weibliche Sexualität (About the Female Sexuality), 1931, ch. III.
551 Reiker, P. and Carmen, E: The Victim to Patient Process: The disconfirmation and transformation of abuse. American Journal for Orthopsychiatry, 56/1986, p.360-370, quoted in: Van der Kolk, Bessel A., The Compulsion to Repeat the Trauma. In: Psychiatric Clinics of North America, Vol. 12, June 1989, No.2, p.389-411 (cirp.org/library/psych/vanderkolk/).

louse on some two hundred Holy Fridays from 9th to 11th century: A Jew was brought to the cathedral "to get a symbolic slap – by the hand of, amazing grace, the Comte in person!" Crossan cannot refrain from an ironic stinger: "No Roman, notabene, was ever granted such an honour." The Irish-Catholic theologian views the Toulouse slapstick scene as a remake of the blind man's bluff game (Mt 26:67-68) played by Roman soldiery and so easily empathizable by children: "Then they spit in his face and hit him. Some slapped him, saying: 'Prophesy to us, you Messiah! Who hit you?'"[552]

To repeat and reenact what hit you, in order to work off the trauma and get rid of it: That is what children do when they are unable to understand experiences, unable to, as Piaget said, "assimilate" them to their still soft and provisory concept of the world. Then they try to, as Gunnar Heinsohn wrote, "work off the outsized impact ... in game by reenacting the situation once more, but taking the main figure's role themselves".[553] Hidden by a Christian couple outside the ghetto of Lvov, Stefa Hasson witnessed German soldiers dragging out an old Jewish woman hiding in the neighborhood. "She was screaming, 'I'm not Jewish! I'm Polish, skin and bones!' That must have been some kind of colloquial expression, but you know how kids mix things up. The next few days, we reenacted that scene in our playing, yelling, 'We're Christians, with half a pound of bones!'"[554]

Swiss public-school teacher Hans Zulliger combined his everyday observations of children with his knowledge as a skilled psychotherapist in a strange comparison: "The child behaves similar to the war-neurotic who in his dreams again and again experiences the magical scene of being buried alive, for the purpose of redaction and coping. I don't make this comparison at random. Freud has said that the child and the neurotic move on the same stage of thinking, as also the 'savage'."[555] In Warsaw ghetto, when Alexander Donat returned home from a work day, he often found his eight-year-old son Wlodek and his same-age friend amidst their game. "My son just shouted '*Juden raus! Alle Juden runter!*' They played the deportation game. Sometimes Wlodek buckled my broad belt on, took his toy rifle in his hand to proclaim in his squeaky child's voice: 'I am a Daitsch! I am Geipel, and I travel to Berlin tonight.' And then he always turned around to his friend and snarled: '*Jude, raus!*'"[556]

In Kovno, gynecologist Dr. Aharon Peretz noted: "The children in the ghetto played and laughed, but their games reflected the tragedy of the Jewish people. They played pall bearer. They digged a grave, put a child in and called him Hitler. They played at the gate of the ghetto, one part of the children being German, the others being Jewish. The Germans reviled the Jews and

552 Crossan (1996, Preface, p. ix), citing Raymond E. Brown, The Death of the Messiah, p.575, note 7. Referring to Toulouse see Patai, p.314.
553 Heinsohn, p.33.
554 Kessel, p.60-61.
555 Zulliger 1972, p.22.
556 Donat, p.106.

pommelled on them ... One could see children who had experienced shootings now play the grave-digging, executing and burying."[557]
To reenact unresolved early trauma is, not by chance, the basic idea of various methods of psychological therapy. Otto Rank recommended to reenact the birth trauma to treat its effects. Virginia Satir invented the Systemic Constellation, a spacial scenic reconstruction of family interrelations; Ivan Böszörményi-Nagy aimed to discover invisible loyalties in family sceneries; Brazilian theater-educator Augusto Boal, himself a torture victim of Brazil's military dictatorship, let his adult groups reenact everyday scenes in which oppressive behavior becomes visible, and encouraged the audience to find and play a new, liberating final act. Both Satir, Böszörményi-Nagy and Boal are strongly inspired by Jacob Levy Moreno,[558] who was born four weeks after Adolf Hitler and later on made personal acquaintance with his postcard-painting contemporary in Vienna.[559] Adolf admired the likewise charismatic and likewise (yet in a different way) Jesus-revering Moreno who at sunshine days attracted children in droves, as well as grandmothers and policemen, in Prater park, simply by telling stories. From the stories emerged first small and then bigger play-scenes, out of which Moreno eventually developped his methods of sociometrics and group-therapy by psychodrama.
Concerning tragedies, Karl Marx once remarked that they can come across much lighter and even witty if they are repeated.[560] Independent of Marx, Moreno in his "reciprocal theater" follows his own experience that the cathartic effect of repetitions often occurs in laughter. Imagine young Jacob had been able to treat young Adolf! Imagine Hitler had confessed not to his friend Helene Hanfstaengl, but to Jacob Levi Moreno how long a time he had needed to "overcome this episode"! Imagine Levi would have had the chance to reenact with Adolf the following key scene which requires but one requisit: a tablecloth!
"During a particularly rebellious phase, one day Adolf resolved to run away from home. His father, however, got to know and locked him in one of the rooms upstairs. At night the boy attempted to escape through a window opening; and when the opening turned out to be too narrow, he took his clothes off. In this moment he heard his father coming up the stair; he quit his attempt and hastily covered his bareness with a tablecloth. This time old Herr Hitler did not reach for the whip; instead, he burst into laughter and summoned his wife to come upstairs and look at the 'Toga youngling'. This derision hit the son harder than any physical castigation. And only to Helene Hanfstaengl he later on confessed that he had 'taken long to get over this episode'."[561] Comment: If someone tries to escape through a narrow roof window, undressing shirt and trousers is not a good idea. It seems more likely that the pubescent boy, failing in Realschule after having been

---

557 Quoted according to Heer 1981, p.482 and Hilberg 1992, p.168.
558 Teixeira, p.98.
559 Journal of Group Psychology, Psychodrama & Sociometry, Vol.42, 1/1989, p.45 (cited by Waintrob Nudel, p.70).
560 Marineau, p.78.
561 Toland, p.12; cf. Miller 1983, p.185.

a leader in his primary school, estranged by his male role model at home, had dealed with his own body in the attic room and taken long to invent the whole absurd frame story; a camouflage which enabled him to tell his life-poisoning father-experience to a listening ersatz mother named Helene Hanfstaengl. His real mother selfsame had been but standing by and beneath back then, like mother Mary had stood beneath the cross, witnessing big father's act of castigation while tacitly suffering with her son. Later on, art lover Hitler compared the eyes of the Medusa in Franz von Stuck's painting with the eyes of his mother, and Erik Erikson feels that Hitler's statements about women reveal his being "deeply disappointed and disillusioned with his mother".[562]

On January 30, 1939, Hitler speaks to microphone and multitude: "Very often in my life I've been a prophet and was laughed at mostly. In the time of my struggle for power it was in first line the Jewish people which but with laughter accepted my prophecies ..."[563] His old guard companions are told by him in Munich, November 8, 1941: "They always laughed at me but I always won my case."[564] Few weeks later, shortly before Christmas 1941, in Berlin Sportpalast Hitler prophesies that in case of war "the whole *Judentum* will have played its part in Europe. They may laugh about that still today, just as they laughed about my prophecies earlier."[565] On September 30, 1942, the Toga youngling bets again to have the last laugh in his Greater German restaging: "Once the Jews have laughed about my prophecies. I don't know whether they still laugh today or the smirk has been wiped off their faces already: Anyhow, I can but reassure now, too: The smirk will be wiped off their faces everywhere."[566] Barely six weeks later, on November 8, laughter was over for the Führer again: "One has always laughed at me as a prophet. Of those who laughed back then, nowadays any numbers laugh no more, and those who keep on laughing maybe will also do no more so in a while."[567] In his testament, in the last but one sentence he wrote in his life, the man who was "extremely sensitive to ridicule"[568] reasoned his suicide: "Moreover, I don't want to fall into the hands of enemies who for the amusement of their hate-incited masses need a new drama staged by Jews."[569]

Hours later he was dead. Had his adjuring "Don't laugh at me!" been helpful? Had he escaped the hands of his two enemies? According to Alfred Adler, the one factor that most strongly promotes the internalisation of aggression is "a sense of helplessness which begins with the helplessness children feel at the hand of all-powerful adults."[570]

---

562   Langer, p.246 and 255.
563   Wistrich 1987, p.164.
564   archive.org/stream/AdolfHitlerRedenDerGrodeutscheFreiheitskampf-BandIii/
MicrosoftWord-Document1_djvu.txt.
565   Wistrich 1987, p.209-210.
566   Steffahn, p.93 and 128.
567   Wistrich 1987, p.217.
568   Wiegand, Karl von: "Hitler Foresses His End", in Cosmopolitan, April/May 1939 (quoted by Langer, p.95).
569   Hilberg 1982, p.670.
570   Swaim 2013, p.265.

"The Führer does not change. He is the same now as he was when he was a boy" asserted his minister Goebbels.[571] Hitler's compatriot, the Viennese historian Friedrich Heer, characterizes him as a personality "who until his last days on earth manifests those imprints and impressions which the child, which young Hitler had absorbed."[572] Deeply had he absorbed the *Laugh-at-toga-youngling* scene, with an laughing father and a probably neither laughing nor protecting mother. The power of the hatred that surfaced in Hitler's rhetoric threats against the "now probably no more" laughing Jews resides in a double identification: of his father with the Jewish scoffers, and of himself with the victim in a toga-youngling scene that every Christian, at least every altar-boy absorbs: "They clothed him in a purple robe and went up to him again and again, saying, 'Hail, king of the Jews!' And they slapped him in the face." (John 19:3). My late professor of pedagogy Kurt Singer cited bio-ethologist Konrad Lorenz: "Laughing is a cruel weapon, apt to harm fatally. Laughing at a child is a crime."[573]
By his father-hate, Hitler became the extreme case of a bimillennial normal case: Laden with anger against the torturers of Jesus, ready to this projecting "mimesis" which "shifts the ready-to-jump interior to the exterior",[574] the cross-impressed children set out on reenacting – without ever being able to cure themselves by acting out. "Freud thought that the aim of repetition was to gain mastery", van der Kolk resumes, "but clinical experience has shown that this rarely happens; instead, repetition causes further suffering for the victims or for people in their surroundings."[575] This is clinical as well as Jewish experience, as Horkheimer and Adorno state: "The Jew, ... ridiculed as ruler, they nail on cross, endlessly repeating the sacrifice in whose power they cannot believe."[576]

The cross on stage
Why do passion plays attract so many viewers? What do these people desire to experience where no romance, dance, no sitcom, chanson, blues song, aria, no gripping climax, no comedy of errors, no unexpected turn and all the more no happy end may be expected – if not a healing by reenactment? Why people pilgrim to Oberammergau Festspielhaus, Bruno Bettelheim explains with undue outspokenness, describing this Passion Play as "nothing but an expression of what has been there all the time, and what people liked to see and hear. My guess is that nobody who is not inherently an anti-Semite would go and watch this performance."[577] Full houses then are no

---

571 Goebbels, Vom Kaiserhof zur Reichskanzlei, Munich 1934, p.27 (cit. by Langer, p.76).
572 Heer 1989, p.16.
573 Singer, Kurt, p.17.
574 Horkheimer/Adorno, p.177.
575 van der Kolk, Bessel A., The Compulsion to Repeat the Trauma. In: Psychiatric Clinics of North America, Vol.12, June 1989, No 2, p. 389-411.
576 Horkheimer/Adorno, p.196.
577 Friedman, Saul S., p.98.

surprise since antisemites are, according to survivor Jules Isaac, "the great majority of Christians – or of those who pass for Christians". [578] Rabbi Krauskopf from Chicago visited the Oberammergau Passion Play in 1900 and was strongly impressed: "When I considered the falsity I had listened to, the hatred and malice I had seen enacted, when I reflected upon the wrong that has been done to us, I could not but ask myself: How will it end? When will justice be done to the Jew?"[579] The Oberammergau event is the worldwide premium product of a genre that began in 1150 with the first complete Passion Play of Monte Cassino, comprising twelve acts but only 320 lines. First act: Judas bargains with Caiaphas. Last act: Virgin Mary bewails her son on the cross. Around 1377 the Wakefield Passion emerged, whose 450 lines almost exclusively deal with the act of crucifixion. Jesus is brought to Pilate by four torturers. Laughing they prepare him for execution: "Hold down his knees!" – "Dryfe a naill there thrughoutt!" At Donaueschingen Passion (after 1470), "the driving-in of every nail is accompanied by a double speech".[580] Compassion must be deepened, also for women and children: "Women, see those nails three/ they must be driven into free/ through your son's hands and feet/ may he feel sour or sweet" – thus explains the oldest text of Oberammergau, and up to 20th century Jesus here was led to crucifixion by a "Jewish boy" who carried a torture toolbox.[581] Mixing like in a messy box, pious feelings blend with the arousing effect of torment: The German *Alsfelder Passionsspiel*, premiered in 1501, dedicates 700 of its 8095 lines to torture. The deepness of compassion excited by torture and the vanishing borderline between stage and audience show up in lethal accidents on stage. A Swedish king once stroke down the legionary Longinus on the boards, because the actor's lance had stabbed the man on cross too hard; another performer of Longinus' role actually stabbed the Jesus-player to death. At Holy Friday 2018, when Longinus perfurates Jesus with his lance, in southern Brazilian city Nova Hartz an angry man jumps onto stage and downs the Roman with his own motorcycle helmet. "I hurt a little, but luckily I had my helmet on", the actor commented while the police said that the attacker is known as a drug-addict and went on stage saying that he had to "save" Jesus. [582] The soul-stirring effects of all these Passion Plays should not be underrated. In a quite modern way, the spectators were integrated into the course of action: as extras of the crowd which shouts its "crucifige"; as consoling bystanders to Mary and the women standing beneath the cross. "Joined in suffering and rejoice, they take part in the action, reacting to it by shared outrage, elation, angst and ire."[583] In 1338, Freiburg authorities prohibited

---

578 Eckardt, p.6.
579 Friedman, Saul S., p.191.
580 Dieckmann, p.73.
581 Queri, G. (ed.): Der älteste Text des Oberammergauer Passionsspieles. Oberammergau 1910, p.96 (cited by Rohrbacher/Schmidt, p.258).
582 "Homem invade encenação de 'Paixao de Cristo e agride ator para 'salvar' Jesus", em: UOL, 31.03.2018.
583 Schmid, R.H.: Raum, Zeit und Publikum des geistlichen Spiels. Aussage und Absicht

anti-Jewish scenes because one had experienced their inciting effects in urban life bitterly. In many places "empathic public anger" forged ahead in a similar return-the-like way as in Prague of 1389, where a "Spiritual Play" had stimulated subsequent "bloodiest riots of the rabble" against the Jews.[584] Saul Friedman compares the back then spectators with the fans filling modern arenas: "Constantly exposed to homilies about the treachery, greed and satanic power of the Jews, they brought with them to the theater a religious zeal not unlike that of today's football fans. Theirs was a world of good pitted against evil. The evil ones were responsible for the bloodied crucifixes which hung in churches from Europe to Latin America. Many Christians brought with them a 'pathological absorption in the physical wounds of Jesus'. Now the Jewish merchants, priests and mob responsible for these hideous torments were reveling before them onstage ..."[585]

In 1435, the "obsession with the violence of the crucifixion" vented in a phantom play imputed to the guilty ones: Rumours spread in Palma de Mallorca that Jews planned to reenact the Stations of the Cross, employing an Arab slave and including the final crucifixion of the protagonist. Four Jews were burned in Palma, even though the bishop's investigation found that the slave was alive and well.[586]

Paris authorities ruled in 1459 that Jews must not leave their houses during the Passion Play; in Frankfurt the city council instituted in 1469 the protection of the ghetto by armed guards during the performances; in Rome all Passion dramas were banned in 1539 because they were regularly followed by the sacking of the ghetto along the Tiber.[587] The public damage was lesser after a triggering incident in Lower-Bavarian Deggendorf: At the Passion Play performance in 1740 the Jews whipped Jesus so brutally that Jesus shortly forgot his part and beat back, thus unleashing a general free-for-all scuffle – this being just another folksy Bavarian tradition.

Yet in 1860 a Scottish Christian viewer wrote that here in Oberammergau he for the first time understood how and why this hatred has provoked "cruelties and barbarities unrivalled in history". In 1900, American visitor Krauskopf heard friends say that this Play would have led them "to hate the Jew ever after" – if they were not Jewish themselves.[588] At the same time, a Bavarian historian explained folksy reactions by drawing connections: "As is well known, in medieval times every Catholic town was an Oberammergau – and likewise every Catholic church is a perpetual Oberammergau where year in, year out the Passion is celebrated, the Saviour captured in the garden of Gethsemane, nailed to the cross and laid into the Holy Grave ... Moreover

eines mittelalterlichen Massenmediums. Munich 1975, p.198 (cited by Dieckmann, p.56).
584 Dieckmann, p.69 (cases of Freiburg in German Black Forest and of Prague).
585 Friedman, Saul S., p.107. He cites ("pathological absorption ...") from a Christian commentary of 1930: "Is the Passion Play Antisemitic?" Christian Century 47 (April 27, 1930), p.1007.
586 Gitlitz, p.23; alemannia-judaica.de/mallorca; Jüdische Allgemeine, October 8, 2008. "Yo soy católico" means "I am Catholic".
587 Paris: Kühner, p.143; Frankfurt and Rome: Friedman, p.108.
588 Scottish Christian: Cohen, p.221; Rabbi Krauskopf: Friedman, p.108-109.

add to this a daily Oberammergau played as often as the mass is read and the sacrifice is offered, which daily repeats the same world-redeeming scene, just symbolically and in form of a mystery. Thanks to these frequent, ever new yet still identical presentations, the *Volk* turns quasi *hypnotisch*, as it stares incessantly at the cross with which the Church confronts it – phantasy just can't help sojourning steadily on Golgotha, envisioning devoutly the *Haupt voll Blut und Wunden ...*" These clear-sighted lines were written by German historian Johannes Kleinpaul in 1900, while ten-year-old Adolf Hitler, the later star guest in Oberammergau, lived 120 miles north-east, serving as an altar boy and choir singer in Lambach Benedictine convent. How deeply the desire for just punishment can worry even adults becomes palpable when Kleinpaul describes how such Passion Plays prompted the spectators to passionately hate not only the Jews but also "the actors who gave the Jewish roles in the Passion Play, and to persecute them as if they were really guilty for the suffering and death of Christ."[589] For example, Andreas Lang who played the character known simply as "Rabbi" told two real rabbis that English women had refused to lodge in his home because he had "persecuted Christ". As this happened to the "Rabbi", what about the "Judas"? Gregor Lechner, who (himself succeeding his father) played this part for two decades, was asked by Krauskopf whether he wanted his son to follow him in this role. "God forbid" said Lechner. "I love my child too much to bring the same sufferings upon him which I and my father before me have been obliged to endure." Role-typical sufferings – and dangers: In 1922, a spectator actually tried to shoot the Judas-player Guido Mayr on stage.[590]

Few years later came the days when Hitler made his celebrated blitz-visit to applaud enactments with eight of twelve apostles holding party member-ship, in a town where "all citizens were Nazis except the one who played the Judas".[591] During election campaign, Hitler visited the performance of 1930; at the Jubilee Passion of 1934 (out of the ten-years-rhythm) the Führer was there again and full of praise: Pilate appeared at this Festspiel "as a racially and in his intelligence superior Roman acting like a rock amidst the Jewish vermin and swarming", the Führer rhapsodized and left no doubt: "Recognizing the enormous importance of these Festival Plays for the en-lightenment of also all coming generations I am a Christian absolutely."[592] It was the German audience of 1934 that shocked an American from Chicago: "These people are all crazy," he said. "This is not a revolution, it's a revival. They think Hitler is God. Believe it or not, a German woman sat next to me at the Passion Play and when they hoisted Jesus on the Cross, she said, 'There he is. That is our Fuehrer, our Hitler.' And when they paid out the

---

589 Kleinpaul, Rudolf: Der Mord von Konitz und der Blutaberglaube des Mittelalters. Leipzig 1900, p.9-13 (cited by Lehr, p.170-171).
590 Friedman, Saul S., p.103.
591 Remark by Simon Wiesenthal after his visit in Oberammergau 1947; Friedman, Saul S., p.XXIV.
592 "Table talk" of July 1, 1942, cited by Heer 1989, p.419.

thirty pieces of silver to Judas, she said: 'That is Roehm, who betrayed the Leader.'"[593]
The only Jew in town, "Jud Meyer", was deported to Dachau camp in 1939. That "back then" the Judas-players got spat at in the street after the plays, actors training for the 2010 Passion related still in 2008. Christian Stückl, producer of the five-hour Passion of 2010, confessed with remarkable openness: "Personally I don't believe in a God in Heaven who somehow demands a bloody sacrifice. That's a God I don't believe in and don't want to believe in. Jesus actually wanted to bring into this world something very different from this suffering on cross. He actually wanted to open people, unclose their minds. But at the end what remains to us is the cross as the most important sign and the suffering and atonement and guilt. And sometimes one thinks: That's a very odd sign, a sign that makes not really free."[594]
Stückl has more courage than freedom of art. Sitting on one of the 4,740 folding chairs, his colleague Tuvia Tenenbom from New York observes: "Part two snaps out of any political correctness. Here Pilate is a driven one, who is coerced by Sanhedrin, High Council and the Priests to kill Jesus. He rages against, he refuses, he shouts, he does all he can. The Jews, however, are cleverer, more scheming, they hold the upper hand. The Let's-be-nice-to-the-Jews-approach of the production goes wholly down the drain."[595]

Nailing again: From Norwich 1144 ...
At the first Monte Cassino Passion Plays in 1150, the start of a different type of reenactments dated just 54 years back. That he would "revenge Christ's blood on Israel" and "leave no single member of the Jewish race alive", crusader Geoffrey of Bouillon had sworn in 1096.[596] Already during the first weeks of the march to Holy Land, 4000 Jews were killed in Rhineland; having conquered Jerusalem on July 15, 1099, the crusaders dragged all Jews into one of the local synagogues and burnt them alive.[597] The noble crusade leaders Guibert de Nogens and Richard de Poitiers had couched their intentions into phrases which all too clearly point to their hurts in childhood: "You are the descendants of those who killed and hanged our God. Moreover, [God] himself has said: 'The day will yet dawn when my children will come and avenge my blood.'"[598]
Forty-five years later, and three years before the second crusade, a Norwich housewife was approached by a man who claimed to be a cook working for

593 Langer, p.63, quoting from Thompson, "Good Bye to Germany", Harper's Magazine, December 1934, p.46. SA leader Ernst Röhm was shot on July 1, 1934 by SS officer Eicke during a cleansing operation which was passed off as defence action against the so called Röhm Putsch.
594 Kopetzky, Helmut: Kruzifix. Das Logo des Abendlands, 2008. NDR-Radio feature, broadcast on Holy Friday 2009 and Easter 2013.
595 Tenenbom 2012, p.121.
596 Carmichael, Joel: The Satanizing of the Jews. New York 1992 (by Wistrich 2010, p.19).
597 Wilensky, p.31; see also Jewishencyclopedia.com.
598 Cohn, N.: Pursuit of the Millennium, p.70 (Michael, p.68); cf. Wilensky, p.122.

the Archdeacon of Norwich. He offered to her twelve-year-old son a job in the Archdeacon's kitchens. William's mother was paid three shillings to let him go. It was Tuesday before Easter, March 19, 1144. This was the last time William, who as a tanner apprentice had been in the habit of frequenting the houses of certain Jews, was seen alive. His body, showing signs of a violent death, was found wearing "a jacket and shoes", lying on the soil of Thorpe Wood forest, on Holy Saturday – the day of tortured Jesus' repose in the grave. And just this psychobsessive combination of three images – Jesus in the manger, Jesus stripped on cross, William abused and stripped lying under trees – was the stabilizing triangle for a new kind of reenactions that would spread quickly over Europe and is rightly tagged by Catholic Encyclopedia as "one of the most notable and disastrous lies of history".

The body was not touched until Monday, when it was buried without any ceremony just where it was found. Shortly after, the grave was opened again by William's uncle, the priest Godwin Stuart, just to have the body recognized, the burial Office read, and earth cover the victim for the second time. The man to whom William's mother had entrusted her son was never seen again.[599] Some days later Stuart, at the diocesan synode, accused the Jews of the murder. But the Sheriff pointed out that since the Jews were the king's men, he had no jurisdiction in the case. The only result of Stuart's action was that the body was exhumed again and buried at Norwich monks' cemetery on April 24.

Poor William's corpse was not to rest in peace, for five years later, in 1149, the Jew Eleazar was murdered by men of his debtor, Sir Simon de Novers. When the Jews demanded just punishment, the murderer's advocate Bishop Turbe tried to counter the accusation by broaching the "Jewish murder" of Little William anew and – what a bother! – in vain again. But the next year – exactly the year when in Monte Cassino the world's first Passion Play was enacted – brought a new constellation: The new Prior of the monks was now Bishop Turbe's friend Richard de Ferraris, whose confrere Thomas of Monmouth now during the Lent before Holy Friday happened to have three visions which ordered him to procure a worthier resting place for Little William. Thus the putrid corpse moved three more times, first into the chapter house, then into the cathedral and eventually in the cathedral's martyr chapel, since meanwhile Brother Thomas had made three discoverings: First, murdered Eleazar was one of Little William's murderers. Second, citing Jewish convert Theobald of Cambridge as witness, Thomas had achieved to shed a first beam of light into the darkness of Jewish international conspiracy: In Spain, Theobald had told him, an annual meeting of Jews of all countries would assign by lot, where the sacrifice of a Christian child was to be fulfilled this year; after French Narbonne it had been Norwich's turn this time. Thomas' third invention for acting out his cross obsession was the fatal mise-en-scène concept of all future ritual murders of Christian children; a concept that a contemporary condensed in one sentence: "The Jews of Norwich brought a child before Easter, and tortured him with all the tortures

---

599 Perry/Schweitzer, p.48.

wherewith our Lord was tortured, and on Long Friday hanged him on a rod in hatred of our Lord ..."[600]

The ritual murder of William of Norwich on Holy Friday 1144. Woodcut from Schedelsche Weltchronik, Nuremberg 1493. The two men applying hammer and driller are tagged on their shoulders by the yellow rings mandatory for German Jews at that time.

No wonder, the Passion of the Christ(ian Child) was reenacted with as many painful details as the concurring Monte Cassino Passion, from "three silver shillings" as payment to William's mother, on to three wounds by nails, many wounds in headskin and one stab wound in the victim's side. The desire to act out is obvious: "The blood libel charges Jews with playing the same role they did during the crucifixion" states Gabriel Wilensky, while Phyllis Goldstein resumes the case concisely: "They reenacted the crucifixion of Jesus [and] mimicked the details of the passion."[601]

Obsessive detailing ramps up in the case of "Little Hugh of Lincoln", described by the poet Matthew Paris in 1255: A "great number" of Jews assembled in Lincoln, "and then they appointed a Jew of Lincoln judge, to take the place of Pilate, by whose sentence, and with the concurrence of all, the boy was subjected to various tortures. They scourged him till the blood

600   Prager/Telushkin, p.81.
601   Wilensky, p.34; Goldstein, Phyllis, p.77 and 82.

flowed, they crowned him with thorns, mocked him, and spat upon him; each of them also pierced him with a knife, and they made him drink gall, and scoffed at him with blasphemous insults, and kept gnashing their teeth and calling him Jesus, the false prophet. And after tormenting him in diverse ways they crucified him, and pierced him to the heart with a spear."
What is true in the story? In fact, many Jews had assembled in Lincoln, not for killing a boy but to attend the marriage of Bellaset, daughter of Berachiah. In fact the little son of (probably unmarried) Christian mother Beatrice had been found in the well shaft of the Jew Jopin. In fact Jopin, under torture and the given promise to be spared himself, had disclosed that Little Hugh had been crucified by the Jews who met in London. In fact, King Henry III had sold his rights to tax the Jews six months before to his brother Richard, the Earl of Cornwall. Having lost this source of income, the King decided that he was eligible for the Jews' money if they were convicted of crimes. So 99 Jews of London were encarcerated, 18 of them executed, Jopin himself bound to the tail of a wild horse, dragged through the streets of London and hanged. The remaining 80 Jews were pardoned and set free, most likely because Richard, who saw a potential threat to his own source of income, intervened on their behalf with his brother.[602]
The well marketed concept of "Little William" inspired not only the profitable follow-up of "Little Hugh", but hundreds of alleged ritual murders which actually cost the lives of innumerable Jewish men, women and children in Europe and Middle East. In 1171 the case in French town Blois lacked any juridical honesty as well as a corpus delicti, but the obdurate 31 Jews and 17 Jewesses, refusing the easy escape through baptismal water, preferred to die in a burning wooden tower, singing the "Aleinu" with their last gasps.[603] At Saragossa in 1182 and at almost all other cases the remakes of crucifixion happened when Christians prepared for Holy Friday and Easter. Only in Fulda 1235 the accusation of having killed five Christian children came on agenda around Christmas or better say the feast day of Herod's massacre (December 28). Emperor Frederic II constituted an inquiry commission and on grounds of the results rejected the accusation, holding the Jews of Fulda and entire Germany "completely absolved of this imputed crime".[604]
The arraigners of the Blois ritual murder defamation were innovative in their imputations to the Jews. In the earlier cases "the murder of the victim was broadly adjusted to the Passion of Christ; the victim allegedly was tortured to death by the Jews, who thus repeated the crime that their ancestors once had committed against Christ himself and for which they were condemned." But here in the Loire valley, famous for it's wines, for the first time rumors spread that Jews committed murder in order to extract blood for their unleavened Passover *matzot*. "By the association of the *Jews*, who anyhow were uncanny to all good Christians, with the magic of the *blood*, which was so common to folkways, the scary story became popular for the first

---

602 jewishencyclopedia, Hugh of Lincoln; Wikipedia, Little Saint Hugh of Lincoln.
603 Michael, p.84.
604 Chazan: Church, State and Jew, p.123-126 (cited by Michael, p.85).

time."[605] And the connection Jew+blood becomes a trias of Jew+cross+corpus in the following three examples of reenactments:

A. In 1265, the *Siete Partidas* code of Spanish King Alfonso the Wise charged the Jews of celebrating Good Friday contemptuously, "stealing children and fastening them to crosses or making images of wax and crucifying them when they cannot obtain children."[606]
B. During Holy Week of 1290 a Christian woman in Paris had pawned her clothing in order to borrow money from a Jewish moneylender. He persuaded her that she instead of paying him back her debt of *30 silver coins* should provide him with a *consecrated wafer*. The woman agrees, steals the host in her mouth and redeems her pledge with it. After shop closing time the Jewish broker starts to work on the wafer, knocking a *nail* into it with his *hammer*, stabbing the holy wafer with his pen knife, causing it to *bleed* profusely. When he throws it whole into the fire, the Host leaps up and flies around the Jew's house, the Jew running after it and *piercing it with a lance*. Submerged into a pot of seething water, the Host again rises of its own accord and appears to the Jew in the form of *crucified Christ*. Fortunately, another woman, "armed with the *sign of the cross*", rescues the tortured and persecuted host from the house of the wicked Jew and delivers it to her parish priest. The Jew is burned at the stake, his wife and children convert to Christianity.[607]
Remind the reminders: While bread was the most important daily food for medieval Europeans, bread was also the center of their daily religious rite: "This is my body, which is for you; do this in remembrance of me ... For whenever you eat this bread and drink this cup, you proclaim *the Lord's death* until he comes" (1 Cor 11:24-26). To sane Christian people, the Pauline myth – which Paul probably didn't understand himself – was simply indigestible, but repugnant enough to activate the hurts and tools they had in mind since childhood: Nails and hammer, wounds and lances, blood and silver coins.
C. The following *cause celebre* brings to stage the whole sequence of images in a reenactment that illustrates the words of British historian David Abulafia: "Jews constantly recrucify Christ in countless ways, of which this [crucifying children] is the most horrible."[608]
He was known as "the hammer of the Jews": In spring 1475, Franciscan monk Bernardino da Feltre (1439-1494), sternly condemning Jewish usury, concluded his Lenten sermons in the Dome of Trento with a portentous prophecy: "Easter will not pass without God having revealed in some way the sad works of the Jews".[609]

605 Trachtenberg, p.135-136 (italics: K.Y.R.).
606 Prinz, p.24.
607 Cohen, p.103; (italics K.Y.R.).
608 "Blood Libels Are Back", in The Times Literary Supplement, February 28, 2007 (quoted by Wistrich 2010, p.90).
609 vivoscuola.it/us/gsignn8659/S.simo/quadro.html: "Concluse l'ammonizione asserendo che non sarebba passata la Pasqua senza che Dio non avesse mostrato attravesso qualche

On Holy Friday, Master Andreas Unferdorben reported to Bishop Hinderbach that his three-year-old son Simon was missing. On Saturday the house of Samuel, the head of the Jewish community, was examined without results. On Easter Sunday, in a basin in his cellar that was connected with his ritual bath as well as with an outward water collector, the boy's corpse was found by Samuel's cook Seligman. Together with his neighbors Engel and Tobias, Samuel went to the Buonconsiglio to report their find. In quite patho-logical consequence, the Christian child's death would lead to the doom of Trento's Jews who were as holistically guilty for killing Simon the son of Maria Unferdorben as their ancestors for killing Jesus the son of Mary. The detailed screenplay of Jesus' agony replayed with Little Simon was reconstructed by Hong Kong born historian Ronnie Po-Chia Hsia on the basis of the protocols of torture.

The most important method of torture consisted, similar to Spanish inquisition, in the *Strappada*: a rope tied the hands of the victim on his back and then lifted the body up to the ceiling by means of a pulley. If the victim refused to confess, the torturer bate on the rope or let it off for a sudden so that the body sagged some inches, one foot, two feet ... The interrogation protocol of October 26 illustrates how this "let jump" was repeated as often as the search for truth required:

Joaff: Let me down, I'll tell the truth.
Podestà: He should tell it on the rope.
Joaff: I have never done any wrong.
One pulled him up and let him fall then.
Joaff: By the death that I will suffer, I am innocent. I haven't seen the child elsewhere than I've said already.
One shaked him for a while on the rope. [...] Then one let him down.
Joaff: Where do you want that I have seen him? ...

"Some of the Jews", Po-Chia Hsia resumes, "kept stalwart and between cries of pain and relentless questions asserted their innocence again and again; others ... in order to escape the torments, probably would have readily made a confession, but did not know the screenplay that went around in the heads of the judges, and hence had to keep suffering." The following nine details are what the hanging ones ought to have known:
(1) The Temple: Saw him in the synagogue? Just one more time Joaff had to be pulled up to have him remember this point. Eight further details show which elements of Jesus' Passion are painful, puzzling and personal enough to call for reenactment:
(2) The Holy Family: This popular subject of 15th century painting showed father Joseph the hardworking carpenter, Mary the diligent housewife and in between their little Jesus, once on his hobby horse, once helping Mummy and Daddy. Both little Simon's father, the master craftsman Andreas *Unferdorben* (literally *untainted*, in German) and his wife Maria fit well to this

---

via, le tristi opere degli Ebrei." Cf. Flannery, p.116.

domestic idyll. And now their son was killed by Herod's people. The more strongly the Holy Family, with two caring parents, contrasted to Paul's outrageous teaching of God the sacrificing Father, the more eagerly the outrage produced by this Father-cross-complex was projected onto the bearded men hanging on the strappada.

(3) Virgin and Mother: Expectably, "faithless" Jews would make sport of this truth of Christian faith. How could a clerical interrogator, feeling inwardly troubled by his own sinful objections to this dogma, avoid to put this question to the script?

According to the process report, the physician Samuel had compared Little Simon with Jesus as both were illegitimate sons; but in the torture chamber it was Samuel's servant Lazarus who provided the interrogators with the requested mixture of Jewish tradition and Trentine inquisition: "The Jews had spoken that the Jesus-child and the Christian God whom they call the hanged one was a bastard born from the shattered or weakened Mary who became pregnant by Joseph who was not her right husband. Her right husband was a priest."

(4) Conspiration: On April 8, Engel confesses that the three house fathers had conspired to rob a Christian child for purpose of his blood. On April 17, the pulled up Tobias admits the international dimension of the scheming, telling about one merchant Abraham from Candia (Crete) who six or seven years ago, in Venice, had "brought to sale a big part of blood and a big part of sugar."

(5) Betrayal: For this role Tobias was chosen, who had treated Jewish and Christian citizens of Trento as physician. During the first examinations he remained steadfast, though he hung for half an hour in the air and the torturer "often bate the rope". On April 7, however, one pulled him so high that he cried he would tell the truth now and begged to be let down. "One let him down", the clerk relates, "as it seemed he almost faded or went to waste". The interrogation had to be postponed. Two days later a broken man named Tobias had found the suitable allegory to Judas' kiss and was able to confess that "with sweet promises" he had enticed Simon to the place of his sufferings.

(6) Mocking: "The men who were guarding Jesus began mocking and beating him. They blindfolded him and demanded, "Prophesy! Who hit you?" And they said many other insulting things to him" (Lk 22:63-65). What things? The young inventive culprit Moses had depicted a joyous scene with stomping and laughter; the others confessed indecent and grotesque gestures, having exposed their butt and penis and poked their tongue out to mock the Christian child.

(7) Circumcision: According to Luke (2:22-24), Jesus had been circumcised on the eighth day. Various blood libel depictions of the epoch show "how the murderers circumcise their victim first."[610] Why must this seemingly minor detail be reenacted? "If Simon's death was to be a replication of Christ's

---

610 Rohrbacher/Schmidt, p.278.

203

crucifixion, the boy had to be circumcised", Po-Chia Hsia opines.[611] Indeed some widespread illustrations of the Trento blood libel produce a strange simultaneity of circumcision and crucifixion. The cut on the male member was momentous because it put the cruel fathers of the old Bible against the loving divine son of the Gospel. The factual lesions that had been found on the child's penis fit perfectly into the screenplay, and on June 11 the judges had Seligman, hanging on the rope, confess how "the old Moses had circumcised the boy, while the others had stretched his arms across to imitate Christ's crucifixion."

Circumcision and "crosswise" torture of Little Simon of Trento. From Hartmann Schedel's Nurembergian World Chronicle (1493).
Right: Jews crucifying a Christian boy. From the collected Vitae sanctorum of Jesuite father Matthäus Rader (1561-1634).

(8) Crosswise: Yet on April 10 the clerk had meticulously transcribed the Hebrew words "which had accompanied the ritual torture of the child who, as is written in the process report [alluding to John 19:30] 'standing crosswise bowed his head and gave up his spirit'."
In the face of such merciless crosswise torture of a Christian child, the punishment to apply on adult Jewish torturers had to be proportionate. "Having inflicted untold torments on a little Christian child, they now, thanks to victorious Christian justice, had to suffer agonies beyond description." Samuel, in whose cellar the little son of Maria Unferdorben had been found, was elected to suffer for what the son of Mary suffered on his way to Golgotha: On order of the Podestá, Samuel's flesh was teared out underway with pincers from his body.
To mention the good things: One of Trento's Jewish men survived, while their women were rescued by the intervention of Pope Sixtus, the open-minded, pleasure-loving patron of fine arts and nepotism. He stopped the torture of twenty-five-year-old Sara and thirty-six-year-old Schönle and

611   Hsia 1997, p.89.

ordered his legate Baptista dei Giudici to examine the entire process. Back in Rome again, dei Giudici reported that the process against the Jews had been performed in a highly inappropriate way. The extorted confessions did not prove anything; all evidence rather pointed to a man called *Schweizer* (Swiss) suspect to be Simon's murderer. [612] The Jewish women and children, so the legate urged in vain, must be released immediately.

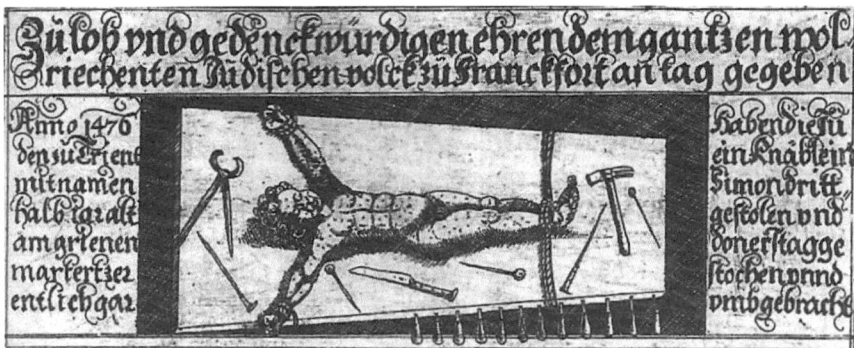

"To praise and memorable honor for the whole sweet-smelling Jewish people displayed at Frankfurt today": Little Simon's "crosswise" torture was painted on Frankfurt Bridge Tower yet around 1476. Side text of this 17th century depiction: "Anno 1476 the Jews at Trento stole a boy with name Simon, third half year old, and on Green Thursday martyred, pricked all over and finally slew him."

(9) Final accord, redeeming faith: One year after the execution of their husbands and fathers-in-law, on January 13, 1477, in front of a big audience, Schönle (Bella), Anna and Sara appeared in the Bishop's chapel. Having approached to the altar, the women "humbly bade for baptism and prayed to the Lord, the Virgin Mary, to the angels, apostles and saints". Bishop Hinderbach, the driving force of the whole process, asked them whether they desired baptism "voluntarily and without any influence of violence, fear, dread or instigation" but rather "by virtue of divine inspiration and free will ... to preserve Catholic faith with sincerity and strength until the end of their lifes?" – "Yes." – And after they had solemnly admitted and regretted the crimes committed by their husbands, Hinderbach performed the rites of exorcism and baptism. Sara became Clara, Schönle Elisabeth and Anna was now Susanna. Together, they had six good reasons to choose life, change faith: Both Anna and Schönle had one child while Sara was a mother of four.[613] Thirteen days after their conversion, the new Christians experienced a special grace: Draped in white garments they were led to the cathedral, where they were allowed to contemplate the wounds of Little Simon and pray for his intercession.

---

612 This theory was defended later on also by Joseph Bloch, Rabbi in Floridsdorf, a suburb of Vienna. (Bloch, Joseph Samuel: Erinnerungen aus meinem Leben. Vienna and Leipzig 1922, Vol.II, p.82-83; cited by Lehr, p.81).
613 Cf. Swaim 2013, p.240-276, about victims' behavior as in Stockholm Syndrome.

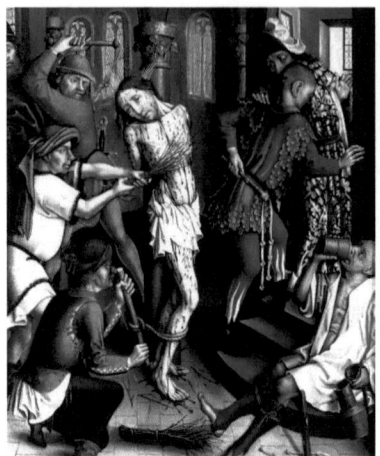

In agonizing detail: Scourging of Christ, painted by the Master of so called Karls-ruhe Passion (ca.1450). Right: *"Ein hübsch new lied von zweyen Juden und einem Kind"*, pamphlet about the Sappenfeld (Bavaria) blood libel of 1540, whose victim was the boy of four years Michael Pisenharter.

Fifteen years later, during his voyage home from his *Camino de Santiago* pilgrimage to Santiago de Compostela, the 60-year-old Spanish Convert Be-nito Garcia had the bad luck to spend a night in tavern together with a bunch of drunken riff-raff. They rummaged his luggage, allegedly found a host, and at the end of 1490 Benito, together with his eighty-year-old father, three other New Christians and six Jews was accused of "abducting a Christian boy from a street in Toledo around Christmas of 1488, then bringing him to a secret cave near La Guardia where they used him to reenact Jesus's cruci-fixion. First they inflicted injuries and abuses ... then they nailed the child to a cross and cut out his heart" which they, together with the host, needed for their black magic.[614]
The accusation against one of the conspirators, Yuce (Joseph) Franco, de-clared: "His soul embittered and depraved, he went in company with several others to crucify a Christian child on a Good Friday, in the same fashion, with the same animosity and cruelty as his forefathers had for our Saviour Jesus Christ, tearing his flesh, beating him and spitting in his face, covering him with wounds, crushing him with blows and turning to ridicule our holy Faith." The last five words became true at least for the former Santiago pilgrim Benito Garcia. Treated with an early version of waterboarding, with a rest of humour he affirmed that "from the time they poured water into his nostrils, he was totally de-Christianized".[615] In 1491 brave Benito's pilgrimage ended on the stake, and in 1492 Torquemada achieved to have the *Reyes Católicos* sign the edict of expulsion. Up to the present day *El*

---

614   Yovel, p.179; as to *El Niño de La Guardia* view also picture on p.277.
615   Poliakov, Vol.II, p.197.

Niño Santo is the church-patron of La Guardia and the arrival point of many pilgrimages, notwithstanding that also this "Holy Child" – like that of Blois in 1171 – neither had a name nor ever existed. What existed and lived on was the cross in Christian minds. In spite of the fact that, besides of Emperor Frederick II and Pope Innocent IV in 13th century, also in later centuries "a long, impressive series of popes, statesmen, theologians and scholars ... protested against the ritual murder and blood libels, the accusations only spread, penetrating deeper and deeper into the mind and culture of Christian Europe".[616]

... to Bavaria 1948

Springtime in Poland, before Easter 1747: A body is found in the melting snow near rural village Zaslav. Easter? Ever after Holy Friday! A peasant makes the connection: "The Jews are feasting in the inn." Indeed, the guests in the Jewish-owned inn are celebrating a boy's circumcision. "The accused were all sentenced to a monstrous death ... their hands and feet amputated and nailed to the gallows."[617]

Springtime in Moscow, Easter 1935, nice weather. In a workers' suburb a Jewish mother sends nursemaid Frosja on a walk with four-year-old Chava and one-year-old Michael. Chava's Christian friend begs insistently, she absolutely wants to accompany them, so let's go. Two hours later the friend's caring sister comes and asks about the child. "She's having a walk with them", Chava's mother answers and the anxious sister returns home. Soon after, dozens of people emerge. "You Jewess! What have you done to the child?" Someone was clued-in on them: "The Jews are celebrating Passover right now, they need the blood of Christian children for their Matze." The crowd keeps growing and gets edgy, stones are hurled and windows clash, the mother tries to flee indoors but the mob tugs her out: "Beat the Jew!" There comes a girl, shoves the men away: It's Frosja. "And then all noticed the two girls standing besides my buggy", Michail Voronov tells: "My sister and the neighbor's girl who allegedly was yet to be consumed with the Matze. Just one hour later, the parents of the 'gone lost' girl urgently entreated my mother to condone their fault and begged her not to file a complaint to the authorities. When my father came home from work, the door and the windows were already repaired completely."[618]

Summertime in Kielce, July 1, 1946. Eight-year-old Henryk Blaszczyk remembers the dainty cherries and his good friends in the village 15 miles from Kielce where he had lived with his parents until Christmas. He jumps onto a horsecart and off goes the story. When Henryk doesn't come home in the evening, his parents get very worried; at 11 p.m. they go to the police station and report their son missing. Two days later, at 7 p.m., Henryk is back again, laden with cherries. All's well that ends well?

---

616 Cohen, p.113-115.
617 Dubnow, S.M.: History of the Jews in Russia and Poland, p.176-177 (quoted by Perry/Schweitzer, p.57).
618 Chrulev, Dmitry: "Ritualmordlegende des 21.Jahrhunderts", in: Jüdische Zeitung, April 2011, p.19.

Fifty years later, a 59-year-old man with sad eyes and heart-aches, living with his wife, a parrot and a dog in a Kielce suburb, is interviewed by German *Der Spiegel* magazine. Still he remembers exactly his father's first words on his return that evening: "Henio, at last! Have the Jews caught you or what?" Fearing to get the stick, Henio nods, his father clicks: his built-up tension has found metal. Later on that evening, Henryk's father Walenty in considerably drunken state goes to the police again, informing the officer that his son had been kidnapped by Jews and brought to the basement of their house but fortunately had managed to escape. The next morning, on their way to the police station, Walenty inculcates his son with what to say. Since almost all of the 200 Jews living in Kielce – camp survivors, ex-soldiers, young Zionists – live in one apartment block in Planty Street No.7, the policemen carry the boy to this address. Was it this house? – Hum, yes. – Was this Jew one of them? – And this ...? The officer calls for back-up, which arrives quickly. Why did you call for us? – Jews have kidnapped ... The militia invades, rushes not to the basement but upstairs, shoots some Jews, delivers the others to the waiting mob. At noon, hundreds of workers from Ludwików steel mill, led by activists of communist party, arrive with clubs and steel rods, beat twenty Jews to death. At 3 p.m. a new unit of security forces, firing few salvos of warning shots, achieves to restore order. Next day, July 4, a Polish Christian named Novak, in the train from Czestochava to Kielce, witnesses the following scene: "At the stop in Wloszcowa station, the passengers called out between two trains the last news, saying that Jews had murdered Christian children and the people of Kielce take revenge now." In Piekoszów station the witness Józef Sztarkman heard how at the arrival of the train from Kielce news got about quickly that Jews had "killed Christian children for Matzo" – the perfect key to trigger a wildfire pogrom at the station. Brunon Piatek, the manager of an iron foundry, and the engineer Elzanowski saw how at the platforms people were pushed and pulled out of the wagons. "The method of killing was to hurl stones on the Jews who helplessly ran over rails and platforms until they fell down. Then the fallen ones were finished with iron hefts." When Piatek and Elzanowski confronted the persecutors, they were threatened by a furiously shouting crowd: "You Jewish rogues! Jews have killed our children and you dare to defend them!" The plural form of "our children" refers to the rumours that in the aforesaid basement little Henryk had eye-witnessed the killing of fifteen Christan children "for their blood".

On July 5 the pogrom ended which had cost the life of 42 Shoah survivors. At the end of August, the British ambassador telegraphed to the secretary of foreign affairs: "Bishop Bieniek, suffragan of Upper Silesia, astonished me yesterday, asserting that there were certain proves for that the allegedly mistreated child was actually mistreated and the Jews had taken blood from his arm." In Cardinal Hlond's view the Jews themselves had provoked the massacre by accepting jobs in Poland's new, communist government. And nearly 700 years after Innocent IV had become the first of many popes to confirm that Jews did not practice ritual murder, Stefan Wyszynski, the

Bishop of Lublin, commented that the question of the Jewish use of Christian blood had "not yet been definitely settled".[619]
Two weeks before the pogrom, the journal *Odrodzenie* had apprehensively stated that "the deep-rooted Polish anti-Semitism has not slackened though more than three million Jews have been murdered by Hitler's inquisition ... One should expect that this historically singular murder would generate in the Polish people, having been tortured and harrowed itself, a shared answer of compassion, a feeling of brotherhood ... Instead, the Jewish blood shed so excessively by the barbaric enemy of Polish nation and of free humanity has but roused the mob's instincts."
Bishop Teodor Kubina of Czestochava was the only one in Polish episcopate who vigorously preached against Jew-hate and blood-libel delusion – and was rebuked by his colleagues. The mere fact that after Auschwitz, Maidanek, Treblinka there were still Jews living in Poland was taken as a proof of their uncanny power; the allegedly disproportional Jewish presence in the communist power-structures created by the Soviet "liberators" provided even stronger evidence to many.
Cardinal Hlond, who before the pogrom had rejected two solicitations to speak out against blood libel defamations, lastly spoke out that "it is the Jews who now occupy leading positions in governmental institutions". Actually however, historian Jan T. Gross states at the end of his book titled "Fear" that during the short timeframe of five years after the war – while communist party consolidated – Poland became *judenrein*.[620]
"I was still a child, wasn't I?" Henryk Blaszczyk, nicknamed the "Kielce Phantom", never got over the black consequences of his childish white lie. "Still decades after the massacre", a friend of his relates, "Henryk went to the house in Planty Street to search for a basement there – although he knew that there is no."[621]

Same year, at German scene: "In order to choose the most suitable forest lot for building the chapel, on April 25, 1946 Parson Humpf, his sister Anna and Bärbel Ruess walked to the forest." For yet at the beginning of allied air raids the young parson of my home village Pfaffenhofen had made the vote with his parish to build a chapel for Mother Mary if the village would be spared from bombs. Since just four farms had been destroyed by fire bombs, the Virgin Mother's chapel was to be built now. "We had just started when Bärbel said: 'Someone has called me ... Come and see what a woman ...'"
Neither the parson nor his sister saw the woman Bärbel talked with: "I don't understand that! – How do you know that? – Yes, this was one year ago when the Americans came." To his bishop the parson later on imparted the "rather cloudy, unintelligible things" the woman had talked about: "Hand out many sacrifices to me! ... I want to load my children with crosses, heavy

619 Goldstein, Phyllis, p.296; Wyszynski: Wikipedia, Kielce pogrom.
620 Gross, p.243; previous citations (after footnote 618) concerning Kielce from his pages 83-84, 103, 105-106, 110, 113, 129 and 135.
621 "Ganz langsam gesteinigt", in: Der Spiegel, July 01, 1996.

and deep as the sea, because I love them in my sacrificed Son. [...] I am the sign of the living God. I press my sign on my children's foreheads. The star will persecute the sign. But my sign will defeat the star ..."[622]

On Holy Friday 1948 – a star now appeared in news about Palestine – the twenty-two-year-old visionary Bärbel did not come home in the evening. Like Henryk, she turned up again three days later, relating that she had been pulled into a car at church hill, abducted and brought to a basement where she experienced terrible things: "When I came to myself again I saw several men standing around me. They conversed in partly foreign and partly German language. I also viewed among them some who looked like Jews. Others stood more in the background, counting money."

Next day: "At awakening, again other ones were standing around me. They undressed me, stretched my arms out and fetched an electrical cable with two illuminable plates which they attached on my hands and feet ... The clutching on hands and feet was very painful. They did not much on the side wound."

Next day: "At awakening I heard a man – holding a host in his hand – blaspheming it terribly. He seemed to be a Jew, talked brokenly, was fat and had black hair. During the blasphemies his face distorted [...] Blankets were fetched inside, men and women – in shameless attire – came in and wreaked terrible things, yelling and shouting. They did so for a long time. At this, many – all consecrated, brightly flashing up – hosts were defiled in unimaginable ways [...] Then they fed ... a dog with hosts. They left but one and told me: 'If you will not consume it – dipped into this poison – we will give this one to the dog as well.' I replied: 'Give it to me!' – 'So you don't believe that this is poison?' they asked mockingly and let the poison drip onto one of the hosts that had fallen down ..."[623]

The Jewish-looking host defilers give the host to the dog who dies immediately, while the poison doesn't harm Bärbel who consumes the host to protect it from desecration.

All this happened three years after the gassings with Zyklon B (cyanide dripped onto a white substrate); it happened to a girl who in 1944 had contracted meningitis while serving as an army flak assistant; happened on Holy Friday of the very year 1948 when Evangelical Church of Germany proclaimed: "In crucifying the Messiah, Israel discarded it's chosenness ... That God's judgement follows Israel in it's reprobation till this day is a sign of His forbearance ... That God is not to be scoffed at is the silent sermon of the Jewish fate, a warning for us, an admonition for the Jews whether they too should convert to the One in which alone their salvation rests as well."[624]

622 Eizereif, p.34; fatherspeaks.net/pdf/ms_Marienfried_Marian-Shrines-Germany.pdf..
623 Eizereif, p.54-56.
624 "Darmstädter Erklärung" ("Wort zur Judenfrage"): Wikipedia, cf. Greenberg 2004, p.113. Note: Still on December 17, 1941 the Lutheran church superiors of Mecklenburg, Thuringia, Saxonia, Hesse-Nassau, Schleswig-Holstein, Anhalt and Lübeck in a joint declaration had urged "to take sharpest measures against the Jews and to expel them from German lands" (cf. Goldhagen 1996, p.143).

Like Little Simon of Trento, Bärbel had been put "crosswise" by the Jews – now in a modern way between two electrical plates, as if roentgenizing her belly. Why? After her mother's early death Bärbel had fled from the new situation in her father's house to the parson's house. Between her and the parson seventeen years her senior a deep mutual attachment existed that did not remain secret to their ambience; the priest himself admitted later on that he had been "not free of feelings" for his pretty clerical assistant. When he baptized my eldest brother in 1948, he told my parents who as a young couple lodged in the parson's house: "If this were my child I'd jump to the ceiling with joy." In 1996 Bärbel died just 22 days after her first love Martin. Not until the year 2000 Bärbel's sister dared to say that a daughter had been the fruit of this forbidden love. In a later photo this daughter is standing two steps behind a park bench where Bärbel sits with her Clopas (a theologian) and the children of a very pious marriage that however put to test her ability of suffering. The dedicated and progressive, sexually just very human parson told me personally that he would have liked to become a physician or architect but submitting to his parents' wish had chosen to become a priest. Eugen Drewermann's insight that anyone apt for being a celibatarian cleric and identifying with the doctrine of sacrifice "must have been sacrificed himself yet in his childhood"[625] shows up exemplarily in this gifted, energetic man who sacrificed his favorite profession and as a priest became the architect of a pilgrim place including subterranean atomic shelter for provident payers, and the creator of a daughter with a much more loving but hardly more present father than Jesus had.

Between two robbers

"Traditionally of sophisticated cruelty", writes historian Peter Schuster, "was the punishment of Jewish culprits." As a *„reverse observance of Jesus' crucifixion"* Cecil Roth interprets the special treatment which Jews facing the gallows deserved from 14th to 16th century in Spain, France, Germany and Switzerland.[626] Contrary to Christian delinquents, the Jewish thieves were hanged head-down between two hungry dogs. Albeit, their suffering could be stopped and finished more humanely at any time – if the culprit showed his readiness to baptism. In Basel for instance, in 1374 a Jew was baptized with water from a bucket on a stick but then left hanging until noble women took him down and nursed him – alas not back to health but at least to baptism anew, death by exhaustion and Christian burial. *"Do hengen die 3 hunde tosamen"*, a chronicler commented the accompanied death of Jewish thief Michael in Dortmund 1486. In August 1558, a Frankfurt Jew hung fully conscious seven days head-down, survived one of the dogs and at last, one day before the second guiltless dog, gave up his guilt-laden soul.[627]

---

625 Drewermann 1989, p.91.
626 Roth, Gleanings, 6-15, 81 n1; thus cited by Michael, p.54; Roth, p.33.
627 Schuster, p.178-183 (chapter "Todesstrafen für Juden").

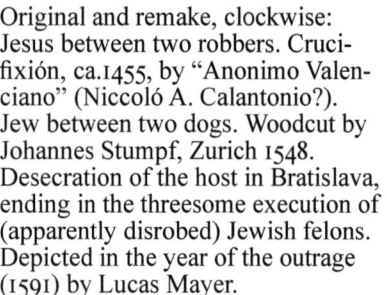

Original and remake, clockwise:
Jesus between two robbers. Cruci-
fixión, ca.1455, by "Anonimo Valen-
ciano" (Niccoló A. Calantonio?).
Jew between two dogs. Woodcut by
Johannes Stumpf, Zurich 1548.
Desecration of the host in Bratislava,
ending in the threesome execution of
(apparently disrobed) Jewish felons.
Depicted in the year of the outrage
(1591) by Lucas Mayer.

His guilt, and what the Jew had to replay between the two canine-baring robbers left and right, the spectators had well in mind: "Those who were crucified with him also taunted him" (Mk 15:32). The head-down reenactment is a Freudian slip also: placing a despised Jewish criminal in the role of suffering Christ – sided by discardable animals – manifests the actual degree of estimation Christian mind conceded to Jews, to dogs – and to Jesus.

The following remake of crucifixion in a threesome did nevermore get out of Eli Wiesel's mind:

All prisoners had been mustered to have to look on the hanging of three fellow prisoners: two adults who had been found with weapons, and an eleven-year-old boy who even under torture had given away no one. The SS seemed to be concerned and more uneasy than normally. To hang a child in front of thousands of spectators was no trifle. The *Lagerkapo* refused to serve as hangman, so three SS-guards had to put the nooses round the necks. The adults shouted "Long live freedom", the child kept silent, and on a sign of the camp commander the chairs rolled over.

Absolute silence reigned over the whole camp. At the horizon the sun sank. The two adults did not live any more. But the third rope moved. Because he was so light, the boy was still alive. For more than half an hour he wrestled with death. "Where is God?" a prisoner standing behind Eli Wiesel asked in a low voice. And Wiesel heard a voice in himself answer: "Where he is? There – hanging on the gallows."

Threesome, why? "Chance is not a kosher word" is one of Wiesel's words. And Pinchas Lapide makes the numerical connection: "The three crosses at Golgotha and the three gallows in Auschwitz: Pagans as tormentors, Jews as victims, and the same question: "My God, my God, why hast Thou forsaken me?"[628]

Bloodless pain in Spain: Autos da fé

After Auschwitz: In the main synagogue of Bosnian capital Sarajevo, Rabbi Joachim Prinz sits on his chair ready to start the sermon he was invited to give. Time passes and nobody wants to open. In Germany, Rabbi Prinz had clairvoyantly propagated mass emigration yet in 1934. In 1963 he had marched with Martin Luther King on Washington. And why here in Sarajevo, the old refuge of Spanish Jews, nobody wants to start at the scheduled time? Eventually Prinz flusters to his neighbor for the cause of the strange delay. "He replied, with some embarrassment, that I was sitting before the altar with my legs crossed, and that reminded the Sephardic community of the cross which their ancestors had been forced to worship many centuries before. It was a great relief to the rabbi and the congregants when I uncrossed my legs. The service began. They were no longer 'in the shadow of the cross'."[629]

In 1492, when the Jewish community of Spain tempted to rescind the expulsion order with an exorbitant bribe, Torquemada is said to have erupted into the royal chamber with crucifix held high: "Behold the *crucifixo* whom the wicked Judas sold for thirty pieces of silver!" And King Ferdinand caved in and the Jews got out of Spain after 2000 years, many of them fleeing to Ottoman Empire, for instance Sarajevo.[630]

In Spanish Inquisition the crucifix conjoined with another, comparably threatful, equally wooden learning device. The image of Jesus' cruellest possible execution was present at all stages of the proceedings that ended in the second cruellest killing, in burning on the stake, alive.

Praying "without making the sign of the cross" was, for instance, one of the denouncable evidences of apostasy which made Maria de Zarate face the crucifix in the interrogation room. The crucifix was needed for swearing oaths and it was present in the torture chamber; there were crucifixes in the procession to and at the stake, green crucifixes in the hands of the con-

---

628 Lapide 1988, p.72.
629 Prinz, p.99-100.
630 Perera, p.54; cf. Gerber, p.135, quoting as first source Luis de Páramo, De Origine et Progressu Officii Sanctae Inquisitionis, Madrid 1598; Alexy, p.266.

demned ones, and crucifixes in the hands of the friars who till the very last moment solicited the stiffnecked ones to take the last minute opportunity of being strangled on the stake instead of burning in the flames alive – simply by kissing what?[631] Tomas Treviño de Sobremonte was among the non-kissers: "When I held the crucifix to his lips, he turned away his head", Father Correño related, "saying ... he was a Jew and wanted to live and die in the Law of Moses."[632]

As eagerly as the absence of crucifixes in converso homes was noted by informers, as proudly the informers showed on their chests and houses the sign of fame they were entitled to display: a cross between a dagger and an olive branch.[633] Nevertheless it would be overstated to say that Inquisition pivoted around the crucifix alone, while actually the machine was fuelled by the money which the Church was entitled to confiscate from the condemned ones and which was, together with the dues of state, shared justly; for instance 11.000 Reis for an inquisitor, 4000 for a notary, 500 for the mayor and each of his guards after an auto in Coimbra, A.D. 1699.[634] Actually the Inquisition did not aim at "real" Jews. A leading motive of the informers was bourgeois social envy against those Jews who by their baptism had found access to all professional careers and now were putting the "old Christians" behind.[635] In case someone had made himself conspicuous by suspicious Judaizing conduct (cooking with oil instead of lard, excessive handwashing, change of bedclothes at the eve of *Sabado* ...), he nevertheless got off unpunished if he was able to prove that he never had been baptized.

All other Jew-baptizers were put behind by Vincent Ferrer, who from his childhood in a noble family fasted rigorously every Friday since "the passion of Christ was always the object of his most tender devotion."[636] Having entered Dominican order in 1367 at age seventeen, he still in 1411, now in his sixties, infatigably traversed Castile from end to end, invading synagogues with a Torah scroll in one arm and a crucifix in the other, "while an unruly mob at his heels added force to his arguments". In this way, "on a single day, in Toledo, he is said to have gained four thousand converts."[637]

Even more successful in his way was Manoel I, the young King of Portugal who in 1497 wanted to marry the daughter of the Spanish royal couple and therefore had a small problem. Spain insisted on the precondition of expulsion of all Jews but Manoel wanted to keep this yielding source of income. On March 19, 1497, he decreed that all children age four to fourteen were to be baptized and separated from their parents – if the adults refused to convert. Those who wanted to leave Portugal could do so only in the port of

631   See Bodian, p.27 and passim.
632   Wachtel, p.151 (Maria de Zarate) and 115 (Tomas Treviño).
633   Wiesenthal, p.46.
634   Nazario, p.144.
635   Cf. Carvalho, Francisco Moreno de: O Antijudaismo e o Problema da Heresia Judaizante nas Inquisições da Espanha e Portugal. In: Fuks, p.229-253.
636   Our Lady of the Rosary Library, olrl.org/lives/ferrer.shtml; wikipedia.org/wiki/Vincent_Ferrer.
637   Poliakov 2003, Vol.II, p.148; 156-157; 165-167.

Lisbon. When thousands of Jews arrived there at the given day, their children too were taken away. There were no boats to transport them to exile but "an army of padres" with baptismal water. "The decree of expulsion did not have to be carried out, because all the Jews of Portugal were now Christians."[638]

But how sincere were those thousands of baptized Jews? In 1506, on April 19, mass was celebrated in a church of Lisbon, to celebrate the Sunday of Easter, this "age-old source of anti-Jewish explosion",[639] imploring for cessation of the pestilence which had begun to spread half a year ago, adding to the miseries of draught and lower-class famine. Suddenly, a crucifix with glass reliquary at the altar was observed to be unusually luminous. A miracle! Tactlessly, a New Christian laughed at the idea, saying that nothing more was in question than the normal refraction of light: "How can a piece of wood do miracles?" He was dragged out of church by a group of women, beaten do death, his body dragged to the Praça do Rocio and burned. The mob was strengthened by German, Dutch and French seamen. Hundreds of New Christians from babies to old men, and also some Old Christians with "Jewish resemblance" were killed. Many New Christians sought refuge in churches, but "the monks dragged women and children from the high altar, violated them and threw them into the flames. One heroic woman slew such a pious priest ... with the killing gear he held in his hand."[640] On Monday evening the mob's anger seemed to chill down, but on Tuesday morning, aided by two confreres, "a Dominican friar with a big wooden cross, brading 'Here, sons! For the faith in Jesus Christ, not one of those Jews shall remain!' roamed the streets till supper" and the crowd replied shouting: "Since the king refused to punish the New Christians, God now must do so." Even a work of charity was organized – giving money to buy wood for the bur-ning of the hardly less than 2,000 dead.[641] As the riot had ended in revolt, the King cracked down: Two of the Dominicans were garroted and burnt at the stake, others expelled from their convent.[642]

Apart from those chaotic outbreaks, the great *Autos-da-Fé* (acts of faith), for which one had to buy tickets in advance, exercised order-confirming functions within the social fabric. To an auto everybody of distinction would endeavour to be present; the women in their best dresses and jewelry, the common people with food baskets like going to a picknick. The small town Logroño with its 4000 inhabitants was inundated in 1610 by 30.000 auto-pilgrims; the great auto-da-fé of Múrcia (20.000 citizens) attracted a mass of 50.000 pious visitors in 1682. By what reason? For the masses "who only think in images", the autos-da-fé operated as "a collective catharsis within

---

638   Gerber, Jane, p.141-142.
639   Yovel, p.198.
640   Kayserling 2009, p.189, quoting Lisbon poet and historian Samuel Usque (~1500-1555): "... desonrrando as molheres e corrõpendo as virgens e sobre ysso tirandolhe a vida".
641   Kayserling 2009, p.185-191; Yovel, p.198-199; Roth, p.64-65.
642   Roth, p.64-65; François Soyer (Universität Southampton): "The Massacre of the New Christians of Lisbon 1506: An Eyewitness Account." (eprints.soton.ac.uk/65962/1/Francois_SoyerLisbon1506.pdf).

a society where women left the house but at their baptism, marriage and burial ... So many emotions concentrated and witnessed on one single day, like a beam of light in their monotony of daily routine, provided for the mass an ersatz for happiness, a befuddling dose of terror and ecstasy."[643] This entertainment was accrued by an element of social justice: The burning of rich and established Judaizers – after confiscation of their assets by the Holy Office – proved to the common people, that here (long before national antisemitism as "socialism of the witless guys") a sound egalitarian justice prevailed without distinction of person. "Viva la fé de Jesus Cristo!" In this motto carpenters worked overtime to construct tribunes, saying: "We must finish this work in time and if the wood runs out we'll dismantle our houses for our holy task!"[644] Looking up to cross-beams and cutting planks for auto tribunes, they experienced blissful solidarity in human sacrifice, and an anonymous poet in northern Portuguese Lamego yet in 1532 is very modern in his diction, praying: "We thank God who lets us view in our days the castigation of this *race* of infidel dogs and heretics ... and we bind brush-wood bundles so wood will not be lacking *na hora do holocausto*".[645]

In this *"teatro pedagogico"*,[646] an important detail of stage construction and social structure was that the inquisitor's chair occupied the highest position – above even the king. When the regent in 1604 cancelled a burning at Sevilla at the last moment, "a general feeling of internal sadness took hold on everyone, as if each were wounded; for the cause of God had such strength that everyone wanted to come to its defense ..." However, the chronicler reports that "the inquisitors protested and the auto was held a few days later, to the great joy of Seville and the whole province."[647] Luiz Nazario gives this joy of burning an interpretation that partly explains the love of crosses also: "The auto-da-fé transpired terror, but the crowd perceived this terror as "good and salutary". Nazario notices that the "sober, appeasing, dispassionate" inquisitorial language "reflects the posture of Pilate"; but the autos-da-fé as "totalitarian rituals" uniting people, Church and State in a "real thanksgiving", also provided space to reenact a Passion detail that in 1476 was presented already in Trento, and that Nazario calls the "Corrida to the burning place":[648] Sometimes delinquents died already on their way to the stake by a mixture of beating, taunting and stoning which the more seems to have been fuelled by the Catholic way to the cross stations as nothing of that kind is reported from the escort of witches to the burning place in 17th century.[649] The Corrida contained a most dramatic element, peaking when the monk Frei Domingo de Rojas went his last walk: "Monks and priests of

---

643 Nazario, p.82 and 102.
644 Nazario, p.116.
645 Herculano, A.: History of the Origin and Establishment of the Inquisition in Portugal. Stanford 1926, p.535; cited by Nazario, p.65, from Poliakov 2003, Vol.II (p.203 in the Portuguese, p.241 in the US-edition).
646 Nazario, p.93.
647 Poliakov 2003, Vol.II, p.205; Nazario p.102-103.
648 Nazario, p.102-104, 161 and 169.
649 Cf. the work of Jesuite priest Friedrich Spee, Cautio Criminalis, especially p.XV-XVI.

Dominican, Franciscan and other orders struggled in a bitter madness for his conversion. More than hundred clerics rushed to accompany and admonish obstinate brother Domingo." The efforts of the accompanying clerics escalated to "a veritable betting" for the salvation of the soul, by the mercy of "last chance. The total impact of the auto-da-fé enactment on the audience did include the spectacular conversion of the condemned ones on their way to the burning-place."[650]

Representação de um Auto da Fé. Lithograph (1822) from Lisbon, where the last *Act of Faith* had been performed in 1765.

Death in fire – why? Poliakov points to Jesus' words in the gospels (for instance John 15:6: "The withered branches are heaped together ... and burnt") from which clerics concluded that the withered heretic should be burnt; he also states that since the Church claimed to abhor the shedding of blood (*Ecclesia abhorret sanguinem*), "the impenitent heretics were burned at the stake so blood would not flow".[651] Nazario, however, reports details reminding German soldiers cutting the old fathers' beards as well as the "amazing rigor" Piaget heard children demand in cases of "just punishment": Yelling "Let's shave the dogs their beards" the mob burned the condemned ones' faces "with roaring cheers of joy", whereas the victims' cries for "Pardon, for God's love" just triggered "fluxes of joy and satisfaction never ut-

---

650   Nazario, p.169.
651   Poliakov 2003, Vol II, p.188.

tered in whatever other occasion."[652] When in 1699 a Jew of Granada refused to convert after 25 months of interrogations, the Jesuit father at the stake shouted at him with fury: *"Pues anda, maldito de mi Padre, a cremar en los infernos para siempre e jamás!"* Nazario comments: "Those burnt alive were literally thrown to the inferno and to rubbish."[653] Images of hell, taken from the gospels and the Apocalypse, played no minor role in Christian preaching; twice the Apocalypse (chapters 2-3) mentions the "synagogue of Satan" and five times (chapters 19-21) the "lake of fire", and every Christian knew that the enemies of the "King of Kings" were to be "thrown alive into the lake of fire" (19:16-20).

In a joint view, the two interpretations of the French and the Brazilian scholar point to the stake as a sophisticated reenactment of crucifixion. On one side, the Church by sheer cross-piety had to avoid not only bloodshed but any too close likeness with crucifixion: no crossbar, no blood red. On the other hand, burning alive almost equals crucifixion in the level of torment, and does so completely in the level of protracted, hopeless suffering, in public visibility and eventually the nakedness of the victim, stripped by the dry red flames.

Consenting with Camilo Castelo Branco, Suzanne Chantal concludes that "the condemned one, tethered very high, was seized by the fire up to somewhat above his knees, to the effect that it took in the best case a half, and in worst case up to two or three hours to expire in atrocious agony, breathing the smell of the own burnt flesh". José Saraiva relates that in the breezy bay of Lisbon "the flames did not burn but rather grill the victim, during a half or two hours before he died. His cries – *'Misericordia, por amor de Deus'* – provoked the jubilance of the spectators".[654] This malicious glee should be seen in the light of recent neurological evidence suggesting that "effective punishment is experienced as rewarding while it is occurring".[655]

What punishment would fit to newly arrived Marrano woman Catherine de Fernandes who in French border town St.-Jean-de-Luz in 1619, watched by a Portuguese priest, after communion removed the consecrated wafer (Christ's holy body) from her mouth? She was imprisoned, but an angry mob hauled her from her cell, dragged her through the streets and burned her alive.[656] The utter disproportion between her bread crime and roasted flesh atonement prompts the conclusion that the angry punishers' relief derived not just from punishment concerning Jesus, but also from watching doubts vanishing in smoke: their doubts about doctrines so far from common sense as virgin-gives-birth, flesh-turns-bread and God-tortures-son; those secret doubts that surfaced when Jews were accused of grave misdemeanours like

---

652 Nazario, p.165-166, quoting Miachael Geddes, Miscellaneous Tracts, London 1714.
653 Nazario, p.165-168; translation: "So go, cursed one of my father, to burn in hell for ever and never!"
654 Chantal, Suzanne: La vie quotidienne de Portugal après le Tremblement de Terre de Lisbonne de 1755. Paris 1981, p.157-159; Saraiva, Antonio José. Inquisição e cristãos-novos. Porto 1969, p.704 (both cited by Nazario, p.168).
655 Lerner/Clayton, p. 232, referring to De Quervain et al., 2004.
656 Gerber, Jane, p.191.

"deleting Ave Maria from the benediction", keeping "absent from communion" and "looking away from the crucifix".[657]

"Here the crucifix has been offended! Let us pray the rosary" a Catholic priest thundered when the judges adjourned for recess in my Munich 2001 trial concerning classroom crosses. Actually I had quoted, concerning god images, some statements of Kant and the Bible.[658]

The hurt of this offense was felt by whom? By the crucifix or by its worshippers? The question is less absurd than psychologically telling.

For one: Compassion for deniers of salvation by Jesus' Passion was punishable, bar none. At the solemn auto of March 6, 1600 in Toledo – performed to celebrate the accession of Philipp III, son of Philipp II with Anna of Austria, to the throne – the chroniclers relate that this 21-year-old next ruler, unable to hold in his compassion with the convicts going to the stake, shed tears for them. These drops did not escape the vigilant eyes of the inquisitors, who classified his crying as a crime. To expiate his teardrops, His Majesty had to undergo a royal blood drawing and assent to the burning of some drops of his blood as atonement for his guilt.[659]

On the other hand, and unlike living human bodies, the wooden crucifix with its carved wood or cast metal corpus truly merited compassion. The Christian expectation that Jews would scourge crucifixes – a frequent accuse in Brazilian Bahia after 1646[660] – enters stage yet around 1543 in Coimbra in a drama directed by Dominican friar Bernardo de Santa Cruz (sic!) harboring a grievous suspicion against rich Simão Alvares and his spouse. Both remained steadfast under torture, but they had a nine-year-old daughter who had been born in Porto six months before their move to Coimbra. Would she help to find the truth? He put the child in front of a basin filled with burning coals and threatened he "would burn off her little hand in the basin instantly if she would not confess having seen with her own eyes that back then in Porto her father and mother had scourged a crucifix". The girl confessed, the parents burned."[661]

Also the skilled interrogators of Madrid found out in 1630 that during their perverse religious services Judaizers used to flagellate a crucifix; in the subsequent auto seven of them were burned in their flesh and four only in effigy because they had escaped.

The scourging of a wooden figure as well as the voodoo-like burning of a puppet attests the psycho-power of the palpable. Inescapably, on their last steps to the stakes the convicts faced the graspable effigy of obedience as

---

657 Perera, p.64; cf. Novinsky 2009, p,121 (João Nunes): "crime: desrespeito ao crucifixo".

658 My maximal insult was stating that according to Immanuel Kant (Religion within the Limits of Reason Alone, 1793) and Bible verses (Ex 20:4 and 34:17; Lev 26:1; Dt 4:15; 5;8; 26:15; Wisdom 13:10-19) one could not refrain from calling crucifixes "products of pseudoreligious, barbaric superstition" and "fetishes which diametrically contradict central statements of Christian doctrine".

659 Mendonça, J. L. and Moreira, A.J.: Histórias dos principais actos e procedimentos da Inquisição em Portugal. Lisbon 1980, p.89 (cited by Nazario, p.113).

660 Novinsky 2009, p.153 (Nuno Fernandes, 1591); after 1646: Novinsky 2013, p.134.

661 Kayserling p. 281-282 (German original print: p. 239-240); Heer 1981, p.168.

their last chance to learn submission and earn the finer end of burning just as a numb, strangled corpse.

"Take that away, Father, it is only a piece of wood that will not save anybody", Diego Diaz, with some personal logic, uttered on his last way. At the same Mexican auto on November 19, 1659 one Francisco Botello, "withstanding all attempts to make him pronounce the name of Jesus and of the Blessed Virgin, went to his death at the stake, burned alive."[662] The stubbornness of many penitents in preferring hot flames instead of true faith sometimes aroused a public anger which law enforcement forces fiercely fought to tame – and understandably, since the Judaizers' defiance endangered the great learning target: the insight that everyone has to submit like Jesus himself, who on cross had visibly "learned obedience" (Hebrews 5:8). At an auto in the colony of Goa, India, at the beginning of 18th century, the preacher compared Inquisition with Noah's Arch, with the difference that the animals which entered the Arch before the deluge, thereafter disembarked with the same nature as before, while Inquisition had an "admirable feature" to dismiss "as sweet as lambs" those who had entered with the cruelty of wolves and the arrogance of lions. The architect of tribunes Joseph del Olmo viewed those defiant ones "throwing crazy glances like flames onto the audience" and accused them of a "guilty contempt of life" which had to entail eternal damnation. So irritating was the existence of human beings who better chose the second most awful death for themselves than to kiss the most awful symbol, that even criticists of Holy Office "were not free of the idea that heresy is a physical contamination, transmitted in the blood".[663] In Spanish Cuenca, on June 29, 1654, ten "New Christians" were chosen for burning because they had "relapsed" into their old faith. Balthasar Lopez, for example, had amassed a considerable fortune as court saddler. Betaking himself to French border city Bayonne, he had returned to Judaism there but then ventured back into Spain with the object of persuading some of his kinsmen to embrace Judaism. Now he joined the ten Judaizers going in their paper-miters and "Sambenitos" – yellow ponchos with painted-on infernal sceneries – to the stake. As they approached the *quemadero*, the priest exhorted him to rejoice, since through a profession of repentence – extremely recommendable – the gates of Paradise would open for him freely. "Freely, say you, Father?" retorted Lopez, indignantly. "The confiscation of my property has cost me 200.000 ducats; am I to believe that I struck a bad bargain?" When the executioner began to fasten his feet, Lopez struggled against this indignity. "If you bind me, I won't believe in your Jesus. Take this crucifix away!" Suiting the action to the word, he threw it from him. Finally, when the priest did not give up asking him whether he was truly repentant, Lopez looked at him in reproof. "Father", he said sadly, "do you think this is a time of joke?"[664]

---

662 Wachtel, p.170.
663 Nazario, p.150 (Goa); 123-124; 107.
664 Roth, p.160-161.

Lopez was one of the innumerable. Roth doubts the earliest (1823) researched number of 32,912 burnt victims given by Canon Juan Antonio Llorente, an ex-secretary of Holy Office, adding that "the intensely Catholic" Amadeo de los Rios estimates 28,540 exclusively Jewish victims just until 1525.[665]

Pedro Berruguete (1450-1504): *Auto de Fé presidido por Santo Domingo de Guzmán*, 1494 (detail). The section presents two phases of the auto: While first (downstairs on the left) the two delinquents are wearing their clothes under their Sambenitos, they then, fixed by grotesque phallic Sediles, are burnt in exact the same nakedness as the (intentiously parallel?) corpus on the friar's crucifix.

The forcedly baptized young couple Abraham and Isabel de Castro had emigrated to France where their son Thomas Luiz, alias Isaac, was born in 1626. The highly gifted young man had studied medicine and philosophy in Paris and Bordeaux before moving with his parents to Amsterdam, from where he sailed to the Dutch possessions in Brazil. On a visit to Bahia, which was in Portuguese hands, he was arrested and sent to Lisbon for trial. When the fire leapt up around him on December 15, 1647, "there was heard from the midst of the flames a strange cry, which was repeated about the town by the populace until the Inquisition ordered them to desist. It was the Jewish confession of faith, the Shemá: 'Hear, O Israel! The Lord, our God, the Lord is One!'"[666]

---

665 Roth, p.143, viewed together with David A. Plaisted: Estimates of the Number Killed by the Papacy in the Middle Ages and later, 2006 (cs.unc.edu/~plaisted/estimates.doc).
666 Kayserling, p.355-356; Roth, p.157-158; cf. Bodian, p.192.

De Castro's westward flight was one of many. "When America opened up for Europeans, also the era of New Christians began. As their world was broken they constructed a new illusion: Brazil, which many of them even viewed as the Promised Land." Anita Novinsky regards the Cristãos Novos in America as "the real precursors of laicist thinking ... two centuries ahead of European 'illuminated' religious criticism." The São Paulo University historian estimates that 30 percent of the immigrants who settled in Brazil during 16th-17th century were baptized Jews. On this basis presumably between 35 and 60 percent of today 204 million Brazilians have Marranos in their multi-ethnic pedigrees.[667]

Three thinkers with Marrano family background[668] shall be mentioned here with their statements concerning the symbol of suffering.

The date of Moses Cordovero's birth in 1522 is not known; his parents were on the run. From 1540 to his death in 1570 he lived in Galilean Safed as teacher, jurist and judge. In his cabalist texts he opposed misguided forms of worship: "These disastrous attitudes toward God come into being if someone connects God with suffering, with dying or with Gehenna. Thus, one views him as a power which lets suffering, execution or infernal torment come upon us; maybe one even makes him essentially a tormenter, hangman or devil."[669]

Paulo Freire (1921-1997) had five children with his wife Elza Maia Costa de Oliveira. Famous worldwide for his down-to-earth method of alphabetisation, the Pernambucano educator, imprisoned and exiled by the military government, in his "Pedagogy of the Oppressed" writes about a "perverted notion of God. Under the influence of magic and myth, the oppressed ones view their sufferings – result of exploration – as God's will, as if God were the creator of this 'organized disorder'. One trait of this necrophilous consciousness of the oppressor is ... sadism." [670]

Freire's pedagogical mentor Anísio Teixeira was born in Bahia in 1900 and died during *ditadura militar* in 1971 in a never cleared up elevator accident. Just as his disciple Paulo, also Anísio, whom his mother had dissuaded from becoming a cleric by her counsel "My son, better become a padre secular", in his struggle for "one school for all children" was strongly oriented at this children-centered, women respecting, social justice promoting rabbi and dissenter Jesus. And it sounds like an echo of the "ancestry demands" on which Hungarian Jewish psychologist Leopold Szondi bases his "Fate

---

667   Citations: Novinsky 2013, p. XVIII f.; 60 percent: Wasserman, Marcos, in: Amazônia Judaica, 2/2010, p.7. In Roth's view (p.283) "Brazil became filled with New Christians, of doubtful orthodoxy." Wachtel (p.249) regards Brazil as "quintessential territory" of the New Christians; as to Novinsky, cf. Elaine Eiger's and Luize Valente's documentary "A Estrela Oculta do Sertão" (2005, Wikimedia); concerning Marranos and Illumination see Yovel.
668   Freire, Costa, Oliveira and Teixeira are common Sephardic surnames; cf. sephardim. com; genealogiafreire.com.br; Roth mentions Teixeiras on p.76, 301-303; heresy trials listed by Novinsky (2009): Teixeira p.90, 201; Freire p.61, 135, 144; Oliveira p.53, 112, 137, 149, 160, 179, 199, 201; Costa p.63, 68, 84, 149, 92, 99, 103, 126, 139, 149, 152, 181, 184, 204, 205.
669   Cordovero, p.249-250. Gehenna is a vague analogue of Christian purgatory or hell.
670   Freire, p.46-48.

Analysis",[671] when Anísio, the probable descendant of Marranos, tries to dissuade his sister Tilinha from becoming a nun: "Due to an extreme interpretation of some passages of the gospels we have accustomed to view life as a permanent inevitable way of sacrifice ... And in this 'madness' for the cross, how some call it, we not only spare ourselves no sacrifices but impose them on others. This theory is monstrous and contrary to the most elementary teachings of Christ ..."[672]

As naked

The "astonishing reality of Christian-Jewish relationships" is to Lawrence Swaim "that 'the Jews' didn't kill Jesus but Christians *did* kill hundreds of thousands (and finally millions) of Jews, symbolically crucifying them because of their own obsession with a God who demands redemption through violence".[673]

Just symbolically? Actually, real crucifixions on real beams of German *KREUZ* were reenacted in *KZ* Auschwitz, *KZ* Majdanek, *KZ* Dachau and *KZ* Sachsenhausen. In her novel "The Seventh Cross", finished in Mexican exile in 1942, Anna Seghers depicts how but one man out of a group of seven fugitives succeeds – thanks to courageous fellow humans – in escaping his persecutors, evading thus the seventh of the crosses that had been placed on the Lager parade ground to welcome the caught runaways. Political prisoner Willi Knoob (1914-1984) has kept a different memory of the events in Sachsenhausen camp, November 1936:

"Golgotha: This idea could come to no one else's mind but to the sick and perverted brain of an SS-officer. The Indian torture stake wouldn't have done it. The Kreuz was the stronger symbol for the tacky power feeling. Boots, black uniform, machine pistol and *Kreuz*. – As far as I remember, all got caught."[674] And all got crucified, in almost as detailed a way as the SS reenacted the antique prototype in Lithuania: "In the Ghetto of Vilnius", Pinchas Lapide remarks, "there was a Jew whom the SS-guards mockingly called *Jud' Jesus*. One day they seized him, frazzled his head with a crown of barbed wire and crucified him at the Lager gate."[675]

This Jew Jesus was spared one detail that came to be a very common feature of Catholic baroque churches in Germany: Stripped to the wooden waist and whipped to the painted blood, this life-size battered body visualized the cruel intermezzo between trial and cross: "So Pilate, wishing to satisfy the crowd, released Barabbas to them. He had Jesus flogged, and handed him over to be crucified" (Mark 15:15).

Unmistakably the flogging was done by Roman soldiers. However, the iconic "Scourging of Christ" which spread wide during a 12th century marked by increasing veneration of Christ's corpus and increasing accusations of

671 Szondi, p.15-21.
672 Viana Filho, p.50.
673 Swaim 2012, p.59.
674 Hilzinger, p.100-102.
675 Lapide 1987, p.99-100.

host-abuse,[676] almost naturally was attributed to scourge-men marked as Jews by their conical hats (portal of San Zeno Maggiore, Verona, 12th century), while the soldier was judaized mainly by his nose on a 19th century German wayside crucifix (chapter VIII).

Jews flogging naked one: Alejo Fernández (ca. 1475-1545), La Flagelación (1500-1505).
Left: Scourging of Christ, lateral panel, by the Master of Strache Altar (probably Master Lorenz Katzheimer of Bamberg), 1490-1500.
Engraving: The ritual murder of little Rudolf of Bern, from Diebold Schilling's Berner Chronik (1483).

In 1260 the flagellant movement arose suddenly. With red crosses on their hats and cloaks and gowns, each flagellant group travelled for 33 ½ days

---

676 Hsia, p.24.

(symbolizing Jesus' life-years) from town to town performing their bloody self-scourging rites. At some places the Scourging Shows enlarged to Passion Plays which excited the spectators so much that they not only clobbered the actors who played the Jews. During the plague, "in every town they entered, the flagellants rushed to the Jewish quarter, trailed by citizens howling for revenge upon 'the poisoners of the wells'. In Freiburg, Augsburg, Nuremberg, Munich, Königsberg, Regensburg, and other centers, the Jews were slaughtered with a thoroughness that seemed to seek the final solution."[677] In their final revenge attempt six centuries later, also the Nazis had a predilection for whips and scourges in maltreating Jews. In February 1940, German Colonel-General Blaskowitz blamed the SS for a "whipping orgy" in Nasielek, going on a whole night long and affecting 1600 Jews. Concerning the Józefów massacre in June 1942, a Policeman of Batallion 101 testified: "I still remember well that on the eve of the action in Józefów whips were handed out ... The whips were to be used for driving the Jews out from their houses. The whips actually were downright bull's pizzles."[678] The reenactment of outright humiliation, however, needs one more detail of unprotected skin. A strange peculiarity which sets the mass murder of Jews apart from other genocides (American Indians, Aborigenes, Armenians, Cambodians, Bosnian Muslims, Tutsi ...) is the previous divestment of the victims.

When Sturmbannführer Dr.juris Bruno Müller in the evening of October 22, 1941 got to know that the Romanian ally troups after the capture of Odessa had started massacring the Jewish population, "he bargained with them to leave 300 Jews for him and led the victims to a disused well where he had them shot. The half or fully unclothed bodies of the men, women and children then were thrown into the well."[679] Obviously, the killing of the Jews in Müller's view had high non-material value which could still be augmented by their disrobing. When on November 8, 1941, two-hundred German and native Belarussian militia, after a celebratory banquet on the eve, had shot 8000 Jews near Borissow, their clothes were delivered to the social welfare organization "Belarussian Self-Help". Serving a good cause? Clothing the naked? Did the "killing naked" apply to Jewish victims only? While later on sometimes gypsies also were shot naked, at the first "test gassings" (beginning of 1942) in Auschwitz 900 Russian POWs had to unclothe – since the shower, so they were told, had the purpose of delousing.[680]

While in April 1942 Slovakian Jews were gassed in Auschwitz "apparently full dressed", the Jews deported from nearby Sosnowitz soon after were ordered to strip in the yard, men and women together. When the victims became suspicious and restive, swearing SS-guards drove men, women and

677 Tuchman, Barbara: A Distant Mirror. The Calamitous 14th Century. New York 1978, p.115 (cited by Nicholls, p.246).
678 Hilberg 1982, p.139 (Nasielek); Goldhagen 1996, p.253 (Józefów).
679 Hilberg 1992, p. 66 and 108. Müller was sentenced in 1947, amnestied in 1953 and died in 1960. Sturmbannführer is the SS equivalent of Major.
680 Gypsies (pejorative German: *Zigeuner*): Hilberg 1982, p.677-678; Russians: Testimony of Lager commander Rudolf Hoess; shoaportalvienna.wordpress.com/1943-3/.

children into the gas chamber, while a squad of prisoners had to store their clothes in the magazines called "Canada". A textile-economic rationale was given by Himmler yet on October 14, 1942: With the Jewish clothes *Volksdeutsche* would be provided: "The garments must arrive at their recipients before Christmas." When killings started in Bogdanovka camp on December 21, 1942, first more than 4000 Jews were burnt in the pigsties where they had lived; then about 43.000 Jews in groups of up to 400 were driven into a forest where at icy temperatures they had to strip and kneel down at a slope to be shot. The shootings were suspended during Christmas holidays and ended on December 30. What would the Germans do with their stripped victims' typhus-infected pigsty-clothes? Economical reasons for robbing the Christ-killers of their clothes appear doubtful since a report of German army's economical supervision already on July 1, 1942 had stated that by German standards Jewish clothes and underwear could be classified as "rags" only. On February 6, 1943, Obergruppenführer (Lieutenant General) Pohl of the SS-Economy-Administration Main Office criticized that a big part of the clothes from the depots of Auschwitz and Lublin had consisted of tatter, while "the best possible valorization of old textiles indeed is of greatest importance". At a shooting in Ponar on April 5, 1943, "the ones with poorer clothes on weren't even undressed". In 1944, due to lack of dresses, thousands of Auschwitz prisoners had to walk around stark naked. When Soviet troops liberated the camp on January 27, 1945, they found 29 of the 35 magazines burnt down by the SS. In the remaining six depots, which represented 20 percent of the storage capacity, the liberators found 368,820 men's suits, 836,255 ladies' coats and dresses, as well as big quantities of children's dresses. [681]

We don't know how many robbed dresses were stored in the 29 burnt magazines. What we have to suppose given these numbers is that "textile economy" was but a pretext to reenact the tenth station of the cross "Jesus bereft of his clothes" with Jewish victims.

If not to textile economy, did the stripping orders aim to extreme humiliation? Conceivably yes; but this "uttermost humiliation" is also, in Martin Hengel's words, the aim of the Roman "public display of a naked victim at ... crucifixion".[682] Textile economy was secondary, for the SS even more than for Roman soldiers. The primary motive of the stripping of Jewish victims is hard to overlook but forbidden to address in Christian *leitkultur*, not because of piety towards the victims but of shunning the fact that the crucified man's nakedness essentially contributed to compassion with him, and to anger against his disrobers, from the beginning.

There were no crucifixes in 2nd century, but Church Father Melito of Sardes (near Smyrna in western Anatolia) probably had repeatedly witnessed the (complete) nakedness of contemporaries hanging on Roman crosses when he bewailed Christ: "He who fixed the heavens is fixed there ... God has been murdered, the king of Israel has been slain by an Israelitish hand. O

---

681 Hilberg 1982, p.258, 266, 615, 646, 657, 665.; Gilbert, p.552 (Ponar) and 773.
682 Hengel, p.87 (cf. Crossan, p.162).

strange murder, strange crime! The Master has been treated in unseemly fashion, his body naked, and not even deemed worthy of a covering, that [his nakedness] might not be seen ..."[683] Melito paints the naked Jesus just with words; physically, the killing of naked Jews began exactly when the new expressive style of carving and painting crucifixes would start to exhibit, instead of a sovereign Christus Pantocrator clad in a long and noble loincloth, now the stripped victim suffering in his bloody nakedness.

Left: "They parted my raiment among them, and for my vesture they cast lots." The verse of John (19:24) is, in Latin and French, the caption of Achille Lemot's cartoon in French Catholic weekly *Le Pelerin* around *L'Affaire Dreyfus* (1894-1906). The right picture (Spain, 18th century) also displays Jews casting dice, while harvesting the heart of crucified Niño de La Guardia.

In May 1096, the crusaders, lead by Count Emicho of Leiningen, seized hundreds of Jews in Mainz, "stripped them naked and dragged them off, granting quarter to none, save those few who accepted baptism", and threw them, "still writhing and convulsing in their blood", from the windows until the dying Jews laid piled in heaps on the ground.[684]
Exactly hundred years later, in Speyer on Rhine the body of a murder victim was found, and Jews were suspected of complicity. "In revenge, some

683 Hengel (p.21) quotes here from O.Perler: Méliton de Sardes, Sur la Paque, Sources Chrétiennes 123, 1996, p. 194-195.
684 Chronicler "Mainz Anonymous", cited in Poliakov 2003, Vol.I, p.44; also in Chazan: European Jewry, p.239, cited by Michael, p.63.

Christian burghers ... desecrated the body of a recently dead Jewish girl" and even found a substitute for the crown of thorns, when they "hung the Jewish corpse naked in the marketplace with a rat strung in its hair".[685] It was exactly in this 12th century that accusations of ritual murder arose on the terrible view of Christian children stripped naked by their sexually deranged murderers. A Flemish poet of the thirteenth century had his poem start with this image:

> *And when they had stripped off his clothes*
> *The dirty Jews, the stinking hounds,*
> *They inflicted on him many wounds ...*[686]

Correspondent treatment happened in 1467 to two conversos of Toledo, where the "New Christians" had put up armed resistance for the first time. "The mob captured the two young commanders, Fernando and Alvaro de La Torre, and hung their naked bodies upside down before sending them by donkey cart to one of the city's squares, where they were kept on display for four days while members of the crowd mutilated them with daggers beyond recognition."[687] The connection between naked Jewish victims and naked Christ on cross which Holocaust historians refuse to see until today was obvious to the Jews of then. "European Jews", notes Jeremy Cohen, "remembered their martyrs of the crusades ... in matching and even in out-performing the sufferings of the crucified Christ [...] Just as the Gospels report about Jesus on the cross, many of these Jewish martyrs had their clothes removed and stolen."[688] In December 1919, during a Polish post-war pogrom Jewish women were exempted from execution, but "stripped naked and flogged" they had to pass down "a passage full of Polish soldiers." Still on April 21, 1946, five Jews were shot by Polish Home Army and "left naked on the highway".[689] Naked to the pit, naked into the chamber, thus millions had gone – urged and hurried by those SS-men who, as Himmler emphasized in his Posen speech, had "remained decent" in all their massacres.[690] Do I have the right to present the victims in this book naked, in the minute before their death? Is this consistent with due respect for them? How near are these photos "to a kind of fascination with Nazi sadism that is very nearly pornographic – or at least voyeuristic"?[691] Counterquestion: Which right entitles Christians to present the victim Jesus for all times and eyes naked and bloody not in books but in churches, public places, court rooms and above the blackboard of public school classrooms? Would anyone hang an image of Pastor Diet-

---

685 Michael, p.74.
686 Vauchez, André: Laity in the Middle Ages, Notre Dame, Indiana, 1993, p.148 (Cohen, p.110. I slightly modified his translation according to medieval German vocabulary).
687 Yovel, p.147.
688 Cohen, p.155.
689 Gilbert, p.22 and 817; as to stripped Jewish victims, cf. p.288, 571, 612, 650 and 753.
690 Himmler, speech in Posen on October 4, 1943: Hilberg 1982, p. 683-685.
691 Swaim, p.177.

rich Bonhoeffer, as naked as he was hanged in Bavarian KZ Flossenbürg, on the classroom walls of Protestant day schools?[692]

Disrobing of Christ by Jews
(left side from top)
Jacquemart de Hesdin (ca.1355-1414).
Workshop of Hans von Aachen (1552-1615).
The 10th Station of Calvary of Wiele, Poland, 1915-1925.

Disrobing of Jews by Christians
(right column)
Women at Liepaja beach, Latvia.
Last photo of Lea Epstein and her brother Max.
Shooting of four men and one boy in German occupied Soviet Union.

Every man of Police Batallion 101 knew that: “They stripped him” (Matthew 27:28), “divided his clothes among them” (Mark 15:24) and “cast lots to divide his clothing” (Lk 23:34). On August 19, 1942, this volunteer Police

692 Together with Bonhoeffer also the other resistance members Wilhelm Canaris, Ludwig Gehre, Hans Oster and Karl Sack had to unclothe completely in the morning of April 9, 1945 in KZ Flossenbürg (Eastern Bavaria) and to walk naked to the gallows (Wikipedia).

Batallion entered the Polish town of Łomazy, gathered all Jews in a holding area, marched them to the execution area "and made them undress once they got there ... Some of them had to wait naked under the strong sun for hours and got severely sun burnt." The company commander made bearded elderly Jews "undress and crawl into the grave ..."[693]

Catholic military chaplain Heinz Keller remembers a conversation with a wounded soldier who had been part of a machine gun commando in Sevastopol: "The guy was completely ruined by this experience. Line up the Jews, clothes off, naked before his eyes, women, children, men, and then the machine guns. He had to man one of the guns himself. 'I can say I did not hit any of them. I always shot in the air.' But the experience, how the people fell backwards, earth over them, and then the next row, until the anti-tank trench was full ... 'What should I have done?' the man wanted to know. He had a wife and family."[694]

A woman with child related at the Eichmann trial: "I had my daughter in my arms and ran after the truck. There were mothers who had two or three children and held them in their arms running after the truck. We ran all the way. There were those who fell – we were not allowed to help them rise. They were shot right there wherever they fell ... When we all reached the destination, the people from the truck were already down and they were undressed – all lined up. All my family was there – undressed, lined up ... When it came to our turn, our father was beaten. We prayed, we begged with my father to undress, but he would not undress, he wanted to keep his underclothes. He did not want to stand naked. Then they tore off the clothing of the old man and he was shot ..."[695]

In 1860 a Scottish writer noted how the Oberammergau Passion Play enacted the original scene: "With strange emotions you gazed upon the executioners as upon the wild beasts when they tore his mantle into shreds, and cast lots for his vesture; and the Jewish race appeared hateful in your eyes, as you watched them gathering around the cross."[696]

Concerning latency and potency of learning contents, German psychologist Hans-Peter Nolting notes: "Model behavior can be learned, i.e. stored in memory, without being displayed. From the difference between learning and performing follows that we know many forms of aggression and virtually could perform them but actually we never do ... This difference also provides the option that model-learning realizes later on in suitable situations."[697]

War is mostly suitable for reenaction of learned violence. The actions described above were exclusively the work of men who grew up in Christian culture and "practically without exception were the baptized children of

693 Wilensky, p.279-280.
694 Heinz Keller: "Ob das der Herrgott von uns will?" In: Brandt, Priester in Uniform, p.130-131 (quoted by Wilensky, p.190).
695 Eichmann Trial, Jerusalem 1961, session Nr.30, according to Ellis 1987, p.81.
696 Shapiro, James: Oberammergau: The Troubling Story of the World's Most Famous Passion Play. New York 2000, p.76-77 (by Perry/Schweitzer, p.4).
697 Nolting, p.108.

Christians".[698] The perpetrators came mostly from rural areas, particularly from southern Germany and Austria which not only have the probably highest spacial density of crucifixes worldwide but statistically provided a far disproportional number of skull troops and an even higher percentage of KZ commanders.[699] The "murderous phantasy of these men and women from 1939-1945" in Friedrich Heer's diagnosis "is visibly stimulated by martyry images in primarily rural places of worship and pilgrimage in Bavarian and Austrian region."[700] Nakedness in these regions was tabooed to a degree which bedevilled cleanliness, hygiene and wellbeing considerably; a naked body was an accepted view almost nowhere else than at the humiliated Jesus; and within the fourteen "stations of the cross" common in Bavaria and Austria, the tenth station "Jesus is stripped of his garments" was expressly explained as special atonement for our "evil desires and sinful inclinations".[701]

Since Christ's nakedness was linked to his humiliation by Jews, the fact of naked Jews humiliated by young men with strict Christian upbringing should not astonish. Resuming this chapter, we first can object to Hannah Arendt's opinion that anti-Semitism explained the choice of the victim but not the *Art und Weise* of the crime.[702] Masked and modernized, the *mode and manner* still was *fac simile* – do it similarly with them. *Modo fac simile*, second, Peter Schuster's statement points to Europe's visual background: "Not the worldly norms have coined the history of death penalty, but the Churches in their changing views on the right of states to kill human beings, and their changing views on crime, sin and their punishment."[703]

698   Wistrich 1987, p.251.
699   Adorno 1971, p.93 (rural areas); Wilensky, p.144-145.
700   Heer 1989, p.572.
701   Cf. ourcatholicfaith.org/stations/menu.html; the Franciscan monks Antonius Daza and Leonard of Porto Maurizio created and propagated this way of 14 stations in 17th century.
702   Bauman 2007, p.248.
704   Schuster, p.34-35.

XI   The cross is the nerve

"A Man with German blood whose only child survives the Jewish mother, even if for but short time (death of mother and child in puerperium), remains Jewish. But if the child dies shortly before the mother, the man becomes German again."[704]

The juridical definition quoted above seems crazy, but its author was considered the "second most powerful man of German Federal Republic", second only to chanceler Konrad Adenauer.[705]

In 1949, the courageous Catholic Konrad Adenauer, having been imprisoned by the Nazis and heard saying in 1946 that "also the Church and the clericals bear big guilt concerning what happened in the concentration camps", had been elected the first chancellor of *Bonner Republik*. On September 10, 1952 (my birthday) he signed the Luxemburg Contract with Israel, providing a three billion marks *Wiedergutmachung* (compensation, making good again) which, imitating Adenauers Rhenanian dialect, was nicknamed *Wiederjudmachung*. Staying in office until 1963, this devout and upright, anti-Nazi Christian personified the tranquillizing view that the Nazis were but a godless gang and their crimes hadn't anything to do with Christian teachings. Adenauer himself discredited this mirage when with the remark "You don't tip away murky water as long you have no clean one"[706] he brought into his chancellor's office a capable administrator whose political engagement had started early in Catholic students' fraternities and Catholic Zentrum Party and who yet in 1932, as solicitor in Prussian Interior Ministery, had suggested that Jews be prohibited to change their names if the purpose was "to veil their Jewish descent"; who in 1935 had participated in mapping the Nuremberg Laws and who in 1938 had initiated the marking of Jewish passports by the name affixes "Israel" and "Sara";[707] who was charged by CIA documents to be partially responsible for the deportation of 20,000 Greek Jews to extermination camps in Poland; who after the war had admitted his early knowledge that the Jews were being "killed systematically", and whose breast in 1963, five days after old Adenauer's demission, was decorated with the *Großkreuz* of German Order of Merit, the highest decoration of democratic Germany. Higher than the *Ehrenkreuz* [Cross of Merit] of front combatants he had received in in 1934, higher than his *Kriegsverdienstkreuz* [War Cross of Merito] and his *Komturkreuz* of the order Star of Romania, both awarded in 1942, higher than the Italian *Croce Grande de Benemerenza* (1956), the *Croix Grande* of the Grand Duchy of Luxemburg (1957) and higher even than his portuguése *Cruz Grande* da Ordem de Cristo (1960). Better seven crosses on your breast than one in your back.

---

704 Essner, Cornelia: Die ‚Nürnberger Gesetze' oder die Verwaltung des Rassenwahns 1933-1945, Paderborn 2002, p.167-168 (quoted by Junginger, p.9).
705 Bevers, p.10.
706 Tagesspiegel, 23.08.2006: "Globke, Filbinger, Fassbinder, Walser, Flick."
707 Hilberg 1982, p.29, 129 and 740.

All these European cross awards remind the sign that marked the crusaders' flags and garments but please not the fact that the campaign of destruction Hitler unleashed in June 1941 against Soviets and Jews was named Operation Barbarossa, honoring Emperor Friedrich I, the red-haired leader of the Third Crusade.

In a culture which, all the more after the cross with hooks, revered the *Kreuzritter* cross of crusaders as the embodiment of pro-societal merits; in a new state which marked its new tanks, ships and bombers again with the black *Kreuz* emblem of two German-dominated world wars, any howsoever tender nexus between Kreuz and Jew-hatred simply never had existed and logically could not have been the basis for godless Nazis' KZ system.

Indeed a German born Jewish lawyer in July 1973 had successfully refused to have his demand for reparation tried under the cross of a Düsseldorf court room, on the grounds that Jews in Germany "for centuries have been persecuted and humiliated also under the crucifix and its – be it falsified and misused – spirit." Tellingly, however, in 1995 this untoward rationale was mentioned neither by the judges of Supreme Court in their classroom cross decision (building expressly on the 1973 precedent) nor in the subsequent media hype, with the one exception of *Der Spiegel* magazine, in an article whose title needs no translation: "*Das Kreuz ist der Nerv*".[708]

Only three breast crosses earned the German boy who went to the same gymnasium as my brother and my sister, became a famous physician, died in Brazil and deserves to be presented here as an exemplar case for the nerval tangles between cross and children.

The doctor as selector

He was born in 1911 and grew up in a place where the Romans in 77/78 built their castellum Guntia and from which innumerous Jews, for example US Supreme Court Judge Ruth Bader Ginzberg, derive their name, though the Günzburgers expulsed their Jews already in 1617.

When I cycled to Günzburg on a warm evening in June 2005, I once again passed those 11 impressing roadside crucifixes on the 13 miles between my home and the place of the event, the Maria-Ward-Gymnasium in Günzburg's center. My teachers' union for Education and Science had invited Eva Mozes Kor, a blond lady of 71 years, to the native city of her dark-haired torturer who in Auschwitz was called the Angel of Death.

The tenor of Mrs. Kor's lecture was that by forgiving the perpetrators she had recovered her vitality and emotional stability. At the end of her lecture, a lean grey-haired Günzburger, slightly her elder, raises his hand and starts what slowly turns out to be an increasingly maddening apology of the torturer. When he plainly asks "What has he done, actually?" I shout "Stop!" So let's stop here and see what, corresponding to the focus of this book, the monstrous doctor did to children and their mothers.

---

708 Der Spiegel, August 14, 1995

"Mengele supervised the birth of a child with meticulous care. Within an hour mother and child were sent to the gas chamber." A warrant of Frankfurt district court accused him of having "thrown the newborn baby of the Jewess Sussmann from Vienna into the fire alive". Once he sewed together gypsy twins back to back and wrist to wrist, connecting their bloodstream for scientific reasons. "Guido and Nina cried day and night. Somehow her mother could get morphine and end the suffering of her children."[709] Without any surgical experience he removed the ovaries of women in view of possible means of population control. He forced twin sisters to have sex with other twins, apparently to discover if twins would reproduce twins. The subject here was to increase the Aryan birthrate. The man who at school "had endured mild taunts from his classmates about his Gypsy looks" certainly knew that "in the past the Gypsies, in popular opinion as well as in scientific research, had always been classified as Jews. In 17th century the German author Johann Christof Wagenseil had tried to prove that the first Gypsies had been Jews born in Germany. The nazis were not sure about the Gypsies' origin, but they supposed a racial kinship between them and the Jews."[710] Once Mengele, who was called "uncle Pepi" by many of "his" twins, killed fourteen Gypsy twins by injections of Evipal and chloroform. During the liquidation of the "Gypsies Camp" a girl of four years is said to have addressed him with the words "Uncle Doctor". Since the girl didn't want to go away, he dropped a hint to a German kapo who grabbed the girl by her feet and smashed her head.[711]

Perhaps most gruesome of all is the allegation that Mengele had 300 children burned alive in an open fire, an event witnessed by several inmates including a Russian named Annani Silovich Pet'ko: "Later I was told that some of these children that were brought and burned were actually taken from their mothers."

Thirty-six twin children he used for his eye tests, which resulted in painful infections and sometimes blindness. After the tests the children served no further use, and so they were gassed.[712]

During the arrival of a train from Lodz there was an incident on the platform when a mother didn't want to be separated from her daughter of thirteen years. Having shot both, the authoritarian doctor, angry about this case of female disobedience, ordered to send those who had been selected for work already to the gas chambers also. The prussic acid gas pellets "Zyklon B" at times the doctor threw himself into the inlet pipes on the roof of the gas chambers, but his favorite place was on the platform, at selection. Why? An inmate, the medical Dr. Martina Puzyna, whom Mengele employed as his anthropologist to measure the external features of twins, saw him "shrieking in a loud voice, 'Twins, out, twins out,'" while running alongside a procession of Hungarian Jews as they streamed off the train. His permanent

709 Posner/Ware, Introduction (birth); Keller, p.63 (warrant), 40 (Guido/Nina), 34 (ovaries).
710 Posner/Ware, p.25 (taunts), Hilberg 1982, p.677-678.
711 Posner/Ware p.37 (twin sisters/brothers), 39 (14 children), 48 (girl age four, cf. Zofka).
712 Posner/Ware p.34.

need of twins for his scientific tests by which he wanted to excel enough for becoming a post-war unversity chairholder was the reason for his eagerness for selection. Most SS doctors considered the selections the most stressful of all their camp duties, but the Günzburger was one of only two doctors who performed the selections without any stimulants. "He really jostled taking part" said Ludwig Wörl, a senior inmate. Another witness, Arie Fuks, said in 1964 that while he worked near the arrival ramps he constantly saw Mengele perform the selections. "But Mengele cannot have been there all of the time?" asked the incredulous judge. "In my opinion, always," responded Fuks. "Night and day."

During his twenty-one months at the Auschwitz concentration camp (April 1943 to January 1945) "four hundred thousand souls, babies, small children, young girls, mothers, fathers, and grandparents are said to have been casually waved to the lefthand side with a flick of the cane clasped in a gloved hand.[713] During this time, the doctor sired, and rejoiced with the birth of, his own son Rolf, on March 16, 1944.

This son visited his father three decades later in Brazil, a land his father disliked since in his view it was filled with "half-monkeys, people of a sick and secondary race." When his anti-nazist son discussed with him in São Paulo, the father's answers were so full of philosophical and pseudo-scientific verbiage that Rolf began to fear that "my mind would be overrun." His father kept straying off the essential points, justifying his racist views, falling back at one stage on a detailed critique of prehistoric evolution. "What precisely", asked the son, is your "evidence for asserting that some races were superior to others? "Here most of his arguments were sociological, historical and political," said Rolf. "They were quite unscientific."[714]

But religious?

The warrant issued by Frankfurt Land Court on January 19, 1981 leaves no doubt about his "contempt" for Jews, which "manifested itself in particular when he made selections on their religious festivals, which was especially painful for them." The German charge goes on: "Thus it is alleged that he selected Jewish children on the Friday before the Jewish New Year festival 1944 from camp section B2D in Birkenau; sending 328 children to their death in the gas chambers on the Jewish festival; on Jewish Yom Kippur 1944 in camp B2E in Birkenau he hung a batten between the goalposts of a football pitch and those approximately 1000 children who were not the required height were sent to the gas chamber." A witness named Kleinmann remembered Mengele's dreadful wording: "I'll show you. Get me a hammer and some nails and a plank." A deathly silence prevailed on the parade ground ... Mengele approached a tall boy ... in the first row. He put the boy near the goalpost and gave orders to nail the plank above the boy's head so that it was like the letter "L" only in reverse [Γ].

Why the heck with nails and hammer when a simple cord between the goalposts would have served the purpose easily? What synapses had linked at

---

713 Posner/Ware, p.29 (Zug); 26-30 (without stimulants, Wörl, Fuks); p.2 (400.000).
714 Posner/Ware, p.159 (half-monkeys); 278 (discussion father-son).

this moment in Mengeles mind? Any young Günzburg soccer player knew that the upper corners of the goal, forming two letters L in reverse, are called the *Kreuzeck* – cross corner. And that's where you have to send the ball. To a cross corner, hammered with nails, Mengele sent thousand balls, thousand heads of Jewish boys, gassed on Yom Kippur 1944. Posner and Ware come to a conclusion that agrees exactly with my theses about the learning of Jew-hate in view of planks and sadistic nailing: "Mengele's combination of anti-Semitism and sadism is probably the explanation for this desecration of Jewish holidays with his games of death."[715]

However, in his boyhood the monster had other games in mind. His neighbors remember this Josef, nicknamed *Beppo* Mengele as a "sunny and fun-loving child." As a teenager he wrote a play he titled "Travels to Lichtenstein", a fairy tale "performed for the benefit of a children's home". Was there a sensitive boy hiding in black uniform? "The strictness of his Catholic up-bringing produced in the teenage Josef a cynical contempt for the Church and its religious festivals, which he viewed as an opportunity merely to fill its coffers." Nevertheless, he didn't leave the Catholic Church as many SS men did, and had his marriage celebrated in church.[716]

Grown up in a "devoutly Catholic home" and "in a house not noted for its warmth or family affection" but rather for its "emotional austerity", he wrote bitterly of his father as "a cold figure" and of his mother as "not much better at loving," although he came to admire her energy and decisive nature. A witness who until 1919 lived in the family's house related that the appearance of the mother in the factory was much more dreaded by the workers than the father's emergence. And nevertheless, in his autobiographi-cal sketches the son depicts a childhood experience in which the parents came to blows, the father left the house fuming and the son consoled the mother promising „Mother, I will always stay with you". For the early part of his life, "a nanny called Monika fulfilled the dominant maternal role, coaxing and at times intimidating Josef into holding fast the Catholic faith". A 1960 Günzburg police report stresses that here "the public at large till this day cannot believe the accusations, as everybody knows how rigidly the proprietor of the machine factory Karl Mengele had educated his three sons" – and now "a model boy from such a good, honest and Christian family" would be a monster? A mass murderer of Jews the man who in his autobiography confessed: "One could feel flattered that the family tradition going back generations was continued with the name of the Father of Christ, Josef"? A "so rigidly educated son" whom the educative floggings received from his father Karl "hardly seem to have impressed", since in a letter to his son he mentions these paternal punishments "only incidentally and without bitterness".[717]

---

715 Posner/Ware, p. 49-50 (religious holidays, cf. Greenberg 1993, p.316); 51 (combination).
716 Posner/Ware, p.5-6 (sunny child, Lichtenstein); Zofka (wedding).
717   Posner/Ware, p.4-5 (Catholic house, Monika); Zofka ("Mother, I ..."); Keller, p.132 (police report); 132-134 and 187 (public opinion);Völklein, p.136 (letters to his son).

"The Mengele family was staunchly Catholic and also the three sons were educated in this sense", states Günzburg born biographer Sven Keller. "If Josef Mengele came into contact with anti-Jewish resentments in his family home, they probably arose from the latent cultural anti-Judaism typical for the Catholic milieu of the time."[718]

Typical for German culture are three cruciform decorations the doctor was awarded: Iron Cross second and first class for his bravery, and the war merit cross for his success in fighting a typhus epidemy: He sent a whole block of 600 Jewish women to the gas chambers, had the empty block desinfected and the other blocks move further along, one at a time. Problem resolved, deserving cross of merit.

By the way, the highest of all crosses of merit (that is, the Knights' Cross of the Iron Cross with Oak Leaves, Sword and Diamonds) deserved the nazi combat pilot Hans-Ulrich Rudel who after the war praised the Catholic Church for having "saved the best ones of our nation and efficiently thwarted the crazy winners' frantic desire for revenge and retaliation"[719] Saved, how? By lending helping hands along the "rat lines" which had been called "cloister lines" before the participation of US secret service: post-war escape lines for nazis from Europe to South America. For example, to verify if Aryans willing to emigrate deserved his help, Pallottine Father Anton Weber used an unfailing test: "I had them recite the Lord's Prayer and the Ave Maria; on that it transpired quickly who was true and who not." Until 1945 Father Weber had led an aid center for "Catholic baptized non-Aryans", but when in 1950 a Protestant who, thanks to the parson of Sterzing, had found shelter in the Franciscan monastery of Bolzano knocked on his door and told him with Austrian accent that he was East-German and didn't like the Bolsheviks, Father Weber let him pass without Ave Maria. Thus the organizer of Final Solution, Adolf Eichmann, in 1950 escaped on Bishop Hudal's rat line to the Buenos Aryans of Argentina's capital.[720]

His friend Josef Mengele had used this line successfully in 1949. In his flight, the most critical point was the moment when he was caught in Genoa and happened to spend few days in prison until the bribable policeman returned from his vacancy. The obscene graffiti adorning his cell walls bothered the chief selector of Auschwitz more than anything else." In Argentina, the two friends were protected by the mentioned ex-colonel Rudel, son of a Lutheran parson, who had arrived there in 1948, without his wife of which the most decorated German hero had divorced because she didn't want to emigrate with him and – how heartlessly! – had wholesaled all his cross decorations. Counseled and helped by Rudel, Mengele chose to live in Paraguay where he, having read reports about himself in German newspapers, commented that "behind all this stands only one thing: that is all the Old Testament hate

---

718 Keller, p.76.
719 Wikipedia, article "Rattenlinien".
720 Klee, p.25.

toward everything in the German consciousness [that is] heroic and truly superior".[721]
Mengele hid much more cautiously than Eichmann who even gave interviews in Buenos Aires. Probably as from 1952, the CIA and the government of Adenauer knew that Eichmann was living there. But the prudent adults obviously didn't want to expose a historical link between Globke and Eichmann. Unfortunately, 12-years-old pretty Silvia Hermann in a cinema of Buenos Aires became acquainted with a boy of 17. "Eichmann or so", she told her father when he asked her for the surname of her new friend. When Silvia invites him to her home, at the dinner table daddy asks him what his father had been doing in Germany. "He`s done a lot of things. The war, you know. We moved around a lot, even living in Prague for some time. He always said, 'we're here to bring German values into the world'." Señor Lothar Hermann had lost most of his family in the holocaust and one eye in Dachau Camp in 1936. Recently he had learned that a certain Eichmann organized extermination. He lets Silvia ask at the front door of her ex-friends house, informs Frankfurt General Public Prosecutor Fritz Bauer, who happens to be Jewish and passes the information concerning Eichmann to the government of Israel which however after a short time surveillance of the suspect leaves him in peace. Not until Bauer in 1959 can present a second informer, the Mossad kidnaps Eichmann in 1960 and flies him, allegedly passing controls drugged and in the uniform of an El-Al-steward, to Tel Aviv. When in Buenos Aires Lothar Hermann tries to reveal the backgrounds of Eichmann's long non-arrestment, on March 21, 1961, three weeks before Eichmann's trial, he himself gets arrested. German special agents had informed the local police that this man is Josef Mengele, and only after the latter's finger prints arrived two weeks later, Lothar Hermann was released. His daughter had received threatening letters and fled to the US in 1959; Lothar Hermann never met her again until his death in 1974.
"When Adolf Eichmann was captured and brought to trial in Israel", George Bailey recalls, "I toured West Germany with a television camera team interviewing old and young for their reactions to the forthcoming Eichmann trial. To my astonishment, among the interviewees over forty years of age as often as not we heard the frankly stated opinion that the Jews had brought the Final Solution on themselves. How so? 'Because they crucified our Lord Jesus Christ!'"[722]
The question whether Eichmann should be executed by and in the "Jewish state" divided Israel in the spring of 1962. While Hannah Arendt agreed to his execution, Martin Buber disapproved since he denied to any state the right to kill. Yeshayahu Leibowitz objected since he denied Eichmann's guilt and deemed the whole trial a faulty action. "I think it was an agreement between Adenauer and Ben-Gurion in order to free the German people of its guilt by turning the spotlight on the completely meaningless person of Eichmann. In return, the Germans paid us billions! After kidnapping Eich-

---

721 Posner/Ware, p.92 (Genoa) and 154 (German consciousness).
722 Bailey, p.158. As to Lothar Hermann, see the article about him in German Wikipedia.

mann and bringing him here, we should have given him the best attorney to prove that this man is not guilty and not responsible for anything." – "Not guilty because he obeyed orders?" – "That's the final point. To begin with, Eichmann is the historical product of two millennia of Christendom whose whole striving aimed to the annihilation of Judaism ... – "I don't understand in this context the link to Christendom. Hadn't Nazism broken with it?" – "This doesn't change anything. The mindset of the world concerning Judaism springs from Christendom, no matter that the Nazis' world yet wasn't Christian any more. The other thing remains, and an old joke expresses it quite well: The secular goy tells you that Jesus is from fairy-tale and never existed, but one thing is sure, the Jews have crucified him."[723]

When Mengele, now living in Brazil, in June of 1962 received the notice that his friend Eichmann had been hanged in Jerusalem, he felt "startled by the reality of the path of history over the last 2000 years. His people have betrayed him [Eichmann] miserably."[724]

They didn't betray many. Of the 14 participants of infamous Wannsee Conference, having planned and resolved Final Solution in January 1942, twelve survived the war. Besides Eichmann only one was indicted – and released early on. Of 8,000 Nazis working in Auschwitz, 22 were brought to court, 17 convicted. Of altogether 500,000 persons involved in the holocaust just 900, that is less than 0.02 percent, were condemned. "German justice failed totally" no less a figure than minister of justice Heiko Maas declared in April 2015, seventy years after Hitler's self-execution.[725]

When the Jews hanged Eichmann, I was age nine and had the distinct feeling that this killing was not right, by reasons which I find today in Buber and Leibowitz. Mengele survived his friend for 17 years and never was caught, because his family in Günzburg supported him through all those years and was warned by an informer within Günzburg's local police station each time federal police arrived with a search warrant. In these three decades, Mengele muted to a monster and mystery. Two movies made much money "with one of the twentieth century's most evil men", this "man who was the very personification of evil" and "the most hated and sought-after man in the world". Print media wasted huge sums for fake news about him; two innocent men lost their lives because they resembled too much with the photos said to show him. On February 7, 1979, the doctor selector drowned at Bertioga beach, having suffered his second stroke while swimming. But only when the nice Günzburg policeman had retired at last and for the first time federal police achieved to search successfully, a São Paulo coroner on June 6, 1985 could present the unearthed skull to the world's cameras. About the day when his death was proved, Michael Berenbaum writes: "I remember feeling that for Mengele to die outside of captivity, it should have been from

---

723 Leibowitz, p.101.
724 Posner/Ware, chapter 9.
725 Gerhard Jauch in TV talkshow "Das kann wieder passieren" (This can happen again), with Auschwitz survivors, Jan. 26, 2015 (t-online.de); Julian Moering: "Die deutsche Justiz hat total versagt", t-online, April 27, 2015.

cancer – long, painful, and slow. Where was God? Why such a quick death, why so painless?"[726]
The last paragraph, from When the Jews ... to ... why so painless, contains three essential facts of this book. The first one, in Hitler's words: "Cruelty impresses, people need the wholesome horror. They want to dread something [...] You talk about cruelty, you're indignant about torments? The mass wants that, needs something to get terrified".[727] The second one is the question of Michael Berenbaum that sheds no murky light on the sad reality that we adults, just as the children of Geneva observed by Jean Piaget, instead of researching motives (the subject of this book) tend to recur to "just" and rigid punishments – in innocent Jesus' as in guilty Josef's case. And the third fact points to our terrible underestimation of experiences which transform a "sunny and fun-loving child", a boy who "wrote a play for the benefit of a children's home" into a monster of daily maltreatment of children who for him, as Posner and Ware state seven times, were *human guinea-pigs* just as animals are guinea-pigs for scientists.

Where was God, asks Berenbaum, saddened since the divine retaliator let Josef die without a dose of adequate torture; let simply die this father and big boy Josef M. who by the way lived in permanent fear, who had a watchtower on his farm, who almost panicked in crowds or supermarkets, who never slept without his Mauser pistol at his bedside, who bit and swallowed so much hair of his moustache that eventually a hair ball blocked his intestines, who thought about suicide and wrote in his diary: "Instead of refreshing sleep, evil appearances and dreams are vexing the one so deeply tired in his soul ... Sleeplessness cites specters"?[728] Maybe the specter of a little gipsy girl who had approached him as "uncle doctor"?

Is Proverb 24:17 an antidote against our quasi sadistic desires for just punishment? "Don't rejoice when your enemy falls."

At this point, let's come back to the lecture of Jewish twin Eva Mozes Kor, given in the Catholic Girls' Gymnasium. After I had shouted "Stop!" the old man went on apparently undeterred, but maybe in a self-protecting way revealed `now that he bears the "priestly robes". "That fits well!" replied my quick female atheist colleague sitting next to me, a native of Günzburg who of course knew the priest. The audience was ruffled, angry with the cleric whose intention no one understood. In this moment, Eva Mozes Kor stood up, stepped down from the podium, went over to the man, embraced him – and the Catholic priest answered her embrace in the awkward ways one would expect from a celibatarian who never was meant to hug a woman. Strong applause for the forgiving victim.

The newspaper report about the incident in Eva Mozes Kor's lecture, written by journalist Alf Geiger who years ago had told me about his college research work about the Jews of his Swabian home town, didn't mention

---

726 Posner/Ware, Preface (most evil, personification of evil), p.195 (most hated); New Introduction (by Michael Berenbaum).
727 Heer 1967, p.389.
728 Posner/Ware, p. 223-231 (tower, market, moustache), 259 (pistol); Keller, p.59 (diary).

that the grey-haired defender of Mengele was a Catholic priest. There's no connection between Christian faith and genocidal racism, is there? Not a priest but a veterinary and natural health professional was the next German lecture actor who surprised me in March 2008. During his lecture on *"Angst und Mobbing"* at the local Natural Medicine Club in Senden, Bavaria, this Dr.Schuhmacher reaped knowing nods consensually woven with decent sighs when he by no discernable motive suddenly remarked: "At the attack on the World Trade Center not a single Jew has been among the victims. These guys have done it right." When I protested, the Club president asked me: "Which remark do you mean?" The healer himself was astonished: "But those facts are well known, right?"

What obviously was well plausible to the speaker and his audience is that Jewish employees of WTC had previous notice of what would happen on this workday and stayed at home this morning of 9/11 to watch their non-Jewish colleagues on TV, jumping from the windows of burning 89th flat. This innovative variant of old Jewish conspirators watching the despair up there with a sardonic smile did not appear as neither abstruse nor offensive to an audience of at least eighty very normal, health-club-healthy Bavarians.

Dr. Schuhmacher, born in 1940, not only had indicated with words and finger that Iranian president Ahmedinedshad who threatened Israel with nuclear extermination was "from above", but on his website sells for instance his *Our Father CD* about "the most powerful prayer *Jesus the Creator and Father* has taught us", or the book *Forgotten Words* with unknown teachings Jesus gave his disciple John, or *The Secrets of the Pyramides*. To the health club members the doctor also had disclosed that he personally had viewed UFOs flying zigzag over his home and that the earth is hollow and inhabited inside. Which seems not a bad metaphor concerning an expanding religious vacuum of German culture, with old incubi still bustling inside.

The teachers as selectors

Religious hazard: Reacting to medical complications after the circumcision of a four-year-old Muslim boy, a Cologne district court jury decided in July 2012 that circumcisions are an illegitimate infringement of a child's integrity and therefore a penal offense. Look, those guys come here from Orient and ... – therefore it was no surprise that a majority of German population agreed with the ban on circumcision and that xenophobic rightists enjoyed their new bounce house. After a TV talkshow including a rabbi, Liberal Munich daily *Süddeutsche Zeitung* even had to beg the reader's pardon for publishing just a small part of the letters to the editor concerning circumcision, while many more readers would have liked to criticize the *Jewish* attack on children publicly. The number of fully signed letters of threat or abuse addressed to Jewish communities increased dashingly. "It's payback time", a young journalist sarcastically noted in view of a young strong Germany where "healthy *Volksgefühl*, alert again like a butcher's dog, is losing patience".[729]

---

729 Stefan Gärtner, in The European/ t-online, 14.09.2012.

If a Muslim circumcision leads to an outburst of sound emotions against Jewish targets this is hardly conceivable without latent energies flowing from piercingly bloody images. The friendly view that this German outrage was really centered in caring for Muslim and Jewish children threatened by an outdated initiation rite cracks at the fact that the same Germans broadly agree with another ritual initiation required for befitting German education: "One type of school prepares you to become a doctor, a second one to become a technician and the third one teaches you how to make a kebab and to clean restrooms." This is Tuvia Tenenbom's view.[730] A Brazilian mother comments: "To see this system in a first-world country was a big shock to me ... The school defines the status of the child as well as of his family; defines early on what the child is going to be and particularly not to be."[731] For in Germany today there are, just as in a German plan of 1739, "1st the studying youth, 2nd the not studying youth who nevertheless shall not become rough populace, 3rd the rough German youth, that is the bad children of common townsmen and peasants".[732] Plus, nowadays, the migrants. Whereas recent studies proved that a child's IQ is subject to changes of 20 points up and 20 downward after the age of twelve,[733] already the ten-year old children in Germany and Austria are selected according to their prospective aptitude for university, with the effect that the daughter or son of middle-class academic parents has more than six times better chances to be selected to *Gymnasium* (which leads to university) than an equally intelligent working-class or immigrant child. The selection stress, permanent fear of decisive tests and rejection that 4th-graders undergo in the procedure even mainstream school directors dare to diagnose as "utter madness": With coaching and psychotropic drugs, children of grade three and four get doped for this rite of passage at the grade 4 "clear point of intersection" as a Realschul teacher lobbyist called it in German sharpness. And once you got in, face daily the Out! In 2004/2005 in North Rhine-Westphalia alone 16,500 losers got demoted from Gymnasium to Real- and Hauptschule, 8,800 from Real- to Hauptschule, while just 1,350 winners were allowed to climb one sieve higher. Why does Germany stick to this "Angstsystem"? Hamburg middle class parents whose plebiscite successfully stopped the shift of selection from grade four to grade six admitted quite openly: "We don't want our children have to learn together with migrant children longer than necessary."[734]

Unsuccessfully UN High Commissioner Vernor Muñoz Villalobos (Costa Rica) called for a structural reform of the "extremely selective" German

730 Tenenbom 2012, p.216.
731 Behrla, p.21-22.
732 Rosenberger, p.37.
733 Cathy Price, London University College London, tested 33 teenagers (age 12-16) for verbal and non-verbal intelligence twice in a distance of four years. Süddeutsche Zeitung, October 20, 2011.
734 North Rhine-Westphalia: Kurt Singer, p.169; point of intersection: Rektor Obert, Bavarian Realschul Teacher's Union, 2005; Angstsystem: Berlin school reformer Margret Rasfeld, t-online, July 29, 2016; plebiscite: Antje Berg, Südwestpresse, Ulm, July 19, 2010.

education system which he said causes "angst and resistance" in the children and implicates a "quite clear link" between social provenance and success in formation. As the pupils' performances are "imposed by the system and not by the child's potential", this early selection discriminates mainly the offspring of migrant parents.[735] That is: mainly Muslim pupils, by coincidence. Selection hits also Austrian fourth graders who graciously get segregated into but two drawers. Ruth Beckermann, documentary film producer and daughter of Shoah survivors, was asked by Vienna daily *Standard* on August 3, 2009 what detail of Austrian education system made her particularly angry. "I wouldn't really call it education system, but social sifting system", she replied. "It's been working in this country for centuries, by way of elites keeping their schools and peergroups occupied in order to let enter as few as possible others. [...] The main focus in Austria is continuation of the status quo. Someone coming from a poor or migrant family shall stay where he is, okay? [...] What happens in Austria to my view is a crime committed on children. [...] One reason why we didn't enroll our son in any state-run Austrian school was the cross on the wall. I didn't want my son to have to sit under Jesus on the cross. Why should he? What is being communicated to him by this permanently is just what the people believe: 'You have killed him'." Incongruously by no means, Beckermann addresses selection of children and charging of Jews in the same breath. "The idea of selection" says social democratic Berlin lawmaker Christoph Ehmann, "arises from a longing for homogeneity – and therefore from the same ideology that views salvation in the uniformity of Volk and language, of race and religion. This inescapably leads to 'ethnical cleansings' or to the incompatibility of Christian-Jewish occident and Islam. Hundred years ago this exclusion which today affects Muslims still applied to Jews, too. Fortunately, this has changed. Even so, what shows up is that German education policy is still grounded on an ideology of homogeneity. This goes with the political will to select and has – something fascistic."[736]
Discouragement, abasement and fear of selection have been and still are core elements of repressive, angst-based German "*Schwarze Pädagogik*". Hitler, the "*enfant humilié*" in George Bernanos' view,[737] left the Realgymnasium of Linz with an "elementary hatred of school" and with his anti-Semitism he created a "socialism for the witless guys" – guys like himself, the dropout underachiever. The aftermaths of previous humiliation recur in Melvin Lerner's and Susan Clayton's study as a reinforcing factor in justified anger acted out in just punishment: "Those participants who had experienced a lowering of their self-esteem ... rated the most extreme responses as considerably more desirable."[738]

735 Zeit online, March 22, 2007; Frankfurter Allgemeine, February 21, 2006, faz.net.
736 Christoph Ehmann (Member of the Bundestag, SPD): Ausgrenzung und Selektion in der Bildung. Tageszeitung (taz), Berlin, December 16, 2009.
737 Heer 1989, p.39; *Schwarze Pädagogik* means "black" (violent, rigid ...) education.
738 Lerner/Clayton, p.240.

Evidently, Sander Gilman's diagnosis "To not a minor degree, Shoa was the result of German fear of heterogeneity"[739] not least applies to German education system whose cardinal fault Vernor Muñoz detects in its "patriarchal frame of reference".[740] The most patriarcal state of Germany doubtlessly is Bavaria, governed since 1954 by Christian Social Union, mostly elected by absolute majorities of the electorate. Here the selection is the most rigid one, Jesus's crucifixion is a classroom obligation and distortion of history was visible in the history textbook of my last Bavarian 8th-graders, devoting three well-earned pages to the resistence group Weisse Rose (six Christian victims) and one and a half pages to the holocaust (six million Jewish). This way pupils grasp easily that Nazi Jew-hate had nothing to do with Christian tradition, that Nazis went after Christians and Jews while Christians used to fight heroically against those godless Nazis.

The editor as disinfector
When one commenter Dr.Dede called these Christian roots the "central taboo of the republic" in *Jüdische Zeitung* (54/2010), one orderly Dr. Ordnung charged him of coming close to *Volksverhetzung* (stirring up the people's hatred) which is a fact of criminal offence, in modern Germany.
For comparison: In Britain, the theologian James Parkes long before had stated that "the Christian Church is responsible for the extermination of six million Jews"; Bishop Christopher Budd had pointed to the charge of God-murder as "the fertile soil of national socialism". In France, the Catholic Bishops in 1997 confessed that until the Second Vatican Council "a tradition of anti-Judaism marked doctrine and education of Christians, theology and apologetics, preaching and liturgy. On this hotbed the poisonous plant of Jew-hate prospered." In the USA, Emil Fackenheim yet in 1978 had interpreted Hitler's Jew-hate as "the nemesis of a two thousand years long pathological aberration within Christianity"; while in 2002 US-historian Daniel Goldhagen stated that the gospels are "the source of the most obnoxious anti-Semitism" and Irving Greenberg in 2004 registered the "record of brutality and Jewish suffering" as "brought on or contributed to by Christianity".[741] The wide gap between well-researched facts and neglected motives must stay open especially in the most Shoah-affected countries since Christian motives of history's most heinous mass murder are not accepted by editions, media, universities and research funding, while (cause or consequence?) discussing those things seems neither interesting nor desirable to a great part of the society. To me this lack of interest became palpable in the variety of holocaust literature I found in bookshops and libraries of Manhattan; a broadness of deepness quite alien to the famous *Land der Dichter und*

---

739 Gilman, p.276.
740 munoz.uri-text.de/VernorMunoz7teJunio9_OL_deutscheUebersetzung.pdf.
741 Budd: Goldhagen 2002, p.298; Parkes: Heer 1981, p.475; French Bishops: Goldhagen 2002, p.296; Fackenheim: Wistrich 1987, p.247; Goldhagen: 2002, p.271; Greenberg: 2004, p.127.

Denker (... of Poets and Thinkers) with its unfathomable *Tiefe* (deepness) of whatsoever. Saul Friedman's work about the Oberammergau Passion Play would have been rejected by any German editor alone for its subtitle "A Lance against Civilization". Robert Wistrich's iridescent statement that Nazi ideology "chose ... human sacrifice as way of salvation" would probably had passed the editorial report, but his statement that "the seed of hate, prepared for years by the clergy, fell on fertile soil" was surely more suitable for a Brazilian edition.[742] James Carroll's brillant "Constantine's Sword", bestseller of New York Times und winner of National Book Award, would well deserve to be a set book of German historians and theologians, the more so since its title rather gently circumscribed Cross by *Sword*. But 756 pages in English make at least 820 in German; how should future theologists cope with this and read that "the cross is meant to be a symbol of love, but looked from below, it can be a symbol only of domination"? And what's worse, that "the cross drives this story, from its beginning at Golgotha to its end at what John Paul II called 'this Golgotha of the modern world'"?[743] If historian Ulrich Herbert calls the "so called *Vergangenheitsbewältigung*" (coping with the past) a decades long "struggle for elucidation – against a conspiracy of silence"[744] he himself conceals that this reticence mainly concealed the compromising Christian roots of hate and haters. Of course the "conspiracy of silence" transpires not as a secret meeting of men in trenchcoats and dark sunglasses, but rather as the preemptive cozy compliance between media and readers concerning what one would want to read. With envy towards rich people, with dumb prejudice and oafish obedience holocaust may have to do – but with religion and good Jesus? *Mein Gott*, there are things one should respect, alright?

"The Germans will never forgive the Jews this Auschwitz",[745] Zvi Rex once predicted. Actually the German not-forgiving points to a trifurcation of "secondary" anti-Semitism. First, national resentments remain because Auschwitz reminds the big stain in the pride-producing image of German culture; second, religious grounds of this stain might underline the innocence of those (rich, exploitative et cetera) Jews and aggravate German guilt. And third: "In the absence of explanatory circumstances, the assumption is made that the members of this group somehow deserve the negative treatment they receive."[746] This is not a statement about post-war Germans' view of Jews as a group but a result of Melvin Lerner's studies. In one of his experiments, 72 female students of University of Kansas had to watch another student receiving electrical shocks under a variety of conditions. Initially, the observers were upset; but as the suffering continued and observers remained unable to intervene, they began to derogate the victim. This shift of guilt is due to a very basic concept of human world-view

---

742 Wistrich 2002, p.56 and 325.
743 Carroll, p.396.
744 "Tüchtig, klug, womöglich sogar charmant" (on occasion of the Eichmann trial's 50th anniversary), Berlin daily taz, April 11, 2011, p.15-16.
745 Cited by Ian Buruma, in: Rabinovici/Speck/Sznaider, p.240.
746 Lerner/Clayton, p.231, referring to Dharmapala/Garoupa/McAdams, 2009.

which Melvin Lerner called the "just world hypothesis": In order to live in a predictable environment, people need to believe that in this world people reap what they sowed. If an injustice seems unlikely to be resolved in reality, people re-evaluate the situation in line with their belief in a just world, confirmed by sayings like "What goes around comes around" and "You get what you deserve and deserve what you get". Lerner's conclusion that "the greater the undeserved suffering, the more negatively they portrayed the victims' character"[747] applies nicely to the German pupils who in the late seventies after a holocaust fact film opined: "The Jews must have been guilty, otherwise they wouldn't have been punished like that."[748]
They will stay guilty because the infamous religious charge remains taboo and therefore concomitantly acting undercover, sustaining the old allegations against those greedy, conspiring Jews behind the sign that's German culture's nerve. While the inclination towards such prejudices is generally stronger among people with poor education, in 1913 a research of Munich University evidenced antisemitic views in 37 % of female and 61% of male citizens in a group of 1127 interviewees consisting of 100 percent urban, 50.1 percent university graduate adults among whom 27 percent pretended to vote for Germany's most anti-racist and multi-cultural faction, that is Green Party.[749]
German mindcuffs and silent German conspiration against Christian holocausality motivated also the last and final example: a very orderly and speaking falsification published by Süddeutsche Zeitung in March 2011; a nice little ellipsis that says all in what it burkes to say:
The journal's series about emancipated Bavarian women of 20th century started with great Munich actress Therese Giehse, who in her role of Brecht's *Mother Courage* had sung the verse *"Wie kreuzbrav waren wir doch schon"* (How cross-obedient we've been already) and who as Dürrenmatt's *"Fräulein Doktor"* had healed *The Physicists* Newton, Einstein, Galilei. Now she was presented to Bavarian left-leaning middle class readers with her childhood memory "I was fat, red-haired and *jüdisch*."
The most telling words in this dull, witless quote are those which were left out in *kreuzbrav* compliance with political correctness. Four years earlier, the hardly left-leaning Catholic "Sunday Journal for Augsburg Diocesis" had cited *die Giehse* with all her subtle humour correctly, having the senior actress enumerate the three reasons why she had been mobbed by her classmates in Munich cross-equipped primary school between the world-wars: "I was fat, red-haired *and had killed Herr Jesus*."[750]

747 Lerner/Clayton, p.225 and en.wikipedia.org/wiki/Just-world_hypothesis.
748 Miller 1983, p.187.
749 Dominik Steinbeißer, Felix Bader, Christian Ganser, Laila Schmitt: Gruppenbezogene Menschenfeindlichkeit in München. Institute of Sociology at Munich Ludwig-Maximilians-Universität, October 8, 2013.
750 Gernot Römer, speech in Hainsfarth Synagogue, in: Sonntagszeitung, Augsburg, May 4, 1997. Falsification until today: Archive of Süddeutsche Zeitung, 08.03.2011: Zum Weltfrauentag. Bayerische Pionierinnen. Als Mann verkleidet, mit Mistgabeln gejagt.

XII Cruzion
Back at the scene

Lana Abuhijleh's mother has been gunned down by Israeli forces in front of her home in Nablus. Today Lana is the country director of an international relief agency operating in the West Bank and Gaza. She lives in Jerusalem and commutes to Ramallah, a short drive if you don't consider the checkpoints. The twenty-five-foot-high separation wall accompanies you on the six-mile journey, dividing the northern suburbs annexed by Israel from (still) Palestinian territory. One day Lana was making the trip with her eight-year-old daughter. "Mummy", the pensative girl suddenly asked her mother, "why do they make the Jews live behind that wall?"[751]

Anti-Zionist Jewish peace activist Mark Braverman who relates this wise child's view of the conflict gives the basic and obvious answer to the girl's question: "Zionism was the answer to the anti-Semitism of Christian Europe." Already in 1979, Palestinian Edward Said stated that the Palestinians who were driven out in 1948 were "victims of the same movement whose whole aim had been to end the victimization of Jews in Christian Europe."[752] This chapter brings the book's core thesis – Jesus' unforgettable crucifixion as the root of collective punishment – back to the scene of the crime. "You know, 'a criminal always goes back to the scene of the crime', isn't that right?"[753] And it brings the following theses to local inspection:
1. The images and imaginations of Jewish-caused Christian suffering have been exported, casually as well as methodically, from Europe into the mainly Muslim Oriental culture.
2. Here they function not only as the rough drawing of several anti-Zionist stereotypes, but also as the mental basis for a kind of media coverage that markets images of Palestinian victims and their Jewish abusers to Christian cultural sphere, replying to the given special receptivity of Christian psyche.
3. Muslim anti-Jewish animosity differs crucially from Christian Jew-hate, this very difference offering hopeful outlooks on a Jewish-Muslim future.
4. Zionism is largely a Christian designed solution for the Jewish question. It served and keeps serving purposes of Christian occident while having regressive effects on Judaism.

---

751 Braverman, p.287-288.
752 Said 1992, p.xxxix.
753 Schützenberger, p.52. She quotes here from Claudine Vegh: I Didn't Say Goodbye. Interviews with Children of the Holocaust (1985) the statement of Robert beginning with the last words of his father ("Robert, don't forget you're Jewish and must remain Jewish!") and ending with "My eldest daughter ... is moving to live in Israel ... The circle is closed ... My father would be proud of her."

Golgotha – Europe and return

"I told him the difference between him and me is that he's a Muslim Arab and I'm a Jewish Arab. Period." Bennett Greenspan, who said this to a "seven percent Jewish" Riyadh resident client, is well known to many Arabs who have their genetics tested at his Texas laboratory, and he insists that 75 percent of all Jews share roots in Arab Middle East.[754] Long before genetical testing, Shlomo D. Goitein viewed a similar closeness in the linguistic aspect that "Arabic, Hebrew and Aramaic were basically one and the same language"; he also perceived an "amazing affinity" between the fully developed systems of the two religions" and stressed as "significant for understanding of the close connection between Muslim and Jewish law" the fact that "Islam later adopted Jewish abhorrence of graven images".[755]

Due to this abhorrence, not the lethal symbol but the rumours of their crime followed the "Jewish Arab" returnees on their heels, disrupting Arab-Jewish affinities by a carriage free European delivery in three stages:

I. Christian hostility to Jews began to trickle into Islam with ex-Christian converts during the High Middle Ages.[756] But not until Christian Constantinople had been conquered by the Turks in 15th century, the accusation of ritual murder – introduced by Christian Greeks now living under Ottoman dominion – found entrance to Islamic culture. The acceptance of the gory phantasm remained low, in lack of its basis: According to Koran, the son of Miriam was not a son of God but "nothing else but an envoy" (Sura 5:79). And not this prophet Jesus was crucified by the "people of the scripture" but "a resembling one" (Sura 4:152-156). Unlike the gospel writers with their fear of Roman power, Mohammed had no interest in highlighting the Jews as guilty ones of crucifixion. Since Islam even tightened the Jewish prohibition of idols and strongly objected to visible nakedness, the Christian minorities nowhere from Morocco to Malaysia achieved to have the naked bleeding corpus displayed in public space.

II. A second wave of blood libel sloshed onto Middle East when in late 18th and early 19th century the Ottoman Empire crumbled and parts of its population began to perceive non-Muslim compatriots as internal menace. The transmission route was once again a Christian one, personified in Christian missionaries and minority groups such as Maronites and Copts. The most infamous case was the Damascus Affair of 1840, when French Capuchin monk Thomás and his Muslim servant disappeared traceless. His confrère Father Tusti alleged that both men's blood would serve the Jews for their Passover six weeks later; the French consul deemed the charge wellfounded, though a Turkish merchant who had heard a mule-merchant utter death-threats against Father Thomás (allegedly the monk had defamed Islam) was

---

754 Judy Maltz, "Genetics Expert Insists 75% of Jews Share Roots in Middle East", in: The Forward, November 14, 2014.
755 Goitein, p.59, 137 and 207.
756 Lewis, p.132.

found hanged shortly after his testimony. The American vice-consul seized on the suspicion calling it "a secret which in these 1840 years [sic!] must have claimed many unfortunate victims". Also the Austrian consul Casper Merlato initially warned about the "Jewish secret" and praised the "zeal and vigor" with which local authorities conducted the case. Only when he had to (and did efficiently) protect the young merchant Isaac Picciotto by having Austrian officials accompany his interrogations, the veneer of torture-forced confessions spalled. Three Jews had already been tortured to death – with the consent of French consul Ratti-Menton whose first dispatch to Paris had ended this way: "Informed of what had happened, I went to the monastery where the street was full of Christians from all the different sects who were shouting that Father Thomás had been slain by the Jews."[757]
Despite this kind of European development assistance, the obsessive Christian nexus of blood+Jew remained alien to Islamic Orient for the next three generations. During the Dreyfus Affair, parts of Arabic press sided with the accused Jewish captain of French army, his infamous condemnation being evidence for Europe's fictive and hypocritous "cultural mastery". At the beginning of 20th century, however, the Ottoman Empire incurred its final crisis and the Jews, who now in growing numbers – many by foot – migrated from Russia to Palestine came under general suspicion. In January 1926 the first Arabic translation of the "Protocols of the Elders of Zion" appeared in *Raqíb Sahyun*, a periodical published in Jerusalem by the Latin Catholic Community, and one year later a Christian Arab published the bogus as a book in Cairo.[758]

III. In the third stage, the old stereotypes of altogether Christian origin became the Third Reich's most important article of exportation into Arabic Orient. At first, anti-Jewish flyers and pamphlets were meant to serve the purpose well; but yet in 1933 the Cairo group of Hitler's Party sent a recommendation to Berlin requiring the central office to desist from such brochures and rather address the point where "real conflicts of interest exist between Arabs and Jews: Palestine. The antagonism between Arabs and Jews at that place must be transplanted to Egypt." Here on the fertile banks of Nile, to wit, there was no talk about Jew-hate so far. Jews were well-esteemed by Egyptian population and influential in economy and politics. The new approach, however, was successful: As early as in May 1936, the Muslim Brotherhood called for boycott of all Jewish shops in Egypt.[759]
In Jerusalem, German News Bureau (DNB) had installed an Arab service yet in 1936. In 1937, two staff members of the *Judenreferat* (Jews Department) within SS Security Service departed for a several weeks exploration trip to Middle East, their names being Herbert Martin Hagen (1913-1999) and Adolf Eichmann.

757 Goldstein, Phyllis, p.183-190, quoting from Frankel, Jonathan: The Damascus Affair: "Ritual Murder", Politics and the Jews in 1840. Cambridge (UK) 1997, p.20 and 67.
758 Lewis, p.199; cf. Schoenfeld, p.35-36.
759 Küntzel, Matthias in: Rabinovici/Speck/Sznaider, p.282.

The strongest effectiveness, however, was soon to be deployed by an Arab radio program that Berlin's minister of propaganda Joseph Goebbels praised as "our long-range-cannon in the airwaves".[760] In Zeesen, a village of 4000 inhabitants south of Berlin, the Reich installed the then most powerful short-wave transmitter worldwide. At that time, in Arabian culture people used to listen to the new medium preferentially in public places, bazaars and coffee houses. And no other transmitter down there in Orient enjoyed greater popularity than the Nazi-channel which since April 25, 1939 sent down infotainment from northern *Almaneea*. Eighty staff members were busy with compiling a daily program in Arabic language, yet also Turks, Persians and Indians were diligently stewarded. In a very catchy way, anti-Jewish agitation was mixed up here with quotings from Koran and Arab popular music. Spicy highlights of the potpourri were the calls for Jihad emitted by the then most popular Arab in Berlin, the Great Mufti of Jerusalem, Amin al-Husseini (1895-1974).

Living in Berlin since 1941, al-Husseini supervised the Arabic broadcasts aired from Zeesen, but also those from Rome and Athens. In an intimate circle (Hitler, al-Husseini, foreign minister Ribbentrop, Arabia-expert Fritz Grobba) the Führer let the Mufti in his plan to continue "the battle until the total destruction of the Jewish-communist empire in Europe" and begged him – few weeks before the infamous Wannsee Conference – to lock this item of their conversation "into his heart's deepest depths". This battle would, as soon as German troops had reached the southern exit of Caucasus, find its further target in the "extermination of the *Judentum* living in Arab space under protection of British power". A special command unit of SS headed by the gassing-expert Walter Rauff had been attached to Rommel's tank divisions providently. After Rommel's defeat at El Alamein, still about 380 miles from Jerusalem, the *Gaswagen* unit was redeployed to Germany.[761]

This defeat of General Rommel in 1942 frustrated also the expectations of Mufti al-Husseini and caused him to write letters to the governments of Italy, Hungary, Romania and the king of Bulgaria, as well as to intervene in Croatia with the purpose of thwarting the emigration of Jewish fugitives to Palestine. "It would be infinitely more desirable", he wrote on June 28, 1943 to Budapest, to send the Hungarian Jews "into other countries where they stand under active control, for instance Poland" – which he knew from his guided visits in Auschwitz and Majdanek camps.[762] In a speech on November 2, 1943, Husseini emphasized the fact that "most of all they [the Ger-

---

760 Küntzel, Matthias in: Rabinovici/Speck/Sznaider, p.276.
761 Wistrich 2010, p.680. Gassing expert Rauff after 1945 spent one year and a half in Catholic convents and escaped probably with the help of Bishop Hudal, who in 1937 had dedicated his book "The Groundworks of National Socialism" to the Austrian "Siegfried of German hope and greatness". He died in 1984 in a Hospital of Santiago de Chile, protected by General Pinochet.
762 Wistrich 2010, p.669-674; concerning El-Husseini's KZ-visits Wistrich refers to Wiesenthal, Simon: Großmufti-Großagent der Achse, Salzburg 1947, p.37.

mans] have definitely solved the Jewish problem."[763] In a broadcast from Berlin on September 21, 1944, Husseini spoke of "the eleven million Jews of the world" while he must have known that there had been seventeen million Jews in 1939.[764]

This third import wave of Jew-hate to Middle East did not end with the Third Reich's doom: Ludwig Heiden, a former official of the Reich's Main-Security-Office and since 1950 one of several Cairo resident Ex-SS-officers, under the meaningful name "Luis Al-Hadj" translated Hitler's *Mein Kampf* (which still in 2000 ranked sixth on the bestseller-list of Palestinian Authonomy Authorities)[765] to Arab language.

"Demand of the Hour: Jews out": With this pamphlet, in which he presented ritual murders as a present danger for Christian children, the estate owner's son Johann von Leers yet in 1933 caused Leiden University Principal Johan Huizinga to exclude the German delegation from a symposion. In 1938 Himmler's long-term friend von Leers became the chairholder for "German history of law, economy and politics on racial basis" at Jena University, where he edited the Nazi monthly *Der Weg*. Since 1943 he took part in a meaningful project of "Research Section Orient" within Reich's Main Security Office, titled "Koran passages allegedly referring to the Führer" (as the predicted Messiah). Johann's religious bent was not unique in his family: In spite of his good rapport with Himmler, von Leer's brother Kurt Mathias, a student of Catholic theology, died in 1945 on the sequelae of his six months detention in Dachau concentration camp, having resisted to torture and refused to renounce Catholic Church as his eldest brother had tried to persuade him in order to ease his release.

Since 1950 living as Adolf Eichmann's friend in Argentine, von Leers moved to Cairo in 1955 to work there in the Ministry of Information. In his public welcome for von Leers in Cairo, the Ex-Mufti thanked him "for venturing to take up the battle with the powers of darkness that have become incarnate in world-Jewry".[766] In his struggle of enlightenment, the polyglot von Leers, now under his Muslim convert name Omer Amin Johannes, revived the charge of ritual murder, organized anti-Jewish broadcasts in numerous languages, was contact man to *ODESSA* (Organization of Erstwhile SS-Associates) and maintained a warm-hearted correspondence in which he encouraged the first generation of Holocaust deniers. Remarkably, his wife, having returned to her home country after his death, puzzled her neo-Nazi German friends by not denying but defending the extermination of the Jews publicly.[767]

One of her husband's greatest achievements during his lifetime was the successful promotion of the "Protocols of the Elders of Zion" in Arab edition:

763 Wistrich 2010, p.52.
764 Lewis, p.157.
765 Wistrich 2010, p.748.
766 Lewis, p.207.
767 Emil L. Fackenheim: To Mend the World: Foundations of Post-Holocaust Jewish Thought. Bloomington and Indianapolis 1994, p.184; quoted in: Fishman, Joel, Das Problem in historischer Perspektive: Israel und der Medienkrieg, haolam.de.

In 1958, Egypt's president Nasser urged a journalist of India: "It is very important that you should read it. I will give you a copy. It proves beyond the shadow of a doubt that three hundred Zionists, every one of whom knows all the others, govern the fate of the European continent." Rathenau himself had asserted in 1909 that "three hundred bankers and economic leaders direct the economic fate of Europe". In Hitler's speech of April 13, 1923 the three hundred became "those 300 Rathenaus of whom each one knows each other, who control the fate of the world". Now they went Zionists.[768]
The Aryan-Arab import of the Protocols from czarist secret kitchen is but one example of various western offers. "Over a period of centuries Europe was a net exporter of homegrown anti-Semitism", Gabriel Schoenfeld resumes. But his view of Europe's "product line enjoying especially strong demand in the Islamic world"[769] needs clarification: Not until European Jew-hate led to growing export of immigrants to Eretz Israel, the long offered supply of hate products found acceptance in Muslim culture. Only now the Orient became a resonating body of anti-Jewish accusations composed during 19 centuries of cross based Christian role-making. If history doesn't repeat, Jewish roles do:

Bankers and usurers: After the interrogations of Germany resident persons acquainted with the main 9/11 terrorists, German General Federal Attorney Kay Nehm stated that all of them were unified by a seamlessly woven "hate against world-Jewry and the United States".[770] According to the witness Shahid Nickels, a member of the innermost circle around Mohammed Atta, his group was "convinced that Jews dominate the American government as much as the media and economy of the USA ... ; that a world-wide conspiration of the Jews exists" and that "America desires to rule the world so that the Jews can pile capital."[771]

Poisoners: No less a figure than Nabil Ramlawi, the ambassador of Palestine at UN-commission for human rights in Geneva, startled the delegates in 1997 with the message that Israeli authorities had "infected by injection 300 Palestinian children with the HIV virus during the Intifada", a purpose they achieved later on (2006) using "HIV-infected mosquitos".[772]
On January 1, 2000, the state-controlled weekly of Syrian-Arab Writers' Association proclaimed that Israel not only spread AIDS in Egypt by attractive Jewish prostitutes, deliberately infecting Egyptian youngsters. "Egyptian authorities also discovered Zionist gifts for children made of animal-shaped chewing gum. An examination revealed that it causes ... sterility. For university students they dispersed chewing gum that arouses sexual lust ... Even the Egyptian soil is not safe from the satanic war waged by Zionism. Tens of

---

768 Nasser: Wistrich 2010, p.611; Rathenau: Wistrich 1987, p.317; Hitler: Boepple, p.48-49.
769 Schoenfeld, p.57.
770 Schoenfeld, p.55.
771 Bartov, Omer, in: Rabinovici/Speck/Sznaider, p.39.
772 Wistrich 2010, p.709; Moskitos: Bremner, Charles: "Gaddafi Faces Outrage ...", in The Times (UK), 20.12.2006.

thousands of seeds were sent [to Egypt] through agricultural deals with the Zionist entity. These seeds destroyed the Egyptian soil."[773]

Icons of Jewish crime and their remake: Above, The Bethlehem Child Murder, in: J.Schnorr v. Carolsfeld, Die Bibel in Bildern, 1860; dead children in Gaza 2014 (Jornal Mercosur, Curitiba, August 2014).
Below: Pietá of Giovanni Bellini, 1505; five centuries later the artist of "Do not kill him twice" copies Michelangelo's 1499 Vatican Pietá.

Child murderers: In 1984, Syrian secretary of defense Mustafa Tlass published his book "The Matzah of Zion" about the Damascus Affair, endorsing the 1840 allegation of ritual murder. On March 25, 2001, Egyptian daily Al-Akhbar taught its readers: "The Talmud, the second holiest book of the Jews, determines that the matzah of Atonement Day must be kneaded with the blood of a non-Jew." Medieval Christian anti-Semites leastwise knew that Jews eat their matzah during Passover, not on Yom Kippur, the Day of Atonement. But Al-Akhbar went one notch higher: "If possible, the blood should stem from youths, after precursory rape."[774] In March 2002, Saudi-Arabian university professor Umayma al-Jahlama had a new version, the blood now being needed for the rambunctious Purim holiday.[775]

---

773 Wistrich 2010, p.793.
774 Mahmoud al-Said al-Kurdi, in Al-Akhbar, March 25, 2011 (Wistrich 2010, p.807); cf. Schoenfeld, p.14.
775 Wistrich 2010, p.802-803.

253

"Listen", the Rabbi tells his pupil, "for the unleavened bread of Passover we need the blood of a Christian child." In the next scene of this episode of Syrian pre-prime-time serial "Al-Shatat", a frightened neighborhood boy is tugged to the scene, the camera zooms and in close-up picture the viewer observes the cut and the blood streaming from the boy's throat into the metal basin.[776]

Also in this case, the export product returns to Europe where few children don't link Bethlehem with the name of a rotten Jewish king whom they imagine as obese as an Israeli head of state (2001-2006). In spring of 2002, anti-Zionist demonstrations in Berlin showed banners with the message "Sharon ist ein Kindermörder"; in Kopenhagen the same Sharon-Herod link was made by a Lutheran bishop.[777]

Crucifiers: The "modern Muslim concern with the crucifixion of Christ – an event entirely outside both the theology and historiography of Islam ... reached its apex during the Second Vatican Council" (1962-1964), when Muslims feared that the Roman Church would "exonerate the Jews from the crime of deicide". Jordan's Foreign Minister predicted that the resolution would be "disastrous", since "history testifies to Jewish intentions of destroying Christ and Christianity". On his arrival in Jordan on January 4, 1964, Pope Paul VI was reminded by Radio Amman that "fifteen years ago, in the most cruel manner, the Jews overran Palestine [thus proving] their responsibility for the infamies of their forebears, and for the crucifixion and humiliation of Christ nineteen centuries ago."[778]

Exactly on September 11, 2001, few hours before the attack on the Twin Towers, Jewish NGO-participants at the World Conference against Racism in Durban (South Africa) got to hear: "Why haven't the Jews taken responsibility for killing Jesus? ...You are all murderers! You have Palestinian blood on your hands!"[779] On April 3, 2002 (Wednesday after Easter) liberal Italian daily La Stampa published a cartoon in which toddler Jesus bobs up in the hay of his manger and looks right into the cannon of an Israeli tank, babbling: "Surely they don't want to kill me again?"[780]

The assertion that Jews had betrayed and murdered Christ "is booming in Arab media", German journalist Michael Borgstede wrote in 2004.[781] Six years later Robert Wistrich states: "The never ending flood of Der Stürmer-like images, depicting Israelis as satanic beings and murderers of God who have crucified Palestine just as the Jews crucified Christ are Christian anti-Semitic motifs that have been thoroughly Arabized and Islamicized." A transparent example of what Wistrich calls the "Christianization of Muslim

776 Matthias Küntzel in: Rabinovici/Speck/Sznaider, p.271.
777 "Thousands March in Germany to Oppose Israeli Incursions"; New York Times, April 14, 2002 (Schoenfeld, p.73); Kopenhagen: Schoenfeld p.84.
778 Lewis, p.220-222.
779 Goldstein, Phyllis, p.340-341.
780 Prager/Telushkin, p.159; tomgrossmedia.
781 Michael Borgstede, Frankfurter Allgemeine Sonntagszeitung, cited by nahost-politik. de/syrien/diaspora.htm.

attitudes toward Jews (at a time of extreme tension between jihadi Islam and the West)" was given by Yasser Arafat at a September 2, 1983 press conference in Geneva: "We were under Roman imperialism. We sent a Palestinian fisherman, called St. Peter, to Rome. He not only occupied Rome, but also won the hearts of the people. We know how to resist imperialism and occupation. Jesus Christ was the first Palestinian militant fedayin who carried his sword along the path on which the Palestinians carry their cross." A path of torture which on December 11, 2000, Palestinian daily newspaper *Intifada* accentuated by feminizing the victim: "A long spear transfixes her body to the cross, its protruding point embossed with a Star of David and an American flag at the shaft end. Blood spurts from her martyred body down upon a trio of huddled, caricatured Oriental Jews, who are looking up and grimacing at the crucified young woman ..."[782] The basic motive of Jew-hate sometimes seems to be more obvious to Arabs than to Christian Europeans. On August 2, 2014, in a Brazilian forum Senhor Elias M. Assad proposed: "What about reminding the Christians that this people killed Jesus? What should one expect from them?" Before I could post my reply, the proposal was vehemently, and with historical awareness, rejected and deleted by my Arab friends of *Instituto Árabe-Israelita Brasileiro*.

Conspirators: "In accordance with the 'Protocols of the Elders of Zion', the Zionists will expand, after having swallowed Palestine, as far as Nile and Euphrates" – as announced in article 32 of the Charta of Hamas."[783] Apparently flourishing here is the seed which was imported by the Protocols, meanwhile translated nine times and available in more than 60 editions in the Islamic world. In 2001, Egyptian TV let 41 episodes of the TV-serial "Horseman without a Horse" grow out of the fertile European bull-shit, explaining to Egyptian families during Ramadan 2001 the Jewish striving for world-dominance. Remarkably, some Arab intellectuals used the occasion of the media hype to dispel the antisemitic myth. "The 'Protocols of the Elders of Zion' are a pamphlet full of nonsense", said Ahmed Dabur, the secretary general of Palestinian Department of Information. Osama al Baz, counselor of Egyptian president Mubarak, classified this "anti-Semitism" as a European phenomenon unknown in the Arab world for centuries. There was also efficient resistence (to some degree, and mainly from the exterior) against the infamous TV-series "*Al-Shatat*" ("Diaspora") of Hizbollah station Al-Manar, produced with support of various Syrian governmental authorities and broadcast during Ramadan of 2003 for the first time. Apart from Jewish ritual murder, the 29 episodes visualize how Jews pulled the wires in almost all major catastrophes of modernity: They have sought to control the world for many centuries, via a secret global Jewish government which was led since the 19th century by the Rothschild family. Under this government's leadership, Jewish wire-pullers were directly responsible for: causing the English stock market to collapse following the Battle of

---

782 Wistrich 2010, p.709-710 (Arafat; Intifada caricature) and 809-810 (Stürmer-like ...).
783 Gehrcke/von Freyberg/Grünberg, p.178.

Waterloo and again during WWI, in order to make millions of pounds (for the Rothschilds); spying for Germany against France (Dreyfus); starting the Kishinev pogroms (1903 and 1905) and inciting the Russo-Japanese war; assassinating Archduke Franz Ferdinand at Sarajevo; starting WWI and deposing Czar Nicholas II in 1917; starting WWII and helping Hitler annihilate the Jews of Europe; helping the Nazis annihilate 800,000 Hungarian Jews in exchange for the release of 2,000 wealthy German Jews; dropping the atomic bombs on Hiroshima and Nagasaki; inventing chemical weapons (Chaim Weizmann) and selling them to both the Germans and the British. To graph the magnitude of infamy in just one point, here's what the trial after the Kishinev pogrom yielded: Highranking officials, including three subsequent mayors and the commander of the garrison, testified that the Jews and Christians in Kishinev had always lived together in harmony, and that the Moldavians even held the Jews in high esteem until the foundation of the newspaper "Bessarabetz", whose editor Krushevan carried on a campaign against the Jews. He availed himself of the opportunity created by the murder of a boy (by his own relatives!) in an adjoining village, and the suicide of a Christian girl in the Jewish hospital of Kishinev; he laid both tragedies at the door of the Jews, describing the "ritual murders" with a wealth of sickening detail, and in inflammatory articles he appealed to the people for vengeance. When the church bells of Kishinev pealed on Easter Sunday 1903, the first pogrom of the twentieth century began with young people hounding Jews to leave Chuflinskii Square, their cause being gradually taken up by adults in an increasing state of holiday drunkenness. "Students and seminarists from the Royal School and the city's religious colleges, iron bars and axes in hand, followed the hooligans. [...] Christian homes, differentiated earlier that morning by large chalked crosses, went unscathed. Passing through the streets in his carriage, Orthodox bishop Iakov blessed the mostly Moldavian attackers" who left 49 murdered, 495 wounded and 2000 homeless Jews.[784] Not by coincidence thirty-eight years later, in June 1941, the safeguarding of Christian homes by chalk crosses was repeated in Romanian town Iaşi (sixty miles west of Kishinev), right before the round-up and killing of the Jewish citizens, this time at the hands of German avengers.[785]

The child, the key
This wall reminded him on the Berlin Wall, and "this is something one does to animals but not to humans" said Cologne Cardinal Meissner in March 2007 in East-Jerusalem, on the Arab side of the security wall. "This morning we saw pictures from the Warsaw ghetto in Yad Vashem and tonight we go to the ghetto of Ramallah. That makes you come unglued", Meissner's travel companion Bishop Gregor Maria Franz remarked after the first historical visit of German Bishops Conference at the Shoah Memorial.[786] Nicaraguan

---

784 Monty Noam Penkower, muse.jhu.edu; and jewishencyclopedia, Kishinev pogrom.
785 Goldhagen 2002, p.102.
786 Eldad Beck, ynetnews.com, June 3, 2007.

Padre Miguel d'Escoto Brockmann, who champions Liberation Theology and presided UN General Assembly from 2008 to 2009, hugged Ahmadinejad after his UN speech in 2008 unabashedly echoing conspiracy theories of Jewish world domination, and demanded international sanctions against this Israel "crucifying" Palestinians.[787]

All three Roman-Catholic clericals start from iconic pictures of sufferers (animals, Jews, Jesus) and in a narrow loop they turn the pity back as anger against the Jewish state maltreating, ghettoizing, crucifying Palestinians. The narrow loop is eased by Israel's location close to the scene of crime, which is crucial also in the following examples.

Conditioned by daily views of cross-fixed corpuses with bleeding thorax wound, the Westerner is open to a bizarre connection of Shylock's "pound of Christian flesh" with Judas's silverlings and Jewish networking: On August 17, 2009, Swedens largest daily *Aftonbladet* spread the news that Israeli soldiers were abducting Palestinians in order to steal their organs for sale on the black market.[788] The modern blood libel story snowballed yet before winter: In late November 2009, a Ukrainian philosophy professor claimed that Israel had brought some 25,000 Ukrainian children into the country over the past two years in order to harvest their organs. Professor Vyacheslav Gudin told the estimated 300 attendees of a Kiev conference about a Ukrainian man's fruitless search for 15 children who had been adopted in Israel. The children, Gudin said, had clearly been taken by Israeli medical centers, where they were used for "spare parts".[789]

Writing in Scotlands best-selling Daily Record, the extremely funny columnist George Galloway, under the headline "Dark Echoes of Holocaust" presented Israel as "playing mini-Mengele" on Palestinians.[790] His column was published in 2009 on December 28 – just by coincidence the Christian "Holiday of Innocent Children" – and rather sounds like a *Dark Echo* on early *Xmas feelings* of a young Scot, stored in the hard X form audible in the speaking Xmas spelling of the holiday of Christ's nativity.

The death of innocent children has been emphasized in many military conflicts to prove the other side's moral depravity. But the reader who went through this book up to here will not doubt that pictures of children have a highly charged meaning whenever Jews are on the drama's stage and Christians in the audience. "A good picture is a dusty teddy bear placed by Hezbollah at the scene of the sites bombed by Israel", explained reporter Giulio Meotti who writes for *Il Foglio*. Otherwise, he says, photos of dead Israelis "just interfere with the story the European media is trying to tell."[791] The exhibit A and the literal poster child for these expectations is the Palestinian boy Muhammad al-Dura, who caught the eyes of French TV-audience and then of whole mankind with the last pictures of his young life, on September

787 Wistrich 2010, p.492;
788 en.wikipedia.org/wiki/2009_Aftonbladet_Israel_controversy.
789 haaretz.com/print-edition, Dec 3, 2009.
790 Diane Weber Bederman, "Part Two: Post-Modern Sounds of Antisemitism", in: Huffingtonpost, September 4, 2013.
791 "How the West Wasn't Won". Yedioth Achronoth, March 17, 2011.

30, 2000. Huddling with his father behind a cement barrel, fear in his face, and then – Cut! Cam! – lying on the sidewalk, pronounced dead by the reporter.

Left: *"Wo ist + der Mörder?"* (Where is the murderer?). Memorial for the 1891 "Xanten Ritual Murder", in "Politischer Bilderbogen", Dresden 1893. Subtext: *"In Xanten lies a little child, God knows where his murderers hide"*. Above: Little Muhammad and his father in crosshairs of the Jewish star. The artist shows the holes in the wall in their real shape, as hit by bullets shot from a straight opposite (i.e. camera) position.

Two days later two Israeli soldiers were lynched in Ramallah, the crowd shouting "Revenge for the blood of Muhammad al-Dura!" Osama bin Laden zoomed big: "In the murder of this child the Israelis have killed every child of this world." The boy was immortalized in epic poems and postage stamps. Streets and schools (more than 150 in Iran alone) were named in his honor. Little Muhammad's canonization reminds those of Little William of Norwich, Little Simon of Trento, the non-existant Niño de La Guardia; but today the proofs and allegations can be analysed. The very video shows round bullet-holes in the wall behind father and son: a sure proof that the bullets were fired from somewhere straight across the street (where the cameraman stood), and by no means from the thirty-six-degrees position of the Israeli soldiers in their tower. It shows that fresh red stains appeared not earlier than the next day – but not on the spot where the child had been lying. It shows that neither father nor son had been hit and that the alleged young victim was hardly identic with the boy whose dead body had been delivered to the hospital yet four hours earlier and had been buried just two hours after, while already on the cemetery the funeral guests were provided with copied posters of the victim Muhammad al-Dura.

Matter of fact, the father showed his real breast wounds in a press conference later on. Wounds that were, however, not caused by Israeli bullets but at first by the knife attack of another Palestinian man and at second by the scalpel of surgeon Dr. David Yehuda who had treated the wounds years before. The "silver bullet" apt to refute any doubts would consist in examining the bullets lodged in the wall or at least in the cement barrell: Are they Israeli M-16, or Palestinian Kalashnikov? Inexplicably, there were no bullets to be found. In a filmed interview, Abu Rahma, the cameraman, admitted to have removed the bullets from the wall. When questioned about what he had discovered – and why a cameraman would be involved in ballistic research in the first place – the man who was repeatedly honoured as Journalist of the Year answered: "We have the bullets, I have photographed them." Esther Schapira: "Can we see them?" Abu Rahma: "Ask the General, he can tell you." – "The General has no bullets." – "France Deux has collected them." – "So France Deux does a better job than the police?" – "No, no, no ... we, we, we have our secrets also. We can not give something ... give everything."[792] Inadvertently disclosing European desires with amazing precision, notable French TV-news anchorwoman Catherine Nay (*1943) commented that "The death of Muhammad annuls, erases that of the Jewish child, his hands in the air before the SS in the Warsaw Ghetto".[793] Alex Joffe rightly diagnosed that Catherine Nay's statement "holds the key to understanding the reception of Palestinian rhetoric in Europe. It is a means to erode *historical and moral* realities regarding the European treatment of the Jews, and it is eagerly embraced in some quarters.[794] It is the child who holds the key to European Jew-hate: the hands-up Warsaw ghetto child, the Palestinian boy in M-16 crosshairs, the Christ-child martyred on the cross, forever anchored in the mind of *la petite Catherine ...*

"The entire goal of the exercise was to manufacture a child martyr, in correct anticipation of the damage this would do to Israel in the eyes of the world", Nahum Shahaf says. "I believe that one day there will be good things in common between us and the Palestinians. But the case of Mohammad al-Dura brings the big flames between Israel and the Palestinians and Arabs. It brings a big wall of hate."

Shahaf is a physicist, medal-rewarded by Israeli Ministry of Science for his work on digital video transmission. As a person dedicated to solving a case of visual defamation, he has something in common with the author of this book: "I left everything for it, because I believe that this is most important." Lifetime is no matter: "It took twelve years for the truth of the Dreyfus case to come out."[795]

---

792   See the extense and verifiable presentation at seconddraft.org; the interview of German television producer Esther Schapira with Abu Rahma at youtube.com/watch?=DzsCBFhCsyY;
793   Pierre-André Taguieff, on debriefing.org/25585.html. Concerning the persons in the photo see commons.wikimedia.org, Stroop Report.
794   Alex Joffe: "Fabricating Palestinian History: The Rhetoric of Nonsense", on: meforum.org/meq/pdfs/3262.pdf.
795   James Fallows, The Atlantic Monthly (theatlantic.com/past/docs/issues/2003/06/fal-

Shahaf does not accuse the Palestinians of killing the boy – he doubts Muhammad was killed at all. The most probable case is: There was a dead child in the morning of this day. There is much indication that it was Muhammad's Cousin Rahmi, whose name was given by the hospital at first. Few indications exist for Israeli bullets having killed Rahmi, since even the Palestinian side declared that the IDF soldiers started shooting only after noon. In this afternoon little Muhammad became, by not very professional enactment and the explainably willing takeover by western media, an icon of just anger arising from compassion, reminding the boy born and killed and buried two millennia before just sixty miles northeast of Gaza.

Remarkably, however, it was Jewish journalist Charles Enderlin who had bought and forwarded and propagated the film sequence Abu Rahma had offered him. Immediately after its publication, IDF had taken up responsibility for the boy's accidental killing. When Shahaf convinced the IDF to start an investigation, Israel's liberal newspaper *Haaretz* complained that "the stupidity of this bizarre investigation ... on such a sensitive issue, is shocking and worrying."[796] Still in 2013, Haaretz claimed that the IDF's initial confession of culpability "was a far wiser course of action than ... an independent investigation" and recommended not to "disturb the dead and remind the world of an incident it was in Israel's own self-interest to let fade in the mists of time". It should be noted that Khaleb Diab, the author of this Haaretz comment, is an Egyptian-Belgian journalist.[797] Nevertheless, the appeasing Jewish role-taking formula "Yes, we are guilty, now tell me of what" appears to reflect the Jewish experience that one cannot fight the power of accusing images.

Hany Farid, a Dartmouth professor and expert on digital photography, explains the cerebral program that underlies the human learning by images: "What's happening in our brain, roughly 30 to 50 percent of our brain is doing visual processing ... Vision is a pretty unique sense for the brain. It's incredibly powerful and is very valuable from an evolutionary point of view. So it's not surprising that it has an emotional effect on us. The Vietnam War, the war abroad and the war at home, has been reduced to a few iconic images – the Napalm girl, the girl at Kent State [kneeling besides a shot down protester]. What seems to emerge from major events and eras are one or two images that effectively embody the emotion and rage, the happiness and anger. The whole thing somehow is enfolded in there. The brain is just very good at processing visual imageries and bringing in memories associated with images."[798]

A picture is worth a thousand words: Surely, this Chinese proverb applies the stronger the more illiterate a culture is. In 15th century, when the Dutch Master I.A.M. of Zwolle engraved his filigree "Last Supper", he not only

lows.htm), June 2003.
796 James Fallows, theatlantic.com, June 2003.
797 Khaleb Diab: "The al-Dura report: A slanderous farce and a 'blood libel' – against Palestinians", in: Haaretz, May 26, 2013.
798 Hany Farid interviewed by Erroll Morris: "Photography as a Weapon", Opinionator Blog/New York Times, August 11, 2008.

identified Judas by his moneybag and the "Jewish" profile of his face. The disciple next to him is holding his nose – visually transmitting to any illiterate viewer the olfactory notion of Jewish stench. "Without the use of words", Maccoby comments, "but by visual indoctrination alone (far more effective) the message was conveyed, 'The stinking Jews are the Judas-nation'."[799] With few words, the following cartoons mark the state of the Jews by their crime of old:

Crosses creatively combined: Clockwise: Lebanese-Brazilian cartoonist Latuff features a speaking swastika-crucifix allusion (2009).
"The Future of the Relationship Between Palestinian Authority and Hamas", previewed in Al-Ahram (Egypt), July 27, 2005.
"Those who crucified the prophets have crucified my people tonight." Ad-Dustour (Jordan), April 4, 2001.

Muslim and Christian Jew-hate: A crucial difference

1942: After the allied victory at El-Alamein, Hitler's and Himmler's friend Al-Husseini calls for Jihad: "I declare a Holy War, my Muslim brothers! Murder the Jews! Murder them all!"
1948: On May 14, shortly after Israel's declaration of independence according to the U.N. partition plan, the Arab League secretary Azzam Pasha announces: "This will be a war of extermination."
1967: On the eve of Six-Day War, PLO-leader Ahmad Shukeiry declares that Jews would not have to remigrate to Europe: "Those who survive will remain in Palestine. I estimate that none of them will survive."

---

799 Maccoby 1992, p.112-113.

2002: The "hoax of holocaust" by now has been debunked by many French studies as "nothing but machination, lie and fraud", writes Al-Akhbar, the second-biggest Egyptian daily. "However, I", the columnist laments, "complain to Hitler ... : If you'd just done it, my brother", so that the world, now free of Jews, "could sigh with relief".[800]

Chapter 9 concluded that while Christian theology concerning the "deicidal race" led to racist extermination, real genocide was alien to a doctrinally anti-racist, moral-based Christendom relying not on burning fire but on the earning waters of baptism. Chapter 12 now aims to show, in spite of voices as those four cited above, that Middle-Eastern anti-Judaism is by far not as exterminatory as the European original that was responsible, between 622 and 1946 CE, for more than 99.8 percent of Jewish victims of religious persecution.[801] Comparing the Muslim with the Christian forms and degrees of Jew-hate, we measure a culture devoid of crucifixes against a culture abounding with; the result will allow for causal and prognostic conclusions. What indeed was common in Muslim culture were varying degrees of humiliation suffered by the Jewish and Christian "religions of the book" in certain ages and regions of Islamic dominion. To begin with, cloth-signs for Jews were not a Christian invention: Already Bagdad's caliph Omar II (634-644) decreed a blue belt for Christians and a yellow one for Jews; in 807, the Abbassid caliph Haroun-Al-Rashid legislated that Jews along with their yellow belt had to wear a tall, conical cap.[802] Until French colonialization, Jews in Marrakesh still had to wear a blue, white-flecked headkerchief, to walk barefoot and to hug the walls when they entered the Arab town. In Iraq, at times the Jews could live in peace and their leaders were even highly respected; at others, the Jewish men had to wear special clothes, badges, yellow hats, and a bell around the neck; the women had to mark themselves by a yellow mantle, one white and one black shoe, and an iron chain around the neck when going to the public bath; the houses had to be marked by wooden figures at the entrance. In Buchara, Jewish houses and shops had to be lower than those of the Muslims and marked by a rag hoisted over the buildings; upon paying his poll tax the Jew received a slap in the face. In Persian Hamadan with a Jewish population share of ten percent, still in 1892 Jewish physicians were forbidden to ride, a Jewish man was never to overtake a Muslim on a public street or speak loudly to him; in case of being insulted by a Muslim, he must drop his head and be silent. No music or singing on Jewish marriages, no plaster for whitewashing Jewish houses, no leaving the house during rain or snowfall, lest Jewish impurity be inadvertently transmitted to pure Shiite Muslims. Jewish women, on the other

800   As to 1942: Wikipedia, Mohammed Amin al-Husseini; 1948: Telushkin 2001, p.316-317; as to 1967: Wistrich 2010, p.712; as to 2002: Küntzel, in: Rabinovici/Speck/Sznaider, p.285.
801   According to Wikipedia, Jewish Virtual Library and discoverthenetworks; the overall numbers of Jewish victims of persecution by Muslims vary between <11,000 (Wikipedia) and <25,000 victims (discoverthenetworks).
802   Nicholls, p.205 and Telushkin 2001, p.165.

hand, were obliged to reveal their faces in public, which "made them the equivalent of prostitutes in Muslim eyes".[803] In the sharply demarcated class system that characterized the Shiite Muslim society of Yemen, the Jew occupied the lowest position. He was not allowed to raise his voice against a Muslim, to discuss religion with him, to ride on horseback, to touch a Muslim in passing, to wear new or good clothes, but obliged to rise in deference whenever a Muslim passed him. However, what hurt the Jews of Yemen most was a decree issued in 1922 according to which every Jewish child under the age of thirteen years whose father had died was taken from his mother and reared as a Muslim. Naturally, the Jewish community did their best to avert those all but rare disasters. S.D. Goitein heard of a particularly wealthy and pious man in lower Yemen who always had eighteen children, "their only common feature being that none was his own child." When the Turks conquered Yemen in 1872 and the Turkish Governor asked an assembly of notables to keep schoolboys from throwing stones at Jews, an old doctor of Muslim law arose and explained that this stone-throwing at Jews was an age-old custom and therefore it was unlawful to forbid it. In spite of all that, Goitein ponders that "as a whole the position of non-Muslims under Arab Islam was far better than that of the Jews in Medieval Christian Europe."[804] "The Jew in Muslim lands", Raphael Patai resumes, "was treated with rude condescension, was cursed to his face, slapped and buffeted, ... compelled to allow any Muslim who commandeered him to jump on his back to be carried across the mud or sewage of the street, and to suffer many more small and greater indignities." However, citing André Chouraqui, Patai annotates that "the lot of the Jews ... was no worse than that of the lowest classes in the Moslem society who were exploited with equal harshness by the dominating feudal system ... They never experienced anything like the Crusaders' massacres, the tortures and stakes of the Inquisition, the countrywide expulsions that hurled Jews from one part of Christian Europe to another and then back again, the bloodbaths of Chmielnitzki's Cossacks, the Russian pogroms, or the Nazi holocaust."[805] In genuine Islamic culture Jews never were accused of Judas' treason and his maniac greed for money, of sheming and heartless intellect, of child murder and blood libel, the poisoning of wells and cruelty to man and animal; of any of these facets of "Christian anti-Semitism, which lite-rally flowed with Christ's blood ..."[806] The anti-Jewish stereotypes within Islamic anti-Zionism are, as shown above, European imports, enrooted very deeply in Christian art, doctrine and tradition, but very weakly in Islam. Antisemitism is, as Jonathan Sacks and Antony Lerman clarify, "not intrinsic" to Islam but derives from "alien origin"; from countries where, as

803 Patai, p.195 (Marrakesh); 225 (Yemen), 238 (Irak), 256-257 (Buchara); Wistrich 2010, p.832 (Hamadan, Jewish women). .
804 Goitein, p.76-79 and 84.
805 Patai, p.170-171; Chouraqui, André: Between East and West: A History of the Jews in North Africa. Philadelphia 1968, p.55.
806 Perry/Schweitzer, p.75.

Matthias Küntzel explains, the Jews were viewed "as a lethal and powerful instance which even achieved to kill God's only son."[807]
Contrarily, in 1987 Bernard Lewis, the distinguished expert of Islamic and Middle-Eastern history, stated the "absence among even anti-Semitic Muslims – with few exceptions – of the kind of deep, intimate hatred characteristic of the classic anti-Semite in Central and Eastern Europe and sometimes elsewhere. Time and time again, European and American Jews travelling in Arab countries have observed that, despite the torrent of broadcast and published anti-Semitism, the only face-to-face experience of anti-Semitic hostility that they suffered during their travels was from compatriots, many of whom feel free, in what they imagine to be the more congenial atmosphere of the Arab world, to make consciously anti-Semitic and incidentally also antifeminist remarks that they would not make at home." The fact that uttering anti-Jewish prejudice "at the personal level" is still rare in the Arab lands, Lewis ascribes to "a certain ingrained courtesy in the Arab cultural tradition" that I, by the way, gratefully enjoyed in countless encounters with Muslims in Germany, France, Brazil, Turkey, Palestine, Israel and Egypt. "But it must also owe something to the absence hitherto of that kind of visceral, personal hostility that marks the European anti-Semite, and which, even in those only mildly affected, can cause an almost physical discomfort in personal encounters with Jews." Already on the first pages of his work Lewis proves to be a sensitive observer when he, using the same expression, points to the "*almost physical* hatred which inspired and directed anti-Semitism in Europe."[808] This European hatred, better say punitive anger, is *physical* and worked out *physically* because it was learnt at the image of a tortured *physical* body. This is why, for instance, a Romanian nationalist newspaper lamented in 1992 that the Jews had brought communism to Romania and "nailed it into our flesh and bone until they crucified us", while Zionists today engage in "crucifying" the Palestinians.[809]
The Koran hardly engages with the cross. The charge that the Jews "uttered a big slander against [Jesus' mother] Miriam" and "murdered and crucified not him but someone similar to him" is nevertheless concluded with the sentence: "For that we cursed them" (Sura 4:155-156). Indeed, verse 5:85 clearly gives preference to the friendly Nazarenes against the hostile Jews, while verse 9:30 lumps both together because the Nazarenes proclaim the "Messiah" and the Jews their "Esra" as "Allah's son". The condemnation is followed by the harsh wish for both: "Allah beat them dead! How reasonless they are!"
Several reasons, however, suggest that Muslims are – apart from genes and geography – also mentally closer to Jews than to Christians. Circumcision, ritual slaughter and food prohibitions are nothing suspicious to Muslims. Since the destruction of the temple, Judaism works fine without a sacerdotal

---

807   Sacks, p.103; Lerman, in: Rabinovici/Speck/Sznaider, p.109; Küntzel, ibidem, p.277.
808   Lewis, p.258 and 21 (italics K.Y.R.).
809   Rumania Mare, March 15, 1992 and Feb. 1991 (Wistrich 2010, p.189-190). Romania had 850,000 Jews in 1939 and has 8,000 now, making for 0.04 percent of the population.

priesthood; there has never been any in Islam. Both groups reject the concept of a God-man as strongly as his bloody sacrifice; both take monotheism as serious as the prohibition of God-images. Encouraging his Moro brethren in Spain, an Algerian mufti wrote to them in 16th century in Isaiah's diction: "Know that their idols are nothing but gilded wood and constructions of stone; they will do nothing for you; they are useless: Royalty belongs to God."[810] Recalling the medieval poet Yehuda Halevy who praised Islam's potential of connecting, Emanuel Lévinas views Muslim culture as a main factor of human development towards solidarity.[811] "Islam ... is from the very flesh and bone of Judaism", S.D. Goitein states. "It is, so to say, a recast, an enlargement of the latter, just as Arabic is closely related to Hebrew."[812] When in December 2010 a forest fire raged on the Karmel near Haifa, Turkey as well as Jordan and Egypt sent airplanes to support the extinguishing efforts. In April 2013, Jerusalem daily Haaretz interviewed Prof. Raphi Walden, vice-president of Israeli Physicians for Human Rights: "In those 20 years, have you ever encountered hostility?"
"Never."
"Really?"
"Not even once. You remember the horrific [1994] murder perpetrated by Baruch Goldstein in the Tomb of the Patriarchs, right? He killed almost 30 people. We were scheduled to go to the territories on the following Shabbat, but we hesitated. The whole region was like a seething cauldron. In the end we decided to go. And even on that day, we were received with boundless warmth and love."[813]

The areal solution of the Jewish question

"What are you doing on our land?" The young settler put this question to the Palestinian Daoud who was on his tractor cultivating a plot bordering the recently constructed Jewish settlement. "This is my land", Daoud answered simply. "No, it is ours", said the boy, nervously fingering his gun. Not a man to be intimidated, Daoud looked the boy in the eyes, saying: "My grandfather bought this land. We have the papers to prove it." The young Jew, pointing to the sky: "You have papers from here. We have papers from God."[814] Pretending that papers or voices come from God is the most common manner of exercising power by religion. Of course most of the Bible papers concerning a divinely promised land reflect the situation of the Jewish elite having returned from Babylonian exile to Jerusalem after 538 BC. But let's take the young lad serious: What's in the old papers?
In Genesis 15, Yahve assigns the land between Nile and Euphrates to Abram's offspring, that is, the Hebrew of Isaac and the Arab of Ishmael,

810 Poliakov 2003, Vol.II, p.330.
811 Lévinas 1996, p.127.
812 Goitein, p.130.
813 Ayelett Shani: "A different kind of Israeli: Prof. Raphi Walden on why the Jewish people stopped caring", Haaretz, April 25, 2013.
814 Braverman, p.76.

his six sons with Ketura and the ten peoples listed in the verses 19-21, for instance the Canaanites. In the land of those Canaanites later on (Genesis 48:4) El Shaddai appears to Jacob, promising "I will make you a community of peoples and give this land to your offspring". Much later (Dt 28:58-64), the Landlord Yahve explains his harsh conditions: "If you fail to observe faithfully all the terms of this Teaching ... you shall be torn from the land that you are about to enter and possess. The Lord will scatter you among all the peoples from one end of the earth to the other ..." .

And what are the moral terms to stick to, not to be evicted from the leasehold? In any conflict "only trees that you know do not yield food may be destroyed" Deuteronomy 20:20 explains, presaging Israeli caterpillars stubbing Palestinian farmers' green olive trees. – "You shall have one law for stranger and citizen alike" says Leviticus 24:22. And 36 Bible verses enjoin to equal rights for strangers, for example this commandment authorized by supreme instance: "When a stranger resides with you in your land, you shall not wrong him. The stranger who resides with you shall be to you as one of your citizens; you shall love him as yourself, for you were strangers in the land of Egypt. [Signature locator:] *I the Lord am your God*" (Lev 19:33-34). Exactly this commandment "to love the stranger (the one who is not like us)", along with "an unusual sensitivity to questions of identity, the dignity of human beings, the primacy of freedom, opposition to coercion, respect for difference", represents to Robert Wistrich "the humanist core of the Judaic message."[815]

In the light of this humanist essence as well as all juridical standards, nothing else but the local population's agreement to the return of old kin's cousins could have endowed – and can endow – moral legitimacy to the Zionist endeavour of return.

Why, after all, did this return not happen earlier in the two millennia of persecution?

To begin with, the widespread notion that after the destruction of the Second Temple (70 CE) or after the defeat of Bar Kokhba's rebels (135 CE) the Jews were "scattered among the nations" (Deuteronomy 28:64), is a thoroughly Christian view engendered by Luke who post factum had Jesus foresee the catastrophe of 70 CE: "They will fall by the edge of the sword and be taken away as captives among all nations" (21:24).

Actually, that's where the great majority then lived already. In Jesus' days about ten percent of the population of Roman Empire were Jewish. Five to seven million Jews lived in the "diaspora" and not more than one million Jews in Palestine.[816] And of this minority living in the Promised Land, after both defeats the great majority of the survivors kept to their fathers's soil, changing rather their religion than their homeland. In 1917, Zionist Ben-Gurion called the Palestinians the *am ha'aretz* (folk of the land) "who chose

815   Wistrich 2010, p.568-569.
816   Sorj, p.33 estimates "five to ten", Klinghoffer six, Entine (p.117) "over 5 million" Jews in the Herodian era, Salo Baron 8, Flannery (p.9) estimates 5 million (of these 1 million in Palestine) and supposes that one of eight inhabitants of Roman Empire was Jewish.

under pressure of the times to deny their faith so long as they would not be uprooted from the soil."[817] In our days, even Yehuda Etzion, one of the founders of the settlers' movement, appreciates the fact "that unlike secular urban Jews, rural Arabs were one with the land."[818] Not unlike Marranos, many of the Muslim Palestinians still maintain vestiges of Jewish customs, and half of this population is conscious of their Jewish ancestry;[819] an ancestry confirmed by modern DNA scrolls yielding that "more than 70% of the Jewish men and 82% of the Arab men whose DNA was studied, had inherited their Y chromosomes from the same paternal ancestors, who lived in the region within the last few thousand years".[820] That is, more than 80 percent of Palestinians descend from Jews who remained on their soil in the hills while parts of the more affluent and mobile urban population chose exile. Dauntless Daoud has probably more DNAbraham than the young gungay sky paper settler whose genes sojourned in Europe. Very rare up there and most typically "Jewish", the Y-DNA haplogroup J1 marks 38.5 percent of Palestinians, 22 percent of Sephardim and 19 percent of Ashkenazi Jews. The globally rare and even more antique-Jewish Middle-Eastern Y-DNA haplogroup T1 scores 7 percent among Palestinians, 6 percent among Sephardim and 2 percent among European Ashkenazim like Tuvia Tenenbom who is told by Shlomo Sand: "A Palestinian born in Hebron is with greater probability a direct descendant of the Jews of antiquity than Tuvia."[821] Genetics defeat sky papers, and the two-pronged "ethnoterritorial mythos that motivated the Zionist enterprise"[822] twice points to the Palestinians as the ethnos of this terra, *am ha'aretz.*

In the tenth century CE, the Jewish scholar Saadia Gaon, born and raised in Egypt, migrated to Tiberias in Galilee but soon left the Holy Land again to accept a teaching job offer in Babylon. He did so without hesitation, lamenting the extensive Islamization of the Holy Land's Jewish inhabitants.[823] In spite of the mantric "Next year in Jerusalem", famous Jewish thinkers from Maimonides and Abulafia in 12th and 13th century up to Hermann Cohen and Raphael Hirsch in 19th century spoke out against attempts of return to the Holy Land or turning it into a homeland. Surely, Jewish practical unwillingness to celebrate the next Rosh Hashana in Jerusalem had to do with costs and dangers of such a relocation at that time. But after the Spanish expulsion decree of 1492, much more Jews fled to Italy and Cyprus, Salonika and Istanbul than to Palestine. When in 1666 the messianic pretender Sabatai

---

817 Misinai, p.263; Sand (2012, p.208) comments that the revolt of 1929 put a quick end to major Zionist activists's (as Belkin, Ben-Gurion, Ben-Zvi) attempts of "ethnoracial unification".

818 Shavit, p.213.

819 Misinai, p.106 and passim; Rabbi Dov Stein and others, in the documentary "Palestinian Jews", youtube.com/watch?v=L1gLziSsIe4.

820 Nebel, Filon, Weiss et al., "High-resolution Y chromosome haplotypes of Israeli and Palestinian Arabs reveal geographic substructure and substantial overlap with haplotypes of Jews", in: Human Genetics, December 2000.

821 eupedia.com/europe/Haplogroup_T_Y-DNA.shtml; Tenenbom 2014, p.397.

822 Sand 2012, p.258.

823 Sand 2012, p.110.

Zevi preferred conversion to Islam instead of execution, the great return he had promised his adherents fell back into the utopian drawer for two hundred years. "Judaism refused to be shackled to a piece of land", Shlomo Sand resumes pre-Zionist era. "With all its veneration for the Holy Land, it refused to be enslaved by it."[824] In 1919, in anticipation of the Paris Peace Conference, some 300 prominent American rabbis and community leaders sent a letter to President Wilson opposing the formation of a Jewish state in Palestine. For such a state could not be democratic since "the keystones of democracy are neither condescension nor tolerance but justice and equality"; a "Jewish State" in Palestine would endanger Jewish diaspora and "evoke bitter controversies" in Middle East.[825]

The 300 rabbis could not presage that besides of Europe's antisemitism, four other Christian factors would make the Zionist project become reality.

1. Christian Zionism: Yet in 1649, when the Hebrew Bible inspired Cromwell's battles, two English Baptists in Dutch exile petitioned their government "that this nation of England, with the inhabitants of the Netherlands, shall be the first and readiest to transport Izraell's sons and daughters in their ships to the Land promised to their forefathers, Abraham, Isaac and Jacob for an everlasting inheritance."[826] Somewhat less caringly, as early as in 1793 Protestant idealist philosopher Johann Gottlieb Fichte presented the two European solutions of the Jewish question. In "sugar-sweet words of tolerance" Fichte takes no stock: "They don't believe in Jesus Christ; this you must not tolerate" he explains to the German reader. Towards the utopic aim of granting Jews civil rights, Fichte in a footnote saw no viable means "except perhaps, if one night we chop off all of their heads and replace them with new ones, in which there would not be one single Jewish idea. And then, I see no other way to protect ourselves from the Jews, except if we conquer their promised land for them and send all of them there."[827]

Lord Shaftesbury (1801-1885), the leader of English 19th century evangelicalism – a man whom Sand would not dislike to label as the Anglican Herzl – not only played an important role in legislation against child labor and slave trade but also cultivated the idea of a Jewish-Christian restoration in the Holy Land. In 1854 he confided to his diary: "There is a country without a nation, and God now, in his wisdom and mercy, directs us to a nation without a country." Auguring the Zionist blinder slogan of "a land without people for a people without land", Shaftesbury actually sought not only the restoration but the conversion of this people: As president of the London Society for Promoting Christianity among the Jews (known as The Jews' Society) he actively campaigned to bring the Jews into the Christian fold.[828]

824   Sand 2012, p.109.
825   David Glick: "Netanyahu Removes the Mask: The Two-State-Solution Is Dead." In: tikkun.org, March 27, 2015.
826   Sand 2012, p.145.
827   J.G. Fichte, Beiträge zur Berichtigung der Urtheile des Publicums über die französische Revolution, 1793, p.191–193; cf. Klug, p.42.
828   Klug, p.78-79.

2. Since a colonialization like in Africa and India was not possible in Middle East under Ottoman rule, "the original Christian Zionist idea of settling Jews in Palestine presented itself" yet in the coal based economy around 1850 "as a means of bypassing this obstacle to the establishment of a [British] imperial foothold in the Middle East."[829]

3. From 1881 until the first world-war, Christian anti-Semitism erupted in pogroms which caused waves of mass emigration from Eastern Europe. The threat of mass immigration "coerced" Christian governments to legislate anti-immigrant laws that detoured Jewish emigrants away from Christian Occident, down to Arab Middle Orient. The same Lord Balfour who told Richard Wagner's widow Cosima that he "shared many of her antisemitic postulates"[830] promoted the British legislation of 1905 regarding (undesired) foreigners. Together with the American Immigration Act of 1924 and the selfsame Lord Balfour's famous letter to Rothschild ("Balfour declaration") this foreign politics meant bypassing Jewish foreigners from Christian West and gently persuading them down to Muslim Orient: "The Western countries found it convenient to get rid of the Jewish refugees by channeling them to the Middle East. This was the hour of opportunity for stagnant Zionism."[831]

4. In November 1947, the distinguished evangelical theologian Reinhold Niebuhr favoured the Zionist project by rather Calvinist reasons: "Whoever approaches the Middle East with even a minimum of objectivity has to admit that thus far there is only one vanguard of progress and modernization in the Middle East, and that is Jewish Palestine. A second factor for progress is Christian Lebanon [...] But for these two islands of Western civilization, Jewish Palestine and Christian Lebanon, the Arab-Moslem Middle East presents a hopeless picture from an American viewpoint." Comments Edward Said: "Herzl used the idea, Weizmann used it, every leading Israeli since has used it: Israel was a device for holding Islam ... at bay."[832]

Again, the Christian Zionism of Protestant and Evangelical Americans – in a 2015 poll, seventy-seven percent of U.S. evangelicals said we right now are living in the End Times, and many of them assume that the trigger event will be a cataclysmic war in the Middle East – holds that the ingathering of Jewry to the Holy Land is the second last, and their subsequent conversion to the Christian faith the very last precondition for Jesus' second coming. This hope for Israel as door opener to apocalypse helps whom exactly? "The leaders of Christian Zionism have an extreme interpretation of Genesis 12:3 ("I will bless those who bless you") that results in massive support for settlement activity in the West Bank."[833]

Although Theodor Herzl's diagnosis of Christian and racist European Jew-hatred was accurate, the medicine he prescribed had "striking resem-

829 Sand 2012, p.154.
830 Leonard Stein, The Balfour Declaration, New York 1961, p.154 (cited by Klug, p.207).
831 Sand 2012, p.230.
832 New York Times, November 21, 1947 (Said 1992, p.29-30).
833 Poll dates and quotation: Jay Michaelson, "Don't Be Shocked by Jewish Honor for Anti-Gay Pastor Charles Stanley. Far Right Views Part of Israel Alliance With Evangelicals." The Forward, April 17, 2015.

blance to the ideological core of modern anti-Jewish sentiment."[834] That is, to *blood and soil*: Didn't Herzl's Zionism fight for the old-new homeland of a blood-related group on biblical soil? Wasn't this exodus from Christian Europe an excellent since extra-European, intro-Oriental and perfectly humane final solution B of the Jewish question? A happy end since those incongruous people finally had got the picture?

Around 1930, "Race Pope" H.F.K.Günther proposed that the Jews emigrate to "Palestine or another region suitable for their inherited dispositions".[835] In January 1933, invited by the *Bund der Köngener*, a Protestant group ostensibly ready to engage in dialogue, Martin Buber gave a lecture titled *Israel und die Völker*. During the subsequent months the leader of this Bund, Lutheran vicar Jakob Wilhelm Hauer (1881-1962) tried to rope unsuspecting Buber in for cooperation in the solution of the "Jewish question". One should take advantage of the Zionist will to make Judaism "a distinctly marked-off people" in Palestine again, vicar Hauer – who concerning this matter in 1934 met with Heinrich Himmler and Reinhard Heydrich – wrote to Werner Best (1903-1989), the contact man between Nazi friendly German Faith Movement and the SS. Buber as a *"Vertreter einer* [representant of] *zionistischen Dissimilation"* might be helpful in releasing the Jews from German *Volkskörper*, Hauer hoped though Buber yet in 1932 had written to him: "I regard the concept of a *völkisch* state problematic and its presently common absolutization the direct way to disaster."[836]

On June 1, 1933, leading Protestant theologian Gerhard Kittel gave a speech in Tübingen about *"Die Judenfrage"*. By their race, Jews are an alien element in Germany, Kittel stated and proposed four possible solutions to the "Jewish Question". Literal quotation:

1. One can try to exterminate the Jews (*Pogrom*);
2. One can reinstall the Jewish State in Palestine or elsewhere and try to gather the Jews of the world there (*Zionismus*);
3. One can make Judentum merge in the other peoples (*Assimilation*);
4. One can decisively and consciously maintain the historical fact of a *Fremdlingsschaft* [foreignership] among the peoples."[837]

On May 15, 1935, the official newspaper of the SS, *Das Schwarze Korps* (The Black Corps) editorialized: "The time should not be all that far distant when Palestine will again receive its sons who have wandered lost for over a thousand years. Our wishes, joined with the good will of the state, accompany them."[838] In 1936, Jewish-owned shops in the Polish town of Piotrkow were daubed with the slogan "Get out to Palestine". Father Maximilian Kolbe, canonized due to his martyrdom in Auschwitz 1941, during the 1930 in his popular Catholic papers demanded Jewish emigration. On

---

834   Sand 2012, p.197.
835   de.wikipedia.org/wiki/Hans_F._K._Günther.
836   Junginger, p.107-109.
837   Junginger, p.161; cf. Goldhagen 1996, p.158-159.
838   Bailey, p.151.

October 27, 1938, when 18,000 Polish-born German Jews were expelled to Poland, one of them, namely Zindel (father of Hershel) Grynszpan, saw the streets of Hanover "black with people shouting 'The Jews out to palestine'".[839] On November 10, 1938, the day after infamous "Kristallnacht", the Jewish inhabitants of Regensburg were marched through the streets of their Bavarian home town under a banner announcing their exodus: *Auszug der Juden*. Theologian Gerhard Kittel who before, during, and after the holocaust called the New Testament the "most anti-Jewish book of world history", indeed already in 1942 categorically rejected a Zionism that pursued the purposes of world Jewry, supported Jewish plans of world dominion and furthermore never had the intention to "mold the parasite's claim into a genuine gestalt of peoplehood and homeland."[840] But already half a century earlier an Austrian cartoon designer who let the sun shine warmly on Jewish departure (announced in German, Slavic and Hungarian terms: *Abreise – Odjazd – Az Elmenet*) from Europe, with eery premonition had pictured the Jewish travellers waiting for their smoking train at the station of Oswiecim – this being the Polish name of Auschwitz.

Exodus from Europe, three times:
Ca. 1890: Austrian picture postcard "Departure" (of Jews) at the train station of Oswiecim (Auschwitz).
Ca. 1900: Munich made "Odinskarte Nr. 16", titled *Die Zukunft* (The Future) with signpost to *Palästina*.
Nov. 1938: *Auszug* [exodus] *der Juden* from Regensburg (the Roman founded *Regentia* where they had settled already before CE).

Some fifteen years after Auschwitz, the Vatican resident Jesuite General Jean Baptiste Janssens, nicknamed the "Black Pope", and Nahum Goldmann, President of Jewish World Congress, sat together for a respectful

---

839   Gilbert, p.53 (Piotrkow) and 67 (Hanover); Kolbe: Ökumenisches Heiligenlexikon.
840   Junginger, p.400; "antijüdischstes Buch": p.154, 155, 405.

conversation. "Our behavior toward the state of Israel and Zionism is one of the most complex problems of the Church", Janssens explained. "Speaking from a theological viewpoint, you are the cursed people, the people that crucified Christ. Your dispersion is your castigation. From this perspective, how could we approve the concept of a Jewish state? Our discussion of this problem lasts seven years now. How to concile the existence of Israel with the theological abomination you Jews have committed? Nonetheless, we came to a conclusion: If God allowed the Jews to establish a state, He thus gives us the proof that your crime has been expiated. This obstacle exists no more and it's up to us to examine what, from a pragmatic viewpoint, is good or bad for Mother Church, taking into account her religious institutions within Arab countries. Two reasons drive us to support your state and I hope, my esteemed President, that expressing them will not offend you. The first one is negative. Along her history, the Church has learned that the dispersion of the Jews is not good for her. Dispersed over almost all countries, the Jews frequently are liberals, atheists, socialists and even communists. It's no good for us having that much anti-religious focuses all over the world, the more so since your people is very influential. Better they are united in but one place. Second reason: the Church can conceive the hope that if the Jews are gathered again in the land of the Lord, the day will come when His spirit will dominate them and they convert to Christendom." To which Goldmann replied: "You're very sanguine. That's a long-term policy."[841]

Actually, Christian Europe's long-term policy of establishing a final ghetto, a last concentration land for Jews outside of Europe and right in the middle of Islamic world, with nice geopolitical, economic and religious side effects, was utterly successful. In Avraham Burg's view, "the West solved its mid-twentieth-century 'Jewish problem' largely as Hitler would have wished, by underwriting the removal of European Jews to Israel".[842]

The result was, at the end of nationalistic era, a national post-traumatic syndrome state that represents a regressive misunderstanding of Jewishness and Jewish history. For what is more *Hebrew* (derived from *ivri*, to pass over) than mobility? In Franz Rosenzweig's diasporic opposition to Zionism, Judaism is fundamentally bound up with waiting and wandering, but neither with the claim of territory nor the aspirations of a state.[843] Sure, Rosenzweig died in 1929. But in 1943, amidst the horrors, Charles Singer stressed what his father Simeon Singer (1846-1906) said to Herzl: "A Jewish Nation! Why, you're fifty years out of date. Only the little half-civilised peoples need an artificial nationality and are busy all over Europe finding their new national consciousness." For Singer senior as well as for his friend Claude Montefiore (1858-1938) and his son-in-law Israel Abrahams (1858-1925), "a national movement was an attempt to throw back Judaism to a Maccabean stage". In their view, "Judaism had as completely outgrown the conception

841 Goldmann, p.169-170.
842 Lynne Segal in Karpf et al., p.16, quoting Avraham Burg according to Ari Shavit's article "Burg: Defining Israel as a Jewish State Is the Key to Its End", Haaretz, June 7, 2007.
843 Butler, p.120.

of a Jewish State as the Jewish liturgy should have outgrown the priestly service of the temple and its sacrifices."[844] – "I would say the best of Jewish culture is bound to the fact of being dispersed, polycentric", Auschwitz survivor Primo Levi said in 1984,[845] concordant with the Christian Palestinian Edward Said (1935-2003) who cast Moses among the refugees, invoking the "irremediably diasporic, unhoused character" of Jewish life.[846] In a very Jewish way, to Ernst Bloch no place in space but only the "working, creating human, transforming and overhauling the conditions in real democracy ... gives birth to something in the world that shines in everybody's childhood and *where no one has ever been: home.*"[847]

"At home" is to Melanie Kaye/Kantrowitz a resolute Jewish diasporism.[848] "Do you know what our true country is?" French historian Nathan Wachtel was asked and told by my Brazilian friend, Marrano descendant Odmar Pinheiro Braga: "It can be found anywhere. Wherever we are, we carry the tradition. The Torah, study, that's where our country is found, and it is the legacy of our ancestors."[849]

Jewish identity is not defined by land but by an ethical constitution founded in the Sinai's no-man's territory. If the progressive task of Jewish culture as "light of the nations" is to "bring forth the true way" (Isaiah 42:3) of right against power, the retreat to the empowered ghetto Israel is a very regressive turn.[850] The "Jewish state" counteracts this ever progressive and transborder essence of Jewishness, for according to Israel's model the future world should consist of tribal areas with a joint state-religion constitution, instead of states defined as "home for all", granting equal rights for all regardless where their mothers lived in Mary's and Sarah's, Eve's and Lucy's days.

In 1929, Einstein had warned Chaim Weizmann: "If Jews cannot coexist peacefully with Arabs, then we have learned absolutely nothing during our 2,000 years of suffering."[851]

In 1967, already one month after Israel's blitz victory, Yeshayahu Leibowitz warned that a continuing occupation of the Westbank would "undermine the social structure we have created, and effect the corruption of individuals, Jews as well as Arabs."[852] Defending his term of "Jew-Nazis" in Israel, he warned in 1987: "If the nation – in Nazi diction the 'race' – and the power

---

844 Charles Singer, p.118-119.
845 Butler, p.202, citing Belpoliti, Marco / Gordon, Robert: The Voice of Memory. Interviews, 1961-1987. Cambridge 2001, p.292-293.
846 Said 2003, p.53.
847 Final words in Ernst Bloch's "The Principle of Hope" (last word in German: *Heimat*).
848 Butler, p.215.
849 Wachtel, p.276.
850 Ellis 1999, p.108: "That is, the National-Israeli culture takes in its Middle-Eastern isolation an almost ghetto-like reality, the fundamental difference being that this ghetto is an empowered one."
851 Rivlin: Naomi Zeveloff: "Reuven Rivlin Questions …", in The Forward, April 22, 2015; Olmert: Brian Klug in Karpf (ed.), p.293; military aid package: The Forward, Sept. 15, 2016; Einstein: Paul Berger, "Einstein's True Relationship …", in The Forward, Nov. 22, 2015.
852 Gorenberg, p.220.

of the national state are elevated to supreme values, then there is no halt any more to the action of people."[853]
In 2005, Israeli Moshe Zimmermann described the failure of Zionism as to its main purpose: "Instead of fighting anti-Semitism effectively, instead of backing up the Jews in the diaspora, Israel endangers, by an occupation policy completely contrary to the Jewish state's strategic and moral interests, exactly these Jews"[854] – enabling antizionists and antisemites to project simplifications like "Warsaw ghetto = Gaza" or "First Jesus, now Arafat". This first-now quip is awfully precise. First, it illumines the transfer of just punitive anger, and second the fact, that the stage itself – the scene of the original crime – permanently activates the mental circuit between two maltreatments: Back then of Jesus, and now of Palestinians, by those Jews who returned, *regressed* to the scene. This word seems appropriate, as regression, in the sense Sigmund Freud and Kurt Lewin gave to the term, means a temporary drawback to an earlier level of development with more primitive options of behavior, with the purpose of fighting fear by new emotional security. The collective return to the ancestral land provided the safety of the power-ghetto and a robust We-and-them worldview, fulfilling a manifest destiny marked by the Almighty's word to Abraham and the flaming sword of Adolf, "the instrument of God's will".[855] For the people's crucifixion in Shoah had to be followed by the people's resurrection and "sitting at the right hand" of Temple Mount forever, right? In a predictable way, Zionism ran into the regression trap: the Jewish huddling together in the majority state almost inevitably must lead to an ethnocentric shrinkage of Jewish ethics. To the great pleasure of all antisemites, exactly where the old murder was committed the Jews now play the role of the ego-people rightly thrown out from most European countries.
"A salesman for the IAI [Israel Aerospace Industries] told me that assassinations and operations in Gaza bring about an increase of tens of percentage points in company sales", says Israeli journalist Yotam Feldman who in his documentary film *The Lab* provides a disturbing look at a country of New Jersey's size that has become, just by beating swords into plowshares, the fourth-largest weapons exporter in the world. "The war in Gaza", Feldman judges, "has become inherent to the Israeli political system, possibly a part of our system of government."
In "Disproportionate Force," a 2008 paper published by the Institute for National Security Studies, Colonel Gabi Siboni declared that with an outbreak of hostilities, Israeli army will need to act "with force that is disproportionate to the enemy's actions ... meting out punishment to an extent that will demand long and expensive reconstruction processes."
December 27, 2008: Israel starts the Gaza operation "Cast Lead" which ends three weeks later. Death balance: 1387 Palestinian, 9 Israeli victims, 154:1.[856]

---

853 Leibowitz, p. 100-101.
854 Zimmermann (p.306), both in: Rabinovici/Speck/Sznaider.
855 Cohn-Sherbok, p.232, quoting British Jewish theologian Ignaz Maybaum.
856 Among the 1387 Palestinian victims 770 were civilians and 320 minors, according to Israeli NGO B'Tselem (ag-friedensforschung.de/; Amnesty International, Gaza-Bericht, Juli

July 1, 2014: Three Jewish youths which had been kidnapped on June 12 on their way home from a Yeshiva school near the Jewish settlement Kfar Etzion south of Jerusalem, are found death.
July 2: Family therapist Sarah Debbie Gutfreund publishes an article on AISH.com, titled "Tears and Shattered Prayers. An open letter to the three boys, *may their blood be revenged*." The same day, sixteen-year-old Mohammad Abu Khdeir is kidnapped, knocked unconscious and burnt alive by three young Jews who on July 6 confess the murder of their Arab peer.
July 8: On grounds of the governmental order to "hit Hamas hard", Israeli military forces start the action "Protecting Edge" against Gaza, ending on August 26 with a score of (according to UN data) 2,220 dead including 1,492 civilians and 551 children (nine of them killed in Gaza by a failed Hamas rocket)[857] on Palestinian, versus 67 fatalities, among them 64 soldiers and one child, on Israeli side. For every one Israeli victim there were 33 Palestinians, the murder of three Jewish youths having led to the 184-fold number of dead youth and children in Gaza.
The moral distinction between killing members of the own tribe versus persons of foreign tribes is viewed by Peter Singer as a feature of tribal societies.[858] Already the Babylonian Talmudist Rabbah bar Nahmani (270-320) rejected such distinctions with his classical response to a Jew who had to choose between killing a man on governmental order or facing his own execution: "Is your blood redder?"
It is. And demographically the situation is getting darker day by day. Of worldwide 14 million Jews, yet 6.3 million live in "Greater Israel", where they face the higher procreation rates of a non-Jewish population that is expected to present the majority between the river Jordan and the coast including Gaza within a few years, or within twenty years if Gaza stays apart. In April 2015, President Rivlin foreboded that it is "not obvious" that Israel will survive "until Israel's Jewish population reaches 12 million, and Palestinians will decide that the best place for them to live is Israel."[859] But yet in 2006 Prime Minister Olmert had insisted that "every Jew in the world" should "make aliyah" (come to live in Israel). This final exodus would realize Hitler's wildest dreams, opposing a finally *judenrein* world to the big kike vac in its optimal location.
In June 2015 only 28 of 100 Israeli teenagers condemned the so called pricetag-actions – attacks against Palestinian objects like mosques with the purpose of promoting árab emigration from occupied Palestine. On July 31, 2015 in one of those arson attacks a Palestinian toddler died in the flames, his father and mother succumbed few days later. Commenting an article "Thousands In Israel Rally Against Jewish Terror" a Latin American named Angel Rodriguez seemed hardly surprised: "If these types, I mean their ancestors, already killed CRISTO, now what would they do with simple mortals?"[860]

2009, p.75-77).
857   The Algemeiner, July 30, 2014: "Italian Journalist Defies Hamas ..."
858   Singer, Peter, 1994, p.117.
859   "Reuven Rivlin Questions Future of Israel ...", in The Forward, April 22, 2015.
860   Comment posted by Angel Rodriguez, in: librered.net/, Aug. 2, 2015: "Si éstos tipos,

On March 30, 2018, the eve of Passover when CRISTO back then was executed, Israeli sharpshooters wound more than 700, and kill 17 simple mortals, unarmed demonstrators at the borderline to Gaza. For an old Israeli born in 1923 as Helmut Ostermann, flown from Germany in 1933, wounded in the war of 1948, member of Knesset for 12 years, fighting for peace, separation of state and religion and Israel without Zionism, this is too much: "I, Uri Avnery, soldier number 44410 of the Israel army, hereby dissociate myself from the army sharpshooters who murder unarmed demonstrators along the Gaza Strip, and from their commanders, who give them the orders, up to the commander in chief.We don't belong to the same army, or to the same state. We hardly belong to the same human race."[861]
Few weeks later the ghetto fires again, hitting 1,500 and killing 60 Palestinians by bullets passing the barbed wire freely. How about a Gaza wall? "Half fascist" Avnery calls, weeks before his death in August 2018, the new Nation State Law that builds a constitutional wall around the "Jewish state". Always a staunch optimist, Avnery never would have viewed Kafka's Little Fable in the sense of Zionist regression to protective national walls, after thousand defenseless years under Europe's crosses:
"Akh" said the mouse, "the world is getting narrower every day. At first it was so broad I got afraid, I kept running and was happy when at last I saw walls in the distance, but those walls hasten so quickly to one another that I am in the last room already and there in the corner is the trap I am running into." – "Just change direction" said the cat and ate her.[862]

"... imposing the cross not only on his Son, but on all creation": Joint humanimal salvific bleeding in Matthias Grünewald's Isenheim altarpiece, ushering in the lamb's own chapter ...

digo sus antepasados, mataron a CRISTO, que no harán con simples mortales."
861 Uri Avnery: Eyeless in Gaza. Tikkun.org, April 14, 2018.
862 Kafka 1976, p.320.

XIII The Lamb on Cross

... is but an animal

> *"The constantly recurring assertion that savages, blacks, Japanese resemble animals, as for example monkeys, is the key to pogrom. The possibility of pogrom is decided in the moment when the gaze of a fatally-wounded animal falls on a human being. The defiance with which he thrusts aside this gaze – 'after all, it's just an animal' – reappears irresistibly in those cruelties towards human beings by which the perpetrators time and again must back up the 'just an animal' to themselves since yet concerning animals they've never been wholly convinced of it."* Th.W. Adorno[863]

Just animals: On April 21, 1933, twelve weeks after having seized power and one day after the new Chancellor's birthday had been celebrated including parades and special church services in his honor, the government of Hitler effectively outlawed ritual slaughter. The new law did not refer to the Jewish religion, but required that "warm-blooded animals must be stunned at slaughter before the beginning of blood withdrawal". By incident, April 21 was the Friday after Holy Friday, the most strictly meat-free Catholic fast day in an ecclesiastical year of (back then) 52 meatless Fridays, in memory of Jesus' crucifixion on the eve of Sabbath.

How mankind incurred the craze of sacrifice is an important subject of this chapter which holds three theses:

1. The image of the anti-natural, animal-torturing Jew is a core infamy of anti-Semitism;
2. The Jew Jesus was much closer to vegetarians and animal liberators than to Paul's pagan-friendly and victorious laissez-faire "eat what is available on the meat-market";
3. The Christian myth of the cruelly sacrificed, salvific Lamb of God tangible in the cross had and still has disastrous effects on the western attitude concerning animals.

Just animals? "Are not two sparrows sold for a cent? And one of them shall not fall on the ground without your Father" (Matthew 10:29). "Consider the ravens: They do not sow or reap, they have no storeroom or barn; yet God feeds them. And of how much more value are you than birds!" (Luke 12:24). Two more times Jesus takes animals as basis for this principle of comparative enhancement: "If any of you has a sheep and it falls into a pit on the Sabbath, will you not take hold of it and lift it out? How much more valuable is a human being than a sheep!" (Matthew 12:11-12). And how much more this woman he healed on Sabbath (Luke 13:16) deserved the healing, as "each of you on the Sabbath [will] untie his ox or his donkey from its manger and lead it away to give it water?" This way of giving evidence by

---

863 Adorno 1982, (Minima Moralia; passage "Menschen sehen dich an"), p.133.

277

enhancement is a common Talmudic figure of argumentation and shows its sophistication for instance in the famous case of Dave Rubin's beautiful but two-timing wife, whose indicted lover argued this way: "Rabbi, is Rubin entitled to have sex with his wife?" – "Of course." – "Am I entitled to have sex with *my* wife?" – "Quite normally!" – "Is Rubin entitled to have sex with my wife?" – "Of course not!" – "Look, Rabbi: If I am entitled to have sex quite normally with a woman that is strictly forbidden to Rubin, how much more am I entitled to, at times, have sex with a woman that even he is allowed to have, quite normally, sex with?"

Anyhow, these four verses of enhancement, four times clearly subordinating animals to humans, are altogether already the ultimate of feelings Jesus ever voiced for animals. Significantly, in his sensitive book "Saints and Animals", the Catholic priest Joseph Bernhart can illustrate the point "Jesus and Animals" only with the passage in Mark (1:13), where Jesus "was in the wilderness forty days, tempted by Satan; and he was with the wild beasts; and the angels attended him.[864] No word of compassion ever comes from Jesus' lips like from Saint Basil's who remembered: "I myself have seen an ox shedding tears when his companion of pasture and yoke had died." No sermon for birds to whom Jesus' most consequent disciple Francesco de Assisi preached; no protection for a persecuted hare like the one Anselm of Canterbury defended; no cohabitation with a hunted deer as Holy Nennoka of Ireland is known for; no holy patience as Saint Kevin showed when he did not close his hand nor draw it back until the blackbird had built her nest, layed her eggs and reared all her fledglings in it; no humanimal friendship as between the grey wolve and Don Bosco, with whom Joseph Bernhart's short collection – "Love of Animals by Saints from two Millennia" – comes to an early end. Thrice significantly, Bernhart had to give up ministry when he married his love Elisabeth Nieland in 1913; he was mercifully allowed to cohabitate with his wife in "sister marriage" in 1939 by the Church; and was banned of publishing by the Nazis in 1941. To some degree, Bernhart's collection disproves the "*totale Nullität*" of the animal in Christianity which the India-inspired philosopher Arthur Schopenhauer asserts.[865]

Involuntarily, however, Bernhart's thorough collection of Christian love to animals demonstrates Peter Singer's Jewish statement that "while ... the Old Testament did at least show flickers of concern for their sufferings, the New Testament is completely lacking in any injunction against cruelty to animals, or any recommendation to consider their interests."[866] The *imitatio Christi* could not expand its love to animals because the master – according to the gospels – nowhere invoked to. If, as I will show, the balance in campassion

---

864 Bernhart, p.43.
865 "The important role animals play throughout in Brahmanism and Buddhism, compared to the total nullity in Christendom, condemns the latter." Schopenhauer, Arthur: Parerga und Paralipomena, Zurich 1977, Vol.II, p.407-408; cited by Streminger, Gerhard: Schopenhauers Kritik am Christentum in Parerga und Paralipomena, in: Aufklärung und Kritik 2/1984, p.3-15 (translation: K.Y.R.).
866 Singer, Peter, 2002, p.191.

with animals plainly leans to Judaism, why does Judaism equal "cruel to-wards animals" to Christians if not by the signal effect of the crucified lamb? "Revealingly", a German freethinker magazine proclaimed in 2011, "there is not one single sentence in the whole Bible that takes the side of animals against human brutalness and greed". When I objected by a letter to the editor, a Leipzig resident "anti-theist" replied with an angry defence based exclusively on quotes collected from ten staunchly Christian Bible schol-ars.[867] Even more irate is the critique of Arthur Schopenhauer (1788-1860), who first postulates that compassion is "the true moral driving force", prov-ing itself not least "because it also comes to the defence of the animals so irresponsibly badly cared for in European systems of ethics. The pretended rightlessness of animals, the delusion that our conduct towards them has no moral significance, or, as it is put in the language of these codes, that 'there are no duties to be fulfilled towards animals, is a downright revolting coarse-ness and barbarism of the occident, whose source is Judaism."[868]

So let's have a look to those basic texts of Judaism which Rabbi Jesus had to be content with. They will illustrate not only his rabbinic stance concerning animals but also the freethinkers' well-versed assertion and Schopenhauer's savant charge.

"Compassion with animals", Schopenhauer claims four pages later, "is in-timately connected with goodness of character, and it may confidently be asserted that he, who is cruel to living creatures, cannot be a good man." Proverbs 12:10 comprises the same issue just more concisely: "The righteous care for the needs of their animals, but the kindest acts of the wicked are cru-el." In accordance with this leitmotiv, in the cases of three prominent loving couples of the Bible (the old collection; there is Passion but no love story in the gospels) the looking for one's soul mate proceeds according to the crite-rion "She/he must be nice with animals": Because Rebecca says "Drink, and I'll water your camels too", she is the right one for Isaac (Genesis 24:14). One generation later, Jacob first cares for the thirsty mouths of Rachel's sheep before he kisses his cousin (Genesis 29:10-11). And Moses, on the run as the detected killer of an Egyptian who hurt a Hebrew, is found worthy to become Ziporah's husband because he unbidden served her thirsty sheep as water-carrier (Exodus 2:17-21).

In quite a modern way these verses don't ask for personal rights but for justified interests. "The borderline of sensitivity [thirst for water, for kisses] is the only one tenable border for respecting the interests of others."[869] In this perspective of Peter Singer, Genesis – written at a time when Palestine was still a biotope for lions – confronts the hard verse "Fill the earth and subdue it; reign over the fish in the sea, the birds in the sky, and all the animals that move along the ground" (1:28) with Noah's Arch (Gen 6-8) as a didactic symbol of human responsibility for all species. And right in the next

867 MIZ, Materialien und Informationen zur Zeit (a political magazine for atheists and un-denominationals), Aschaffenburg 1/2010 – 3/2010; antitheismus.de/categories/16-Leserbriefe.
868 Schopenhauer 1881, p.233 and 238.
869 Singer, Peter, 1996, p.85 (chapter "Equality for Animals?").

verse (1:29), the human sovereigns are given an exclusively vegetable diet of "every seed-bearing plant ... and every tree with seed-bearing fruit", while the animals get a free choice menu of "all the green plants". The eventual Messianic perfection of this-wordly life will be even more symbiotic, as Isaiah announces: "The wolf shall dwell with the lamb, the leopard lie down with the kid" (11:6). Louis Berman comments: "Meat-eating, like polygamy, fit into an earlier stage of human history." But isn't the forecast "The cow and the bear shall graze, their young shall lie together" just a metaphor for peace in human societies? "How remarkable", Berman replies, "that a pastoral people should give the world a vision of a time of Creation when there was no eating of meat, and of a time of the Messiah when 'the lion will eat straw like the ox' (when all the world would be vegetarian?)."[870]

The same concern for all sensitive beings transpires in the Psalms: God preserves them (36:6), gives them water (104:10); feeds them (145:16) and does not desire their sacrifice (40:7). At least in his misery, Job becomes "a brother to jackals, a companion to Ostriches" (30:29), confronted now with his restrictions compared to the worldly wisdom which bear and lioness, hind and raven, mountain goat and wild ass, onager and wild ox, ostrich and stork, horse and locust, hawk and eagle are gifted with (38:32-39:27).

"My beloved is like a gazelle" romances the Song of Songs. "Your eyes are like doves, your hair is like a flock of goats and like a flock of ewes your teeth ... O maidens of Jerusalem, like gazelles and hinds of the fields, do not wake up love, until it wakes up alone." Neither for such love nor any humanimal beauty the gospels dare to waste a word.

"Then the Lord opened the ass's mouth, and she said to Balaam: 'What have I done to you that you have beaten me three times?'" The ass had swerved from the road and refused to move forward because only she, not Balaam, had seen the angel of death standing on the way (Num 22). While no one doubts that migrating birds sense magnetic fields, scientific evidence attests that animals can have fine antennas for upcoming catastrophies, from room fire to earthquake. And Françoise Dolto wasn't joking when she affirmed: "In a family, children and house dogs know everything, and particularly when it's left unsaid."[871] Since the beaten she-ass shows "that at a given moment an animal may be more sensitive" than humans, Maimonides took her as basis for the "rule laid down by our Sages, that it is directly prohibited in the Torah to cause pain to an animal"[872] This conclusion is shared by the Talmud, as well as by the comprising *Shulchan Aruch* in 18th century. In the same epoch, Rabbi Ezekiel Landau of Prague was asked by a Jew, whether he was allowed to go hunting with his Christian friends provided that he wouldn't eat the meat. "According to the Talmud", the Rabbi answered, "it is permitted to slay wild animals only when they invade human settlements,

---

870   Berman, p.XV.
871   Schützenberger, p.61.
872   Soncino Pentateuch, p.673, cited by Berman, p.5;

but to pursue them in the woods, their own dwelling place, ... is prohibited."[873]
An effect of the prohibition of "tzaar baalei hayim" – of causing unnecessary "pain to living beings" is for instance the commandment "You shall not
plow with an ox and a donkey yoked together" (Deuteronomy 22:10). This
would be economical for small farms, but compassionate farmers knew that
mainly the weaker donkey would suffer in this unbalanced cooperation.
"You shall not muzzle the ox while he is threshing the grain." Alan Young
interprets this verse (Deuteronomy 25:4; cf. 24:19) as sensitively as it is:
"Imagine yourself out picking strawberries on a warm day and not being
tempted to pop one into your mouth. Animals have the same desires to eat
as we do."[874] Paul, however, misused the verse to justify his travel expenses
and counters it (1 Corinthians 9:9) by the rhetorical question which informed
the Christian culture's relation to oxen and other soulless beings: "Is it for
oxen that God is concerned?" Thus asks this Paul who claimed to descend
from Benjamin but forgot that already father Jacob (in Genesis 49:6-7) was
concerned and chose to disown his sons Simeon and Levy by two reasons:
"May I never join their company. For in their anger they murdered men, and
they crippled oxen just for sport"?

This Jewish quirk of Animal Rights
Romanian buffalos were used as draft animals by German army in WW I,
and how they were treated Rosa Luxemburg describes in a letter to Sonja
Liebknecht: "The escorting soldier, a brutal fellow, began to strike at the
animals with the thick end of his scourge in such a way that the supervisor
called out on him in disgust, whether he felt no pity for the animals. 'For us
people nobody feels pity either!' he replied to her with an evil glimpse, and
stroke the stronger ... At last the animals pulled on and came over the mountain, but one of them bleeded ... Sonitschka, the hide of buffalos is proverbially thick and tough, and it was teared. During unloading, the animals then
stood dead calm, exhausted, and one, the bleeding one, stared ahead with
an expression in the black face and the gentle eyes like a weeping child."[875]
This German socialist Rosa Luxemburg, murdered in 1919, saw a buffalo
shedding children's tears. The ethnologist Claude Lévi-Strauss proposed to
view human rights not as a privilege of man but rather "a special case of
rights which befit all species".[876] To Paul's cynical question "Is it for oxen
that God is concerned?" which she regards as "fundamental to Christianity's
later attitude towards animals", feminist writer Roberta Kalechofsky has an
answer that is religious in the term's best sense: "It is indeed 'for oxen that
God is concerned'... The Mosaic law does envisage animal interest, does

873 Telushkin 1994, p.448.
874 Young, p.85.
875 Letter to Sonja Liebknecht, mid-December 1917, in: Linnemann 2000, p.279-281.
876 Linnemann 2000, p.339.

legislate animal rights, and to that extent, does represent animals as moral objects."[877]
Lewis Gompertz (1779-1861), the British pioneer of social justice, women's right and animal rights (and moreover inventor of a front-drive bicycle), in his book "Moral Inquiries. On the Situation of Man and of Brutes" (1824) repeatedly uses the term "men and other animals" – decades before Darwin's theory of evolution. Also Peter Singer equals animals to humans, with respect to Jeremy Bentham's criterion "Are they able to suffer?" Singer's book "Animal Liberation" ranks as the Bible of the Animal Rights Movement. The Australian philosopher does not deny "important differences between humans and other animals", but asserts that these differences are no barrier "for extending the basic principle of equality to nonhuman animals ... The basic principle of equality does not require equal or identical treatment; it requires equal consideration."[878] Lewis Gompertz was forced to retreat in 1832 from his office as secretary of the Society for the Prevention of Cruelty to Animals – due to his secular-moralist argumentation and his Jewishness.[879] Singer and Lévi-Strauss, Luxemburg and Kalechofsky, all four blurring the human-animal fence line, are Jewish. Rather than coincidence, there's one feature in which their world-views coincide: The anti-speciesist, non-separate unity of man and animal in Jewish tradition. "As regards men," Ecclesiastes decides "to face the fact that they are animals [...] For the fate of the sons of man and animals, there is one fate to them: as this dies that dies, one breath is to all and there is no superiority of man over animal ..." (3:18-20).
What basically unites human and non-human animals is what emerges first in the *néfesh hayá*, the soul of life brought forth, to note, by the waters that covered the earth some billions of years ago, or as soon as Genesis 1:20. This soul spreads from aquatic to flying and terrestrial animals (1:21/24/30) and to Adam who, introducing symbolic representation, starts to name his fellow beings (2:19). *Néfesh* signifies the vitality and own will common to all living, sentient beings, and since man and beast own *néfesh*, both own the ability to enter into treaties. Already Genesis 9 practises this egalité: Here God establishes his covenant "with you and your offspring to come, and with every living thing [*kol néfesh hahayá*] that is with you – birds, cattle and every wild beast as well – all that have come out of the ark, every living thing on earth." Not only do all these beings merit salvation, be it in the ark or later in Ninive with its "more than 120.000 persons who do not know their right hand from their left, and so many animals" (Jonah 4:11); they all have also, long before a workers' movement, a right for free Sabbath: "But the seventh day is a Sabbath for the Lord your God: not any work shall do, you and your son and daughter, your male or female worker, your animals and your stranger in your settlement" (Ex 20:10); "... in order that your ox and

---

877   Kalechofsky 1992, p.52, citing James Gaffney in his article "The Relevance of Animal experimentation to Roman Catholic Ethical Methodology".
878   Singer, Peter, 2002, p.2.
879   vegan.at/veganelebensweise/buchbesprechungen/lewis_gomperz.html.

your ass may rest, and respire [*yinéfesh*] the son of your maidservant and the stranger" (Ex 23:12). On this seventh day "you shall not do any work; you, your son and your daughter and your worker and your maidservant and your ox and your ass and all your cattle and your stranger ... will rest like you" (Dt 5:13-14). On grounds of these three commandments, the medieval Talmudist and winegrower Rashi (1040-1105) declared that on Sabbath animals are entitled to roam around, to graze freely and to enjoy the beauties of nature – which would go against the factual restraints of livestock industry, be it "kosher" or capitalist cost-sensitive simply. Livestock industry might calculate even more tightly, and Noah's ark have to carry eatable passengers only, according to Kant's enlightened view of 1780 that "so far as animals are concerned, we have no direct duties" because "animals are not self-conscient". In the same year, Jeremy Bentham countered Kant: "The question is not, Can they reason? Nor Can they talk? But, Can they suffer?" Dryly rebutting the sacrificers' motto "Better you suffer, and die, than I", Bentham's contemporary, the English cleric Humphrey Primatt, gave the answer concisely: "Pain is pain no matter who suffers it."[880]

How can we, after this collection of Jewish Bible verses advocating for animals, now interpret Schopenhauer's accusation that disrespect for animals is a "barbarism of the occident, whose source is Judaism"? Schopenhauer nowhere proves his imputation but spices it with sharp phrases against always the same guys: "One must really be blind in all senses, or totally chloroformed by *foetor judaicus* [Jewish stench] not to perceive that the essence and substance in animal and man is the same."

Exactly this sameness in suffering, dignity and interests is, as shown above, not just perceived but implemented within the culture of *foetor judaicus*.

Yet on the next page Schopenhauer rants: "One must remind such an *occidentalischen, judaisirten* despiser of animals and idolator of reason that he has been wet-nursed by his, just like the dog by his mother ..."

Right this is reminded by the Thorah's commandment not to boil the kid in his mother's milk.

"That the moral of Christendom does not regard the animals" Schopenhauer ascribes back to bad humus sickening a good plant, since Christian moral shows "the greatest conformance with the moral of Brahmanism and Buddhism ... and may have come to Judea via Egypt, so that Christendom might be a reflection of Indian primal light from the ruins of Egypt; a light which, alas, has fallen on Jewish soil."[881]

What a pity! Why the young philosopher views bright Christendom as the victim of Jewish soil and why he so physically and sensorily can't stand smelling anything Judaish shows up in the following sequence of sensitive insights pointing altogether to one scaring sight:

"We suffer with him, so within him: we feel his pain as his pain and don't have the imagination that it's our pain."

"Treason ...belonging to the category of double injustices, is despised deeply."

880 Kalechofsky 2003, p.6; cf. Spiegel, p.6.
881 Schopenhauer 1881, p.238, 240, 241 (archive.org/stream/diebeidengrund ...).

"How is it possible then, that a suffering that is not mine and does not affect me should become a motive for me and cause me to act as directly as otherwise only my own suffering does? [What shows up here is] what yet Calderon speaks out: *que entre el ver padecer y el padecer ninguna distancia habia* (that there's no difference between the viewing of suffering and the suffering). This, however, implies that I have identified with the other in a certain way ..." – "Nothing appalls in so deep a sense our moral feeling like cruelty. Every other crime we can pardon, except for cruelty. The reason of this is that cruelty is the downright contrary of compassion."[882]

Legalize by sacrifice

Next German thinker: "Be warned about compassion", Nietzsche wrote in 1882, "from that a heavy cloud will come to mankind!" Seven years later the long repressed cloud came over him and first drops fell: Sobbingly he hugged a horse maltreated by the carter and lived the remaining eleven years of his life in mental derangement.[883]

Compassion as mankind's cloud of problems: Very slowly, Lucy's prehistorical East African gatherers had learned to kill animals and use them for food, clothing and tools. Neolithic farmers had domesticated animals and used them for many more purposes including milk, riding, pulling, hunting. The more northern the Eurasian living-place, the lesser a completely plant-based nutrition was a realistic option. Synchronously however, due mostly to children's steadily extending need of parental care, the ability to feel compassion and to empathize with other living beings increased in humans steadily. Therefore, to these increasingly empathic humans the killing of animals posed an emotional problem growing inexorably. "If one preyed on animals, one at least had a bad conscience", German agro-economist Franz Kromka states, reminding the antique Greek rites of apology; "we've lost that completely."[884] We, the bank card brandishing Walmart hunters, look down on "primitive" hunter cultures while among the still existing ones there is none "that would not suffer by the necessity to kill"[885] or wouldn't attempt to mitigate their guilt feelings by certain rites of exculpation. "Cherish us no grudge because we have killed you", an Ottawa tribe of American Indians in 18th century implored the spirit of the bear. "You have sense; you see that our children are hungry." Indians of the Great Plains "wept with remorse for the buffalos they were about to kill". African tribes, when they had killed an elephant in a hunt, offered an apology to the animals's spirit, "pretending its death was quite accidental". The Ainus of Sakhalin, before slaughtering one of the bear cubs they raised as meat animals, informed the

---

882   Schopenhauer 1881, p.221, 222, 229 und 232.
883   Nietzsche quote from: Also sprach Zarathustra, chapter "Von den Mitleidigen"; breakdown: Weischedel, p.259.
884   Franz Kromka: Eine Idylle gab es noch nie. In: Tageszeitung (taz), Berlin, January 16, 2001, p.13.
885   Drewermann, E., in: Kaplan, p.28.

bear "that he will be shot by the best archer so its death will be as quick and painless as possible [and] that it will now go to the 'god of the forest'".[886] After humans had overcome the stage of gatherer-hunters, their emotional need to reduce feelings of blood-guilt seems to have exacerbated further when pastoral tribes day after day lived face to face, eye to eye with a multitude of next victims. The psychic solution was to transform the killing into a sacral act which brought the victim not down to death but up to God.

The Jewish way to cope with the guilt of killing animals resembles the Ainu way: offering the animal to God and killing it as painlessly as possible. As an act "pleasing to God" the sacrifice of animals is introduced – with risks and side effects disclaimer – at three points of the Torah. First step, Genesis chapter 4: Plant grower Cain offers the vegetable products of his soil-tilling work, while Eve's second son Abel burns the firstborns of his flock. "And the Lord paid heed to Abel and his offering", but rejected Cain's and thus revoked the vegetable diet he had commanded to both brothers' parents. But the green plant eater Cain strikes Abel dead.

Why is here the gardener the murderer, the vegan the villain? "Abel killed an animal, Cain killed Abel" – thus Roberta Kalechofsky deduces the human killing from the animal, while Mark M. Braunstein outlines the learning process: "When Cain (a tiller of the ground) saw Abel (a keeper of sheep) sacrifice an animal, he assumed killing was good; it is well known, what Cain did to Abel – but it was Abel, not Cain, who was the first killer", having learnt this skill at animal guinea-pigs. Jacques Derrida ponders why God promises protection to the murderer Cain: "As if he repented. As if he felt shame or confessed to have preferred the animal sacrifice. As if he thus confessed remorse concerning the animal."[887]

Second step: Having just disembarked from the ark, "Noah built an altar to the Lord and ... offered burnt offerings" from among the flood surviving ark passengers. God is fond of the "pleasing odor", writes the priestly scribe by understandable reasons of profession, hinting at how victims fare in temple routine: "Fear and dread of you shall be upon all the living beings of the earth." Remarkably, God makes little distinction between the killers, announcing he will now "require a reckoning for shedding life-blood, from every animal and from every human being." The prohibition of eating "flesh with its life-blood in it" (Gen 9:4) from now on is the permanent reminder (and weak placation) of whatsoever residual guilt pangs.

The third step signifies an essential stage in the humanizing of God or sanctification of human life: In the story of Isaac's prevented sacrifice, the animal – a ram – is the substitute for Sarah's and Abraham's son. Significantly, the abolition of human sacrifice is attributed to God – while the vicarious sacrifice of the casually found animal is exclusively Abraham's invention. More precisely, it is man who wanted meat, in Abraham's lifetimes as well as shortly after the exodus (Numbers 11), when "the riffraff in their midst felt a gluttonous craving; and then the Israelites wept and said: If only we

886 Berman, p.11.
887 Kalechofsky 1992, p.247; Braunstein, p.117; Derrida, p.82.

had meat to eat! We remember the fish that we used to eat free in Egypt, the cucumbers, the melons, the leeks, the onions, and the garlic ..." And now: nothing but manna. Moses argues ecologically: "Could enough flocks and herds be slaughtered to suffice them? Or could all the fish of the sea be gathered ...?" God is sick of all the griping, lets the wind sweep quail from the sea, real delicatessen food, but "the meat was still between their teeth" when Yahve's anger "struck the people with a very severe plague" so lethal that the place was named "the graves of craving". But still the craving was not stilled, and one book later (Deuteronomy 12:20) the Lord confirmed that "when ... you have the urge to eat meat, you may eat meat whenever you wish."

But not of all beasts! The choice of allowed meat reflects the pragmatism of an agricultural-artisan religion. Allowed was the meat of those animals which provided human culture also with other and much more indispensable substances: wool from sheep, leather from cattle, cymbal strings and drumheads from goats, parchment from their hides, feathers from fowl and milk from cows; nothing from pigs since they were food concurrents to man, inapt to arid climate and could have been exploited only for their more unhealthy meat and less useful leather. The kosher selection of non-prohibited animals (ruminant cloven hoofed mammals, scaled fish, fowl and locusts) refers to health, economy and ecology, and Lea Fleischmann is right in calling kashrut "the first wildlife conservation program of mankind".[888]

An essential motive, however, is the eschewal of the meat of carnivore animals: "Here is a protest against an apparent law of nature" Birnbaum and Rosenberg observe: "The altar repels those who live thanks to the death of other animals. At the end of days, nature herself will be altered."[889]

In the mid of days, the critical French theologian Jean Meslier (1664-1729) deemed it yet "awful to merely see the slaughterhouses", and with revulsion he imagines "that horrible sacrifice and bloodbath ... which King Solomon, on occasion of the consecration of his temple, committed against innocent animals by ordering the slaughter of twenty-two thousand cattle and twenty thousand sheep."[890] Indeed, Solomon's temple not too slightly resembled a slaughterhouse. And as such it deserved its destruction by the Romans, which Maccoby deems "no great shock" for the Jewish sacrificial system that already "had moved in the direction of seeing sacrifices as gifts to God, rather than as vicarious sufferers for the sacrificer's sins."[891] Jonathan Sacks even appreciates the fall of the temple as "one of the most creative moments of Jewish history, a triumph of renewal in the midst of tragedy".[892] The break of the temple allowed, after the break of Isaac's sacrifice, now the second phase of liberation from delusional blood-bribery, a liberation Yahve Himself had demanded again and again: "When I brought your ancestors out of Egypt, I did not tell them anything about burnt offerings and sacrifices",

---

888   Lea Fleischmann in her speech at Haus der Begegnung, Ulm, January 27, 2004.
889   Birnbaum/Rosenberg, p.69.
890   Linnemann, p.99.
891   Maccoby 1992, p.13.
892   Quoted by Sergio Margulies in Fuks, p.182.

Jeremiah (7:22) had heard Him say from where to get off, and where to go to She told Hosea: "I desire mercy, not sacrifice, and knowledge of God rather than burnt offerings" (6:6). That the burnt sacrifices were abolished only by the Roman destroyers of the temple illustrates the persistence of archaic costumes, shameful for judaism since "a whole galaxy of central rabbinic and spiritual leaders ... has been affirming vegetarianism as the ultimate meaning of Jewish moral teaching". This is the central rabbinic viewpoint of Israel's former Chief Rabbi Isaac Halevi Herzog.[893] "Everything indicates that the biblical ideal is vegetarianism" distinguished Brazilian Rabbi Nilton Bonder clarifies, while in the US modern orthodox Rabbi Irving Greenberg balances that "Judaism's ideal world is vegetarian but halacha permits eating meat, with restrictions." Their conservative colleagues Dennis Prager and Joseph Telushkin make the same conflict hearable: "According to Judaism, the ideal is that we should be vegetarians."[894]

An apparently narrow but far-reaching commandment packs ideal and reality into six Hebrew words: "*Lo tebashel gedi ba hálav imó*" – "Not cook kid in milk his mother's" (Ex 23:19 and 34:26; Dt 14:21). The six old words are the basis for a whole system of separating "milchig" from "fleishig" in Jewish kitchen, cupboards, daily diet, with the sole purpose of keeping Jews alert about the fact that meat, as result of killing, does not combine with life, whose symbol is the mother's milk. Naive and effectless? Anyhow, three millennia later the feminist Carol Adams calls for reinserting the "absent referent", i.e. the killed animal, into the discourse, "acting as a reminder of what process is used to produce meat", while feminist Roberta Kalechofsky confirms practical efficiency: "Kashrut has prepared the Jew for vegetarianism."[895]

Nevertheless Spinoza's mannish opinion that "not to slaughter animals has its foundation more in vain superstition and womanish tenderness than in sound reason"[896] apparently still prevails in the "most feminine of all nations" which animal rights activist Gary Yourofsky attempts to turn into "the first vegan nation". With 13 percent vegetarians Israel – with some distance to India's 40 percent – ranked second worldwide in 2014 (third now maybe behind Brazil's 14 percent). And outdoing even Argentine, the land of milk and honey ranked ninth worldwide in its disillusioning meat consumption of 99.2 kilogram (220 lbs) per year and person, as against 27 kg in Palestine, 5 in India, 4.5 in Congo and 3 in Bangladesh.[897] Thanks to this meat consumption, every Israeli needs 4.82 "global hectares" (11,9 acres) for his self

893   brook.com/jveg/; I.H.Herzog (1888-1959) was Ireland's chief rabbi and the father of Israel's president (1983-1993) Chaim Herzog.
894   Bonder: 2004, p.66; Greenberg: 1993, p.95 (halacha, literally "the going" is the practical ethics based on Torah and Talmud); Prager/Telushkin: Birnbaum/Rosenberg, p.31.
895   Kalechofsky 2006, p.186.
896   Adams, p.112 and 109; citing Spinoza, Ethics, Fourth Part, prop.XXXVII, Note 1.
897   13 percent: The Jewish Vegetarian, London, 1/2014; meat consumption per country: vegetarian.procon.org/view.resource.php?resourceID=004716; in Israel: Abigail Klein Leichman:The (halachic) case for veganism, Jpost.com Magazine, November 13, 2015.

supply whereas the Promised Land provides just 0.32 gha (0,79 acres) for him or her. The storm troopers' marching for Chaplin's Great Dictator sang "We Aryans, are fighting any folk of vegetarians" just for the rhyme. But let's return from ending slaughter to the slaughtered Holy Lamb: not the least important objective of this book is fathoming the deep psychological – and political – motives in the sacrifice complex. Obviously, sacrifice happens within an asymmetric triad consisting of Power + offerer + victim, its purpose being appeasement of the former by the latter's death. The central discrepancy between Abraham's and Paul's religion, that is Isaac's prevented sacrifice *with* the proxy ram of atonement versus Jesus' executed proxy sacrifice *as* our lamb of atonement, provides us with two leitmotivs which I will investigate in a strictly humanist manner: **(A)** Why do humans seek to appease almighty Power by the sacrifice of a living being? And **(B)** Why did Christian humans, heeding Paul's *Anything goes* in meat consumption, grasp his presentation of Jesus as the slaughtered Lamb?

A. The basic motive for a group of human beings to sacrifice the life of a howsoever ordained individual is the fear for their own lives, ingrained in them during seven million years of survival as small edible bipeds. "The original trauma" of hominids and early humans "was the trauma of being hunted by animals, and eaten", Barbara Ehrenreich exposed in Blood Rites (1997).[898] But yet in 1960, Elias Canetti had stated that "an active mass-fear is the great collective experience of all animals that live in herds and as good runners save themselves together."[899] We could go back by time machine to a group of pre-human primates whose only chance is rushing up the next tree; or to a tribe of early humans who live in open bushland and already are good runners. Let's imagine a mighty feline predator approaches. A sudden shout of warning; frightened all the fellows flee in panic from the mighty one announcing death. Who will be stroken? Alas, one has to bite the dust, será, the roaring one collars one of us, poor guy, the great one roars and bares his canines, pulls poor boy up to a branch fork, eats him, roars satisfied once more and leaves, the group calms down again and life goes on, now safer than before, because *the lion sleeps tonight*.
A drama of four acts, a sequence of four emotional experiences has happened: Peaceful group life – fear of fatal power – sacrifice of good guy – new peaceful group life. A resuming logic, repeating rhythmically for 400,000 generations of steppe inhabitant early humans, infixed itself to each one: We have to give HIM someone HE can kill, pull up and eat; the victim – mostly a young venturesome male – has saved us, brought us peace and took our angst away with him into the nothing he has vanished in. "The stroken one is a sacrifice, offered to the danger", Canetti says. "It provides repose for the other herd comrades. As soon as the lion has got what he wanted and as soon as they notice, their fear subsides ... If the gazelles had a faith, the lion being their god, they could, in order to satisfy his greed, voluntarily deliver

898   Hart/Sussman, p.83.
899   Canetti, p.23.

a gazelle to him on their own accord. Exactly this is what happens among humans: from the condition of their mass fear derives religious sacrifice." In Ehrenreich's words: "We are still handling things as if we were prey."[900] Already in groups of hominids the fallen one, this poor guy, is mourned as he deserves – at him the Mighty One had aimed – and the gratefulness of reverent mourning joins the joyful relief of survival. From now on, whenever survival depended from the heavenly power's benevolence, sacrifice was scheduled: For good spring weather after a hard winter, some *sacre du printemps*; for good winds when Greek warriors sail to Troy, some virgin; and when the king of Moab is trapped in his fortress, he burns his son on the wall, successfully – since after the boy's death "there was great indignation in [or against] Israel, so they withdrew from him" (2 Kings 3:27).

Paul's myth, with the divine Power appeasing itself and releasing mankind by human-divine sacrifice, is to Maccoby "a powerful version of a means of exorcising guilt that had been practiced by mankind since Neolithic times". Paul's regression apparently corresponded to old and powerful human dispositions, too powerful for "a revolutionary religion that attempted to eschew both human and divine sacrifice, and sought to lay moral responsibility on the community itself and on the individuals who compose it".[901]

B. However, the stroken one for whom the ruler had it – let's call him our Reliever – is important also for relieving guilt feelings when the survivors cut into foreign flesh themselves. The following passage of Canetti exposes why crucifixes hang above dinner tables and in Bavarian butcher's shops, while the Lamb with cross banner stands in the crest of German butcher guild: "The hunt- and chase-mob absolves itself as mourning mob. As persecutors the human beings have been living, and as persecutors they continue living in their way ever. They search for foreign flesh and they cut into it and they feed on the weak creatures' torment. In their eye the victim's breaking eye is reflected, and the last scream on which they feast trenches deeply in their soul. Maybe most of them don't sense that along with their body they feed the darkness in themselves. But guilt and angst within themselves increase incessantly, and so they unwittingly yearn for redemption. Hence they attach themselves to someone who dies for them, and in the mourning for him they feel as persecuted ones themselves. Whatever they have done, however they have raged, for this moment they put themselves on the side of suffering. It is a sudden and far-bearing change of parties. It relieves them of the accumulated guilt of killing and of the angst that death will hit themselves. Whatever they have done to others, all this now another one takes onto himself; and by adhering to him trustily and unreserved they will, so they do hope, escape revenge ... It runs out that the religions of mourning are indispensable to the psychic economy of human beings, as long as they cannot forgo the killing in mobs."[902]

---

900 Canetti, p.56 (up to "offered to the danger") and 343; Ehrenreich: Hart/Sussman, p.83.
901 Maccoby 1992, p.12-13.
902 Canetti, p.158-161.

In this view the crucifix has, besides of the oedipal meaning of the sacri-ficed son and the appeasement of the power that threatens with death, a third psycho-physical effect: The crucified lamb relieves the meat-eater from his dimly felt blood-guilt, fulfilling the same function which "sanctifying" slaughter rituals exercise in Islam and Judaism. "The angst that death will hit themselves" shows up, for instance, in a superstitious ritual by which some retrodox Jews until today run afoul to the atonement day of Yom Kippur. A rooster (in case of women a hen) is swung three times above the head of the person, while one recites: "This is my exchange, my substitute, my atonement. This rooster (this hen) shall go to its death, but I shall go to a good, long life, and to peace."[903] Then the condemned animal is donated to needy people who have it slaughtered. The delayed ritual of sacrifice came up around the eighth century CE – that is, 700 years after the Jews had abandoned animal sacrifice – in the ambience of Christian Europe. Called *"Kappores schlagen"* in Yiddish idiom and *Kapparot* in Hebrew, this eery *his-blood-upon-me* rite found metaphorical expression in the *Rotwelsch* idiom of German vagrant population where the phrase *"Du wirst gehen kappores"* signified "You are done, going down". Apropos down: The vocabulary of this *Rotwelsch* jargon is by thirty percent of Hebrew-Yiddish origin because, in disaccord to proverbial Jewish wealth, before 1780 estimated "sixty to seventy-five percent" of Germany's Jews belonged to this lowest ten-percent stratum of vagrant marginals.[904] The background of the "Beating Kappores" is no less power-laden. In the psychic background of this ritual lurks a God who wants to kill – if not you, then but the animal. At this low point of religious imagination, a killer-god can be enticed by a bait animal in order to have Him sidetracked from oneself – according to the mentioned ethics-free maxim: Better you suffer, and die, than I.

Leon Festinger coined the term of "cognitive dissonance", meaning the discomforting inconsistence between two contradictory behaviors practiced simultaneously. Caring for pets and chewing pig-meat; caressing children with big eyes and eating lambs with equally big innocent eyes; imputing maternal feelings to she-goats but frying their kids: these are strident dissonances, rather muffled than harmonized by holy sacrifice. The function of animal sacrifice "ranks among the most misunderstood points in the Bible", Richard E. Friedman remarks from within a modern civilization of industrialized slaughter and of meat portions that are just as shrink-wrapped and deep-frozen as the consumers' willingness to see the background reality. Richard Friedman admits that in the world of Torah most animal sacrifices served eating. Nevertheless, the psychic background of these rituals ap-parently was "the conviction that humans should recognize that they destroy life if they wanted to eat meat. For them this was not a simple act of the profane daily life. It was a sacred act, performed by a commissioned person (a priest) at an altar."[905]

903 Schwartz 2011, p.313.
904 Gerber, Barbara, p.63, quoting Jacob Toury, Der Eintritt der Juden ..., p.145-414.
905 Friedman, Richard E., p.119.

Abraham took his son from the altar and put the ram on it. Paul put God's son on the altar, and since this sacrifice was virtual, the Lamb's flesh became virtual in the plant-based, sin-free host, this last souvenir of the sacrificed vegetarian. Since "Christ, our Passover Lamb, has been sacrificed" (I Cor 5:7) above in lofty spirit, the fleshly animal beneath could slip into unworthiness: Pauline tradition emphasized the Holy Spirit as opposed to sinful flesh; by the divine gift of soul man belonged to the spiritual category – high above those soulless animals in the lower realm of matter. Why should soulless beings escape from what the world principle exacted so visibly from the highest (hanging) human being: to suffer, die and offer his flesh as food? Why should they be spared from what was exacted so visibly by a Western world principle "defined as a Father who revealed himself most fully by imposing the cross not only on his Son, but on all creation"?[906]

Since Paul offered relief for the meat-eaters' guilt feelings by and through identifying with God's slaughtered Holy Lamb, he easily could claim that God does not care for oxen (I Cor 9:9) and Christians must not care about what meat they eat (I Cor 10:25). Western culture's relation to animals was shaped by Paul's first letter to Corinth. Consequently, while all verses of the Jewish Bible that somehow point to animal rights were overlooked by the Church Fathers, their master mind Thomas Aquinas, starting from the Torah's sixth commandment "You shall not kill", arrives at conclusions which deny to animals the dignity granted by Torah: "No one commits a sin by using a thing to what it is destined for ... Animals and plants don't have the life of reason by which they could lead their lives, but due to their natural drives they always are quasi 'lived' by someone else. This signifies that they by nature are destined to serve for and get used by other beings."[907]
Mainly two passions dominated the life of Dominican monk Thomas: to study and to eat. Allegedly, from his writing desk a semi-circular segment had to be cut out for convenience.[908] However, this-worldly obesity was nothing special among clerics. In 1500, the Benedictine monks of Westminster Abbey consumed 7,735 calories per day. This diet included, according to Oxford historian Barbara Harvey, up to three pounds of meat per lunch, which makes the rate of one gallon of beer (4.5 litres) per day and monk understandable.[909] I mention these data only to shed light on the motives of meat-friendly priestly castes in all religions. No one has articulated these motives more clearly than church father Clement of Alexandria: "Sacrifices were invented by men to be a pretext for eating flesh."[910] Universally, all pre-Christian world religions showed a tendency to start with animal-friendly primal narrations and to decline, once the cult was established, into flesh-friendly systems favorable to the priestly castes which called the shots

906 Carroll, p.277.
907 Thomas Aquinas, Summa Theologica (cited by Linnemann 2000, p.43-44).
908 Weischedel, p.90.
909 Paul Beckett: "Eat Pounds of Meat, Drink Gallons of Ale, and Be a Very Merry Monk." In: Wall Street Journal, November 23, 1994, p.1 (Berry 1998, p.213).
910 Clemens of Alexandria: On Sacrifices, book VII (Berry 1998, p.193).

and changed the texts. In Judaism, the priestly writers inserted their boring texts of sacrifice and privilege mainly into Leviticus and Numbers. These texts prohibited sacrifice outside the temple of Jerusalem (centralization) and restricted the priestly profession to the Levites (monopolization). At the same time the sacral service "animal sacrifice" was offered in no less than six different products (diversification), ranging from burned/food/sin/ guilt offering to the offering of ordination and the sacrifice of well-being (Leviticus 7:37).[911]
But there was also another worldwide tendency, one of rebellion against the transformation of Gods into grill-gourmets and their temples into slaughterhouses. Around 600 BCE, when Jeremiah (8:8) asked: "How can you say we are wise, we have God's law? Actually it is falsified by the lying pen of scribes"; when Aristophanes satirized the friends of animal sacrifice in his drama "The Birds" and the Pythagoreans formed a vegetarian school of philosophy, in India the Jains rebelled against the well-fed Brahmins, in China the Taoists and Buddhists spoke out against the sacrifice-friendly authoritarian state religion of Confucius, while in the promised land of milk and honey the prophets bashed the Levite establishment that had turned the temple into a high volume slaughter center flushing with blood and meat, urine and last feces. How could a sensitive, impulsive, *rebelligious* man like Jesus have stayed passive with all this? Ernest Renan, in the first biography of Jesus that treated him as a man rather than a god, declared that Jesus was an Essene (i.e. vegetarian) who "sought the abolition of sacrifices that had caused him so much disgust" since "the worship he had conceived for his Father had nothing in common with scenes of butchery."[912]

The usual torturers

During the Passover week anno domini 1451, the Jews on the island of Crete were accused by a nun named Orsa of "having crucified a lamb, for the mockery of Jesus, on Holy Friday". As Crete was under Venetian dominion, nine notables of the Jewish community were placed in shackles, shipped in chains to Venice, where they docked after a 49-day voyage and were thrown into prison, separated from each other. Two of the prisoners died as a result of torture, while the survivors remained in custody awaiting the decisions of the Major Council of Venice, which met on Saturday, July 15, 1452. Whereas the investigation of the inquisitor had yielded that the Jews had used to crucify a suckling lamb each year before Easter, to everyone's great surprise the defendants were absolved, with 220 votes in favor, 130 against and 80 "not convinced", i.e., abstaining; on August 9 following, the defendants were re-leased and left Venice. They landed in Candia (Crete) after a 13-day voyage and were joyfully received by the entire Jewish community on the island.[913]

---

911   Cf. Friedman, R.E., particularly p.132-133, 222-227 and 259.
912   Renan, Ernest: The Life of Jesus. New York, undated, p.173 and 169 (Berry 1998, p.193).
913   Toaff, Ariel: Blood Passover [Original title: Sangue di Pasquoa]. The Jews of Europe and Ritual Murder. Complete English text translated by Gian Marco Lucchese and Pietro

Remarkably, the accusation had suspected that "maybe because faithful boys could not be captured" the Jews had crucified lambs. Four centuries later, in 1893, Jewish ritual murder of animals was subject of a referendum in Switzerland. Initiated by the Swiss Union for Animal Protection, the referendum against ritual slaughter became a plain issue of sound popular feeling, of *gesundes Volksgefühl*. The seventy scientific defenders of ritual slaughter were discredited as callous vivisectionists, being *"rabbinisch"* in their scholarship and having been paid for their expert statements by the Jews. The Swiss animal welfarists combined three popular images of un-christian cruelty – King of Jews, ritual slaughter, ritual murder – in a cartoon that showed King David slitting the throat of Goliath Schweizervolk. Distinctly more cultivated Weinländer Gazette offered freedom of choice: "If the Jews are not content with the meat that Christians have to eat, they can leave." The referendum was successful due mainly to the voters in the cantons closest to Germany, and Jewish butchers now had to import their kosher meat from German Reich.[914]

In Norway, anti-shechitah legislation was adopted in 1929, and similar to Switzerland, the Agrarian Party newspaper *Nationen* had suggested that if Jews were not content with the meat of animals "slaughtered in good Norwegian fashion, they should leave Norway". Exempted from the ban of killing animals without preceding stunning was the "Danish-American" method of killing pigs by gouging a hole in the heart of the animal hoisted by its hind leg. Exempt was also the method (argued to be "gruesome" by Christian Norwegians) which the Lapps used to kill their reindeer, involving 15,000 head of Santa Claus' draft animals a year, compared to 300 cattle killed according to shechita. "We have no obligation", proclaimed one Agrarian Party member, "to expose our domestic animals to the cruelty of the Jews; we did not invite the Jews to this country, and we are under no obligation to supply the Jews with animals for their religious orgies."[915]

In Germany, the law forbidding ritual slaughter adopted one day after Hitler's 44th birthday, on April 21, 1933, can hardly be separated from Reich Secretary of Propaganda Joseph Goebbels' aim to give Hitler the image of a selflessly dedicated, ascetic animal lover and vegetarian. None of his other-wise slavishly obeying Aryans followed the Führer in this diet, but Goebbels' imaging was successful enough that still today, and well in line with Godwin's Law ("As a discussion grows longer, the probability that someone makes a comparison with Hitler approaches 100 percent") the veget-Aryan mass murderer is thrown in as the trumping joker whenever a debate touches the relation of meat and human ethics.

Just to settle the issue: Actually some of the "most virulent forms of anti-Semitism" in Imperial Germany (ending in 1919) have been propagated by "reform of life movements, vegetarians, antivivisectionists, back-to-nature-

Gianetti, 2007, p.49-54. bloodpassover.com/index1.htm. (Note: The website and probably the translaters are anti-Jewish and gratefully view Toaff's work (which the author withdrew quickly from the market) as a proof for the historical reality of Jewish ritual murder).
914 Michael F. Metcalf in Kalechofsky 1992, p.117.
915 Quotations in this passage from Metcalf, Michael F., in: Kalechofsky 1992, p.114-133.

cults".[916] In fact Hitler at times kept a meatless diet in order to alleviate his intense sweating, his embarrassing flatulence and his stomach aches, while continuing to take the pills of pulverized bull testicles his quack gave him for other ailments. And if his favorite dishes, such as Bavarian white sausages and liver dumplings, pork ham and stuffed pigeon are vegetarian and also the roasted game *Herr Wolf* did not disdain, then the man who shortly after January 1933 prohibited all vegetarian societies was a real veggie.[917] Concerning his kindness to animals, young Hitler's Munich short-term date Maria Reiter had a strong experience when during a walk in the evening Adolf's dog attacked her own dog: "Hitler raised his whip and lashed. One, two, three lashes, again and again, like a madman. He whipped and kicked this dog like his father had whipped and kicked. The dog yelped. Minutes before, Hitler had told me that the dog is his truest friend and he couldn't live without him. And now he seized the animal on its collar and almost shaked it dead. When Hitler had calmed down, I asked him: 'How can one be that brutal, beating one's dog this way?' – 'This was necessary', Hitler replied. With this, for him the issue was settled."[918]

Indeed, Hitler owed his part-time vegetarianism to the influence of another great artist with whom Hitler shared the propensity to sudden volcanic outbursts including "tiger-like leaps" as well as the terrible suspicion of being a Jew's offspring: Hitler's favorite composer Richard Wagner. "This violent character could not see a bird in a cage; a cut flower made him grow pale, and when he found a sick dog in the street, he took it home." With these words Wagner was described by his leading French apostle Edouard Schuré; the maestro himself disclosed to Mathilde Wesendonck what he had suffered as an adult ear-witness of the slaughter of a chicken: "The terrible scream of the animal, and the pitiful weaker wailing during the act of violence, entered my soul with horror." Contrarily, Wagner rejoiced on the death of his former sponsor, the composer Giacomo Meyerbeer (Jakob Liebmann Meyer Beer) in 1864, and showed no regret when 800 visitors died in a fire during a performance of composer Jacques Offenbach (son of cantor Isaac Ben-Juda Eberst) in the Ringtheater of Vienna in 1882. While in this data I gratefully rely on Léon Poliakov, my analysis of vegetarian Jew-hate and anti-vivisectionist anti-Judaism is much shorter than Poliakov's attempt "to bare the final sources of anti-Semitic passion" by examining Wagner's case.[919]

First, I state that ethical vegetarians assumably are people with above-average sensitivity. By this reason, second, they are affected above-average by the crucifix. And third, this primary impression of a fixing "Jewish" cruelty is transferred to, charged and incited anew by every experience of cruelty towards animals fixed in cages, hoisted by the butcher or pinned down by the

---

916   Poliakov 2003, Vol.IV, p.20, quoting Paul Massing, Rehearsal for Destruction. A Study of Political Anti-Semitism in Imperial Germany, New York 1949, p.75.
917   Langer, p.266 (bull testicles); Patterson, Charles, p.152-153; Waite, p.19 and 25-26; cf. Berry 2004, p.58-60.
918   Peis, Günter: "Hitlers unbekannte Geliebte"; in: Stern (weekly), No.24/1959, p.28, quoted by Schaake.
919   Poliakov 2003, Vol.III, p.431-442 and 462.

vivisector – reminding the lamb on cross. As sons of unloved fathers whom they both suspected to have been Jewish, both Hitler and Wagner had a particularly strong compassion with this Holy Lamb that an unsparing father had delivered to Jewish hangmen. Listen to how Wagner tried to substitute Wotan for the Christian God-Son: "For in him was found the striking likeness to Christ himself, the Son of God, that he too died, was mourned and avenged – as we still avenge Christ on the Jews of today."[920] In Wagner's *Parsifal* which Hitler called the "key-opera par excellence", the essential requisits are the Holy Spear that pierced Jesus on the cross and the chalice called Holy Gral that collected his dripping blood. With every new unveiling of the Gral that gives energy to the whole knighthood, the never-healing wound of King Amfortas breaks open again, being curable only "by the spear that bate it". With this spear the hero Parsifal makes the cross sign that destroys the hateful schemer Klingsor together with his machinations. In the end the same spear is to "cure the wound of King Amfortas, whom Wagner invested with all his anxieties", while the seductive female Kundry sinks down lifelessly, redeemed now from her guilt of having laughed at Jesus carrying his cross to Golgotha. We may suppose that Wagner tried to cure primarily his own energy-supplying "conflict of early childhood" by re-enacting the mind-piercing myth of Christ's Passion but also by describing his young hero Parsifal as "knowing by compassion, the chaste fool" and turning the Last Supper into "a sort of vegetarian banquet".[921] Pondering on Parsifalian mythematics since 1845 and making the first rough-draw in 1857, the empathic child Wagner (1813-1883) indeed composed a veritable key-opera, focusing on the impact of cruelty Kierkegaard had described in 1850: "For this the child *Richard* would have determined inwardly for later on when he'd grown up: to smash to pieces all those *scheming Klingsor* people who had behaved so wickedly against the one man full of love, against whom they had shouted "crucify him, crucify him!""

This sensitive child who for decades had demanded the departure from meat consumption and vivisection but became a vegetarian only in the wisdom of his old age, in his revulsion at Jewish cruelty to animals accords with the following two omnivore contemporaries:

"Boys and Girls! Look back once more to ... the world war. One single people remained victorious in this dreadful war, a people of whom Christ said their father is the devil. Boys and Girls! If one tells you that once the Jews have been a chosen people, don't believe it! ... A chosen people does not slay and torture animals to death. Boys and girls! For you we've taken upon us scoff and revilement and became fighters against the Judenvolk, against this world-wide organization of criminals against whom yet Christ has struggled, the greatest anti-Semite of all times."[922]

920 Wagner, Die Nibelungen. Wagner's Prose Works, London 1897 (by Poliakov 2003/III, p.435).
921 Poliakov 2003, Vol.III, p.452-455; de.wikipedia.org/wiki/Parsifal.
922 Michael, p.175, quoting the English edition of Hilberg 1982, p.12; cf..German ed., p.21.

295

This was, in his Nuremberg speech of June 22, 1935, the same Julius Streicher who referred to the holocaust as "Jewish punishment for Golgotha".[923]
At the same time, the renowned Italian writer Giovanni Papini depicted even
more graphically how the ritually slaughtering Jews fuse with the Jews who
nailed the Holy Lamb in cross-fixed imaginations: "Look, in the hangman's
hand the nails are gleaming", Papini has the Jews at Golgotha rejoice in the
rough metal spikes. "Their blaze is more agreeable to our eyes than all the
pearls with which the daughters of Zion adorn themselves at the holidays.
Listen, the hammer knocks: the sound is music to our ears, more pleasant
even than the sounds of psaltry ... our eyes gloat over the blood of this blas-
phemer! If we yet delight to see the sacrificing priest sinking his knife into
the throats of lambs, how much may we rejoice today, observing how those
idolaters nail their victim onto the gallows!"[924]
Jesus' nails, the *shochet*'s knife and Herod's lambs in Bethlehem: this chain
of images yielded imaginations of Jewish *ritual* murder – the term *ritual*
itself yet reminding archaic, prescribed procedures, stubbornly repeated for
a sacrificing Godhead's sake.
However, exactly the ritualization must be rated as a Jewish attempt to pre-
define the killing of animals in the most painstaking, pain avoiding way.
The quick and smooth cut through windpipe, gullet and all brain-supplying
arteries with a sharpest possible knife was for millennia doubtless the least
painful and fastest stunning method, perhaps less cruel than electric tongs,
gas gondolas or bolt guns of today. The latter, rather gruesome method I had
to watch several times during my apprenticeship on an organic milk farm.
With German thoroughness, the butcher's apprentice induced a wire into the
hole he had shot on the calf's forehead and stirred his brain, thus avoiding
problems of the kind US meat inspector Luther Johnson points to: "I've seen
them put twenty to twenty-five holes in a hog's head trying to knock her
and she was still on her feet. Her head looked like Swiss cheese." The other
stunning option, electric shocks without preceding stunning, belongs to the
most dreadful torture methods. The fact that slaughterhouses have to cope
with an extremely high rate of staff turnover is a hopeful sign: Most humans
are too sensitive to do this job for a long time. "Every sticker I know carries
a gun", the sticker Van Winkle told Gail Eisnitz, "and every one of them
would shoot you. Most stickers I know have been arrested for assault. A lot
of them have problems with alcohol. They have to drink, they have no other
way of dealing with killing live, kicking animals all day long."
In German vocational schools the "butcher classes" are the nightmare of
many teachers, since according to the shirker motto "Let George do it" and
Brecht's angry "I order a steak and the brute of a butcher kills an ox" the
profession of butcher is viewed as menial and defiling in most cultures –
except the Jewish, where the office of *shochet* requires high mental quali-

---

923 Michael, p.174, quoting A. Roy Eckardt: Your People, My People, p.24.
924 Isaac, p.445; Papini (1881-1956) after a Church-critical phase returned to Catholicism
in 1921. In 1942 he became the vice president of European Writers Association (Europäische
Schriftsteller-Vereinigung), founded on Goebbels' instigation in Weimar (Wikipedia).

fications and in eastern European shtetls often ranked in reputation equal to a cantor or even a rabbi. Knowing that one who feels despised will be inclined to despise the living beings he is concerned with, the sanctification of slaughter and the high respect for persons charged with kosher slaughtering were Judaism's two attempts to safeguard respect for animals condemned to death.

Contrarily, US meat packing plants, where "a shackler out there don't have no choice but to hang hogs alive in order to keep his job and everything else go smooth" (sticker Nathan Price); where the hoisted cattle "go wild" when the legger cuts off their legs; where workers suffer a six times higher risk of injury or illness than workers in a coal-mine and risk their job when they go to the bathroom; where "at the end of the line" the slaughtered animals "are no cleaner than if they had been dipped in a toilet"; these streamlined plants indeed are "reminders of a system that places nearly as little value on human life as it does on animal life."[925]

The hanging and heaving of living corpuses – "Running a meat hook through the rabbit's leg muscle and sometimes into bone" – is completely legal although some rabbits are fully conscious when they get hanged this way "because rabbits are classified as poultry by USDA and are therefore excluded from Humane Slaughter Act enforcement." – "Nobody likes to see animals hung up alive, but Tim 's too sensitive to the animals' suffering", Ronnie criticised his former co-worker whose whistleblowing about cattle skinned alive had got things rolling. "In the morning the big holdup was the calves ... As soon as they start going in, you start shooting, the calves are jumping, they're all piling up on top of each other. You don't know which ones got shot ... and you forget to do the bottom ones. They're hung anyway, and down the line they go, wriggling and yelling" (stunner Alberto Cabrera). "Okay, when they turn their heads around when they're hanging upside down and they look at you, I guess that's one way you can tell they're alive. See, once they regain consciousness they start bellowing. They're hanging there going Oooaaah!" (Ken, beef-kill-knocker). Quoting the "second-legger" Ramon Moreno, the Washington Post headlined: "They die piece by piece".[926] "Limb by limb, exhaling life drop by drop": this is how Seneca described crucifixion.

But should we compare the two cruelties? The first one happens when stunning fails, the second is fully intentional; the first one's purpose is meat, the second one's terror; the still alive animals hang in slaughterhouses in eyesight of tough adult males many of whom don't stand it for long; the still alive man is inevitably put before the eyes of European schoolkids.

To finish with words of compassion: Larry once got a light stroke from the electric prod his co-worker used to drive the animals onward: "Holy shit does that hurt ... Even a hog don't deserve that". In spite of which heinous crimes the hog had committed and got the chair for?

---

925 Eisnitz, p.200; 266; 128; 271-272; 275; 169.
926 Joby Warrick, Washington Post, April 10, 2001; Tuttle, p.171.

Anyhow, Gail Eisnitz gratefully remembers "more than two dozen Latino employees, among the most courageous people I've ever known. They all signed sworn affidavits describing how, for decades, they had been forced to skin and dismember hundreds of thousands of fully conscious, live cows at the beef plant owned by the largest meat producer in the world."[927]
Day by day, thousands of "stunned" animals get skinned this way: fully conscious but invisible. "If slaughterhouses had glasswalls ...", the vegan Paul McCartney muses. For pity comes from pictures.
Particularly if the slaughterers are Jewish: When the vegan Brazilian website Olhar Animal (eye for animals) reported an action of radical right-wing Israelis for reintroduction of temple sacrifice, displaying the photo of an unsuspecting kid carried by a notorious grandson of racist rabbi Meir Kahane dressed in the old white priestly garb of Cohanim, one Theophilo Gomes commented: "As to those wretched ones who tolerate the butchering of Palestinians I'm not surprised they regress to such idiotic practices that involve sacrifice. These people seem to enjoy viewing bloodshed. Should we have to admit that Hitler was right?"
And an animal lover with the fitting name Lion Wolf applauded via facebook: "*Exatamente*, as I always thought, in my view he was *totalmente* right in decimating those poor miserables."
Posted on April 23, 2016, the first day of Jewish Passover.

Fending off compassion
"For our paschal lamb has been sacrificed, Christ": Paul's "animalization" of crucified Jesus (1 Cor 5:7) is inspired by Isaiah (53:7) who compares the suffering servant with a "sheep being led to slaughter". But what drives Paul to morph the son of a God who yet doesn't care for oxen now into a lamb? Since Paul identified with this son of God the father, how tenderly must we assume Paul's father cared for his child?
Ducklings, chicken, calves, foals, puppies, kittens or kids – are there young animals whose child-like charm awakes protective instincts more disarmingly than lambs? Anyhow, for more than thousand years western exploitation of animals developed under the image of a tortured human being called Holy Lamb, nailed on beams but numb because it's wooden.
Doubtlessly the reification of animals in occidental culture has much to do with technical rationality and the factual constraints of capitalist markets. But where does the factual and allegedly rational view of animals as soulless objects root? Is this reification of sentient beings a genuine sprout of the "absolute nullity of the animal" Schopenhauer held against Christendom and which is a doubtless aspect of New Testament? Is it an aspect of Jesus, too? As an opponent of animal sacrifice, he hardly can be imputed with having tried to devalue animals by a pattern of argumentation à la "how much worth are you than animals". But the gospels had this effect since Paul had

---

927 Eisnitz p.31 (Tim), 43 (Albert), 129-130 (Ken), 299 (Washington Post), 311, 124 (Larry) and 295 (Eisnitz herself).

built Greek body-soul duality into his transformation of Jesus, and thus into the human-animal relation of Christendom. "We see and hear by their cries", Augustine explained, "that animals die with pain, although man disregards this in a beast, with which as not having a rational soul, we have no community of rights."[928]

In his distinction between insensate fruit plants, unreasoning animals and rational man, Thomas Aquinas refers to Augustine and Aristotle: "On grounds of divine order the life of plants and animals is being maintained, but not for themselves but for man. Therefore Augustine says: 'By the thoroughly just order of the creator life and death of these beings are at our disposal.'"[929]

This power of disposal gets absolutized when René Descartes' (1566-1650) views the animal as a soulless "clockwork of wheels and springs", whose sounds must be taken as seriously as those of the wooden bird shouting out of a cuckoo clock. Francis Bacon (1561-1626), a contemporary of Descartes and Spanish Inquisition, called for an "inquisition of nature". Scientific knowledge of natural things, Bacon says, is best elicited with "nature under constraint and vexed; that is to say, when by art and the hand of man she is forced out of her natural state, and squeezed and molded".[930] In his "New Atlantis" he describes in 1627 the progressive civilization on the Island Bensalem in Pacific Ocean. Here Bacon anticipates submarines, flying machines, laser beams, the telephone, hearing aids, and artificial flavoring for food. In the island's cultural centre called "Salomon's house" a man who is both priest and scientist explains: "We have also parks, and inclosures of all sorts of beasts and birds, which we use not only for view or rareness, but likewise for dissections and trials; that thereby we may take light what may be wrought on the body of man ... We try also all poisons and other medicines upon them, as well of chirurgery as physic." Summarizing the influence of Bacon, who allegedly was related to the Rosicrucians, Brian Klug states that "secular science was conceived in a Christian crucible". In order to "take lightly what may be wrought *on the body of man*", in Bacon's science "the inquisition of nature and of animals proceeds apace; and we have ways of making them talk."

Bensalem culture excels by three traits: good and happy people, established scientific research and – it's Christian. The liberating faith came to the island in form of a small ark containing the holy Bible. How? Disarmingly Bacon mixes Noah, Moses, exodus and Jesus: The small ark was all that could be found when one night the boats went out to approach to a strange phenomenon: "At sea a pillar of light was seen, bearing upon it a large cross also formed of light."[931] The light of western science, or just the pillar dominating Bacon's mind?

Since his era, among the students of all disciplines particularly the future physicians – whose professional work depends on their ability to empathize

928 Young (p.137) quoting from Augustine: On the Morals of the Manichaeans, 17:59 (see full text on newadvent.org).
929 Augustine, Summa Theologica, quoted by Linnemann 2000, p.43-44.
930 Bacon, Francis: New Atlantis, III, 29 (quoted by Klug, p.282).
931 Brian Klug in Kalechofsky 1992, p.264-279; and in Klug, p.277.

– were taught in this scientifixed crucible to repress inhibiting compassion. The famous Professor Magendie (1783-1855) performed deliberately cruel experiments to prove that "the sentimental instincts" were extinct in him to the degree which he believed was "necessary".[932] Carl Jung (1875-1961) noted in his student diary that he was sickened by a vivisection experiment in lecture hall and vowed never to go again: "Horrible, barbarous and above all unnecessary." Concentration camp physicians like Dr.med.Dr.phil. Mengele (1911-1979) had learned the skills they applied in experiments on humans – including children – in vivisection of animals.

A quite different Christian physician – the famous Albert Schweitzer (1875-1965) – once compared European moral philosophy to "a housewife who, having cleaned the living room, makes sure that the door is closed so the dog won't dare to come in and blemish the done work by the traces of his paws. Thus the European thinkers keep watch that no beasts would run across their ethics."[933] The housewife metaphor has some involuntary irony insofar as the dominant thinkers, vivisectors and Lager doctors were generally male. And not too accidentally this *nature* that should be kept *under constraint and vexed, that is to say, when by art and the hand of man she is forced out of her natural state, and squeezed and molded* – this *natura* is female.

Whereas Carol Adams in 1990 stated a "direct relationship between child and animal abuse, and woman-battering and animal abuse"[934] one year later Luise Schottroff in "Dictionary of Feminist Theology" pointed to another connection: "Continuing the charge ... that the preaching of the cross serves the oppression of humans, feminist critique works out the specifically wo-men-oppressive character of cross theologies: The image of God projects the despotic patriarchal father into heaven. Redemption happens by sacrifice, enforcing the societal demand on women to sacrifice themselves for fami-ly."

In 2002, Regula Strobel in the Dictionary's second edition criticizes the concept of sacrifice in general: "Doesn't the idea that one gets sacrificed for the sake of others imply an anticipation and justification of a behavior that today is paying the costs of our wealth with the death of thousands in so called Third World countries?" With this theology of "instrumentalizing the son for the salvation plans of God ... a sadistic, sacrifice-addicted image of God ... and eventually divine child abuse is being promulgated." Even those interpretations of the cross that emphasize divine solidarity foster the acceptance of violence." Christa Mulack's judgement is rigorous: "For me he wouldn't have had to die!"[935]

Neither did he save animals from crucifixion.

Was the cultural sphere of crucifixes just by coincidence the region where animals were nailed on boards by their four paws for scientific reasons?[936] Until today, test animals get fixed by their four paws to prevent them from

932 Brian Klug in Kalechofsky 1992, p.286.
933 albert-schweitzer-stiftung.de/tierschutzinfos/zitate-von ... /philosophiekritik.
934 Adams, p.20.
935 Three feminist voices: Gunda Schneider-Flume in Zimmemann/Annen, p.164-167.
936 Rosenfield, Leonarda Cohen, cited by Kalechofsky 2006, p.37.

rubbing the chemical test solutions out of their aching eyes, somehow reminding the crucified victims in Mel Gibson's Passion movie who are prevented by nails from protecting their eyes against the satanic raven's sharp beak. The parallel is sixfold. (1) Both animal testing and salvific crucifixion base on the principle of vicarious suffering. Animal testing and crucifix coincide in three coordinates: (2) *Fixing* and (3) *torment* bring (4) *healing* for mankind's sins and ailments: Add (5) to this the side effect of splitting off: The same splitting apart of emotion from rational function that Bacon and Magendie deemed necessary for scientists and physicians, the same busy overlooking of pain is being trained by crucifixes above dinner tables, school blackboards and conjugal beds. "Once I saw in a bedroom the cross above the pillow", Shoah survivor Andermann remarked, "and didn't understand how one could sleep with the hanged one over him. Didn't he hear his cries of pain before falling asleep and in his dreams?"[937] And the man with crown of thorns meets the monkey with brain electrodes in (6) the perspective of necessity: The credo of animal testing necessary for the health of mankind and the credo of the Lamb's cross necessary for healing mankind – these two diverge but at the very end: When "it is finished", the son of monkey ends up in the waste bin, the son of man in heaven.

Impious? Absolutely! Or where's the piety concerning God's creatures in the laboratory's waste bin? Where was this piety when "they nailed poor animals up on boards by their four paws to vivisect them and see the circulation of the blood which was a great subject of controversy" as Nicholas Fontaine wrote in 1738?[938]

Almost hundred years and thousands of paws later, impious Cardinal John Henry Newman in 1842 preached a sermon that begins with the biblical metaphor of Christ as the Lamb of God and points out how Christ is identified with the unprotected, defenseless and vulnerable. Newman went on to argue that there is something "Satanic" in the infliction of suffering upon innocents and claimed that the suffering inflicted upon innocent creatures is morally equivalent to the suffering inflicted upon Christ himself. "Think then, my brethren, of the suffering inflicted upon brute animals and you will gain one sort of feeling which the history of Christ's Cross and Passion ought to incite within you."[939] Newman had converted from Anglican to Catholic Church and was suspected here – also due to his theological stance – to be of Jewish descent.

Still seventy years later, shortly before WWI, Pope Pius IX prohibited the foundation of an animal protection society in Rome, because man has no duties concerning animals. Another thirty years later, incidentally at the time when Auschwitz and Treblinka worked at full speed, the otherwise taciturn Pius XII declared that if animals are killed in slaughterhouses and laborato-

---

937 Andermann, p.39.
938 Spiegel, p.65; cf. Peter Singer (2002, p.202) who quotes Voltaire on the same issue of nailing a dog "down to a table and dissect him alive, to show you the mesaraic veins".
939 Cited by Oxford theologian Andrew Linzey in Berry 1998, p.295.

ries, "their screams should not arouse more of unreasonable pity than red-hot iron under the blacksmith's hammer".[940]

This awful enticement to kindness

It sounds like half-hearted pity when Leviticus 22:28 forbids to kill an animal from the flock "on the same day with its young". But quite contrarily to Pius (who also knew Leviticus), Maimonides (1135-1214) took from this verse that there is no difference in this case between the pain of humans and the pain of animals to see their children die, "because the love and tenderness of a mother for her young ones is not produced by reasoning but by feeling, and this faculty exists not only in people but in most living things".[941]

How it exists in children, Warsaw orphanage director Janusz Korczak observed: "The child's clear-sighted mind acknowledges no hierarchies. The child suffers in view of the sweat-dripping worker as well as of the hungry other child, the freight-horse's misery, the beheaded chicken's torture. Dog and sparrow are his kin, butterfly and flower are his friends, pebble and shell his brothers."[942]

Their dismay when children discover how meat is made resembles their reaction to how men have made Jesus suffer. Harvard philosopher Robert Nozick was converted to vegetarianism by his two-and-a-half-year-old daughter. Viewing the Thanksgiving turkey she asked: "This turkey wanted to live. Why was it killed?" One three-year-old vegetarian demanded that he and his mother confront the local marketpersons with the literal truth that they were selling "poor dead mommie and baby animals". Lynn Meyer tells a different passion story that made her a vegetarian yet in her childhood: "It all goes back to a duckling I had when I was a kid. It grew up to be a duck, and then we killed it and cooked it. And I wouldn't eat it. Couldn't. From that, it was all obvious and logical."[943]

In Sigmund Freud's analysis the child seems to adhere to the primitive nefesh concept of the Jewish Bible: "The child's relationship with the animal has much resemblance with that of primitive man. The child still doesn't show any hint of the haughtiness which then makes the adult *kulturmensch* delimitate his own nature by a sharp borderline from all that is animallike."[944] This "advanced" exclusion collides with the principle of universalization Lawrence Kohlberg and Jürgen Habermas postulated for the human sphere: If animals resemble us in feeling and conceiving so much that they fit as ersatz test persons for our pills and social ersatz partners for our psyche, how come we divest them of all rights? If Harsanyi and Rawls ground their ethics on the "veil of ignorance" i.e. of not knowing which role you will pick in the next legal system – how can we condemn a young fellow player in Madame

---

940 Braunstein, p.78.
941 Schwartz 2001, p.22-23.
942 Korczak, O Direito da Criança ao Respeito (The Child's Right to Respect), in: Dallari, p.73.
943 All three stories related by Adams, p.106-107.
944 Freud 1973 (Totem und Tabu), p.131.

Nature's ensemble who by chance entered stage as calve instead of child, to lifelong dark cell confinement on seven square feet of concrete floor – as if s/he had chosen this role?

And our choice? In an amazingly happy coincidence after tens of thousands of years of meat consumption, modern science and technology have enabled us to substitute all materials of animal origin by artificial ones including flesh substitutes that even gourmets will have a hard time to recognize. Lucky we are with this progress coming just in time, since we will have no choice. For an estimated world population of 9.1 billion humans in 2050, the United Nations Environment Programme (UNEP) predicted in May 2014: "Mankind can find alternatives for fossil fuel but not for food: people need to eat. A substantial reduction of the impacts is possible but with a substantial change in nutrition, eliminating products of animal origin."[945] For yet in August 2012 the World Watch Institute estimated the input for the production of a steak with 500 calories at 20,000 calories of fossil energy and 9,500 litres of drinkable water. At that, the steak provides half as much proteins as 500 calories of broccoli.[946] And if the meat-eater after dinner walks home meat powered he consumes more fossil energy per distance than a vegan in a car burning seven litres of gasoline per 100 kilometers.[947] Meat and milk, produced on an 83 percent slice of all cultivable land, give us 18 percent of our calories and 38 percent of our proteins in exchange for 58 percent of our greenhouse gases, more than twice as much as the whole transport sector with all fossil powered ships, planes, vehicles exhales together. If he renounced on a pound of steak just one time, the meat eater would save more water than he spends by daily showers the whole year round. And at that he occupies for his nutrition the agricultural area sufficient to feed 39 vegans much healthier. For now, no vegan saves the world by her nutrition but spares it 1.5 tons of carbon dioxide per year.[948] How much illness would we forgo meatlessly? The ABC of meat&milk related diseases goes from Alzheimer, Botulism and Cancer (60 percent higher risk) to Diabetes, E.coli, Fatness, Gout, Heart diseases (100 percent higher risk), Immuno deficiencies and Kidney diseases, Listeriosis, Multiple Sclerosis, Norovirus, Osteoporosis, Parkinson, Q fever, Rheumatism, Salmonellosis, Trichinosis, Urinary tract diseases, Vibrio infection and Yersiniosis, to end in the wide range of Zoonoses like Aids, Ebola, SARS, avian flu and all the other originally animal diseases 75 percent of which jumped onto man by meat consumption and livestock industry. "Post-antibiotic era" means that along with this we soon will cease to have on hand antibiotics, because their routine application in livestock farming (80 percent of antibiotics production) has bred resistencies.[949] Oops, I left out (in spite of Morbus Wilson)

945 The Guardian, June 2, 2010 (theguardian.com/ … un-report-meat-free-diet).
946 Colb, p.26, referring to Joel Furmann, Eat To Live (2005), p.138.
947 Dr. David Pimentel, Cornell University, bicycleuniverse.info/transpo/energy.html.
948 Quoted from two studies of Oxford University: a) Poore and Nemecek, 2018 (The Guardian, 31.Mai 2018); b) Peter Scarborough, 2014 (New Scientist, June 26, 2014).
949 Health: cf. Greger, passim; antibiotics: Roberts, p.89, 185; Francione, p.19.

the W! Why must, for this Wonderous World of human Wellness, calves be pressed into dark boxes and hens into cage batteries for their whole lives? Why must the testicles and tails of pigs, the beaks of hens and the horns of cattles be cut to prevent the neurotic inmates to hurt other prisoners? Why must pre-fried chicken be bred for breast-meat so intensely that they hardly can walk but yet after 40 days will be grasped at their legs by an exploited migrant worker – few thousand leg-pairs daily – and hanged into a band conveyer that runs straightly to a rotating cutter? Mind you, none of the inmates was ever convicted of any crime or minor infraction.

Contrarily, mankind owes immense gratefulness to animals. Where would we be without them? We needed them for food, sinews, needles, clothes and tents when we were gatherers and hunters; we had them pull the ploughs and carts, extract the minerals and carry our warriors. They were our cultural sponsors by their ivory, their strings for Mozart's violins, their hides for Samba drumheads and Holy Book parchments. Thus animals have helped us to develop our intelligence and sensitivity, or didn't they? And with these two haunting abilities mankind will not escape the two questions whether (1) in our relation to animals might makes right, and whether (2) we in our own interest should, as Suzanne Goldenberg proposed in British daily Guardian, come "until 2050" to drastic changes "at the dinner table".

Take a glass of milk – as example for our conservative bodies: After 8,000 years of humans drinking "silly" cows' maternal milk (nutritionally specialized for calves' needs) still three quarters of mankind, 78 percent of Arabs, 78 percent of Jews, 85 percent of Japanese, 90 percent of Native Americans and Sub-Sahara Africans can stomach lactose only in infancy.[950] Similarly, our hominid bodies remained biologically herbivorous in every aspect. Our well-developed facial muscles, our jaw type and motion, our small mouth opening, the form and order of our incisors as well as our canine and molar teeth, our chewing instead of swallowing type of eating, the chemistry of our saliva and stomach liquids, the length of our small intestine and the structure of our colon, the function of our liver and kidney, our loathing for the smell and sight of corpses: all this proves that our herbivore physics have overcome the carnivore intermezzo unscathed.[951]

Spiritually all "great" religions invest considerable portions of their energies in the philosophical and ritual mastering of human relation to other animals. The vegan turn will have immense impacts on the religions that during the last 200 generations tried in different ways to appease the cognitive dissonance between solidarity with humans and lethal enmity with mostly gentle subhumans. The cleavage between rightless animals and respect deserving humans simply does not work. Leo Tolstoi was sure that "as long as there will be slaughterhouses, there will be battlefields", I.B.Singer declared that "slaughter and justice cannot dwell together", and Leonardo da Vinci

---

950 Felipe, p.160.
951 Cf. Hart/Sussman, chapter 11; The Comparative Anatomy of Eating, by Milton R. Mills, M.D.; michaelbluejay.com/veg/natural.html; Dr.Acosta Navarro at Vegfest Curitiba, September 2013.

prophesied that "time will come when people will look down at the murder of animals just as we today look down at the murder of people."[952] In all probability, we are entitled to expect that renouncing on blood and meat will promote peace and justice – and make exculpation devices abdicable. By all means, mankind should set even more hope in changes of nutrition than in fighting violent myths of sacrifice.

"On the beach there was a man, a model case of unlikeable, bony paper-pusher", my Munich professor of philosophy observed. "When he, with his lame leg, had waded hundred meters into the water he stopped, fished out an insect condemned to death from the waves and carried it back to a bush. Then he hobbled out again and swam into deep water."[953] And if he rescued the animal to feel good himself, what's bad in it? Grusche, the maid and protagonist in Brecht's *Caucasian Chalk Circle* realizes what would happen if she overlooked the abandoned baby of the fat governor; how one who fends off her compassion is bound to go down in a human sense:

> *"Know this, woman: one who doesn't hear a cry for help*
> *But passes by, with deafened ears: nevermore*
> *Will such one hear the lover's low-voiced call,*
> *The blackbird in the morning's dawn,*
> *The sighs of weary vineyard pickers at the chime of angelus."*

In Grusche's case seduction wins to open ears, and Brecht's songster is as brief as Nietzsche in "Be warned about compassion": *"Awful is the enticement to kindness."*
How awful must be the enticement to open our ears for animals that still so few succumb to it? Though it would spare nameless pain, improve the health and social condition of innumerable humans and safeguard better environment for countless generations? And at that would liberate mankind from morbid rituals and symbols of sacrifice which fail to deafen ears, for "the silenced voices are not really silent"?[954]
Concerning this temptation Jesus was literally two millennia ahead of our time. In their "dogmatic vegetarianism", the Ebionites as "real heirs" of real Jesus[955] seem to have viewed the connections as clearly as Max Horkheimer in his metaphor of the skyscraper (written in 1933), viewing on the top "the trust magnates of the different capitalist power groups and at the bottom, "below the spaces where the coolies of this world are perishing per millions, there would be to depict the indescribable, unimaginable suffering of the animals, the hell of animals in human society, the sweat, the blood, the despair of animals."[956]

---

952 Kaplan, p.54 (Leonardo) and p.115 (Tolstoi); Telushkin 1994, p.450 (I.B. Singer).
953 Neuhäusler, p.57.
954 Young, p.33.
955 Schoeps, Hans-Joachim, p.100 and 133.
956 Horkheimer: Dämmerung. Notizen in Deutschland (1931-1934), by Linnemann, p.327.

XIV The Strasbourg Passion
Direction: Silvio Berlusconi

*"At first I thought it was bound to end well," said K., "but now
I have my doubts about it. I don't know how it will end. Do you
know?" – "I don't," said the priest, "but I fear it will end badly.
You are considered guilty. Your case will probably not even go
beyond a minor court."*   Franz Kafka, The Trial

Unfounded fear: The case went up to the European Supreme Court where it
was judged two times and ended very well for Cross and Children! Though
the first judgment was unanimous, 7:0 against, the 17:2 judges of Strasbourg
Court for Human Rights' Grand Chamber on March 18, 2011 legalized obligatory crosses in the continent's classrooms. The Kafkaesque judgement
revealed Europe's uncanny persistence to sacrifice – and even its own legal
culture, if the cross requires. The judgement happened in the city whose
gothic dome juxtaposes a triumphant Ecclesia holding the chalice in her
left and steadying proudly on the cross-staff in her right hand, casting a
withering glance at a bowed down Synagoga with thrice broken lance and
bandaged eyes who lowers and almost drops the parchments of her voided
law. But besides of dropping legal standards, the new process even more
revealingly reenacted the trial related in the gospels – in its outcome as well
as in its cast of roles. As protagonist figured ...

The mannish Roman
Admittedly, his reverence for the cross is not so over-spiritual. But how
should one who considers the following notice about a nightly devotions
meeting in his modest house – reported by a journal not subject to his dic-
tates – call this man impious?
"The men are sitting in a half-circle. A nun comes in, attractive, sexy. She
dances and slowly opens her robe. The men in the Villa Arcore in Milan
enjoy it. Now the nun is naked. Berlusconi takes the crucifix she wears on
her necklace, caresses her breasts and thighs with it. Tenderly he says: 'God
bless you'."
This, as Swiss journalist Heiner Hug relates, was lastly overmuch to the
Catholic Church. As policewomen, stewardesses or nurses with short little
skirts and full cups, okay. As "Prosecutor Ilda Boccassini", occasionally,
why not? As "President Barack Obama" turning sexy round the pole, against
racism, okay! But as a nun?[957]
Of course Nicole Minetti has not yet taken final vows. She was Berlusconi's
dental hygienist or so. In reward for having introduced to the Prime Minister
more than hundred young ladies (including a 17-year-old Moroccan) who
were kept on hand in Milanese luxury apartments, he made Nicole a member

---

957 Heiner Hug, journal21.ch, October 19, 2011.

of Lombardy's Regional Council; no problem with her time schedule since merely once per month, as witness Imane F. declared, "Italy's Dragon" needed his *croce-sulla-pelle-nuda* scene.
The holy cross abused as ...? "Basta", the Vatican now said, "enough with this religious porno". And even "Via Berlusconi!" – Away with him! This was a painful worsening of the "best relationship with the Church" Berlusconi had boasted to have out of all Italian heads of state; sad for the Church, whose silence Berlusconi used to reward with good lines in his media, for instance *pro crocifisso*. The "Cavaliere" thus continued best Roman tradition, achieving in four steps whatever *Buon Gesú* looked forward to:

Pilate's job was just judicial,
to Paul He owed divinization.
Constantine made him official
and Silvio? The must of education!

More precisely: a legal, indefeasible learning object in Europe's classrooms! How come that 15 honest judges turn a 7:0 decision contra classroom crucifixes into a 15:2 home run pro Berlusconi?
Not to convey a false impression: "This is an honest man, write that", Vittorio Mangano, sentenced to twice life in prison for murder, narcotraffic and Mafia activities as Godfather of *Famiglia di Porta Nuova*, assured in 2000, adding: "To me Berlusconi was like a member of the family."
A Turin Court President was told by the honest member in 1996: "Listen, through all these years I had occasion to work in other countries. In France, for instance, the under-the-table-practice is completely current: The market has accepted this ..." When the judge asked him: "What is 200 million? As much as 20,000 Lira are to me?" Berlusconi explained: "Bah! You know ... even lesser than that!"[958]
Two years after the Strasbourg miracle, in March 2013, center-left politician Sergio de Gregorio confessed to have accepted three years before Strasbourg the nice present of three million Euro from *Forza Italia*, just to change sides to Berlusconi's parliamentary alliance: an act of betrayal that led first to the breakdown of Romano Prodi's government in 2008, then to a subsequent electoral victory of Berlusconi's *Forza Italia*, and eventually to his Strasbourg transformation wonder.[959]
Anyhow, Berlusconi doesn't know what's all the fuss about. Bribes are necessary, he says, to make certain deals. Be it with politicians or lawyers or please not too chatty prostitutes, or be it his huge sums for Cosa Nostra between 1974 and 1992: All those payments are by no means indecent, he says, but kind of "commissions".[960]

---

958 Veltri/Travaglio, p.7 (Mangano), 274 and 284 (Turin).
959 zeit.de/politik/ausland/2013-03/berlusconi-gregorio-bestechung.
960 deutsche-wirtschafts-nachrichten.de/2013/02/15/berlusconi-korruption-ist-nicht-unan-staendig-sondern-hilft-der-politik; bribing prostitutes: t-online news, November 29, 2013, referring to a Milan court charge; Cosa Nostra: de.wikipediaorg/wiki/Silvio_Berlusconi, referring to ilfattoquotidiano.it, September 5, 2013.

Let's take the Cavaliere just for a a slightly indecent kind of action artist. Which sado-sexist content of vulgar *nailing* (if not of the symbol itself) does he reveal in stroking below the vagina and above two nipples with a phallic sculpture that very correspondingly is marked by one nail below and two above?

And if Freud is right in stating that "man's self-disclosure transpires from all his pores"[961] – what is it that transpires when a politician legally sentenced for bribing court personal and now attempting to win the Church's favour by making another court legalize the abuse of crucifixes, has the female roles of Justitia and Ecclesia (public prosecutor and nun) in his nightly enactments played by very pliable actresses?

The proxy of Jesus

"The smoke of Satan which invaded the Vatican forty years ago meanwhile seems to have spread in all chambers. Is Pope Benedict still getting enough air to breath in this poisoned atmosphere?"[962] This question was put by La Stampa journalist Andrea Tornielli in German Christian weekly *Christ und Welt* late in 2012, at the end of an article about the scandals around the Bank of Vatican. Tornielli's colleagues of *Deutsche Wirtschafts Nachrichten* (German Economy News) found his smoky metaphor trenchant enough to use it months later headlining the news that Vatileaks affair "for the first time promulgated documents that exposed the Vatican as stronghold of criminal machinations ... The Bank [of Vatican] rates as center of money laundering – for the Mafia, for tax evading wealthy Italians and all others interested in discrete black accounts. Joseph Ratzinger wanted to end this role of the Bank once and for all."[963]

His demission at his own request in the same year 2013 Pope Benedict reasoned with no longer having "sufficient strength for the ministry". In 2009 the Vatican had called the judgment against compulsory classroom crosses "schocking, wrong and myopic" and in March 2011 the Pope had still the strength and air to speak out loudly enough to be heard in Strasbourg, demanding to maintain divine presence "by the cross symbol in private homes as well as in public buildings".[964] This divine presence had always been the Vatican's concern. In April 1897 one Father Ballerini had regretted in the Vatican journal "Civiltá Cattolica" what had happened in the schools of Vienna: "In deference to the offspring of this race ... the effigies of the crucified Christ had to be removed from the walls, lest they might harm the tender feelings of the children of his crucifiers."[965] Nine months later, on January 19, 1898, the journal "La Croix" was pointing at more antique culprits: "You don't have to be a great scholar to understand that this law which ... removes

---

961 Zulliger, p.137.
962 "Der Kirchenstaat steht Kopf", in: Christ & Welt, 23/2012.
963 "Papst-Rücktritt: Vatikan-Bank im Visier der Ermittler", in: Deutsche Wirtschafts Nachrichten, February 14, 2013.
964 Christian Rath, "Sisyphus in Straßburg", taz.de/!76559/, August 19, 2011.
965 Kertzer, p.263.

the Crucifix from hospitals and schools comes from the same Pharisees who underhandedly persuaded people to free Barabbas and to vote for the death of the innocent Jesus."[966]
When not a Pharisee but Bavarian nazi secretary of education Adolf Wagner ordered on April 23, 1941, since "crucifixes are out of place in school" to remove them "gradually", the son of a policeman was 14 years old, and probably more occupied with Jesus' enemies than charming girlfriends. For yet seven years earlier Joseph's mother, herself an illegitimate child and very pious, had tailored for him and his then ten-year-old brother Georg "beautiful paraments", so both future priests could play their favorite game. Paraments are not for playing cops and robbers, nor pirates or cowboys and Apaches, but Holy Mass. Joseph remembers: "We even had compiled sermon booklets and little sermons already. That's always been adventurous also, to accomplish such a thing there." In 1939 the lonesome and eccentric, in his own description "fragile" boy entered the Episcopal seminary which he was to experience as "torture". Now his favorite reading is the "Schott", the Catholic Mass book, and again "it was a captivating adventure to penetrate slowly into the mystery world of liturgy." Which secret is the center of his liturgy? His biographer and former student Christian Feldmann perceives "creatural angst" and abysmal pessimism as thriving forces in Ratzinger's life; Alan Posener discerns a "deficit of hunger for life which leads one to think on early injuries."[967]
The deficit of action and information which Cardinal Ratzinger, as head of Catholic doctrinal commission and subsequently as Pope, displayed concerning injuries of children by abusive clerics worldwide is upsetting. This systemical abuse is causally connected with the cross: by Paul's crucification of the flesh and by the celibate in following the heavenly father's unmarried and childless sacrifice; a celibate that, by estimate of Anselm Bilgri, former prior of famous Bavarian abbey Andechs, one third of the clerics seriously tries to keep chastely while one third lives in homo- and one third in a heterosexual relationships.
And the pedophiles? "7000 trials": So many processes against Catholic clericals the Führer had dropped, Hitler's foreign minister Ribbentrop said on March 11, 1938 in audience with Pius XII. According to the German protocol, the Pope "definitely showed understanding towards these statements of the foreign minister and admitted the mentioned facts straightforward".[968]
70 years later, governmental understanding showed up in Canada where the Church payed 80 million of recompense to the victims of her (state-funded) schools, while the government put up 2,2 billion dollars. Cases of abuse "are subject to papal secrecy", Cardinal Ratzinger on May 18, 2001 wrote to the world's bishops; nine months later his proxy Tarcisio Bertone demanded respect for the "professional secrecy" of priests. By decision of Pope Ratzinger, Bishop Müller of Regensburg, who by cover-up had caused the 22-fold

966   La Croix (January 19, 1898): Wilensky, p.124-125.
967   Posener, p.261-263.
968   Heer 1989, p.366 f.

rape of an altar boy by a previously convicted priest, was put in charge of the henhouse, or better say appointed prefect of Congregation for the Doctrine of the Faith. Kirsten Sandberg, chairperson of the investigating UN committee, accused the Vatican of having "systematically placed preservation of the reputation of the Church ... over the protection of child victims". This applies to clerical abusers disregarded by, and to classroom crosses required by Jesus' German proxy Joseph. This abismal gap, together with his "panic fear of gays"[969] and his pastoral counsel that Christians should not practice yoga because "it brings you too much in contact with your body",[970] maybe adumbrates how the view of the tortured male body formed the successful career of a sensitive Bavarian boy, held captive by the sacrifice he reenacted in his adventurous Holy Mass game: the violent sacrifice of the violated mother's son whose carved image he demanded to hang above children, while he looked away when clerics came violently over the little ones.

His voluntary and responsible resignation owes respect. It brought the task of being Deputy of Christ back into the range of human fallibility.

The first aid Jew

No kidding: It was the distinguished lawyer Professor Joseph Halevi Horovitz Weiler (Universities of New York – Florence – Jerusalem) who had put his best black velvet kippá on his head before he entered the Strasbourg court room to plead for legalizing crucifixes in all classrooms of the continent where Jews were murdered under crucifixes in all countries except Scotland and Scandinavia. Weiler was the star of the day, of course. And it speaks volumes about European taboos that Berlusconi shrewdly had prepared his play to pivot around a Jewish joker as *advocatus crucifixi*.

Weiler's aptness for the job was proved by his 2003 bestseller "A Christian Europe", in which he encouraged Europe to stand by its "Christian inheritance". Good news! And evidence that good Jews exist.

After his pleading for classroom crosses, Weiler was interviewed by the National Catholic Reporter (January 21, 2011). Here Weiler mentions "very harsh reactions, especially from the European Jewish community in Italy, France, Germany", citing also the question which the author of this book (and surely not he alone) had asked him: "How can the son of a Lithuanian rabbi do this?" Weiler admits that laicity and secularism are strong Jewish positions because they mean emancipation. He even mentions the book *Libres et Egaux* of Robert Badinter (former president of French Constitutional Court) and his wife Elisabeth, wherein the Jewish couple expounds how the Jews gained civil rights in France not until the separation of state and religion.[971] However, Weiler discloses how he uses to counter any Jewish

---

969   Sandberg: AP, Feb.05, 2014; cf. Kübli et alii, p.608; panic fear: Posener, p.143-144.
970   Matthew Fox, "Pope Benedict XVI's Legacy": tikkun.org, February 12, 2013.
971   Badinter's father, deported on order of Klaus Barbie, was murdered in Sobibor. His son was Minister of Justice in the government of Mitterrand and until 1995 President of the Constitutional Council. The abolition of death penalty in France (2006) owes decisively to his efforts. His wife, a prominent university professor, author and women's rights activist, is

critics: "In every Israeli school there's a sign of the menorah, which is the official symbol of the State of Israel. Would you have it removed? On every door, there's a mezuzah. Would you have it removed?"

Counter question: How naive may a Jewish lawyer be? Sure, you can compare everything. Apples and oranges? Comparing apples with planets Isaac Newton found a rather plausible law of nature. But what is it that this favorite Jew of European law schools – allegedly "it would be easier to list the elite European universities from which he doesn't hold honorary doctorates" – is equating here in his breathtaking logic of "symbol is symbol"? A small tube hiding a piece of parchment with the Hebrew wording of the Shemá Israel ("Hear, Israel ... God is one") equals the picture of a man tortured dead and exposed on beams? A seven-branched candelabrum (menorah) equals the dark accuse that led to millionfold murder revenging a murdered Godson?

But also in this murder case the lawyer Weiler – "I'm really an expert" – has come to exciting new insights. The Rabbi's son at last confesses everything: Yup, the Jews have done it, and they did it because God wanted to test them, as Weiler concludes from Deuteronomy 13:1-5. Indeed this passage deals with one who says "Let us follow and worship another God" and therefore is killed. Not fully the Jesus-Pilate story, but: "My thesis is that Jesus is the person referred to in Deuteronomy." This thesis, Weiler says, will be the heart of the book he is writing right now – not his cookbook "Kosher but delicious" which runs alongside – but this eye-opening book in which "I want to be able to say, yes, we Jews put Christ to death, because that's what the Lord required us to do. Of course personally I'm not responsible, I'm not Caiaphas. But as a Jew, I want to be able to say that when somebody came as a prophet working signs and wonders and trying to change the law [which one, please?] we did what God asked us to do."

At this point, the National Catholic Reporter can't help uttering his less inspired amazement: "I can imagine a Jew saying: We spent 2,000 years trying to escape the charge of deicide, and here you are embracing it."

Weiler, patiently: "In the trial, God achieves two things in one stroke. It's a trial of the Jews, to remind the Jews that they have their covenant and their salvation lies in it. It's also a trial of Jesus, in which he dies innocently because in that way he expiates the sins of everybody else. His death is the way of redemption for the world. At the end of the day, according to this vision, everybody is following the path of God." At this point Weiler's disclaimer seems indispensable: "Make no mistake – I am no 'Jews for Christ'. I abhor that. But even as an observant Jew, it is not for me to exclude any possible plan the Holy One, Blessed Be He, may have had for the rest of the nations." Or for Europe's classrooms.

I admit that my blood pressure soars to quite un-vegan levels whenever someone speaks of God's plans as if he'd discussed them with HIM at breakfast – because if human history follows God's plans Eichmann's plans did also. But what is more upsetting is that Mr. Weiler (his five children went to expensive Jewish dayschools) doesn't use the words "child" and

---

not mentioned as co-author of this book.

"children" a single time in the seven pages of his interview and just as often in his successful plea for pupils' crucifixes.
To me personally he explained that his father, the Rabbi, had taught him the meaning of *"tsedek, tsedek tirdof"* – "justice, justice you shall seek" this way: "The reason tsedek is mentioned twice is that you have to pursue it when it is in your interest, but also when it is not in your interest."
The facts that since early Talmudic times "all that was marked with a cross sign was considered as forbidden to Jews"[972] and some Jews by harmful reasons even avoided the harmless plus symbol in maths makes sufficiently clear that Weiler did not act in Jewish interest. So in whose? The interest of the weak ones, in this case the children? The right of the Italian plaintiff family who was threatened with murder? The rights of Europe's religious minorities? Or the rights, better say, the might of the strong men, the main-stream faith, the populists alla Berlusconi whose applause Weiler the Zionist desired and who found in him their perfect problem fixer?
Honor to whom honor is due! His next honorary degree Weiler received from Opus Dei, by its own definition a "Catholic combat unit" whose foun-der Josemaría Escrivá preached "blind obedience" and mortification of the flesh. And now, interviewed after the ceremony at Universidad de Navarra in Spanish Pamplona, November 2011, Weiler did mention children! "How can a practicing Jew defend the crucifixes in Italy's schools?" – "I didn't do it as a Jew but as a practicing constitutionalist. In a deep sense the question is offensive. Imagine a poor Christian child run over by a car and I am a physician? Will I refuse to help him cause I'm a Jew? That's the same ..."[973] More or less! And now we know that in his first aid action of helping to hang legions of Jesuses in European classrooms, Doctor Weiler succoured to Europe's children, not to Europe's most corrupt silverback.
Tellingly, the cream of European judges was, as a Munich newspaper observed, "very impressed" by an oral pleading mentally based on the Israeli non-separation of state and religion which Hannah Arendt deemed "disastrous".[974] As veteran commander of a tank unit Halevi Weiler doesn't seem to notice a contradiction in his steely-tender approach to Palestinian Muslims versus European Christians, slightly reminding Herzl's Vienna Christmas tree. What counts, is European sympathy for Zion: "Every Jew in the world is an Israeli" – says Fiamma Nirenstein, Berlusconi's long term journalist and member of Italian parliament from 2008-2013. Designated by Netanyahu as ambassador in Rome, she renounced in March 2016 due to a security conflict: Her son is working in Italian secret service. Her party leader was Netanyahu's staunchest supporter among the European heads of state, which was why Jewish Anti-Defamation League honored the *Cavaliere* as Statesman of the Year 2003.[975]

---

972 Lapide 1988, p.89.
973 caraacara.blogspot.com.br/2011/11/joseph-halevi-horowitz-weiler.html, Nov. 5, 2011.
974 Butler, p.51.
975 Ruth Ellen Gruber: Pro-Israel-Berlusconi Loses In Italy (Jewish Telegraph Agency, April 17, 2006); Anna Momigliano: The Strange Relationship Between Silvio Berlusconi and Italian Jews (972mag.com, February 6, 2013); Fiamma Nirenstein: Wikipedia.

Weiler's action shows not only what Jewish Zionists are willing to sacrifice for a little love from their Christian friends. It also proves that in their view Jews must not live in Europe. They have their homeland now, just as the wooden Jew on cross has his. Thus it happened that after the "European project" as German historian Götz Aly defines Shoah, after "1900 years of revenge for the death of the Jew Jesus"[976] (Simon Wiesenthal) an Israeli put his blackest kippá on and promoted blackest pedagogy, extending the chuppah of the Mussolini-Vatican-treaty of 1929 – ordering crucifixes in class- and courtrooms – to Europe as a whole.[977] Kudos!

The shouting crowd
If the poll in 2010 was confidable, 85 percent of Italian citizens – the population that reelected a figure like Berlusconi three times – espoused that the cross be upon their children in all public school classrooms.
However, 82 percent of Italian Jews survived the German occupation, many of them "because of aid received from the Italian population and the local Catholic priesthood", while an Italian military commander, contrasting pleasantly with German generals, made it quite clear to a German official that anti-Jewish measures are "incommensurate with the honour of Italian Army".[978] Italians had hardly less motives to cooperate with the German occupiers than their French or Slavic neighbors had, but Jew-hatred was clearly less intense between the Alpes and Sicily. To explain this difference, historians offer the facts that Italy was traditionally multicultural, to the point that at least southern Italy has a strong "crypto-Jewish past";[979] that Italian racists could not point at the Jews' black hair and long noses, that the stereotype of "Jewish usurer" was hardly applicable in the land of contos, saldos, bancos and Lombardos (the latter ones called "the Pope's usurers")[980] and that "the close proximity of the Papacy bred scepticism".[981]
To me four other traditions seem more important: First, Italian artists used to emphasize much more the *nobiltá divina* of Christ than his compassion-arousing pains. Second, while "it may rate as Hitler's real big time having offered to Germans, who were trained from so early on in hardness, obedience and repression of feelings, the Jews for their projections",[982] Italian education is as little known for its hardness as Italians are for their blind obedience and repression of feelings; few *bambini* had reason to project their built up father-hate on the people of the evil father. Italian religiosity is, third, much

---

976 Wiesenthal, p.233.
977 The "Patti Lateranensi" of 1929 indeed determined that "State and Church, each in his domain, are independent and sovereign" (Art.7), but also required the affixing of "crucifixes in every classroom and court room". The chuppah is the Jewish wedding canopy.
978 Bauer, Yehuda, p.334. Surviving Jews in comparable other occupied countries: Denmark 99 %; France 78 %, Belgium 56 %, Netherlands 29 %, Yugoslavia 19 %, Greece 14 %; statement of Italian commander of Mostar, Yugoslavia: Hilberg 1982, p.488.
979 Dr. Mario Rende, Puglia (Calabria) in HaLapid, Fall/Winter 2013, p.54.
980 Perry/Schweitzer, p.125.
981 Maccoby 1992, p.118.
982 Miller 1983, p.110.

more a folklore accessory to human life than the notorious, abysmal German *Tiefe* (deepness) would tolerate also in religious affairs. And fourth, most of all: "He suffered under Pontius Pilate, was crucified, died and buried": This verse in the Catholic credo, connected with popular experiences concerning ruthless Godfathers, peccant Papas and corrupt Principes, let the anyway not surf-eligible hate-waves break at the quay wall of the notion that rather the Romans, or even we Italians, or *semplicemente* we sinful humans were the guilty ones. Living in such a glass house of history, one would at least throw smaller bricks. By these reasons, Jew-hate had a burlesque, almost playful touch here. An annual highlight of Roman medieval carnival was to have an old Jew roll down the Monte Testaccio in a barrel, and when he arrived dead, cheerfulness was not diminished.[983] In 1466 Pope Paul II forced young Jews to have a race every day of the carnival, between the Arco Domiziano and the church of San Marco.[984] This merriment called "Via Lata" became a tradition requiring eight Jews each year, almost naked running the gauntlet between the Christian spectators who would "throw anything they could get their hands on" at the runners. "The racers were often killed and rabbis were forced to follow them simply to listen to the crowd, and then kiss the statue of a pig at the end of the corso" while the Holy Father, watching the *calvario del carnevale* on a richly ornamented balcony "laughed heartily".[985]

In 2009, after Strasbourg's first-instance decision against classroom crosses, an Italian cartoon had depicted Jesus in a deeply disappointed attitude (since hanging is what he wants) carrying his cross out of the court building with a bystander commenting "They have decided for Barabbas again".

But the fact that the jury was attacked as "Turk judges" at the same time points to a strong instrumentality of the ancient cross in modern Europe: Useful as a warning defense against the Islamic South-East, it marks the banners of the xenophobous English Defence League (EDL) as well as of neo-Nazi Hungarian Jobbik-party. "Hands off from the crucifix!" the fascist youth movement Gioventú Italiana warned with the same words as the extreme rightist students of Forza Nuova, while recently (2018) Bavarian Christian Social Union (CSU) decreed – in spite of severe critiques issued by Cardinal Marx and Bishop Wolfgang Bischof – crosses in all administrative buildings in order to win back voters from xenophobous and increasingly antisemitic AfD (Action for Deutschland). Severe critique came from Cardinal Marx who, clearly against the judges of Strasbourg, denied the right of state authorities to define the meaning of the cross. Bishop Bischof added that the cross is neither a symbol of Baviera nor an emblem for political campaigns, and recommended to practise Christian faith rather by actions of solidarity with fugitives.

---

983   Kühner, p.107; David Freedberg, Cassiano on the Jewish Races, footnote on p.53, co-lumbia.edu/cu/arthistory/faculty/Freedberg/Cassiano-on-the-Jewish-Races.pdf.
984   David Freedberg, ibid., p.53-55.
985   Wilensky, p.103; Michael, p.53; Kertzer, p.100, quoting Gregorovius: The Ghetto and the Jews in Rome, p.33-34.

The honest judges

In 1014, anointed by Pope Benedict VIII, Emperor Heinrich II was the first European ruler to hold a symbol inspired by the Roman *globus*, the imperial orb, now *globus cruciger*, in his hand. In 2011, this European culture, as if not haunted enough by faithful formulae like Torquemada's "One People, One Kingdom, One Faith" or Hitler's "Ein Volk, ein Reich, ein Führer" now takes the One Symbol and makes it's school *escola cruciger*, no matter what had happened meanwhile.[986]

What had changed since 2002, when not only "Italy's Muslims, it's Jewish community and the country's Protestant Church ... protested forcefully against the plans of governmental politicians" but also "Catholic Bishop's Conference pronounced against a governmental decree for the attachment of crucifixes", and Bishop Riboldi warned that coercion would be "contraproductive and might result in hate of crosses"?[987]

What had changed since 2009, the year when the jury of first instance had reasoned their unanimous decision for the plaintiff Mrs. Lautsi so clearly? "The presence of the crucifix – which it was impossible not to notice in the classrooms ... could be encouraging for religious pupils, but also disturbing for pupils who practised other religions or were atheists, particularly if they belonged to religious minorities ... The State was to refrain from imposing beliefs in premises where individuals were dependent on it. In particular, it was required to observe confessional neutrality in the context of public education, where attending classes was compulsory irrespective of religion, and where the aim should be to foster critical thinking in pupils. The Court was unable to grasp how the display, in classrooms in State schools, of a symbol that could reasonably be associated with Catholicism (the majority religion in Italy) could serve the educational pluralism that was essential to the preservation of a 'democratic society' ... The compulsory display of a symbol of a given confession in premises used by the public authorities, and especially in classrooms, thus restricted the right of parents to educate their children in conformity with their convictions, and the right of children to believe or not to believe."[988]

Why had Italian Protestants welcomed this judgment unanimously? "Because it serves religious freedom", the President of FCEI, the Federation of Italian Evangelical Christians stated. "To defend the crucified Christ like a national symbol means to warp Christian belief", Baptist president Anna Maffei cautioned. "This judgement safeguards the rights of everyone" declared Maria Bonafede, speaker of the Waldensians. Because Adventists "actively commit to conserving the principles of freedom of religion", their speaker Dora Bognan di Pellegrini acclaimed the judgment. "Public space is not the place to display arrogations", Lutheran Dean Holger Milkau opined. Waldensian Professor Paolo Rocca even recommended to apply

---

986 Torquemada: Perera, p.53.
987 „Italien: Bischöfe gegen Staats-Kruzifix ...", Die Tagespost, Sept.24, 2002, p.5.
988 ECHR Strasbourg, (echr.coe.int/), Chamber judgment Lautsi vs. Italy (application no. 30814/06), 03.11.2009, press release issued by the Registrar.

the no-cross-decision to public administration and court rooms, too.[989] And speaking for the Italian Jewish communities, their president Amos Luzzato had proposed to waive crosses in schools in respect of the diversity of their pupils.[990]

All this, actually, would be in best accord with European Convention whose Article 9 guarantees freedom of thought, conscience and religion and whose Article 14 prohibits discrimination by reasons of religion. On grounds of the thereby consequent "duty of neutrality and impartiality"[991] the European Court of Human Rights had denied Swiss Muslim teacher Lucia Dahlab in 2001 and Istanbul student Leyla Sahin in 2005 the right to wear a headscarf in classroom and university. In the 2007 case of humanistic Norwegian family Folgerø (concerning Christian details in normative curriculum) the court had emphasized this duty of state neutrality as "far-reaching" and "comprising all functions of the state". Now in 2011, the crucifix erased this duty of the state together with the rights of children, parents, teachers. While the judges expressly confirmed the court's former decision in the case of Mrs. Dahlab's unbearable headscarf, with "regard above all to the tender age of the children for whom the applicant was responsible", now millions of European children where not too tender to have a bleeding thorn-crowned victim of sadistic torture put before their eyes.

No less double-standard are the judges' rationales for their return to the old principle *cuius regio, eius religio*.[992] First, they gratefully took up Weiler's argument that the question of crucifixes in state-school classrooms should be "a matter falling within the margin of appreciation of the respondent State", the more so as "there is no European consensus on the question of the presence of religious symbols in State schools". So a court should, first, assess only questions on which there is a general consensus? And why does, of all matters, just *this* one fall within the margin of appreciation of every single state, though according to European Convention freedom of religion is subject only to limitations that are "necessary in a democratric society"? And while German Supreme Court had expressly stressed the symbol's influence on pupils and its "appellative character",[993] why did European Supreme Court now see no violation of neutrality since "a crucifix on a wall is an essentially passive symbol"?

The last photo of Jewish journalist Vladimir Herzog (born in Osijek in 1937, his parents fled with him to Italy and Brazil) was an absolutely passive symbol. Suicide by hanging, the media were told by São Paulo military torture center. But Rabbi Henri Sobel refused to bury Herzog as a suicide. The badly faked photo incensed Brazilians, eight thousand went to the funeral service celebrated by Cardinal Arns, Archbishop Helder Câmara and Rabbi

---

989 reformiert-info.de/4641-0-12-2.html.
990 European Jewish Press, ejpress.org/article/2490.
991 Overview of the Court's case-law on freedom of religion (October 31, 2013), echr.coe.
int/Documents/Research_report_religion_ENG.pdf.
992 Charles Singer, (p.103) translates this principal of the 1555 Peace of Augsburg after thirty years of war (1618-1648) as "Of whom the government, his be the religion".
993 BVerfG, 16.05.1995 - 1 BvR 1087/91. Full text in NJW 1995, Heft 38, p.2477-2483.

Sobel in the Cathedral. Precisely by the passive picture, Sobel resumes, the death of this Jew became a "catalyst for the restitution of democracy."

Essentially passive:
1. Vlado Herzog in São Paulo torture center, Oct 25, 1975;
2. Vlado with beach shirt and lemonade, in Carlos Latuff's cartoon satirizing "soft dictatorship", in 2009;
3. Vlado's memorial, being inaugurated in São Paulo 2016.

And the other hanging Jew was catalyst – and is – for what? Don't Strasbourg's judges know? "Every prejudice and hatred that led to persecutions and illegal discriminations is – particularly in our days of growing consciousness of human rights and condemnation of racial or religious partiality – the task of educators, sociologists and lawyers" judge Haim Cohn wrote in 1968 on the last pages of "The Trial and Death of Jesus".[994] Now Strasbourg's judges, claiming that "the question whether the crucifix is charged with any other meaning beyond its religious symbolism is not decisive at this stage of the Court's reasoning" closed their eyes discreetly. "There is no evidence before the Court that the display of a religious symbol on classroom walls may have an influence on pupils and so it cannot reasonably be asserted that it does or does not have an effect on young persons ..."[995] No influence, no effect, but the learning tool must hang, no question! How can highly intelligent judges take such a scandalous decision, such an "ultimate MCA of European law culture" on such awkward figleaf reasonings without having suffered the kind of influence "internationally notorious" Berlusconi is well-known for?[996]

---

994 Cohn, Haim, p.344.
995 ECHR, Case of Lautsi and others v. Italy (hudoc.echr.coe.int/ ...).
996 Both terms by Gerhard Czermak, in Humanistischer Pressedienst, March 23, 2011. Dr. jur. Czermak is a retired judge, an expert on "State-Church-right" and author of the book "Christen und Juden".
Remarkably, my own application concerning classroom crucifixes, after having gathered dust in Strasbourg for 37 months, was rejected (without reasoning) exactly when I had engaged a renowned attorney and he had solicited the court for deferral until the filing of his

Vatican minister of culture Cardinal Ravasi welcomed the judgement eulogizing the unique image: "The cross is a symbol of our civilization, one of the greatest in the West." Well said, as since the crusades Europe's love for a picture radiating lesser civilized than effective brutality of Roman state terrorism is inseparable from Europe`s way of civilizing all other continents – "sword and cross marched together in conquest and colonies"[997] – and of cleansing the own condo. "Today the popular feeling of Europe has won", Berlusconi's foreign minister Frattini exulted. "I hope that after this judgment Europe will tackle with the same courage the issue of tolerance and freedom of religion."[998]

"Not a good sound" one could comment to this, echoing the British Guardian who condensed his opinion about the European Court's pro-cross-lapse into the stark headline "Not a good sign".

But the Guardian was a singular exception within a widespread Strasbourg syndrome characterized by European media's free speech disorder, miosis and urbane smile whenever Europe's logo is on stage. The compact majority of continental media kept a disturbing but significant indifference. Munich's liberal *Süddeutsche Zeitung* commented: "A prudent judgment, for this is not the point."

So what *is* the point? To this question, I imagine, the Munich columnist would answer with Prague style goodwill:

"Oh, my God!" said the guard. "In a position like yours, and you think you can start giving orders, do you? It won't do you any good to get us on the wrong side, even if you think it will – we're probably more on your side than anyone else you know!"[999]

"I say", said K. "Please pardon my book. But may I ask your Reverence to answer some childishly simple questions?"

---

memoire. The rejection in "single-judge-decision" was signed by Judge Lorenzen, one of the 15 pro-crucifix among 47 ECHR judges in total.

997   Galeano, p.41.
998   derStandard.at, March 18, 2011.
999   Kafka, Franz: Der Proceß. Stuttgart 1995, p.11.

Exam: Why Johanna fed him vanilla cake
and other child's play questions

"This is the first Jesus on the cross that I'm not afraid of."

A boy of seven years viewing this crucifix in Marl, Westphalia.

Cui bono? Who is it good for?
In this final chapter, I will try to apply this key and standard question of Roman jurisdiction to the crucifix: *Cui bono*? Is it good for Christians? Jews? Children? Educators? State? Society? For the victim? Good for *God*? What kind of God? Wherever I used this latter, weighty word in 14 stations I was well aware of the "legitimate demands of atheism" Jewish philosophers like Jacques Derrida and Emanuel Lévinas have pointed to; demands I view as valid, however, in but one of the following two cases:
a) When sewer worker and rescuer Leopold Socha shortly after the war was run down by a truck in Polish Gliwice, some townsmen said God had him punished for saving Jews;
b) Annie P., who at age six suffered crippling kicks to her spine rather than tell the Nazi guard about the Jews her parents hid in their Dutch horticulturist nursery, told Eva Fogelman that her childhood experiences with hidden ones and rescuers strengthened her belief in God. The faith of these people was "astonishing" to her. "It comforted me then and became a guiding light and an integral part of my life."[1000]
In Lévinas' view, ethical monotheism – which Bloch described as the "reinterpretation of God's features into models for humans" – is "sheer *a*-theism" as compared to the "divine" revered in images of God.[1001]

1000 Fogelman, p.274-275.
1001 Bloch, Ernst: Die Gestalt der unkonstruierbaren Frage (ca.1918). In: Bloch 1967, p.27; Lévinas 1996, p.25 and 110.

Lèvinas illustrates his view by an old story about a young atheist. In Ur of the Chaldeans, Abram's father Terah ran a flourishing trade with clay-made Gods. The lesson young pensative Abram taught his business-minded father shows chutzpah and destiny of Judaism – and the concrete fixation it never accepted – yet in the patriarch's teenage. One day, when Terah was out and Abram had to mind the store, he took a hammer, smashed all the clay gods except the largest one, placed the hammer in the solid hands of the big boss and waited for daddy to come home. When Terah saw the mess and, not amused, asked his son what happened, Abram said, "The idols got into a fight, and the big one smashed all the other ones." Now dad was hopping mad: "Are you crazy? A hollow clay-made figure? As if ceramics could do anything!" That was exactly what Abram had wanted to hear. After the incident, however, his life at the family seat Ur in Chaldea turned unpleasant to a degree that made him hear God or Sarai or himself saying: "Go forth from your native land and from your father's house ..."

A God-image may serve to mark a territory, believers in and dissidents out: „You are suing against the cross, so why do you live in our Christian Germany?" a German anonymus wrote to me counseling: "Emigrate to Turkey, Iran, or Iraq." – "Go to another place", Frau Theodora Seidl advised me, „your best bet is the Orient". – „Nobody coerces you to earn your living in this country any longer", School Board Director Anton Müller assured me, "if you think that the view of crosses strains you psychically" – "Herr Riggemann your name does not sound very Bavarian and maybe in your home country you'd be in greater demand" I was counseled by someone who excused his weak spelling with having gone to school "when Volksschul teachers acquired their little knowledge in seminaries to forward it with pandy sticks and slaps to the unfortunate pupils." – "Do you want to suffer untold never ending torments during the whole eternity?" one *Südtiroler W.* asked me avering that "Jesus died also for you on KREUZ so you too may be happy forever."

"Give it up", Frau Elisabeth Schwarz advised me almost as friendly as the policeman in *Give it up!* whom Kafka had breathlessly asked the way. "Give it up", she wrote, "for finally you'll draw the short straw." She enclosed a psychologically interesting booklet published by Parson A.M.Weigl in St.Grignion Edition 1977, titled *God Intervenes*. A document of angst-ridden cruci-captivity, teaching in thirteen stories „to see Your love in everything" and showing thirteen times how God steps in whenever the symbol of his love suffers offense. "Never shall my child view this sign of superstition ..." the expecting mother tells the nurse and doctor in the delivery ward, and the fondly awaited baby consequently is born blind. "Your stubborn head will get smashed one day", a Protestant father warns his "unfaithful" son who wants to remove his Catholic mother's crucifix from the kitchen, and soon after gets smashed by a ton of bedrock in the coal mine. "Was no good one anyway, else he wouldn't have got burned", a young manufactory worker during morning break sneers at a crucifix destroyed in a church fire the night before, and after the break a machine tears off his left arm.

Punishment for what? Wasn't the worker's sarcasm about the wooden symbol's impotence just the short form of the following Bible passage? "A carpenter may cut down a suitable tree and ... produce something fit for daily use, and use the scraps from his handiwork in preparing his food, and have his fill. But the good-for-nothing refuse from these remnants, crooked wood grown full of knots ... is what he takes and carves ... and forms to the image of a human being ... He makes a fitting shrine for it and puts it on the wall, fastening it with a nail. Thus he provides for it lest it fall down, knowing that it cannot help itself; for, truly, it is an image and needs help. But when he prays about his goods or marriage or children, he is not ashamed to address the thing without a soul. For vigor he invokes the powerless; for life he entreats the dead; for aid he beseeches the wholly incompetent ... (Wisdom 13:11-18).

The book of Wisdom in the Catholic Bible was authored probably by a Jewish contemporary of Jesus living in Alexandria on Egypt's coast. How, so one may ask, would our Galilean rabbi evaluate the Christian God image that presents his own tortured body? Did he ever put his innovative "But I tell you" behind Moses' warnings "Molten gods you shall not make" (Ex 34:17) and "Do not become corrupt and make for yourselves an image in any likeness whatever, the form of a man or a woman ..." (Dt 4:15)? Or did he comment the "You shall not make yourself a sculptured image, ... You shall not bow down to them and serve them" (Dt 5:8-9) with his well-known "But I ..."?

If one purpose of these antique God images was to establish relations of power, then Immanuel Kant, as a representative of autonomous rational ethics, can be but praiseful here: "Maybe there is no passage in the legal code of the Jews that is more sublime than the commandment: You shall not make an image for yourself."[1002]

And the most sublime one for Jesus? To the question which commandment is the greatest he responds: "The first is: Hear, O Israel: the Lord our God, the Lord is one" (**Mark 12:29**). And he goes on: "δευτέρα αὕτη" – *deutera aute*, literally "the second is the same" – and this second, equal law he cites is Leviticus 19:18: "You shall love your neighbor as yourself, I am Yahve." In John Dewey's words: "All moral is social."[1003] In Kant's words: "Everything that, besides of good moral conduct, man deems he can do in order to become complacent to God is sheer religious delusion and counterfeit service of God." And in the same Fourth Piece of his Critique of Religion, Kant rejects the "fetish making ... since the sensual representation [of God] is against the reasonable prohibition 'You shall not make an image', and so on". In this, Kant aims exactly at Constantinian state church, at a "fetish faith by which the crowd is ruled and, by obedience to a Church (not to religion) is robbed

---

1002   J. Assmann in "Dresdner Vortrag", aroumah.net/agora/assmann2-dresdner vortrag ...
1003   Dewey: Ethical Principles Underlying Education. In: Third Yearbook of the Herbart Society, Chicago 1907, p.12-13.

of its moral freedom ... Thus the Church eventually rules the state, not by violence exactly but by influence on the minds ..."[1004]
Why is this moral freedom threatened by *fetish faith*? Because not with looking up to, speaking to and bowing down to wooden models and clay figures one reveres the social You of moral responsibility but with word and deed, regard and respect for fellow sentient beings. "I will be who I will be": the undefined God of Moses is not an object of worship by frankincense and bending knees in front of golden thrones but "of honoring by social behavior in all spheres of life", as Wikipedia frames it.

"If someone would ask me about the sense of Judaism", Nahum Goldmann ponders, "I would say: nonconformism."[1005] The Latin word relates to formed conventions and prevalent views, but inconvenient stubbornness starts with the Jewish "No, thanks" to God as hardware and utility value. The physical value of Jews, including nine months hard work up to death and subsequent valorization of their hair, bones, ash and gold teeth German bookkeepers reckoned in 1942 at medium 1.631 Reichsmark. Gassing cost less than 0.015 Reichsmark per victim in 1944 but in order to save that expense children, God's non-wooden images, were thrown alive into the ovens.[1006] Today the Christian God image sells cheap in good shops, provided that supply from China arrived in time, at a price per God unit of some Euro ninety.[1007]
If someone would object that the crucifix in Christian living-rooms and Austrian landscapes is not comparable to pagan idols of 700 BCE, read Jeremiah 10:3-5: "The customs of the peoples are delusion; because it is wood cut from the forest, the work of the hands of a craftsman with a cutting tool. They decorate it with silver and with gold; They fasten it with nails and with hammers so that it will not totter. Like a scarecrow in a cucumber field are they, and they cannot speak." (See also Ex 20:4; Lev 26:1; Isaiah 44:9-19).
No matter which harmless god images Jeremiah cartooned here: The fact that exactly the Jews who abolished god images were pestered with a god image depicting a Jew for thousand years implies an awful irony – but no unfathomable depth. For pain is power. The "company sign of Christians", as Cardinal Meissner called it, energized the company's triumphant victory by a corporate identity of pain, by the socially unifying pity with the poor one and the impetus of justice for the victim all Christians sympathized with. The symbol anchored in the souls because "pain is a more terrible lord ... than even death proper", as the physician Albert Schweitzer knew.[1008] It anchored because it provoked insoluble questions and gave the creeps of a crucifying superfather conceived by Paul in glaring contradiction to Jesus' way of addressing God as a kind, loving father. "Without the trauma bond of an inexplicable and brutal God who sacrifices his son, the Church would

1004 Kant, Die Religion ..., 4.Stück, §2, until Allgemeine Anmerkung, p.225, 235-239, 265.
1005 Goldmann, p.70.
1006 Greenberg 2004, p.169.
1007 Chinese competitors do challenge Oberammergau woodcarving industry! (Helmut Kopetzky, radio feature "Kruzifix. Das Logo des Abendlands" (NDR Easter 2009/ 2013).
1008 Tuttle, p.147.

almost surely lose its mass base."[1009] Exactly because of this psychopathic, pathogeneous discrepancy between human Jesus and inhuman cross, the latter worked as an anchor in the child's mind; an anchor which like an inverted question mark would snag deep down in this "fathomless secret of faith" recommended against the dangers of too deep pondering.

In 1794 the great thinker Kant had argued against fetish-making and fetish-faith; in 1795 a descendant of crusade prisoner Mehmet Sadık Selim Sultan (1270-1328) and decided opponent of crosses [1010] named Johann Wolfgang Goethe, together with Friedrich Schiller started his "Tame Xenias" one of which warns:

Foolish stuff you well may talk and pen
Will kill no body and no soul, as all will stay as now and then
But foolery imposed to eyes is magic, strong and grave
For as it shackles senses, the spirit stays a slave.

"This complies exactly with the Jewish view", Jan Assmann comments Goethe's warning about enslaving pictures.[1011] But foolish stuff (German *Dummes,* related with dumb, dimwitted) the symbol never was, neither in the rational nor in the sensitive, emotional or the political meaning. Contrarily, it was functional for marking the peak of a social pyramid, above which but the heavenly guarantor hovered. It suited as the bodily symbol of the subservient obedience to which the serf, the day labourer, the underdog was entitled. It suited for an authoritarian society, as symbol of a hierarchy that sacrificed humans in battlefields and animals in slaughterhouses. The crucifix suited for a patriarchal bellicose society that demanded emotionally tough and sturdy individuals. Is it by coincidence that the holocaust was performed by males of the two most repressive, most obedient, most rigidly educating national cultures of Europe, namely Austria and Germany? Holocaust is past, the Churches could argue, and we've cleaned theology from anti-Judaism, and since today no responsible Christian connects the crucifix to Jewish guilt, the symbol is neutral and we can go on with it, okay? – First, the argument ignores that the connection incessantly is made in gospel texts which no one will change or renounce of. Second, it ignores that the impact of the cruel symbol instills the need to make the connection, to find out who's done that. And third, the transformation of compassion into justified anger is automatic, as Lerner and Clayton taught us.

By good reasons Christians may surmise that a second holocaust of Nazi thoroughness must not be feared: by six million reasons. And what has caused the first one? "The source of Jewish-Christian violent conflict lay entirely on the Christian side of the hyphen" says James Carroll, pointing to

---

1009   Swaim 2012, p.113.
1010   German Wikipedia, Sadok Seli Sultan. As to Goethe's stance against crosses, see his Venezianische Epigramme (66); Werner Keller: "The cross symbolism was a nuisance to Goethe, the doctrine of original sin a debasement of creation, the deification of Jesus in the trinity a blasphemy of the one God." (Goethe-Jahrbuch. Band 130, 2013, p.47).
1011   J. Assmann, Dresdner Vortrag: Was ist so schlimm an den Bildern? aroumah.net.

a cause "so plain that we can hardly see it as such, and it has been there all along. A miscarried cult of the cross is ubiquitous in this story, from Milvian Bridge to Auschwitz."[1012]

However, one who deems the cult of the cross now harmless since Auschwitz will not repeat anyway is, first, making use of just those six million victims who impede repetition currently. And second, he ignores the right of present-day and future children not to get inoculated with hate, not laden with resentments. Only people callous enough to think that hate doesn't hurt the hater will fail to recognize this right of children.

To illustrate the cult's efficiency, let's review the story quickly, starting not with Constantine's first battle under the new sign but with the liturgy of the cross-centered holiday:

In 1928, the "Amici Israel" approached Pope Pius XI bidding for an alteration of the Holy Friday liturgy, particularly the rogation "for the perfidious Jews", arguing that these words were quoted whenever Christians "seek arguments for anti-Semitism". The Amici Israel counted no less than 3000 priests, 280 bishops and 18 cardinals among their members. But then Cardinal Merry de Val, head of the Vatican faith congregation, entered stage. If these Amici had their way, he warned, in future one could neither call the Jewish people deicidal nor speak about their usury and ritual murders. On March 25, 1928, the Amici Israel were dismantled.[1013]

On April 26, 1933, Bishop Berning of Osnabrück and vicar general Steinmann of Berlin visit the new chancellor Adolf Hitler who explains: "During 1500 years the Catholic Church has seen the Jews as vermin, confined them to ghettoes and so on. ... I view the vermin in the representants of this race for State and Church, and maybe I am doing the greatest service to Christendom."[1014]

For Easter 1941, Freiburg Archbishop Gröber described the Jewish people in a pastoral letter: "Their eyes were blinded by Jewish greed of global dominion. Seduced by the Pharisees, now also the people rises against him ... The beast has smelled human blood and wants to quench its wildly burning thirst on it, not being satisfied until he dies nailed to the cross beam ... Over Jerusalem meanwhile yells the crazy but prophesying self-curse of the Jews: 'His blood be on us and on our children!' The curse has fulfilled terribly till this day."

On July 26, 1941, Munich Cardinal Faulhaber intervened against the order of Nazi Secretary of Culture Adolf Wagner to have the crosses "gradually" removed from schools. "How shall our people understand", the Cardinal asked, "that from German public schools cross images get removed while the fathers and brothers of these school children are standing afield against bolshevism and overthrowing with incomparable double-quick pace the sworn enemies of the cross?" In his letter of protest, the cardinal built on Wagner himself who still in 1937 had declared: "Why, then, should one re-

---

1012   Carroll, p.250; cf. Goldhagen 2002, p.100-101.
1013   Posener, p.107-108.
1014   Klee 1989, p.32.

move the crucifixes from the schools? Why? Leave the crosses hanging! If I were a teacher, I would say every morning: Boys and girls! Look at that, thus the Jew has nailed Christ on the cross! I wouldn't even think about removing the crucifix."

Apparently Faulhaber agreed with Wagner's view of the cross as learning tool for Jew-hatred, since taking up this view he goes on highlighting that the cross image indicates to "really everyone" who enters a school with crosses: "Here you are not in a *Juden* school, here you are not in a pagan school, but in the public school of a people who owes his great culture to Christian religion."

Due to Bavarian population's resistance and to the leverage given by Martin Bormann, the second most powerful figure of nazi state and driving force of Jewish persecution, Wagner stopped the removal of crosses on August 28, 1941."[1015]

On October 5, 1941, five weeks after invasion, Bavarian Bishop Rackl canonized the war against the Soviet Union as "a real crusade", this being a "holy war for home and people, for faith and Church, for Christ and his Holy Cross."[1016] In 1942, Vatican informed Slovakian Prime Minister Tuka that the Jews were deported to Poland not for forced labor, but that they were being exterminated there.[1017] "How is it conceivable", Saul Friedlander asks, "that at the end of 1943 the pope and the highest dignitaries of the Church were still wishing for victorious resistance by the Nazis in the east and therefore seemingly accepted by implication the maintenance, however temporary, of the entire nazi extermination machine?"[1018]

In vain the Catholic writer Jacques Maritain, married to a Jewish born Russian, had begged the world in 1944 not to be blind to "the most appalling mystery of contemporary history – the mass crucifixion of the Jewish people".[1019] In 1947, Pope Pius decried any "crucifixes so designed that the Redeemer's body shows no traces of his cruel sufferings" as a "straying from the straight path".[1020]

In April 1948, in their "Word to the Jewish Question" the Brother's Council (Bruderrat) of German Lutheran Churches cleared what was still valid and what was to add for correction:

Still Jewish question, now less race: "Since the Church recognizes in the Jew the erring brother who nevertheless is destined for Christ ... she is prohibited from viewing the Jewish question as a racial or *völkisch* Problem."

1015 Gröber: Fricke, p.270; Faulhaber: Pfister/Kornacker/Laube, p. 294-299. In 1943, Charles Singer (p.86) wrote: "Cardinal Faulhaber, least timid of the clerics – the standard of courage is not high – in his well-known sermons of 1933, most significantly omits to touch upon the treatment of the Jews."
1016 Rackl: de.wikipedia.org/wiki/Michael_Rackl.
1017 Hilberg 1982, p.501 (affidavit by Hans Gmelin of German embassy in Bratislava, June 15, 1948.
1018 Friedländer, Saul: Pius XII and the Third Reich, p.210 and 237 (Phayer, p.60 and Weiss, Chicago 1997, p.354).
1019 Jacques Maritain, Pour la Justice. New York, undated, p.311 (cit. by Phayer, p.178).
1020 Encyclical "Mediator Dei", November 20, 1947.

No longer valid: "By crucifying the Messiah, Israel rejected it's chosenness and destiny". Valid now: "We all are complicit in the cross of Christ. Therefore the Church is prohibited from branding the Jew as the only culprit of the cross of Christ." Because "Christ was crucified and has risen also for the people of Israel. This is the hope for Israel after Golgotha."
Still valid, now newly evidenced: "Israel standing trial is the indissoluble confirmation of the truth, the reality of the divine word and the constant warning to his community. That God cannot be mocked is the silent sermon of the Jewish fate, a warning to us and an admonition to the Jews, whether they shouldn't turn towards the one who alone grants their salvation, too."
In 1953, Pius was followed by the rescuer of thousands, John XXIII, who now described the very fact which Pius had "knowingly ignored" as "sei miglione crocifissione"[1021] and summoned a council which abrogated the Holy Friday rogation "pro perfidis Judaeis". Anticipating his early death in 1963, he had entrusted the task of preparing a "declaration on the Jewish people" to Cardinal Bea. However, not only the Arab delegates at the council railed against the proposed declaration; conservative Catholics including Italian bishop Luigi Carli insisted that Jews today still "participate objectively in the responsibility for *deicide*". So the council, now presided by Paul VI, finally proclaimed that "the *crucifixion* of Christ can not be held neither against all Jews then living indiscriminately, nor against the Jews living today": a revealingly trite declaration, never improved since, but blamed as a "victory for the international Jewish conspiracy" by traditionalists, and even as a "permission given to the enemies of Church to *crucify* the Church".[1022]
It does not matter much whether the Churches have, in well couched declarations, departed from anti-Judaism already. The obsession with terms like *deicide, crucify* and *crucifixion* again attests to the much stronger visual than textual impact of the passion traditions. This is also proved by the odd phenomenon of charging the Jewish people for an execution that was indispensable for redemption. The textual fact that according to Luke (23:34) Jesus himself prays on the cross "Father, forgive them; for they do not know what they are doing" was taken by Jews as inducement to astute questions. For instance: If the Jews didn't know what they did, have they been morally guilty at all? If Jesus would not have been crucified due to this purported Jewish instigation, but stayed alive and passed away peacefully in old Magdalene's arms, what then about our redemption? Put more simply, shouldn't Christians thank the alleged crucifiers profusely for having promoted redemption?
And one more point: Did God will the crucifixion? If not, how could it have occurred? If yes, why blame the Jews? Yet the twelfth-century Jewish "Polemic of Nestor the Priest" left no escape for Christian theology: "If you say according to his will, [then] everything which the Jews did to him was good and just according to your word, since they did his will. If you say they did to him that which he did not want, can someone who cannot save

---

1021   Wilensky, p.197; "knowingly ignored": Hans Küng, sueddeutsche.de, May17, 2010.
1022   Cohen, p.172-176; original: "... to crucify it".

himself from the hands of the Jews, the Greeks, and the infidels possibly be a God?"[1023]
But what chances does sound logic have, when the visual brunt of crucifixes lashes into human emotion? Martin Luther stated that the warning dream of Pilate's wife Procula (Mt 27:19) must have been sent by Satan who desperately wanted to avert getting doomed by Jesus' holy crucifixion – and at the same time Luther raged against the Jews for having achieved this crucifixion.[1024] The logic in the absurd is that the Christian teaching of redemption by the crucified one's love requires the Jews as visible, accusable and indictable perpetrators, as objects of hate and dark countervailing power. The black and white of Christian-Manichean dualism has its speaking dualist symbol in the crucifix: The good almighty father above the son he had to sacrifice was compelled to do this by the evil countervailing power – His goodness needs the evil Jews down there, satanically destructive and mighty enough to kill the divine son against the divine father's will. In societal practice, this dualist constellation of a good majority against an evil minority provided hate-mongers of all crucifaithful centuries with the needed objects. Hence Maccoby regards textual alterations and "minor bowdlerizations" in school textbooks as "merely cosmetic. It is the sheer power of the myth itself, moulding the minds of children too young to be affected by well-meaning interpretations, that implants the archetype of the Jews for life. Only a solution that prevents this imprinting of infants can work on a large scale ... The real and only permanent solution to the problem of anti-Semitism is to dismantle the Pauline Christian myth of atonement. When Jesus is revered as a teacher, rather than worshipped as a sacrifice – when he is valued for his life and deeds, and not for his death and mythic resurrection – antisemitism will cease."[1025]
Paul's myth, shortly: Since Adam listened to his wife and became disobedient like her, obedient Jesus – the second, wifeless Adam – had to come and let himself be tortured dead, to reconcile the offended heavenly father with his mankind (Romans 4:25, 5:9-10, 8:32; Eph 5:3; Phil 2:8; Gal 1:4; Col 1:19). Psychopathy was never easier to recognize. One just has to put human questions: Who, exactly, required this sacrifice of Jesus? If the father, so what a character is he? How would modern policemen, lawyers, psychiatricians deal with a father like this one? And how has this paragon (Eph 3:15) of monstrous fatherhood, with the power to sire, hire, fire his son for dad's good ends, influenced Christian parents' and educators' attitudes concerning children?
Who or what entitles the cross-exposers to depict God as a psychopathic monster and to exhibit this picture everywhere, preferably at places where innocent children are learning? Who entitles them to turn their big and small contemporaries into viewers and bystanders of an extremely painful execution that they, by whatever reasons, deem edifying and healthful?

1023 Cohen, p.148.
1024 Procula's dream: de.wikipedia.org/wiki/Claudia_Procula.
1025 Maccoby 1992, p.163 resp.166.

In 1996, the Church of England unreservedly admitted that the Christian concepts of hell as eternal torment amidst of flames have been "expressions of sadistic kind" and that such "terrorizing theologies, which transform God into a monster" left "burning sores" in many persons. When will such insight apply to crucifixes, too?

Dear respectful Christians, can you deny that the crucifix reproduces the cruelty, debasement and inhumanity of a Roman act of state terrorism that aimed to the single purpose of deterring terrified people from disobedience, in order to stabilize the power of the authorities? Could anyone expect that a symbolic reproduction of this motif would reproduce something else but cruelty, debasement, inhumanity and fear of authority?

Has the Roman world record in cruellest execution, or the Christian record in cruellest symbol ever been broken? If the respect for a gone person mandates – in Judaism – to never exhibit the corpse but to bed it in the earth at least the next day – as Jesus' friends probably did yet on the evening of his death – what would the Rabbi Jesus say in view of a symbol of his hanging body that is nicknamed "corpse drier" in German youth slang? If someone lost a loved person by a traffic accident or even by sadistic murder, would the mourner, in her mourning, frame the first foto that policemen took at the scene and place it in her living-room? Above the dining table?

What my book constantly shows in fourteen stations is the simple fact of the crucifix being the tap root and learning device of Jew hate. Anyone who wants to refute this thesis should warm up with the following set of more historic questions:

Why did the genesis of murderous Jew-hate synchronize so exactly with the coming up and spreading of the crucifix? Why did the increasingly realistic, pain expressive, compassion arousing design of crucifixes after 1000 CE so coincidentally go along with the increase of charges concerning cross-linked crimes (ritual murder, treason, conspiration, poisoning) and their atonement by cross-inspired kinds of punishment?

How come that while until 1700 the majority of Jews lived within Islamic culture, 99.8 percent of Jewish victims of persecution during Christian/Islamic era died in the most richly cross-adorned countries of Europe, whereas the wealthy Jewish communities in China and Japan, as well as the farmer and artisan *Beni Israel* in India "have provoked no hatred and experienced no persecution"[1026] and also in Islamic culture the Jews lived incomparably safer than where no child escapes the view of crucifixes?

Why was "anti-Semitism without Jews" present in many Christian regions, but "anti-Semitism without crucifixes" in none? Whence the coincidence that Hitler came from crucifix-abundant Austria, made his career in crucifix-abundant Bavaria and located most death camps in crucifix-abundant Poland?

Whence the connection between "Nowhere are crucifixes bigger, bloodier, more explicit than in Spain", and the fact that just here up to the 1980s children used to play "Killing Jews" on Easter mornings; and that just here

---

1026 Until 1700: Malka, p.24; Beni Israel: Poliakov 2003, Vol.I, p.16.

where most of the 46 million citizens hardly ever meet one of their thirty thousand (0.07 percent) Jewish compatriots, nonetheless in 2005 still 55 percent believed they nourish "dark intentions", 69 percent thought they are too powerful and 75 percent would not accept one of them as neighbor, and more than fifty percent of all students between 12 and 18 years would reject a Jewish desk neighbor?[1027]

Why are all anti-Jewish stereotypes invariably connected with and derived from the Passion stories of the gospels that ended in what is presented in the crucifix?

Why are Kierkegaard, Coudenhove-Kalergi, Runes and all others wrong who described how the child, out of his compassion with Jesus, develops hate for his torturers? Has anyone yet tried to refute this terrible indictment of child maltreatment and incitement to hate?

And if a skeptic then admits that the crucifix, if anything, could have a marginal share in the causes of Shoah: What is a marginal share of, say, one per mille, out of "6,000,000 crucifixions" in Pope John's account?

"A beautiful crucifix": Also this esthetical opinion uttered so often in Bavaria and Austria moots questions: How can murder by torture be esthetical? And how much content must be repressed if artistical skill leads to such an assessment concerning the execution of a death sentence?

Could there be a more esthetical, more respectful, and less expensive way of changing history for the better than to renounce on crucifixes?

If you have a pro-cross point for any of the up to here 28 questions, please tell me (kyriggenmann@gmail.com) and help me if you can with the rest, ending at the Our Father question which in my counting is number 49.

Is the Catholic mother "Dembara" (see chapter 1) right when she states that "a crucifix is one of the few symbols that are valid for all Christians equally? So why is there no crucifix or cross in the great Dome of Basel, a temple of Reformed Lutheran Church? How do Quakers and Adventists, Mormons and Jehova's Witnesses without crucifixes?

Is Susan Sontag right when, starting from the fact that some people look at pain "with satisfaction, with *schadenfreude*, with the perennial interest that grotesquery invites", she ends with the conclusion that "*love of cruelty* is as natural to human beings as is sympathy"?[1028] Doesn't she declare sadist sickness as the natural condition here on this planet?

Are Catholics "naturally cruel"? Or do they really love the crucifix? Then how come that tough Bavarian Catholics so loudly use to utter the life-affirming words "*Ja Krutzificks!*" whenever they want to vent anger and rage? Why do they nickname the crucified Jesus as "*Balkensepp*" (Beam Joe) or "*Lattengustl*" (Slat Gustav)? Because they love the picture or because they understandably try to play down the symbol's cruelty and the dark "cosmi-

---

1027 Crucifixes and Easter game: Alexy, p.267 and 96, quoting a Catholic ex-priest of Marrano descent respectively Jewish refugee Nina Mitrani; poll data: Goldstein, Phyllis, p.346, referring to European Monitoring Centre on Racism and Xenophobia. Students poll: Carvajal, p.153.
1028 Susan Sontag: Regarding the Pain of Others, 2003; cited by Kalechofsky 2003, p.9.

cal sadist" in its background, who has to sacrifice his son to save the world from his own anger?

Doesn't Gabriele Schwab reflect our visual susceptibility much more precisely than Susan Sontag when she writes: „Looking at raw horror, terror, or violence can appall, but we also know of its inevitable attraction"? Didn't Augustine perceive this attraction even more precisely in his unbiased days when Christians never had to look at crucifixes? "Why does man want to see mournful scenes full of misery which he would not himself care to live through in reality? And yet the spectator wants to be dolefully affected, nay the pain itself is what he relishes."[1029] Does the love of crucifixes base on a confusion of emotions, as the symbol arouses affects which Christians have learned to interpret as wholesome though they are the contrary?

"That God needs a human sacrifice to reconcile his own creation with himself; that he, the ruler of the world, cannot justify anyone without a bloody sacrifice, is as incomprehensible to Jews as it is contrary to the Bible", Pinchas Lapide marvels, and James Carroll comments: "Where is the Good News in such appeasement? This paradoxical and tragic idea of God's mercy, bound to the cross, is profoundly violent. Whatever the feudal origins of the system, however tenderly meant its composition, and however glibly we invoke the word 'love', the God of such atonement can appear, in a certain light, to be a monster."[1030] Children, free of whatevers and howevers, need no *certain light* to perceive the violence instantly. Carroll's adult theologist conclusion is decisive: "A new Christology will banish from Christian faith the blasphemy that God wills the suffering of God's beloved ones, and the inhuman idea that anyone's death can be the fulfillment of a plan of God's." Aware of the blasphemy's lethal effects in history, Carroll demands: "The penitential rite would consist of a dismantling of this cross, a removal of the horizontal beam, an uprooting of the vertical, a reversal of the instruction Constantine gave to his soldiers. In this way, the cross would be returned to Jesus, and returned to its place as the cause of his death, not the purpose of his life. For Jesus, the cross could have been nothing of conquest or power. For Jesus, therefore, the cross could not conceivably have become a symbol of triumphalism, nor a sign of defamation of his own people. To remove this cross is to begin the reversal of all that we Christians here confess."[1031]

What is intolerant in rejecting a symbol that arouses hatred?

What is wrong with me when I can't help imagining that the man who "overturned the tables of the money changers and the benches of those selling doves", would snatch the crucifixes off the walls of Munich classrooms or Vienna kindergartens and send them flying out of the window?

What is wrong with people who dislike sadism, as for instance my Munich professor of philosophy Anton Neuhäusler with his aphorism "The history of sadism arouses the desire to efface mankind"?[1032] Aren't we, those kooky

---

1029   Schwab, p.63; Augustine, Confessions, book 3, chapter 2 (by Eisler, p.23-24 and 77).
1030   Carroll, p.288-289, citing Lapide from Hans Küng SJ, Judaism, p.389.
1031   Carroll, p.587 and 604.
1032   Neuhäusler, p.54.

sissies scared by sadism, just closer to our inner child, and closer, – yes, really – closer to the crucified one?

For didn't this book's key figure – this Jesus bar Abbas who out of traumatic childhood experiences became the women's and the sinner's rabbi, and especially the children's rabbi – didn't he teach an especially respectful awareness of children and put them really in the center, as all synoptic gospels relate? Did he mean children approaching the crucifix when he said "Let the little children come to me, and do not hinder them, for the kingdom of heaven belongs to such as these" (**Mk 10:14; Mt 19:14**)?

Did he mean wooden arms and nail-fixed hands when "he took the children in his arms, placed his hands on them and blessed them" (**Mk 10:16**)?

Big boys and girls, still mesmerized, by what? The Five Wounds of Christ, painted about 1525 by Simon Bening (~1483-1561), the Flamish minaturist who was praised as "the best master of book illustration in Europe" by the later victim of the Inquisition Damião de Góis (1502-1574).

Did he dream of crucifixes in European kindergartens when he "called a child and set him in their midst and said: 'Unless you change and become like little children, you will never enter the kingdom of heaven'"? (**Mt 18:3; ThEV 22:1-2**). Unless you change: Do you really change yourselves or

rather change the souls of children by your ordealove picture? Shouldn't maybe rather your "religion of the adults", as Erik Erikson characterized the Christian doctrine, revise its visual education?[1033]

"This is the first Jesus on the cross that I'm not afraid of." Note that the **boy of seven years** at the beginning of this chapter refers to a modern crucifix that is rather a cruci-non-fix as Jesus is not fixed to it. The artist did just what in 1654 a Lisbon maidservant told the inquisitor about the New Christian Luis Lopez Franco: "... that Luis, one day before an auto-da-fé, had unfixed Christ from a crucifix."[1034] Also in Marl Jesus is unfixed, freed of nails and obedience: an acrobatic genie from Orient who enjoys his liberation after 1001 night years of Europe. Why did this cross bring hundreds of visitors, "fierce and contentious" discussions and in February 2015 a television service to Marl's Protestant Kreuzkirche which was shut down, due to general depletion of churches, on January 22, 2017 with a last Sunday service?[1035]

Stauros is the Greek term for the Roman terror-generator, and staurophobia denotes an "abnormal" fear of the Christian symbol of love, accompanied by symptoms like breathlessness, excessive sweating, dry mouth, heart palpitations, fear of dying, panic attacks, trembling, crying, screaming and nausea. One of many help-offering websites assures all help-seeking persons: "You are not the only one to suffer from this phobia. Most sufferers are surprised to learn that they are far from alone in this surprisingly common, although often unspoken, phobia."[1036]
Under the alias "**robskater**", for instance, a teenager speaks out at catholic-forum.com in February 2008: "I am new to the forums and have come here for help. I have been raised Catholic and am 17 years old. Today I just found out there is a name for something I have suffered for a long time. Staurophobia. The fear of crosses or crucifixes. I myself am not afraid of crosses, just crucifixes. It's horrible and messes with me a lot. I believe in the bible and I believe in God being great and all. It just scares me. I know I can go into a lot of churches and be okay because they do not have very realistic crucifixes, but the one I went to all of my life up until I was about 11 had one. This is messing up the way I want to be and live my life. I have come here for help that all. I'm not sure if this is in the right section but if anyone could help me or just do anything I would be very grateful."
Ben, a young Belgian cleric, replies: "Hello Robskater, First of all: Pray. The Rosary would be a good idea. Let the Blessed Virgin Mary pray for you so that you may overcome this fear. Since this is a 'phobia' and thus a psychological issue, I would seek help from a psychologist for this as well.

1033 Erik Erikson, cited by Ernst Lange in his preface to Freire, Pädagogik der Unterdrückten, p.17.
1034 Novinsky 2013, p.138-139.
1035 rundfunk.evangelisch.de... das-kreuz-mit-dem-kreuz-der-kreuzkirche; radiovest.de/vest/lokalnachrichten ... .
1036 phobiasource.com/staurophobia-fear-of-crosses-or-the-crucifix; phobia-fear-release.com/staurophobia.html.

It is a fear, so it has to be confronted. Fleeing from it only makes it worse. I know this as I suffer from OCD [obsessive-compulsive disorder] which is also tied with lots of fear and anxiety. When you see a crucifix, I suggest you try and meditate on the deep meaning of the symbol. It is the sign of Christ's immeasurable ocean of love and mercy for us and He endured this painful death completely for our sake. What was first an image of death becomes the standard of Life's sweet victory over death. His death has opened for us the gates to Paradise, which was closed to us by Adam. Meditate these deep mysteries of the Cross, and the Lord will start healing you and freeing you from this terrible fear. (...) God bless and much strength, Ben."

Note: This is about a symbol that causes phobias not in the minds of the wicked but in sensitive persons; a symbol mandatory in primary school classrooms of Bavaria and Italy, as well as in the public kindergartens of Hitler's home country. In the USA with their relatively low frequency of crucifixes in public space, a team of therapists who offer help in case of staurophobia can explain their method online this way: "It is essential to re-orient your unconscious newly. On the conscious level you know that your dread of crucifixes is illogical. But it continues existing because your unconscious has linked a whole load of powerful negative emotions – mainly dread – yet with the mere thought of crosses."[1037]

In Germany by contrast, with an ubiquitary presence of the symbol from delivery room and kindergarten to wayside, mountain peak and court room, staurophobia is ridicularized – probably as a means of psychic defence – quite frequently: "The typical staurophobic is probably a vampire ..." one graduate psychologist Christian Hilscher quips in the phobia listing of psylex.de. The distress signal "I have fear of crosses. At that I don't know why" was followed on yahoo by such funny German comments like "You aren't a vampire, are you?" – "You aren't a devil, right?" – "Maybe you're a Satanist and fear what is good ..." and "always shut your eyes good boy if you discover one, and cross yourself thrice, oh no that won't do ..."

Are staurophobous people simply HSPs, i.e. highly sensitive personalities? Or are they rather stauroconscious, i.e. aware of what the cross did to those who hung on it, and of what the symbol did in history? Nicholls writes: "I still remember vividly a friend whose childhood was spent in Poland saying to me years ago that he could not even pass a building with a cross on it without a shudder of fear."[1038]

Is staurophobia a neurosis, or does societal neurosis consist in the fact that fear of crosses is considered kooky and staurophilia as normal?

When Tyrolian **School Director Thomas Köhle** removed the five feet high crucifixes from the classrooms of Nassereit primary school and replaced them by simple larch wood crosses without corpus, Catholic website kreuz. net attacked him in September 2011, saying he "ridicularized himself when he asserted that the children had been afraid of the crosses".

1037 changethatsrightnow.com/fear-of-crucifix/.
1038 Nicholls, p.XXVI.

Contrarily, in his "Virtuelle Exerzitien" **Father Nicolas Schwizer** openly speaks of the "grace of overcoming the fear of the cross". For instance, **Sister Emilie Engel**, who was "characterized by fears from childhood on" had suffered from this fear, the only cure of which consists, as Schwizer assures, in guiding the angst-ridden person "radically back to God and harbor her in His loving father's heart".[1039]

"Who could speak of a father-god here in all seriousness?" **Renate Elian** asks in 1985. She remembers how outraged she rebelled in her childhood "against a father-god whose anger can be assuaged but by the blood of his own son ... Not even the worst human father has a debit account as high as this man-eating monster which ... so to say from high observatory, watches with sadistic pleasure." [1040]

"Thinking of the Holocaust and all that led to it, what kind of God presides over such a history?" **James Carroll** asks in 2002. "What kind of God shows favor to a beloved Son by requiring him to be nailed to a cross in the first place?"[1041]

The **anonymous poet** of the following old songtext was not a theologian like James Carroll. He just looked closely. Living in a Bavarian language enclave in the mountain region of Slovenia, the village poet put in his Holy Friday song[1042] the pity even adults feel with a victim clearly connoted as a child; like Kierkegaard's child he wonders "why God in Heaven had not done everything to prevent that this has happened ..."; he protests in a pious permissible way against the symbol of an inhuman torture that should stop now, or better: never have happened:

In the entire town, there is burning no light,
But the carpenter's house has its windows so bright,
Where they're timbering for Jesus the bar and the joist,
When from heavenly heights sounds a tenuous voice:
Don't you please, don't you please make so heavy those beams!
The Lord Jesus, behold, is still young in his years.

In the entire town, there is burning no light,
But the blacksmithe's house has its windows so bright,
Where they're forging for Jesus the iron to nails,
That will fix his small hands on the carpenter's rail.
Don't you forge, don't you forge Jesus'nails so much long!
For those nails the Lord Jesus is still all too young.

In the entire town, there is burning no light,
But the wreathmakers house has its windows so bright,

1039 cmsms.schoenstatt.de, online-version of a text of Father Schwizer of March 15, 2008.
1040 Until "son ..." quoted by Mynarek, p.176 (cf. Elian, p.131); rest of quote: Elian, p.130.
1041 Carroll, p.23.
1042 Words (and melody) from the Gottschee region near Ljubljana, Slovenia; arranged by Annette Thoma, translated by the author (K.Y.R.) using original and arranged version from two sources: a) heimat-bayern.de/uploads/; b) volksmusik-archiv.de/vma/files/infohefte/...

Where they're weaving Lord Jesus his prickely crown
And a voice is heard calling from heaven-high down:
Don't you please, don't you please weave this crown very strong!
For this crown the Lord Jesus is still all too young.

Will you please, will you please now extinguish your light,
Oh please spare the Lord Jesus, don't you rack him with might.

"I just came here to ask you when I will be allowed to take down the class-room crucifixes", a young **teacher of Catholic religion** told me during a meeting of Green Party where I reported on my recently finished lawsuit of seven years. "Because always before Easter children burst into tears when we speak about Jesus' crucifixion."

"Hallo my dear friends, once more I got a question concerning my **two-year-old daughter**. My parents-in-law are very devout Catholic faithful. In their dining-room they've always had this big and heavy, dark wooden cross hanging with Jesus on it. My daughter all along had angst of this cross. When she was age one and a half I was totally amazed because she always said that the man is hurt by hanging there, though one can hardly spot Jesus because the cross is that dark. For some time now it's getting really terrible. She no more dares to enter the room where it hangs; only if I go along she would follow and only shortly and reluctantly at that. To my in-laws this is completely absurd since they are so faithful. It always seems to me as if they view a little devil in her because of that. But why oh why can she have such angst? Do you have an answer for that? Lots of love, Kiwi."
My answer as an educator and psychologist consists in the questions a child will ask concerning dark crucifixes: That's what people use to do to other people? Can that happen to me also? What a world have I come to?
Since the puzzled mother Kiwi put her question (*Warum hat sie Angst davor*, July 19, 2007) in "esoterikforum.net", she gets an answer that supposes memories of a life before life:
"Hallo Kiwi, actually your daughter says very plainly that 'the man is hurt by hanging there', so to her this cross is the picture of an act of violence and that is what it has been. It was an execution and it is beyond dispute that it was very painful. Maybe she once has lived in a time when such methods of execution were still common. These experiences she took along into her new life. This cross then is like a dejavú. And children have, if there's no vision defect since birth, an incredible acuteness of vision. So it's well possible that she recognizes everything on this dark cross. Lots of love, Sascha."

Acuteness of vision: Brazilian children sitting on a lawn, watching something that bustles between the grass stalks, proudly name the little insects: "Formigas! Formigas!" Their pride of knowing, naming their bustling little

world colleagues reminded my on the eye-sight of Kiwi's daughter. And of same-age Johanna.

When two-year-old **Johanna** was visiting her grandparents, grandma put her delicious vanilla cake on the afternoon coffee table. While Johanna was parting the piece of cake with her fork, on a sudden something crossed her mind. In her caring and empathic way, Johanna took a piece of cake between her fingers, climbed up the corner bench and fed hungry Jesus, putting the cake to his pain-twisted wooden mouth.

"You are mistaken", Janusz Korczak warned. Not "descending" to the child's point of view, not "bowing down, declining, making ourselves smaller" is our task as adults, but "climbing up, stretching out, tiptoeing, extending. In order not to hurt."[1043]

At this child-centered end of of my book, I venture to consolidate its matter by very personal aspects, descending time-wise – first into my childhood: When I myself at age four asked my father "Papa, what's that up there?" I pointed to the same wooden Jesus whom my niece Johanna would try to feed four decades later and that my parents had received as a wedding gift in 1947. What my father replied to me I remember but vaguely; what I'm sure about is that the word "Juden" did not occur.

My own way of testing whether an artificial body has feelings differed scari-ly from Johanna's. One morning, before leaving for school, my sister had bedded her doll on the dresser besides the crucifix corner. Alone now in the room, I lighted a match and put it to the doll's right foot. Terribly quick the cellophane foot caught fire, panicking I took the plastic girl by her tiny hand and whirled her around in desperation, threw her under the piano, ran out by the veranda door and hid in the garden. Alarmed by the smell of burning, my mother found the burned out doll dresses beneath the smoldering piano, thought on first sight it was me, ran out and called her neighbor women one of whom found me behind a shrub. My sister shed bitter tears when she came home from school, my sister with her green eyes and brown braids whom family and friends never called by her name Elisabeth but always by the name my oldest brother had invented for her in the cradle: Haia, almost like the sister with black braids recalled by Binem Heller in his song: "Main shvester Chaye mit di oygn grine, a daytsh hot in treblinke si farbrent."

On Friday, April 29, 1966 I was alone at home at night, my younger brothers sleeping already, and I, age thirteen, watching at TV a drama that I not until 2005, in the library of Porto Alegre's Instituto Goethe, recognized as *The Investigation* of Peter Weiss, staging the Frankfurt Auschwitz Trial, with a scene that shaped my life. The witness Number 5, Dunia Wasserstrom, related how outside the window a truck transporting children arrived, a little boy jumped down with an apple in his hand, and SS guard Boger went over to the boy and grabbed him at his feet and smashed his head against the wall

---

1043 Korczak, Janusz: Wenn ich wieder klein bin und andere Geschichten von Kindern. Göttingen 1973, p.13 (Wikipedia, Janusz Korczak).

and told the witness she should "wipe down that" and an hour later she saw him "... eating the apple.' Attorney: '*Frau Zeugin*, during the preliminary hearings you never mentioned this incident.' Zeugin 5: 'I was not able to talk about it ... By personal reasons ... Since then I never wanted to have an own child."

And I made the same decision right in this moment, considering a world in which fathers are not able to protect their children from such monsters.

This strange kind of celibate seven years later became the passage in mined area that led me, after local leadership activity in Catholic Youth and military service, to the entrance of Augsburg sacerdotal seminary. There, reality caught me up soon. "How can Jesus say about Judas that this man better never had been born? For a Godson this is a declaration of bankruptcy" I explained to our wise old spiritual trainer Father Waldmann who used to start his exercises with Martin Buber's Chassidic Tales and who, unable to clear my doubts, asked me to accept his blessing.

So I became a blessed teacher, and my first 8th-graders, by whatever reason, nicknamed me Moses. While my father had brought the Hollywood movie *Ben Hur* to stage with his young choir, my pupils enjoyed their voyage to the past in our *Time Machine*, escaping Roman soldiers and burning of witches before stopping in 1993 to warn a Jewish girl, as well as in 1987 they liked reviving the tragicomical life of famous eighteenth-century pickpocket Elisabeth Gassner (known as *Schwarze Lis*), who later on proved to have been the Jewish ancestor of two boyhood friends and two pupils of mine. After our Jesus-birth-play *Miriam under the Palm Tree* according to the Koran, my Turkish, German and Ghanaian pupils in our stage version of John Landis' cult movie *Blues Brothers*, touring in service of the Lord (and of their Catholic orphanage mother), made Chicago Nazis feel the Blues. My prize-awarded drama *New Heimat* about German US-immigrants in the aftermath of 1848 March Revolution focused on Jewish seamstress Gitele Ullmann as protagonist, whereas the *Dragonburghers*, my young actors' version of Jewish writer Evgeny Shvarts's *The Dragon*, satirized human sacrifice as means of corrupt authoritarianism. Two months later, the coincidence of viewing the German "crucifix judgement" headlines exactly at a newsstand in Prague's former Jewish ghetto triggered my henceforth dedication to an issue – the issue of this book – that seems to have been subthreshold present in my family.

Present – how? Let's come back to the family's afternoon coffee table with vanilla cake for crucified Jesus. Johanna's father, my brother Johannes Riggenmann, is a church painting master with own company. Three times I helped him hang up life-size corpuses, standing on the ladder embracing Jesus' bloody legs. Once in the 1990s, he was performing the restoration of the townhall in nearby village Waldstetten, when an old resident watched him painting and remarked that here in Waldstetten yet in 17th century a church painter named Johannes Riggenmann (1682-1767) had lived. Old Mr. König even provided my brother with church register documents yielding that this master Riggenmann the Elder was the grandson of the shoemaker

Jacob Rikheman (1627-1687) who around 1653 – when the Chmielnitzky pogroms raged in Eastern Europe – had settled here and reared 14 children with his first wife Anna Maria N.N. and his second wife Maria Mandel. One grandson and one great-grandson of his became church painters; a family crest confirmed the Riggenmann clan's descendence from "a good old lineage" of Lower Rhinelands, so good and noble that generations of Riggenmann had this usurped family crest of Dutch family Rukem adorn their farmhouse parlors.

For instance my grandfather who was the nephew of an Innsbruck entrepreneur with Jewish partner, while he in Swabia farmed with his wife 23 acres for seven children, and his neighbors looked askant at him because of his Jewish friend, the textile peddler Jakob Koschland of Ichenhausen. In 1937 my gifted father, just seventeen, painted a tableau "Madonna with Jesus boy" which was placed on one of my grandfather's fields at the country road to Ichenhausen. Ready painted, the boy and his mother had pitch-black curled hair like Mr. Koschland. In this way my father – as my youngest uncle Joseph told me – protested at a time when Jesus and his mother had to be blond Aryans. The Koschland family was deported to Poland in 1943, when my grandfather died on stomach ulcer and my father earned his two Iron Crosses in service as lieutenant of artillery in Ukraine and Crimea while his brother Alois died near Moscow, and though the death letter told my grandmother that the shell had killed him instantly her beautiful voice never again was heard in church. In 1945 my father came home, read Eugen Kogon's *Der SS-Staat*, married the young woman with whom he had exchanged more than 500 letters, became a father of five children, the master of the church choir, a theatre group and two amateur choirs; a busy school director and village mayor of Christian Social Party.

In spite of his increasing symptoms of Alzheimer, my father still in 2000 had contributed to my book *Kruzifix und Holocaust*, providing me with cut-out articles, for instance concerning Russian neo-nazis, of his staunch Catholic *Tagespost* weekly. "Auschwitz, this is a question that must occupy every good-willing human": With these words I had quoted in my book the Jesuite Father Alfred Welker fighting in the slums of Cali, Colombia against the structural violence of our days.[1044]

At my father's burial in January 2004 – with five priests concelebrating and a CSU lawmaker praising the humanistic stance of the beloved school director – hardly anyone of the many funeral guests will not have pondered about the estrangement that the devout Catholic apparently had suffered by his strayed and wayward son, the infamous, and alas successful, objector against classroom crosses. Two weeks later, one morning my daily newspaper had an article about Padre Welker. No sooner than I had cut out the article from my daily, I perceived what was right on its back: Johann Riggenmann. Card of Thanks, to all who took part in our father's burial.

1044 "Warum riskiert Alfred Welker sein Leben in Agua Blanca?", 3sat TV broadcast, April 14, 2000.

Chance is not a kosher word, said Eli Wiesel. I read the front side article again. At its end, Father Welker explained his concept of Imitation of Christ by a Colombian legend: "A woman took the vow to donate a crucifix. When she had saved up the money, she spent it for ransoming her brother from jail. Jesus appeared to her in a dream and said: "You have understood what I want."

Not far from Colombia, in a street play in Brazilian São Luis, some months later I heard an actor say *"Andamos com os mortos nas costas"* – We walk with the dead ones on our back. In 1943, Charles Singer said: "We carry our history in our very bowels. Both spiritually and biologically the dead live in each of us", and in 1993, highlighting "coincidence in time and space" as means of transmission between generations, Anne Ancelin Schützenberger stressed drily: "The dead pass down to the living."[1045]

In 2012 I had to know it: what I carry not on my back but in my chromosomes. A genetical test confirmed my deeply engrained intuition as clearly as such tests can. According to Oxford genetician Bryan Sykes, European women descend from but seven prehistoric mothers only one of whom lived outside Europe, more precisely around Lebanon. Twelve millennia later her mtDNA is "common in the Near East, Europe, the Caucasus, North Africa and the Middle East and among Jews."[1046] Whether 1790 born Maria Anna Kössinger came from Franconian town Kissingen (where Jews were first mentioned during the Rintfleisch pogrom of 1298) is not verifiable, but surely she passed her Libanese genes down to my grandmother, a girl with "nothing but A" in her Volksschul report, a farmer's wife who in her late life had fear of crucifixes.

Romantically I could say: Few millennia ago somewhere between Lebanon and Sinai my maternal genes said goodbye to my paternal ones and married again in Swabia in 1947. For plain-talking is the Y-DNA of 1627 born shoemaker Jacob Rikheman which I share with even more Arab than Jewish relatives, the latter bearing many Spanish-Portuguese surnames like Enriques and Rodrigues. Recent research links my paternal genetic signature with its "very low frequency in the world" to "demographic processes such as ... the Assyrian and Babylonian exiles and the Jewish Diaspora. The Median-Joining network for T1 haplotypes links these lineages to *Israel, Lebanon and Palestine"*, while its high frequencies in border-near Northern Portugal, on the Balear Islands, the Azores and among Colombians of Spanish descent "may reflect migration of Sephardic Jews during the Inquisition".[1047] The high frequency of my male lineage among Sephardic Levites, Iraqi, Curd, and Galilean Jews, among Somalian Cushites, Palestinians and the Black Jewish Lemba of South Africa evinces racism once more as "science of the witless guys" and stresses the impact of carnally transmitted mental dispositions, maybe even this "hereditary aversion against the cult of

1045 Singer, Charles, p.68; Schützenberger, p.6 and 146.
1046 oxfordancestors.com/content/view/35/55; Entine, p.357.
1047 Bennett Greenspan, quoted by Carvajal, p.161/162.

images" Anita Novinsky attests to Portuguese Marranos.[1048] Which leaves me with the question what went portably along from Riques to Riggenmann or better: from Nile and Euphrates to Rio Tejo and Danube where my first Swabian 8th-graders nicknamed me Moses: Is it in the genes that Jews abolished God images, Arabs introduced the number zero and both can do without concrete representations of divinity?

Anyhow, Little Johanna acted out a brilliant idea when she climbed up to serve cake to the wooden *Herrgott* Jesus, enacting after 3000 years the Deuteronomy (4:28) verse of Moses "There you will serve man-made gods of wood and stone that cannot see or hear or eat or smell". Her spontaneous action is as witty and provoking as Abram's god smashing coup, and more economical at that: Offering sweet cake to a woodcarved mouth, artful little Johanna put the senseful human reality of taste, smell and caring against the insensivity of the wooden idol her uncle *Moses* wrote this book about.

"Quién me presta una escalera, para subir al madero, para quitarle los clavos a Jesús el Nazareno?"

This verse from a classic Spanish saeta song asks: "Who will lend me a ladder to climb the wood, remove the nails from Jesus the Nazarene?"[1049] Jesus' freeing never foundered on a lack of ladders. The gripping image held Christian culture captive since it docks within the viewer's mind at the three most important relations of this viewer's personal life, i.e. his body, his core family (father) and his fellow humans (justice, punishing maltreatment). It held us captive by its extremely bipolar tension between visible cruelty and the love we'd love to believe in. It held us tight by the core of humanity it appeals to: compassion. And many a good Christian is held captive because "unresolved justice concerns may have a lingering effect on the best-intentioned actors."[1050]

And that's why even religious persons with the best intentions, focused on a Jew with best intentions, developed the worst intentions concerning the Jewish people. Focused on this *filho da mãe*[1051] from Nazareth who, thrice ahead of his time, acted against animal sacrifice, called for women's rights and put children to the center – and who, following his own advice, remained the outraged child of his outset till his end. His *Love your neighbor as yourself* is the precise reverse image to the radical evil of sadistic *Your neighbor's pain won't hurt yourself* (or even save you), depicted detailed in the symbol by which his cause is reversed into its opposite.

His moral principle of equal respect for all human beings links the Christians with the Jews who shaped this principle around 500 BC in Babylon, as well as with the Indian Mahabharata which likewise resumed some 500 years before Jesus: "This is the sum of all real probity – treat others as you wish to get treated ... – man acquires a right guideline for his behavior if he views his neighbor as himself."[1052]

1048 Novinsky 2013, p.37-38.
1049 Carvajal, p.117.
1050 Learner/Clayton, p.221.
1051 Portuguese "son of mother", also softer synonym for "filho da puta" (son of a bitch).
1052 Vasudev, Jyotsna: "Kohlbergs Universalitätspostulat aus indischer Sicht"; in:

The past 340 pages showed the crucifix as learning tool for hatred against Jewish neighbors, allowing now two Christian answers: (1) Let's protect our neighbors like ourselves, by taking Jesus from the tool; or (2) "Am I my brother's keeper?

The cute little baby in this book's last picture (taken in 1890) grew up to be a man who, impressed by Jesus but intrigued by the cross, became the global epitome of mass murderer. When the grown-up toddler was already called Führer, the later Nobel-Prize awarded psychologist Daniel Kahneman was a teenager in occupied France and struggled with the thought "that the monstrous Hitler enjoyed flowers and was tender to babies. If there was some good even in Hitler, then evil could not be described simply ..."[1053]

An image of utter evil, done to the good one, held this child captive until the last day of his life on which he wrote he didn't want to assume the role of the laughed at culprit in a "new drama enacted by Jews."

Maybe the baby on the next page could have ended his life as an Austrian grandfather, proudly painting portraits of his grandchildren, all charming big-eyed toddlers.

Why not?

Edelstein /Nunner-Winkler, p.156.
1053   Pearl, p.234.

Acknowledgements

I am indebted to the authors of all the books and whatever verbal expressions I could quote in this book, including all the persons from infancy to old age who ventured to disclose their feelings concerning the picture. Gratefully I remember all who gave me support during my now 25 years of questioning the most momentous symbol of mankind: Christians, Muslims, atheists, freethinkers and humanists.

Special thanks I owe to two out of fourteen million Jews on this planet who backed my efforts: My Curitiban friend Fabiano Amaral of Judaismo Humanista helped me tirelessly with the layout while being triply stretched by his postgraduate studies, his job at a Baptist faculty and as a young father of his Maria's sons Yosef and David.

Equally obliged I am to old Munich resident Jonathan Wolff who after my trial called me in January 2002, thanking me for having brought this subject to the table. "So you agree", I asked him, "with my thesis that the cross is the tap root of Jew-hate?" – "Of course", Herr Wolff replied. "What else?"

Curitiba, October 26, 2018   K.Y. Riggenmann

Bibliography

Abunimah, Ali: One Country. A bold proposal to end the Israeli-Palestine impasse. New York 2006.

Adams, Carol J.: The Sexual Politics of Meat. New York 2010.

Adorno, Theodor W.: Erziehung zur Mündigkeit, Frankfurt on Main 1971.

Adorno, Theodor W.: Minima Moralia, Frankfurt on Main 1982.

Akers, Keith: The Lost Religion of Jesus. Simple Living and Nonviolence in Early Christianity. New York 2000.

Alberti, Bettina: Die Seele fühlt von Anfang an. Wie pränatale Erfahrungen unsere Beziehungsfähigkeit prägen. Munich 2005.

Alexy, Trudi: The Mezuzah in the Madonna's Foot. Marranos and Other Secret Jews: A Woman Discovers Her Hidden Identity. Lincoln, NE 2006.

Amery, Jean: Jenseits von Schuld und Sühne. Bewältigungsversuche eines Überwältigten. Munich 1966.

Andermann, Frank: Das große Gesicht. Roman. Munich 1970.

Arendt, Hannah: Eichmann in Jerusalem. Ein Bericht von der Banalität des Bösen. Munich 1976.

Aron, Elaine N.: The Highly Sensitive Person. New York 1997.

Askenasy, Hans: Sind wir alle Nazis? Zum Potential der Unmenschlichkeit. Frankfurt on Main 1971.

Aslan, Reza; Zealot. The Life and Times of Jesus of Nazareth. New York 2013.

Bailey, George: Germans. The Biography of an Obsession. New York 1991.

Barbet, Pierre: Die Passion Jesu Christi aus der Sicht des Chirurgen. Karlsruhe 1953.

Bauer, Joachim: Das Gedächtnis des Körpers. Wie Beziehungen und Lebensstile unsere Gene steuern. Munich 2005.

Bauer, Yehuda: A History of the Holocaust. Danbury, CT, 1982.

Bauman, Zygmunt: Modernity and the Holocaust. Maldon, Massachusetts 2007.

Behrla, Carolina: Minha Vida na Alemanha. São Paulo 2011.

Ben-Chorin, Shalom: Überwindung des christlichen Antisemitismus. Rothenburg on Tauber, 1962.

Ben-Chorin, Shalom: Bruder Jesus. Der Nazarener in jüdischer Sicht. Munich 1967.

Ben-Chorin, Shalom: Paulus. Der Völkerapostel in jüdischer Sicht. Munich 1980.

Berman, Louis: Vegetarianism and the Jewish Tradition. New York 1982.

Bernhart, Joseph: Heilige und Tiere. Munich 1937.

Berry, Rynn: Food For The Gods. Vegetarianism and the World Religions. New York 1998.

Berry, Rynn: Hitler: Neither Vegetarian Nor Animal-Lover. New York 2004.

Bevers, Jürgen: Der Mann hinter Adenauer. Hans Globkes Aufstieg vom NS-Juristen zur Grauen Eminenz der Bonner Republik. Berlin 2009.

Birnbaum, Eliahu and **Rosenberg**, Shalom: O que é Cashrut? Antologia do Pensamento Judaico sobre as Leis Dieteticas Judaicas. São Paulo 2003.

Bloch, Ernst: Wegzeichen der Hoffnung. Eine Auswahl aus seinen Schriften: Mythos, Dichtung, Musik. Freiburg i.B. 1967.

Bloch, Ernst: Atheismus im Christentum. Frankfurt on Main 1973.

Bloch, Ernst: Das Prinzip Hoffnung. Frankfurt on Main 1985.

Bodian, Miriam: Dying in the Law of Moses. Crypto-Jewish Martyrdom in the Iberian World. Bloomington, IN, 2007.

Boepple, Ernst (ed.): Adolf Hitlers Reden. Munich 1925/1933.

Bonder, Nilton: A Alma Imoral. Rio de Janeiro 1998.

Bonder, Nilton: A Cabala da Comida, Rio de Janeiro 2004.

Bonnin, Pere: Sangre Judía. Españoles de ascendencia hebrea y anti-semitismo cristiano. Barcelona 2006.

Boyarin, Daniel: The Jewish Gospels. New York 2012.

Brackmann, Andrea: Jenseits der Norm – hochbegabt und hoch sensibel? Stuttgart 2005.

Braunstein, Mark Mathew: Radical Vegetarianism. Quaker Hill, CT, 1993.

Braverman, Mark: Fatal Embrace. Christians, Jews, and the Search for Peace in the Holy Land. New York 2010.

Brecht, Bertolt: Die Dreigroschenoper. Frankfurt on Main 1973.

Broszat, Martin (ed.): Kommandant in Auschwitz. Autobiographische Aufzeichnungen von Rudolf Höß. Stuttgart 1958.

Burg, Avraham: The Holocaust Is Over. We Must Rise From the Ashes. New York 2008.

Butler, Judith: Parting Ways. Jewishness and the Critique of Zionism. New York 2012.

Bytwerk, Randall L.: Julius Streicher. New York 1983.

Cain, Susan: Quiet. The Power of Introverts in a World That Can't Stop Talking. New York 2013.

Callsen, Brigitta et al.: Das jüdische Leben Jesu, Toldot Jeschu. Die älteste lateinische Übersetzung in den Falsitates Judaeorum von Thomas Ebendorfer. Kritisch herausgegeben, eingeleitet, übersetzt und mit Anmerkungen versehen von Brigitta Callsen, Fritz Peter Knapp, Manuela Niesner und Martin Przybilski. Vienna and Munich 2003.

Canetti, Elias: Masse und Macht, Frankfurt on Main 1994.

Capps, Donald: The Child's Song. Religious Abuse of Children. Louisville, Kentucky 1995.

Carroll, James: Constantine's Sword. The Church and the Jews. Boston and New York 2001.

Carvajal, Doreen: The Forgetting River. A Modern Tale of Survival, Identity and the Inquisition. New York 2012.

Cohen, Jeremy: Christ Killers. The Jews and the Passion from the Bible to the Big Screen. New York 2007.

Cohn, Haim: O Julgamento e a Morte de Jesus. Rio de Janeiro 1994.

Cohn, Norman: Die Protokolle der Weisen von Zion. Der Mythos von der jüdischen Weltverschwörung. Cologne and Berlin 1969.

Cohn-Sherbok, Dan: The Crucified Jew. Twenty Centuries of Christian Anti-Semitism. Grand Rapids, Michigan 1997.

Colb, Sherry F.: Mind If I Order the Cheeseburger? And Other Questions People Ask Vegans. New York 2013.

Cordovero, Moses: Tomer Deborah – Der Palmbaum der Deborah. Eine mystische Ethik radikalen Erbarmens, übersetzt von Shulamith Zemach-Tendler und Klaus Schäfer, mit einer Einführung und Anmerkungen von Klaus Schäfer. Freiburg i.B. 2003.

Coudenhove-Kalergi, Richard (ed.) and Heinrich: Judenhaß von heute – Das Wesen des Antisemitismus. Vienna and Zurich 1935.

Crossan, John Dominic: Who killed Jesus? New York 1996.

Czermak, Gerhard: Christen gegen Juden. Geschichte einer Verfolgung. Reinbek 1997.

Dallari, Dalmo de Abreu and **Korczak**, Janusz: O Direito da Criança ao Respeito. São Paulo 1986.

Dawkins, Richard: Der Gotteswahn. [The God Delusion]. Berlin 2007.

Deal, James Robert: What to Serve a Goddess When She Comes For Dinner. A Theology of Food. Lynnwood, Washington 2007.

deMause, Lloyd: Hört ihr die Kinder weinen? Eine psychogenetische Geschichte der Kindheit. Frankfurt on Main 1982.

Derrida, Jacques: O animal que logo sou. São Paulo 2011.

de Rosa, Peter: Der Jesus-Mythos. Über die Krise der katholischen Kirche. Munich 1993.

Deselaers, Manfred: Und Sie hatten nie Gewissensbisse? Die Biografie von Rudolf Höß, Kommandant von Auschwitz. Leipzig 1997.

Dieckmann, Bernhard: Judas als Sündenbock. Eine verhängnisvolle Geschichte von Angst und Vergeltung. Munich 1991.

Dimont, Max: Jews, God and History. New York 1962.

Donat, Alexander: The Holocaust Kingdom. New York 1965.

Drewermann, Eugen: Kleriker. Olten 1989.

Durant, Will: Caesar und Christus. Eine Kulturgeschichte Roms und des Christentums von den Anfängen bis zum Jahr 325 n.Chr. Bern 1949.

Eberle, Henrik (ed.): Briefe an Hitler. Bergisch Gladbach 2007.

Eckardt, A.Roy: Elder and Younger Brothers. The Encounter of Jews and Christians. New York 1967.

Edelstein, W./ **Nunner-Winkler**, G.: Zur Bestimmung der Moral. Frankfurt on Main 1986.

Einstein, Albert (ed. Carl Seelig): Mein Weltbild. Berlin 2014.

Eisenman, Robert: Jakobus, der Bruder von Jesus. Munich 2000.

Eisler, Robert: Man Into Wolf. An Anthropological Interpretation of Sadism, Masochism and Lycanthropy. London 1951.

Eisnitz, Gail: Slaughterhouse. The Shocking Story of Greed, Neglect, and Inhumane Treatment Inside the U.S. Meat Industry. New York 2007.

Eizereif, Heinrich: Das Zeichen des lebendigen Gottes. Muttergottes-Erscheinungen in Marienfried. Ausgabe B ohne Anmerkungen. Stein on Rhine 1976.

Elian, Renate: Lobe den Schöpfer ... und vergiß fast alles, was man dir von ihm gesagt hat. Stuttgart 1985.

Ellis, Marc H.: Toward a Jewish Theology of Liberation. Maryknoll, NY, 1987.

Ellis, Marc H.: O, Jerusalem! The Contested Future of the Jewish Covenant. Minneapolis 1999.

Ellis, Marc H.: Burning Children. A Jewish View of the War in Gaza. Newdiasporabooks (s.l.), 2014.

Entine, Jon: Abraham's Children. Race, Identity and the DNA of the Chosen People. New York and Boston, 2007.

Epstein, Lawrence J. (ed.): Readings on Conversion to Judaism. Northvale 1995.

Erikson, Erik: Kindheit und Gesellschaft, Stuttgart 1999.

Felipe, Sônia: Galactolatria – mau deleite. Implicações eticas, ambientais e nutricionais do consumo de leite bovino. São José, SC, Brazil 2012.

Ferenczi, Sandor: Schriften zur Psychoanalyse II, Frankfurt on Main 1972.

Finguerman, Ariel: A Eleição de Israel. A polemica entre judeus e cristãos sobre a doutrina do "povo eleito". São Paulo 2005.

Flannery, Edward: The Anguish of the Jews. Twenty-Three Centuries of Antisemitism. Mahwah, New Jersey 2004.

Flusser, David: Jesus in Selbstzeugnissen und Bilddokumenten. Reinbek 1968.

Fogelman, Eva: Conscience & Courage. Rescuers of Jews During the Holocaust. New York 1995.

Fraenkel, Heinrich and **Manvell**, Roger: Goebbels. Der Verführer. Munich 1992.

Francione, Gary L. and **Charlton**, Anna: Eat Like You Care. An Examination of the Morality of Eating Animals. Exempla Press (s.l.), 2013.

Freire, Paulo: Pädagogik der Unterdrückten. Reinbek 1991.

Freud, Sigmund: Jenseits des Lustprinzips (Beyond the Pleasure Principle, 1921), CW Vol. XIII, Frankfurt on Main 1999.

Freud, Sigmund: Hemmung, Symptom und Angst (Inhibitions, Symptoms and Anxiety. Leipzig/Vienna/Zurich 1926; CW Vol. XIV, Frankfurt on Main 1999.

Freud, Sigmund: Freud, S., Über die weibliche Sexualität (1931). CW Vol. XIV, Frankfurt on Main 1999.

Freud, Sigmund: Totem und Tabu. Frankfurt on Main 1973.

Freud, Sigmund: Der Mann Moses und die monotheistische Religion. Frankfurt on Main 1990.

Freud, Sigmund: O Mal-Estar na Civilização [Civilization and Its Discontents]. Obras completas, volume 18. São Paulo 2010.

Freyre, Gilberto: Herrenhaus und Sklavenhütte. Stuttgart 1982.
Friedman, Richard Elliott: Wer schrieb die Bibel? Cologne 2007.
Friedman, Saul S.: The Oberammergau Passion Play. A Lance Against Civilization. Carbondale and Edwardsville 1984.
Fricke, Weddig: Standrechtlich gekreuzigt. Person und Prozeß des Jesus aus Galiläa. Reinbek 1991.
Fromm, Erich: Über den Ungehorsam [On Disobedience]. Munich 1993.
Fuks, Saul (org.): Tribunal da Historia. Vol. II - Processo de formação da identidade judaica e do anti-semitismo. Rio de Janeiro 2008.
Galeano, Eduardo: As Veias Abertas da América Latina. Rio de Janeiro 2016.
Gamm, Hans Jochen: Pädagogische Studien zum Problem der Judenfeindschaft. Berlin 1966.
Gehrcke, Wolfgang / **von Freyberg,** Jutta / **Grünberg,** Harri: Die deutsche Linke, der Zionismus und der Nahost-Konflikt. Cologne 2009.
Gerber, Barbara: Jud Süß. Aufstieg und Fall im frühen 18.Jahrhundert. Ein Beitrag zur historischen Antisemitismus- und Rezeptionsforschung. Hamburg 1990.
Gerber, Jane S.: The Jews of Spain. A History of the Sephardic Experience. New York 1994.
Giehse, Therese: Ich hab nichts zum Sagen. Reinbek 1976.
Gilbert, Martin: The Holocaust. The Human Tragedy. Rosetta Books 2014.
Gilman, Sander L.: Die schlauen Juden. Über ein dummes Vorurteil. Hildesheim 1998.
Gitlitz, David M.: Secrecy and Deceit: The Religion of the Crypto-Jews. Philadelphia 1996.
Glick, Caroline: The Israeli Solution: A One-State-Plan for Peace in the Middle East. New York 2014.
Goitein, S.D. (Shlomo Dov): Jews and Arabs. A Concise History of Their Social and Cultural Relations. Mineola, NY, 2005.
Gold, Helmut / **Heuberger,** Georg (ed.): Abgestempelt. Judenfeindliche Postkarten; auf der Grundlage der Sammlung Wolfgang Haney [Catalogue to the exhibition in Jewish Museum, Frankfurt] Frankfurt on Main 1999.
Goldhagen, Daniel Jonah: Hitlers willige Vollstrecker. Ganz gewöhnliche Deutsche und der Holocaust. Berlin 1996.
Goldhagen, Daniel Jonah: Die katholische Kirche und der Holocaust. Eine Untersuchung über Schuld und Sühne. Berlin 2002.
Goldmann, Nahum: O Paradoxo Judeu. Memorias pessoais dos encontros históricos que moldaram o drama do Judaismo moderno. São Paulo 1984.
Goldstein, Morris: Jesus in the Jewish Tradition. New York 1950.
Goldstein, Phyllis: A Convenient Hatred: The History of Antisemitism. Brookline, MA, 2012.
Goleman, Daniel: Emotionale Intelligenz. Munich 1999.
Gorenberg, Gershom: The Unmaking of Israel. New York 2011.

Greenberg, Irving: The Jewish Way. Living the Holidays. New York 1993.
Greenberg, Irving: For the Sake of Heaven and Earth. The New Encounter Between Judaism and Christianity. Philadelphia 2004.
Greger, Michael, M.D. / **Stone**, Gene: How Not to Die. New York 2015.
Gritschneder, Otto: Bewährungsfrist für den Terroristen Adolf H. Der Hitler-Putsch und die bayerische Justiz. Munich 1990.
Gross, Jan T.: Fear. An Essay In Historical Interpretation. Princeton, NJ 2006.
Hamann, Brigitte: Hitlers Wien. Munich and Zurich 1996.
Häsing, Helga and **Janus**, Ludwig: Ungewollte Kinder. Reinbek 1994.
Hart, Donna and **Sussman**, Robert W.: Man the Hunted. Primates, Predators and Human Evolution. Philadelphia 2009.
Heer, Friedrich: Gottes erste Liebe. Die Juden im Spannungsfeld der Geschichte. Berlin 1981.
Heer, Friedrich: Der Glaube des Adolf Hitler. Anatomie einer politischen Religiosität. Berlin 1989.
Heer, Friedrich: Abschied von Höllen und Himmeln. Vom Ende des religiösen Tertiär. Frankfurt and Berlin 1990.
Heine, Heinrich: Gedichte. Ausgewählt und eingeleitet von Ludwig Marcuse. Zurich 1977.
Heinsohn, Gunnar: Was ist Antisemitismus? Der Ursprung von Monotheismus und Judenhaß – Warum Antisemitismus? Frankfurt on Main 1988.
Hengel, Martin: Crucifixion – In the ancient world and the folly of the message of the cross. Philadelphia 1977.
Henning, Max (translator): Der Koran. Einleitung und Anmerkungen von Annemarie Schimmel. Stuttgart 1960.
Herzog, Hal: Some We Love, Some We Hate, Some We Eat. Why It's So Hard to Think Straight About Animals. New York 2010.
Hilberg, Raul: Die Vernichtung der europäischen Juden. Berlin 1982.
Hilberg, Raul: Täter, Opfer, Zuschauer. Frankfurt on Main 1992.
Hilzinger, Sonja: Anna Seghers, Das siebte Kreuz. Erläuterungen und Dokumente. Stuttgart 2004.
Hirschberger, Johannes: Kleine Philosophiegeschichte. Freiburg i.B. 1961.
Hitler, Adolf: Mein Kampf. Munich 1935.
Hordes, Stanley M.: To the End of the Earth. A History of the Crypto-Jews of New Mexico. New York and Chichester (UK) 2005.
Horkheimer, Max and **Adorno**, Theodor W.: Dialektik der Aufklärung. Philosophische Fragmente. Frankfurt on Main 2008.
Horsley, Richard A. and **Silberman**, Neil Asher.: The Message and the Kingdom. How Jesus and Paul Ignited a Revolution and Transformed the Ancient World. New York 1997.
Hsia, Ronnie Po-Chia: Trient 1475. Geschichte eines Ritualmordprozesses. Frankfurt on Main 1997.
Isaac, Jules: Jesus und Israel. Vienna and Zurich 1968.

Jacobs, Wilhelm G.: Johann Gottlieb Fichte. Reinbek 1984.
Jammer, Max: Einstein e a Religião. Física e Teologia. Rio de Janeiro 2000.
Janus, Ludwig: Der Seelenraum des Ungeborenen. Pränatale Psychologie und Therapie. Düsseldorf and Zurich 2000.
Josephus, Flavius: Geschichte des Jüdischen Krieges, Wiesbaden 1982.
Jüdisches Museum der Stadt Wien (ed.): Die Macht der Bilder. Antisemitische Vorurteile und Mythen. Vienna 1995.
Jung, Carl Gustav: Gesamtwerk (Collected Works), Olten and Freiburg i.B. 1985.
Junginger, Horst: Die Verwissenschaftlichung der „Judenfrage" im Nationalsozialismus. Darmstadt 2011.
Jungreis, Esther: Life Is A Test. How to meet life's challenges successfully. New York 2006.
Kafka, Franz: Der Proceß. Stuttgart 1995.
Kafka, Franz: Sämtliche Erzählungen. Frankfurt on Main, 1976.
Kant, Immanuel: Die Religion innerhalb der Grenzen der bloßen Vernunft. Königsberg 1793/ Stuttgart 1974.
Kant, Immanuel: Zum ewigen Frieden. Ein philosophischer Entwurf. Stuttgart 2002.
Kalechofsky, Roberta: Judaism & Animal Rights. Marblehead 1992.
Kalechofsky, Roberta: Animal Suffering and the Holocaust: The Problem With Comparison. Marblehead 2003.
Kalechofsky, Roberta: Vegetarian Judaism. Marblehead 2006.
Kaplan, Helmut F. (ed.): Warum ich Vegetarier bin. Reinbek 1995.
Karpf, Anne (ed., with Brian Klug, Jacqueline Rose, Barbara Rosenbaum): A Time to Speak Out. Independent Jewish Voices On Israel, Zionism and Jewish Identity. London 2008.
Kaye/Kantrowitz, Melanie: The Colors of Jews. Racial Politics and Radical Diasporism. Bloomington, IN 2007.
Kayserling, Meyer: História dos Judeus em Portugal (Geschichte der Juden in Portugal, Bonn-Leipzig-Braunschweig 1867). São Paulo 2009.
Kertzer, David I.: Die Päpste gegen die Juden. Der Vatikan und die Entstehung des modernen Antisemitismus. Munich 2004.
Kessel, Barbara: Suddenly Jewish. Jews raised as gentiles discover their Jewish roots. Hanover, NH (Brandeis University Press) 2000.
Kierkegaard, Søren: Einübung im Christentum. In: Gesammelte Werke, Vol. 26, Düsseldorf and Cologne 1951.
Kierkegaard, Søren: Auswahl aus dem Gesamtwerk. Wiesbaden 1982.
Klausner, Joseph: Jesus von Nazareth. Jerusalem 1952.
Klee, Ernst: Die SA Jesu Christi. Die Kirche im Banne Hitlers. Frankfurt on Main 1989.
Klee, Ernst: Persilscheine und falsche Pässe. Wie die Kirchen den Nazis halfen. Frankfurt on Main 1992.
Kligsberg, Bernardo: Einstein. Humanismo e Judaismo. São Paulo 2002.

Klinghoffer, David: Why the Jews Rejected Jesus. The Turning Point in Western History. Doubleday/Random House (s.l.) 2005.

Klug, Brian: Being Jewish and Doing Justice. Bringing Argument to Life. Edgware, Middlesex (UK), 2012.

Krogmann, Angelica: Simone Weil. Reinbek 1971.

Kübli, Martin / **Potzel**, Dieter / **Seifert**, Ulrich: Die Rehabilitation des Christus Gottes. Marktheidenfeld 2015.

Kühner, H.: Der Antisemitismus der Kirche. Zurich 1976.

Langer, Walter C.: The Mind of Adolf Hitler. The Secret Wartime Report. New York and London 1972.

Lanzmann, Claude: Shoah. Düsseldorf 1986.

Lapide, Pinchas: Der Rabbi von Nazareth. Wandlungen des jüdischen Jesusbildes. Trier 1974.

Lapide, Pinchas: Er wandelte nicht auf dem Meer. Ein jüdischer Theologe liest die Evangelien. Gütersloh 1984.

Lapide, Pinchas: Ist das nicht Josephs Sohn? Jesus im heutigen Judentum. Gütersloh 1985.

Lapide, Pinchas: Wer war schuld an Jesu Tod? Gütersloh 1987.

Lapide, Pinchas: Warum kommt er nicht? Gütersloh 1988.

Lehr, Stefan: Antisemitismus – religiöse Motive im sozialen Vorurteil (dissertation). Munich 1974.

Leibowitz, Jeshajahu: Gespräche über Gott und die Welt. Mit Michael Shashar. Frankfurt on Main 1990.

Lerner, Melvin J. and **Clayton**, Susan: Justice and Self-Interest. Two Fundamental Motives. New York 2011.

Lerner, Michael: Embracing Israel/Palestine. A Strategy to Heal and Transform the Middle East. Berkeley 2012.

Levend, Helga and **Janus**, Ludwig (ed.): Drum hab ich kein Gesicht. Kinder aus unerwünschten Schwangerschaften. Würzburg 2000.

Lévinas, Emmanuel: Schwierige Freiheit. Versuch über das Judentum. Frankfurt on Main 1996.

Lévinas, Emmanuel: Ethik und Unendliches. Vienna 2008.

Levy, Vera: Prata de Casa. Vida e cultura brasileiras. Vol.4. São Paulo 1991.

Lewis, Bernard: Semites and Anti-Semites. An Inquiry Into Conflict and Prejudice. New York 1999.

Ley, Michael / **Schoeps**, Julius H.: Der Nationalsozialismus als politische Religion. Mainz 1997.

Ley, Michael: Holokaust als Menschenopfer. Vom Christentum zur politischen Religion des Nationalsozialismus. Münster, Hamburg, London 2002.

Liebman Jacobs, Janet: Hidden Heritage. The Legacy of the Crypto-Jews. Berkeley/Los Angeles/London 2002.

Linnemann, Manuela (ed.): Brüder, Bestien, Automaten. Erlangen 2000.

Longerich, Peter: Heinrich Himmler. Oxford 2012.

Lüdemann, Gerd: Jesus nach 2000 Jahren. Was er wirklich sagte und tat. Lüneburg 2000.

Luther, Martin: CW, Vol. 53. Weimar 1920, unchanged reprint 1968.

Maccoby, Hyam: The Day God Laughed. Sayings, Fables and Entertainments of the Jewish Sages. London 1987.

Maccoby, Hyam: Judas Iscariot and the Myth of Jewish Evil. New York 1992.

Maccoby, Hyam: Jesus und der Jüdische Freiheitskampf. Freiburg i.B. 1996.

Maccoby, Hyam: Der Mythenschmied. Paulus und die Erfindung des Christentums. Freiburg i.B. 2007.

Malka, Jeffrey S.: Sephardic Genealogy. Bergenfield, New Jersey, 2002.

Mallet, Carl-Heinz: Untertan Kind. Nachforschungen über Erziehung. Frankfurt on Main and Berlin 1990.

Marineau, René F.: Jacob Levy Moreno 1889-1974. Pai do psicodrama, da sociometria e da psicoterapia de grupo. São Paulo 1989.

Maser, Werner: Adolf Hitler, Mein Kampf. Der Fahrplan eines Welt-eroberers. Esslingen 1974.

Maybaum, Ignaz: The Face of God after Auschwitz. Amsterdam 1965.

Michael, Robert: Holy Hatred. Christian Antisemitism and the Holocaust. New York 2006.

Milgram, Stanley: Das Milgram-Experiment. Zur Gehorsamsbereitschaft gegenüber Autorität. Reinbek 1997.

Mill, John Stuart: Essays on Ethics, Religion and Society. In: Collected Works, Vol.X, Toronto 1969.

Miller, Alice: Du sollst nicht merken, Frankfurt on Main 1981.

Miller, Alice: Am Anfang war Erziehung. Frankfurt on Main 1983.

Misinai, Tsvi: Brother Shall Not Lift Sword Against Brother. The Roots and Solution to the Problem in the Holy Land. Liad Publishing 2008, printed in Lexington, KY, 2014.

Moor, Paul: Jürgen Bartsch: Opfer und Täter. Reinbek 1991.

Moreno, Jacob L.: Gruppenpsychotherapie und Psychodrama. Stuttgart 1973.

Much, Theodor: Zwischen Mythos & Realität. Judentum, wie es wirklich ist. Vienna-Klosterneuburg 2008.

Mynarek, Hubertus: Erster Diener seiner Heiligkeit. Ein kritisches Porträt des Kölner Erzbischofs Joachim Meisner. Cologne 1993.

Myrowitz, Catherine Hall: Finding a Home for the Soul. Interviews with converts to Judaism. Northvale, NJ 1995.

Nazario, Luiz: Autos-de-Fé como Espetáculos de Massa. São Paulo 2005.

Neuhäusler, Anton: Fragmente keines Vorsokratikers. Philosophisches Brevier. Munich 1968.

Neill, A.S.: Antiautoritäre Erziehung. Reinbek 1969.

Nicholls, William: Christian Antisemitism. A History of Hate. Lanham (Maryland) 2004.

Nolting, Hans-Peter: Lernfall Aggression. Wie sie entsteht – wie sie zu vermindern ist. Reinbek 1978.

Norman, Asher: Twenty-Six Reasons Why Jews Don't Believe In Jesus. Los Angeles 2007.

Novinsky, Anita Waingort: Inquisição: Prisioneiros do Brasil, Séculos XVI a XIX. São Paulo 2009.

Novinsky, Anita Waingort: Cristãos Novos na Bahia: A Inquisição no Brasil. São Paulo 2013.

Oberman, Heiko A.: Wurzeln des Antisemitismus. Christenangst und Judenplage im Zeitalter von Humanismus und Reformation. Berlin 1981.

Ostrer, Harry: Legacy. A Genetic History of the Jewish People. New York 2012.

Pappe, Ilan: The Idea of Israel: A History of Power and Knowledge. London 2014.

Patai, Raphael: Tents of Jacob. The Diaspora – Yesterday and Today. Englewood Cliffs (NJ) 1971.

Patterson, David: Pilgrimage of a Proselyte. From Auschwitz to Jerusalem. Middle Village, NY, 1993.

Patterson, Charles: Für die Tiere ist jeden Tag Treblinka. Über die Ursprünge des industrialisierten Tötens. Frankfurt on Main 2004.

Pearl, Judea and Ruth (ed.): I Am Jewish. Personal Reflections Inspired By the Last Words of Daniel Pearl. Woodstock (VT), 2013.

Perera, Victor: The Cross and the Pear Tree. A Sephardic Journey. London 1995.

Perry, Marvin / **Schweitzer**, Frederick M.: Antisemitism: Myth and Hate from Antiquity to the Present. New York and Basingstoke (UK), 2002.

Pfister, Peter / **Kornacker**, Susanne / **Laube**, Volker: Kardinal Michael von Faulhaber. 1869-1952. Munich 2002.

Phayer, Michael: The Catholic Church and the Holocaust, 1930-1965. Bloomington 2000.

Piaget, Jean: Das moralische Urteil beim Kinde. Frankfurt 1973.

Picker, Henry: Hitlers Tischgespräche. Newly edited by Percy Ernst Schramm. Stuttgart 1963.

Pilhofer, Susanne: Romanisierung in Kilikien? Das Zeugnis der Inschriften. Munich 2006.

Poliakov, Léon / **Delacampagne**, Christian / **Girard**, Patrick: Über den Rassismus. Sechzehn Kapitel zur Anatomie, Geschichte und Deutung des Rassenwahns. Stuttgart 1979.

Poliakov, Leon: The History of Anti-Semitism (4 volumes), Philadelphia 2003.

Posener, Alan: Der gefährliche Papst. Eine Streitschrift gegen Benedikt XVI. Berlin 2012.

Posner, Gerald und **Ware**, John: Mengele. Die Jagd auf den Todesengel. Berlin 1993.

Prager, Dennis / **Telushkin**, Joseph: Why the Jews? The Reason for Antisemitism. New York 2003.
Primor, Avi / **von Korff**, Christiane: An allem sind die Juden und die Radfahrer schuld. Deutsch-jüdische Missverständnisse. Munich and Zurich 2010.
Prinz, Joachim: The Secret Jews. New York 1973.
Rabinovici, Doron: Credo und Credit. Frankfurt on Main 2001.
Rabinovici, Doron/ **Speck**, Ulrich/ **Sznaider**, Natan (ed.): Neuer Antisemitismus? Eine globale Debatte. Frankfurt 2005.
Rauschning, Hermann: Gespräche mit Hitler. Zurich 2005.
Riggenmann, Konrad: Escola nova - escola ativa! John Dewey's Pädagogik am Beispiel ihrer Rezeption in Brasilien. Oldenburg 2001.
Riggenmann, Konrad: Kruzifix und Holocaust. Über die erfolgreichste Gewaltdarstellung der Weltgeschichte. Berlin 2002.
Riggenmann, Konrad: So gut warst du, Jeschu Barabbas. Der Nazarener nach der Frau aus Migdal. Wien 2007.
Riggenmann, Konrad: Jesus. Vom Mißbrauch des Menschensohns. Wien-Klosterneuburg, 2009.
Roberts, Paul: The End of Food. Boston and New York 2009.
Roggenkamp, Viola: Erika Mann. Eine jüdische Tochter. Frankfurt on Main 2008.
Rohrbacher, Stefan / **Schmidt**, Michael: Judenbilder. Kulturgeschichte antijüdischer Mythen und antisemitischer Vorurteile. Reinbek 1991.
Rohman, Fernand: Hitler, Le Juif et le Troisième Homme. Presses Universitaires de France, 1983.
Römer, Gernot (ed.) and **Erlanger**, Arnold: Ein Schwabe überlebt Auschwitz. Augsburg 2002.
Rosenzweig, Franz: Der Stern der Erlösung. Frankfurt on Main 1988.
Rosenberger, Erich: Schulsystem im Kollaps. Plädoyer für eine neue Schule. Remshalden (author's edition) 2005.
Roth, Cecil: A History of the Marranos. New York 1974.
Rubenstein, Richard L.: After Auschwitz. Radical Theology and Contemporary Judaism. Indianapolis/New York/Kansas City 1966.
Rubenstein, Richard E.: Assim disse o Senhor. A visão revolucionaria dos profetas. Rio de Janeiro 2009.
Rudin, James: Christians & Jews – Faith to Faith. Woodstock 2011.
Runes, Dagobert D.: The Jew and the Cross. New York 1966 (1st ed.1955).
Sacks, Jonathan: Future Tense. Jews, Judaism and Israel in the Twenty-First Century. New York 2009.
Said, Edward: The Question of Palestine. New York 1992.
Said, Edward: Freud and the Non-European. London 2003.
Sand, Shlomo: Die Erfindung des jüdischen Volkes. Israels Gründungsmythos auf dem Prüfstand. Berlin 2010.
Sand, Shlomo: The Invention of the Land of Israel. London and NY 2012.
Sand, Shlomo: How I Stopped Being a Jew. London 2014.
Sartre, Jean-Paul: Drei Essays. Frankfurt on Main and Berlin 1986.

Schaake, Erich: Hitlers Frauen. Munich 2000.
Schaberg, Jane: The Illegitimacy of Jesus. A Feminist Theological Interpretation of the Infancy Narratives. San Francisco, ca. 1994.
Schatzman, Morton: Die Angst vor dem Vater. Langzeitwirkungen einer Erziehungsmethode. Eine Analyse am Fall Schreber. Reinbek 1974.
Schoenfeld, Gabriel: The Return of Anti-Semitism. San Francisco 2004.
Schönberger, Heinrich / **Pleticha**, Otto: Die Römer. Gütersloh 1977.
Schoeps, Hans-Joachim: Jewish Christianity: Factional Disputes in the Early Church. Philadelphia 1969.
Schoeps, Julius H. / **Schlör**, Joachim (ed.): Antisemitismus. Vorurteile und Mythen. Munich and Zurich 1995.
Scholem, Gershom: On the Mystical Shape of the Godhead. Basic Concepts in the Kabbalah. New York 1991.
Schopenhauer, Arthur: Die beiden Grundprobleme der Ethik, behandelt in zwei akademischen Preisschriften. Leipzig 1881 (archive.org).
Schuster, Peter: Verbrecher, Opfer, Heilige: Eine Geschichte des Tötens 1200-1700. Stuttgart 2015.
Schützenberger, Anne Ancelin: The Ancestor Syndrome. Transgenerational Psychotherapy and the Hidden Link in the Family Tree. New York 1998.
Schwab, Gabriele: Haunting Legacies. Violent Histories and Transgenerational Trauma. New York 2010.
Schwartz, Richard H.: Judaism and Vegetarianism. New York 2001.
Schwartz, Richard H.: Who Stole My Religion? Revitalizing Judaism and applying Jewish values to help heal our imperilled planet. Raleigh (SC) 2011.
Schwarz-Bart, André: The Last of the Just. New York 2000.
Schweitzer, Albert: Die psychiatrische Beurteilung Jesu. Hildesheim, Zurich, New York 2005.
Sezgin, Hilal: Artgerecht ist nur die Freiheit. Eine Ethik für Tiere oder warum wir umdenken müssen. Munich 2014.
Shavit, Ari: My Promised Land. The Triumph and Tragedy of Israel. New York 2013.
Shoham, Giora S.: Walhalla, Golgotha, Auschwitz. Über die Interdependenz von Deutschen und Juden. Vienna 1995.
Singer, Charles: The Christian Failure. London 1943.
Singer, Kurt: Die Schulkatastrophe. Weinheim and Basel 2009.
Singer, Peter: Praktische Ethik. Stuttgart 1994.
Singer, Peter: Animal Liberation. New York 2002.
Sorj, Bernardo: Judaísmo Para Todos. Rio de Janeiro 2010.
Spee, Friedrich: Cautio Criminalis. Munich 1982/2007.
Spiegel, Marjorie: The Dreaded Comparison. Human and Animal Slavery. New York 1996.
Stangneth, Bettina: Eichmann before Jerusalem. New York 2014.
Steffahn, Harald: Hitler. Reinbek 1983.
Stierlin, Helm: Adolf Hitler. Familienperspektiven. Frankfurt o.M. 1975.

Strauss Feuerlicht, Roberta: The Fate of the Jews. A People Torn Between Israeli Power and Jewish Ethics. New York 1983.

Sussman, Robert Wald: The Myth of Race. The troubling persistence of an unscientific idea. Cambridge (Massachusetts) and London 2014.

Swaim, Lawrence: The Death of Judeo-Christianity. Religious Aggression and Systemic Evil in the Modern World. Alresford (UK) 2012.

Swaim, Lawrence: Trauma Bond. An Inquiry into the Nature of Evil. Winchester and Washington 2013.

Szondi, Leopold: Schicksalsanalyse. Wahl in Liebe, Freundschaft, Beruf, Krankheit und Tod. Basel 2004.

Tabor, James D.: Die Jesus-Dynastie. Das verborgene Leben von Jesus und seiner Familie und der Ursprung des Christentums. Munich 2007.

Teixeira, Tânia: Dimensões Educativas do Teatro do Oprimido. Barcelona 2007 (dissertation).

Telushkin, Joseph: Jewish Humor. What the Best Jewish Jokes Say About the Jews. New York 1992.

Telushkin, Joseph: Jewish Wisdom. Ethical, Spiritual and Historical Lessons from the Great Works and Thinkers. New York 1994.

Telushkin, Joseph: Jewish Literacy. The most important things to know about the Jewish religion, its people, and its history. New York 2001.

Tenenbom, Tuvia: Allein unter Deutschen. Eine Entdeckungsreise. Berlin 2012.

Tenenbom, Tuvia: Allein unter Juden. Eine Entdeckungsreise durch Israel. Berlin 2014.

Tobin, Diane and Gary A. & **Rubin**, Scott: In Every Tongue. The Racial & Ethnic Diversity of the Jewish People. San Francisco 2005.

Torrejoncillo, Francisco de: Centinela contra Judios, puesta en la Torre de la Iglesia de Dios. Pamplona 1720 (Google-books).

Trachtenberg, Josua: The Devil and the Jews. The Medieval Conception of the Jew and its Relation to Modern Antisemitism. Philadelphia 1983 (first edition 1943).

Travers Herford, Robert: Christianity in Talmud and Midrash. London 1903; reprint 2012 (forgottenbooks).

Tucker, Jim B.: Vida antes da Vida. Uma pesquisa científica das lembranças que as crianças têm de vidas passadas. São Paulo 2007.

Tuttle, Will: The World Peace Diet. Eating for Spiritual Health and Social Harmony. New York 2005.

Veltri, Elio / **Travaglio**, Marco: L'odeur de L'argent. Les origines et les dessous de la fortune de Silvio Berlusconi. Édition Fayard, s.l., 2001.

Vermes, Geza: Die Geburt Jesu. Geschichte und Legende. Darmstadt 2007.

Viana Filho, Luis: Anísio Teixeira. A Polemica da Educação. Rio de Janeiro 1990.

Völklein, Ulrich: Josef Mengele – Der Arzt von Auschwitz. Göttingen 1999.

Wabbel, T.D. (ed.): Das Heilige Nichts. Gott nach dem Holocaust. Düsseldorf 2007.

355

Wachtel, Nathan: The Faith of Remembrance. Marrano Labyrinths. Philadelphia 2013.
Waintrob Nudel, Benjamin: Moreno e o Hassidismo. São Paulo 1993.
Waite, Robert G.L.: The Psychopathic God Adolf Hitler. New York 1977.
Fraenkel, Heinrich / **Manvell**, Roger: Goebbels. Der Verführer. Munich 1992.
Weischedel, Wilhelm: Die philosophische Hintertreppe. 34 große Philosophen in Alltag und Denken. Munich 1973.
Weiss, John: Ideology of Death. Why the Holocaust Happened in Germany. Chicago 1997.
Weiss, John: Der lange Weg zum Holocaust: die Geschichte der Judenfeindschaft in Deutschland und Österreich. Hamburg 1997.
Weiss, Peter: Die Ermittlung (Docudrama). Frankfurt on Main 2005.
Wiesenthal, Simon: Segel der Hoffnung. Christoph Columbus auf der Suche nach dem gelobten Land. Berlin 1991.
Wilensky, Gabriel: Six Million Crucifixions. How Christian Teachings About Jews Paved the Road to the Holocaust. San Diego 2010.
Wistrich, Robert: Der antisemitische Wahn. Von Hitler bis zum Heiligen Krieg gegen Israel. Ismaning 1987.
Wistrich, Robert S.: Hitler e o Holocausto, Rio de Janeiro 2002.
Wistrich, Robert: A Lethal Obsession. Anti-Semitism from Antiquity to the Global Jihad. New York 2010.
Yerushalmi, Yosef Hayim: Freud's Moses. Judaism Terminable and Interminable. New Haven and London 1991.
Young, Richard Alan: Is God a Vegetarian? Christianity, Vegetarianism and Animal Rights. Chicago and La Salle, Illinois, 1999.
Yovel, Yirmiyahu: The Other Within. The Marranos: Split Identity and Emerging Modernity. Princeton and Oxford 2009.
Zimmermann, Béatrice Acklin and **Annen**, Franz: Versöhnt durch den Opfertod Christi? Die christliche Sühneopfertheologie auf der Anklagebank. Zurich 2009.
Zulliger, Hans: Schwierige Kinder. Bern and Stuttgart 1951.
Zulliger, Hans: Heilende Kräfte im kindlichen Spiel. Frankfurt o.M. 1972.

Bible editions used:

Arenhoevel, Diego (ed.): Jerusalemer Bibel. Freiburg, Basel, Vienna 1968.
Biblehub.com.
Jewish Publication Society: Hebrew-English Tanach. Philadelphia 1999.
Levine, Amy-Jill and **Brettler**, Marc Zvi (editors): The Jewish Annotated New Testament. Oxford 2011.

Pictures and their sources

Cover:
On the left, "La Virgen del huso" (ca.1501-1513, modelled on Leonardo da Vinci's painting), Museo Soumaya, Mexico City: Wikimedia Commons.
Christian children: "Der Giftpilz" (The Poisonous Mushroom) by Ernst Hiemer, Stürmerverlag, Nuremberg 1938, p.40; courtesy archive.org ("a non-profit library of millions of free books ...").
Right side (and p.6): Auschwitz, May 1944, Jewish women and children mostly from Szombathely, with non-Jewish nanny Edith, all selected for and going to the gas chambers: Courtesy Yadvashem archive.
Boy at Warsaw Ghetto Umschlagplatz, from the Stroop Report, May 1943: Courtesy Yadvashem archive.

Pages:
23: Brazilian boy jams street Passion Play: Courtesy (my facebook friend) Amaury Echeverria, Antonina/Paraná, December 21, 2013.

41: Tombstone of Roman legionary Pantera: Flusser, p.40, courtesy Rowohlt Verlag; tombstone of Pintaius Pedilici (Signifer): Wikimedia Commons.

62: James Tissot (1836-1902), Barabbas: Wikimedia Commons.

96: Ku-Klux-German: Courtesy Badische Zeitung, BZ October 17, 2012.

101: Left: "Crucifixion of Christ", Irish bookpainting, 8th century, Stifts Library St. Gallen, Switzerland; published in: Erziehung zur Kunst, plate 6, Schuler Verlagsgesellschaft Stuttgart, about 1960.
Center: Master of Lucca, around 1250: zeno.org/Kunstwerke (courtesy Sven and Katrin Lohmann, kirchengucker.de).
Right: Matthias Grünewald, Isenheim Altar, Alsacia, ca. 1512-1516: Wikimedia Commons.

105: "Der Giftpilz" (The Poisonous Mushroom): See cover illustration.
Hitler's watercolor (1923-1925): Courtesy nobeliefs.com/mementoes.htm.

107: From Julius Streicher's smearsheet "Der Stürmer":
a) Issue 15, Easter 1933: Varga, William P.: The Number One Nazi Jew-Baiter [about Julius Streicher]. New York 1981, p.193 (in Riggenmann 2002, p.22); now courtesy humanist.de/kriminalmuseum.
b) Issue 13/1929: research.calvin.edu/german-propaganda-archive/.

109: The stigmatized mystic Anna-Katharina Emmerick, painting by Gabriel von Max, 1885: de.wikipedia.org/wiki//Anna_Katharina_Emmerick.
Dreyfus at martial court: Wikimedia Commons.

117: Circumcision of J.: Schoeps/Schlör, p.90, ©Hubert Walder, Bozen. Photo album of Police Battalion 101: Goldhagen 1996, p.292, courtesy Bundesarchiv, no. B 162 Bild-0207 / Foto: o.Ang.

127: Stürmer poster 1937: courtesy Bundesarchiv, Plak 003-020-028-T1, Fips. Stropkov: courtesy H.E.A.R.T., holocaustresearchproject.org.

138: Hieronymus Wierix, Christ in the Wine Press: Wikimedia Commons.

142: Stürmer cartoon "Young Plan": nobeliefs.com/mementoes.html (site deactivated), cf. research.calvin.edu/german-propaganda-archive/. Stürmer cartoon "Kreuzigung"; Courtesy HolocaustResearchProject.org.

153: Folio from the Rabbula Gospel: Wikipedia. Crucifixion, bookpainting in an evangeliar of late 9th century: Rohrbacher/ Schmidt, p.227, courtesy Rowohlt Verlag.

155: Wayside crucifix near Meßkirch: Schoeps/Schlör, p.64, © Reiner Löbe, www.fotoloebe.de, with kind permission. "The Nuremberg Jew ...": Courtesy Jüdisches Museum der Stadt Wien (ed.: Die Macht der Bilder, p.182).

158: Leonardo da Vinci (1452-1519) and helper, Madonna dei fusi (also Madonna dell'Aspo, Madonna of the Yarnwinder), 1501: Wikimedia Commons. Lorenzo Lotto (1480-1557), Natività (Adoration), 1523: Wikimedia Commons (see also wikiart.org/en/lorenzo-lotto/nativity-of-christ-1523). Russian icone, displayed in a Bavarian field chapel: author's archive, K.Y.R. I.A.M. of Zwolle (ca.1440-1504): The Madonna Seated, the Christ Child Holding a Cross: Wikimedia Commons.

184: Burning of chief Hatuey, Capitol of Havanna; Ku-Klux-Klan meeting, Gainesville, Florida, Dec. 31, 1922; Poster of an 1938 exhibit in Düsseldorf: all Wikimedia Commons.

199: William of Norwich, his murder on Holy Friday 1144. Woodcut from the Schedelsche Weltchronik, Nuremberg 1493: Rohrbacher/Schmidt, p.19, courtesy Rowohlt Verlag.

204: The circumcision and torture "crosswise" of Little Simon of Trento, from Hartmann Schedel's Nürnberger Weltchronik (1493): Hsia 1997, p.87; Wikimedia Commons. Jews crucifying a Christian boy, from the Vitae Sanctorum (1615-1628) of Jesuite Father Matthäus Rader: Rohrbacher/Schmidt, p.277, courtesy Rowohlt Verlag.

205: Little Simon of Trento, a detail of "Frankfurter Judensau" (cf. Cohen, p.209): Courtesy Historisches Museum Frankfurt, photo Horst Ziegenfusz.

206: Scourging of Christ, by the Master of so called Karlsruhe Passion (around 1450): Wikimedia Commons.
"Ein hübsch new lied von zweyen Juden und einem Kind", 1540: Rohrbacher/Schmidt, p.301, courtesy Rowohlt Verlag.

212: Anonymous Valencian artist (possibly the Neapolitan Niccoló Antonio Calantonio, 1420-1460), Crucifixion, ca. 1450-1460: Wikimedia Commons.
A Jew hanging between two dogs, woodcut by Johannes Stumpf, Zurich 1548: reproduced courtesy Rare Books Division, The New York Public Library, Astor, Lenox and Tilden Foundations, in: Carlebach, Elisheva: Divided Souls. Converts from Judaism in Germany, 1500-1750. Yale University 2001, p.41; Riggenmann 2009, p.191.
Lucas Mayer, copper engraving "Desecration of the host by Jews in Bratislava", 1591: Courtesy of bpk / Kupferstichkabinett Staatliche Museen zu Berlin – Preußischer Kulturbesitz; (cf. badnewsaboutchristianity.com).

217: Representação de um Auto da Fé, Portuguese lithograph: Wikipedia (português).

221: Pedro de Berruguete, Auto de Fé: Wikimedia Commons.

224: Alejo Fernández (1475-1545), La Flagelación (detail): Wikimedia Commons.
Scourging of Christ, from the Master of Strache Altar: Wikimedia Commons (commons.wikimedia.org/wiki/Category:Master_L._Cz).
The ritual murder of little Rudolf of Bern, from Diebold Schilling's Berner Chronik (1483): Wikimedia Commons.

227: L'histoire se recommence", caricature of Valentin Achille Lemot: Jüdisches Museum Frankfurt am Main (Abgestempelt, p.354); courtesy Museum für Kommunikation, Frankfurt.
Crucifican al Santo Niño ... [de La Guardia], Spain, anonymous, 18th century: Wikimedia Commons.

229: Jacquemart de Hesdin, book painting from the Grandes Heures de Jean de Berry: Wikimedia Commons.
Workshop Hans von Aachen, Divestment of Christ: Wikimedia Commons.
10th Station of Calvary of Wiele, Poland: Wikimedia Commons.
Jewish women, Liepaja/Latvia: Courtesy H.E.A.R.T., Holocaust Education Archive and Research Team). (holocaustresearchproject.org ...)
Lea and Max Epstein: Courtesy Yad Vashem archive.
Jewish men and boy before execution: english.illinois.edu/maps/holocaust/ photo (not accessible any more).

253: The Bethlehem Child Murder: Julius Schnorr von Carolsfeld, Die Bibel in Bildern, 1860, Wikimedia Commons.
Jornal Mercosur, Curitiba, numero 32, Agosto 2014: Personal archive, K.Y.R.
Pietá (dated 1505) of Giovanni Bellini, 1430-1516: Wikipedia.
"Do not kill him twice": Courtesy badnewsaboutchristianity.com.

258: Xanten Ritual Murder 1891: Jüdisches Museum Frankfurt am Main (ed.: Abgestempelt, p.39); courtesy Museum für Kommunikation, Frankfurt.
Mohammed al-Dura: extremecentre.org/2007/10/01/.

261: Cartoon from Al-Hayat al Jadida, April 17, 2005: wikiislam.net.
Cartoon of Carlos Latuff, "Holocaust Remembrance Day 2009": Wikimedia Commons.org/wiki/File:Holocaust_Remembrance_Day.jpg), courtesy Carlos Latuff, (commons.wikimedia.org/wiki/User:555/Latuff).
Cartoon in Ad-Dustour, April 14, 2001: Courtesy Semit (Independent Jewish Magazine, Neu-Isenburg, Germany, issue 1/2010).

271: "Abreise": Courtesy Jüdisches Museum Vienna (ed.: Die Macht der Bilder, p.162).
"Die Zukunft. Palästina." Münchner Odinskarte Nr.16: Jüdisches Museum Frankfurt on Main (Abgestempelt, p.107), courtesy Bildarchiv Foto Marburg.
"Auszug der Juden", Regensburg, November 1938 (Goldhagen 1996, p.130): Courtesy bpk Bildarchiv Preußischer Kulturbesitz, Berlin, no. 30006107.

276: Lamb with cross, detail from Matthias Grünewald's Isenheim Altarpiece (ca. 1512-1516): Wikimedia Commons.

317: Vladimir Herzog, last photo: Courtesy Marcus Vinícius Assis da Costa, Universidade de São Paulo (lemad.fflch.usp.br/node/7885).
Cartoon Latuff, 2009 (Pinterest.com): courtesy Carlos Latuff, (commons.wikimedia.org/wiki/User:555/Latuff).
Inauguration of Vlado Herzog's memorial, 2016: Wikipedia.

319: Cross in Lutheran Kreuzkirche, Marl: Courtesy Parson Thomas Damm.

331: Simon Bening, The worship of the five wounds of Christ (1525-1530): Wikimedia Commons.

340: Hitler as baby: wikipedia.org/wiki/Hitler_family.